THE

HISTORIES

OF

CAIUS CORNELIUS TACITUS:

WITH

NOTES FOR COLLEGES,

BY

W. S. TYLER,

PROFESSOR OF LANGUAGES IN AMHERST COLLEGE

Auguror, nec me fallit augurium, historias tuas immortales futuras.
PLIN. ad Tac. Epist. 7, 33.

Respondit Cornelius Tacitus eloquentissime et, quod eximium orationi ejus inest, σεμνῶς. PLIN. Epist. 2, 11.

NEW YORK:
D. APPLETON & CO., 443 & 445 BROADWAY.
1864

PREFACE.

THE text of this edition follows, for the most part, Orelli's, Zurich, 1848, which, being based on a new and most faithful recension of the Medicean MS. by his friend Baiter, may justly be considered as marking a new era in the history of the text of Tacitus. In several passages, however, where he has needlessly departed from the MS., I have not hesitated to adhere to it in company with other editors, believing, that not unfrequently "the most corrected copies are the least correct." The various readings have been carefully compared throughout, and, if important, are referred to in the notes.

The editions which have been most consulted, whether in the criticism of the text or in the preparation of the notes, are, besides Orelli's, those of Walther, Halle, 1831; Ruperti, Hanover, 1839; and Döderlein, Halle, 1847. The notes of Orelli are judicious and tasteful. Walther is sagacious, shrewd and independent, sometimes to a fault. Ruperti's edition is chiefly valuable as a repository of facts and opinions, selected with no great care and put together with little skill. Döderlein is concise and discriminating, but is excessively fond of originality and bold conjecture. His Essay on the Style of Tacitus, besides this fault in the matter, is also wanting in ease and elegance of language; yet it has been esteemed worthy to be translated for this edition, as on the whole one of the best treatises on that subject. Bötticher's Lexicon Taciteum, Berlin, 1830, is marked by a felicitous expression, as well as a just appreciation, of our author's merits as a historian and of his peculiarities as a writer; and its most valuable results have been freely incorporated with the notes. Freund's Wörterbuch der Lateinischen Sprache, and Smith's Dictionaries, of Greek and Roman Antiquities, and of Biography and Mythology, the former republished in this country under the supervision of Dr. Anthon, and the latter still issuing in numbers from a London press, have been found very useful, and are often referred to. References are also made to Becker's Gallus, and to the Roman Histories of Niebuhr, Arnold and Schmitz.

It will be seen, that there are not unfrequent references to my edition of the Germania and Agricola. These are not of such a nature, as to render this incomplete without that, or essentially dependent upon it. Still, if both editions are used, it will be found advantageous to read the Germania and Agricola first. The Treatises were written in that order, and in that order they best illustrate the history of the author's mind. The editor has found in his experience as a teacher, that students generally read them in that way with more facility and pleasure, and he has constructed his notes accordingly.

The notes on the Histories have been prepared with the same general views and principles, as those on the Germania and Agricola. In accordance with suggestions in some of the public journals, they have been made somewhat more grammatical. Their value in this respect has been enhanced by more copious references to the excellent grammar of Zumpt in addition to that of Andrews and Stoddard. It is chiefly by way of such references, that the general principles of grammar have been illustrated. Sometimes, however, a concise statement of the principle referred to has been added; and in regard to such idioms and constructions as are more or less peculiar to Tacitus, it has been found necessary to enter into more extended comments. It is hoped, that the notes will be found to contain not only the grammatical, but likewise all the geographical, archæological and historical illustrations, that are necessary to render the author intelligible. The editor has at least endeavored to avoid the fault, which Lord Bacon says "is over usual in annotations and commentaries, viz. to blanch the obscure places, and discourse upon the plain." But it has been his constant, not to say his chief aim, to carry students beyond the dry details of grammar and lexicography, and introduce them into a familiar acquaintance and lively sympathy with the author and his times, and with that great empire, of whose degeneracy and decline, in its beginnings, he has bequeathed to us so profound and instructive a history. It was for this end, that the Preliminary Remarks were composed; and if they accomplish this result in any considerable degree, though long, they will hardly be thought too long, and they will not have been written in vain.

The Indexes have been prepared with much labor and care, and, it is believed, will add materially to the value of the work.

The editor takes this opportunity to express his grateful sense of the kind reception which has been given to his edition of the Germania and Agricola, and his thanks especially for such notices, whether by letter or in the public journals, as, while they fully appreciate its merits, point out its faults for correction. If this edition is in any degree more meritorious or less faulty, the superiority will be owing, in no small measure, to such acts of kindness. Besides his obligations to those who have thus favored him, he acknowledges his particular indebtedness to Professor B. B. Edwards of Andover, and Professor H. B. Hackett of Newton, for the aid and encouragement, which they have in various ways extended to him. He has been aided in the correction of the press by Mr. Marshall Henshaw, whose accurate and patient scholarship well fit him to render such and still higher services to classical learning.

With these explanations, the editor takes leave of a work, on which he has bestowed much time and toil, and which, he would fain hope, may contribute in some humble measure to the better understanding and appreciation by his youthful countrymen of an author, a language and a people, formed by nature beyond most, if not beyond all others, to be severally the writer, the vehicle and the subject of history.

AMHERST, 1848.

PREFACE TO THE REVISED EDITION.

IN this Revised Edition, the text and the notes have been carefully collated with those of Ritter in his new edition (Bonn and Cambridge, 1848), and such corrections and additions, as were deemed just and important, have been adopted from this source. I cannot, however, by any means, accept the many gratuitous emendations and dogmatic assertions which disfigure and depreciate this otherwise excellent commentary. Other corrections and improvements have also been made, which have been suggested by use of the book in classes, or to which my attention has been called, whether by private correspondence, or by notices and reviews in the public journals. I have been especially indebted to the critical acumen and accurate scholarship of my friend, Mr. Charles Short, of Roxbury, writing in the Bibliotheca Sacra, for not a few valuable suggestions and amendments.

AMHERST, JULY, 1851.

ESSAY

ON THE STYLE OF TACITUS.*

1. TACITUS was the inventor of an entirely new style of historic composition; or rather he did not himself designedly form it, but, while he applied himself to writing history with a different design and spirit from other authors, a new style of expression was the natural and necessary result. For formerly it had been a prevalent custom among writers of history, not only to defer writing till they had arrived at a mature age, but also to compose with calm and tranquil feelings; differing in this respect from orators, who were wont to believe that the effect of their speaking would correspond with the degree of energy and emotion with which they spoke. Hence the calm, smooth and flowing style of the ancient historians, even of those who desired to be distinguished from the others by a sort of peculiar dignity.

Now Tacitus was the first to depart from the rules of these writers. For it was the natural bent of his genius, not so much to narrate the mere facts and events of history, which are often fortuitous, but he labored especially to exhibit the character and spirit of the actors in his scenes. Hence his chief merit, his great power, is seen in the delineation of character: whether he labors by description to place before us the image of some distinguished man; or so relates his deeds, that the reader, by his own discernment, forms an opinion of his secret motives and principles of action.

But since constant reflection upon virtue or vice has a very great influence over the passions, he came to write in an excited rather than a tranquil state of mind, so that he seems to possess more of the ardor of youth than of the maturity of age. Now of such a state of mind, a rapid and energetic style is the natural expression and the necessary result. In a word, his style is impetuous, always hastening on to the issue, impatient of delay. And this arose not merely

* Abridged from the Prolegomena of L. Döderlein to his edition of Tacitus, tom. ii., Halle, 1847, and translated from the Latin by Mr. Marshall Henshaw, A. M., Tutor in Amherst College.

from his own natural disposition, but he adapted the style of his narrative to the taste of his age. For, as is usually the case in a time of great moral declension, not only lassitude and listlessness, but also, at the same time, a sort of morbid desire for haste, had taken possession of the spirits of men; while those qualities which are a proper mean between them—calmness of spirit and a healthy activity—are the characteristic of but few. Hence what was formerly considered simplicity and dignified repose, then began to appear dull, spiritless and insipid. Tacitus was therefore impelled at the same time by his own genius, and by the taste of his age, to a hurried style of expression.

But rapidity is opposed to dignity,—a grace which cannot be separated from equability and moderation. And since dignity, in ancient times, was the peculiar characteristic and requisite of a good history, so skill was necessary in the later historians to temper rapidity with dignity. To accomplish this purpose, Tacitus employed the utmost diligence in producing an ornamented diction.

Now since I must briefly treat of the style of Tacitus, I will first show by what arts, nay, even by what artifices, he attained to that brevity which we admire as appropriate and peculiar to this writer; secondly, by what means he made his style at the same time dignified and beautiful.*

2. The conciseness of Tacitus is proverbial. But an incorrect notion has prevailed among some, viz. that this consists mostly in the brevity of single expressions, such as resemble the responses of oracles. And this style of writing does indeed prevail in the treatise on Germany, inasmuch as it is best adapted to description; and while John Mueller and others, who seek a reputation for the same, imitate it, they think they are rivalling Tacitus. But, on the contrary, the acute judgment and the consummate skill of this writer are seen in this very thing, that he adopted this style, so rare, only in treating those subjects, the nature of which demanded it, while in other connections he is scarcely less fond of full and rounded periods, not being inferior, in this respect, to Cicero and Livy. At the commencement of the Annals, he hastens, in a series of very brief propositions, to premise whatever was important, from which he passes to a very full and brilliant period, and thus introduces the history itself, as if he would show the difference between the preface and the real history, by a sudden change of diction. The orations, inserted in the narrative, consist, according to the character of the speaker, sometimes of con-

* I have been assisted much in this Essay by the Prolegomena of G. Boetticher to the Lexicon on Tacitus, Berlin, 1830; and by the Excursus ad Tac. Agricolam of C. L. Roth, Norimb. 1833.

cise sentences, sometimes of rounded periods. And in the narration of heroic deeds, battles and debates, he varies his style, according as he himself hastens on to more important matters, or desires to urge and hurry forward the minds of his readers, or to delay them and persuade them to a calmer examination of the subject. Therefore he never wearies us by a series of concise sentences, continued beyond proper limits, which is a fault of Seneca.

Tacitus has omitted nothing which would contribute to brevity of style. In this he chose to imitate, not so much the oracles, as the ancient Roman writers. For as the language of the Greeks was naturally adapted to express grace (χάριτα), so that of the Romans contained in it the elements of dignity, and, as it were, imperial brevity. In its own nature it was fitted to illustrate that common saying: *quot verba, tot pondera.* I might mention the want of the article—a thing to be regretted in other respects—as among the chief reasons and sources of this merit, although this is not the place for examining this subject more fully. Now Cicero, and the writers of his time, disregarded, in a manner, this natural character of the Latin tongue, while they attempted to soften the rough power and strength of the Roman language by the polish and refinement of the Greek. But those writers who adorned the age of the Cæsars after the time of Tiberius—Seneca and Tacitus—again departed from this elegance of style. For they carefully and intelligently cherished that style of expression, which the ancient Romans, almost without cultivation and under the impulse of their nature, had employed. Besides other advantages, they labored to preserve the power of the ancient style, in such a way as both to avoid the antique rudeness of an uncultivated age, and drop the effeminate verbosity of a subsequent period.

While therefore Tacitus strove to speak so that every word might have its weight, he made use of many, or rather of all kinds of ingenious contrivances, not neglecting even the most minute. Nor, while I am pursuing this subject, do I entertain any fear of seeming to depreciate the ability of Tacitus, as if it were the mark of a weak and narrow mind, in so earnest a narration of the most important events, to choose his words with a sort of scholarlike care and anxiety. The foundation and source of so rich a diction was the sublime genius of Tacitus, the greatness of his mind, and the strength and fervor of his emotions. At the same time, it is well known with what almost religious scrupulosity the ancients elaborated, each one for himself, their style and language; and, in so doing, attributed less to a sort of divine power and inspiration, (as if words would flow from a subject spontaneously,) than to industry and care. Remarkable sto ries are told even about Thucydides, of such a careful choice respecting substantives and infinitives; but Tacitus lived at an age which was much richer in the rules of grammar and rhetoric, and, as was natural for a Roman, he strove more earnestly than the Greeks to render his style as effective as possible. Wherefore to that hurried breviloquence, to which he was led by the impulses of his nature, he superadded all the ornaments of learning, art and taste, not fearing the appearance or the reproach of a labored brevity, but freely rejecting the merit of a plain, pure and natural style. Now this brevity is seen in choosing the shortest words which will express the thoughts, in omitting as many words as possible, and finally in condensing the sentences themselves within the smallest possible compass.

3. To commence with the smallest matters, he generally prefers the shorter forms of words to the longer, sometimes contrary to common usage. Few, I think, use simple *ut* for *velut*, *as if*, as he does in Ann. II., 34; III., 9; or for *prout*, Ann. I., 61; Hist. II., 46: *qua* for *quatenus*, *since*, even at the hazard of obscurity, Ann. VI., 10; XI., 8; XV., 72; Hist. II., 31: *super* for *insuper*, Hist. II., 34. For the same reason he often used *ne*, where the common rule required *ut non*, e. g., Ann. II., 29. *Ita moderans ne lenire neve asperare crimina videretur*, Add. XI., 15, 29; XII., 47; XVI., 4; Hist. III., 11. If we can put confidence in the MSS. he also often used *que* for *quoque*. See in Ann. IV., 74; VI., 33; XII., 35.

Tacitus often manifests a sort of dislike for substantives ending in *tio;* for besides their length they are somewhat barren of meaning. He therefore prefers *aemulatus*, *dispositus*, *advectus*, and such like words, to *aemulatio*, and those of a similar form. Hence I have defended *diversus* in Ann. XIII., 9; and *pulsus* in Hist. IV., 18, as the true reading. Elsewhere he is wont also to employ the primitive noun in place of the derivative, as in Ann. VI., 5, Dial. 3, *fabulae* for *confabulationes;* G. 26, *fenus* for *feneratio;* Hist. II., 2, *audentioribus spatiis* for *spatiationibus*. And since the use of deponent verbs had long prevailed, by which means the language was virtually robbed of an equal number of passive verbs and thereby impoverished, Tacitus did not hesitate to return to the ancient signification of such words, and to use passives that were obsolete in his age, gaining the advantage of brevity, and, at the same time, the appearance of antiquity. Hence *adipisci* is used passively in Ann. XV., 12; *opperiri*, Ann. XI., 26; *ulcisci*, Ann. I., 9; and *palari*, Hist. III., 80; perhaps also *fateri*, Dial. 25.

4. The use of simple words instead of compound is very extensive, in which Tacitus vies with poets. The principle of this license is no other than to substitute the genus for the species; for instance,

quaerere instead of *acquirere*, Ann. I., 35; instead of *conquirere*, Ann. VI., 1; instead of *exquirere*, Ann. II., 53; instead of *requirere* = *desiderare*, Hist. IV., 6. Hence this exchange is usually made with a loss of definiteness, but with advantage in regard to brevity. I will mention a few examples, unique indeed, but yet allowed by all. Hist. I., 84, *congestu lapidum stare* = *constare*.—Ann. XIV., 21, *struere* = *destruere*.—Ann. XV., 14, *cernerent* = *decernerent*.—G., 2, *tristem cultu* = *ad incolendum*.—Ann. XIV., 4, *pectori haerens* = *inhaerens*.—Hist. III., 57, *miscebant* = *immiscebant*.—Hist. III., 25, *pulsos* = *impulsos*.—Hist. I., 35, *sistens* = *obsistens*.—Ann. XV., 50, *cepisse* = *suscepisse*. In many other places I have restored this usage from the MSS., where other editors have not ventured to do so: e. g., Agr. 4, *Sublime et rectum ingenium*, i. e., *erectum*.—Hist. IV., 20, *Omnibus portis rumpunt*, where the common editions have *erumpunt*.—Hist. IV., 81, *Postremo aestimari a medicis jubet*, where Ernesti has preferred *existimari*.—Hist. IV., 48, *Si pauca supra petiero ab initio*, Edd. *repetiero*. Perhaps also *cursaturus* should be preferred to *incursaturus* in A. 1.

5. The dignity of the Latin language is impaired by nothing more than by a frequent use of particles, pronouns, or auxiliary verbs; on the other hand it is increased when nouns follow nouns or verbs directly, so that the sentence seems to consist of mere solid and weighty matter. Thus originate those sentences which strike our ears, and those of the Greeks, as too cumbrous and heavy, since there is no pause allowed after the separate parts and words. But the same expressions had a very pleasing sound to the Romans, and especially to Tacitus, as the following: *Agrippina aequi impatiens, dominandi avida, virilibus curis feminarum vitia exuerat*, Ann. VI., 25. In this example, whatever is heavy was produced spontaneously without any design or study. But weight and stateliness may be promoted by an intentional effort of the writer. With this view Tacitus omits the more unimportant words oftener, and with more studious design, than any other writer. And first he refrains from the use of *prepositions*, satisfied with the power of the case alone. Hence *ab* or *ex* is omitted contrary to common usage. Hist. V., 23, *Commeatus Gallia adventantes*, cf. III., 15.—Agr. 18, *Cujus possessione revocatum*.—G. 14, *Exigunt principis sui liberalitate illum bellatorem equum*.—Hist. I., 55, *Non tamen quisquam in modum concionis aut* *s u g g e s t u* *locutus*.—III., 29, *Cum superjacta tela* *t e s t u d i n e* *laberentur*.

Hence I have restored the shorter reading of the manuscripts in Agr. 19: *Ut civitates proximis hibernis in remota et avia deferrent*, and Hist. III., 74: *Clamore proximis orto*. In both places the editions have *a proximis*.

In the same way the dative is very often used for the ablative with *ab*, e. g., Hist. III., 70: *Ne militibus interficeretur.* Moreover, *in* is omitted, e. g., Hist. V., 5: *Vitisque aurea templo reperta.* Hist. I., 13: *Hi discordes et rebus minoribus sibi quisque tendentes.*

Hence I have erased *in* of the common editions as often as it is wanting in the MSS. Hist. II., 33: *Imperia ducum incerto reliquerat.* Hist. I., 68: *Ipsi* (in) *medio vagi*, as Ann. II., 52. Hist. II., 59: *Appulsu litoris trucidatus.*

Moreover, *ad* or *in* is used or omitted promiscuously before the accusative. I pass by those examples in which a preposition enters into the composition of the verb, as, *advolvi genua;* although even such have given offence, as Hist. III., 43, *Stoechadas insulas affertur;* and c. 50, *Omniaque quae agenda forent . . . aderat;* for in both these places the old editions inserted *ad.* Very often the early editors silently inserted a preposition, which, upon the authority of the manuscripts, I have either erased, or advised to erase, or ought myself to have erased. Hist. III., 7: (in) *majus accipitur.* Agr. 10: (in) *universum aestimanti.* The following are more peculiar to Tacitus: Hist. I., 45: *Marium Celsum . . .* (ad) *supplicium expostulabant.* Hist. II., 36: *Macer* (ad) *exitium poscebatur.*

I suspect that I shall hardly persuade many that Tacitus makes use of this license; but, at all events, it was worth while to set forth a number of examples, and the unanimity of the MSS. And surely it would be wonderful harmony between books, if the same error were so often repeated. Each one, according to his own taste, will concede to Tacitus more or less of this liberty of accomplishing, by the power of the cases alone, most purposes for which other writers think prepositions necessary. I only add, Hist. II., 63: *Ne periculo principis famam clementiae affectaret;* cf. IV., 69. Hist. II., 70: *Vulgus clamore et gaudio deflectere via.*

6. The use of the *genitive* is likewise somewhat more extensive with Tacitus than with other Latin authors, since, by its assistance he could dispense with prepositions. What other writer has used *jus libertorum*, Hist. II., 92, or *jus militum*, Ann. XI., 33, for *in libertos, in milites?*

Tacitus seeks the same brevity in the use of the *dative*, which he is wont to substitute, with far greater freedom than other writers, for the preposition *ad*, with the accusative. He says, in the same sense, Ann. II., 58, *Neu proceres . . . ad discordias traheret*, and Agr. 12, *Per principes factionibus et studiis trahuntur;* or, Hist. II., 45, *In lacrimas effusus*, and I., 69, *lacrimis effusus;* or, Hist. IV., 5, *Ut firmior adversus fortuita*, and, A. 35, *firmus* ADVERSIS. With characteristic love of variety he has brought together both constructions in

Ann. XIV., 38, *Adversa pravitati ipsius, prospera ad fortunam referebat.*

I will add some instances in which the more unwonted use of the dative has, from its unfrequency, escaped the notice of commentators, or may, from its resemblance to the ablative, escape the notice of the reader; Hist. I., 89, *Pacis adversa reipublicae pertinuere;* G., 38, *Propriis nationibus discreti;* as, Hist. IV., 16, *Propriis cuneis componit;* Hist. I., 77, *Sacerdotiis recoluit,* i. e., *in sacerdotia restituit;* Hist. I., 55. 76, *Sacramento adigere.* Moreover, he uses the dative for *adversus,* with the accusative; A. 30, *famae defendit,* i. e., *adversus famam.* On the contrary, he sometimes prefers a preposition to the ordinary dative, when it will serve his purpose; Ann. II., 39, *Forma haud dissimili in dominum erat;* and he substitutes *in vulgus* for the dative *vulgo,* see in Hist. I., 71.

7. He is no less sparing in the use of *conjunctions,* and is peculiarly fond of *asyndeta.* The style of the Latins differs very much in the use of asyndeta from that of the Greeks. For since the Greeks make use of very many exceedingly small conjunctions, and such as often do not even form a syllable, as in elision δέ and τέ, they were not accustomed, merely for the sake of brevity or convenience, to omit conjunctions, but they omit them as often as it will subserve the purposes of rhetoric. It is different with the Latins; since their conjunctions have a fuller sound, and, in their length, equal many nouns and verbs, as *autem, quidem, igitur,* it was worth while, for the sake of rapidity and conciseness, to be sparing in the use of them. Thence the books of the Latins abound in asyndeta, even where they have no peculiar significance or rhetorical power. Owing to the unprecedented frequency with which he uses this liberty, the style of Tacitus is considered, for the most part, concise, and similar to that which the French call *style coupé.* For its character is seen, not only in its refraining from the longer forms of propositions, but also in its generally omitting connectives between the separate propositions.

The peculiarity of Tacitus is seen in his frequent omission of the two conjunctions *et* and *sed.* Most Latin writers omit the copulative *et* as often as, by the rhetorical figure asyndeton, three or more separate parts of a sentence are connected together, since they dislike to use many conjunctions in the same sentence. But Tacitus joins two members in the same way, in accordance with a custom of the ancient Romans, which Niebuhr has noticed.* Examples are too numerous to require specification. Moreover, it is customary with Tacitus to omit *sed,* especially after negative propositions. Ann. IV.,

* Röm. Gesch., T. i., p. 326, ed. third.

35, *Non modo libertas, etiam libido impunita;* Add. III., 19; XVI., 29; Hist. II., 27. Hence, without reason, Lipsius has urged the insertion of *sed* in Dial. 8. *Nec hoc illis alterius ter mille sestertium praestat; ipsa eloquentia*, evidently like Agr. 37. Some MSS. also omit *sed* in G. 10, *Non solum apud plebem sed apud proceres, apud sacerdotes.*

Of relative conjunctions *ut* is sometimes omitted by asyndeton, and not by ellipsis. For, in Ann. III., 10, *Petitum est, cognitionem reciperet*, is not properly an ellipsis. And the same construction is found in many other passages.

8. At this day, indeed, when the science of grammar has begun to be so much improved, no one will call such examples ellipses. I now pass to ellipses proper.

Tacitus omits auxiliary verbs almost without any distinction of tense or mode. A. 16, *Ac velut pacti;* ibid. 1, *ni incursaturus*, scil. *essem.* Add. Hist. II., 42; Hist. II., 76, *quod inchoaturi*, scil. *sunt*, where the editions have *inchoatur.* The following may justly be considered somewhat harsh; Hist. IV., 7, *Satis Marcello* (sit) *quod Neronem in exitium tot innocentium impulerit.* Hist. IV., 55, *Socius* (esse) *jactabat.*

He is also accustomed to omit many other words, and the more general the signification of each, the more frequently it is omitted, as words of *doing*. Hist. I., 36, *Omnia serviliter pro dominatione.* Thus must be explained without correction, Agr. 27, *At Brittanni non virtute sed occasione et arte ducis* (factum esse) *rati*; coll. Hist. II., 19. Numberless ellipses of this kind might be mentioned of words of *speaking*, *thinking*, *fearing*, and *going*, not entirely peculiar to Tacitus, since Cicero also has a similar usage, e. g., N. D. II., 4, *Augures rem ad senatum*, (tulerunt); *senatus ut abdicarent consules* (decrevit); *abdicarunt.* There are many more in his letters to Atticus which exhibit even some appearance of haste. Wherefore, I do not understand why any one should wish to change, A. 9, *Nullam ultra potestatis personam*, scil. *agebat.* Much less has Ernesti rightly forced *agere* into c. 19, *Nihil per libertos servosque publicae rei.*

I pass by other common ellipses, as, of *causa* and *potius.* One that is rare has escaped the notice of commentators, in Hist. III., 10, *Et ut proditionis* (scil. *reum*) *ira militum in Flavianum incubuit.*

9. Brachylogy (βραχυλογία) resembles ellipsis very closely. In ellipsis, words must be supplied evidently from some external source; these which are omitted through brachylogy are implied in the adjoining words, and must be supplied from what either precedes or follows. Of this figure there are three kinds. The first is when the

same word, that has been once expressed, must be understood again; as, Hist. III., 70, *Simulationem prorsus et imaginem deponendi imperii* (scil. imaginem, speciem) *fuisse;* G. 19, *Ne* (scil. maritum) *tanquam maritum, sed tanquam matrimonium ament.* See in Hist. IV., 5; Agr. 20. Also words must often be understood again after a longer distance, though the obvious meaning of the sentence requires the repetition. Hist. II., 21, *Moles perfringendis* (scil. pluteis et vineis,) *obruendisque hostibus expediunt,* unless for the sake of concinnity, *operibus* must be supplied. Hist. V., 6, *Praecipuum montium Libanon erigit,* scil. *Judaea;* A. 10, *Dispecta est et Thule, quam hactenus,* scil. *invenit domuitque.*

Another kind of brachylogy is when, in some word, a similar word, springing from the same root, is implied, so that one case must be supplied from another, one mode from another, a verb from a noun, and *vice versa,* and in fine, homogeneous words from homogeneous, for the purpose of completing the sense. Hist. III., 9, *In Vitellium ut inimici* (scil. inimica) *praesumpsere;* G. 20, *Pares* (paribus) *validaeque* (validis) *miscentur;* Hist. I., 37, *Plus rapuit Icelus quam quod Polycliti . . .* (scil. rapientes *or* praedati) *perierunt;* Hist. I., 32, *Tradito more quemcumque principem adulandi licentia acclamationem,* scil. *adulabantur;* Hist. IV., 24, *Flaccus lectos . . . legato tradit ut quam maximis per ripam itineribus celeraret, ipse navibus* (sc. celeraturus,) *invalidus corpore, invisus militibus.*

Also simple words are supplied from compound, and one compound word from another. Ann. I., 17, *Hinc . . . tentoria* (scil. emi) *hinc vacationes munerum redimi;* Hist. I., 8, *Cluvius Rufus, vir facundus et pacis artibus,* (scil. expertus,) *bellis inexpertus.* To the same head must be referred the following: Hist. III., 46, *Castra legionum exscindere parabant,* (scil. et exscidissent,) *ni Mucianus sextam legionem opposuisset;* A. 13, *Agitasse Caium Caesarem de intranda Brittannia, satis constat,* (et intraturum fuisse) *ni velox ingenio . . . et ingentes adversus Germaniam conatus frustra fuissent;* Hist. II., 68; A. 4, *Se studium philosophiae acrius . . . . . hausisse,* (et porro hausturum fuisse,) *ni prudentia matris coercuisset.* Those who would translate such expressions briefly and clearly into the English, should substitute for the hypothetical clauses *but* with the indicative. Finally, in the third kind of brachylogy, a word conveying an idea in contrast with some adjoining word must be supplied. Hist. II., 30, *Hinc aemulatio ducibus: Caecina* (Valentem) *ut foedum et maculosum; ille,* (Caecinam) *ut tumidum et vanum irridebant;* Hist. II., 74, *Esse privatis cogitationibus progressum* (et regressum) *et prout velint plus minusve sumi ex fortuna.* See Ann. I., 55; Hist. II., 87; IV., 80.

10. *Zeugma* approaches quite nearly to brachylogy. The following are examples: Hist. II., 80, *Caesarem* (vocare) *et omnia principatus vocabula cumulare*. See C. Roth, in Agr. Exc. XXXII.

There is a species of the same zeugma in that custom, surprising to our ears, and scarcely imitable in our language, of uniting the same verb or word in one sense with one, and in another sense with another part of the sentence. Pindar took the lead in this: ἕλεν δ' Οἰνομάου βίαν παρθένον τε σύνευνον, *he slew Œnomaus and (married) the virgin;* and in like manner Soph. Trach., 353. Like this is Hist. I., 67, *Plus sanguinis ac praedae Caecina hausit;* Hist. II., 32, *Britannicum militem hoste et mari distineri;* Agr. 25, *Silvarum et montium profunda;* Agr. 45, *Nos Maurici Rusticique visus, nos innocenti sanguine Senecio perfudit.*

11. Another means of conciseness is that grammatical figure which we, at this day, are beginning to call *prægnantia*—a word quite recently formed and a barbarous substantive—but yet appropriate, and withal necessary, which the more strict, if they choose, may call *structura praegnans.* Very often a secondary idea lies concealed in some noun or verb, unseen indeed, but breathing like the fœtus in the womb, and frequently also very forcible. I could wish that some one of the great grammarians had defined, in an appropriate treatise, the compass and limits of this figure, that I might have some authority to follow; but now each, according to his own humor, is accustomed to use a vague and undefined word; a privilege which I shall claim for myself. Both nouns and verbs, and likewise adverbs, are employed *prægnanter.* Thus he says *cupido* for *pecuniae cupido*, in Ann. XII., 57; Hist. I., 66; and on the other hand *pecunia* in the same sense, Hist. III., 41. The following come under the same class, Hist. I., 85, *Occulto habitu*, scil. *animi;* for it ought not to be understood of the assumption of a false dress; Hist. 3., 19, *Cumulos*, scil. *corporum;* Hist. IV., 86, *Modestiae imagine in altitudinem* (silentii) *conditus;* Hist. IV., 72, *Stare integram sedem*, scil. *belli;* Dial. 6, *Publico*, scil. *judicio; Ingenium = commentum ingenii*, in Hist. III., 28; *Gaudio fungi = gaudii significatione* or *gratulatione*, Hist. II., 55; *Reposcentibus prospera*, i. e., *prosperorum rationem*, Hist. III., 13; *Qui naves, qui classem, qui mare expectabant*, Agr. 18, i. e., *aggressionem per mare apertum ac non per fretum.* In like manner with these words: Hist. I., 76, *mansit*, scil. *in fide;* Agr. 45, *perfudit*, scil. *horrore;* Agr. 25, *complecti*, scil. *bello*, as, Hist. I., 36, Agr. 18, *praesumpsere*, scil. *spe.*

Frequently also adverbs or ablatives, datives or accusatives used like adverbs, bear some attributive, either adjective or participle, as it were, concealed in them. This is evidently contrary to Cicero's custom, who preferred to call his work *libri de officiis scripti*, rather than to omit the participle. Now Tacitus, for the sake of rapidity in his narrative, left such words to be supplied by the reader, as often as he thought there could be no danger of mistake: Hist. I., 31, *Longinum exarmant, quia non ordine militiae* (superior) *sed e Galbae amicis . . . erat;* Hist. III., 82, *Vitelliani sola desperatione* (adjuti) *ruebant;* Hist. IV., 84, *Plurimi Ditem patrem insignibus, quae in ipso manifesta aut per ambages* (significata) *conjectant;* Hist. V., 5, *Judaei mente sola* (visibile) *unumque numen intelligunt;* Hist. I., 80, *Pessimus quisque in occasionem praedae*, scil. intentus; Agr. 30, *Spem in nostris manibus* (positum) *habebant;* Hist. III. 62, *Exercitus immane quantum* (aucto) *animo exitium valentis ut finem belli accepit;* Hist. I., 83, *Pietas vestra acrius quam considerate* (demonstrata) *excitavit.*

A few of these examples have escaped the notice of commentators; others, through a forgetfulness of this license, have been incorrectly understood: Agr. 5, *Electus quem contubernio* (dignum) *existimaret;* Hist. III., 33, *Defossa eruere, faces in manibus* (gerentes), like the English "torch in hand." Nor ought the following to be thought harsh, Hist. I., 31, *Alexandriam praemissos atque inde rursus* (revocatos) *refovebat.*

Frequent also is that kind of prægnantia to which I may venture to give the name *structura contracta*, of which the most familiar examples are *Olympia vincere*, or *pontem jungere.* In Tacitus I find *navare bellum*, i. e., operam navare bello; Hist. IV., 37, *ad liberandum obsidium;* Hist. II., 60, *Fidem absolvit;* Hist. V., 11, *Proelia serebant*, i. e., manus conserebant proeliis; Hist. II., 34, *Ne miles segne otium tereret*, i. e., segni otio tempus. Sometimes he has the same, even when he gains nothing in brevity. Hist. III., 56, *Ut nube atra diem obtenderent*, which differs not more from the common *ut nubem atram diei obtenderent*, than *urbem muris circumdare* differs from *urbi muros.* See Hist. II., 2, *Formam deae paucis disserere.* Editors ought to have recognised the same usage in Hist. III., 3, *Huc illuc tracturus interpretationem*, i. e., res interpretatione. To the same head I refer, Hist. I., 42, *In utrumque latus transverberatus.*

12. By *attraction* not brevity indeed, but rapidity is favored; the number of *words* is not diminished, but of *pauses*, and the members of the sentences are more closely connected together. Nouns are attracted from their state of apposition, and are forced into the relation of adjectives. Hist. I., 65, *Uno amne discretis*, i. e., *una re, amne*; Hist. IV., 56, *Ceterum vulgus*, i. e., *ceteri, vulgus;* Hist. III. 41, *Aderant vis et pecunia et ruentis fortunae novissima libido.*

To the same class belong, Agr. 17, *Cum Cerialis quidem alterius successoris curam . . . obruisset*, and, G. 25, *Cetera domus officio uxor ac liberi exsequuntur.* To destroy the attraction by inserting a comma here, may adapt the construction to our ears, but would not exhibit the thought in the light in which it was viewed by the ancients. In the same way I read, Hist. II., 27, *Quam altiore ab initio repetam*, i. e., *altius, ab initio.*

To a similar attraction belong nominatives with infinitives, after the example of the Greek and Latin poets: Hist. IV., 55, *Socius* (esse) *jactabat;* Hist. IV., 40, *Cognitus est confugisse;* Hist. II., 74, *Legiones secuturae sperabantur;* Hist. IV., 23, *Vis et arma satis placebant*, i. e., *vim et arma satis fore placebat*; and, II., 76, *Ipse qui suadet considerandus est adjiciatne*, etc. Agr. 43, has been correctly restored, *Momenta ipsa deficientis . . . nunciata constabant;* Hist. I., 84, *Muta ista et inanima intercidere ac reparari promiscua sunt.*

Of the same class the following is a very common specimen: Hist. II., 82, *Sufficere videbatur . . . pars copiarum et dux Mucianus et Vespasiani nomen et nihil arduum fatis*, i. e., *et quod nihil arduum esset fatis;* Hist. V., 21, *Obstitit formido et remiges per alia militiae munia dispersi.*

13. Thus far I have examined those sources of brevity which may be referred to the established rules of grammar. There are other examples which cannot be explained under a grammatical term. For example, sometimes the narrative hastens forward so rapidly that it includes two different events in the same expression: Hist. I., 46, *Laco praefectus tanquam in insulam seponeretur ab evocato quem ad caedem ejus Otho praemiserat confossus;* Ann. XVI., 13, *Qui dum assident, dum deflentis saepe eodem rogo cremabantur.* In the latter, *the state of disease*, and in the former, *the act of going forth*, which were intermediate, are passed by in silence. Add Hist. III., 29. Also Hist. II., 68, is obscure for the same reason: *Ludicro initio, ni numerus caesorum invidiam Vitellio* (MS. *bello*) *auxisset.* For the primary idea, *ni numerus caesorum magnus fuisset*, lurks concealed as it were in a single word. And Tacitus quite often did not condescend to relate those things the knowledge of which was necessary for clearly understanding the order of events, provided that readers, sufficiently attentive and discerning, could follow him by their own judgment or sagacity. Thus in Hist. I., 77, it is said that when Otho assigned the consulship to Vopiscus, *plerique Viennensium honori datum interpretabantur*, where the reason for such a construction cannot be clearly seen, unless we decide that Vopiscus was an inhabitant of Vienna. Yet that fact is nowhere

stated. I have noticed a similar example in Hist. II., 71. But I know of no more remarkable instance than Agr. 24, where the words *nave prima transgressus* were obscure, until it was discovered that Agricola had gone over (the previous autumn) from Britain to the continent, or even to Rome, a fact which Tacitus does not mention.

14. Since now such a studied brevity seems to involve a departure from usage, and to favor a copiousness of matter rather than to subserve the beauties of style, Tacitus makes a compensation by laboring intently to adorn his language, in order that he may not lose the praise of eloquence.

Of the ancient authors of history, Cæsar wrote in a style, pure, graceful and devoid of all ornament, not departing from the ordinary modes of expression on the one part, and yet on the other avoiding the vulgarity of colloquial language by a somewhat artificial composition. Sallust was fond of antiquated expressions and wrote in a style of peculiar gravity, still carefully preserving simplicity. Livy applied ornament to his diction, and sought the praise of eloquence. But Tacitus believed that a kind of magnificence and sublimity of style was peculiarly adapted to the dignity of history. And in this, indeed, he resembled Thucydides, who himself also had cultivated a style widely removed from the ordinary eloquence of other writers; not for want of genius, or through ignorance of letters, as some suppose, but intentionally and understandingly, that he might not seem to have furnished the lovers of pleasure with a mere ἀγώνισμα ἐς τὸ παραχρῆμα.* In other respects there is almost a greater difference between these writers, than resemblance.† For the Grecian writer, in discussions and orations, is especially and peculiarly condensed and bold, though in his boldness approaching nearer to the austerity of philosophers than to the ornament of poets; while in narration his style is very clear and flowing. Tacitus, on the contrary, shaped his narrative to the cast of his own mind, therein rivalling the vigor and boldness of poets; but as often as he interwove orations, he contented himself with obeying the ordinary rules of eloquence. In fine, there is no essential difference between his style and that of poetry; and strangely inconsistent are they, who refuse to Tacitus the use of any word or construction, while they freely grant the same to poets. And rarely indeed does he, while laboring to be brief, become obscure, as is usually the case in a

* *I. e.*, "a mere prize essay for temporary applause." The expression is quoted from the Introduction of Thucydides' History, in which, as he says, he gives to the public κτῆμα ἐς ἀεὶ μᾶλλον, ἢ ἀγώνισμα ες τὸ παραχρῆμα. Ed.

† Fried. Roth has written an excellent essay upon these writers, Vergleichende Betrachtungen über Thucydides und Tacitus, Munchen, 1812.

matter so difficult and hazardous, (and when he seems to be so, it happens oftener through the fault of transcribers than through his own): though not unfrequently when he strives to be sublime, he becomes, not bombastic indeed, but he is thought to depart too far from a proper simplicity.

15. And first, the style of Tacitus is terse, polished and elaborate. Rarely, in comparison with his frequent use of other idioms, do we find in his works those *anacolutha*, the use of which with other writers presents the appearance, sometimes of a pleasing negligence, sometimes of a disagreeable carelessness. I have noticed a few, e. g., in Ann. XII., 52; Hist. III., 60; IV., 12, etc.

If he sometimes so arranged his words as to appear to have mingled different constructions, it ought not to be supposed that he did this without a design: Ann. III., 5, *Perferre non toleravit*, as Dial. 3, *Maturare editionem festino*, or, G. 30, *Initium inchoare*. This appeared to him somewhat stronger than that common accumulation of words, *pertulit ac toleravit*, which Cicero would prefer, as if this latter would add to the *number* of words, while his own arrangement would increase their power.

The concurrence of genitives, which is so annoying wherever it is found, he carefully avoided, by employing the figure Hendiadys. Of the nature and advantage of this figure C. Roth has treated in a learned and critical manner.

16. Moreover he paid a tribute of regard to ornament, in that he did not use special or trite words, particularly those which are called *technical terms*. He avoided these even when he thus lost something in brevity. Hence, by a sort of circumlocution, he preferred to write, Hist. III., 62, *ludicrum juvenum* rather than *Juvenalia*. In Dial. 32, he says, almost obscurely, *jus civitatis* for *jure civili;* whence has arisen confidence in the conjecture of Bach, which proposes as a correction, in Hist. IV., 4, *de bello civium* for the corrupt *civilium*, and the common correction *civili*. Perhaps the Medicean MS. reads correctly, in Hist. II., 89, *ponte Mulvi*, where the editions have *Mulvio;* since in Ann. I., 8; III., 4., he says *campus Martis*.

Hence in the distinction of Latin synonyms, the authority of Tacitus is more suspicious than that of poets. For he disregards (particularly in antitheses) and spurns set and trite words.

Kindred to this peculiarity is his rejection of foreign words, particularly from the Greek, even though they had been naturalized by the Latins. Nowhere, except in the Dialogue, does he use the term *philosophi:* he says, *sapientes*, although the ideas are unlike. He rarely uses the term *poeta:* he generally says *vates*. Rejecting *asylum*, he says *subsidium*. There is a remarkable example of this kind in

Ann. XV., 71, *Milichus praemiis ditatus, Conservatoris nomen Graeco ejus rei vocabulo assumpsit.* Yet he does not maintain so rigid and offensive an observance of this peculiarity as to avoid the use of whatever has a foreign sound; he admits some such words, as *tropaea, asylum, chlamys, catapulta, acinaces.*

17. He hesitated not to revive *ancient words*, and forms of words, which had been condemned by the refinement of the Ciceronian and the Augustan age, believing that there is more brilliancy in that which savors of antiquity. Editors have retained the datives *senatu, nuru, luxu*, as also in Ann. IV., 55, *Persi* for *Persei;* but at the same time they have rejected many ancient forms, lest Tacitus should appear too unlike Cicero. In Ann. IV., 32, the Medicean MS. has *compossivere*, and not *composuere;* and Ann. XIII., 40; Hist. III., 22, *cornum* not *cornu.* It is easy indeed to correct such expressions according to the usage of Cicero, and to ridicule and charge with superstition those who rest their judgment upon the authority of a single MS. But if it is right carefully to pursue truth even in the smallest matters, if it is right to reverence even with pious feeling not only the sentiments but the literary tastes and little preferences of great geniuses, there is nothing—in matters which cannot be settled by any laws of human reason nor decided by any acuteness of judgment—there is nothing which I will trust sooner than even a single MS. It should, therefore, be well considered, whether, as in Germ. 24, *juvenior* is retained without any other example; so in Ann. VI., 17, *venditio et emitio* ought not to be retained, for which *emptio* is now read; and in Ann. IV., 66, I have preferred to change the corrupt *telerant* into *tetulerant* rather than into *tulerant.* Editors have retained other readings also, which had long since gone out of date, as Hist. I., 31, *necdum* for *nondum;* and Ann. III., 2, *munera fungi.* Nay, even the genitive *vis* has succeeded in maintaining its place, Dial. 26. And yet Ann. XIV., 7, *expergens;* Ann. I., 1, *false;* Ann. II., 14, the singular *sacri* for *hostiae;* Hist. I., 53, *decori juventa*, which are in no respect more unusual, have not obtained the same indulgence. It is surely a questionable scrupulosity which refuses such words to a writer who desired to be unique, and who did not even obtain an imitator, by a comparison with whom one can determine what he did and what he did not approve.

On the other hand, Tacitus, in my opinion, coined few new words; unless, perchance, some one may think that all those words, which are found in his writings alone, were of course originated by him. But it is extremely difficult to decide whether Tacitus was the first to use any word, or whether we read it for the first time in his writings. So long as he corresponds to all the rules for forming words, so far at least I think we ought to grant the indulgence to a writer who is universally acknowledged to have entertained no very great horror of the charge of novelty. *Irreverentia*, *improsper*, do indeed savor of novelty, as the *invidentia* of Cicero does, but they are conceded to Tacitus by all. I have not hesitated to propose by way of correction, in Hist. II., 21, the strange frequentative *retortant.* In Ann. XVI., 21, *expectabilis* is sufficiently defended by the authority of Tertullian; and I do not regret having recommended *confestinantius* in Ann. XV., 3, and *exapertae* in Hist. V., 13; or having defended *indictus favor* in Hist. III., 44.

18. But as an *innovator in the construction of words* he was exceedingly fruitful. He delighted in the unusual, as if itself an ornament, even though he gained nothing either in brevity or grace of style; as if he remembered the precept of Horace,

> Dixeris egregie, notum si callida verbum
> Reddiderit junctura novum.

I know not what other Latin author would have said *utilis pro nobis*, Agr. 12. I refrain from other examples, as they are obvious in every part of his works. In the use of the *historical infinitive* also, he differs from other writers by transferring it to present circumstances and customs of long standing. I would not have believed it, had not three instances conspired to prove it, still unchanged by all the pertinacious industry of editors, who, while they dispose of separate examples, have forgotten the others. These are Germ. 7, *audiri;* Agr. 34, *ruere;* and Dial. 30, *insumere.* I am inclined to think a fourth ought to be added, Ann. III., 54, *Tot a majoribus repertae leges . . . contemptu abolitae securiorem luxum facere*, where editors have *fecere;* not to mention those places in which I have recalled the usual infinitives from the MSS., Ann. I., 20; II., 2. 38; VI., 18; Hist. IV., 20; to which I ought to add Hist. II., 95, *Facem Augustales subdere;* and III., 17, *Quo pudore haud plures quam centum equites resistere;* and V., 10, *Pace per Italiam parta et externae curae redire*, where editions have *subdidere*, and *restitere*, and *rediere.* For no peculiarity of the Latin language might be expected to be more pleasing to Tacitus, none can be imagined better adapted to his style, so that I do not wonder that, in using it, he sometimes dared to go beyond proper limits. He may have shown audacity, and almost violence, but it would be a mark of even greater audacity and extravagance for us, who were born so many ages after him, in opposition to so many examples, which are defended by the authority of the MSS., and which not even the genius of the language convicts of fault, to attempt forcibly to abridge this license, merely from a comparison with other writers, to whom our author intended to be unlike.

Tacitus indulges in *Greek constructions*, such as are used only by a few, or by himself alone. For ancient writers, from the commencement of the Græco-Latin literature, had introduced many Græcisms into the Latin language, most of which the following age dropped in order to introduce others in their stead. See Agr. 34, *Ceterorum Britannorum fugacissimi*, an expression which the elder Pliny had used before. Also Hist. IV., 28, *Id nomen appellantur;* and Dial. 18, the words, *pro Catone magis*, resemble the Greek.

19. Tacitus exerted himself particularly to secure *concinnity*, so much so that he rarely neglected it, and some portions he adorned with exquisite art by the use of this rhetorical beauty. He even added superfluous words, provided they would contribute to concinnity; as Hist. II., 72, *Quidam militum errore* VERI *seu turbarum studio certatim aggregabantur.* He even disregarded the rules of grammar in his fondness for this ornament: e. g., Ann. IV., 3, *Ad conjugii spem, consortium regni et necem mariti impulit*, where the idea of *consortium* ought to depend upon *spem*, and therefore would regularly be in the genitive.

He was careful to close his periods with well-chosen clausules, whence that disagreement with grammatical rules in Ann. XIV., 16, *Species carminum . . . non uno fluens;* and Germ. 5, *Pecorum fecunda sed plerumque improcera.* Furthermore he observed the law of variety with solicitous care, sometimes for the sake of euphony, as Ann. II., 20, *quibus—quis;* sometimes to avoid the appearance of poverty in forms of expression. In this way he has sometimes troubled the reader, Ann. XV., 71, *Verginium Rufum claritudo nominis expulit; nam Verginius studia juvenum eloquentia, Musonius praeceptis sapientiae fovebat.* In Hist. II., 87, he employs the same artifice, *Calonum numerus amplior, procacissimis etiam inter servos lixarum ingeniis;* where he puts *lixae* instead of *calones*, in the last clause, for variety, both classes (cooks and campboys) being embraced under each name. But he is particularly fond of varying the *construction* by enallage; e. g., Hist. II., 79, *Illa Syriae, hoc Judaeae caput est;* Agr. 33, *ut . . decorum in frontem, ita fugientibus periculosissima.*

Very often he shows his love of variety in passing from the active to the passive, and *vice versa:* Hist. IV., 77; Germ. 29, *Nam nec tributis contemnuntur, nec publicanus adterit;* and Hist. III., 56, *Ignarus militiae, improvidus consiliis*, where editions have *consilii.*

Frequently he varies the form of construction, as if for no other purpose than to exhibit the richness of his mother tongue, and to show that the freedom of Latin writers could be abridged by no rigid and arbitrary rules: e. g., Ann. I., 18, *Plurimi detrita tegmina et nudum corpus exprobantes;* Hist. IV. 77, *Neque aliud excusandum habeo, quam quod vos Gallici foederis oblitos praedixerim, memoriam Romani sacramenti tenere credidi.* C. Roth has collected and explained many examples in Agr. Ex. XIII.

He also makes frequent use of the figures of rhetoric, in order to render his style brilliant, particularly of the *antithesis:* Hist. I., 36, *Omnia* SERVILITER *pro* DOMINATIONE; Ann. II., 52, *Spe* VICTORIAE *inducti sunt ut* VINCERENTUR; Hist. I., 65, *Uno amne* DISCRETIS CONNEXUM *odium.* *Alliterations* also, to which Latin authors are somewhat tempted by the very nature of their language: e. g., Ann. I., 51, *si poenitentiam, quam perniciem malebat;* A. 1, *virtus .... vicit vitium.* Moreover he abounds in what we call in barbarous Latin *allusiones.* No one is ignorant into what absurdities the scrupulousness of commentators has fallen, who, as often as they find certain words, similar to those of some former writer, cry out at once, "imitation." But Tacitus often does not imitate others, but rather alludes to them, especially the poets, by repeating some words, remarkable either for beauty of sentiment or felicity of expression, and thus exciting a pleasing recollection in his readers. And it is often doubtful whether he did this wittingly or unwittingly. Now none of the poets was better known, or more celebrated at that age, than Virgil, whose words, *Haec ubi dicta dedit,* Livy long ago had not hesitated to introduce into his narrative. Numberless expressions from the same author may be found in Tacitus, scattered here and there. More rarely will you find the words of Horace; as, Ann. XV., 37, *Ex illo contaminatorum grege,* coll. Carm. I., 37, 9, for I do not believe, that, in common prose, eunuchs come under the term *contaminati.* Nowhere, so far as I know, does he allude to Ovid, a writer entirely unlike himself in taste and style, for I am not of the opinion that the words in Agr. 44, were drawn from Ovid. Of prose writers he quoted Sallust most frequently. From a comparison with Livy, Trillerus has made a good correction in Hist. II., 80. Near the close of Agricola he manifestly refers his readers to a most beautiful passage of Cicero de Oratore. If I have rightly corrected Agr. 42, he has there quoted verbatim the language of Seneca. It were easy also to trace resemblances between Tacitus, Demosthenes, Thucydides, and Plato; and the verses of Homer are recognised in Hist. I., 80; and Agr. 34.

Thus much concerning the style of Tacitus. If I had undertaken to write a book on Tacitus, many topics would still remain to be discussed touching the genius of the writer, and his political and religious opinions; touching his learning, his fidelity, and his skill as an historian. But now, since I have no other purpose than to write a preface to my edition, I have briefly discussed some subjects and have passed by others, particularly those which it is evidently better to omit, than to treat briefly and therefore unsatisfactorily. And it is better that those who start such questions should consult those books, (and they are not a few), in which the ideas of men of pre-eminent talent have been ably and fully unfolded. But concerning the style of our author I have treated a little more extensively, in order to compensate for the small number and briefness of my notes; and, at the same time, if I should seem to have used too great boldness in either expressing an opinion or making a correction, to defend my position by bringing together under a single view the scattered examples. For this I have chiefly labored, and not with the more ambitious aim to set forth a sort of image and picture of the style of Tacitus. Whoever shall undertake this, will find not a few who will repeat to him these lines of Goethe:

> Nosciturо, descripturo, quod animo et vita viget,
> Hoc tibi providendum est, animum et vitam ut evites prius;
> Proinde partes exanimatas facili tractabis manu.

CHRONOLOGIA HISTORIARUM

EX

ZUMPTII POTISSIMUM ANNALIBUS DESUMPTA.*

A. U. C.	P. CHR.	COSS.		HIST
822	69	Ex Kal. Jan. Imp. Galba II. T. Vinius (Rufinus). Ex a. d. XVII. Kal. Febr. Imp. Otho, L. Salvius Otho Titianus. Ex Kal. Mart. T. Verginius Rufus, L. Pompeius Vopiscus.	Ineunte anno a superiore exercitu defectio coepit, mox ab utroque Germanico exercitu *A. Vitellius Imperator* salutatur. Eo nuntio accepto Galba Romae L. Pisonem Licinianum, nobilem et modestum adolescentem, sibi adoptat, sed praetorianorum animos omisso donativo magis etiam irritat. Itaque *M. Salvius* OTHO, qui et ipse adoptionem speraverat, conjurationem init, et *Imperator* a militibus declaratur: Galba, Piso, Vinius, Cornelius Laco, praefectus praetorio, aliique foede trucidantur, a. d. XVIII. Kal. Febr.	LIB. I. CAP. 1–49.
		Ex Kal. Maiis M. Caelius Sabinus, T. Flavius Sabinus. Ex Kal. Jul. T. Arrius Antoninus, P. Marius Celsus II. Ex Kal. Sept. C. Fabius Valens, A. Licinius Caecina. Ex pr. Kal. Nov. (pro Caecina) Rosius Regulus.	Paratur ingens de imperio certamen. A. Caecina, a Vitellio praemissus, Alpes Penninas Galliamque Transpadanam occupat: sequitur, subacta Gallia, cum altero exercitu C. Fabius Valens. Eis Otho suum exercitum apud *Bedriacum* opponit, duce fratre Titiano, neque Moesicas legiones jam appropinquantes exspectans, neque Suetonii Paullini prudentioribus consiliis utens. Vincuntur Othoniani, quo nuntio audito *Otho*, infelix bellum ducere nolens, Brixelli XII. Kal. Mai. nonagesimo quinto Imp. die *semet ipse interficit.* Ceteri Vitellio se dedunt, homini non malo, sed *ita gulae dedito, ut paucissimis mensibus novies millies* HS *consumpserit.*	LIB. I. CAP. 50 — LIB. II CAP. 72.
		Ex Kal. Nov. Cn. Caecilius Simplex, C. Quinctius Atticus.	Vixdum Romae honorem inierat, cum *T. Vespasianus*, prope confecto bello Judaico clarus, Muciano Syriae proconsule et Tito filio adhortantibus, principatum concupiscit. Kal. Juliis Alexandriae *Imperator* declaratur a Tiberio Alexandro, Aegypti praefecto; sequuntur Judaicae et Syriacae legiones, continuo, dimissis nuntiis, tres Moesicae, duae Pannonicae, auctore Antonio Primo, acerrimo partium defensore. Is injussu Vespasiani neque exspectato Muciani adventu legiones in Italiam rapit: con-	LIB. II. CAP. 73 — LIB. IV CAP. 11.

* We have copied this table from Orelli's Edition of the Historiae of Tacitus, Zurich, 1848.

A. U. C	P. Chr.	Coss.		Hist
			silia Vitellianorum proditione Caecinae (tum Consulis suffecti cum Valente) perturbantur, et novem legiones a paucioribus adversariis inter Bedriacum et Cremonam nocturno proelio profligantur; castris ad Cremonam vi captis, reliqui Vitelliani deduntur, urbs direpta incenditur. Jam Romam ducitur victor exercitus, sed lente: Apennini angustiae praesidiaque urbium produntur, dum Vitellius Romae, inter spem metumque haesitans, militum et vulgi studiis regitur. Hi Flavium Sabinum, Consularem, praefectum urbis, Vespasiani fratrem, cum reliquis Flavianarum partium sociis in Capitolium compellunt, nolente Vitellio, et templo incenso opprimunt. Sed adventu hostilis exercitus urbs caedibus impletur. Vitellius, latebris protractus, IX. Kal. Jan., quinquaginta septem annos natus, foede trucidatur; frater ejus L. cum reliquiis partium in Campania deditus et ipse interficitur. Omnia haec absente Vespasiano, qui Alexandriae substiterat, acta, sed urbanae res a Muciano et Domitiano, minore Vespasiani filio, utcunque componuntur.	
			Interea fortissima gens Batavorum a Romanis defecerat, duce Julio Civile, proximosque Germanos in partes traduxerat.	Lib. IV Cap 12–37.
823	70	Ex Kal. Jan. Imp. Vespasianus II. Titus Caesar Augusti filius. Ex Kal. Jul. C. Licinius Mucianus II. P. Valerius Asiaticus. Ex Kal. Nov. L. Annius Bassus, C. Caecina Paetus.	Kalendis Januariis absentibus consulibus senatum habet *Julius Frontinus*, praetor urbanus, cui cum ejurasset, succedit Fl. Domitianus cum potestate consulari. Etiam Lingones ac Treveri. Batavorum exemplum secuti, a Romanis deficiunt, ducibus Classico Julioque Tutore, et ipsas legiones Romanas, seditionibus perturbatas, ad sacramentum pro imperio Galliarum faciendum adigunt. Sed mox Petilius Cerialis, a Vespasiano missus, Treveros in potestatem redigit; etiam Civilis duobus proeliis victus ad pacem petendam compellitur Julius Sabinus, Lingonus, in monumento quodam abditus per novem annos latet.	Lib. IV Cap. 38-86. Lib. V. Cap. 14-26.
			Eodem tempore Titus Caesar cum valido exercitu haud procul Hierosolymis castra facit et sexcenta milia Judaeorum obsidet. (Urbe capta atque eversa Judaeis per totum Imp. Rom. tributum annuum binarum drachmarum imponitur, ex quo templum Jovis Capitolini restituatur. Sed regnum Ituraeae Agrippae minori servatum est, cujus sororem Berenicen Titus deperit.)	Lib. V Cap. 1–13.

C. CORNELII TACITI

HISTORIARUM

LIBER PRIMUS.

BREVIARIUM LIBRI.

Cap. I. Praefamen. Auctoris dignitas, aetas, institutum. II, III. Praesentis historiae summa capita. IV, V. Status urbis, mens exercituum, habitus provinciarum, occiso Nerone. Nymphidius, imperium affectans, oppressus. VI, VII. Galbam crudelitas sua, aetas, corporis forma et amicorum vitia reddunt invisum. VIII, IX. Status Hispaniae, Galliae, Germanicorum exercituum, Britanniae, Illyrici. X. In Syria Muciani virtutes et vitia. Fl. Vespasiani, Judaicum bellum administrantis, animus in Galbam. XI. Aegypti, Africae, Mauretaniae, Rhaetiae, Norici, Thraciae, Italiae status COSS. Galba et Vinio.

XII. Deficiente superioris Germaniae milite, Galba de adoptando Caesare cogitat. XIII. Vinius Othoni favet, non ita Laco et Icelus. XIV. Galba, transactis imperii comitiis, Pisonem eligit, hominem antiqui moris et severum, cui, XV, XVI, adoptionis causas et imperii administrandi consilium aperit. XVII. Pisonis inter haec moderatio. XVIII. Adoptio in castris nuncupata, XIX, tum in senatu. Legati ad defectores missi. XX. Neronis prodigae donationes rescissae.

XXI. Othoni spe lapso consilium in turbido, XXII, instigantibus libertis, servis, mathematicis; XXIII, XXIV, paratis jam ante militum studiis per blanditias et largitiones, oscitante ad id praefecto. XXV, XXVI. Ergo jam legiones et auxilia pro Othone. XXVII. Mox consalutatus imperator, XXVIII, castris praetorianis infertur.

XXIX, XXX. Piso cohortem, quae in palatio stationem agit, hortatur ad fidem. XXXI. Illa parat signa, reliquis copiis deficientibus. XXXII, XXXIII. Plebis adulatio et levitas. Fluctuat Galba cum amicis, an occurrendum? XXXIV. Praemittitur in castra Piso. Falsus de occiso Othone rumor. XXXV. Populus et senatus Galbae; XXXVI, castra Othoni favent. XXXVII, XXXVIII. Hic militum animos oratione sibi conciliat, Galbae et Pisoni reddit infensos. Arma militi dividit. XXXIX. Agitat Laco de caede Vinii. XL. Galba fluctuat. Plebs nutat. Othoniani forum irrumpunt. XLI. Galba desertus, occisus, XLII, sic et Vinius. XLIII. Sempronii fides. Piso caesus, XLIV, magna Othonis laetitia. Caedium praemia poscentes jussu Vitellii postea interfecti. XLV. Adulantur senatus et populus victorem Othonem, qui coercendo militum furori impar: XLVI, hi vacationes sibi remitti petunt. Laco et Icelus caesi. XLVII. Pisonis et T. Vinii sepultura, XLVIII, elogia, testamenta. XLIX. Galbae sepultura, aetas, nobilitas, mores, honores.

L. Trepidam urbem novus de Vitellio nuntius exterret. Vespasianum nonnulli augurantur. LI. Initia Vitelliani motus ex bello Julii Vindicis, et secutis inde discordiis inter legiones et Gallos. LII, LIII. Vitellius, suo ingenio ignavus, ad res novas stimulatur a Valente et Caecina Legatis. LIV, LV. Legiones utriusque Germaniae fidem in Galbam exuunt, LVI, segni spectatore Hordeonio Flacco legato. LVII. Valens Vitellium imperatorem consalutat, magno militum studio; LVIII, quibus poscentibus multi caesi. LIX. Julius Civilis periculum evadit. Undique viribus auctus, LX, inter foedas legatorum discordias, LXI, duos exercitus in Italiam mittit. LXII. Torpet Vitellius; ardor et vis militum ultro ducis munia implet. LXIII. Subito furore correptus miles ab excidio Divoduri aegre temperat. Gallias terror invadit. LXIV. Vitellio adhaerent. LXV. Lugdunenses ex vetere odio milites in eversionem Viennensium impellunt; LXVI, isti tamen donis placantur et precibus. Valentis avaritia et libido. LXVII, LXVIII. Helvetios, Vitellii imperium abnuentes, Caecina belli avidus caedit. LXIX. Aventicum aegre impunitatem salutemque impetrat. LXX. In Vitellii partes transgressa Italiae parte, Caecina Alpes superat.

LXXI. Otho prudenter se gerit; Mario Celso ignoscit. LXXII. Tigellinus infamem vitam exitu inhonesto foedat. LXXIII. Galvia Crispinilla cum mala Othonis fama periculo exempta. LXXIV. Principes mutuo sibi conditiones offerunt; mox rixantes flagitia invicem objectant, et LXXV, insidiatores immittunt. LXXVI. Distractis inter utrumque exercitibus ac provinciis, bello opus. LXXVII. Otho imperatorem agit; honores, LXXVIII, civitatem, jura dilargitur: de celebranda Neronis memoria agitat.

LXXIX. Sarmatae Roxolani Moesiam irrumpentes caesi. LXXX—LXXXII. Seditio gravis, in ipsa urbe temere orta, cum magno metu atque discrimine primorum civitatis, precibus et lacrimis Othonis componitur, qui LXXXIII, LXXXIV, milites ad concordiam et modestiam hortatur. LXXXV. Istis compositis, omnia suspicionum et formidinis plena, praecipuo patrum metu. LXXXVI. Prodigia Othonis cladem praesagientia. LXXXVII. Is, lustrata urbe, Narbonensem Galliam aggredi statuit, et LXXXVIII, cum multis nobilibus L. Vitellium aemuli fratrem secum ducit. LXXXIX. Inde varii animorum motus. XC. Commendata patribus republica Otho festinat ad bellum. Trachali eloquentia usus Otho, in quem studia et voces vulgi. Gesta haec paucis mensibus,

IMP. SERV. GALBA ET T. VINIO COSS.

INITIUM mihi operis Ser. Galba iterum, T. Vinius consules erunt. Nam, post conditam urbem octingentos et viginti prioris aevi annos multi auctores retulerunt, dum res populi Romani memorabantur, pari eloquentia ac libertate: postquam bellatum apud Actium atque omnem potentiam ad unum conferri pacis interfuit, magna illa ingenia cessere; simul veritas pluribus modis infracta, primum inscitia reipublicae ut alienae, mox libidine assentandi, aut rursus odio adversus dominantes: ita neutris cura posteritatis, inter infensos vel obnoxios. Sed ambitionem scriptoris facile adverseris, obtrectatio et livor pronis auribus accipiuntur: quippe adulationi foedum crimen servitutis, malignitati falsa species libertatis inest. Mihi Galba, Otho, Vitellius nec beneficio nec injuria cogniti. Dignitatem nostram a Vespasiano inchoatam, a Tito auctam, a Domitiano longius provectam non abnuerim: sed incorruptam fidem professis nec amore quisquam et sine odio dicendus est. Quod si vita suppeditet, principatum divi Nervae, et imperium Trajani, uberiorem securioremque materiam, senectuti seposui, rara temporum felicitate, ubi sentire quae velis, et quae sentias dicere, licet.

II. Opus aggredior opimum casibus, atrox proeliis, discors seditionibus, ipsa etiam pace saevum. Quatuor principes ferro interempti: trina bella civilia, plura externa ac plerumque permixta: prosperae in Oriente, adversae in Occidente res: turbatum Illyricum: Galliae nutantes: perdomita Britannia et statim missa: coortae in nos Sarmatarum ac Suevorum gentes: nobilitatus cladibus mutuis Dacus: mota etiam prope Parthorum arma, falsi Neronis ludibrio. Jam vero Italia novis cladibus, vel post longam saeculorum seriem repetitis, afflicta. Haustae aut obrutae urbes, fecundissima Campaniae ora: et urbs incendiis vastata, consumptis antiquissimis delubris, ipso Capitolio civium manibus incenso: pollutae caerimoniae; magna adulteria; plenum exsiliis mare; infecti caedibus scopuli. Atrocius in Urbe saevitum. Nobilitas, opes, omissi gestique honores pro crimine, et ob virtutes certissimum exitium. Nec minus praemia delatorum invisa, quam scelera; cum alii sacerdotia et consulatus ut spolia adepti, procurationes alii et interiorem potentiam, agerent verterent cuncta odio et terrore. Corrupti in dominos servi, in patronos liberti; et, quibus deerat inimicus, per amicos oppressi.

III. Non tamen adeo virtutum sterile saeculum, ut non et bona exempla prodiderit. Comitatae profugos liberos matres, secutae maritos in exsilia conjuges; propinqui audentes, constantes generi; contumax etiam adversus tormenta servorum fides: supremae clarorum virorum necessitates; ipsa necessitas fortiter tolerata, et laudatis antiquorum mortibus pares exitus. Praeter multiplices rerum humanarum casus coelo terraque prodigia, et fulminum monitus et futurorum praesagia, laeta, tristia, ambigua, manifesta. Nec enim unquam atrocioribus populi Romani cladibus magisve justis indiciis approbatum est, non esse curae deis securitatem nostram, esse ultionem.

IV. Ceterum antequam destinata componam, repetendum videtur, qualis status urbis, quae mens exercituum, quis habitus provinciarum, quid in toto terrarum orbe validum, quid aegrum fuerit; ut non modo casus eventusque rerum, qui plerumque fortuiti sunt, sed ratio etiam causaeque noscantur. Finis Neronis ut laetus primo gaudentium impetu fuerat, ita varios motus animorum, non modo in urbe apud patres aut populum aut urbanum militem, sed omnes legiones ducesque conciverat, evulgato imperii arcano posse principem alibi, quam Romae fieri. Sed patres laeti, usurpata statim libertate licentius ut erga principem novum et absentem; primores equitum proximi gaudio patrum; pars populi integra et magnis domibus annexa, clientes libertique damnatorum et exsulum in spem erecti: plebs sordida et circo ac theatris sueta, simul deterrimi servorum, aut qui, adesis bonis, per dedecus Neronis alebantur, maesti et rumorum avidi.

V. Miles urbanus, longo Caesarum sacramento imbutus et ad destituendum Neronem arte magis et impulsu quam suo ingenio traductus, postquam neque dari donativum, sub nomine Galbae promissum, neque magnis meritis ac praemiis eundem in pace quem in bello locum, praeventamque gratiam intelligit apud principem a legionibus factum, pronus ad novas res, scelere insuper Nymphidii Sabini praefecti imperium sibi molientis agitatur. Et Nymphidius quidem in ipso conatu oppressus: sed, quamvis capite defectionis ablato, manebat plerisque militum conscientia; nec deerant sermones, senium atque avaritiam Galbae increpantium. Laudata olim et militari fama celebrata severitas ejus angebat aspernantes veterem disciplinam, atque ita quatuordecim annis a Nerone assuefactos, ut haud minus vitia principum amarent, quam olim virtutes verebantur. Accessit Galbae vox, pro republica honesta, ipsi anceps, "legi a se militem, non emi." Nec enim ad hanc formam cetera erant.

VI. Invalidum senem T. Vinius et Cornelius Laco, alter deterrimus mortalium, alter ignavissimus, odio flagitiorum oneratum contemptu inertiae destruebant. Tardum Galbae iter et cruentum, interfectis Cingonio Varrone consule designato et Petronio Turpiliano consulari: ille, ut Nymphidii socius, hic, ut dux Neronis, inauditi atque indefensi, tanquam innocentes, perierant. Introitus in urbem, trucidatis tot millibus inermium militum, infaustus omine, atque ipsis etiam qui occiderant formidolosus. Inducta legione Hispana, remanente ea quam e classe Nero conscripserat, plena urbs exercitu insolito: multi ad hoc numeri e Germania ac Britannia et Illyrico, quos idem Nero electos praemissosque ad claustra Caspiarum et bellum quod in Albanos parabat, opprimendis Vindicis coeptis revocaverat: ingens novis rebus materia, ut non in unum aliquem prono favore, ita audenti parata.

VII. Forte congruerat, ut Clodii Macri et Fonteii Capitonis caedes nuntiarentur. Macrum in Africa haud dubie turbantem, Trebonius Garutianus procurator, jussu Galbae, Capitonem in Germania cum similia coeptaret Cornelius

Aquinus et Fabius Valens legati legionum interfecerant, antequam juberentur. Fuere qui crederent, Capitonem, ut avaritia et libidine foedum ac maculosum, ita cogitatione rerum novarum abstinuisse; sed a legatis, bellum suadentibus, postquam impellere nequiverint, crimen ac dolum ultro compositum: at Galbam mobilitate ingenii, an ne altius scrutaretur, quoquo modo acta, quia mutari non poterant, comprobasse. Ceterum utraque caedes sinistre accepta; et inviso semel principe, seu bene seu male facta premunt. Jam afferebant venalia cuncta praepotentes liberti; servorum manus subitis avidae, et tanquam apud senem festinantes; eademque novae aulae mala, aeque gravia, non aeque excusata. Ipsa aetas Galbae irrisui ac fastidio erat assuetis juventae Neronis et imperatores forma ac decore corporis, ut est mos vulgi, comparantibus.

VIII. Et hic quidem Romae, tanquam in tanta multitudine, habitus animorum fuit. E provinciis, Hispaniae praeerat Cluvius Rufus, vir facundus et pacis artibus, bellis inexpertus. Galliae, super memoriam Vindicis, obligatae recenti dono Romanae civitatis et in posterum tributi levamento. Proximae tamen Germanicis exercitibus Galliarum civitates non eodem honore habitae, quaedam etiam finibus ademptis, pari dolore commoda aliena ac suas injurias metiebantur. Germanici exercitus, quod periculosissimum in tantis viribus, solliciti et irati superbia recentis victoriae et metu, tanquam alias partes fovissent. Tarde a Nerone desciverant; nec statim pro Galba Verginius: an imperare voluisset, dubium; delatum ei a milite imperium conveniebat. Fonteium Capitonem occisum, etiam qui queri non poterant, tamen indignabantur. Dux deerat, abducto Verginio per simulationem amicitiae: quem non remitti atque etiam reum esse tanquam suum crimen accipiebant.

IX. Superior exercitus legatum Hordeonium Flaccum spernebat, senecta ac debilitate pedum invalidum, sine constantia, sine auctoritate: ne quieto quidem milite, regimen; adeo furentes infirmitate retinentis ultro accendebantur. Inferioris Germaniae legiones diutius sine consulari fuere, donec missu Galbae A. Vitellius aderat, censoris Vitellii ac ter consulis filius: id satis videbatur. In Britannico exercitu nihil irarum. Non sane aliae legiones per omnes civilium bellorum motus innocentius egerunt, seu quia procul et Oceano divisae, seu crebris expeditionibus doctae hostem potius odisse. Quies et Illyrico, quanquam excitae a Nerone legiones, dum in Italia cunctantur, Verginium legationibus adissent. Sed longis spatiis discreti exercitus, quod saluberrimum est ad continendam militarem fidem, nec vitiis nec viribus miscebantur.

X. Oriens adhuc immotus. Syriam et quatuor legiones obtinebat Licinius Mucianus, vir secundis adversisque juxta famosus. Insignes amicitias juvenis ambitiose coluerat: mox, attritis opibus, lubrico statu, suspecta etiam Claudii iracundia, in secretum Asiae repositus, tam prope ab exsule fuit, quam postea a principe. Luxuria, industria, comitate, arrogantia, malis bonisque artibus mixtus: nimiae voluptates, cum vacaret; quotiens expedierat, magnae virtutes: palam laudares; secreta male audiebant. Sed apud subjectos, apud proximos, apud collegas, variis illecebris potens, et cui expeditius fuerit tradere imperium, quam obtinere. Bellum Judaicum Flavius Vespasianus (ducem eum Nero delegerat) tribus legionibus administrabat. Nec Vespasiano adversus Galbam votum aut animus. Quippe Titum filium ad venerationem cultumque ejus miserat, ut suo loco memorabimus. Occulta lege fati et ostentis ac responsis destinatum Vespasiano liberisque ejus imperium, post fortunam credidimus.

XI. Aegyptum copiasque, quibus coerceretur, jam inde a divo Augusto, equites Romani obtinent loco regum. Ita visum expedire, provinciam aditu difficilem, annonae fecundam, superstitione ac lascivia discordem ac mobilem, insciam legum, ignaram magistratuum, domi retinere. Regebat tum Tiberius Alexander, ejusdem nationis. Africa ac legiones in ea, interfecto Clodio Macro, contenta qualicumque principe, post experimentum domini minoris. Duae Mauretaniae, Raetia, Noricum, Thracia, et quae aliae procuratoribus cohibentur, ut cuique exercitui vicinae, ita in favorem aut odium contactu valentiorum agebantur. Inermes provinciae, atque ipsa in primis Italia, cuicunque servitio exposita, in pretium belli cessurae erant. Hic fuit rerum Romanarum status, cum Ser. Galba iterum, Titus Vinius consules inchoavere annum sibi ultimum, reipublicae prope supremum.

XII. Paucis post Kalendas Januarias diebus Pompeii Propinqui procuratoris e Belgica literae afferuntur: "superioris Germaniae legiones, rupta sacramenti reverentia, imperatorem alium flagitare, et senatui ac populo Romano arbitrium eligendi permittere;" quo seditio mollius acciperetur. Maturavit ea res consilium Galbae jam pridem de adoptione secum et cum proximis agitantis. Non sane crebrior tota civitate sermo per illos menses fuerat, primum licentia ac libidine talia loquendi, dein fessa jam aetate Galbae. Paucis judicium aut reipublicae amor: multi stulta spe, prout quis amicus vel cliens, hunc vel illum ambitiosis rumoribus destinabant, etiam in T. Vinii odium, qui in dies quanto potentior, eodem actu invisior erat. Quippe hiantes in magna fortuna amicorum cupiditates ipsa Galbae facilitas intendebat: cum apud infirmum et credulum minore metu et majore praemio peccaretur.

XIII. Potentia principatus divisa in T. Vinium consulem et Cornelium Laconem praetorii praefectum. Nec minor gratia Icelo Galbae liberto, quem annulis donatum equestri nomine Marcianum vocitabant. Hi discordes, et rebus minoribus sibi quisque tendentes, circa consilium eligendi successoris in duas factiones scindebantur. Vinius pro M. Othone: Laco atque Icelus consensu non tam unum aliquem fovebant quam alium. Neque erat Galbae ignota Othonis ac T. Vinii amicitia; et rumoribus nihil silentio transmittentium, quia Vinio vidua filia, caelebs Otho, gener ac socer destinabantur. Credo et reipublicae curam subisse, frustra a Nerone translatae, si apud Othonem relinqueretur. Namque Otho pueritiam incuriose, adolescentiam petulanter egerat, gratus Neroni aemulatione luxus: eoque jam Poppaeam Sabinam, principale scortum, ut apud conscium libidinum, deposuerat, donec Octaviam uxorem amoliretur; mox suspectum in eadem Poppaea in provinciam

Lusitaniam specie legationis seposuit. Otho, comiter administrata provincia, primus in partes transgressus, nec segnis, et, donec bellum fuit, inter praesentes splendidissimus, spem adoptionis statim conceptam acrius in dies rapiebat, faventibus plerisque militum, prona in eum aula Neronis ut similem.

XIV. Sed Galba, post nuntios Germanicae seditionis, quanquam nihil adhuc de Vitellio certum, anxius quonam exercituum vis erumperet, ne urbano quidem militi confisus, quod remedium unicum rebatur, comitia imperii transigit; adhibitoque, super Vinium ac Laconem, Mario Celso consule designato ac Ducennio Gemino praefecto urbis, pauca praefatus de sua senectute, Pisonem Licinianum arcessi jubet, seu propria electione, sive, ut quidam crediderunt, Lacone instante, cui apud Rubellium Plautum exercita cum Pisone amicitia; sed callide ut ignotum fovebat, et prospera de Pisone fama consilio ejus fidem addiderat. Piso M. Crasso et Scribonia genitus, nobilis utrimque, vultu habituque moris antiqui, et aestimatione recta severus, deterius interpretantibus tristior habebatur: ea pars morum ejus, quo suspectior sollicitis, adoptanti placebat.

XV. Igitur Galba, apprehensa Pisonis manu, in hunc modum locutus fertur: "Si te privatus lege curiata apud pontifices, ut moris est, adoptarem, et mihi egregium erat Cn. Pompeii et M. Crassi sobolem in penates meos asciscere, et tibi insigne Sulpiciae ac Lutatiae decora nobilitati tuae adjecisse. Nunc me deorum hominumque consensu ad imperium vocatum praeclara indoles tua et amor patriae impulit, ut principatum, de quo majores nostri armis certabant, bello adeptus quiescenti offeram, exemplo divi Augusti, qui sororis filium Marcellum, dein generum Agrippam, mox nepotes suos, postremo Tiberium Neronem privignum, in proximo sibi fastigio collocavit. Sed Augustus in domo successorem quaesivit, ego in republica; non quia propinquos aut socios belli non habeam; sed neque ipse imperium ambitione accepi, et judicii mei documentum sint non meæ tantum necessitudines, quas tibi postposui, sed et tuae. Est tibi frater pari nobilitate, natu major, dignus hac fortuna, nisi tu potior esses. Ea aetas tua, quae cupiditates adolescentiae jam effugerit: ea vita, in qua nihil praeteritum excusandum habeas. Fortunam adhuc tantum adversam tulisti; secundae res acrioribus stimulis animos explorant, quia miseriae tolerantur, felicitate corrumpimur. Fidem, libertatem, amicitiam, praecipua humani animi bona, tu quidem eadem constantia retinebis, sed alii per obsequium imminuent. Irrumpet adulatio, blanditiae, pessimum veri affectus venenum, sua cuique utilitas. Et jam ego ac tu simplicissime inter nos hodie loquimur: ceteri libentius cum fortuna nostra quam nobiscum. Nam suadere principi, quod oporteat, multi laboris: assentatio erga principem quemcumque sine affectu peragitur.

XVI. "Si immensum imperii corpus stare ac librari sine rectore posset, dignus eram a quo respublica inciperet: nunc eo necessitatis jam pridem ventum est, ut nec mea senectus conferre plus populo Romano possit quam bonum successorem, nec tua plus juventa, quam bonum principem. Sub Tiberio et Caio et Claudio, unius familiae quasi hereditas fuimus: loco libertatis erit, quod eligi coepimus. Et, finita Juliorum Claudiorumque domo, optimum quemque adoptio inveniet. Nam generari et nasci a principibus fortuitum, nec ultra aestimatur: adoptandi judicium integrum, et, si velis eligere, consensu monstratur. Sit ante oculos Nero, quem longa Caesarum serie tumentem, non Vindex cum inermi provincia aut ego cum una legione, sed sua immanitas, sua luxuria, cervicibus publicis depulere; neque erat adhuc damnati principis exemplum. Nos bello et ab aestimantibus asciti, cum invidia, quamvis egregii, erimus. Ne tamen territus fueris, si duae legiones in hoc concussi orbis motu nondum quiescunt. Ne ipse quidem ad securas res accessi: et, audita adoptione, desinam videri senex, quod nunc mihi unum objicitur. Nero a pessimo quoque semper desiderabitur: mihi ac tibi providendum est, ne etiam a bonis desideretur. Monere diutius neque temporis hujus, et impletum est omne consilium, si te bene elegi. Utilissimus idem ac brevissimus bonarum malarumque rerum delectus est cogitare, quid aut volueris sub alio principe aut nolueris. Neque enim hic, ut gentibus quae regnantur, certa dominorum domus et ceteri servi; sed imperaturus es hominibus, qui nec totam servitutem pati possunt nec totam libertatem." Et Galba quidem haec ac talia, tanquam principem faceret; ceteri tanquam cum facto loquebantur.

XVII. Pisonem ferunt statim intuentibus, et mox conjectis in eum omnium oculis, nullum turbati aut exsultantis animi motum prodidisse. Sermo erga patrem imperatoremque reverens, de se moderatus; nihil in vultu habituque mutatum, quasi imperare posset magis quam vellet. Consultatum inde, pro rostris an in senatu an in castris adoptio nuncuparetur. Iri in castra placuit: honorificum id militibus fore, quorum favorem, ut largitione et ambitu male acquiri, ita per bonas artes haud spernendum. Circumsteterat interim palatium publica expectatio magni secreti impatiens; et male coercitam famam supprimentes augebant.

XVIII. Quartum Idus Januarias, foedum imbribus diem, tonitrua et fulgura et coelestes minae ultra solitum turbaverant. Observatum id antiquitus comitiis dirimendis non terruit Galbam, quo minus in castra pergeret, contemptorem talium ut fortuitorum, seu quae fato manent, quamvis significata, non vitantur. Apud frequentem militum concionem, imperatoria brevitate, adoptari a se Pisonem more divi Augusti et exemplo militari, quo vir virum legeret, pronuntiat. Ac ne dissimulata seditio in majus crederetur, ultro asseverat quartam et duodevicesimam legiones, paucis seditionis auctoribus, non ultra verba ac voces errasse, et brevi in officio fore. Nec ullum orationi aut lenocinium addit aut pretium. Tribuni tamen centurionesque et proximi militum grata auditu respondent: per ceteros maestitia ac silentium, tanquam usurpatam etiam in pace donativi necessitatem bello perdidissent. Constat potuisse conciliari animos quantulacumque parci senis liberalitate: nocuit antiquus rigor et nimia severitas, cui jam pares non sumus.

XIX. Inde apud senatum non comptior Galbae, non longior quam apud militem sermo: Pisonis comis oratio.

Et patrum favor aderat; multi voluntate effusius; qui noluerant medie; ac plurimi obvio obsequio, privatas spes agitantes sine publica cura. Nec aliud sequenti quatriduo, quod medium inter adoptionem et caedem fuit, dictum a Pisone in publico factumve. Crebrioribus in dies Germanicae defectionis nuntiis et facili civitate ad accipienda credendaque omnia nova, cum tristia sunt, censuerant patres mittendos ad Germanicum exercitum legatos: agitatum secreto, num et Piso proficisceretur majore praetextu; illi auctoritatem senatus, hic dignationem Caesaris laturus. Placebat et Laconem praetorii praefectum simul mitti: is consilio intercessit. Legati quoque (nam senatus electionem Galbae permiserat) foeda inconstantia nominati, excusati, substituti, ambitu remanendi aut eundi, ut quemque metus vel spes impulerat.

XX. Proxima pecuniae cura: et cuncta scrutantibus justissimum visum est inde repeti, ubi inopiae causa erat. Bis et vicies millies sestertium donationibus Nero effuderat. Appellari singulos jussit, decuma parte liberalitatis apud quemque eorum relicta. At illis vix decumae super portiones erant, iisdem erga aliena sumptibus, quibus sua prodegerant, cum rapacissimo cuique ac perditissimo non agri aut fenus, sed sola instrumenta vitiorum manerent. Exactioni triginta equites Romani praepositi; novum officii genus et ambitu ac numero onerosum: ubique hasta et sector; et inquieta urbs actionibus. Attamen grande gaudium, quod tam pauperes forent, quibus donasset Nero, quam quibus abstulisset. Exauctorati per eos dies tribuni, e praetorio Antonius Taurus et Antonius Naso, ex urbanis cohortibus Aemilius Pacensis, e vigiliis Julius Fronto. Nec remedium in ceteros fuit, sed metus initium, tanquam per artem et formidinem singuli pellerentur omnibus suspectis.

XXI. Interea Othonem, cui compositis rebus nulla spes, omne in turbido consilium, multa simul exstimulabant, luxuria etiam principi onerosa, inopia vix privato toleranda, in Galbam ira, in Pisonem invidia. Fingebat et metum, quo magis concupisceret. "Praegravem se Neroni fuisse, nec Lusitaniam rursus et alterius exsilii honorem expectandum: suspectum semper invisumque dominantibus, qui proximus destinaretur. Nocuisse id sibi apud senem principem: magis nociturum apud juvenem ingenio trucem et longo exsilio efferatum: occidi Othonem posse; proinde agendum audendumque, dum Galbae auctoritas fluxa, Pisonis nondum coaluisset. Opportunos magnis conatibus transitus rerum; nec cunctatione opus, ubi perniciosior sit quies quam temeritas. Mortem omnibus ex natura aequalem, oblivione apud posteros vel gloria distingui. Ac si nocentem innocentemque idem exitus maneat, acrioris viri esse merito perire."

XXII. Non erat Othonis mollis et corpori similis animus. Et intimi libertorum servorumque, corruptius quam in privata domo habiti, aulam Neronis et luxus, adulteria, matrimonia, ceterasque regnorum libidines avido talium, si auderet, ut sua ostentantes, quiescenti, ut aliena, exprobrabant, urgentibus etiam mathematicis, dum novos motus, et clarum Othoni annum observatione siderum affirmant, genus hominum potentibus infidum, sperantibus fallax, quod in civitate nostra et vetabitur semper et retinebitur. Multos secreta Poppaeae mathematicos, pessimum principalis matrimonii instrumentum, habuerant; e quibus Ptolemaeus Othoni in Hispania comes, cum superfuturum eum Neroni promisisset, postquam ex eventu fides, conjectura jam et rumore senium Galbae et juventam Othonis computantium persuaserat fore, ut in imperium asscisceretur. Sed Otho tanquam peritia et monitu fatorum praedicta accipiebat, cupidine ingenii humani libentius obscura credendi.

XXIII. Nec deerat Ptolemaeus, jam et sceleris instinctor, ad quod facillime ab ejusmodi voto transitur. Sed sceleris cogitatio incertum an repens: studia militum jam pridem spe successionis aut paratu facinoris affectaverat; in itinere, in agmine, in stationibus, vetustissimum quemque militum nomine vocans, ac memoria Neroniani comitatus contubernales appellando; alios agnoscere, quosdam requirere et pecunia aut gratia juvare, inserendo saepius querelas et ambiguos de Galba sermones, quaeque alia turbamenta vulgi.

Labores itinerum, inopia commeatuum, duritia imperii atrocius accipiebantur, cum Campaniae lacus et Achaiae urbes classibus adire soliti Pyrenaeum et Alpes et immensa viarum spatia aegre sub armis eniterentur.

XXIV. Flagrantibus jam militum animis velut faces addiderat Maevius Pudens e proximis Tigellini. Is mobilissimum quemque ingenio aut pecuniae indigum et in novas cupiditates praecipitem alliciendo, eo paulatim progressus est, ut per speciem convivii, quotiens Galba apud Othonem epularetur, cohorti excubias agenti viritim centenos nummos divideret; quam velut publicam largitionem Otho secretioribus apud singulos praemiis intendebat, adeo animosus corruptor, ut Cocceio Proculo speculatori de parte finium cum vicino ambigenti, universum vicini agrum sua pecunia emptum dono dederit, per socordiam praefecti, quem nota pariter et occulta fallebant.

XXV. Sed tum e libertis Onomastum futuro sceleri praefecit, a quo Barbium Proculum tesserarium speculatorum et Veturium optionem eorundem perductos, postquam vario sermone callidos audacesque cognovit, pretio et promissis onerat, data pecunia ad pertentandos plurium animos. Suscepere duo manipulares imperium populi Romani transferendum; et transtulerunt. In conscientiam facinoris pauci asciti: suspensos ceterorum animos diversis artibus stimulant, primores militum per beneficia Nymphidii ut suspectos, vulgus et ceteros ira et desperatione dilati totiens donativi; erant, quos memoria Neronis ac desiderium prioris licentiae accenderet: in commune omnes metu mutandae militiae terrebantur.

XXVI. Infecit ea tabes legionum quoque et auxiliorum motas jam mentes, postquam vulgatum erat labare Germanici exercitus fidem: adeoque parata apud malos seditio, etiam apud integros dissimulatio fuit, ut postero iduum dierum redeuntem a coena Othonem rapturi fuerint, ni incerta noctis et tota urbe sparsa militum castra nec facilem inter temulentos consensum timuissent, non reipublicae cura, quam foedare principis sui sanguine sobrii parabant, sed ne per tenebras, ut quisque Pannonici vel Germanici exercitus militibus oblatus esset, ignorantibus plerisque, pro Othone destinaretur. Multa erumpentis seditionis indicia per conscios oppressa; quaedam apud Galbae aures praefectus Laco elusit, ignarus militarium animorum, consiliique quamvis egregii, quod non ipse afferret, inimicus, et adversus peritos pervicax.

XXVII. Octavodecimo Kalendas Februarii, sacrificanti pro aede Apollinis Galbae haruspex Umbricius tristia exta et instantes insidias ac domesticum hostem praedicit, audiente Othone (nam proximus astiterat) idque ut laetum e contrario et suis cogitationibus prosperum interpretante. Nec multo post libertus Onomastus nuntiat exspectari eum ab architecto et redemptoribus; quae significatio coeuntium jam militum et paratae conjurationis convenerat. Otho, causam digressus requirentibus, cum emi sibi praedia vetustate suspecta eoque prius exploranda finxisset, innixus liberto per Tiberianam domum in Velabrum, inde ad milliarium aureum sub aedem Saturni pergit. Ibi tres et viginti speculatores consalutatum imperatorem ac paucitate salutantium trepidum et sellae festinanter impositum strictis mucronibus rapiunt. Totidem ferme milites in itinere aggregantur, alii conscientia, plerique miraculo, pars clamore et gaudiis, pars silentio, animum ex eventu sumpturi.

XXVIII. Stationem in castris agebat Julius Martialis tribunus. Is magnitudine subiti sceleris, an corrupta latius castra et, si contra tenderet, exitium metuens, praebuit plerisque suspicionem conscientiae. Anteposuere ceteri quoque tribuni centurionesque praesentia dubiis et honestis: isque habitus animorum fuit, ut pessimum facinus auderent pauci, plures vellent, omnes paterentur.

XXIX. Ignarus interim Galba et sacris intentus fatigabat alieni jam imperii deos, cum affertur rumor rapi in castra incertum quem senatorem; mox, Othonem esse, qui raperetur: simul ex tota urbe, ut quisque obvius fuerat, alii formidine augentes, quidam minora vero, ne tum quidem obliti adulationis. Igitur consultantibus placuit pertentari animum cohortis, quae in palatio stationem agebat, nec per ipsum Galbam, cujus integra auctoritas majoribus remediis servabatur. Piso pro gradibus domus vocatos in hunc modum allocutus est: "Sextus dies agitur, commilitones, ex quo ignarus futuri et sive optandum hoc nomen sive timendum erat, Caesar ascitus sum; quo domus nostrae aut reipublicae fato in vestra manu positum est: non quia meo nomine tristiorem casum paveam ut qui adversas res expertus cum maxime discam ne secundas quidem minus discriminis habere; patris et senatus et ipsius imperii vicem doleo, si nobis aut perire hodie necesse est aut, quod aeque apud bonos miserum est, occidere. Solatium proximi motus habebamus incruentam urbem et res sine discordia translatas. Provisum adoptione videbatur, ut ne post Galbam quidem bello locus esset.

XXX. "Nihil arrogabo mihi nobilitatis aut modestiae: neque enim relatu virtutum in comparatione Othonis opus est. Vitia, quibus solis gloriatur, evertere imperium, etiam cum amicum imperatoris ageret. Habitune et incessu, an illo muliebri ornatu mereretur imperium? Falluntur, quibus luxuria specie liberalitatis imponit. Perdere iste sciet, donare nesciet. Stupra nunc et comissationes et feminarum coetus volvit animo: haec principatus praemia putat, quorum libido ac voluptas penes ipsum sit, rubor ac dedecus penes omnes. Nemo enim unquam imperium, flagitio quaesitum, bonis artibus exercuit. Galbam consensus generis humani, me Galba, consentientibus vobis, Caesarem dixit. Si respublica et senatus et populus vana nomina sunt, vestra, commilitones, interest, ne imperatorem pessimi faciant. Legionum seditio adversus duces suos audita est aliquando: vestra fides famaque illaesa ad hunc diem mansit: et Nero quoque vos destituit, non vos Neronem. Minus triginta transfugae et desertores, quos centurionem aut tribunum sibi eligentes nemo ferret, imperium assignabunt? Admittitis exemplum? et quiescendo commune crimen facitis? Transcendet haec licentia in provincias; et ad nos scelerum exitus, bellorum ad vos pertinebunt. Nec est plus, quod pro caede principis quam quod innocentibus datur: sed perinde a nobis donativum ob fidem, quam ab aliis pro facinore accipietis.

XXXI. Dilapsis speculatoribus, cetera cohors non aspernata concionantem, ut turbidis rebus evenit, forte magis et nullo adhuc consilio parat signa quam, quod postea creditum est, insidiis et simulatione. Missus et Celsus Marius ad electos Illyrici exercitus, Vipsania in porticu tendentes. Praeceptum Amulio Serenio et Domitio Sabino primipilaribus, ut Germanicos milites e Libertatis atrio arcesserent. Legioni classicae diffidebat infestae ob caedem commilitonum, quos primo statim introitu trucidaverat Galba. Pergunt etiam in castra praetorianorum tribuni, Cetrius Severus, Subrius Dexter, Pompeius Longinus, si incipiens adhuc et necdum adulta seditio melioribus consiliis flecteretur. Tribunorum Subrium et Cetrium milites adorti minis, Longinum manibus coercent exarmantque, quia non ordine militiae, sed e Galbae amicis, fidus principi suo et desciscentibus suspectior erat. Legio classica nihil cunctata praetorianis adjungitur. Illyrici exercitus electi Celsum ingestis pilis proturbant. Germanica vexilla diu nutavere, invalidis adhuc corporibus et placatis animis, quod eos a Nerone Alexandriam praemissos atque inde rursus longa navigatione aegros impensiore cura Galba refovebat.

XXXII. Universa jam plebs palatium implebat, mixtis servitiis et dissono clamore caedem Othonis et conjuratorum exitium poscentium, ut si in circo ac theatro ludicrum aliquod postularent: neque illis judicium aut veritas, quippe eodem die diversa pari certamine postulaturis, sed tradito more quemcumque principem adulandi licentia acclamationum et studiis inanibus. Interim Galbam duae sententiae distinebant. Titus Vinius "manendum intra domum, opponenda servitia, firmandos aditus, non eundum ad iratos" censebat: "daret malorum poenitentiae, daret bonorum consensui spatium: scelera impetu, bona consilia mora valescere. Denique eundi ultro, si ratio sit, eandem mox facultatem: regressus, si poeniteat, in aliena potestate."

XXXIII. "Festinandum" ceteris videbatur, "antequam cresceret invalida adhuc conjuratio paucorum. Trepidaturum etiam Othonem, qui furtim digressus, ad ignaros illatus, cunctatione nunc et segnitia terentium tempus imitari principem discat. Non exspectandum, ut compositis castris forum invadat et prospectante Galba Capitolium adeat, dum egregius imperator cum fortibus amicis janua ac limine tenus domum cludit, obsidionem nimirum toleraturus. Et praeclarum in servis auxilium, si consensus tantae multitudinis, et, quae plurimum valet, prima indignatio elanguescat. Proinde intuta quae indecora; vel si cadere necesse sit, occurrendum discrimini. Id Othoni invidiosius, et ipsis honestum." Repugnantem huic sententiae Vinium Laco minaciter invasit, stimulante Icelo privati odii pertinacia in publicum exitium.

XXXIV. Nec diutius Galba cunctatus, speciosiora suadentibus accessit. Praemissus tamen in castra Piso, ut juvenis magno nomine, recenti favore, et infensus T. Vinio, seu quia erat, seu quia irati ita volebant; et facilius de odio creditur. Vix dum egresso Pisone, occisum in castris Othonem, vagus primum et incertus rumor: mox, ut in magnis mendaciis, interfuisse se quidam et vidisse affirmabant, credula fama inter gaudentes et incuriosos. Multi arbitrabantur compositum auctumque rumorem mixtis jam Othonianis, qui ad evocandum Galbam laeta falso vulgaverint.

XXXV. Tum vero non populus tantum et imperita plebs in plausus et immodica studia, sed equitum plerique ac senatorum, posito metu incauti, refractis palatii foribus ruere intus, ac se Galbae ostentare, praereptam sibi ultionem querentes. Ignavissimus quisque et, ut res docuit, in periculo non ausurus, nimii verbis, linguae ferocis: nemo scire, et omnes affirmare, donec inopia veri et consensu errantium victus, sumpto thorace, Galba, irruenti turbae neque aetate neque corpore sistens, sella levaretur. Obvius in palatio Julius Atticus speculator, cruentum gladium ostentans, occisum a se Othonem exclamavit. Et Galba, "Commilito," inquit, "quis jussit?" insigni animo ad coercendam militarem licentiam, minantibus intrepidus, adversus blandientes incorruptus.

XXXVI. Haud dubiae jam in castris omnium mentes; tantusque ardor, ut non contenti agmine et corporibus, in suggestu, in quo paulo ante aurea Galbae statua fuerat, medium inter signa Othonem vexillis circumdarent. Nec tribunis aut centurionibus adeundi locus: gregarius miles caveri insuper praepositos jubebat. Strepere cuncta clamoribus et tumultu et exhortatione mutua, non tanquam in populo ac plebe, variis segni adulatione vocibus, sed, ut quemque affluentium militum aspexerant, prensare manibus, complecti armis, collocare juxta, praeire sacramentum, modo imperatorem militibus, modo milites imperatori commendare. Nec deerat Otho protendens manus adorare vulgum, jacere oscula, et omnia serviliter pro dominatione. Postquam universa classicorum legio sacramentum ejus accepit, fidens viribus et quos adhuc singulos exstimulaverat, accendendos in commune ratus, pro vallo castrorum ita coepit:

XXXVII. "Quis ad vos processerim, commilitones, dicere non possum: quia nec privatum me vocare sustineo princeps a vobis nominatus, nec principem alio imperante. Vestrum quoque nomen in incerto erit, donec dubitabitur imperatorem populi Romani in castris an hostem habeatis. Auditisne, ut poena mea et supplicium vestrum simul postulentur? adeo manifestum est, neque perire nos neque salvos esse nisi una posse. Et cujus lenitatis est Galba, jam fortasse promisit, ut qui, nullo exposcente, tot millia innocentissimorum militum trucidaverit. Horror animum subit, quotiens recordor feralem introitum et hanc solam Galbae victoriam, cum in oculis urbis decumari deditos juberet, quos deprecantes in fidem acceperat. His auspiciis urbem ingressus, quam gloriam ad principatum attulit nisi occisi Obultronii Sabini et Cornelii Marcelli in Hispania, Betui Chilonis in Gallia, Fonteii Capitonis in Germania, Clodii Macri in Africa, Cingonii in via, Turpiliani in urbe, Nymphidii in castris? Quae usquam provincia, quae castra sunt, nisi cruenta et maculata, aut, ut ipse praedicat, emendata et correcta? Nam quae alii scelera, hic remedia vocat, dum falsis nominibus severitatem pro saevitia, parcimoniam pro avaritia, supplicia et contumelias vestras disciplinam appellat. Septem a Neronis fine menses sunt, et jam plus rapuit Icelus, quam quod Polycliti et Vatinii et Aegiali paraverunt. Minore avaritia ac licentia grassatus esset T.

Vinius, si ipse imperasset: nunc et subjectos nos habuit tanquam suos, et viles ut alienos. Una illa domus sufficit donativo, quod vobis nunquam datur et quotidie exprobratur.

XXXVIII. "Ac ne qua saltem in successore Galbae spes esset, arcessit ab exsilio, quem tristitia et avaritia sui simillimum judicabat. Vidistis, commilitones, notabili tempestate etiam deos infaustam adoptionem adversantes. Idem senatus, idem populi Romani, animus est. Vestra virtus exspectatur, apud quos omne honestis consiliis robur, et sine quibus, quamvis egregia, invalida sunt. Non ad bellum vos nec ad periculum voco: omnium militum arma nobiscum sunt. Nec una cohors togata defendit nunc Galbam, sed detinet. Cum vos aspexerit, cum signum meum acceperit, hoc solum erit certamen, quis mihi plurimum imputet. Nullus cunctationis locus est in eo consilio, quod non potest laudari nisi peractum." Aperire deinde armamentarium jussit: rapta statim arma sine more et ordine militiae, ut praetorianus aut legionarius insignibus suis distingueretur: miscentur auxiliaribus galeis scutisque; nullo tribunorum centurionumve adhortante, sibi quisque dux et instigator: et praecipuum pessimorum incitamentum, quod boni maerebant.

XXXIX. Jam exterritus Piso fremitu crebrescentis seditionis et vocibus in urbem usque resonantibus, egressum interim Galbam et foro appropinquantem assecutus erat: jam Marius Celsus haud laeta retulerat; cum alii in palatium redire, alii capitolium petere, plerique rostra occupanda censerent, plures tantum sententiis aliorum contradicerent, utque evenit in consiliis infelicibus, optima viderentur, quorum tempus effugerat. Agitasse Laco, ignaro Galba, de occidendo T. Vinio dicitur, sive ut poena ejus animos militum mulceret, seu conscium Othonis credebat, ad postremum vel odio. Haesitationem attulit tempus ac locus, quia, initio caedis orto, difficilis modus: et turbavere consilium trepidi nuntii ac proximorum diffugia, languentibus omnium studiis qui primo alacres fidem atque animum ostentaverant.

XL. Agebatur huc illuc Galba vario turbae fluctuantis impulsu, complètis undique basilicis ac templis, lugubri prospectu: neque populi aut plebis ulla vox, sed attoniti vultus et conversae ad omnia aures: non tumultus, non quies, quale magni metus et magnae irae silentium est. Othoni tamen armari plebem nuntiabatur. Ire praecipites et occupare pericula jubet. Igitur milites Romani, quasi Vologesen aut Pacorum avito Arsacidarum solio depulsuri, ac non imperatorem suum inermem et senem trucidare pergerent, disjecta plebe, proculcato senatu, truces armis, rapidi equis forum irrumpunt: nec illos capitolii aspectus et imminentium templorum religio et priores et futuri principes terruere, quo minus facerent scelus, cujus ultor est quisquis successit.

XLI. Viso cominus armatorum agmine, vexillarius comitatae Galbam cohortis (Atilium Vergilionem fuisse tradunt) dereptam Galbae imaginem solo afflixit. Eo signo manifesta in Othonem omnium militum studia, desertum fuga populi forum, destricta adversus dubitantes tela. Juxta Curtii lacum, trepidatione ferentium Galba projectus e sella ac provolutus est. Extremam ejus vocem, ut cuique odium aut admiratio fuit, varie prodidere. Alii, suppliciter interrogasse, quid mali meruisset? paucos dies exsolvendo donativo deprecatum: plures, obtulisse ultro percussoribus jugulum: agerent ac ferirent, si ita e republica videretur: non interfuit occidentium, quid diceret. De percussore non satis constat: quidam Terentium evocatum, alii Lecanium; crebrior fama tradidit Camurium quintaedecimae legionis militem, impresso gladio, jugulum ejus hausisse. Ceteri crura brachiaque (nam pectus tegebatur) foede laniavere: pleraque vulnera feritate et saevitia trunco jam corpori adjecta.

XLII. Titum inde Vinium invasere; de quo et ipso ambigitur, consumpseritne vocem ejus instans metus, an proclamaverit, non esse ab Othone mandatum, ut occideretur. Quod seu finxit formidine, seu conscientia conjurationis confessus est: huc potius ejus vita famaque inclinat, ut conscius sceleris fuerit, cujus causa erat. Ante aedem divi

Julii jacuit, primo ictu in poplitem, mox ab Julio Caro legionario milite in utrumque latus transverberatus.

XLIII. Insignem illa die virum Sempronium Densum aetas nostra vidit. Centurio is praetoriae cohortis, a Galba custodiae Pisonis additus, stricto pugione occurrens armatis et scelus exprobrans, ac modo manu, modo voce, vertendo in se percussores, quamquam vulnerato Pisoni effugium dedit. Piso in aedem Vestae pervasit, exceptusque misericordia publici servi et contubernio ejus abditus, non religione nec caerimoniis, sed latebra imminens exitium differebat; cum advenere, missu Othonis, nominatim in caedem ejus ardentes, Sulpicius Florus e Britannicis cohortibus nuper a Galba civitate donatus, et Statius Murcus speculator: a quibus protractus Piso, in foribus templi trucidatur.

XLIV. Nullam caedem Otho majore laetitia excepisse, nullum caput tam insatiabilibus oculis perlustrasse dicitur, seu tum primum levata omni solicitudine mens vacare gaudio coeperat, seu recordatio majestatis in Galba, amicitiae in T. Vinio, quamvis immitem animum imagine tristi confuderat: Pisonis, ut inimici et aemuli, caede laetari, jus fasque credebat. Praefixa contis capita gestabantur inter signa cohortium juxta aquilam legionis, certatim ostentantibus cruentas manus, qui occiderant, qui interfuerant, qui vere, qui falso, ut pulchrum et memorabile facinus, jactabant. Plures quam centum et viginti libellos praemium exposcentium ob aliquam notabilem illa die operam Vitellius postea invenit: omnesque conquiri et interfici jussit, non honore Galbae, sed tradito principibus more, munimentum ad praesens, in posterum ultionem.

XLV. Alium crederes senatum, alium populum: ruere cuncti in castra, anteire proximos, certare cum praecurrentibus, increpare Galbam, laudare militum judicium, exosculari Othonis manum; quantoque magis falsa erant, quae fiebant, tanto plura facere. Non aspernabatur singulos Otho, avidum et minacem militum animum voce vultuque temperans. Marium Celsum consulem designatum et Galbae usque in extremas res amicum fidumque, ad supplicium expostulabant, industriae ejus innocentiaeque, quasi malis artibus, infensi. Caedis et praedarum initium et optimo cuique perniciem quaeri apparebat: sed Othoni nondum auctoritas inerat ad prohibendum scelus; jubere jam poterat. Ita simulatione irae, vinciri jussum et majores poenas daturum affirmans, praesenti exitio subtraxit.

XLVI. Omnia deinde arbitrio militum acta. Praetorii praefectos sibi ipsi legere, Plotium Firmum e manipularibus quondam, tum vigilibus praepositum et, incolumi adhuc Galba, partes Othonis secutum. Adjungitur Licinius Proculus, intima familiaritate Othonis, suspectus consilia ejus fovisse. Urbi Flavium Sabinum praefecere, judicium Neronis secuti, sub quo eandem curam obtinuerat, plerisque Vespasianum fratrem in eo respicientibus. Flagitatum, ut vacationes praestari centurionibus solitae remitterentur: namque gregarius miles ut tributum annuum pendebat. Quarta pars manipuli sparsa per commeatus aut in ipsis castris vaga, dum mercedem centurioni exsolveret; neque modum oneris quisquam, neque genus quaestus pensi habebat: per latrocinia et raptus aut servilibus ministeriis militare otium redimebant. Tum locupletissimus quisque miles labore ac saevitia fatigari, donec vacationem emeret: ubi sumptibus exhaustus socordia insuper elanguerat, inops pro locuplete et iners pro strenuo in manipulum redibat: ac rursus alius atque alius, eadem egestate ac licentia corrupti, ad seditiones et discordias, et ad extremum bella civilia ruebant. Sed Otho, ne vulgi largitione centurionum animos averteret, fiscum suum vacationes annuas exsoluturum promisit, rem haud dubie utilem et a bonis postea principibus perpetuitate disciplinae firmatam. Laco praefectus, tanquam in insulam seponeretur, ab evocato, quem ad caedem ejus Otho praemiserat, confossus: in Marcianum Icelum, ut in libertum, palam animadversum.

XLVII. Exacto per scelera die, novissimum malorum fuit laetitia. Vocat senatum praetor urbanus: certant adulationibus ceteri magistratus. Accurrunt patres: decernitur Othoni tribunicia potestas et nomen Augusti et omnes principum honores, annitentibus cunctis abolere convicia ac probra, quae promiscue jacta haesisse animo ejus nemo sensit. Omisisset offensas an distulisset, brevitate imperii in incerto fuit. Otho, cruento adhuc foro, per stragem jacentium in capitolium atque inde in palatium vectus, concedi corpora sepulturae cremarique permisit. Pisonem Verania uxor ac frater Scribonianus, T. Vinium Crispina filia composuere, quaesitis redemptisque capitibus, quae venalia interfectores servaverant.

XLVIII. Piso unum et tricesimum aetatis annum explebat, fama meliore quam fortuna. Fratres ejus Magnum Claudius, Crassum Nero interfecerant. Ipse diu exsul, quatriduo Caesar, properata adoptione ad hoc tantum majori fratri praelatus est, ut prior occideretur. T. Vinius quinquaginta septem annos variis moribus egit. Pater illi praetoria familia, maternus avus e proscriptis. Prima militia infamis, legatum Calvisium Sabinum habuerat; cujus uxor mala cupidine visendi situm castrorum, per noctem militari habitu ingressa, cum vigilias et cetera militiae munia eadem lascivia temperasset, in ipsis principiis stuprum ausa: et criminis hujus reus T. Vinius arguebatur. Igitur jussu C. Caesaris oneratus catenis, mox mutatione temporum dimissus, cursu honorum inoffenso legioni post praeturam praepositus probatusque: servili deinceps probro respersus est, tanquam scyphum aureum in convivio Claudii furatus: et Claudius postera die soli omnium Vinio fictilibus ministrari jussit. Sed Vinius proconsulatu Galliam Narbonensem severe integreque rexit: mox Galbae amicitia in abruptum tractus, audax, callidus, promptus, et, prout animum intendisset, pravus aut industrius, eadem vi. Testamentum T. Vinii magnitudine opum irritum: Pisonis supremam voluntatem paupertas firmavit.

XLIX. Galbae corpus diu neglectum et licentia tenebrarum plurimis ludibriis vexatum, dispensator Argius e prioribus servis, humili sepultura in privatis ejus hortis contexit. Caput, per lixas calonesque suffixum laceratumque, ante Patrobii tumulum (libertus is Neronis punitus a Galba fuerat) postera demum die repertum et cremato jam corpori admixtum est. Hunc exitum habuit Ser. Galba, tribus et septuaginta annis quinque principes prospera fortuna emensus et alieno imperio felicior quam suo. Vetus in familia nobilitas, magnae opes: ipsi medium ingenium, magis extra vitia, quam cum virtutibus. Famae nec incuriosus nec venditator. Pecuniae alienae non appetens, suae parcus, publicae avarus. Amicorum libertorumque, ubi in bonos incidisset, sine reprehensione patiens; si mali forent, usque ad culpam ignarus. Sed claritas natalium et metus temporum obtentui, ut, quod segnitia erat, sapientia vocaretur. Dum vigebat aetas, militari laude apud Germanias floruit. Pro consule Africam moderate; jam senior citeriorem Hispaniam pari justitia continuit, major privato visus, dum privatus fuit, et omnium consensu capax imperii, nisi imperasset.

L. Trepidam urbem, ac simul atrocitatem recentis sceleris, simul veteres Othonis mores paventem, novus insuper de Vitellio nuntius exterruit, ante caedem Galbae suppressus, ut tantum superioris Germaniae exercitum descivisse crederetur. Tum duos, omnium mortalium impudicitia, ignavia, luxuria deterrimos velut ad perdendum imperium fataliter electos non senatus modo et eques, quis aliqua pars et cura reipublicae, sed vulgus quoque palam maerere. Nec jam recentia saevae pacis exempla, sed repetita bellorum civilium memoria captam totiens suis exercitibus urbem, vastitatem Italiae, direptiones provinciarum, Pharsaliam, Philippos, et Perusiam ac Mutinam, nota publicarum cladium nomina, loquebantur. Prope eversum orbem, etiam cum de principatu inter bonos certaretur: sed mansisse C. Julio, mansisse Caesare Augusto victore imperium; mansuram fuisse sub Pompeio Brutoque rempublicam. Nunc pro Othone, an pro Vitellio, in templa ituros? Utrasque impias preces, utraque detestanda vota, inter duos, quorum bello solum id scires, deteriorem fore qui vicisset. Erant, qui Vespasianum et arma Orientis augurarentur: et ut potior utroque Vespasianus, ita bellum aliud atque alias clades horrebant. Et ambigua de Vespasiano fama; solusque omnium ante se principum in melius mutatus est.

LI. Nunc initia causasque motus Vitelliani expediam. Caeso cum omnibus copiis Julio Vindice, ferox praeda gloriaque exercitus, ut cui sine labore ac periculo ditissimi belli victoria evenisset, expeditionem et aciem, praemia quam stipendia malebat. Diu infructuosam et asperam militiam toleraverant ingenio loci coelique et severitate disciplinae, quam in pace inexorabilem discordiae civium resolvunt, paratis utrimque corruptoribus et perfidia impunita. Viri, arma, equi ad usum et ad decus supererant: sed ante bellum centurias tantum suas turmasque noverant; exercitus finibus provinciarum discernebantur. Tum adversus Vindicem contractae legiones, seque et Gallias expertae, quaerere rursus arma novasque discordias; nec socios, ut olim, sed hostes et victos vocabant. Nec deerat pars Galliarum, quae Rhenum accolit, easdem partes secuta, ac tum acerrima instigatrix adversus Galbianos: hoc enim nomen, fastidito Vindice, indiderant. Igitur Sequanis Aeduisque ac deinde, prout opulentia civitatibus erat, infensi, expugnationes urbium, populationes agrorum, raptus penatium hauserunt animo, super avaritiam et arrogantiam, praecipua validiorum vitia, contumacia Gallorum irritati, qui remissam sibi a Galba quartam tributorum partem et publice donatos in ignominiam exercitus jactabant. Accessit callide vulgatum, temere creditum, decumari legiones et promptissimum quemque centurionum dimitti: undique atroces nuntii, sinistra ex urbe fama: infensa Lugdunensis colonia, et, pertinaci pro Nerone fide, fecunda rumoribus. Sed plurima ad fingendum credendumque materies in ipsis castris, odio, metu et, ubi vires suas respexerant, securitate.

LII. Sub ipsas superioris anni Kalendas Decembres Aulus Vitellius, inferiorem Germaniam ingressus, hiberna legionum cum cura adierat: redditi plerisque ordines, remissa ignominia, allevatae notae, plura ambitione, quaedam judicio, in quibus sordem et avaritiam Fonteii Capitonis adimendis assignandisve militiae ordinibus integre mutaverat. Nec consularis legati mensura, sed in majus omnia accipiebantur: et Vitellius apud severos humilis; ita comitatem: bonitatemque faventes vocabant, quod sine modo, sine judicio donaret sua, largiretur aliena; simul aviditate imperandi ipsa vitia pro virtutibus interpretabantur. Multi in utroque exercitu sicut modesti quietique, ita mali et strenui; sed profusa cupidine et insigni temeritate legati legionum Alienus Caecina et Fabius Valens: e quibus Valens infensus Galbae tanquam detectam a se Verginii cunctationem, oppressa Capitonis consilia ingrate tulisset, instigare Vitellium, ardorem militum ostentans. "Ipsum celebri ubique fama, nullam in Flacco Hordeonio moram; affore Britanniam, secutura Germanorum auxilia: male fidas provincias, precarium seni imperium et brevi transiturum: panderet modo sinum et venienti Fortunae occurreret. Merito dubitasse Verginium equestri familia, ignoto patre, imparem, si recepisset imperium, tutum, si recusasset. Vitellio tres patris consulatus, censuram, collegium Caesaris imponere jampridem imperatoris dignationem, auferre privati securitatem." Quatiebatur his segne ingenium, ut concupisceret magis quam ut speraret.

LIII. At in superiore Germania Caecina decora juventa, corpore ingens, animi immodicus, scito sermone, erecto incessu, studia militum illexerat. Hunc juvenem Galba, quaestorem in Baetica impigre in partes suas transgressum, legioni praeposuit; mox compertum publicam pecuniam avertisse ut peculatorem flagitari jussit. Caecina aegre passus, miscere cuncta et privata vulnera reipublicae malis operire statuit. Nec deerant in exercitu semina discordiae, quod et bello adversus Vindicem universus affuerat, nec nisi occiso Nerone translatus in Galbam, atque in eo ipso sacramento vexillis inferioris Germaniae praeventus erat. Et Treveri ac Lingones, quasque alias civitates atrocibus edictis aut damno finium Galba perculerat, hibernis legionum propius miscentur. Unde seditiosa colloquia, et inter paganos corruptior miles, et in Verginium favor, cuicumque alii profuturus.

LIV. Miserat civitas Lingonum vetere instituto dona legionibus, dextras, hospitii insigne. Legati eorum in squalorem maestitiamque compositi, per principia, per contubernia, modo suas injurias, modo vicinarum civitatium praemia, et, ubi pronis militum auribus accipiebantur, ipsius exercitus pericula et contumelias conquerentes, accendebant animos. Nec procul seditione aberant, cum Hordeonius Flaccus abire legatos, utque occultior digressus esset, nocte castris excedere jubet. Inde atrox rumor, affirmantibus plerisque interfectos, ac, nisi ipsi consulerent, fore, ut acerrimi militum, et praesentia conquesti, per tenebras et inscitiam ceterorum occiderentur. Obstringuntur inter se tacito foedere legiones. Asciscitur auxiliorum miles, primo suspectus, tanquam circumdatis cohortibus alisque impetus in legiones pararetur, mox eadem acrius volvens, faciliore inter malos consensu ad bellum quam in pace ad concordiam.

LV. Inferioris tamen Germaniae legiones solenni Kalendarum Januariarum sacramento pro Galba adactae, multa cunctatione et raris primorum ordinum vocibus: ceteri silentio proximi cujusque audaciam exspectantes, insita mortalibus natura propere sequi quae piget inchoare. Sed ipsis legionibus inerat diversitas animorum. Primani quintanique turbidi adeo ut quidam saxa in Galbae imagines jecerint: quintadecima ac sextadecima legiones, nihil ultra fremitum et minas ausae, initium erumpendi circumspectabant. At in superiore exercitu quarta ac duodevicesima legiones, iisdem hibernis tendentes, ipso Kalendarum Januariarum die dirumpunt imagines Galbae, quarta legio promptius, duodevicesima cunctanter, mox consensu. Ac ne reverentiam imperii exuere viderentur, senatus populique Romani obliterata jam nomina sacramento advocabant, nullo legatorum tribunorumve pro Galba nitente, quibusdam, ut in tumultu, notabilius turbantibus. Non tamen quisquam in modum concionis aut suggestu locutus: neque enim erat adhuc, cui imputaretur.

LVI. Spectator flagitii Hordeonius Flaccus consularis legatus aderat, non compescere ruentes, non retinere dubios, non cohortari bonos ausus, sed segnis, pavidus et socordia innocens. Quatuor centuriones duodevicesimae legionis, Nonius Receptus, Donatius Valens, Romilius Marcellus, Calpurnius Repentinus, cum protegerent Galbae imagines, impetu militum abrepti vinctique. Nec cuiquam ultra fides aut memoria prioris sacramenti, sed quod in seditionibus accidit, unde plures erant, omnes fuere. Nocte, quas

Kalendas Januarias secuta est, in coloniam Agrippinensem aquilifer quartae legionis epulanti Vitellio nuntiat, quartam et duodevicesimam legiones, projectis Galbae imaginibus, in senatus ac populi Romani verba jurasse. Id sacramentum inane visum: occupari nutantem fortunam, et offerri principem placuit. Missi a Vitellio ad legiones legatosque, qui descivisse a Galba superiorem exercitum nuntiarent: proinde aut bellandum adversus desciscentes, aut, si concordia et pax placeat, faciendum imperatorem; et minore discrimine sumi principem, quam quaeri.

LVII. Proxima legionis primae hiberna erant, et promptissimus e legatis Fabius Valens. Is die proximo coloniam Agrippinensem cum equitibus legionis auxiliariorumque gressus, imperatorem Vitellium consalutavit. Secutae ingenti certamine ejusdem provinciae legiones; et superior exercitus, speciosis senatus populique Romani nominibus relictis, tertium Nonas Januarias Vitellio accessit: scires illum priore biduo non penes rempublicam fuisse. Ardorem exercituum Agrippinenses, Treveri, Lingones aequabant, auxilia, equos, arma, pecunias offerentes, ut quisque corpore, opibus, ingenio validus. Nec principes modo coloniarum aut castrorum, quibus praesentia ex affluenti et parta victoria magnae spes: sed manipuli quoque et gregarius miles viatica sua et balteos phalerasque, insignia armorum argento decora, loco pecuniae tradebant, instinctu et impetu et avaritia.

LVIII. Igitur laudata militum alacritate, Vitellius ministeria principatus per libertos agi solita in equites Romanos disponit; vacationes centurionibus ex fisco numerat; saevitiam militum plerosque ad poenam exposcentium saepius approbat, partim simulatione vinculorum frustratur. Pompeius Propinquus procurator Belgicae statim interfectus. Julium Burdonem Germanicae classis praefectum astu subtraxit. Exarserat in eum iracundia exercitus, tanquam crimen ac mox insidias Fonteio Capitoni struxisset. Grata erat memoria Capitonis; et apud saevientes occidere palam, ignoscere non nisi fallendo licebat. Ita in custodia habitus, et post victoriam demum, stratis jam militum odiis, dimissus est. Interim, ut piaculum, objicitur centurio Crispinus: sanguine Capitonis se cruentaverat; eoque et postulantibus manifestior et punienti vilior fuit.

LIX. Julius deinde Civilis periculo exemptus, praepotens inter Batavos, ne supplicio ejus ferox gens alienaretur. Et erant in civitate Lingonum octo Batavorum cohortes, quartaedecimae legionis auxilia, tum discordia temporum a legione digressae, prout inclinassent, grande momentum sociae aut adversae. Nonium, Donatium, Romilium, Calpurnium centuriones, de quibus supra retulimus, occidi jussit, damnatos fidei crimine, gravissimo inter desciscentes. Accessere partibus Valerius Asiaticus Belgicae provinciae legatus, quem mox Vitellius generum ascivit, et Junius Blaesus Lugdunensis Galliae rector, cum Italica legione et ala Taurina, Lugduni tendentibus. Nec in Raeticis copiis mora, quo minus statim adjungerentur.

LX. Ne in Britannia quidem dubitatum. Praeerat Trebellius Maximus, per avaritiam et sordes contemptus exercitui invisusque. Accendebat odium ejus Roscius Caelius legatus vicesimae legionis, olim discors, sed occasione civilium armorum atrocius proruperat. Trebellius seditionem et confusum ordinem disciplinae Caelio, spoliatas et inopes legiones Caelius Trebellio objectabat, cum interim foedis legatorum certaminibus modestia exercitus corrupta, eoque discordiae ventum, ut auxiliarium quoque militum conviciis proturbatus et, aggregantibus se Caelio cohortibus alisque, desertus Trebellius ad Vitellium perfugerit: quies provinciae, quanquam remoto consulari, mansit: rexere legati legionum, pares jure, Caelius audendo potentior.

LXI. Adjuncto Britannico exercitu, ingens viribus opibusque Vitellius duos duces, duo itinera bello destinavit. Fabius Valens allicere vel, si abnuerent, vastare Gallias, et Cottianis Alpibus Italiam irrumpere, Caecina propiore transitu, Peninis jugis degredi jussus. Valenti inferioris exercitus electi cum aquila quintae legionis et cohortibus alisque, ad quadraginta millia armatorum data: triginta millia Caecina e superiore Germania ducebat, quorum robur legio una, primaetvicesima, fuit: addita utrique Germanorum auxilia, e quibus Vitellius suas quoque copias supplevit, tota mole belli secuturus.

LXII. Mira inter exercitum imperatoremque diversitas. Instare miles, arma poscere, dum Galliae trepident, dum Hispaniae cunctentur: non obstare hiemem neque ignavae pacis moras: invadendam Italiam, occupandam urbem: nihil in discordiis civilibus festinatione tutius, ubi facto magis quam consulto opus esset. Torpebat Vitellius, et fortunam principatus inerti luxu ac prodigis epulis praesumebat, medio diei temulentus et sagina gravis, cum tamen ardor et vis militum ultro ducis munia implebat, ut si adesset imperator et strenuis vel ignavis spem metumque adderet. Instructi intentique signum profectionis exposcunt. Nomen Germanici Vitellio statim additum: Caesarem se appellari etiam victor prohibuit. Laetum augurium Fabio Valenti exercituique, quem in bellum agebat, ipso profectionis die aquila leni meatu, prout agmen incederet, velut dux viae praevolavit: longumque per spatium is gaudentium militum clamor, ea quies interritae alitis fuit, ut haud dubium magnae et prosperae rei omen acciperetur.

LXIII. Et Treveros quidem, ut socios, securi adiere. Divoduri (Mediomatricorum id oppidum est) quanquam omni comitate exceptos subitus pavor terruit, raptis derepente armis ad caedem innoxiae civitatis, non ob praedam aut spoliandi cupidinem, sed furore et rabie et causis incertis eoque difficilioribus remediis, donec precibus ducis mitigati ab excidio civitatis temperavere; caesa tamen ad quatuor millia hominum. Isque terror Gallias invasit, ut venienti mox agmini universae civitates cum magistratibus et precibus occurrerent, stratis per vias pueris feminisque, quaeque alia placamenta hostilis irae, non quidem in bello, sed pro pace tendebantur.

LXIV. Nuntium de caede Galbae et imperio Othonis, Fabius Valens in civitate Leucorum accepit. Nec militum animus in gaudium aut formidinem permotus: bellum volvebat. Gallis cunctatio exempta, et in Othonem ac Vitellium odium par, ex Vitellio et metus. Proxima Lingonum civitas erat, fida partibus: benigne excepti, modestia certa-vere; sed brevis laetitia fuit cohortium intemperie, quas a legione quartadecima, ut supra memoravimus, digressas exercitui suo Fabius Valens adjunxerat. Jurgia primum, mox rixa inter Batavos et legionarios, dum his aut illis studia militum aggregantur, prope in proelium exarsere, ni Valens animadversione paucorum oblitos jam Batavos imperii admonuisset. Frustra adversus Aeduos quaesita belli causa. Jussi pecuniam atque arma deferre, gratuitos insuper commeatus praebuere: quod Aedui formidine, Lugdunenses gaudio fecere. Sed legio Italica et ala Taurina abductae. Cohortem duodevicesimam Lugduni, solitis sibi hibernis, relinqui placuit. Manlius Valens legatus Italicae legionis, quanquam bene de partibus meritus, nullo apud Vitellium honore fuit: secretis eum criminationibus infamaverat Fabius ignarum et, quo incautior deciperetur, palam laudatum.

LXV. Veterem inter Lugdunenses Viennensesque discordiam proximum bellum accenderat: multae invicem clades crebrius infestiusque, quam ut tantum propter Neronem Galbamque pugnaretur. Et Galba reditus Lugdunensium occasione irae in fiscum verterat; multus contra in Viennenses honor: unde aemulatio et invidia et uno amne discretis connexum odium. Igitur Lugdunenses exstimulare singulos militum et in eversionem Viennensium impellere, obsessam ab illis coloniam suam, adjutos Vindicis conatus, conscriptas nuper legiones in praesidium Galbae referendo: et ubi causas odiorum praetenderant, magnitudinem praedae ostendebant. Nec jam secreta exhortatio, sed publicae preces: "Irent ultores, exscinderent sedem Gallici belli: cuncta illic externa et hostilia; se coloniam Romanam et partem exercitus et prosperarum adversarumque rerum socios: si fortuna contra daret, iratis ne relinquerentur."

LXVI. His et pluribus in eundem modum perpulerant, ut ne legati quidem ac duces partium restingui posse iracundiam exercitus arbitrarentur, cum haud ignari discriminis sui Viennenses, velamenta et infulas praeferentes, ubi agmen incesserat, arma, genua, vestigia prensando flexere militum animos. Addidit Valens trecenos singulis militibus sestertios: tum vetustas dignitasque coloniae valuit, et verba Fabii salutem incolumitatemque Viennensium commendantis aequis auribus accepta: publice tamen armis mulctati, privatis et promiscuis copiis juvere militem. Sed fama constans fuit ipsum Valentem magna pecunia emptum. Is diu sordidus, repente dives, mutationem fortunae male tegebat, accensis egestate longa cupidinibus immoderatus, et inopi juventa senex prodigus. Lento deinde agmine per fines Allobrogum et Vocontiorum ductus exercitus, ipsa itinerum spatia et stativorum mutationes venditante duce, foedis pactionibus adversus possessores agrorum et magistratus civitatum, adeo minaciter, ut Luco (municipium id Vocontiorum est) faces admoverit, donec pecunia mitigaretur: quotiens pecuniae materia deesset, stupris et adulteriis exorabatur. Sic ad Alpes perventum.

LXVII. Plus praedae ac sanguinis Caecina hausit. Irritaverant turbidum ingenium Helvetii, Gallica gens, olim armis virisque, mox memoria nominis clara, de caede Galbae ignari et Vitellii imperium abnuentes. Initium bello fuit avaritia ac festinatio unaetvicesimae legionis: rapuerant pecuniam missam in stipendium castelli, quod olim Helvetii suis militibus ac stipendiis tuebantur: aegre id passi Helvetii, interceptis epistolis quae nomine Germanici exercitus ad Pannonicas legiones ferebantur, centurionem et quosdam militum in custodia retinebant. Caecina belli avidus proximam quamque culpam, antequam poeniteret, ultum ibat. Mota propere castra, vastati agri, direptus longa pace in modum municipii exstructus locus, amoeno salubrium aquarum usu frequens: missi ad Raetica auxilia nuntii, ut versos in legionem Helvetios a tergo aggrederentur.

LXVIII. Illi ante discrimen feroces, in periculo pavidi, quanquam primo tumultu Claudium Severum ducem legerant, non arma noscere, non ordines sequi, non in unum consulere: exitiosum adversus veteranos proelium, intuta obsidio dilapsis vetustate moenibus: hinc Caecina cum valido exercitu; inde Raeticae alae cohortesque et ipsorum Raetorum juventus, sueta armis et more militiae exercita: undique populatio et caedes: ipsi in medio vagi, abjectis armis, magna pars saucii aut palantes in montem Vocetium perfugere. Ac statim immissa cohorte Thracum depulsi et, consectantibus Germanis Raetisque, per silvas atque in ipsis latebris trucidati. Multa hominum millia caesa, multa sub corona venundata; cumque dirutis omnibus Aventicum gentis caput justo agmine peteretur, missi qui dederent civitatem; et deditio accepta. In Julium Alpinum e principibus, ut concitorem belli, Caecina animadvertit: ceteros veniae vel saevitiae Vitellii reliquit.

LXIX. Haud facile dictu est, legati Helvetiorum minus placabilem imperatorem an militem invenerint: civitatis excidium poscunt, tela ac manus in ora legatorum intentant. Ne Vitellius quidem minis ac verbis temperabat, cum Claudius Cossus, unus ex legatis, notae facundiae, sed dicendi artem apta trepidatione occultans atque eo validior, militis animum mitigavit, ut est mos vulgo, mutabilem subitis et tam pronum in misericordiam quam immodicus saevitia fuerat: effusis lacrimis et meliora constantius postulando, impunitatem salutemque civitati impetravere.

LXX. Caecina paucos in Helvetiis moratus dies, dum sententiae Vitellii certior fieret, simul transitum Alpium parans, laetum ex Italia nuntium accipit, alam Silianam circa Padum agentem sacramento Vitellii accessisse. Proconsulem Vitellium Siliani in Africa habuerant; mox a Nerone, ut in Aegyptum praemitterentur, exciti et ob bellum Vindicis revocati, ac tum in Italia manentes, instinctu decurionum, qui Othonis ignari, Vitellio obstricti robur adventantium legionum et famam Germanici exercitus attollebant, transiere in partes: et, ut donum aliquod novo principi, firmissima Transpadanae regionis municipia Mediolanum ac Novariam et Eporediam ac Vercellas adjunxere. Id Caecinae per ipsos compertum; et quia praesidio alae unius latissima pars Italiae defendi nequibat, praemissis Gallorum Lusitanorum Britannorumque cohortibus et Germanorum vexillis cum ala Petrina, ipse paululum cunctatus, num Raeticis jugis in Noricum flecteret, adversus Petronium ibi procuratorem, qui concitis auxiliis et interruptis fluminum pontibus fidus Othoni putabatur. Sed metu, ne amitteret praemissas jam cohortes alasque, simul reputans plus gloriae retenta Italia et, ubicumque certatum foret, Noricos in cetera victoriae praemia cessuros, Penino itinere subsignanum militem, et grave legionum agmen hibernis adhuc Alpibus traduxit.

LXXI. Otho interim contra spem omnium non deliciis neque desidia torpescere: dilatae voluptates, dissimulata luxuria, et cuncta ad decorem imperii composita: eoque plus formidinis afferebant falsae virtutes et vitia reditura. Marium Celsum consulem designatum, per speciem vinculorum saevitiae militum subtractum, acciri in capitolium jubet: clementiae titulus e viro claro et partibus inviso petebatur. Celsus constanter servatae erga Galbam fidei crimen confessus, exemplum ultro imputavit. Nec Otho quasi ignosceret, sed, ne hostis metum reconciliationis adhiberet, statim inter intimos amicos habuit, et mox bello inter duces delegit: mansitque Celso velut fataliter etiam pro Othone fides integra et infelix. Laeta primoribus civitatis, celebrata in vulgus Celsi salus, ne militibus quidem ingrata fuit, eandem virtutem admirantibus cui irascebantur.

LXXII. Par inde exsultatio disparibus causis consecuta, impetrato Tigellini exitio. Sophonius Tigellinus obscuris parentibus, foeda pueritia, impudica senecta, praefecturam vigilum et praetorii et alia praemia virtutum quia velocius erat vitiis adeptus, crudelitatem mox, deinde avaritiam et virilia scelera exercuit, corrupto ad omne facinus Nerone, quaedam ignaro ausus ac postremo ejusdem desertor ac proditor. Unde non alium pertinacius ad poenam flagitavere, diverso affectu, quibus odium Neronis inerat et quibus desiderium. Apud Galbam T. Vinii potentia defensus, praetexentis servatam ab eo filiam: et haud dubie servaverat, non clementia, quippe tot interfectis, sed effugium in futurum, quia pessimus quisque, diffidentia praesentium mutationem pavens, adversus publicum odium privatam gratiam praeparat; unde nulla innocentiae cura, sed vices impunitatis. Eo infensior populus, addita ad vetus Tigellini odium recenti T. Vinii invidia, concurrere e tota urbe in palatium ac fora, et ubi plurima vulgi licentia, in circum ac theatra effusi seditiosis vocibus obstrepere, donec Tigellinus, accepto apud Sinuessanas aquas supremae necessitatis nuntio, inter stupra concubinarum et oscula et deformes moras, sectis novacula faucibus, infamem vitam foedavit etiam exitu sero et inhonesto.

LXXIII. Per idem tempus expostulata ad supplicium Galvia Crispinilla variis frustrationibus et adversa dissimulantis Principis fama periculo exempta est: magistra libidinum Neronis, transgressa in Africam ad instigandum in arma Clodium Macrum, famem populo Romano haud obscure molita, totius postea civitatis gratiam obtinuit, consulari matrimonio subnixa et apud Galbam, Othonem, Vitellium illaesa, mox potens pecunia et orbitate, quae bonis malisque temporibus juxta valent.

LXXIV. Crebrae interim et muliebribus blandimentis infectae ab Othone ad Vitellium epistolae offerebant pecuniam et gratiam et quemcumque quietis locum prodigae vitae legisset. Paria Vitellius ostentabat, primo mollius, stulta utrimque et indecora simulatione: mox, quasi rixantes, stupra et flagitia invicem objectavere, neuter falso. Otho, revocatis quos Galba miserat legatis, rursus alios ad utrumque Germanicum exercitum et ad legionem Italicam easque, quae Lugduni agebant, copias specie senatus misit. Legati apud Vitellium remansere, promptius quam ut retenti viderentur. Praetoriani, quos per simulationem officii legatis Otho adjunxerat, remissi antequam legionibus miscerentur. Addidit epistolas Fabius Valens, nomine Germanici exercitus, ad praetorias et urbanas cohortes, de viribus partium magnificas et concordiam offerentes. Increpabat ultro, quod tanto ante traditum Vitellio imperium ad Othonem vertissent. Ita promissis simul ac minis tentabantur, ut bello impares, in pace nihil amissuri: neque ideo praetorianorum fides mutata.

LXXV. Sed insidiatores ab Othone in Germaniam, a Vitellio in urbem missi: utrisque frustra fuit, Vitellianis impune, per tantam hominum multitudinem, mutua ignorantia fallentibus: Othoniani novitate vultus, omnibus invicem gnaris, prodebantur. Vitellius literas ad Titianum fratrem Othonis composuit, exitium ipsi filioque ejus minitans, ni incolumes sibi mater ac liberi servarentur. Et stetit domus utraque, sub Othone, incertum an metu; Vitellius victor clementiae gloriam tulit.

LXXVI. Primus Othoni fiduciam addidit ex Illyrico nuntius, jurasse in eum Dalmatiae ac Pannoniae et Moesiae legiones. Idem ex Hispania allatum, laudatusque per edictum Cluvius Rufus; et statim cognitum est conversam ad Vitellium Hispaniam. Ne Aquitania quidem, quanquam a Julio Cordo in verba Othonis obstricta, diu mansit. Nusquam fides aut amor; metu ac necessitate huc illuc mutabantur. Eadem formido provinciam Narbonensem ad Vitellium vertit, facili transitu ad proximos et validiores. Longinquae provinciae, et quicquid armorum mari dirimitur, penes Othonem manebant, non partium studio, sed erat grande momentum in nomine urbis ac praetexto senatus, et occupaverat animos prior auditus. Judaicum exercitum Vespasianus, Syriae legiones Mucianus sacramento Othonis adegere. Simul Aegyptus omnesque versae in Orientem provinciae nomine ejus tenebantur. Idem Africae obsequium, initio a Carthagine orto. Neque exspectata Vipstani Aproniani proconsulis auctoritate, Crescens Neronis libertus (nam et hi malis temporibus partem se reipublicae faciunt) epulum plebi ob laetitiam recentis imperii obtulerat, et populus pleraque sine modo festinavit. Carthaginem ceterae civitates secutae.

LXXVII. Sic distractis exercitibus ac provinciis, Vitellio quidem ad capessendam principatus fortunam bello opus erat. Otho, ut in multa pace, munia imperii obibat, quaedam ex dignitate reipublicae, pleraque contra decus ex praesenti usu properando. Consul cum Titiano fratre in Kalendas Martias ipse: proximos menses Verginio destinat ut aliquod exercitui Germanico delenimentum. Jungitur Verginio Pompeius Vopiscus praetexto veteris amicitiae; plerique Viennensium honori datum interpretabantur. Ceteri consulatus ex destinatione Neronis aut Galbae mansere, Caelio ac Flavio Sabinis in Julias, Arrio Antonio et Mario Celso in Septembres; quorum honori ne Vitellius quidem victor intercessit. Sed Otho pontificatus auguratusque honoratis jam senibus cumulum dignitatis addidit, aut recens ab exsilio reversos nobiles adolescentulos avitis ac paternis sacerdotiis in solatium recoluit. Redditus Cadio Rufo, Pedio Blaeso, Sevino Pomptinio senatorius locus; repetundarum criminibus sub Claudio ac Nerone ceciderant. Placuit ignoscentibus verso nomine, quod avaritia fuerat, videri majestatem, cujus tum odio etiam bonae leges peribant.

LXXVIII. Eadem largitione civitatum quoque ac provinciarum animos aggressus, Hispaliensibus et Emeritensibus familiarum adjectiones, Lingonibus universis civitatem Romanam, provinciae Baeticae Maurorum civitates dono dedit; nova jura Cappadociae, nova Africae, ostenta magis quam mansura. Inter quae necessitate praesentium rerum et instantibus curis excusata, ne tum quidem immemor amorum, statuas Poppaeae per senatus consultum reposuit. Creditus est etiam de celebranda Neronis memoria agitavisse spe vulgum alliciendi: et fuere, qui imagines Neronis proponerent; atque etiam Othoni quibusdam diebus populus et miles, tanquam nobilitatem ac decus adstruerent, Neroni Othoni acclamavit. Ipse in suspenso tenuit vetandi metu vel agnoscendi pudore.

LXXIX. Conversis ad civile bellum animis, externa sine cura habebantur. Eo audentius Rhoxolani, Sarmatica gens, priore hieme caesis duabus cohortibus, magna spe ad Moesiam irruperant, novem millia equitum, ex ferocia et successu praedae magis quam pugnae intenta. Igitur vagos et incuriosos tertia legio, adjunctis auxiliis, repente invasit: apud Romanos omnia proelio apta; Sarmatae dispersi aut cupidine praedae graves onere sarcinarum, et lubrico itinerum adempta equorum pernicitate, velut vincti caedebantur. Namque mirum dictu, ut sit omnis Sarmatarum virtus velut extra ipsos: nihil ad pedestrem pugnam tam ignavum: ubi per turmas advenere, vix ulla acies obstiterit. Sed tum humido die et soluto gelu neque conti neque gladii, quos praelongos utraque manu regunt, usui, lapsantibus equis et cataphractarum pondere. Id principibus et nobilissimo cuique tegimen, ferreis laminis aut prae-duro corio consertum, ut adversus ictus impenetrabile, ita impetu hostium provolutis inhabile ad resurgendum: simul altitudine et mollitia nivis hauriebantur. Romanus miles facilis lorica et missili pilo aut lanceis assultans, ubi res posceret, levi gladio inermem Sarmatam (neque enim scuto defendi mos est) cominus fodiebat, donec pauci, qui proelio superfuerant, paludibus abderentur. Ibi saevitia hiemis et vi vulnerum absumpti. Postquam id Romae compertum, M. Aponius Moesiam obtinens triumphali statua, Fulvius Aurelius et Julianus Titius ac Numisius Lupus legati legionum consularibus ornamentis donantur, laeto Othone et gloriam in se trahente, tanquam et ipse felix bello et suis ducibus suisque exercitibus rempublicam auxisset.

LXXX. Parvo interim initio, unde nihil timebatur, orta seditio prope urbi excidio fuit. Septimam decimam cohortem e colonia Ostiensi in urbem acciri Otho jusserat: armandae ejus cura Vario Crispino tribuno e praetorianis data. Is quo magis vacuus quietis castris jussa exsequeretur, vehicula cohortis incipiente nocte onerari, aperto armamentario, jubet. Tempus in suspicionem, causa in crimen, affectatio quietis in tumultum evaluit; et visa inter temulentos arma cupidinem sui movere. Fremit miles, et tribunos centurionesque proditionis arguit, tanquam familiae senatorum ad perniciem Othonis armarentur, pars ignari et vino graves, pessimus quisque in occasionem praedarum, vulgus, ut mos est, cujuscumque motus novi cupidum; et obsequia meliorum nox abstulerat. Resistentem seditioni tribunum et severissimos centurionum obtruncant: rapta arma, nudati gladii, insidentes equis urbem ac palatium petunt.

LXXXI. Erat Othoni celebre convivium primoribus feminis virisque: qui trepidi, fortuitusne militum furor an dolus imperatoris, manere ac deprehendi an fugere et dispergi periculosius foret, modo constantiam simulare, modo formidine detegi, simul Othonis vultum intueri: utque evenit inclinatis ad suspicionem mentibus, cum timeret Otho, timebatur. Sed haud secus discrimine senatus quam suo territus, et praefectos praetorii ad mitigandas militum iras statim miserat, et abire propere omnes e convivio jussit. Tum vero passim magistratus, projectis insignibus, vitata comitum et servorum frequentia, senes feminaeque, per tenebras diversa urbis itinera, rari domos, plurimi amicorum tecta, et, ut cuique humillimus cliens, incertas latebras petivere.

LXXXII. Militum impetus ne foribus quidem palatii coercitus, quo minus convivium irrumperent, ostendi sibi Othonem expostulantes, vulnerato Julio Martiale tribuno et Vitellio Saturnino praefecto legionis, dum ruentibus obsistunt. Undique arma et minae, modo in centuriones tribunosque, modo in senatum universum, lymphatis caeco pavore animis et, quia neminem unum destinare irae poterant, licentiam in omnes poscentibus, donec Otho contra decus imperii toro insistens, precibus et lacrimis aegre cohibuit, redieruntque in castra inviti neque innocentes. Postera die, velut capta urbe, clausae domus, rarus per vias populus, maesta plebs; dejecti in terram militum vultus, ac plus tristitiae quam poenitentiae. Manipulatim allocuti sunt Licinius Proculus et Plotius Firmus praefecti, ex suo quisque ingenio mitius aut horridius. Finis sermonis in eo, ut quina millia nummum singulis militibus numerarentur. Tum Otho ingredi castra ausus: atque illum tribuni centurionesque circumsistunt, abjectis militiae insignibus otium et salutem flagitantes. Sensit invidiam miles, et compositus in obsequium auctores seditionis ad supplicium ultro postulabat.

LXXXIII. Otho, quanquam turbidis rebus et diversis militum animis, cum optimus quisque remedium praesentis licentiae posceret, vulgus et plures seditionibus et ambitioso imperio laeti per turbas et raptus facilius ad civile bellum impellerentur, simul reputans non posse principatum scelere quaesitum subita modestia et prisca gravitate retineri, sed discrimine urbis et periculo senatus anxius, postremo ita disseruit. "Neque ut affectus vestros in amorem mei accenderem, commilitones, neque ut animum ad virtutem cohortarer (utraque enim egregie supersunt), sed veni postulaturus a vobis temperamentum vestrae fortitudinis et erga me modum caritatis. Tumultus proximi initium non cupiditate vel odio, quae multos exercitus in discordiam egere, ac ne detrectatione quidem aut formidine periculorum: nimia pietas vestra acrius quam considerate excitavit. Nam saepe honestas rerum causas, ni judicium adhibeas, perniciosi exitus consequuntur. Imus ad bellum: num omnes nuntios palam audiri, omnia consilia cunctis praesentibus tractari ratio rerum aut occasionum velocitas patitur? Tam nescire quaedam milites quam scire oportet. Ita se ducum auctoritas, sic rigor disciplinae habet, ut multa etiam centuriones tribunosque tantum juberi expediat. Si, ubi jubeantur, quaerere singulis liceat, pereunte obsequio etiam imperium intercidit. An et illic nocte intempesta rapientur arma? Unus alterve perditus ac temulentus (neque enim plures consternatione proxima insanisse crediderim) centurionis ac tribuni sanguine manus imbuet? Imperatoris sui tentorium irrumpet?

LXXXIV. "Vos quidem istud pro me: sed in discursu ac tenebris et rerum omnium confusione patefieri occasio etiam adversus me potest. Si Vitellio et satellitibus ejus eligendi facultas detur, quem nobis animum, quas mentes imprecentur, quid aliud quam seditionem et discordiam optabunt? ne miles centurioni, ne centurio tribuno obsequatur, hinc confusi pedites equitesque in exitium ruamus. Parendo potius, commilitones, quam imperia ducum sciscitando res militares continentur; et fortissimus in ipso discrimine exercitus est, qui ante discrimen quietissimus. Vobis arma et animus sit: mihi consilium et virtutis vestrae regimen relinquite. Paucorum culpa fuit, duorum poena erit. Ceteri abolete memoriam foedissimae noctis: nec illas adversus senatum voces ullus usquam exercitus audiat. Caput imperii et decora omnium provinciarum ad poenam vocare, non hercule illi, quos cum maxime Vitellius in nos ciet, Germani audeant. Ulline Italiae alumni et Romana vere juventus, ad sanguinem et caedem depoposcerint ordinem, cujus splendore et gloria sordes et obscuritatem Vitellianarum partium praestringimus? Nationes aliquas occupavit Vitellius, imaginem quandam exercitus habet: senatus nobiscum est. Sic fit, ut hinc respublica, inde hostes reipublicae constiterint. Quid? vos pulcherrimam hanc urbem domibus et tectis et congestu lapidum stare creditis? Muta ista et inanima intercidere ac reparari promiscua sunt: aeternitas rerum et pax gentium et mea cum vestra salus incolumitate senatus firmatur. Hunc auspicato a parente et conditore urbis nostrae institutum, et a regibus usque ad principes continuum et immortalem, sicut a majoribus accepimus, sic posteris tradamus. Nam, ut ex vobis senatores, ita ex senatoribus principes nascuntur."

LXXXV. Et oratio ad perstringendos mulcendosque militum animos, et severitatis modus (neque enim in plures quam in duos animadverti jusserat) grate accepta, compositique ad praesens, qui coerceri non poterant. Non tamen quies urbis redierat: strepitus telorum et facies belli, et militibus, ut nihil in commune turbantibus, ita sparsis per domos, occulto habitu, et maligna cura in omnes, quos nobilitas aut opes aut aliqua insignis claritudo rumoribus objecerat. Vitellianos quoque milites venisse in urbem ad studia partium noscenda, plerique credebant. Unde plena omnia suspicionum, et vix secreta domuum sine formidine. Sed plurimum trepidationis in publico, ut quemque nuntium fama attulisset, animum vultumque conversis, ne diffidere dubiis ac parum gaudere prosperis viderentur. Coacto vero in curiam senatu, arduus rerum omnium modus, ne contumax silentium, ne suspecta libertas. Et privato Othoni nuper atque eadem dicenti nota adulatio. Igitur versare sententias, et huc atque illuc torquere, hostem et parricidam Vitellium vocantes, providentissimus quisque vulgaribus conviciis; quidam vera probra jacere, in clamore tamen et ubi plurimae voces, aut tumultu verborum sibi ipsi obstrepentes.

LXXXVI. Prodigia insuper terrebant, diversis auctoribus vulgata. "In vestibulo capitolii omissas habenas bigae, cui Victoria institerat: erupisse cella Junonis majorem humana speciem: statuam divi Julii in insula Tiberini amnis sereno et immoto die ab Occidente in Orientem conversam: prolocutum in Etruria bovem: insolitos animalium partus:" et plura alia, rudibus saeculis etiam in pace observata, quae nunc tantum in metu audiuntur. Sed praecipuus et cum praesenti exitio etiam futuri pavor, subita inundatione Tiberis; qui immenso auctu, proruto ponte sublicio, ac strage obstantis molis refusus, non modo jacentia et plana urbis loca, sed secura hujusmodi casuum implevit. Rapti e publico plerique, plures in tabernis et cubilibus intercepti. Fames in vulgus, inopia quaestus et penuria alimentorum. Corrupta stagnantibus aquis insularum fundamenta, dein remeante flumine dilapsa. Utque primum vacuus a periculo animus fuit, id ipsum, quod paranti expeditionem Othoni campus Martius et via Flaminia iter belli esset obstructum a fortuitis vel naturalibus causis, in prodigium et omen imminentium cladium vertebatur.

LXXXVII. Otho, lustrata urbe et expensis belli consiliis, quando Peninae Cottiaeque Alpes et ceteri Galliarum aditus Vitellianis exercitibus claudebantur, Narbonensem Galliam aggredi statuit, classe valida et partibus fida, quod reliquos caesorum ad pontem Mulvium et saevitia Galbae in custodiam habitos, in numeros legionis composuerat, facta et ceteris spe honoratioris in posterum militiae. Addidit classi urbanas cohortes et plerosque e praetorianis, vires et robur exercitus, atque ipsis ducibus consilium et custodes. Summa expeditionis Antonio Novello, Suedio Clementi primipilaribus, Aemilio Pacensi, cui ademptum a Galba tribunatum reddiderat, permissa. Curam navium Oscus libertus retinebat, ad observandam honestiorum fidem comitatus. Peditum equitumque copiis Suetonius Paulinus, Marius Celsus, Annius Gallus, rectores destinati. Sed plurima fides Licinio Proculo praetorii praefecto: is urbanae militiae impiger, bellorum insolens, auctoritatem Paulini, vigorem Celsi, maturitatem Galli, ut cuique erat, criminando, quod facillimum factu est, pravus et callidus bonos et modestos anteibat.

LXXXVIII. Sepositus per eos dies Cornelius Dolabella in coloniam Aquinatem neque arcta custodia neque obscura nullum ob crimen, sed vetusto nomine et propinquitate Galbae monstratus. Multos e magistratibus, magnam consularium partem Otho, non participes aut ministros bello, sed comitum specie secum expedire jubet; in quis et L. Vitellium, eodem quo ceteros cultu, nec ut Imperatoris fratrem, nec ut hostis. Igitur motae urbis curae: nullus ordo metu aut periculo vacuus; primores senatus aetate invalidi et longa pace desides, segnis et oblita bellorum nobilitas, ignarus militiae eques, quanto magis occultare et abdere pavorem nitebantur, manifestius pavidi. Nec deerant e contrario, qui ambitione stolida conspicua arma, insignes equos, quidam luxuriosos apparatus conviviorum et irritamenta libidinum, ut instrumenta belli, mercarentur. Sapientibus quietis et reipublicae cura; levissimus quisque et futuri improvidus, spe vana tumens; multi afflicta fide in pace ac turbatis rebus alacres et per incerta tutissimi.

LXXXIX. Sed vulgus et magnitudine nimia communium curarum expers populus sentire paulatim belli mala, conversa in militum usum omni pecunia, intentis alimentorum pretiis; quae motu Vindicis haud perinde plebem attriverant, secura tum urbe et provinciali bello, quod inter legiones Galliasque velut externum fuit. Nam ex quo divus Augustus res Caesarum composuit, procul et in unius sollicitudinem aut decus populus Romanus bellaverat. Sub Tiberio et Caio, tantum pacis adversa reipublicae pertinuere. Scriboniani contra Claudium incepta simul audita et coercita. Nero nuntiis magis et rumoribus quam armis depulsus. Tum legiones classesque et, quod raro alias, praetorianus urbanusque miles in aciem deducti; Oriens Occidensque et quicquid utrimque virium est a tergo; si ducibus aliis bellatum foret, longo bello materia. Fuere, qui proficiscenti Othoni moras religionemque nondum conditorum ancilium afferrent. Aspernatus est omnem cunctationem ut Neroni quoque exitiosam; et Caecina jam Alpes transgressus exstimulabat.

XC. Pridie Idus Martias, commendata patribus republica, reliquias Neronianarum sectionum, nondum in fiscum conversas, revocatis ab exsilio concessit. Justissimum donum et in speciem magnificum, sed festinata jam pridem exactione usu sterili. Mox vocata concione, majestatem urbis et consensum populi ac senatus pro se attollens, adversum Vitellianas partes modeste disseruit, inscitiam potius legionum quam audaciam increpans, nulla Vitellii mentione; sive ipsius ea moderatio, seu scriptor orationis sibi metuens contumeliis in Vitellium abstinuit, quando ut in consiliis militiae Suetonio Paulino et Mario Celso, ita in rebus urbanis Galerii Trachali ingenio Othonem uti credebatur: et erant, qui genus ipsum orandi noscerent, crebro fori usu celebre et ad implendas aures latum et sonans. Clamor vocesque vulgi, ex more adulandi, nimiae et falsae: quasi dictatorem Caesarem, aut imperatorem Augustum prosequerentur, ita studiis votisque certabant, nec metu aut amore, sed ex libidine servitii; ut in familiis, privata cuique stimulatio et vile jam decus publicum. Profectus Otho quietem urbis curasque imperii Salvio Titiano fratri permisit.

C. CORNELII TACITI

HISTORIARUM

LIBER SECUNDUS.

BREVIARIUM LIBRI.

Cap. I. Titus ad Galbam missus, nuntio mortis ejus accepto, vertit iter. II. Paphiae Veneris templum adit. III Hujus origo et deae cultus. IV. Ibi futura edoctus, aucto animo, ad patrem, qui bellum Judaicum profligaverat, redit. V. Vespasiani Mucianique ingenium ac mores diversi. Hi duces, positis odiis, in medium consulunt. Inde VI, VII, civilis belli occasio, intumescentibus Orientis legionibus. VIII, IX. Falsi Neronis ludibrium, ab Asprenate compressum. X. In urbe parvae res magnis motibus actae. Vibius Crispus Annium Faustum, delatorem fratris sui, pervertit.

XI. Laeta Othoni principia belli. XII. Miles ejus in Alpinos saevit, XIII, in Albium Intemelium iras vertit. Egregium maternae pietatis exemplum. XIV. Imminet provinciae Narbonensi Othoniana classis. Vitelliani caesi, XV, nec Othonianis incruenta victoria. XVI. Pacarium procuratorem, juvare Vitellium Corsorum viribus parantem, insulani necant. XVII. Vitellianorum res secundae in Italia. XVIII, XIX. Spurinna Placentiam munit contra Vitellianos: XX, eam Caecina dum oppugnat, XXI, amphitheatrum urbi proximum conflagrat. XXII. Obsidione soluta, Cremonam Caecina petit, ubi XXIII. Othoniani prospere pugnant. Vincentium impetum reprimunt duces, inde suspecti fiunt suis. XXIV. Caecinae insidias in ipsum vertit Suetonius Paulinus, cujus XXV, cunctatione Vitelliani servantur. XXVI. Utrimque tumultuantur milites.

XXVII. Valens in Italiam copias ducit. XXVIII, XXIX. Gravis in ejus exercitu orta Batavorum seditio Alpheni Vari consilio composita. XXX. Junctis armis, aemulatione suppressa, Caecina ac Valens Vitellium fovent, Othoni probra objectant. Eorum XXXI. Othonisque et Vitellii comparatio. Otho consultat de ratione belli. XXXII. Suetonius Paulinus moram suadet. XXXIII. Titiani fratris et Proculi consilia praevalent. Otho cum valida manu Brixellum concedit. XXXIV. Vitelliani transitum Padi simulant;

XXXV, XXXVI, quem prohibentes Othoniani caeduntur. XXXVII. Vanus rumor, pavore belli fastidiove utriusque principis, pacis consilia inter exercitus fuisse agitata. XXXVIII. Excursus de prioribus P. R. civilibus bellis, XXXIX, XL. Titianus et Proculus ad quartum a Bedriaco castra imperite promovent. Ducibus dubiis, rem in discrimen mitti Otho jubet. XLI—XLIII. Bedriacensis pugna. XLIV. Othonianorum fuga et adversus duces suos ira. XLV. Induciae. Victi cum victoribus, in lacrimas effusi, civilia bella detestantur. XLVI—XLIX. Accepto cladis nuntio, Otho, consilii certus, spretis amicorum militumque solatiis, seditionem compescit et in ferrum pectore incumbit. Funus maturatum. Ad rogum quidam militum se interficiunt. L. Othonis aetas, origo, fama.

LI. Novata luctu ac dolore militum seditio. LII—LIV. Pars senatus Othonem secuta, extremum discrimen adit. LV. Romae trepidationis nihil, spectantur ludi; audita Othonis morte, Vitellio plauditur LVI. Gravis Italiae victor exercitus. LVII. Vitellius nuntium de victoria sua accipit, LVIII, simulque de transgressa in partes suas utraque Mauretania. LIX. Blaesi verniles blanditias odiis pensat LX. Othonianorum promptissimos centuriones interficit, duces absolvit. LXI. Maricci, inserere sese fortunae ausi, supplicium. LXII. Vitellii gula, leges. Spretum Augusti Caesarisque praeconium. Pulsi mathematici. Equites arena prohibiti. LXIII, LXIV. Dolabellae caedes. Triariae licentia; Galeriae et Sextiliae modestia. LXV. Cluvius absolvitur; Trebellius removetur. LXVI. Victae legiones ferociunt. Quartadecimanorum et Batavorum discordia. LXVII. Praetorianorum honesta missio. Sparguntur legiones. LXVIII. Luxuriam principis aemulatur exercitus. Ticini tumultus alio tumultu sedatus. Verginii periculum. LXIX. Cohortes Batavorum in Germaniam remissae: amputati legionum auxiliorumque numeri: miles luxu corruptus. LXX. Vitellius Bedriacenses campos laetus lustrat, propinquae sortis ignarus. LXXI. Neronis libidines aemulatur. Consulatus partitur. LXXII. Falsus Scribonianus cruci suffixus.

LXXIII. Vitellius, ob adactum in verba ejus Orientem superbus et vecors, Vespasiani ad nomen excitatur. LXXIV. Hic bellum armaque parat. LXXV—LXXVIII. Nutantem firmant Mucianus, legati alii, vatum responsa et Carmeli dei sacerdos. LXXIX, LXXX. Imperatorem salutant Aegyptus et Syria. LXXXI. Accedunt ad partes ejus reges Sohemus, Antiochus, Agrippa; regina Berenice LXXXII. Belli consilia. Titus instat Judaeae. Vespasianus claustra Aegypti obtinet. LXXXIII, LXXXIV. Mucianus, cum exercitu praemissus, nervum belli conquirit. LXXXV, LXXXVI. Moesicae Pannonicaeque legiones, in partes transgressae, Dalmaticum militem trahunt. Belli faces Antonius Primus, Cornelius Fuscus.

LXXXVII. Vitellius, contemptior in dies, gravi urbem agmine petit, eamque, LXXXVIII, LXXXIX, patrata multa militum paganorumque caede, ut captam, ingressus, XC, magnificam de semetipso orationem promit, XCI, humani divinique juris expers, nonnulla tamen popularia usurpat. XCII. Munia imperii Caecina ac Valens obeunt. Vitellio auctoritas nihil. XCIII. Militis in urbe otium, libidines, morbi, mortes, XCIV, insolentia, paucitas. Vitellii inopia, prodigentia. Duces Galliarum postulati ad supplicium. Militiae ordo confusus. XCV. Natalis Vitellii ingenti paratu celebratus, Inferiae Neroni factae. Urbis miseria. XCVI. Defectionis Flavianae rumores male coercet Vitellius. XCVII, XCVIII. Excita tamen auxilia, sed necessitas dissimulata. XCIX. Irrumpentibus hostibus, Caecina ad bellum praemittitur; sed is C, CI, cum Lucilio Basso classibusque Ravennate Misenensique proditionem componit, et ad partes Vespasiani transit. Gesta haec sunt paucis mensibus anno eodem, consulibus iisdem et aliis suffectis, de quibus videsis 1, 77.

Struebat jam fortuna in diversa parte terrarum initia causasque imperio, quod varia sorte laetum reipublicae aut atrox, ipsis principibus prosperum aut exitio fuit. Titus Vespasianus e Judaea, incolumi adhuc Galba, missus a patre, causam profectionis officium erga principem et maturam petendis honoribus juventam ferebat. Sed vulgus fingendi avidum disperserat accitum in adoptionem. Materia sermonibus senium et orbitas principis et intemperantia civitatis, donec unus eligatur, multos destinandi. Augebat famam ipsius Titi ingenium, quantaecunque fortunae capax, decor oris cum quadam majestate, prosperae Vespasiani res, praesaga responsa, et inclinatis ad credendum animis, loco ominum etiam fortuita. Ubi Corinthi, Achaiae urbe, certos nuntios accepit de interitu Galbae, et aderant qui arma Vitellii bellumque affirmarent, anxius animo, paucis amicorum adhibitis, cuncta utrimque perlustrat. Si pergeret in urbem, nullam officii gratiam, in alterius honorem suscepti: ac se Vitellio sive Othoni obsidem fore. Sin rediret, offensam haud dubiam victoris; sed incerta adhuc victoria, et concedente in partes patre, filium excusatum. Sin Vespasianus rempublicam susciperet, obliviscendum offensarum de bello agitantibus.

II. His ac talibus inter spem metumque jactatum spes

vicit. Fuere, qui accensum desiderio Berenices reginae vertisse iter crederent. Neque abhorrebat a Berenice juvenilis animus; sed gerendis rebus nullum ex eo impedimentum: laetam voluptatibus adolescentiam egit, suo quam patris imperio moderatior. Igitur oram Achaiae et Asiae ac laeva maris praevectus, Rhodum et Cyprum insulas, inde Syriam audentioribus spatiis petebat. Atque illum cupido incessit adeundi visendique templum Paphiae Veneris, inclitum per indigenas advenasque. Haud fuerit longum initia religionis, templi ritum, formam deae (neque enim alibi sic habetur) paucis disserere.

III. Conditorem templi regem Aerian vetus memoria, quidam ipsius deae nomen id perhibent. Fama recentior tradit a Cinyra sacratum templum, deamque ipsam conceptam mari huc appulsam. Sed scientiam artemque haruspicum accitam, et Cilicem Tamiram intulisse; atque ita pactum, ut familiae utriusque posteri caerimoniis praesiderent. Mox, ne honore nullo regium genus peregrinam stirpem antecelleret, ipsa quam intulerant scientia hospites cessere: tantum Cinyrades sacerdos consulitur. Hostiae, ut quisque vovit, sed mares deliguntur. Certissima fides haedorum fibris. Sanguinem arae offundere vetitum: precibus et igne puro altaria adolentur, nec ullis imbribus, quanquam in aperto, madescunt. Simulacrum deae non effigie humana, continuus orbis latiore initio tenuem in ambitum metae modo exsurgens; et ratio in obscuro.

IV. Titus spectata opulentia donisque regum, quaeque alia laetum antiquitatibus Graecorum genus incertae vetustati affingit, de navigatione primum consuluit. Postquam pandi viam et mare prosperum accepit, de se per ambages interrogat, caesis compluribus hostiis. Sostratus (sacerdotis id nomen erat) ubi laeta et congruentia exta magnisque consultis annuere deam videt, pauca in praesens et solita respondens, petito secreto, futura aperit. Titus, aucto animo ad patrem pervectus; suspensis provinciarum et exercituum mentibus, ingens rerum fiducia accessit. Profligaverat bellum Judaicum Vespasianus, oppugnatione Hierosolymorum reliqua, duro magis et arduo opere ob ingenium montis et pervicaciam superstitionis, quam quo satis virium obsessis ad tolerandas necessitates superesset. Tres, ut supra memoravimus, ipsi Vespasiano legiones erant, exercitae bello: quatuor Mucianus obtinebat in pace; sed aemulatio et proximi exercitus gloria repulerat segnitiam, quantumque illis roboris discrimina et labor, tantum his vigoris addiderat integra quies et inexperti belli labor: auxilia utrique cohortium alarumque, et classes regesque, ac nomen dispari fama celebre.

V. Vespasianus acer militiae anteire agmen, locum castris capere, noctu diuque consilio ac, si res posceret, manu hostibus obniti, cibo fortuito, veste habituque vix a gregario milite discrepans; prorsus, si avaritia abesset, antiquis ducibus par. Mucianum e contrario magnificentia et opes et cuncta privatum modum supergressa extollebant: aptior sermone, dispositu provisuque civilium rerum peritus; egregium principatus temperamentum, si, demptis utriusque vitiis, solae virtutes miscerentur. Ceterum hic Syriae, ille Judaeae praepositus, vicinis provinciarum administrationibus, invidia discordes, exitu demum Neronis positis odiis in medium consuluere, primum per amicos; dein praecipua concordiae fides Titus prava certamina communi utilitate aboleverat, natura atque arte compositus alliciendis etiam Muciani moribus. Tribuni centurionesque et vulgus militum industria, licentia, per virtutes, per voluptates, ut cuique ingenium, asciscebantur.

VI. Antequam Titus adventaret, sacramentum Othonis acceperat uterque exercitus, praecipitibus, ut assolet, nuntiis, et tarda mole civilis belli, quod longa concordia quietus Oriens tunc primum parabat. Namque olim validissima inter se civium arma in Italia Galliave viribus Occidentis coepta; et Pompeio, Cassio, Bruto, Antonio, quos omnes trans mare secutum est civile bellum, haud prosperi exitus fuerant, auditique saepius in Syria Judaeaque Caesares quam inspecti. Nulla seditio legionum: tantum adversus Parthos minae, vario eventu. Et proximo civili bello, turbatis aliis, inconcussa ibi pax: dein fides erga Galbam. Mox, ut Othonem ac Vitellium scelestis armis res Romanas raptum ire vulgatum est, ne penes ceteros imperii praemia, penes ipsos tantum servitii necessitas esset, fremere miles et vires suas circumspicere. Septem legiones statim et cum ingentibus auxiliis Syria Judaeaque: inde continua Aegyptus duaeque legiones, hinc Cappadocia Pontusque et quicquid castrorum Armeniis praetenditur. Asia et ceterae provinciae nec virorum inopes et pecuniae opulentae: quantum insularum mari cingitur, et parando interim bello secundum tutumque ipsum mare.

VII. Non fallebat duces impetus militum: sed bellantibus aliis placuit exspectari belli exitum: victores victosque nunquam solida fide coalescere: nec referre, Vitellium an Othonem superstitem fortuna faceret. Rebus secundis etiam egregios duces insolescere: discordiam his, ignaviam, luxuriem; et suismet vitiis alterum bello, alterum victoria periturum. Igitur arma in occasionem distulere, Vespasianus Mucianusque nuper, ceteri olim mixtis consiliis; optimus quisque amore reipublicae: multos dulcedo praedarum stimulabat, alios ambiguae domi res. Ita boni malique causis diversis, studio pari, bellum omnes cupiebant.

VIII. Sub idem tempus Achaia atque Asia falso exterritae, velut Nero adventaret, vario super exitu ejus rumore eoque pluribus vivere eum fingentibus credentibusque. Ceterorum casus conatusque in contextu operis dicemus: tunc servus e Ponto sive, ut alii tradidere, libertinus ex Italia, citharae et cantus peritus (unde illi super similitudinem oris propior ad fallendum fides) adjunctis desertoribus quos inopia vagos ingentibus promissis corruperat, mare ingreditur: ac vi tempestatum Cythnum insulam detrusus et militum quosdam ex Oriente commeantium ascivit vel abnuentes interfici jussit, et spoliatis negotiatoribus, mancipiorum valentissimum quemque armavit; centurionemque Sisennam, dextras, concordiae insignia, Syriaci exercitus nomine ad praetorianos ferentem, variis artibus aggressus est, donec Sisenna, clam relicta insula, trepidus et vim metuens aufugeret: inde late terror, multis ad celebritatem nominis erectis, rerum novarum cupidine et odio praesentium.

IX. Gliscentem in dies famam fors discussit. Galatiam ac Pamphyliam provincias Calpurnio Asprenati regendas Galba permiserat: datae e classe Misenensi duae triremes ad prosequendum, cum quibus Cythnum insulam tenuit. Nec defuere, qui trierarchos nomine Neronis accirent: is in maestitiam compositus et fidem suorum quondam militum invocans, ut eum in Syria aut Aegypto sisterent, orabat. Trierarchi nutantes, seu dolo, alloquendos sibi milites et paratis omnium animis reversuros firmaverunt. Sed Asprenati cuncta ex fide nuntiata; cujus cohortatione expugnata navis et interfectus quisquis ille erat. Corpus, insigne oculis comaque et torvitate vultus, in Asiam atque inde Romam pervectum est.

X. In civitate discordi et ob crebras principum mutationes inter libertatem ac licentiam incerta, parvae quoque res magnis motibus agebantur. Vibius Crispus pecunia, potentia, ingenio inter claros magis quam inter bonos, Annium Faustum equestris ordinis qui temporibus Neronis delationes factitaverat, ad cognitionem senatus vocabat. Nam recens Galbae principatu censuerant patres, ut accusatorum causae noscerentur. Id senatusconsultum varie jactatum et, prout potens vel inops reus inciderat, infirmum aut validum retinebatur. Ad hoc terroris et propria vi Crispus incubuerat, delatorem fratris sui pervertere; traxeratque magnam senatus partem, ut indefensum et inauditum dedi ad exitium postularent. Contra apud alios nihil aeque reo proderat quam nimia potentia accusatoris: dari tempus, edi crimina, quamvis invisum ac nocentem more tamen audiendum censebant. Et valuere primo, dilataque in paucos dies cognitio: mox damnatus est Faustus, nequaquam eo assensu civitatis quem pessimis moribus meruerat quippe ipsum Crispum easdem accusationes cum praemio exercuisse meminerant, nec poena criminis sed ultor displicebat.

XI. Laeta interim Othoni principia belli, motis ad imperium ejus e Dalmatia Pannoniaque exercitibus. Fuere quatuor legiones, e quibus bina millia praemissa; ipsae modicis intervallis sequebantur, septima a Galba conscripta, veteranae undecima ac tertiadecima et praecipui fama quartadecumani, rebellione Britanniae compressa. Addiderat gloriam Nero, eligendo ut potissimos; unde longa illis erga Neronem fides et erecta in Othonem studia. Sed quo plus virium ac roboris, e fiducia tarditas inerat: agmen legionum alae cohortesque praeveniebant, et ex ipsa urbe haud spernanda manus, quinque praetoriae cohortes et equitum vexilla cum legione prima, ac deforme insuper auxilium, duo millia gladiatorum, sed per civilia arma etiam severis ducibus usurpatum. His copiis rector additus Annius Gallus, cum Vestricio Spurinna ad occupandas Padi ripas praemissus, quoniam prima consiliorum frustra ceciderant transgresso jam Alpes Caecina, quem sisti intra Gallias posse speraverat. Ipsum Othonem comitabantur speculatorum lecta corpora cum ceteris praetoriis cohortibus, veterani e praetorio, classicorum ingens numerus. Nec illi segne aut corruptum luxu iter; sed lorica ferrea usus est, et ante signa pedester, horridus, incomptus famaeque dissimilis.

XII. Blandiebatur coeptis fortuna, possessa per mare et naves majore Italiae parte penitus usque ad initium maritimarum Alpium: quibus tentandis aggrediendaeque provinciae Narbonensi Suedium Clementem, Antonium Novellum, Aemilium Pacensem duces dederat. Sed Pacensis per licentiam militum vinctus: Antonio Novello nulla auctoritas: Suedius Clemens ambitioso imperio regebat, ut adversus modestiam disciplinae corruptus, ita praeliorum avidus. Non Italia adiri nec loca sedesque patriae videbantur; tanquam externa littora et urbes hostium urere, vastare, rapere, eo atrocius quod nihil usquam provisum adversum metus. Pleni agri, apertae domus: occursantes domini juxta conjuges et liberos securitate pacis et belli malo circumveniebantur. Maritimas tum Alpes tenebat procurator Marius Maturus. Is concita gente (nec deest juventus) arcere provinciae finibus Othonianos intendit. Sed primo impetu caesi disjectique montani, ut quibus temere collectis, non castra, non ducem noscitantibus, neque in victoria decus esset neque in fuga flagitium.

XIII. Irritatus eo praelio Othonis miles vertit iras in municipium Albium Intemelium: quippe in acie nihil praedae; inopes agrestes et vilia arma: nec capi poterant, pernix genus et gnari locorum: sed calamitatibus insontium expleta avaritia. Auxit invidiam praeclaro exemplo femina Ligus, quae filio abdito, cum simul pecuniam occultari milites credidissent eoque per cruciatus interrogarent. ubi filium occuleret, uterum ostendens latere respondit. Nec ullis deinde terroribus aut morte constantiam vocis egregiae mutavit.

XIV. Imminere provinciae Narbonensi, in verba Vitellii adactae, classem Othonis trepidi nuntii Fabio Valenti attulere. Aderant legati coloniarum, auxilium orantes. Duas Tungrorum cohortes, quatuor equitum turmas, universam Treverorum alam cum Julio Classico praefecto misit; e quibus pars in colonia Forojuliensi retenta, ne omnibus copiis in terrestre iter versis vacuo mari classis acceleraret. Duodecim equitum turmae et lecti e cohortibus adversus hostem iere: quibus adjuncta Ligurum cohors, vetus loci auxilium, et quingenti Alpini, qui nondum sub signis. Nec mora praelio, sed acie ita instructa, ut pars classicorum, mixtis paganis, in colles mari propinquos exsurgeret, quantum inter colles ac littus aequi loci praetorianus miles expleret, in ipso mari ut annexa classis et pugnae parata conversa et minaci fronte praetenderetur. Vitelliani, quibus minor peditum vis, in equite robur, Alpinos proximis jugis, cohortes densis ordinibus post equitem locant. Treverorum turmae obtulere se hosti incaute, cum exciperet contra veteranus miles, simul a latere saxis urgeret apta ad jaciendum etiam paganorum manus, qui sparsi inter milites, strenui ignavique, in victoria idem audebant. Additus perculsis terror invecta in terga pugnantium classe. Ita undique clausi; deletaeque omnes copiae forent, ni victorem exercitum attinuisset obscurum noctis, obtentui fugientibus.

XV. Nec Vitelliani, quanquam victi, quievere: accitis auxiliis securum hostem ac successu rerum socordius agentem invadunt: cæsi vigiles, perrupta castra, trepidatum apud naves, donec sidente paulatim metu, occupato juxta colle defensi, mox irrupere. Atrox ibi caedes, et Tungrarum cohortium praefecti, sustentata diu acie, telis obruuntur. Ne Othonianis quidem incruenta victoria fuit, quorum improvide secutos conversi equites circumvenerunt. Ac velut pactis induciis, ne hinc classis, inde eques subitam formidinem inferrent, Vitelliani retro Antipolim Narbonensis Galliae municipium, Othoniani Albigaunum interioris Liguriae revertere.

XVI. Corsicam ac Sardiniam ceterasque proximi maris insulas, fama victricis classis in partibus Othonis tenuit. Sed Corsicam prope afflixit Decumi Pacarii procuratoris temeritas tanta mole belli nihil in summam profutura, ipsi exitiosa. Namque Othonis odio juvare Vitellium Corsorum viribus statuit, inani auxilio etiam si provenisset. Vocatis principibus insulae consilium aperit, et contradicere ausos, Claudium Pyrrhicum trierarchum Liburnicarum ibi navium, Quintium Certum equitem Romanum interfici jubet: quorum morte exterriti qui aderant, simul ignara et alieni metus socia imperitorum turba, in verba Vitellii juravere. Sed ubi delectum agere Pacarius et inconditos homines fatigare militiae muneribus occepit, laborem insolitum perosi infirmitatem suam reputabant: insulam esse quam incolerent, et longe Germaniam viresque legionum: direptos vastatosque classe etiam quos cohortes alaeque protegerent. Et aversi repente animi; nec tamen aperta vi, aptum tempus insidiis legere. Digressis, qui Pacarium frequentabant, nudus et auxilii inops balineis interficitur; trucidati et comites. Capita, ut hostium, ipsi interfectores ad Othonem tulere; neque eos aut Otho praemio affecit aut puniit Vitellius, in multa colluvie rerum majoribus flagitiis permixtos.

XVII. Aperuerat jam Italiam bellumque transmiserat, ut supra memoravimus, ala Siliana, nullo apud quenquam Othonis favore, nec quia Vitellium mallent; sed longa pax ad omne servitium fregerat, faciles occupantibus et melioribus incuriosos. Florentissimum Italiae latus, quantum inter Padum Alpesque camporum et urbium, armis Vitellii (namque et praemissae a Caecina cohortes advenerant) tenebatur.

Capta Pannoniorum cohors apud Cremonam. Intercepti centum equites ac mille classici inter Placentiam Ticinumque: quo successu Vitellianus miles non jam flumine aut ripis arcebatur. Irritabat quin etiam Batavos Transrhenanosque Padus ipse: quem repente contra Placentiam transgressi, raptis quibusdam exploratoribus, ita ceteros terruere, ut adesse omnem Caecinae exercitum trepidi ac falsi nuntiarent.

XVIII. Certum erat Spurinnae (is enim Placentiam obtinebat) nec dum venisse Caecinam, et, si propinquaret, coercere intra munimenta militem nec tres praetorias cohortes et mille vexillarios cum paucis equitibus veterano exercitui objicere. Sed indomitus miles et belli ignarus, correptis signis vexillisque, ruere et retinenti duci tela intentare, spretis centurionibus tribunisque; quin prodi Othonem, et accitum Caecinam clamitabant. Fit temeritatis alienae comes Spurinna, primo coactus, mox velle simulans, quo plus auctoritatis inesset consiliis, si seditio mitesceret.

XIX. Postquam in conspectu Padus et nox appetebat, vallari castra placuit. Is labor, urbano militi insolitus, contundit animos. Tum vetustissimus quisque castigare credulitatem suam, metum ac discrimen ostendere, si cum exercitu Caecina, patentibus campis, tam paucas cohortes circumfudisset: jamque totis castris modesti sermones et, inserentibus se centurionibus tribunisque, laudari providentia ducis, quod coloniam virium et opum validam robur ac sedem bello legisset. Ipse postremo Spurinna, non tam culpam exprobrans quam ratione ostendens, relictis exploratoribus, ceteros Placentiam reduxit, minus turbidos et imperia accipientes. Solidati muri, propugnacula addita, auctae turres, provisa parataque non arma modo, sed obsequium et parendi amor; quod solum illis partibus defuit, cum virtutis haud poeniteret.

XX. At Caecina, velut relicta post Alpes saevitia ac licentia, modesto agmine per Italiam incessit. Ornatum ipsius municipia et coloniae in superbiam trahebant, quod versicolori sagulo, braccas barbarum tegmen indutus, togatos alloqueretur. Uxorem autem ejus Saloninam, quanquam in nullius injuriam insigni equo ostroque veheretur, tanquam laesi gravabantur, insita mortalibus natura recentem aliorum felicitatem acribus oculis introspicere, modumque fortunae a nullis magis exigere quam quos in aequo viderunt. Caecina Padum transgressus, tentata Othonianorum fide per colloquium et promissa, iisdem petitus, postquam pax et concordia speciosis et irritis nominibus jactata sunt, consilia curasque in oppugnationem Placentiae magno terrore vertit, gnarus, ut initia belli provenissent, famam in cetera fore.

XXI. Sed primus dies impetu magis quam veterani exercitus artibus transactus: aperti incautique muros subiere, cibo vinoque praegraves. In eo certamine pulcherrimum amphitheatri opus, situm extra muros, conflagravit, sive ab oppugnatoribus incensum, dum faces et glandes et missilem ignem in obsessos jaculantur, sive ab obsessis, dum retorta ingerunt. Municipale vulgus, pronum ad suspiciones, fraude illata ignis alimenta credidit a quibusdam e vicinis coloniis, invidia et aemulatione, quod nulla in Italia moles tam capax foret: quocumque casu accidit, dum atrociora metuebantur, in levi habitum; reddita securitate, tanquam nihil gravius pati potuissent, maerebant. Ceterum multo suorum cruore pulsus Caecina, et nox parandis operibus assumpta. Vitelliani pluteos cratesque et vineas suffodiendis muris protegendisque oppugnatoribus; Othoniani sudes et immensas lapidum ac plumbi aerisque moles perfringendis obruendisque hostibus expediunt. Utrimque pudor, utrimque gloria et diversae exhortationes, hinc legionum et Germanici exercitus robur, inde urbanae militiae et praetoriarum cohortium decus attollentium; illi ut segnem et desidem et circo ac theatris corruptum militem, hi peregrinum et externum increpabant: simul Othonem ac Vitellium celebrantes culpantesve uberioribus inter se probris quam laudibus stimulabantur.

XXII. Vix dum orto die plena propugnatoribus moenia, fulgentes armis virisque campi; densum legionum agmen, sparsa auxiliorum manus, altiora murorum sagittis aut saxis incessere, neglecta aut aevo fluxa cominus aggredi. Ingerunt desuper Othoniani pila librato magis et certo ictu adversus temere subeuntes cohortes Germanorum cantu truci et more patrio nudis corporibus super humeros scuta quatientium. Legionarius pluteis et cratibus tectus subruit muros, instruit aggerem, molitur portas. Contra praetoriani dispositos ad id ipsum molares ingenti pondere ac fragore provolvunt: pars subeuntium obruti; pars confixi et exsangues aut laceri, cum augeret stragem trepidatio eoque acrius e moenibus vulnerarentur, rediere infracta partium fama. Et Caecina pudore coeptae temere oppugnationis, ne irrisus ac vanus iisdem castris assideret, trajecto rursus Pado Cremonam petere intendit. Tradidere sese abeunti Turulius Cerialis cum compluribus classicis et Julius Briganticus cum paucis equitum, hic praefectus alae, in Batavis genitus, ille primipilaris et Caecinae haud alienus, quod ordines in Germania duxerat.

XXIII. Spurinna, comperto itinere hostium, defensam Placentiam, quaeque acta et quid Caecina pararet, Annium Gallum per literas docet. Gallus legionem primam in auxilium Placentiae ducebat, diffisus paucitate cohortium, ne longius obsidium et vim Germanici exercitus parum tolerarent: ubi pulsum Caecinam pergere Cremonam accepit, aegre coercitam legionem et pugnandi ardore usque ad seditionem progressam Bedriaci sistit. Inter Veronam Cremonamque situs est vicus, duabus jam Romanis cladibus notus infaustusque. Iisdem diebus a Marcio Macro haud procul Cremona prospere pugnatum: namque promptus animi Marcius transvectos navibus gladiatores in adversam Padi ripam repente effudit. Turbata ibi Vitellianorum auxilia et, ceteris Cremonam fugientibus, caesi qui restiterant. Sed repressus vincentium impetus, ne novis subsidiis firmati hostes fortunam proelii mutarent. Suspectum id Othonianis fuit omnia ducum facta prave aestimantibus. Certatim, ut quisque animo ignavus, procax ore, Annium Gallum et Suetonium Paulinum et Marium Celsum (nam eos quoque Otho praefecerat) variis criminibus incesserant. Acerrima seditionum ac discordiae incitamenta interfectores Galbae: scelere et metu vecordes miscere cuncta, modo palam turbidis vocibus, modo occultis ad Othonem literis, qui humillimo cuique credulus, bonos metuens trepidabat, rebus prosperis incertus et inter adversa melior. Igitur Titianum fratrem accitum bello praeposuit. Interea Paulini et Celsi ductu res egregiae gestae.

XXIV. Angebant Caecinam nequicquam omnia coepta et senescens exercitus sui fama: pulsus Placentia, caesis nuper auxiliis, etiam per concursum exploratorum, crebra magis quam digna memoratu proelia, inferior, propinquante Fabio Valente, ne omne belli decus illuc concederet, reciperare gloriam avidius quam consultius properabat. Ad duodecimum a Cremona (locus Castorum vocatur) ferocissimos auxiliarium imminentibus viae lucis occultos componit: equites procedere longius jussi, et irritato proelio sponte refugi festinationem sequentium elicere, donec insidiae coorirentur. Proditum id Othonianis ducibus; et curam peditum Paulinus, equitum Celsus sumpsere. Tertiaedecimae legionis vexillum, quatuor auxiliorum cohortes et quingenti equites in sinistro locantur; aggerem viae tres praetoriae cohortes altis ordinibus obtinuere; dextra fronte prima legio incessit cum duabus auxiliaribus cohortibus et quingentis equitibus. Super hos e praetorio auxiliisque mille equites, cumulus prosperis aut subsidium laborantibus, ducebantur.

XXV. Antequam miscerentur acies, terga vertentibus Vitellianis, Celsus doli prudens repressit suos. Vitelliani temere exsurgentes, cedente sensim Celso, longius secuti ultro in insidias praecipitantur: nam a lateribus cohortes, legionum adversa frons, et subito discursu terga cinxerant equites. Signum pugnae non statim a Suetonio Paulino pediti datum: cunctator natura, et cui cauta potius consilia cum ratione quam prospera ex casu placerent, compleri fossas, aperiri campum, pandi aciem jubebat; satis cito incipi victoriam ratus, ubi provisum foret ne vincerentur. Ea cunctatione spatium Vitellianis datum in vineas nexu traducum impeditas refugiendi. Et modica silva adhaerebat; unde rursus ausi promptissimos praetorianorum equitum interfecere: vulneratur rex Epiphanes, impigre pro Othone pugnam ciens.

XXVI. Tum Othonianus pedes erupit: protrita hostium acie, versi in fugam etiam qui subveniebant; nam Caecina non simul cohortes sed singulas acciverat: quae res in proelio trepidationem auxit, cum dispersos nec usquam validos pavor fugientium abriperet. Orta et in castris seditio, quod non universi ducerentur. Vinctus praefectus castrorum Julius Gratus, tanquam fratri apud Othonem militanti proditionem ageret, cum fratrem ejus, Julium Frontonem tribunum, Othoniani sub eodem crimine vinxissent. Ceterum ea ubique formido fuit apud fugientes, occursantes, in acie, pro vallo, ut deleri cum universo exercitu Caecinam potuisse, ni Suetonius Paulinus receptui cecinisset, utrisque in partibus percrebruerit. Timuisse se Paulinus ferebat tantum insuper laboris atque itineris, ne Vitellianus miles recens e castris fessos aggrederetur et perculsis nullum retro subsidium foret: apud paucos ea ducis ratio probata, in vulgus adverso rumore fuit.

XXVII. Haud perinde id damnum Vitellianos in metum compulit quam ad modestiam composuit; nec solum apud Caecinam, qui culpam in militem conferebat seditioni magis quam proelio paratum: Fabii quoque Valentis copiae (jam enim Ticinum venerat) posito hostium contemptu, et recuperandi decoris cupidine, reverentius et aequalius duci parebant. Gravis alioquin seditio exarserat, quam altiore initio (neque enim rerum a Caecina gestarum ordinem interrumpi oportuerat) repetam. Cohortes Batavorum, quas bello Neronis a quartadecima legione digressas, cum Britanniam peterent, audito Vitellii motu in civitate Lingonum Fabio Valenti adjunctas retulimus, superbe agebant, ut cujusque legionis tentoria accessissent, coercitos a se quartadecimanos, ablatam Neroni Italiam, atque omnem belli fortunam in ipsorum manu sitam jactantes. Contumeliosum id militibus, acerbum duci; corrupta jurgiis aut rixis disciplina: ad postremum Valens e petulantia etiam perfidiam suspectabat.

XXVIII. Igitur nuntio allato pulsam Treverorum alam Tungrosque a classe Othonis et Narbonensem Galliam circumiri, simul cura socios tuendi et militari astu cohortes turbidas ac, si una forent, praevalidas dispergendi, partem Batavorum ire in subsidium jubet. Quod ubi auditum vulgatumque, maerere socii, fremere legiones: orbari se fortissimorum virorum auxilio: veteres illos et tot bellorum victores, postquam in conspectu sit hostis, velut ex acie abduci: si provincia urbe et salute imperii potior sit, omnes illuc sequerentur; sin victoriae sanitas, sustentaculum, columen in Italia verteretur, non abrumpendos, ut corpori, validissimos artus.

XXIX. Haec ferociter jactando, postquam immissis lictoribus Valens coercere seditionem coeptabat, ipsum invadunt, saxa jaciunt, fugientem sequuntur, spolia Galliarum et Viennensium aurum et pretia laborum suorum occultare clamitantes, direptis sarcinis, tabernacula ducis ipsamque humum pilis et lanceis rimabantur: nam Valens servili veste apud decurionem equitum tegebatur. Tum Alfenus Varus praefectus castrorum, deflagrante paulatim seditione, addit consilium, vetitis obire vigilias centurionibus, omisso tubae sono quo miles ad belli munia cietur. Igitur torpere cuncti, circumspectare inter se attoniti et id ipsum, quod nemo regeret, paventes: silentio, patientia, postremo precibus ac lacrimis veniam quaerebant. Ut vero deformis et flens et praeter spem incolumis Valens processit, gaudium, miseratio, favor: versi in laetitiam, ut est vulgus utroque immodicum, laudantes gratantesque circumdatum aquilis signisque in tribunal ferunt. Ille utili moderatione non supplicium cujusquam poposcit: ac ne dissimulans suspectior foret, paucos incusavit, gnarus civilibus bellis plus militibus quam ducibus licere.

XXX. Munientibus castra apud Ticinum de adversa Caecinae pugna allatum, et prope renovata seditio, tanquam fraude et cunctationibus Valentis proelio defuissent. Nolle requiem, non exspectare ducem, anteire signa, urgere signiferos: rapido agmine Caecinae junguntur. Improspera Valentis fama apud exercitum Caecinae erat: expositos se tanto pauciores integris hostium viribus querebantur, simul in suam excusationem et adventantium robur per adulationem attollentes, ne ut victi et ignavi despectarentur. Et quanquam plus virium, prope duplicatus legionum auxiliorumque numerus erat Valenti, studia tamen militum in Caecinam inclinabant, super benignitatem animi, qua promptior habebatur, etiam vigore aetatis, proceritate corporis et quodam inani favore. Hinc aemulatio ducibus. Caecina ut foedum ac maculosum, ille ut tumidum ac vanum irridebant. Sed condito odio eandem utilitatem fovere, crebris epistolis sine respectu veniae probra Othoni objectantes, cum duces partium Othonis quamvis uberrima conviciorum in Vitellium materia abstinerent.

XXXI. Sane ante utriusque exitum, quo egregiam Otho famam, Vitellius flagitiosissimam meruere, minus Vitellii ignavae voluptates quam Othonis flagrantissimae libidines timebantur. Addiderat huic terrorem atque odium caedes Galbae; contra illi initium belli nemo imputabat. Vitellius ventre et gula sibi inhonestus; Otho luxu, saevitia, audacia reipublicae exitiosior ducebatur. Conjunctis Caecinae ac Valentis copiis, nulla ultra penes Vitellianos mora, quin totis viribus certarent. Otho consultavit, trahi bellum an fortunam experiri placeret. Tunc Suetonius Paulinus dignum fama sua ratus, qua nemo illa tempestate militaris rei callidior habebatur, de toto genere belli censere, festinationem hostibus, moram ipsis utilem disseruit.

XXXII. "Exercitum Vitellii universum advenisse, nec multum virium a tergo, quoniam Galliae tumeant, et deserere Rheni ripam, irrupturis tam infestis nationibus, non conducat: Britannicum militem hoste et mari distineri: Hispanias armis non ita redundare: provinciam Narbonensem incursu classis et adverso proelio contremuisse: clausam Alpibus, et nullo maris subsidio Transpadanam Italiam, atque ipso transitu exercitus vastam: non frumentum usquam exercitui, nec exercitum sine copiis retineri posse. Jam Germanos, quod genus militum apud hostes atrocissimum sit, tracto in aestatem bello, fluxis corporibus, mutationem soli coelique haud toleraturos. Multa bella, impetu valida, per taedia et moras evanuisse. Contra ipsis omnia opulenta et fida: Pannoniam, Moesiam, Dalmatiam, Orientem cum integris exercitibus, Italiam et caput rerum urbem, senatumque et populum nunquam obscura nomina, etsi aliquando obumbrentur; publicas privatasque opes et immensam pecuniam, inter civiles discordias ferro validiorem; corpora militum aut Italiae sueta aut aestibus: objacere flumen Padum, tutas viris murisque urbes; e quibus nullam hosti cessuram, Placentiae defensione exploratum. Proinde duceret bellum: paucis diebus quartamdecimam legionem, magna ipsam fama, cum Moesiacis copiis affore: tum rursus deliberaturum et, si proelium placuisset, auctis viribus certaturos."

XXXIII. Accedebat sententiae Paulini Marius Celsus: idem placere Annio Gallo, paucos ante dies lapsu equi afflicto, missi qui consilium ejus sciscitarentur retulerant. Otho pronus ad decertandum; frater ejus Titianus et praefectus praetorii Proculus, imperitia properantes, fortunam et deos et numen Othonis adesse consiliis, affore conatibus testabantur: neu quis obviam ire sententiae auderet, in adulationem concesserant. Postquam pugnari placitum, interesse pugnae Imperatorem an seponi melius foret dubitavere. Paulino et Celso jam non adversantibus, ne principem objectare periculis viderentur, iidem illi deterioris consilii auctores perpulere ut Brixellum concederet ac dubiis proeliorum exemptus summae rerum et imperii se ipsum reservaret. Is primus dies Othonianas partes afflixit: namque et cum ipso praetoriarum cohortium et speculatorum equitumque valida manus discessit, et remanentium fractus animus, quando suspecti duces, et Otho, cui uni apud militem fides, dum et ipse non nisi militibus credit, imperia ducum in incerto reliquerat.

XXXIV. Nihil eorum Vitellianos fallebat, crebris, ut in civili bello, transfugiis; et exploratores, cura diversa sciscitandi, sua non occultabant. Quieti intentique Caecina ac Valens, quando hostis imprudentia rueret, quod loco sapientiae est, alienam stultitiam opperiebantur, inchoato ponte transitum Padi simulantes adversus oppositam gladiatorum manum, ac ne ipsorum miles segne otium tereret. Naves pari inter se spatio validis utrimque trabibus connexae, adversum in flumen dirigebantur jactis super ancoris, quae firmitatem pontis continerent. Sed ancorarum funes non extenti fluitabant, ut augescente flumine inoffensus ordo navium attolleretur. Claudebat pontem imposita turris et in extremam navem educta, unde tormentis ac machinis hostes propulsarentur. Othoniani in ripa turrim struxerant, saxaque et faces jaculabantur.

XXXV. Et erat insula amne medio, in quam gladiatores navibus molientes, Germani nando praelabebantur. Ac forte plures transgressos, completis Liburnicis, per promptissimos gladiatorum Macer aggreditur. Sed neque ea constantia gladiatoribus ad proelia, quae militibus, nec perinde nutantes e navibus quam stabili gradu e ripa vulnera dirigebant. Et cum variis trepidantium inclinationibus mixti remiges propugnatoresque turbarentur, desilire in vada ultro Germani, retentare puppes, scandere foros aut cominus mergere: quae cuncta in oculis utriusque exercitus quanto laetiora Vitellianis, tanto acrius Othoniani causam auctoremque cladis detestabantur.

XXXVI. Et proelium quidem, abreptis quae supererant navibus, fuga diremptum: Macer ad exitium poscebatur; jamque vulneratum eminus lancea strictis gladiis invaserant, cum intercursu tribunorum centurionumque protegitur. Nec multo post Vestricius Spurinna jussu Othonis, relicto Placentiae modico praesidio, cum cohortibus subvenit. Dein Flavium Sabinum consulem designatum Otho rectorem copiis misit, quibus Macer praefuerat, laeto milite ad mutationem ducum et ducibus ob crebras seditiones tam infestam militiam aspernantibus.

XXXVII. Invenio apud quosdam auctores, pavore belli seu fastidio utriusque principis, quorum flagitia ac dedecus apertiore in dies fama noscebantur, dubitasse exercitus, num posito certamine vel ipsi in medium consultarent, vel senatui permitterent legere imperatorem; atque eo duces Othonianos spatium ac moras suasisse, praecipua spe Paulini, quod vetustissimus consularium et militia clarus gloriam nomenque Britannicis expeditionibus meruisset. Ego ut concesserim apud paucos tacito voto quietem pro discordia, bonum et innocentem principem pro pessimis ac flagitiosissimis ex-petitum, ita neque Paulinum, qua prudentia fuit, sperasse corruptissimo saeculo tantam vulgi moderationem reor, ut, qui pacem belli amore turbaverant, bellum pacis caritate deponerent, neque aut exercitus linguis moribusque dissonos in hunc consensum potuisse coalescere, aut legatos ac duces, magna ex parte luxus, egestatis, scelerum sibi conscios, nisi pollutum obstrictumque meritis suis principem passuros.

XXXVIII. Vetus ac jam pridem insita mortalibus potentiae cupido cum imperii magnitudine adolevit erupitque. Nam rebus modicis aequalitas facile habebatur: sed ubi subacto orbe et aemulis urbibus regibusve excisis securas opes concupiscere vacuum fuit, prima inter patres plebemque certamina exarsere: modo turbulenti tribuni, modo consules praevalidi, et in urbe ac foro tentamenta civilium bellorum. Mox e plebe infima C. Marius et nobilium saevissimus L. Sulla victam armis libertatem in dominationem verterunt. Post quos Cn. Pompeius occultior, non melior. Et nunquam postea, nisi de principatu quaesitum. Non discessere ab armis in Pharsalia ac Philippis civium legiones; nedum Othonis ac Vitellii exercitus sponte posituri bellum fuerint: eadem illos deum ira, eadem hominum rabies, eaedem scelerum causae in discordiam egere. Quod singulis velut ictibus transacta sunt bella, ignavia principum factum est. Sed me veterum novorumque morum reputatio longius tulit: nunc ad rerum ordinem venio.

XXXIX. Profecto Brixellum Othone, honor imperii penes Titianum fratrem, vis ac potestas penes Proculum praefectum. Celsus et Paulinus, cum prudentia eorum nemo uteretur, inani nomine ducum alienae culpae praetendebantur. Tribuni centurionesque ambigui, quod spretis melioribus deterrimi valebant: miles alacer; qui tamen jussa ducum interpretari quam exsequi mallet. Promoveri ad quartum a Bedriaco castra placuit, adeo imperite, ut quanquam verno tempore anni et tot circum amnibus, penuria aquae fatigarentur. Ibi de proelio dubitatum, Othone per literas flagitante ut maturarent, militibus ut imperator pugnae adesset poscentibus; plerique copias trans Padum agentes acciri postulabant. Nec perinde dijudicari potest, quid optimum factu fuerit, quam pessimum fuisse, quod factum est.

XL. Non ut ad pugnam sed ad bellandum profecti, confluentes Padi et Adduae fluminum, sedecim inde millium spatio distantes, petebant. Celso et Paulino abnuentibus militem itinere fessum, sarcinis gravem objicere hosti, non admissuro quo minus expeditus et vix quatuor millia passuum progressus aut incompositos in agmine aut dispersos et vallum molientes aggrederetur. Titianus et Proculus, ubi consiliis vincerentur, ad jus imperii transibant. Aderat sane citus equo Numida cum atrocibus mandatis, quibus Otho increpita ducum segnitia rem in discrimen mitti jubebat, aeger mora et spei impatiens.

XLI. Eodem die ad Caecinam operi pontis intentum duo praetoriarum cohortium tribuni, colloquium ejus postulantes, venerunt. Audire conditiones ac reddere parabat, cum praecipites exploratores adesse hostem nuntiavere. Interruptus tribunorum sermo; eoque incertum fuit, insidias an proditionem vel aliquod honestum consilium coeptaverint. Caecina dimissis tribunis revectus in castra, datum jussu Fabii Valentis pugnae signum et militem in armis invenit. Dum legiones de ordine agminis sortiuntur, equites prorupere: et, mirum dictu, a paucioribus Othonianis quo minus in vallum impingerentur, Italicae legionis virtute deterriti sunt: ea strictis mucronibus redire pulsos et pugnam resumere coegit. Disposita Vitellianarum legionum acies sine trepidatione; etenim, quanquam vicino hoste, aspectus armorum densis arbustis prohibebatur: apud Othonianos pavidi duces, miles ducibus infensus, mixta vehicula et lixae et praeruptis utrimque fossis via quieto quoque agmini angusta. Circumsistere alii signa sua, quaerere alii: incertus undique clamor accurrentium, vocitantium; ut cuique audacia vel formido, in primam postremamve aciem prorumpebant aut relabebantur.

XLII. Attonitas subito terrore mentes falsum gaudium in languorem vertit, repertis qui descivisse a Vitellio exercitum ementirentur. Is rumor, ab exploratoribus Vitellii dispersus, an in ipsa Othonis parte seu dolo seu forte surrexerit, parum compertum. Omisso pugnae ardore Othoniani ultro salutavere, et hostili murmure excepti, plerisque suorum ignaris quae causa salutandi, metum proditionis fecere. Tum incubuit hostium acies integris ordinibus, robore et numero praestantior: Othoniani, quanquam dispersi, pauciores, fessi, proelium tamen acriter sumpsere: et per locos arboribus ac vineis impeditos non una pugnae facies: cominus eminus catervis et cuneis concurrebant: in aggere viae collato gradu corporibus et umbonibus niti, omisso pilorum jactu gladiis et securibus galeas loricasque perrumpere: noscentes inter se, ceteris conspicui, in eventum totius belli certabant.

XLIII. Forte inter Padum viamque, patenti campo, duae legiones congressae sunt; pro Vitellio unaetvicesima, cui cognomen Rapaci, vetere gloria insignis; e parte Othonis, prima Adjutrix, non ante in aciem deducta, sed ferox et novi decoris avida. Primani stratis unaetvicesimanorum principiis aquilam abstulere: quo dolore accensa legio et impulit rursus primanos, interfecto Orfidio Benigno legato, et plurima signa vexillaque ex hostibus rapuit. A parte alia propulsa quintanorum impetu tertiadecima legio; circumventi plurium accursu quartadecimani. Et ducibus Othonis jam pridem profugis Caecina ac Valens subsidiis suos firmabant. Accessit recens auxilium Varus Alfenus cum Batavis, fusa gladiatorum manu, quam navibus transvectam oppositae cohortes in ipso flumine trucidaverant: ita victores latus hostium invecti.

XLIV. Et media acie perrupta fugere passim Othoniani, Bedriacum petentes. Immensum id spatium: obstructae strage corporum viae; quo plus caedis fuit: neque enim civilibus bellis capti in praedam vertuntur. Suetonius Paulinus et Licinius Proculus diversis itineribus castra vitavere. Vedium Aquilam tertiaedecimae legionis legatum irae militum inconsultus pavor obtulit: multo adhuc die vallum ingressus clamore seditiosorum et fugacium circumstrepitur: non probris, non manibus abstinent: desertorem proditoremque increpant, nullo proprio crimine ejus, sed more vulgi suum quisque flagitium aliis objectantes. Titianum et Celsum nox juvit, dispositis jam excubiis compressisque militibus, quos Annius Gallus consilio, precibus, auctoritate flexerat, ne super cladem adversae pugnae suismet ipsi caedibus saevirent: sive finis bello venisset seu resumere arma mallent, unicum victis in consensu levamentum. Ceteris fractus animus. Praetorianus miles non virtute se sed proditione victum fremebat. Ne Vitellianis quidem incruentam fuisse victoriam, pulso equite, rapta legionis aquila: superesse cum ipso Othone militum quod trans Padum fuerit; venire Moesicas legiones; magnam exercitus partem Bedriaci remansisse: hos certe nondum victos, et si ita ferret, honestius in acie perituros. His cogitationibus truces aut pavidi, extrema desperatione ad iram saepius quam in formidinem stimulabantur.

XLV. At Vitellianus exercitus ad quintum a Bedriaco lapidem consedit, non ausis ducibus eadem die oppugnationem castrorum; simul voluntaria deditio sperabatur. Sed expeditis et tantum ad proelium egressis munimentum fuere arma et victoria. Postera die, haud ambigua Othoniani exercitus voluntate et, qui ferociores fuerant, ad poenitentiam inclinantibus, missa legatio: nec apud duces Vitellianos dubitatum, quo minus pacem concederent. Legati paulisper retenti: ea res haesitationem attulit ignaris adhuc an impetrassent. Mox remissa legatione patuit vallum. Tum victi victoresque in lacrimas effusi, sortem civilium armorum misera laetitia detestantes. Iisdem tentoriis, alii fratrum, alii propinquorum vulnera fovebant. Spes et praemia in ambiguo, certa funera et luctus. Nec quisquam adeo mali expers, ut non aliquam mortem maereret. Requisitum Orfidii legati corpus honore solito crematur; paucos necessarii ipsorum sepelivere; ceterum vulgus super humum relictum.

XLVI. Opperiebatur Otho nuntium pugnae nequaquam trepidus et consilii certus: maesta primum fama, dein profugi e proelio perditas res patefaciunt. Non exspectavit militum ardor vocem imperatoris: bonum haberet animum jubebant: superesse adhuc novas vires, et ipsos extrema passuros ausurosque: neque erat adulatio. Ire in aciem, excitare partium fortunam furore quodam et instinctu flagrabant: qui procul astiterant, tendere manus, et proximi prensare genua, promptissimo Plotio Firmo. Is praetorii praefectus identidem orabat, ne fidissimum exercitum, ne optime meritos milites desereret: majore animo tolerari adversa, quam relinqui; fortes et strenuos etiam contra fortunam insistere spei, timidos et ignavos ad desperationem formidine properare. Quas inter voces ut flexerat vultum aut induraverat Otho, clamor et gemitus. Nec praetoriani tantum, proprius Othonis miles, sed praemissi e Moesia eandem obstinationem adventantis exercitus, legiones Aquileiam ingressas nuntiabant: ut nemo dubitet potuisse renovari bellum atrox, lugubre, incertum victis et victoribus.

XLVII. Ipse aversus a consiliis belli, "Hunc," inquit, "animum, hanc virtutem vestram ultra periculis objicere, nimis grande vitae meae pretium puto. Quanto plus spei ostenditis, si vivere placeret, tanto pulchrior mors erit. Experti invicem sumus, ego ac Fortuna: nec tempus computaveritis: difficilius est temperare felicitati, qua te non putes diu usurum. Civile bellum a Vitellio coepit, et ut de principatu certaremus armis, initium illic fuit: ne plusquam semel certemus, penes me exemplum erit: hinc Othonem posteritas aestimet. Fruetur Vitellius fratre, conjuge, liberis: mihi non ultione neque solatiis opus est. Alii diutius imperium tenuerint: nemo tam fortiter reliquerit. An ego tantum Romanae pubis, tot egregios exercitus, sterni rursus et reipublicae eripi patiar? Eat hic mecum animus, tanquam perituri pro me fueritis; sed este superstites: nec diu moremur, ego incolumitatem vestram, vos constantiam meam. Plura de extremis loqui pars ignaviae est: praecipuum destinationis meae documentum habete, quod de nemine queror: nam incusare deos vel homines ejus est, qui vivere velit."

XLVIII. Talia locutus, ut cuique aetas aut dignitas, comiter appellatos, irent propere neu remanendo iram victoris asperarent, juvenes auctoritate, senes precibus movebat, placidus ore, intrepidus verbis, intempestivas suorum lacrimas coercens. Dari naves ac vehicula abeuntibus jubet; libellos epistolasque studio erga se aut in Vitellium contumeliis insignes abolet; pecunias distribuit, parce, nec ut periturus. Mox Salvium Cocceianum fratris filium, prima juventa, trepidum et maerentem ultro solatus est, laudando pietatem ejus, castigando formidinem: "an Vitellium tam immitis animi fore ut pro incolumi tota domo ne hanc quidem sibi gratiam redderet? mereri se festinato exitu clementiam victoris. Non enim ultima desperatione, sed poscente proelium exercitu, remisisse reipublicae novissimum casum. Satis sibi nominis, satis posteris suis nobilitatis quaesitum: post Julios, Claudios, Servios, se primum in familiam novam imperium intulisse: proinde erecto animo capesseret vitam, neu patruum sibi Othonem fuisse aut oblivisceretur unquam aut nimium meminisset."

XLIX. Post quae, dimotis omnibus, paulum requievit: atque illum, supremas jam curas animo volutantem, repens tumultus avertit, nuntiata consternatione ac licentia militum: namque abeuntibus exitium minitabantur, atrocissima in Verginium vi, quem clausa domo obsidebant. Increpitis seditionis auctoribus regressus vacavit abeuntium alloquiis, donec omnes inviolati digrederentur. Vesperascente die sitim haustu gelidae aquae sedavit: tum allatis pugionibus, cum utrumque pertentasset, alterum capiti subdidit: et explorato jam profectos amicos, noctem quietam, utque affirmatur, non insomnem egit. Luce prima in ferrum pectore incubuit. Ad gemitum morientis ingressi liberti servique et Plotius Firmus praetorii praefectus unum vulnus invenere. Funus maturatum: ambitiosis id precibus petierat, ne amputaretur caput ludibrio futurum. Tulere corpus praetoriae cohortes, cum laudibus et lacrimis, vulnus manusque ejus exosculantes. Quidam militum juxta rogum interfecere se, non noxa neque ob metum, sed aemulatione decoris et caritate principis: ac postea promiscue Bedriaci, Placentiae aliisque in castris, celebratum id genus mortis. Othoni sepulcrum exstructum est modicum et mansurum.

L. Hunc vitae finem habuit septimo et tricesimo aetatis anno. Origo illi e municipio Ferentio. Pater consularis, avus praetorius, maternum genus impar nec tamen indecorum. Pueritia ac juventa, qualem monstravimus; duobus facinoribus, altero flagitiosissimo, altero egregio, tantundem apud posteros meruit bonae famae, quantum malae. Ut conquirere fabulosa et fictis oblectare legentium animos procul gravitate coepti operis crediderim, ita vulgatis traditisque demere fidem non ausim. Die quo Bedriaci certabatur, avem invisitata specie apud Regium Lepidum celebri luco consedisse incolae memorant, nec deinde coetu hominum aut circumvolitantium alitum territam pulsamve, donec Otho se ipse interficeret; tum ablatam ex oculis: et tempora reputantibus, initium finemque miraculi cum Othonis exitu competisse.

LI. In funere ejus, novata luctu ac dolore militum seditio, nec erat, qui coerceret. Ad Verginium versi, modo ut reciperet imperium, nunc ut legatione apud Caecinam ac Valentem fungeretur, minitantes orabant. Verginius, per aversam domus partem furtim degressus, irrumpentes frustratus est. Earum, quae Brixelli egerant, cohortium preces Rubrius Gallus tulit. Et venia statim impetrata, concedentibus ad victorem per Flavium Sabinum iis copiis, quibus praefuerat.

LII. Posito ubique bello, magna pars senatus extremum discrimen adiit, profecta cum Othone ab urbe, dein Mutinae relicta. Illuc adverso de proelio allatum: sed milites ut falsum rumorem aspernantes, quod infensum Othoni senatum arbitrabantur, custodire sermones, vultum habitumque trahere in deterius; conviciis postremo ac probris causam et initium caedis quaerebant, cum alius insuper metus senatoribus instaret, ne, praevalidis jam Vitellii partibus, cunctanter excepisse victoriam crederentur: ita trepidi et utrimque anxii coeunt, nemo privatim expedito consilio, inter multos societate culpae tutior. Onerabat paventium curas ordo Mutinensis arma et pecuniam offerendo, appellabatque Patres Conscriptos intempestivo honore.

LIII. Notabile jurgium inde fuit, quo Licinius Caecina Marcellum Eprium ut ambigua disserentem invasit. Nec ceteri sententias aperiebant: sed invisum memoria delationum expositumque ad invidiam Marcelli nomen irritaverat

Caecinam, ut novus adhuc et in senatum nuper ascitus magnis inimicitiis claresceret. Moderatione meliorum dirempti. Et rediere omnes Bononiam, rursus consiliaturi: simul medio temporis plures nuntii sperabantur. Bononiae, divisis per itinera qui recentissimum quemque percunctarentur, interrogatus Othonis libertus causam digressus, habere se suprema ejus mandata respondit: ipsum viventem quidem relictum, sed sola posteritatis cura, et abruptis vitae blandimentis. Hinc admiratio et plura interrogandi pudor; atque omnium animi in Vitellium inclinavere.

LIV. Intererat consiliis frater ejus L. Vitellius, seque jam adulantibus offerebat, cum repente Coenus libertus Neronis atroci mendacio universos perculit, affirmans superventu quartaedecimae legionis, junctis a Brixello viribus, caesos victores, versam partium fortunam. Causa fingendi fuit, ut diplomata Othonis, quae negligebantur, laetiore nuntio revalescerent. Et Coenus quidem rapide in urbem vectus, paucos post dies jussu Vitellii poenas luit. Senatorum periculum auctum, credentibus Othonianis militibus vera esse, quae afferebantur. Intendebat formidinem, quod publici consilii facie discessum Mutina, desertaeque partes forent. Nec ultra in commune congressi, sibi quisque consuluere, donec missae a Fabio Valente epistolae demerent metum. Et mors Othonis, quo laudabilior, eo velocius audita.

LV. At Romae nihil trepidationis: Cereales ludi ex more spectabantur. Ut cessisse Othonem, et a Flavio Sabino praefecto urbis, quod erat in urbe militum, sacramento Vitellii adactum certi auctores in theatrum attulerunt, Vitellio plausere: populus cum lauru ac floribus Galbae imagines circum templa tulit, congestis in modum tumuli coronis, juxta lacum Curtii, quem locum Galba moriens sanguine infecerat. In senatu cuncta longis aliorum principatibus composita statim decernuntur. Additae erga Germanicum exercitum laudes gratesque, et missa legatio, quae gaudio fungeretur. Recitatae Fabii Valentis epistolae, ad consules scriptae haud immoderate: gratior Caecinae modestia fuit, quod non scripsisset.

LVI. Ceterum Italia gravius atque atrocius quam bello afflictabatur: dispersi per municipia et colonias Vitelliani spoliare, rapere, vi et stupris polluere; in omne fas nefasque avidi aut venales non sacro, non profano abstinebant. Et fuere, qui inimicos suos specie militum interficerent. Ipsique milites regionum gnari refertos agros, dites dominos in praedam aut, si repugnatum foret, ad excidium destinabant, obnoxiis ducibus et prohibere non ausis: minus avaritiae in Caecina, plus ambitionis: Valens ob lucra et quaestus infamis, eoque alienae etiam culpae dissimulator. Jam pridem attritis Italiae rebus, tantum peditum equitumque, vis damnaque et injuriae aegre tolerabantur.

LVII. Interim Vitellius victoriae suae nescius, ut ad integrum bellum, reliquas Germanici exercitus vires trahebat. Pauci veterum militum in hibernis relicti, festinatis per Gallias delectibus, ut remanentium legionum nomina supplerentur. Cura ripae Hordeonio Flacco permissa; ipse e Britannico delectu octo millia sibi adjunxit: et paucorum dierum iter progressus, prosperas apud Bedriacum res ac morte Othonis concidisse bellum accepit. Vocata concione, virtutem militum laudibus cumulat. Postulante exercitu ut libertum suum Asiaticum equestri dignitate donaret, inhonestam adulationem compescuit. Dein mobilitate ingenii, quod palam abnuerat, inter secreta convivii largitur; honoravitque Asiaticum annulis, foedum mancipium et malis artibus ambitiosum.

LVIII. Iisdem diebus accessisse partibus utramque Mauretaniam, interfecto procuratore Albino, nuntii venere. Lucceius Albinus a Nerone Mauretaniae Caesariensi praepositus, addita per Galbam Tingitanae provinciae administratione, haud spernendis viribus agebat. Decem novem cohortes, quinque alae, ingens Maurorum numerus aderat, per latrocinia et raptus apta bello manus. Caeso Galba in Othonem pronus, nec Africa contentus, Hispaniae angusto freto diremptae imminebat. Inde Cluvio Rufo metus: et decimam legionem propinquare littori, ut transmissurus, jussit: praemissi Centuriones, qui Maurorum animos Vitellio conciliarent: neque arduum fuit, magna per provincias

Germanici exercitus fama. Spargebatur insuper, spreto Procuratoris vocabulo, Albinum insigne regis et Jubae nomen usurpare.

LIX. Ita mutatis animis, Asinius Pollio alae praefectus, e fidissimis Albino, et Festus ac Scipio cohortium praefecti opprimuntur. Ipse Albinus, dum e Tingitana provincia Caesariensem Mauretaniam petit, appulsu littoris trucidatus; uxor ejus, cum se percussoribus obtulisset, simul interfecta est, nihil eorum, quae fierent, Vitellio anquirente: brevi auditu quamvis magna transibat, impar curis gravioribus. Exercitum itinere terrestri pergere jubet: ipse Arare flumine devehitur, nullo principali paratu, sed vetere egestate conspicuus, donec Junius Blaesus, Lugdunensis Galliae rector, genere illustri, largus animo et par opibus, circumdaret principi ministeria, comitaretur liberaliter, eo ipso ingratus, quamvis odium Vitellius vernilibus blanditiis velaret. Praesto fuere Lugduni victricium victarumque partium duces. Valentem et Caecinam, pro concione laudatos, curuli suae circumposuit. Mox universum exercitum occurrere infanti filio jubet: perlatumque et paludamento opertum sinu retinens Germanicum appellavit, cinxitque cunctis fortunae principalis insignibus: nimius honos inter secunda, rebus adversis in solatium cessit.

LX. Tum interfecti centuriones promptissimi Othonianorum; unde praecipua in Vitellium alienatio per Illyricos exercitus. Simul ceterae legiones contactu, et adversus Germanicos milites invidia, bellum meditabantur. Suetonium Paulinum ac Licinium Proculum, tristi mora squalidos tenuit, donec auditi necessariis magis defensionibus quam honestis uterentur. Proditionem ultro imputabant, spatium longi ante proelium itineris, fatigationem Othonianorum, permixtum vehiculis agmen, ac pleraque fortuita, fraudi suae assignantes: et Vitellius credidit de perfidia, et fidem absolvit. Salvius Titianus Othonis frater nullum discrimen adiit, pietate et ignavia excusatus. Mario Celso consulatus servatur: sed creditum fama, objectumque mox in senatu Caecilio Simplici, quod eum honorem pecunia mercari, nec sine exitio Celsi, voluisset. Restitit Vitellius, deditque postea consulatum Simplici innoxium et inemptum. Trachalum adversus criminantes Galeria uxor Vitellii protexit.

LXI. Inter magnorum virorum discrimina (pudendum dictu) Mariccus quidam, e plebe Boiorum, inserere sese fortunae et provocare arma Romana simulatione numinum ausus est. Jamque assertor Galliarum et deus (nam id sibi indiderat) concitis octo millibus hominum, proximos Aeduorum pagos trahebat, cum gravissima civitas, electa juventute, adjectis a Vitellio cohortibus, fanaticam multitudinem disjecit. Captus in eo proelio Mariccus ac mox feris objectus, quia non laniabatur stolidum vulgus inviolabilem credebat, donec spectante Vitellio interfectus est.

LXII. Nec ultra in defectores aut bona cujusquam saevitum: rata fuere eorum qui acie Othoniana ceciderant testamenta, aut lex intestatis: prorsus, si luxuriae temperaret, avaritiam non timeres. Epularum foeda et inexplebilis libido: ex urbe atque Italia irritamenta gulae gestabantur, strepentibus ab utroque mari itineribus; exhausti conviviorum apparatibus principes civitatum; vastabantur ipsae civitates: degenerabat a labore ac virtute miles, assuetudine voluptatum et contemptu ducis. Praemisit in urbem edictum, quo vocabulum Augusti differret, Caesaris non reciperet, cum de potestate nihil detraheret. Pulsi Italia mathematici. Cautum severe, ne equites Romani ludo et arena polluerentur. Priores id principes pecunia et saepius vi perpulerant: ac pleraque municipia et coloniae aemulabantur corruptissimum quemque adolescentium pretio illicere.

LXIII. Sed Vitellius adventu fratris et irrepentibus dominationis magistris superbior et atrocior, occidi Dolabellam jussit, quem in coloniam Aquinatem sepositum ab Othone retulimus. Dolabella, audita morte Othonis, urbem introierat: id ei Plancius Varus, praetura functus, ex intimis Dolabellae amicis, apud Flavium Sabinum praefectum urbis objecit, tanquam rupta custodia ducem se victis partibus ostentasset: addidit tentatam cohortem, quae Ostiae ageret: nec ullis tantorum criminum probationibus, in poenitentiam versus seram, veniam post scelus quaerebat. Cunctantem super tanta re Flavium Sabinum, Triaria L. Vitellii uxor ultra feminam ferox terruit, ne periculo Principis famam clementiae affectaret. Sabinus suopte ingenio mitis, ubi formido incessisset facilis mutatu, et in alieno discrimine sibi pavens, ne allevasse videretur, impulit ruentem.

LXIV. Igitur Vitellius, metu et odio, quod Petroniam uxorem ejus mox Dolabella in matrimonium accepisset, vocatum per epistolas, vitata Flaminiae viae celebritate, devertere Interamnium atque ibi interfici jussit. Longum interfectori visum: in itinere ac taberna projectum humi jugulavit, magna cum invidia novi principatus, cujus hoc primum specimen noscebatur. Et Triariae licentiam modestum e proximo exemplum onerabat, Galeria imperatoris uxor, non immixta tristibus, et pari probitate mater Vitelliorum Sextilia, antiqui moris. Dixisse quin etiam ad primas filii sui epistolas ferebatur, non Germanicum a se, sed Vitellium genitum. Nec ullis postea fortunae illecebris aut ambitu civitatis in gaudium evicta, domus suae tantum adversa sensit.

LXV. Digressum a Lugduno Vitellium M. Cluvius Rufus assequitur omissa Hispania, laetitiam et gratulationem vultu ferens, animo anxius et petitum se criminationibus gnarus. Hilarius Caesaris libertus detulerat, tanquam, audito Vitellii et Othonis principatu, propriam ipse potentiam et possessionem Hispaniarum tentasset, eoque diplomatibus nullum principem praescripsisset. Interpretabatur quaedam ex orationibus ejus contumeliosa in Vitellium, et pro se ipso popularia. Auctoritas Cluvii praevaluit, ut puniri ultro libertum suum Vitellius juberet. Cluvius comitatui Principis adjectus, non adempta Hispania, quam rexit absens exemplo L. Arruntii: eum Tiberius Caesar ob metum, Vitellius Cluvium nulla formidine retinebat. Non idem Trebellio Maximo honos; profugerat Britannia ob iracundiam militum: missus est in locum ejus Vettius Bolanus e praesentibus.

LXVI. Angebat Vitellium victarum legionum haudquaquam fractus animus: sparsae per Italiam et victoribus permixtae, hostilia loquebantur, praecipua quartadecimanorum ferocia, qui se victos abnuebant: quippe Bedriacensi acie, vexillariis tantum pulsis, vires legionis non affuisse.

Remitti eos in Britanniam, unde a Nerone exciti erant, placuit, atque interim Batavorum cohortes una tendere ob veterem adversus quartadecimanos discordiam. Nec diu in tantis armatorum odiis quies fuit. Augustae Taurinorum, dum opificem quendam Batavus ut fraudatorem insectatur, legionarius ut hospitem tuetur, sui cuique commilitones aggregati a conviciis ad caedem transiere: et proelium atrox arsisset, ni duae praetoriae cohortes, causam quartadecimanorum secutae, his fiduciam et metum Batavis fecissent: quos Vitellius agmini suo jungi ut fidos; legionem, Graiis Alpibus traductam, eo flexu itineris ire jubet, quo Viennam vitarent: namque et Viennenses timebantur. Nocte qua proficiscebatur legio, relictis passim ignibus, pars Taurinae coloniae ambusta: quod damnum, ut pleraque belli mala, majoribus aliarum urbium cladibus obliteratum. Quartadecimani postquam Alpibus degressi sunt, seditiosissimus quisque signa Viennam ferebant: consensu meliorum compressi, et legio in Britanniam transvecta.

LXVII. Proximus Vitellio e praetoriis cohortibus metus erat: separati primum, deinde, addito honestae missionis lenimento, arma ad tribunos suos deferebant, donec motum a Vespasiano bellum crebresceret; tum, resumpta militia, robur Flavianarum partium fuere. Prima classicorum legio in Hispaniam missa, ut pace et otio mitesceret: undecima ac septima suis hibernis redditae: tertiadecimani struere amphitheatra jussi: nam Caecina Cremonae, Valens Bononiae, spectaculum gladiatorum edere parabant, nunquam ita ad curas intento Vitellio, ut voluptatum oblivisceretur.

LXVIII. Et quidem partes modeste distraxerat: apud victores orta seditio, ludicro initio, nisi numerus caesorum invidiam bello auxisset. Discubuerat Vitellius Ticini, adhibito ad epulas Verginio. Legati tribunique, ex moribus imperatorum, severitatem aemulantur vel tempestivis conviviis gaudent: perinde miles intentus aut licenter agit. Apud Vitellium omnia indisposita, temulenta, pervigiliis ac bacchanalibus quam disciplinae et castris propiora. Igitur duobus militibus, altero legionis quintae, altero e Gallis auxiliaribus, per lasciviam ad certamen luctandi accensis, postquam legionarius prociderat, insultante Gallo et iis qui ad spectandum convenerant in studia diductis, erupere legionarii in perniciem auxiliorum, ac duae cohortes interfectae. Remedium tumultus fuit alius tumultus: pulvis procul et arma aspiciebantur; conclamatum repente, quartamdecimam legionem verso itinere ad proelium venire: sed erant agminis coactores: agniti dempsere solicitudinem. Interim Verginii servus forte obvius ut percussor Vitellii insimulatur: et ruebat ad convivium miles, mortem Verginii exposcens. Ne Vitellius quidem, quanquam ad omnes suspiciones pavidus, de innocentia ejus dubitavit: aegre tamen cohibiti, qui exitium consularis et quondam ducis sui flagitabant. Nec quenquam saepius quam Verginium, omnis seditio infestavit: manebat admiratio viri et fama: sed oderant, ut fastiditi.

LXIX. Postero die Vitellius, senatus legatione quam ibi opperiri jusserat audita, transgressus in castra ultro pietatem militum collaudavit, frementibus auxiliis tantum impunitatis atque arrogantiae legionariis accessisse. Cohortes Batavorum, ne quid truculentius auderent, in Germaniam remissae, principium interno simul externoque bello parantibus fatis. Reddita civitatibus Gallorum auxilia, ingens numerus, et prima statim defectione inter inania belli assumptus. Ceterum ut largitionibus affectae jam imperii opes sufficerent, amputari legionum auxiliorumque numeros jubet, vetitis supplementis: et promiscuae missiones offerebantur. Exitiabile id reipublicae, ingratum militi, cui eadem munia inter paucos, periculaque ac labor crebrius redibant: et vires luxu corrumpebantur contra veterem disciplinam et instituta majorum, apud quos virtute quam pecunia res Romana melius stetit.

LXX. Inde Vitellius Cremonam flexit, et, spectato munere Caecinae, insistere Bedriacensibus campis ac vestigia recentis victoriae lustrare oculis concupivit. Foedum atque atrox spectaculum: intra quadragesimum pugnae diem lacera corpora, trunci artus, putres virorum equorumque formae, infecta tabo humus, protritis arboribus ac frugibus dira vastitas: nec minus inhumana pars viae, quam Cremonenses lauru rosisque constraverant, exstructis altaribus caesisque victimis regium in morem; quae, laeta in praesens, mox perniciem ipsis fecere. Aderant Valens et Caecina, monstrabantque pugnae locos: hinc erupisse legionum agmen, hinc equites coortos: inde circumfusas auxiliorum manus. Jam tribuni praefectique, sua quisque facta extollentes, falsa, vera aut majora vero miscebant. Vulgus quoque militum clamore et gaudio deflectere via, spatia certaminum recognoscere, aggerem armorum, strues corporum intueri, mirari. Et erant, quos varia fors rerum lacrimaeque et misericordia subiret: at non Vitellius flexit oculos, nec tot millia insepultorum civium exhorruit: laetus ultro et tam propinquae sortis ignarus instaurabat sacrum dis loci.

LXXI. Exin Bononiae a Fabio Valente gladiatorum spectaculum editur, advecto ex urbe cultu. Quantoque magis propinquabat, tanto corruptius iter, immixtis histrionibus et spadonum gregibus et cetero Neronianae aulae ingenio; namque et Neronem ipsum Vitellius admiratione celebrabat, sectari cantantem solitus, non necessitate, qua honestissimus quisque, sed luxu et saginae mancipatus emptusque. Ut Valenti et Caecinae vacuos honoris menses aperiret, coarctati aliorum consulatus, dissimulatus Marcii Macri, tanquam Othonianarum partium ducis; et Valerium Marinum, destinatum a Galba consulem, distulit, nulla offensa, sed mitem et injuriam segniter laturum. Pedanius Costa omittitur, ingratus principi, ut adversus Neronem ausus et Verginii exstimulator: sed alias protulit causas: actaeque insuper Vitellio gratiae, consuetudine servitii.

LXXII. Non ultra paucos dies, quanquam acribus initiis coeptum, mendacium valuit. Exstiterat quidam, Scribonianum se Camerinum ferens, Neronianorum temporum metu in Histria occultatum, quod illic clientelae et agri veterum Crassorum ac nominis favor manebat. Igitur deterrimo quoque in argumentum fabulae assumpto, vulgus credulum et quidam militum, errore veri seu turbarum studio, certatim aggregabantur, cum pertractus ad Vitellium interrogatusque, quisnam mortalium esset, postquam nulla dictis fides, et a domino noscebatur, conditione fugitivus, nomine *Geta*, sumptum de eo supplicium in servilem modum.

LXXIII. Vix credibile memoratu est, quantum superbiae socordiaeque Vitellio adoleverit, postquam speculatores e Syria Judaeaque, adactum in verba ejus Orientem nuntiavere. Nam etsi vagis adhuc et incertis auctoribus, erat tamen in ore famaque Vespasianus, ac plerumque ad nomen ejus Vitellius excitabatur. Tum ipse exercitusque, ut nullo aemulo, saevitia, libidine, raptu in externos mores proruperant.

LXXIV. Et Vespasianus bellum armaque et procul vel juxta sitas vires circumspectabat. Miles ipsi adeo paratus ut praeeuntem sacramentum et fausta Vitellio omnia precantem per silentium audierint. Muciani animus nec Vespasiano alienus et in Titum pronior. Praefectus Aegypti, Tiberius Alexander, consilia sociaverat. Tertiam legionem, quod de Syria in Moesiam transisset, suam numerabat: ceterae Illyrici legiones secuturae sperabantur. Namque omnes exercitus flammaverat arrogantia venientium a Vitellio militum, quod truces corpore, horridi sermone, ceteros ut impares irridebant. Sed in tanta mole belli plerumque cunctatio: et Vespasianus, modo in spem erectus, aliquando adversa reputabat: "Quis ille dies foret, quo sexaginta aetatis annos et duos filios juvenes bello permitteret? Esse privatis cogitatonibus progressum, et prout velint, plus minusve sumi ex fortuna: imperium cupientibus nihil medium inter summa et praecipitia."

LXXV. Versabatur ante oculos Germanici exercitus robur, notum viro militari: "Suas legiones civili bello inexpertas, Vitellii victrices; et apud victos plus querimoniarum quam virium: fluxam per discordias militum fidem, et periculum ex singulis. Quid enim profuturas cohortes alasque, si unus alterque praesenti facinori paratum ex diverso praemium petat? Sic Scribonianum sub Claudio interfectum: sic percussorem ejus Volaginium e gregario ad summa militiae provectum. Facilius universos impelli quam singulos vitari."

LXXVI. His pavoribus nutantem et alii legati amicique firmabant, et Mucianus post multos secretosque sermones jam et coram ita locutus: "Omnes qui magnarum rerum consilia suscipiunt, aestimare debent, an quod inchoatur, reipublicae utile, ipsis gloriosum, aut promptum effectu, aut certe non arduum sit. Simul ipse qui suadet considerandus est, adjiciatne consilio periculum suum, et si fortuna coeptis affuerit, cui summum decus acquiratur. Ego te, Vespasiane, ad imperium voco tam salutare reipublicae quam tibi magnificum. Juxta deos in tua manu positum est. Nec speciem adulantis expaveris: a contumelia quam a laude propius fuerit, post Vitellium eligi. Non adversus divi Augusti acerrimam mentem, nec adversus cautissimam Tiberii senectutem, ne contra Caii quidem aut Claudii vel Neronis fundatam longo imperio domum exsurgimus: cessisti etiam Galbae imaginibus. Torpere ultra et polluendam perdendamque rempublicam relinquere, sopor et ignavia videretur, etiam si tibi, quam inhonesta, tam tuta servitus esset. Abiit jam et transvectum est tempus, quo posses videri concupisse: confugiendum est ad imperium. An excidit trucidatus Corbulo? splendidior origine, quam nos sumus, fateor: sed et Nero nobilitate natalium Vitellium anteibat. Satis clarus est apud timentem, quisquis timetur. Et posse ab exercitu principem fieri, sibi ipse Vitellius documento, nullis stipendiis, nulla militari fama, Galbae odio provectus. Ne Othonem quidem ducis arte aut exercitus vi, sed praepropera ipsius desperatione victum, jam desiderabilem et magnum principem fecit. Cum interim spargit legiones, exarmat cohortes, nova quotidie bello semina ministrat: si quid ardoris ac ferociae miles habuit, popinis et commissationibus et principis imitatione deteritur. Tibi e Judaea et Syria et Aegypto novem legiones integrae, nulla acie exhaustae, non discordia corruptae, sed firmatus usu miles et belli domitor externi, classium, alarum, cohortium robora, et fidissimi reges, et tua ante omnes experientia.

LXXVII. "Nobis nihil ultra arrogabo, quam ne post Valentem et Caecinam numeremur. Ne tamen Mucianum socium spreveris, quia aemulum non experiris: me Vitellio antepono, te mihi. Tuae domui triumphale nomen, duo juvenes, capax jam imperii alter, et primis militiae annis apud Germanicos quoque exercitus clarus. Absurdum fuerit non cedere imperio ei, cujus filium adoptaturus essem, si ipse imperarem. Ceterum inter nos non idem prosperarum adversarumque rerum ordo erit. Nam, si vincimus, honorem, quem dederis, habebo: discrimen ac pericula ex aequo patiemur: immo, ut melius est, tuos exercitus rege, mihi bellum et proeliorum incerta trade. Acriore hodie disciplina victi quam victores agunt: hos ira, odium, ultionis cupiditas ad virtutem accendit: illi per fastidium et contumaciam hebescunt. Aperiet et recludet contecta et tumescentia victricium partium vulnera bellum ipsum. Nec mihi major in tua vigilantia, parsimonia, sapientia, fiducia est, quam in Vitellii torpore, inscitia, saevitia. Sed et meliorem in bello causam quam in pace habemus: nam qui deliberant, desciverunt."

LXXVIII. Post Muciani orationem ceteri audentius circumsistere, hortari, responsa vatum et siderum motus referre. Nec erat intactus tali superstitione, ut qui mox rerum dominus Seleucum quendam mathematicum rectorem et praescium palam habuerit. Recursabant animo vetera omina: cupressus arbor in agris ejus, conspicua altitudine, repente prociderat, ac postera die eodem vestigio resurgens procera et latior virebat: grande id prosperumque consensu haruspicum, et summa claritudo juveni admodum Vespasiano promissa. Sed primo triumphalia et consulatus et Judaicae victoriae decus implesse fidem ominis videbantur: ut haec adeptus est, portendi sibi imperium credebat. Est Judaeam inter Syriamque Carmelus, ita vocant montem deumque: nec simulacrum deo aut templum; sic tradidere majores, aram tantum et reverentiam. Illic sacrificanti Vespasiano, cum spes occultas versaret animo, Basilides sacerdos, inspectis identidem extis, "Quicquid est," inquit, "Vespasiane, quod paras, seu domum exstruere seu prolatare agros sive ampliare servitia, datur tibi magna sedes, ingentes termini, multum hominum." Has ambages et statim exceperat fama et tunc aperiebat: nec quicquam magis in ore vulgi: crebriores apud ipsum sermones, quanto sperantibus plura dicuntur.

LXXIX. Haud dubia destinatione discessere, Mucianus Antiochiam, Vespasianus Caesaream: illa Syriae, haec Judaeae caput est. Initium ferendi ad Vespasianum imperii Alexandriae coeptum, festinante Tiberio Alexandro, qui Kalendis Juliis sacramento ejus legiones adegit. Isque primus principatus dies in posterum celebratus, quamvis Judaicus exercitus quinto Nonas Julias apud ipsum jurasset eo ardore, ut ne Titus quidem filius exspectaretur, Syria remeans et consiliorum inter Mucianum ac patrem nuntius: cuncta impetu militum acta, non parata concione, non conjunctis legionibus.

LXXX. Dum quaeritur tempus locusque, quodque in re tali difficillimum, prima vox, dum animo spes, timor, ratio, casus obversantur, egressum cubiculo Vespasianum pauci milites, solito assistentes ordine ut legatum salutaturi, imperatorem salutavere. Tum ceteri accurrere, Caesarem et Augustum et omnia principatus vocabula cumulare: mens a metu ad fortunam transierat. In ipso nihil tumidum, arrogans, aut in rebus novis novum fuit. Ut primum tantae mutationis offusam oculis caliginem disjecit, militariter locutus laeta omnia et affluentia excepit: namque id ipsum opperiens Mucianus, alacrem militem in verba Vespasiani adegit. Tum Antiochensium theatrum ingressus, ubi illis consultare mos est, concurrentes et in adulationem effusos alloquitur, satis decorus etiam Graeca facundia, omniumque, quae diceret atque ageret, arte quadam ostentator. Nihil aeque provinciam exercitumque accendit, quam quod asseverabat Mucianus statuisse Vitellium, ut Germanicas legiones in Syriam ad militiam opulentam quietamque transferret, contra Syriacis legionibus Germanica hiberna coelo ac laboribus dura mutarentur. Quippe et provinciales sueto militum contubernio gaudebant, plerique necessitudinibus et propinquitatibus mixti; et militibus vetustate stipendiorum nota et familiaria castra in modum penatium diligebantur.

LXXXI. Ante Idus Julias Syria omnis in eodem sacramento fuit. Accessere cum regno Sohemus haud spernendis viribus, Antiochus vetustis opibus ingens et inservientium regum ditissimus: mox per occultos suorum nuntios excitus ab urbe Agrippa, ignaro adhuc Vitellio, celeri navigatione properaverat: nec minore animo regina Berenice partes juvabat, florens aetate formaque, et seni quoque Vespasiano magnificentia munerum grata. Quicquid provinciarum alluitur mari Asia atque Achaia tenus, quantumque introrsus in Pontum et Armenios patescit, juravere: sed inermes legati regebant, nondum additis Cappadociae legionibus. Consilium de summa rerum Beryti habitum: illuc Mucianus cum legatis tribunisque et splendidissimo quoque centurionum ac militum venit, et e Judaico exercitu lecta decora. Tantum simul peditum equitumque et aemulantium inter se regum paratus speciem fortunae principalis effecerant.

LXXXII. Prima belli cura agere delectus, revocare veteranos; destinantur validae civitates exercendis armorum officinis; apud Antiochenses aurum argentumque signatur: eaque cuncta per idoneos ministros, suis quaeque locis, festinabantur. Ipse Vespasianus adire, hortari, bonos laude, segnes exemplo incitare saepius quam coercere, vitia magis amicorum quam virtutes dissimulans. Multos praefecturis et procurationibus, plerosque senatorii ordinis honore percoluit, egregios viros et mox summa adeptos; quibusdam fortuna pro virtutibus fuit. Donativum militi neque Mucianus prima concione, nisi modice, ostenderat; ne Vespasianus quidem plus civili bello obtulit quam alii in pace, egregie firmus adversus militarem largitionem, eoque exercitu meliore. Missi ad Parthum Armeniumque legati, provisumque, ne, versis ad civile bellum legionibus, terga nudarentur. Titum instare Judaeae, Vespasianum obtinere claustra Aegypti placuit. Sufficere videbantur adversus Vitellium pars copiarum et dux Mucianus et Vespasiani nomen ac nihil arduum fatis. Ad omnes exercitus legatosque scriptae epistolae, praeceptumque, ut praetorianos Vitellio infensos, reciperandae militiae praemio invitarent.

LXXXIII. Mucianus cum expedita manu, socium magis imperii quam ministrum agens, non lento itinere, ne cunctari videretur, neque tamen properans, gliscere famam ipso spatio sinebat, gnarus modicas vires sibi, et majora credi de absentibus. Sed legio sexta et tredecim vexillariorum millia ingenti agmine sequebantur. Classem e Ponto Byzantium adigi jusserat, ambiguus consilii, num, omissa Moesia, Dyrrhachium pedite atque equite, simul longis navibus versum in Italiam mare clauderet, tuta pone tergum Achaia Asiaque; quas inermes exponi Vitellio, ni praesidiis firmarentur; atque ipsum Vitellium in incerto fore, quam partem Italiae protegeret, si sibi Brundisium Tarentumque et Calabriae Lucaniaeque littora infestis classibus peterentur.

LXXXIV. Igitur navium, militum, armorum paratu strepere provinciae. Sed nihil aeque fatigabat quam pecuniarum conquisitio: eos esse belli civilis nervos dictitans Mucianus, non jus aut verum in cognitionibus, sed solam magnitudinem opum spectabat. Passim delationes; et locupletissimus quisque in praedam correpti: quae gravia atque intoleranda, sed necessitate armorum excusata, etiam in pace mansere, ipso Vespasiano inter initia imperii ad obtinendas iniquitates haud perinde obstinante, donec indulgentia fortunae et pravis magistris didicit aususque est. Propriis quoque opibus Mucianus bellum juvit, largus privatim, quod avidius de republica sumeret. Ceteri conferendarum pecuniarum exemplum secuti: rarissimus quisque eandem in reciperando licentiam habuerunt.

LXXXV. Accelerata interim Vespasiani coepta Illyrici exercitus studio transgressi in partes. Tertia legio exemplum ceteris Moesiae legionibus praebuit. Octava erat ac septima Claudiana, imbutae favore Othonis, quamvis proelio non interfuissent. Aquileiam progressae, proturbatis qui de Othone nuntiabant laceratisque vexillis nomen Vitellii praeferentibus, rapta postremo pecunia et inter se divisa, hostiliter egerant. Unde metus, et ex metu consilium: posse imputari Vespasiano, quae apud Vitellium excusanda erant. Ita tres Moesicae legiones per epistolas alliciebant Pannonicum exercitum, aut abnuenti vim parabant. In eo motu Aponius Saturninus Moesiae rector pessimum facinus audet, misso centurione ad interficiendum Tertium Julianum septimae legionis legatum, ob simultates, quibus causam partium praetendebat. Julianus, comperto discrimine et gnaris locorum ascitis, per avia Moesiae ultra montem Haemum profugit: nec deinde civili bello interfuit, per varias moras susceptum ad Vespasianum iter trahens, et ex nuntiis cunctabundus aut properans.

LXXXVI. At in Pannonia tertiadecima legio ac septima Galbiana, dolorem iramque Bedriacensis pugnae retinentes, haud cunctanter Vespasiano accessere, vi praecipua Primi Antonii. Is legibus nocens et tempore Neronis falsi damnatus, inter alia belli mala, senatorium ordinem reciperaverat. Praepositus a Galba septimae legioni scriptitasse Othoni credebatur, ducem se partibus offerens; a quo neglectus in nullo Othoniani belli usu fuit: labantibus Vitellii rebus, Vespasianum secutus grande momentum addidit, strenuus manu, sermone promptus, serendae in alios invidiae artifex, discordiis et seditionibus potens, raptor, largitor, pace pessimus, bello non spernendus. Juncti inde Moesici ac Pannonici exercitus Dalmaticum militem traxere, quanquam consularibus legatis nihil turbantibus. Titus Ampius Flavianus Pannoniam, Pompeius Silvanus Dalmatiam tenebant, divites senes. Sed procurator aderat Cornelius Fuscus, vigens aetate, claris natalibus. Prima juventa quietis cupidine senatorium ordinem exuerat: idem pro Galba dux coloniae suae, eaque opera procurationem adeptus, susceptis Vespasiani partibus, acerrimam bello facem praetulit: non tam praemiis periculorum quam ipsis periculis laetus, pro certis et olim partis nova, ambigua, ancipitia malebat. Igitur movere et quatere, quicquid usquam aegrum foret, aggrediuntur. Scriptae in Britanniam ad quartadecimanos, in Hispaniam ad primanos epistolae, quod utraque legio pro Othone, adversa Vitellio fuerat. Sparguntur per Gallias literae; momentoque temporis flagrabat ingens bellum, Illyricis exercitibus palam desciscentibus, ceteris fortunam secuturis.

LXXXVII. Dum haec per provincias a Vespasiano ducibusque partium geruntur, Vitellius contemptior in dies segniorque, ad omnes municipiorum villarumque amoenitates resistens, gravi urbem agmine petebat. Sexaginta millia armatorum sequebantur, licentia corrupta; calonum numerus amplior, procacissimis etiam inter servos lixarum ingeniis; tot legatorum amicorumque comitatus inhabilis ad parendum, etiam si summa modestia regeretur. Onerabant multitudinem obvii ex urbe senatores equitesque, quidam metu, multi per adulationem, ceteri ac paulatim omnes, ne, aliis proficiscentibus, ipsi remanerent. Aggregabantur e plebe, flagitiosa per obsequia Vitellio cogniti, scurrae, histriones, aurigae, quibus ille amicitiarum dehonestamentis mire gaudebat. Nec coloniae modo aut municipia congestu copiarum, sed ipsi cultores arvaque, maturis jam frugibus, ut hostile solum vastabantur.

LXXXVIII. Multae et atroces inter se militum caedes, post seditionem Ticini coeptam manente legionum auxiliorumque discordia; ubi adversus paganos certandum foret, consensu. Sed plurima strages ad septimum ab urbe lapidem. Singulis ibi militibus Vitellius paratos cibos, ut gladiatoriam saginam, dividebat; et effusa plebes totis se castris miscuerat. Incuriosos milites (vernacula utebantur urbanitate) quidam spoliavere, abscisis furtim balteis, an accincti forent rogitantes. Non tulit ludibrium insolens contumeliae animus: inermem populum gladiis invasere: caesus inter alios pater militis, cum filium comitaretur; deinde agnitus, et vulgata caede temperatum ab innoxiis. In urbe tamen trepidatum, praecurrentibus passim militibus. Forum maxime petebant cupidine visendi locum, in quo Galba jacuisset. Nec minus saevum spectaculum erant ipsi, tergis ferarum et ingentibus telis horrentes, cum turbam populi per inscitiam parum vitarent, aut ubi lubrico viae vel occursu alicujus procidissent, ad jurgium, mox ad manus et ferrum transirent. Quin et tribuni praefectique cum terrore et armatorum catervis volitabant.

LXXXIX. Ipse Vitellius a ponte Mulvio, insigni equo, paludatus accinctusque, senatum et populum ante se agens, quo minus, ut captam, urbem ingrederetur, amicorum consilio deterritus, sumpta praetexta et composito agmine incessit. Quatuor legionum aquilae per frontem, totidemque circa e legionibus aliis vexilla, mox duodecim alarum signa, et post peditum ordines, eques: dein quatuor et triginta cohortes, ut nomina gentium aut species armorum forent, discretae. Ante aquilam praefecti castrorum tribunique et primi centurionum, candida veste; ceteri juxta suam quisque centuriam, armis donisque fulgentes. Et militum phalerae torquesque splendebant: decora facies, et non Vitellio principe dignus exercitus. Sic Capitolium ingressus, atque ibi matrem complexus, Augustae nomine honoravit.

XC. Postera die, tanquam apud alterius civitatis senatum populumque, magnificam orationem de semetipso prompsit, industriam temperantiamque suam laudibus attollens, consciis flagitiorum ipsis qui aderant omnique Italia, per quam somno et luxu pudendus incesserat. Vulgus tamen vacuum curis, et sine falsi verique discrimine solitas adulationes edoctum, clamore et vocibus astrepebat; abnuentique nomen Augusti expressere, ut assumeret, tam frustra quam recusaverat.

XCI. Apud civitatem cuncta interpretantem, funesti ominis loco acceptum est, quod maximum pontificatum adeptus Vitellius de caerimoniis publicis quintodecimo Kalendas Augusti edixisset antiquitus infausto die Cremerensi Alliensique cladibus: adeo omnis humani divinique juris expers, pari libertorum, amicorum socordia, velut inter temulentos agebat. Sed comitia consulum cum candidatis civiliter celebrans, omnem infimae plebis rumorem, in theatro ut spectator, in circo ut fautor, affectavit: quae grata sane et popularia, si a virtutibus proficiscerentur, memoria vitae prioris indecora et vilia accipiebantur. Ventitabat in senatum, etiam cum parvis de rebus patres consulerentur. Ac forte Priscus Helvidius praetor designatus contra studium ejus censuerat. Commotus primo Vitellius, non tamen ultra quam tribunos plebis in auxilium spretae potestatis advocavit. Mox mitigantibus amicis, qui altiorem iracundiam ejus verebantur, nihil novi accidisse respondit, quod duos senatores in republica dissentirent: solitum se etiam Thraseae contradicere. Irrisere plerique impudentiam aemulationis; aliis id ipsum placebat, quod neminem ex praepotentibus, sed Thraseam ad exemplar verae gloriae legisset.

XCII. Praeposuerat praetorianis P. Sabinum a praefectura cohortis, Julium Priscum tum centurionem: Priscus Valentis, Sabinus Caecinae gratia pollebant. Inter discordes Vitellio nihil auctoritatis; munia imperii Caecina ac Valens obibant, olim anxii odiis, quae bello et castris male dissimulata, pravitas amicorum et fecunda gignendis inimicitiis civitas auxerat, dum ambitu, comitatu et immensis salutantium agminibus contendunt comparanturque, variis in hunc aut illum Vitellii inclinationibus. Nec unquam satis fida potentia, ubi nimia est. Simul ipsum Vitellium, subitis offensis aut intempestivis blanditiis mutabilem, contemnebant metuebantque. Nec eo segnius invaserant domos, hortos opesque imperii, cum flebilis et egens nobilium turba, quos ipsos liberosque patriae Galba reddiderat, nulla principis misericordia juvarentur. Gratum primoribus civitatis etiam plebs approbavit, quod reversis ab exsilio jura libertorum concessisset, quanquam id omni modo servilia ingenia corrumpebant, abditis pecuniis per occultos aut ambitiosos sinus; et quidam in domum Caesaris transgressi, atque ipsis dominis potentiores.

XCIII. Sed miles, plenis castris et redundante multitudine, in porticibus aut delubris et urbe tota vagus, non principia noscere, non servare vigilias neque labore firmari: per illecebras urbis et inhonesta dictu, corpus otio, animum libidinibus imminuebant. Postremo, ne salutis quidem cura, infamibus Vaticani locis magna pars tetendit: unde crebrae in vulgus mortes. Et adjacente Tiberi, Germanorum Gallorumque obnoxia morbis corpora fluminis aviditas et aestus impatientia labefecit. Insuper confusus pravitate vel ambitu ordo militiae. Sedecim praetoriae, quatuor urbanae cohortes scribebantur, quis singula millia inessent. Plus in eo delectu Valens audebat, tanquam ipsum Caecinam periculo exemisset: sane adventu ejus partes convaluerant, et sinistrum lenti itineris rumorem prospero proelio verterat: omnisque inferioris Germaniae miles Valentem assectabatur: unde primum creditur Caecinae fides fluitasse.

XCIV. Ceterum non ita ducibus indulsit Vitellius, ut non plus militi liceret: sibi quisque militiam sumpsere; quamvis indignus, si ita maluerat, urbanae militiae ascribebatur; rursus bonis remanere inter legionarios aut alares volentibus permissum: nec deerant, qui vellent, fessi morbis et intemperiem coeli incusantes. Robora tamen legionibus alisque subtracta: convulsum castrorum decus, viginti millibus e toto exercitu permixtis magis quam electis. Concionante Vitellio postulantur ad supplicium Asiaticus et Flavius et Rufinus duces Galliarum, quod pro Vindice bellassent. Nec coercebat ejusmodi voces Vitellius, super insitam inerti animo ignaviam, conscius sibi instare donativum et deesse pecuniam, omnia alia militi largiebatur. Liberti principum conferre pro numero mancipiorum, ut tributum, jussi. Ipse sola perdendi cura stabula aurigis exstruere, circum gladiatorum ferarumque spectaculis opplere, tanquam in summa abundantia pecuniae illudere.

XCV. Quin et natalem Vitellii diem Caecina ac Valens, editis tota urbe vicatim gladiatoribus, celebravere ingenti paratu et ante illum diem insolito. Laetum foedissimo cuique, apud bonos invidiae fuit, quod exstructis in campo Martio aris inferias Neroni fecisset: caesae publice victimae cremataeque: facem Augustales subdidere; quod sacerdotium, ut Romulus Tatio regi, ita Caesar Tiberius Juliae genti sacravit. Nondum quartus a victoria mensis, et libertus Vitellii Asiaticus Polyclitos, Patrobios et vetera odiorum nomina aequabat. Nemo in illa aula probitate aut industria certavit: unum ad potentiam iter, prodigis epulis et sumptu ganeaque satiare inexplebiles Vitellii libidines. Ipse abunde ratus, si praesentibus frueretur, nec in longius consultans, novies millies sestertium paucissimis mensibus intervertisse creditur. Magna et misera civitas, eodem anno Othonem Vitelliumque passa, inter Vinios, Fabios, Icelos, Asiaticos, varia et pudenda sorte agebat, donec successere Mucianus et Marcellus, et magis alii homines quam alii mores.

XCVI. Prima Vitellio tertiae legionis defectio nuntiatur, missis ab Aponio Saturnino epistolis, antequam is quoque

Vespasiani partibus aggregaretur. Sed neque Aponius cuncta, ut trepidans re subita, perscripserat, et amici adulantes mollius interpretabantur: unius legionis eam seditionem, ceteris exercitibus constare fidem. In hunc modum etiam Vitellius apud milites disseruit, praetorianos nuper exauctoratos insectatus, a quibus falsos rumores dispergi, nec ullum civilis belli metum asseverabat, suppresso Vespasiani nomine et vagis per urbem militibus, qui sermones populi coercerent: id praecipuum alimentum famae erat.

XCVII. Auxilia tamen e Germania Britanniaque et Hispaniis excivit, segniter et necessitatem dissimulans. Perinde legati provinciaeque cunctabantur, Hordeonius Flaccus, suspectis jam Batavis, anxius proprio bello, Vectius Bolanus nunquam satis quieta Britannia, et uterque ambigui. Neque ex Hispaniis properabatur, nullo tum ibi consulari: trium legionum legati, pares jure, et prosperis Vitellii rebus certaturi ad obsequium, adversam ejus fortunam ex aequo detrectabant. In Africa legio cohortesque, delectae a Clodio Macro, mox a Galba dimissae, rursus jussu Vitellii militiam cepere: simul cetera juventus dabat impigre nomina: quippe integrum illic ac favorabilem proconsulatum Vitellius, famosum invisumque Vespasianus egerat: perinde socii de imperio utriusque conjectabant: sed experimentum contra fuit.

XCVIII. Ac primo Valerius Festus legatus studia provincialium cum fide juvit: mox nutabat, palam epistolis edictisque Vitellium, occultis nuntiis Vespasianum fovens, et haec illave defensurus, prout invaluissent. Deprehensi cum literis edictisque Vespasiani per Raetiam et Gallias militum et centurionum quidam, ad Vitellium missi necantur: plures fefellere fide amicorum aut suomet astu occultati. Ita Vitellii paratus noscebantur, Vespasiani consiliorum pleraque ignota, primum socordia Vitellii; deinde Pannonicae Alpes praesidiis insessae nuntios retinebant: mare quoque Etesiarum flatu in Orientem navigantibus secundum, inde adversum erat.

XCIX. Tandem irruptione hostium, atrocibus undique nuntiis exterritus, Caecinam ac Valentem expedi[?]e ad bellum jubet. Praemissus Caecina: Valentem, e gravi corporis morbo tum primum assurgentem, infirmitas tardabat. Longe alia proficiscentis ex urbe Germanici exercitus species: non vigor corporibus, non ardor animis; lentum et rarum agmen, fluxa arma, segnes equi: impatiens solis, pulveris, tempestatum, quantumque hebes ad sustinendum laborem miles, tanto ad discordias promptior. Accedebat huc Caecinae ambitio vetus, torpor recens nimia fortunae indulgentia soluti in luxum; seu perfidiam meditato infringere exercitus virtutem inter artes erat. Credidere plerique Flavii Sabini consiliis concussam Caecinae mentem, ministro sermonum Rubrio Gallo: rata apud Vespasianum fore pacta transitionis. Simul odiorum invidiaeque erga Fabium Valentem admonebatur, ut impar apud Vitellium, gratiam viresque apud novum Principem pararet.

C. Caecina complexu Vitellii multo cum honore digressus, partem equitum ad occupandam Cremonam praemisit: mox vexilla quartae, quintaedecimae et sextaedecimae legionum; dein quinta et duoetvicesima secutae; postremo agmine unaetvicesima Rapax et prima Italica incessere, cum vexillariis trium Britannicarum legionum et electis auxiliis. Profecto Caecina, scripsit Fabius Valens exercitui, quem ipse ductaverat, ut in itinere opperiretur; sic sibi cum Caecina convenisse; qui praesens eoque validior, immutatum id consilium finxit, ut ingruenti bello tota mole occurreretur. Ita accelerare legiones Cremonam, pars Hostiliam petere jussae: ipse Ravennam devertit, praetexto classem alloquendi: mox Patavii secretum componendae proditionis quaesitum. Namque Lucilius Bassus post praefecturam alae Ravennati simul ac Misenensi classibus a Vitellio praepositus, quod non statim praefecturam praetorii adeptus foret, iniquam iracundiam flagitiosa perfidia ulciscebatur: nec sciri potest, traxeritne Caecinam, an (quod evenit inter malos, ut et similes sint) eadem illos pravitas impulerit.

CI. Scriptores temporum, qui potiente rerum Flavia domo monumenta belli hujusce composuerunt, curam pacis et amorem reipublicae, corruptas in adulationem causas, tradidere. Nobis, super insitam levitatem, et, prodito Galba, vilem mox fidem, aemulatione etiam invidiaque, ne ab aliis apud Vitellium anteirentur, pervertisse ipsum videntur. Caecina legiones assecutus, centurionum militumque animos obstinatos pro Vitellio variis artibus subruebat: Basso eadem molienti minor difficultas erat, lubrica ad mutandam fidem classe ob memoriam recentis pro Othone militiae.

C. CORNELII TACITI

HISTORIARUM

LIBER TERTIUS.

BREVIARIUM LIBRI.

Cap. I. Flavianis de ratione belli deliberantibus moram alii, II, festinationem Antonius Primus suadet, III, et obtinet. IV. Proxima Corn. Fusci auctoritas. V. Principes Sarmatarum Iazygum in commilitium asciti. Sido et Italicus Suevorum reges tracti in partes VI, VII. Antonio, Italiam invadenti, comes est Arrius Varus. Multas urbes occupant. VIII. Verona fit belli sedes. Moras frustra aut sero nectunt Vespasianus et Mucianus. IX. Interim duces mutuis epistolis bellum gerunt. X. T. Ampius Flavianus, militi suspectus, ab Antonio servatur. XI. Hic alteram quoque seditionem, odio Aponii Saturnini ortam, comprimit. XII. Lucilius Bassus, et XIII, XIV, Caecina, a Vitellio deficientes, a militibus suis conjiciuntur in vincula. XV. Discordes Vitellianos ad Bedriacum aggredi statuit Antonius. XVI. Aviditate navandae operae Arrius Varus rem in discrimen adducit; XVII, eam Antonius constantia et virtute restituit, XVIII, victoria potitur. XIX. Vespasiani, ea freti, Cremonam expugnare deposcunt. XX. Inconsultum eorum ardorem frustra retinet Antonius. XXI. Sed adventantis hostis terror obstructas mentes consiliis ducis aperit. XXII—XXV. Proelium atrox, anceps. Antonius egregii ducis munia implet, victoriam aufert. XXVI—XXXIII. Cremona obsessa, capta, cremata, XXXIV, postea restituta. XXXV. Victae legiones dispersae.

XXXVI. Vitellius luxu torpet. XXXVII. In urbem revectus Caecinam condemnat; ei Rosium Regulum in unum diem consulem sufficit. XXXVIII, XXXIX. Junius Blaesus fraude L. Vitellii veneno tollitur. XL, XLI. Fabius Valens libidine et cunctatione Vitellianorum res subruit et, XLII, Flavianis Italiam occupantibus, XLIII, ad Stoechadas delatus, capitur. XLIV. Hispaniae, Galliae, Britannia, cuncta ad Vespasiani opes conversa. XLV. Turbat tamen Britanniam Venutius. Ibi varia sorte pugnatum. XLVI. Turbata quoque Germania. Mota et Dacorum gens, a Muciano ex Oriente reduce, repressa. XLVII, XLVIII. Anicetus Polemonis libertus, Pontum infestans, capitur. Vespasianus Alexandriam pergit, ut urbem fame urgeat. XLIX. Antonius, post Cremonam superbior, L, partem copiarum Veronae relinquit, partem in Vitellianos expedit. LI. Nefarium facinus militis, ob occisum a se fratrem praemium petentis. LII. Festinationem Antonii apud Vespasianum criminatur Mucianus. LIII. Is jactantius quam ad principem literas componit, Mucianum insectatus. Inde graves ducum simultates.

LIV. Vitellius stulta dissimulatione cladis ad Cremonam remedia malorum differt. Notabilis constantia Julii Agrestis. LV. Vitellius, ut e somno excitus, Apenninum obsideri jubet; honores largitur; in castra venit. LVI. Prodigia. Praecipuum ipse Vitellius ostentum, ignarus militiae, improvidus consilii, Romam revertit, perculsus defectione Misenensis classis. LVII. Puteolani Vespasiano; Capua Vitellio favet. Cl. Julianus in partes Vespasiani transit, qui Tarracinam occupat. LVIII. Vitellius fratrem Lucium bello per Campaniam opponit. Ipse Romae ex plebe et servitiis exercitum corradit, qui brevi dilabitur. LIX. Flaviani Apenninum transeunt; ad eos Cerialis, Vitellii custodias elapsus, venit et inter duces assumitur. LX. Pugnae avidos milites aegre cohibet Antonius. LXI. Jam crebra fiunt ad Vespasianum transfugia. Priscus et Alphenus castra deserunt, ad Vitellium regressi. LXII, LXIII. Caeso Valente, desperabundus miles sub signis vexillisque ad Vespasianum transit. Pax et salus offeruntur Vitellio, si se dedat.

LXIV. Flavius Sabinus, urbis praefectus frustra incitatur ad arma; LXV, pacis amans, de pace agit cum Vitellio, LXVI, cedere parato, ni sui reniterentur. LXVII, LXVIII. Hi, pullo amictu palatio degressum, et pro concione cedere se imperio testantem, eo redire cogunt. LXIX. Interim Sabinus rempublicam susceperat, eique aderant Romani omnis ordinis, frementibus Germanicis cohortibus. Modicum proelium, Vespasianis prosperum. Sabinus capitolium occupat, quod, LXX, Corn. Martiale frustra ad Vitellium misso, LXXI, Vitelliani oppugnant, incendunt. LXXII. De prioribus capitolii fatis digressio. LXXIII. Vitelliani cuncta sanguine, ferro, flammis miscent. Flavium Sabinum et Atticum consulem capiunt. LXXIV. Domitianus sacricolae habitu delitescit. Sabinus, invito Vitellio, trucidatur. LXXV. Sabini laudes. Atticus servatur.

LXXVI, LXXVII. Tarracina a L. Vitellio obsessa et capta. Julianus jugulatur. Triariae immodestia. LXXVIII. Flaviani, incertum Antonii an Muciani culpa cunctantes, obsessi capitolii fama exciti, LXXIX, ad urbem properant. Ibi equestre proelium, Ceriali adversum. LXXX, LXXXI. Vitellius legatos et Vestales virgines pro pace aut induciis mittit, nec obtinet. LXXXII. Flaviani tripartito agmine urbi propinquant. Varia ibi fortuna pugnatur. LXXXIII. Foeda lascivientis urbis facies, spectatore populo et plausu diversas partes fovente. LXXXIV. Castra praetoria expugnantur. LXXXV.

Vitellius, e pudenda latebra protractus et contumeliis affectus, ad Gemonias propellitur. LXXXVI. Vita Vitellii moresque. Domitianus Caesar consalutatur. Gesta uno eodemque anno.

Meliore fato fideque partium Flavianarum duces consilia belli tractabant. Poetovionem in hiberna tertiaedecimae legionis convenerant: illic agitavere, placeretne obstrui Pannoniae Alpes, donec a tergo vires universae consurgerent, an ire cominus et certare pro Italia constantius foret. Quibus opperiri auxilia et trahere bellum videbatur, Germanicarum legionum vim famamque extollebant, "et advenisse mox cum Vitellio Britannici exercitus robora: ipsis nec numerum parem pulsarum nuper legionum; et quanquam atrociter loquerentur, minorem esse apud victos animum. Sed insessis interim Alpibus, venturum cum copiis Orientis Mucianum. Superesse Vespasiano mare, classes, studia provinciarum, per quas velut alterius belli molem cieret. Ita salubri mora novas vires affore, et praesentibus nihil periturum."

II. Ad ea Antonius Primus (is acerrimus belli concitator) festinationem ipsis utilem, Vitellio exitiosam disseruit: "plus socordiae quam fiduciae accessisse victoribus: neque enim in procinctu et castris habitos; per omnia Italiae municipia desides, tantum hospitibus metuendos, quanto ferocius ante se egerint, tanto cupidius insolitas voluptates hausisse. Circo quoque ac theatris et amoenitate urbis emollitos, aut valetudinibus fessos. Sed addito spatio, rediturum et his robur meditatione belli, nec procul Germaniam, unde vires; Britanniam freto dirimi; juxta Gallias Hispaniasque; utrimque viros, equos, tributa: ipsamque Italiam et opes Urbis: ac si inferre arma ultro velint, duas classes vacuumque Illyricum mare. Quid tum claustra montium profutura? quid tractum in aestatem aliam bellum? unde interim pecuniam et commeatus? Quin potius eo ipso uterentur, quod Pannonicae legiones, deceptae magis quam victae, resurgere in ultionem properent, Moesici exercitus integras vires attulerint. Si numerus militum potius quam legionum putetur, plus hinc roboris, nihil libidinum; et profuisse disciplinae ipsum pudorem. Equites vero ne tum quidem victos, sed quanquam rebus adversis disjectam Vitellii aciem.

Duae tunc Pannonicae ac Moesicae alae perrupere hostem: nunc sedecim alarum conjuncta signa pulsu sonituque et nube ipsa operient ac superfundent oblitos proeliorum equites equosque. Nisi quis retinet, idem suasor auctorque consilii ero. Vos, quibus fortuna in integro est, legiones continete: mihi expeditae cohortes sufficient. Jam reseratam Italiam, impulsas Vitellii res audietis: juvabit sequi et vestigiis vincentis insistere."

III. Haec ac talia flagrans oculis, truci voce, quo latius audiretur (etenim se centuriones et quidam militum consilio miscuerant), ita effudit, ut cautos quoque ac providos permoveret, vulgus et ceteri unum virum ducemque, spreta aliorum segnitia, laudibus ferrent. Hanc sui famam ea statim concione commoverat, qua recitatis Vespasiani epistolis non, ut plerique, incerta disseruit, huc illuc tracturus interpretatione, prout conduxisset: aperte descendisse in causam videbatur: eoque gravior militibus erat, culpae vel gloriae socius.

IV. Proxima Cornelii Fusci procuratoris auctoritas: is quoque inclementer in Vitellium invehi solitus nihil spei sibi inter adversa reliquerat. T. Ampius Flavianus, natura ac senecta cunctatior, suspiciones militum irritabat, tanquam affinitatis cum Vitellio meminisset; idemque, quod coeptante legionum motu profugus, dein sponte remeaverat, perfidiae locum quaesisse credebatur. Nam Flavianum, omissa Pannonia, ingressum Italiam et discrimini exemptum, rerum novarum cupido legati nomen resumere et misceri civilibus armis impulerat, suadente Cornelio Fusco, non quia industria Flaviani egebat, sed ut consulare nomen surgentibus cum maxime partibus honesta specie praetenderetur.

V. Ceterum ut transmittere in Italiam impune et usui foret, scriptum Aponio Saturnino, cum exercitu Moesico celeraret. Ac ne inermes provinciae barbaris nationibus exponerentur, principes Sarmatarum Iazygum, penes quos civitatis regimen, in commilitium asciti; plebem quoque et vim equitum, qua sola valent, offerebant: remissum id munus, ne inter discordias externa molirentur, aut majore ex diverso mercede jus fasque exuerent. Trahuntur in partes

Sido atque Italicus reges Suevorum, quis vetus obsequium erga Romanos, et gens fidei commissae patientior: posita in latus auxilia, infesta Raetia, cui Portius Septiminus procurator erat, incorruptae erga Vitellium fidei. Igitur Sextilius Felix cum ala Auriana et octo cohortibus ac Noricorum juventute ad occupandam ripam Aeni fluminis, quod Rhaetos Noricosque interfluit, missus: nec his aut illis proelium tentantibus, fortuna partium alibi transacta.

VI. Antonio vexillarios e cohortibus et partem equitum ad invadendam Italiam rapienti comes fuit Arrius Varus, strenuus bello; quam gloriam et dux Corbulo et prosperae in Armenia res addiderant. Idem secretis apud Neronem sermonibus ferebatur Corbulonis virtutes criminatus. Unde infami gratia primum pilum adepto, laeta ad praesens male parta, mox in perniciem vertere. Sed Primus ac Varus, occupata Aquileia, in proxima quaeque et Opitergii et Altini laetis animis accipiuntur: relictum Altini praesidium adversus classem Ravennatem, nondum defectione ejus audita: inde Patavium et Ateste partibus adjunxere: illic cognitum tres Vitellianas cohortes et alam, cui Sebonianae nomen, ad forum Allieni, ponte juncto, consedisse. Placuit occasio invadendi incuriosos; nam id quoque nuntiabatur: luce prima inermos plerosque oppressere. Praedictum, ut paucis interfectis ceteros pavore ad mutandam fidem cogerent; et fuere, qui se statim dederent: plures, abrupto ponte, instanti hosti viam abstulerunt.

VII. Vulgata victoria, post principia belli secundum Flavianos, duae legiones, septima Galbiana, tertiadecima Gemina, cum Vedio Aquila legato Patavium alacres veniunt: ibi pauci dies ad requiem sumpti, et Minucius Justus praefectus castrorum legionis septimae, quia adductius quam civili bello imperitabat, subtractus militum irae ad Vespasianum missus est. Desiderata diu res, interpretatione gloriaque in majus accipitur, postquam Galbae imagines discordia temporum subversas in omnibus municipiis recoli jussit Antonius, decorum pro causa ratus, si placere Galbae principatus et partes revirescere crederentur.

VIII. Quaesitum inde, quae sedes bello legeretur. Verona potior visa, patentibus circum campis ad pugnam equestrem, qua praevalebant: simul coloniam copiis validam auferre Vitellio in rem famamque videbatur. Possessa ipso transitu Vicetia; quod per se parum (etenim modicae municipio vires) magni momenti locum obtinuit, reputantibus illic Caecinam genitum et patriam hostium duci ereptam. In Veronensibus pretium fuit; exemplo opibusque partes juvere. Et interjectus exercitus per Raetiam Juliasque Alpes, ac ne pervium illa Germanicis exercitibus foret, obsepserat; quae ignara Vespasiano, aut vetita: quippe Aquileiae sisti bellum exspectarique Mucianum jubebat, adjiciebatque imperio consilium, quando Aegyptus, claustra annonae, vectigalia opulentissimarum provinciarum obtinerentur, posse Vitellii exercitum egestate stipendii frumentique ad deditionem subigi. Eadem Mucianus crebris epistolis monebat, incruentam et sine luctu victoriam et alia hujuscemodi praetexendo, sed gloriae avidus atque omne belli decus sibi retinens. Ceterum ex distantibus terrarum spatiis consilia post res afferebantur.

IX. Igitur repentino incursu Antonius stationes hostium irrumpit, tentatisque levi proelio animis, ex aequo discessum. Mox Caecina inter Hostiliam, vicum Veronensium, et paludes Tartari fluminis, castra permuniit, tutus loco, cum terga flumine, latera objectu paludis tegerentur: quod si affuisset fides, aut opprimi universis Vitellianorum viribus duae legiones, nondum conjuncto Moesico exercitu, potuere, aut retro actae, deserta Italia, turpem fugam conscivissent. Sed Caecina per varias moras prima hostibus prodidit tempora belli, dum quos armis pellere promptum erat, epistolis increpat, donec per nuntios pacta perfidiae firmaret. Interim Aponius Saturninus cum legione septima Claudiana advenit: legioni tribunus Vipstanus Messalla praeerat, claris majoribus, egregius ipse, et qui solus ad id bellum artes bonas attulisset. Has ad copias nequaquam Vitellianis pares (quippe tres adhuc legiones erant) misit epistolas Caecina, temeritatem victa arma tractantium incusans: simul virtus Germanici exercitus laudibus attollebatur, Vitellii modica et vulgari mentione, nulla in Vespasianum contumelia: nihil prorsus, quod aut corrumperet hostem aut terreret. Flavianarum partium duces, omissa prioris fortunae defensione, pro Vespasiano magnifice, pro causa fidenter, de exercitu securi, in Vitellium ut inimici praesumpsere, facta tribunis centurionibusque retinendi, quae Vitellius indulsisset, spe: atque ipsum Caecinam non obscure ad transitionem hortabantur. Recitatae pro concione epistolae addidere fiduciam, quod submisse Caecina, velut offendere Vespasianum timens, ipsorum duces contemptim, tanquam insultantes Vitellio, scripsissent.

X. Adventu deinde duarum legionum, e quibus tertiam Dillius Aponianus, octavam Numisius Lupus ducebant, ostentare vires et militari vallo Veronam circumdare placuit. Forte Galbianae legioni in adversa fronte valli opus cesserat, et visi procul sociorum equites vanam formidinem ut hostes fecere. Rapiuntur arma, et ut proditionis ira militum in T. Ampium Flavianum incubuit, nullo criminis argumento, sed jam pridem invisus turbine quodam ad exitium poscebatur: propinquum Vitellii, proditorem Othonis, interceptorem donativi clamitabant. Nec defensioni locus, quanquam supplices manus tenderet, humi plerumque stratus, lacera veste, pectus atque ora singultu quatiens; id ipsum apud infensos incitamentum erat, tanquam nimius pavor conscientiam argueret. Obturbabatur militum vocibus Aponius, cum loqui coeptaret; fremitu et clamore ceteros aspernantur: uni Antonio apertae militum aures: namque et facundia aderat, mulcendique vulgum artes et auctoritas. Ubi crudescere seditio, et a conviciis et probris ad tela et manus transibant, injici catenas Flaviano jubet. Sensit ludibrium miles, disjectisque qui tribunal tuebantur, extrema vis parabatur. Opposuit sinum Antonius, stricto ferro, aut militum se manibus aut suis moriturum obtestans: ut quemque notum et aliquo militari decore insignem aspexerat, ad ferendam opem nomine ciens. Mox conversus ad signa et bellorum deos, hostium potius exercitibus illum furorem, illam discordiam injicerent, orabat, donec fatisceret seditio, et extremo jam die sua quisque in tentoria dilaberentur. Profectus eadem nocte Flavianus, obviis Vespasiani literis, discrimini exemptus est.

XI. Legiones, velut tabe infectae, Aponium Saturninum Moesici exercitus legatum eo atrocius aggrediuntur, quod non ut prius labore et opere fessae, sed medio diei exarserant, vulgatis epistolis, quas Saturninus ad Vitellium scripsisse credebatur. Ut olim virtutis modestiaeque, tunc procacitatis et petulantiae certamen erat, ne minus violenter Aponium quam Flavianum ad supplicium deposcerent. Quippe Moesicae legiones adjutam a se Pannonicorum ultionem referentes, et Pannonici, velut absolverentur aliorum seditione, iterare culpam gaudebant. In hortos, in quibus devertebatur Saturninus, pergunt, nec tam Primus et Aponianus et Messalla, quanquam omni modo nisi, eripuere Saturninum, quam obscuritas latebrarum quibus occulebatur, vacantium forte balnearum fornacibus abditus: mox, omissis lictoribus, Patavium concessit. Digressu consularium uni Antonio vis ac potestas in utrumque exercitum fuit, cedentibus collegis et obversis militum studiis: nec deerant, qui crederent, utramque seditionem fraude Antonii coeptam, ut solus bello frueretur.

XII. Ne in Vitellii quidem partibus quietae mentes, exitiosiore discordia, non suspicionibus vulgi, sed perfidia ducum turbabantur. Lucilius Bassus classis Ravennatis praefectus ambiguos militum animos, quod magna pars Dalmatae Pannoniique erant, quae provinciae Vespasiano tenebantur, partibus ejus aggregaverat. Nox proditioni electa, ut ceteris ignaris soli in principia defectores coirent. Bassus pudore, seu metu quisnam exitus foret, intra domum opperiebatur. Trierarchi magno tumultu Vitellii imagines invadunt, et paucis resistentium obtruncatis ceterum vulgus rerum novarum studio in Vespasianum inclinabat. Tum progressus Lucilius auctorem se palam praebet: classis Cornelium Fuscum praefectum sibi destinat, qui propere accucurrit. Bassus honorata custodia Liburnicis navibus Atriam pervectus, a praefecto alae Vivennio Rufino praesidium illic agitante vincitur. Sed exsoluta statim vincula interventu Hormi Caesaris liberti: is quoque inter duces habebatur.

XIII. At Caecina, defectione classis vulgata, primores centurionum et paucos militum, ceteris per militiae munera dispersis, secretum castrorum affectans in principia vocat. Ibi Vespasiani virtutem viresque partium extollit: transfugisse classem; in arcto commeatum, adversas Gallias Hispaniasque, nihil in urbe fidum; atque omnia de Vitellio in deterius. Mox incipientibus qui conscii aderant, ceteros re nova attonitos in verba Vespasiani adigit: simul Vitellii imagines dereptae, et missi qui Antonio nuntiarent. Sed ubi totis castris in fama proditio, recurrens in principia miles praescriptum Vespasiani nomen, projectas Vitellii effigies aspexit, vastum primo silentium, mox cuncta simul erumpunt: "Huc cecidisse Germanici exercitus gloriam, ut sine proelio, sine vulnere, vinctas manus et capta traderent arma? Quas enim ex diverso legiones? Nempe victas; et abesse unicum Othoniani exercitus robur, primanos quartadecimanosque; quos tamen iisdem illis campis fuderint straverintque, ut armatorum millia, velut grex venalium, exsuli Antonio donum darentur; octo nimirum legiones unius classis accessionem fore. Id Basso, id Caecinae visum: postquam domos, hortos, opes principi abstulerint, etiam militibus principem auferre. Integros incruentosque, Flavianis quoque partibus viles, quid dicturos reposcentibus aut prospera aut adversa?"

XIV. Haec singuli, haec universi, ut quemque dolor impulerat, vociferantes, initio a quinta legione orto, repositis Vitellii imaginibus, vincla Caecinae injiciunt: Fabium Fabullum quintae legionis legatum et Cassium Longum praefectum castrorum duces deligunt: forte oblatos trium Liburnicarum milites, ignaros et insontes, trucidant: relictis castris, abrupto ponte, Hostiliam rursus, inde Cremonam pergunt, ut legionibus primae Italicae et unietvicesimae Rapaci jungerentur, quas Caecina ad obtinendam Cremonam cum parte equitum praemiserat.

XV. Ubi haec comperta Antonio, discordes animis, discretos viribus hostium exercitus aggredi statuit, antequam ducibus auctoritas, militi obsequium et junctis legionibus fiducia rediret: namque Fabium Valentem profectum ab urbe acceleraturumque cognita Caecinae proditione conjectabat; et fidus Vitellio Fabius, nec militiae ignarus. Simul ingens Germanorum vis per Raetiam timebatur: et Britannia Galliaque et Hispania auxilia Vitellius acciverat, immensam belli luem, ni Antonius, id ipsum metuens, festinato proelio victoriam praecepisset. Universo cum exercitu, secundis a Verona castris, Bedriacum venit: postero die, legionibus ad muniendum retentis, auxiliares cohortes in Cremonensem agrum missae, ut specie parandarum copiarum civili praeda miles imbueretur. Ipse cum quatuor millibus equitum ad octavum a Bedriaco progressus, quo licentius popularentur: exploratores (ut mos est) longius curabant.

XVI. Quinta ferme hora diei erat, cum citus eques adventare hostes, praegredi paucos, motum fremitumque late audiri nuntiavit. Dum Antonius quidnam agendum consultat, aviditate navandae operae Arrius Varus cum promptissimis equitum prorupit, impulitque Vitellianos, modica caede: nam plurium accursu versa fortuna, et acerrimus quisque sequentium fugae ultimus erat: nec sponte Antonii properatum et fore, quae acciderant, rebatur. Hortatus suos, ut magno animo capesserent pugnam, diductis in latera turmis, vacuum medio relinquit iter, quo Varum equitesque ejus reciperet: jussae armari legiones: datum per agros signum, ut qua cuique proximum, omissa praeda, proelio occurreret. Pavidus interim Varus turbae suorum miscetur, intulitque formidinem: pulsi cum sauciis integri, suometipsi metu et angustiis viarum conflictabantur.

XVII. Nullum in illa trepidatione Antonius constantis ducis aut fortissimi militis officium omisit: occursare paventibus; retinere cedentes: ubi plurimus labor, unde aliqua spes, consilio, manu, voce insignis hosti, conpicuus suis: eo postremo ardoris provectus est, ut vexillarium fugientem hasta transverberaret: mox raptum vexillum in hostem vertit: quo pudore haud plures quam centum equites restitere. Juvit locus, arctiore illic via et fracto interfluentis rivi ponte, qui incerto alveo et praecipitibus ripis fugam impediebat: ea necessitas seu fortuna lapsas jam partes restituit. Firmati inter se densis ordinibus excipiunt Vitellianos temere effusos; atque illi consternantur. Antonius instare perculsis, sternere obvios. Simul ceteri, ut cuique ingenium, spoliare, capere, arma equosque abripere: et exciti prospero clamore, qui modo per agros fuga palabantur, victoriae se miscebant.

XVIII. Ad quartum a Cremona lapidem fulsere legionum signa Rapacis atque Italicae, laeto inter initia equitum suorum proelio illuc usque provecta. Sed ubi fortuna contra fuit, non laxare ordines, non recipere turbatos, non obviam ire ultroque aggredi hostem, tantum per spatium cursu et pugnando fessum. Forte victi haud perinde rebus prosperis ducem desideraverant, atque in adversis deesse intelligebant. Nutantem aciem victor equitatus incursat; et Vipstanus Messalla tribunus cum Moesicis auxiliaribus assequitur, quos militiae legionariis, quanquam raptim ductos, aequabant. Ita mixtus eques pedesque rupere legionum agmen. Et propinqua Cremonensium moenia, quanto plus spei ad effugium, minorem ad resistendum animum dabant.

XIX. Nec Antonius ultra institit, memor laboris ac vulnerum, quibus tam anceps proelii fortuna, quamvis prospero fine, equites equosque afflictaverat. Inumbrante vespera universum Flaviani exercitus robur advenit: utque cumulos super et recentia caede vestigia incessere, quasi debellatum foret, pergere Cremonam et victos in deditionem accipere aut expugnare deposcunt. Haec in medio, pulchra dictu. Illa sibi quisque: "Posse coloniam plano sitam impetu capi. Idem audaciae per tenebras irrumpentibus, et majorem rapiendi licentiam: quod si lucem opperiantur, jam pacem, jam preces et pro labore ac vulneribus clementiam et gloriam, inania laturos: sed opes Cremonensium in sinu praefectorum legatorumque fore. Expugnatae urbis praedam ad militem, deditae ad duces pertinere." Spernuntur centuriones tribunique, ac ne vox cujusquam audiatur, quatiunt arma, rupturi imperium, ni ducantur.

XX. Tum Antonius inserens se manipulis, ubi aspectu et auctoritate silentium fecerat: "Non se decus, neque pretium eripere tam bene meritis" affirmabat; "sed divisa inter exercitum ducesque munia: militibus cupidinem pugnandi convenire; duces providendo, consultando, cunctatione saepius quam temeritate prodesse. Ut pro virili portione armis ac manu victoriam juverit, ratione et consilio, propriis ducis artibus, profuturum. Neque enim ambigua esse, quae occurrant, noctem et ignotae situm urbis, intus hostes et cuncta insidiis opportuna: non, si pateant portae, nisi explorato, nisi die intrandum. An oppugnationem inchoaturos, adempto omni prospectu, quis aequus locus, quanta altitudo moenium, tormentisne et telis an operibus et vineis aggredienda urbs foret?" Mox conversus ad singulos, "num secures dolabrasque et cetera expugnandis urbibus secum attulissent,"rogitabat. Et cum abnuerent, "gladiisne," inquit, "et pilis perfringere ac subruere muros ullae manus possunt? Si aggerem struere, si pluteis cratibusve protegi necesse fuerit, ut vulgus improvidum, irriti stabimus, altitudinem turrium et aliena munimenta mirantes? Quin potius mora noctis unius, advectis tormentis machinisque, vim victoriamque nobiscum ferimus?" Simul lixas calonesque cum recentissimis equitum Bedriacum mittit, copias ceteraque usui allaturos.

XXI. Id vero aegre tolerante milite prope seditionem ventum, cum progressi equites sub ipsa moenia vagos ex Cremonensibus corripiunt: quorum indicio noscitur sex Vitellianas legiones omnemque exercitum, qui Hostiliae egerat, eo ipso die triginta millia passuum emensum, comperta suorum clade in proelium accingi ac jam affore. Is terror obstructas mentes consiliis ducis aperuit. Sistere tertiam decimam legionem in ipso viae Postumiae aggere jubet, cui juncta a laevo septima Galbiana patenti campo stetit, dein septima Claudiana agresti fossa (ita locus erat) praemunita; dextro octava per apertum limitem, mox tertia densis arbustis intersepta: hic aquilarum signorumque ordo: milites mixti per tenebras, ut fors tulerat: praetorianum vexillum proximum tertianis, cohortes auxiliorum in cornibus, latera ac terga equite circumdata: Sido atque Italicus Suevi cum delectis popularium primori in acie versabantur.

XXII. At Vitellianus exercitus, cui acquiescere Cremonae et reciperatis cibo somnoque viribus confectum algore atque inedia hostem postera die profligare ac proruere ratio fuit, indigus rectoris, inops consilii, tertia ferme noctis hora paratis jam dispositisque Flavianis impingitur. Ordinem agminis disjecti per iram ac tenebras asseverare non ausim, quanquam alii tradiderint quartam Macedonicam dextro suorum cornu, quintam et quintamdecimam cum vexillis nonae secundaeque et vicesimae Britannicarum legionum mediam aciem, sextadecimanos duoetvicesimanosque et primanos laevum cornu complesse. Rapaces atque Italici omnibus se manipulis miscuerant. Eques auxiliaque sibi ipsi locum legere. Proelium tota nocte varium, anceps, atrox, his, rursus illis exitiabile. Nihil animus aut manus, ne oculi quidem provisu juvabant: eadem utraque acie arma; crebris interrogationibus notum pugnae signum; permixta vexilla, ut quisque globus capta ex hostibus huc vel illuc raptabat. Urgebatur maxime septima legio, nuper a Galba conscripta. Occisi sex primorum ordinum centuriones; abrepta quaedam signa: ipsam aquilam Atilius Verus primipili centurio multa cum hostium strage et ad extremum moriens servaverat.

XXIII. Sustinuit labantem aciem Antonius accitis praetorianis; qui ubi excepere pugnam, pellunt hostem, dein pelluntur. Namque Vitelliani tormenta in aggerem viae contulerant, ut tela vacuo atque aperto excuterentur, dispersa primo et arbustis sine hostium noxa illisa. Magnitudine eximia quintaedecimae legionis balista ingentibus saxis hostilem aciem proruebat, lateque cladem intulissent, ni duo milites praeclarum facinus ausi, arreptis e strage scutis ignorati, vincla ac libramenta tormentorum abscidissent: statim confossi sunt, eoque intercidere nomina: de facto haud ambigitur. Neutro inclinaverat fortuna, donec adulta nocte luna surgens ostenderet acies falleretque. Sed Flavianis aequior a tergo: hinc majores equorum virorumque umbrae, et falso, ut in corpora, ictu tela hostium citra cadebant: Vitelliani adverso lumine collucentes velut ex occulto jaculantibus incauti offerebantur.

XXIV. Igitur Antonius, ubi noscere suos noscique poterat, alios pudore et probris, multos laude et hortatu, omnes spe promissisque accendens, "cur rursus sumpsissent arma," Pannonicas legiones interrogabat: "illos esse campos, in quibus abolere labem prioris ignominiae, ubi reciperare gloriam possent." Tum ad Moesicos conversus, "principes auctoresque belli" ciebat: "frustra minis et verbis provocatos Vitellianos, si manus eorum oculosque non tolerarent." Haec, ut quosque accesserat: plura ad tertianos, veterum recentiumque admonens: ut "sub M. Antonio Parthos, sub Corbulone Armenios, nuper Sarmatas pepulissent." Mox infensus praetorianis: "Vos" inquit, "nisi vincitis, pagani, quis alius imperator, quae castra alia excipient? illic signa armaque vestra sunt, et mors victis: nam ignominiam consumpsistis." Undique clamor; et orientem solem (ita in Syria mos est) tertiani salutavere.

XXV. Vagus inde, an consilio ducis subditus rumor, advenisse Mucianum, exercitus invicem salutasse: gradum inferunt, quasi recentibus auxiliis aucti, rariore jam Vitellianorum acie, ut quos nullo rectore suus quemque impetus vel pavor contraheret diduceretve. Postquam pulsos sensit Antonius, denso agmine obturbabat: laxati ordines abrumpuntur; nec restitui quivere, impedientibus vehiculis tormentisque. Per limitem viae sparguntur festinatione consectandi victores. Eo notabilior caedes fuit, quia filius patrem interfecit. Rem nominaque, auctore Vipstano Messalla, tradam. Julius Mansuetus ex Hispania, Rapaci legioni additus, impubem filium domi liquerat: is mox adultus, inter septimanos a Galba conscriptus, oblatum forte patrem et vulnere stratum, dum semianimem scrutatur, agnitus agnoscensque et exsanguem amplexus, voce flebili precabatur placatos patris manes, neve se ut parricidam aversarentur: publicum id facinus; et unum militem quotam civilium armorum partem? Simul attollere corpus, aperire humum, supremo erga parentem officio fungi. Advertere proximi, deinde plures: hinc per omnem aciem miraculum et questus et saevissimi belli exsecratio: nec eo segnius propinquos, affines, fratres trucidatos spoliant; factum esse scelus loquuntur faciuntque.

XXVI. Ut Cremonam venere, novum immensumque opus occurrit. Othoniano bello Germanicus miles moenibus Cremonensium castra sua, castris vallum circumjecerat, eaque munimenta rursus auxerat: quorum aspectu haesere victores, incertis ducibus quid juberent. Incipere oppugnationem, fesso per diem noctemque exercitu, arduum, et nullo juxta subsidio anceps: sin Bedriacum redirent, intolerandus tam longi itineris labor, et victoria ad irritum revolvebatur: munire castra, id quoque, propinquis hostibus, formidolosum, ne dispersos et opus molientes subita eruptione turbarent. Quae super cuncta terrebat ipsorum miles periculi quam morae patientior: quippe ingrata quae tuta, ex temeritate spes; omnisque caedes et vulnera et sanguis aviditate praedae pensabantur.

XXVII. Huc inclinavit Antonius, cingique vallum corona jussit: primo sagittis saxisque eminus certabant, majore Flavianorum pernicie, in quos tela desuper librabantur: mox vallum portasque legionibus attribuit, ut discretus labor fortes ignavosque distingueret, atque ipsa contentione decoris accenderentur. Proxima Bedriacensi viae tertiani septimanique sumpsere, dexteriora valli octava ac septima Claudiana; tertiadecimanos ad Brixianam portam impetus tulit. Paulum inde morae, dum ex proximis agris ligones, dolabras, et alii falces scalasque convectant: tum elatis super capita scutis, densa testudine succedunt. Romanae utrimque artes: pondera saxorum Vitelliani provolvunt, disjectam fluitantemque testudinem lanceis contisque scrutantur, donec, soluta compage scutorum, exsangues aut laceros prosternerent multa cum strage.

XXVIII. Incesserat cunctatio, ni duces fesso militi et velut irritas exhortationes abnuenti Cremonam monstrassent. Hormine ingenium, ut Messalla tradit, an potior auctor sit C. Plinius qui Antonium incusat, haud facile discreverim, nisi quod neque Antonius neque Hormus a fama vitaque sua, quamvis pessimo flagitio, degeneravere. Non jam sanguis neque vulnera morabantur, quin subruerent vallum quaterentque portas, innixi humeris et super iteratam testudinem scandentes prensarent hostium tela brachiaque: integri cum sauciis, semineces cum exspirantibus volvuntur, varia pereuntium forma et omni imagine mortium.

XXIX. Acerrimum septimae tertiaeque legionum certamen; et dux Antonius cum delectis auxiliaribus eodem incubuerat. Obstinatos inter se cum sustinere Vitelliani nequirent et superjacta tela testudine laberentur, ipsam postremo balistam in subeuntes pepulere, quae ut ad praesens disjecit obruitque quos inciderat, ita pinnas ac summa valli ruina sua traxit: simul juncta turris ictibus saxorum cessit; qua septimani dum nituntur cuneis, tertianus securibus gladiisque portam perfregit. Primum irrupisse C. Volusium tertiae legionis militem inter omnes auctores constat: is in vallum egressus, deturbatis qui restiterant, conspicuus manu ac voce capta castra conclamavit. Ceteri, trepidis jam Vitellianis seque e vallo praecipitantibus, perrupere: completur caede quantum inter castra murosque vacui fuit.

XXX. Ac rursus nova laborum facies; ardua urbis moenia, saxeae turres, ferrati portarum obices, vibrans tela miles, frequens obstrictusque Vitellianis partibus Cremonensis populus, magna pars Italiae stato in eosdem dies mercatu congregata; quod defensoribus auxilium ob multitudinem, oppugnantibus incitamentum ob praedam erat. Rapi ignes Antonius inferrique amoenissimis extra urbem aedificiis jubet, si damno rerum suarum Cremonenses ad mutandam fidem traherentur: propinqua muris tecta et altitudinem moenium egressa fortissimo quoque militum complet: illi trabibus tegulisque et facibus propugnatores deturbant.

XXXI. Jam legiones in testudinem glomerabantur et alii tela saxaque incutiebant, cum languescere paulatim Vitellianorum animi. Ut quis ordine anteibat, cedere fortunae, ne Cremona quoque excisa, nulla ultra venia, omnisque ira victoris non in vulgus inops, sed in tribunos centurionesque, ubi pretium caedis erat, reverteretur. Gregarius miles, futuri socors et ignobilitate tutior, perstabat: vagi per vias, in domibus abditi, pacem ne tum quidem orabant, cum bellum posuissent. Primores castrorum nomen atque imagines Vitellii amoliuntur: catenas Caecinae (nam etiam tum vinctus erat) exsolvunt orantque, ut causae suae deprecator assistat: aspernantem tumentemque lacrimis fatigant, extremum malorum, tot fortissimi viri proditoris opem invocantes: mox velamenta et infulas pro muris ostentant. Cum Antonius inhiberi tela jussisset, signa aquilasque extulere: maestum inermium agmen, dejectis in terram oculis, sequebatur. Circumstiterant victores, et primo ingerebant probra, intentabant ictus: mox, ut praeberi ora contumeliis et, posita omni ferocia, cuncta victi patiebantur, subit recordatio illos esse qui nuper Bedriaci victoriae temperassent. Sed ubi Caecina, praetexta lictoribusque insignis, dimota turba, consul incessit, exarsere victores: superbiam saevitiamque, (adeo invisa scelera sunt) etiam perfidiam objectabant. Obstitit Antonius, datisque defensoribus ad Vespasianum dimisit.

XXXII. Plebs interim Cremonensium inter armatos conflictabatur: nec procul caede aberant, cum precibus ducum mitigatus est miles. Et vocatos ad concionem Antonius alloquitur, magnifice victores, victos clementer, de Cremona in neutrum. Exercitus praeter insitam praedandi cupidinem vetere odio ad excidium Cremonensium incubuit: juvisse partes Vitellianas Othonis quoque bello credebantur: mox tertiadecimanos ad exstruendum amphitheatrum relictos, ut sunt procacia urbanae plebis ingenia, petulantibus jurgiis illuserant. Auxit invidiam editum illic a Caecina gladiatorum spectaculum, eademque rursus belli sedes; et praebiti in acie Vitellianis cibi, caesae quaedam feminae studio partium ad proelium progressae: tempus quoque mercatus ditem alioqui coloniam majorum opum specie complebat. Ceteri duces in obscuro: Antonium fortuna famaque omnium oculis exposuerat: is balneas abluendo cruori propere petit: excepta vox est, cum teporem incusaret, statim futurum, ut incalescerent. Vernile dictum omnem invidiam in eum vertit, tanquam signum incendendae Cremonae dedisset, quae jam flagrabat.

XXXIII. Quadraginta armatorum millia irrupere, calonum lixarumque amplior numerus et in libidinem ac saevitiam corruptior. Non dignitas, non aetas protegebat, quo minus stupra caedibus, caedes stupris miscerentur. Grandaevos senes, exacta aetate feminas, viles ad praedam, in ludibrium trahebant. Ubi adulta virgo aut quis forma conspicuus incidisset, vi manibusque rapientium divulsus ipsos postremo direptores in mutuam perniciem agebat: dum pecuniam vel gravia auro templorum dona sibi quisque trahunt, majore aliorum vi truncabantur. Quidam obvia aspernati, verberibus tormentisque dominorum abdita scrutari, defossa eruere, faces in manibus, quas, ubi praedam egesserant, in vacuas domos et inania templa per lasciviam jaculabantur: utque exercitu vario linguis, moribus, cui cives, socii, externi interessent, diversae cupidines et aliud cuique fas, nec quicquam illicitum. Per quatriduum Cremona suffecit. Cum omnia sacra profanaque in igne considerent, solum Mefitis templum stetit ante moenia, loco seu numine defensum.

XXXIV. Hic exitus Cremonae anno ducentesimo octogesimo sexto a primordio sui. Condita erat Tiberio Sempronio et Cornelio consulibus, ingruente in Italiam Hannibale, propugnaculum adversus Gallos trans Padum agentes, et si qua alia vis per Alpes rueret. Igitur numero colonorum, opportunitate fluminum, ubere agri, annexu connubiisque gentium adolevit floruitque bellis externis intacta, civilibus infelix. Antonius pudore flagitii, crebrescente invidia, edixit, ne quis Cremonenses captivos detineret: irritamque praedam militibus effecerat consensus Italiae, emptionem talium mancipiorum aspernantis. Occidi coepere: quod ubi enotuit, a propinquis affinibusque occulte redemptabantur: mox rediit Cremonam reliquus populus: reposita fora templaque munificentia municipum; et Vespasianus hortabatur.

XXXV. Ceterum assidere sepultae urbis ruinis noxia tabo humus haud diu permisit; ad tertium lapidem progressi, vagos paventesque Vitellianos, sua quemque apud signa, componunt. Et victae legiones, ne manente adhuc civili bello ambigue agerent, per Illyricum dispersae. In

Britanniam inde et Hispanias nuntios famamque, in Galliam Julium Calenum tribunum, in Germaniam Alpinum Montanum praefectum cohortis, quod hic Trevir, Calenus Aeduus, uterque Vitelliani fuerant, ostentui misere. Simul transitus Alpium praesidiis occupati, suspecta Germania tanquam in auxilium Vitellii accingeretur.

XXXVI. At Vitellius, profecto Caecina, cum Fabium Valentem paucis post diebus ad bellum impulisset, curis luxum obtendebat: non parare arma, non alloquio exercitioque militem firmare, non in ore vulgi agere; sed umbraculis hortorum abditus, ut ignava animalia, quibus si cibum suggeras, jacent torpentque, praeterita, instantia, futura pari oblivione dimiserat. Atque illum in nemore Aricino desidem et marcentem proditio Lucilii Bassi ac defectio classis Ravennatis perculit. Nec multo post de Caecina affertur mixtus gaudio dolor, et descivisse, et ab exercitu vinctum. Plus apud socordem animum laetitia quam cura valuit: multa cum exsultatione in urbem revectus, frequenti concione pietatem militum laudibus cumulat. P. Sabinum praetorii praefectum ob amicitiam Caecinae vinciri jubet, substituto in locum ejus Alfeno Varo.

XXXVII. Mox senatum composita in magnificentiam oratione allocutus, exquisitis patrum adulationibus attollitur. Initium atrocis in Caecinam sententiae a L. Vitellio factum; dein ceteri, composita indignatione, quod consul rempublicam, dux imperatorem, tantis opibus, tot honoribus cumulatus amicum prodidisset, velut pro Vitellio conquerentes, suum dolorem proferebant. Nulla in oratione cujusquam erga Flavianos duces obtrectatio: errorem imprudentiamque exercituum culpantes, Vespasiani nomen suspensi et vitabundi circumibant. Nec defuit, qui unum consulatus diem (is enim in locum Caecinae supererat) magno cum irrisu tribuentis accipientisque eblandiretur. Pridie Kalendas Novembris Rosius Regulus iniit ejuravitque. Annotabant periti nunquam antea, non abrogato magistratu neque lege lata, alium suffectum: nam consul uno die et ante fuerat Caninius Rebilus, C. Caesare dictatore, cum belli civilis praemia festinarentur.

XXXVIII. Nota per eos dies Junii Blaesi mors et famosa fuit; de qua sic accepimus. Gravi corporis morbo aeger Vitellius Servilianis hortis turrim vicino sitam collucere per noctem crebris luminibus animadvertit. Sciscitanti causam, apud Caecinam Tuscum epulari multos, praecipuum honore Junium Blaesum nuntiatur: cetera in majus de apparatu et solutis in lasciviam animis: nec defuere, qui ipsum Tuscum et alios, sed criminosius Blaesum incusarent, quod, aegro principe, laetos dies ageret. Ubi asperatum Vitellium et posse Blaesum perverti satis patuit iis, qui principum offensas acriter speculantur, datae L. Vitellio delationis partes. Ille infensus Blaeso aemulatione prava, quod eum omni dedecore maculosum egregia fama anteibat, cubiculum imperatoris reserat, filium ejus sinu complexus et genibus accidens: causam confusionis quaerenti, "non se proprio metu nec sui anxium, sed pro fratre, pro liberis fratris preces lacrimasque attulisse. Frustra Vespasianum timeri, quem tot Germanicae legiones, tot provinciae virtute ac fide, tantum denique terrarum ac maris immensis spatiis arceat. In urbe ac sinu cavendum hostem, Junios Antoniosque avos jactantem, qui se stirpe imperatoria, comem ac magnificum militibus ostentet. Versas illuc omnium mentes, dum Vitellius amicorum inimicorumque negligens fovet aemulum principis labores e convivio prospectantem. Reddendam pro intempestiva laetitia maestam et funebrem noctem, qua sciat et sentiat vivere Vitellium et imperare et, si quid fato accidat, filium habere."

XXXIX. Trepidanti inter scelus metumque, ne dilata Blaesi mors maturam perniciem, palam jussa atrocem invidiam ferret, placuit veneno grassari. Addidit facinori fidem nobili gaudio, Blaesum visendo: quin et audita est saevissima Vitellii vox, qua se (ipsa enim verba referam) pavisse oculos spectata inimici morte jactavit. Blaeso, super claritatem natalium et elegantiam morum, fidei obstinatio fuit. Integris quoque rebus, a Caecina et primoribus partium jam Vitellium aspernantibus ambitus, abnuere perseveravit: sanctus, inturbidus, nullius repentini honoris, adeo non principatus appetens, parum effugerat, ne dignus crederetur.

XL. Fabius interim Valens, multo ac molli concubinarum spadonumque agmine segnius quam ad bellum incedens, proditam a Lucilio Basso Ravennatem classem pernicibus nuntiis accepit. Et si coeptum iter properasset, nutantem Caecinam praevenire aut ante discrimen pugnae assequi legiones potuisset. Nec deerant, qui monerent, ut cum fidissimis per occultos tramites, vitata Ravenna, Hostiliam Cremonamve pergeret. Aliis placebat accitis ex urbe praetoriis cohortibus valida manu perrumpere. Ipse, inutili cunctatione, agendi tempora consultando consumpsit: mox utrumque consilium aspernatus, quod inter ancipitia deterrimum est, dum media sequitur, nec ausus est satis nec providit.

XLI. Missis ad Vitellium literis, auxilium postulat. Venere tres cohortes cum ala Britannica, neque ad fallendum aptus numerus neque ad penetrandum. Sed Valens ne in tanto quidem discrimine infamia caruit, quo minus rapere illicitas voluptates, adulteriisque ac stupris polluere hospitum domus crederetur: aderant vis et pecunia et ruentis fortunae novissima libido. Adventu demum peditum equitumque pravitas consilii patuit, quia nec vadere per hostes tam parva manu poterat etiam si fidissima foret, nec integram fidem attulerant. Pudor tamen et praesentis ducis reverentia morabatur, haud diuturna vincula apud avidos periculorum et dedecoris securos. Eo metu et paucis, quos adversa non mutaverant, comitantibus, cohortes Ariminum praemittit, alam tueri terga jubet: ipse flexit in Umbriam atque inde Etruriam, ubi cognito pugnae Cremonensis eventu non ignavum et, si provenisset, atrox consilium iniit, ut arreptis navibus in quamcumque partem Narbonensis provinciae egressus, Gallias et exercitus et Germaniae gentes novumque bellum cieret.

XLII. Digresso Valente trepidos, qui Ariminum tenebant, Cornelius Fuscus, admoto exercitu et missis per proxima littorum Liburnicis, terra marique circumvenit. Occupantur plana Umbriae et qua Picenus ager Adria alluitur; omnisque Italia, inter Vespasianum ac Vitellium, Apennini jugis dividebatur. Fabius Valens e sinu Pisano, segnitia maris aut adversante vento portum Herculis Monoeci depellitur: haud procul inde agebat Marius Maturus Alpium maritimarum procurator, fidus Vitellio, cujus sacramentum, cunctis circa hostilibus, nondum exuerat. Is Valentem comiter exceptum, ne Galliam Narbonensem temere ingrederetur, monendo terruit: simul ceterorum fides metu infracta: namque circumjectas civitates procurator Valerius Paulinus, strenuus militiae et Vespasiano ante fortunam amicus, in verba ejus adegerat.

XLIII. Concitisque omnibus, qui exauctorati a Vitellio bellum sponte sumebant, Forojuliensem coloniam, claustra maris, praesidio tuebatur, eo gravior auctor, quod Paulino patria Forum Julii et honos apud praetorianos, quorum quondam tribunus fuerat. Ipsique pagani favore municipali et futurae potentiae spe juvare partes annitebantur: quae ubi paratu firma et aucta rumore apud varios Vitellianorum animos increbruere, Fabius Valens cum quatuor speculatoribus et tribus amicis, totidem centurionibus ad naves regreditur; Maturo ceterisque remanere et in verba Vespasiani adigi volentibus fuit. Ceterum ut mare tutius Valenti quam littora aut urbes, ita futuri ambiguus et magis quid vitaret quam cui fideret certus, adversa tempestate Stoechadas Massiliensium insulas affertur: ibi eum missae a Paulino Liburnicae oppressere.

XLIV. Capto Valente cuncta ad victoris opes conversa, initio per Hispaniam a prima Adjutrice legione orto, quae memoria Othonis infensa Vitellio decimam quoque ac sextam traxit. Nec Galliae cunctabantur. Et Britanniam inditus erga Vespasianum favor, quod illic secundae legioni a Claudio praepositus et bello clarus egerat, non sine motu adjunxit ceterarum, in quibus plerique centuriones ac milites a Vitellio provecti expertum jam principem anxii mutabant.

XLV. Ea discordia et crebris belli civilis rumoribus Britanni sustulere animos auctore Venutio, qui super insitam ferociam et Romani nominis odium propriis in Cartismanduam reginam stimulis accendebatur. Cartismandua Brigantibus imperitabat, pollens nobilitate; et auxerat potentiam, postquam capto per dolum rege Caractaco, instruxisse triumphum Claudii Caesaris videbatur. Inde opes et rerum secundarum luxus: spreto Venutio (is fuit maritus) armigerum ejus Vellocatum, in matrimonium regnumque accepit. Concussa statim flagitio domus. Pro marito studia civitatis; pro adultero libido reginae et saevitia. Igitur Venutius accitis auxiliis, simul ipsorum Brigantum defectione, in extremum discrimen Cartismanduam adduxit. Tum petita a Romanis praesidia: et cohortes alaeque nostrae, variis proeliis, exemere tamen periculo reginam. Regnum Venutio, bellum nobis relictum.

XLVI. Turbata per eosdem dies Germania et socordia ducum et seditione legionum. Externa vi, perfidia sociali prope afflicta Romana res. Id bellum cum causis et eventibus (etenim longius provectum est) mox memorabimus. Mota et Dacorum gens nunquam fida, tunc sine metu abducto e Moesia exercitu. Sed prima rerum quieti speculabantur: ubi flagrare Italiam bello, cuncta invicem hostilia accepere, expugnatis cohortium alarumque hibernis utraque Danubii ripa potiebantur. Jamque castra legionum exscindere parabant, ni Mucianus sextam legionem opposuisset, Cremonensis victoriae gnarus, ac ne externa moles utrimque ingrueret, si Dacus Germanusque diversi irrupissent. Affuit, ut saepe alias, fortuna populi Romani, quae Mucianum viresque Orientis illuc tulit, et quod Cremonae interim transegimus. Fonteius Agrippa ex Asia (pro consule eam provinciam annuo imperio tenuerat) Moesiae praepositus est, additis copiis e Vitelliano exercitu, quem spargi per provincias et externo bello illigari pars consilii pacisque erat.

XLVII. Nec ceterae nationes silebant. Subita per Pontum arma barbarum mancipium, regiae quondam classis praefectus, moverat: is fuit Anicetus Polemonis libertus, praepotens olim, et postquam regnum in formam provinciae verterat, mutationis impatiens. Igitur Vitellii nomine ascitis gentibus quae Pontum accolunt, corrupto in spem rapinarum egentissimo quoque, haud temnendae manus ductor, Trapezuntem, vetusta fama civitatem a Graecis in extremo Ponticae orae conditam, subitus irrupit. Caesa ibi cohors, regium auxilium olim, mox donati civitate Romana, signa armaque in nostrum modum, desidiam licentiamque Graecorum retinebant. Classi quoque faces intulit, vacuo mari eludens, quia lectissimas Liburnicarum omnemque militem Mucianus Byzantium adegerat. Quin et barbari contemptim vagabantur, fabricatis repente navibus; camaras vocant, arctis lateribus latam alvum sine vinculo aeris aut ferri connexam; et tumido mari, prout fluctus attollitur, summa navium tabulis augent, donec in modum tecti claudantur. Sic inter undas volvuntur, pari utrimque prora et mutabili remigio, quando hinc vel illinc appellere indiscretum et innoxium est.

XLVIII. Advertit ea res Vespasiani animum, ut vexillarios e legionibus ducemque Virdium Geminum, spectatae militiae, deligeret. Ille incompositum et praedae cupidine vagum hostem adortus, coegit in naves; effectisque raptim Liburnicis assequitur Anicetum in ostio fluminis Cohibi, tutum sub Sedochezorum regis auxilio, quem pecunia donisque ad societatem perpulerat. Ac primo rex minis armisque supplicem tueri: postquam merces proditionis aut bellum ostendebatur, fluxa, ut est barbaris, fide pactus Aniceti exitium, perfugas tradidit belloque servili finis impositus. Laetum ea victoria Vespasianum, cunctis super vota fluentibus, Cremonensis proelii nuntius in Aegypto assequitur. Eo properantius Alexandriam pergit, ut, fracto Vitellii exercitu, urbem quoque externae opis indigam fame urgeret. Namque et Africam eodem latere sitam terra marique invadere parabat, clausis annonae subsidiis inopiam ac discordiam hosti facturus.

XLIX. Dum hac totius orbis nutatione fortuna imperii transit, Primus Antonius nequaquam pari innocentia post Cremonam agebat, satisfactum bello ratus et cetera ex facili, seu felicitas in tali ingenio avaritiam, superbiam ceteraque occulta mala patefecit: ut captam, Italiam persultare; ut suas, legiones colere; omnibus dictis factisque viam sibi ad potentiam struere; utque licentia militem imbueret, interfectorum centurionum ordines legionibus offerebat: eo suffragio turbidissimus quisque delecti; nec miles in arbitrio ducum, sed duces militari violentia trahebantur. Quae seditiosa et corrumpendae disciplinae mox in praedam vertebat, nihil adventantem Mucianum veritus, quod exitiosius erat quam Vespasianum sprevisse.

L. Ceterum propinqua hieme et humentibus Pado campis, expeditum agmen incedere. Signa aquilaeque victricium legionum, milites vulneribus aut aetate graves, plerique etiam integri, Veronae relicti: sufficere cohortes alaeque et e legionibus lecti, profligato jam bello, videbantur. Undecima legio sese adjunxerat, initio cunctata, sed prosperis rebus anxia, quod defuisset. Sex millia Dalmatarum, recens delectus, comitabantur. Ducebat Pompeius Silvanus consularis: vis consiliorum penes Annium Bassum legionis legatum: is Silvanum, socordem bello et dies rerum verbis terentem, specie obsequii regebat, ad omniaque, quae agenda forent, quieta cum industria aderat. Ad has copias e classicis Ravennatibus legionariam militiam poscentibus optimus quisque asciti: classem Dalmatae supplevere. Exercitus ducesque ad Fanum Fortunae iter sistunt de summa rerum cunctantes, quod motas ex urbe praetorias cohortes audierant, et teneri praesidiis Apenninum rebantur: et ipsos in regione bello attrita inopia et seditiosae militum voces terrebant, clavarium (donativi nomen est) flagitantium: nec pecuniam aut frumentum providerant; et festinatio atque aviditas praepediebant, dum quae accipi poterant rapiuntur.

LI. Celeberrimos auctores habeo tantam victoribus adversus fas nefasque irreverentiam fuisse, ut gregarius eques occisum a se proxima acie fratrem professus, praemium a ducibus petierit. Nec illis aut honorare eam caedem jus hominum aut ulcisci ratio belli permittebat. Distulerant tanquam majora meritum quam quae statim exsolverentur; nec quicquam ultra traditur. Ceterum et prioribus civium bellis par scelus inciderat; nam proelio, quo apud Janiculum adversus Cinnam pugnatum est, Pompeianus miles fratrem suum, dein cognito facinore seipsum interfecit, ut Sisenna memorat: tanto acrior apud majores, sicut virtutibus gloria, ita flagitiis poenitentia fuit. Sed haec aliaque ex veteri memoria petita, quotiens res locusque exempla recti aut solatia mali poscet, haud absurde memorabimus.

LII. Antonio ducibusque partium praemitti equites omnemque Umbriam explorari placuit, si qua Apennini juga clementius adirentur; acciri aquilas signaque et quicquid Veronae militum foret, Padumque et mare commeatibus compleri. Erant inter duces, qui necterent moras: quippe nimius jam Antonius, et certiora ex Muciano sperabantur. Namque Mucianus tam celeri victoria anxius et, ni praesens urbe potiretur, expertem se belli gloriaeque ratus, ad Primum et Varum media scriptitabat, instandum coeptis aut rursus cunctandi utilitates edisserens, atque ita compositus ut ex eventu rerum adversa abnueret vel prospera agnosceret. Plotium Griphum nuper ab Vespasiano in senatorium ordinem additum ac legioni praepositum ceterosque sibi fidos apertius monuit: hique omnes de festinatione Primi ac Vari sinistre, et Muciano volentia rescripsere. Quibus epistolis Vespasiano missis effecerat, ut non pro spe Antonii consilia factaque ejus aestimarentur.

LIII. Aegre id pati Antonius, et culpam in Mucianum conferre, cujus criminationibus eviluissent pericula sua: nec sermonibus temperabat, immodicus lingua et obsequii insolens: literas ad Vespasianum composuit jactantius quam ad principem, nec sine occulta in Mucianum insectatione: "se Pannonicas legiones in arma egisse; suis stimulis excitos Moesiae duces, sua constantia perruptas Alpes, occupatam Italiam, intersepta Germanorum Raetorumque auxilia. Quod discordes dispersasque Vitellii legiones equestri procella, mox peditum vi per diem noctemque fudisset, id pulcherrimum et sui operis. Casum Cremonae bello imputandum: majore damno, plurium urbium excidiis veteres civium discordias reipublicae stetisse. Non se nuntiis neque epistolis, sed manu et armis imperatori suo militare: neque officere gloriae eorum, qui Asiam interim composuerint: illis Moesiae pacem, sibi salutem securitatemque Italiae cordi fuisse. Suis exhortationibus Gallias Hispaniasque, validissimam terrarum partem, ad Vespasianum conversas. Sed cecidisse in irritum labores, si praemia periculorum soli assequantur, qui periculis non affuerint." Nec fefellere ea Mucianum: inde graves simultates, quas Antonius simplicius, Mucianus callide eoque implacabilius nutriebat.

LIV. At Vitellius, fractis apud Cremonam rebus, nuntios cladis occultans, stulta dissimulatione remedia potius malorum quam mala differebat. Quippe confitenti consultantique supererant spes viresque: cum e contrario laeta omnia fingeret, falsis ingravescebat. Mirum apud ipsum de bello silentium: prohibiti per civitatem sermones eoque plures, ac, si liceret, vere narraturi, quia vetabantur, atrociora vulgaverant. Nec duces hostium augendae famae deerant, captos Vitellii exploratores circumductosque, ut robora victoris exercitus noscerent, remittendo; quos omnes Vitellius secreto percunctatus interfici jussit. Notabili constantia centurio Julius Agrestis, post multos sermones quibus Vitellium ad virtutem frustra accendebat, perpulit, ut ad vires hostium spectandas quaeque apud Cremonam acta forent ipse mitteretur. Nec exploratione occulta fallere Antonium tentavit, sed mandata imperatoris suumque animum professus, ut cuncta viseret, postulat. Missi, qui locum proelii, Cremonae vestigia, captas legiones ostenderent. Agrestis ad Vitellium remeavit, abnuentique vera esse quae afferret, atque ultro corruptum arguenti, "quandoquidem," inquit, "magno documento opus est, nec alius jam tibi aut vitae aut mortis meae usus, dabo cui credas:" atque ita digressus voluntaria morte dicta firmavit. Quidam jussu Vitellii interfectum; de fide constantiaque eadem tradidere.

LV. Vitellius, ut e somno excitus, Julium Priscum et Alfenum Varum cum quatuordecim praetoriis cohortibus et omnibus equitum alis obsidere Apenninum jubet. Secuta e classicis legio. Tot millia armatorum lecta equis virisque, si dux alius foret, inferendo quoque bello satis pollebant. Ceterae cohortes ad tuendam urbem L. Vitellio fratri datae. Ipse nihil e solito luxu remittens et diffidentia properus festinare comitia, quibus consules in multos annos destinabat; foedera sociis, Latium externis dilargiri; his tributa dimittere, alios immunitatibus juvare; denique nulla in posterum cura lacerare imperium. Sed vulgus ad magnitudinem beneficiorum aderat; stultissimus quisque pecuniis mercabatur; apud sapientes cassa habebantur, quae neque dari neque accipi salva republica poterant. Tandem flagitante exercitu qui Mevaniam insederat, magno senatorum agmine, quorum multos ambitione, plures formidine trahebat, in castra venit, incertus animi et infidis consiliis obnoxius.

LVI. Concionanti (prodigiosum dictu) tantum foedarum volucrum supervolitavit, ut nube atra diem obtenderent. Accessit dirum omen, profugus altaribus taurus, disjecto sacrificii apparatu, longe nec ubi feriri hostias mos est confossus. Sed praecipuum ipse Vitellius ostentum erat, ignarus militiae, improvidus consilii, quis ordo agminis, quae cura explorandi, quantus urgendo trahendove bello modus, alios rogitans, et ad omnes nuntios, vultu quoque et incessu trepidus, dein temulentus. Postremo taedio castrorum, et audita defectione Misenensis classis, Romam revertit, recentissimum quodque vulnus pavens, summi discriminis incuriosus. Nam cum transgredi Apenninum integro exercitus sui robore et fessos hieme atque inopia hostes aggredi in aperto foret, dum dispergit vires, acerrimum militem et usque in extrema obstinatum trucidandum capiendumque tradidit, peritissimis centurionum dissentientibus et, si consulerentur, vera dicturis. Arcuere eos intimi amicorum Vitellii, ita formatis principis auribus, ut aspera quae utilia, nec quicquam nisi jucundum et laesurum acciperet.

LVII. Sed classem Misenensem (tantum civilibus discordiis etiam singulorum audacia valet) Claudius Faventinus centurio per ignominiam a Galba dimissus ad defectionem traxit, fictis Vespasiani epistolis pretium proditionis ostentans. Praeerat classi Claudius Apollinaris, neque fidei constans neque strenuus in perfidia: et Apinius Tiro praetura functus ac tum forte Minturnis agens ducem se defectoribus obtulit: a quibus municipia coloniaeque impulsae, praecipuo Puteolanorum in Vespasianum studio, contra Capua Vitellio fida, municipalem aemulationem bellis civilibus miscebant. Vitellius Claudium Julianum (is nuper classem Misenensem molli imperio rexerat) permulcendis militum animis delegit: data in auxilium urbana cohors et gladiatores, quibus Julianus praeerat. Ut collata utrimque castra, haud magna cunctatione Juliano in partes Vespasiani transgresso Tarracinam occupavere, moenibus situque magis quam ipsorum ingenio tutam.

LVIII. Quae ubi Vitellio cognita, parte copiarum Narniae cum praefectis praetorii relicta, L. Vitellium fratrem cum sex cohortibus et quingentis equitibus ingruenti per Campaniam bello opposuit. Ipse aeger animi studiis militum et clamoribus populi arma poscentis refovebatur, dum vulgus ignavum et nihil ultra verba ausurum falsa specie exercitum et legiones appellat. Hortantibus libertis (nam amicorum ejus quanto quis clarior, minus fidus) vocari tribus jubet. Dantes nomina sacramento adigit: superfluente multitudine curam delectus in consules partitur. Servorum numerum et pondus argenti senatoribus indicit. Equites Romani obtulere operam pecuniasque, etiam libertinis idem munus ultro flagitantibus. Ea simulatio officii a metu profecta verterat in favorem; ac plerique haud perinde Vitellium quam casum locumque principatus miserabantur: nec deerat ipse vultu, voce, lacrimis misericordiam elicere, largus promissis, et quae natura trepidantium est, immodicus. Quin et Caesarem se dici voluit, aspernatus antea, sed tunc superstitione nominis, et quia in metu consilia prudentium et vulgi rumor juxta audiuntur. Ceterum ut omnia inconsulti impetus coepta, initiis valida, spatio languescunt, dilabi paulatim senatores equitesque primo cunctanter et ubi ipse non aderat, mox contemptim et sine discrimine, donec Vitellius pudore irriti conatus, quae non dabantur, remisit.

LIX. Ut terrorem Italiae possessa Mevania ac velut renatum ex integro bellum intulerat, ita haud dubium erga Flavianas partes studium tam pavidus Vitellii discessus addidit. Erectus Samnis Pelignusque et Marsi aemulatione, quod Campania praevenisset, ut in novo obsequio, ad cuncta belli munia acres erant. Sed foeda hieme per transitum Apennini conflictatus exercitus, et vix quieto agmine nives eluctantibus patuit, quantum discriminis adeundum foret, ni Vitellium retro fortuna vertisset, quae Flavianis ducibus non minus saepe quam ratio affuit. Obvium illic Petilium Cerialem habuere, agresti cultu et notitia locorum custodias Vitellii elapsum. Propinqua affinitas Ceriali cum Vespasiano, nec ipse inglorius militiae, eoque inter duces assumptus est. Flavio quoque Sabino ac Domitiano patuisse effugium multi tradidere. Et missi ab Antonio nuntii per varias fallendi artes penetrabant, locum ac praesidium monstrantes. Sabinus inhabilem labori et audaciae valetudinem causabatur: Domitiano aderat animus; sed custodes a Vitellio additi, quanquam se socios fugae promitterent, tanquam insidiantes timebantur. Atque ipse Vitellius, respectu suarum necessitudinum, nihil in Domitianum atrox parabat.

LX. Duces partium ut Carsulas venere, paucos ad requiem dies sumunt, donec aquilae signaque legionum assequerentur; et locus ipse castrorum placebat, late prospectans, tuto copiarum aggestu, florentissimis pone tergum municipiis: simul colloquia cum Vitellianis decem millium spatio distantibus et proditio sperabatur. Aegre id pati miles, et victoriam malle quam pacem: ne suas quidem legiones opperiebantur, ut praedae quam periculorum socias. Vocatos ad concionem Antonius docuit "esse adhuc Vitellio vires, ambiguas, si deliberarent; acres, si desperassent. Initia bellorum civilium fortunae permittenda; victoriam consiliis et ratione perfici. Jam Misenensem classem et pulcherrimam Campaniae oram descivisse: nec plus e toto terrarum orbe reliquum Vitellio, quam quod inter Tarracinam Narniamque jaceat. Satis gloriae proelio Cremonensi partum, et exitio Cremonae nimium invidiae; nec concupiscerent Romam capere potius quam servare: majora illis praemia et multo maximum decus, si incolumitatem senatui populoque Romano sine sanguine quaesissent."

LXI. His ac talibus mitigati animi: nec multo post legiones venere. Et terrore famaque aucti exercitus Vitellianae cohortes nutabant, nullo in bellum adhortante, multis ad transitionem, qui suas centurias turmasque tradere, donum victori et sibi in posterum gratiam, certabant. Per eos cognitum est, Interamnam proximis campis praesidio quadringentorum equitum teneri. Missus extemplo Varus cum expedita manu paucos repugnantium interfecit: plures abjectis armis veniam petivere: quidam in castra refugi cuncta formidine implebant, augendo rumoribus virtutem copiasque hostium, quo amissi praesidii dedecus lenirent. Nec ulla apud Vitellianos flagitii poena, et praemiis defectorum versa fides, ac reliquum perfidiae certamen: crebra transfugia tribunorum centurionumque; nam gregarius miles induruerat pro Vitellio, donec Priscus et Alfenus desertis castris ad Vitellium regressi, pudore proditionis cunctos exsolverent.

LXII. Iisdem diebus Fabius Valens Urbini in custodia interficitur. Caput ejus Vitellianis cohortibus ostentatum, ne quam ultra spem foverent: nam pervasisse in Germanias Valentem et veteres illic novosque exercitus ciere credebant. Visa caede in desperationem versi; et Flavianus exercitus immane quantum animo exitium Valentis ut finem belli accepit. Natus erat Valens Anagniae, equestri familia: procax moribus, neque absurdus ingenio, famam urbanitatis per lasciviam petere. Ludicro juvenum sub Nerone, velut ex necessitate, mox sponte mimos actitavit, scite magis quam probe. Legatus legionis et fovit Virginium et infamavit. Fonteium Capitonem corruptum, seu quia corrumpere nequiverat, interfecit. Galbae proditor, Vitellio fidus et aliorum perfidia illustratus.

LXIII. Abrupta undique spe, Vitellianus miles transiturus in partes, id quoque non sine decore, sed sub signis vexillisque in subjectos Narniae campos descendere. Flavianus exercitus, ut ad proelium intentus ornatusque, densis circa viam ordinibus adstiterat. Accepti in medium Vitelliani, et circumdatos Primus Antonius clementer alloquitur: pars Narniae, pars Interamnae subsistere jussi: relictae simul e victricibus legiones, neque quiescentibus graves, et adversus contumaciam validae. Non omisere per eos dies Primus ac Varus crebris nuntiis salutem et pecuniam et secreta Campaniae offerre Vitellio, si positis armis seque ac liberos suos Vespasiano permisisset. In eundem modum et Mucianus composuit epistolas; quibus plerumque fidere Vitellius ac de numero servorum, electione littorum loqui. Tanta torpedo invaserat animum, ut, si principem eum fuisse ceteri non meminissent, ipse oblivisceretur.

LXIV. At primores civitatis Flavium Sabinum praefectum urbis secretis sermonibus incitabant, "victoriae famaeque partem capesseret: esse illi proprium militem cohortium urbanarum, nec defuturas vigilum cohortes, servitia ipsorum, fortunam partium et omnia prona victoribus. Ne Antonio Varoque de gloria concederet. Paucas Vitellio cohortes, et maestis undique nuntiis trepidas: populi mobilem animum: et si ducem se praebuisset, easdem illas adulationes pro Vespasiano fore. Ipsum Vitellium ne prosperis quidem parem: adeo ruentibus debilitatum. Gratiam patrati belli penes eum, qui urbem occupasset. Id Sabino convenire, ut imperium fratri reservaret; id Vespasiano, ut ceteri post Sabinum haberentur."

LXV. Haudquaquam erecto animo eas voces accipiebat, invalidus senecta. Erant, qui occultis suspicionibus incesserent, tanquam invidia et aemulatione fortunam fratris moraretur. Namque Flavius Sabinus aetate prior, privatis utriusque rebus auctoritate pecuniaque Vespasianum anteibat, et credebatur affectam ejus fidem praejuvisse, domo agrisque pignori acceptis. Unde quanquam manente in speciem concordia, offensarum operta metuebantur. Melior interpretatio, mitem virum abhorrere a sanguine et caedibus, eoque crebris cum Vitellio sermonibus de pace ponendisque per conditionem armis agitare. Saepe domi congressi, postremo in aede Apollinis, ut fama fuit, pepigere. Verba vocesque duos testes habebant, Cluvium Rufum et Silium Italicum. Vultus procul visentibus notabantur, Vitellii projectus et degener, Sabinus non insultans et miseranti propior.

LXVI. Quod si tam facile suorum mentes flexisset Vitellius quam ipse cesserat, incruentam Urbem Vespasiani exercitus intrasset. Ceterum ut quisque Vitellio fidus, ita pacem et conditiones abnuebant, discrimen ac dedecus ostentantes, "et fidem in libidine victoris. Nec tantam Vespasiano superbiam, ut privatum Vitellium pateretur: ne victos quidem laturos. Ita periculum ex misericordia. Ipsum sane senem, et prosperis adversisque satiatum. Sed quod nomen, quem statum filio ejus Germanico fore? Nunc pecuniam et familiam et beatos Campaniae sinus promitti: sed ubi imperium Vespasianus invaserit, non ipsi, non amicis ejus, non denique exercitibus securitatem, nisi exstincto aemulatore, redituram. Fabium illis Valentem, captivum et casibus dubiis reservatum, praegravem fuisse: nedum Primus ac Fuscus et specimem partium Mucianus ullam in Vitellium nisi occidendi licentiam habeant. Non a Caesare Pompeium, non ab Augusto Antonium incolumes relictos: nisi forte Vespasianus altiores spiritus gerat, Vitellii cliens, cum Vitellius collega Claudio foret. Quin ut censuram patris, ut tres consulatus, ut tot egregiae domus honores deceret, desperatione saltem in audaciam accingeretur: perstare militem, superesse studia populi. Denique nihil atrocius eventurum quam in quod sponte ruant: moriendum victis, moriendum deditis: id solum referre, novissimum spiritum per ludibrium et contumelias effundant an per virtutem."

LXVII. Surdae ad fortia consilia Vitellio aures. Obruebatur animus miseratione curaque, ne pertinacibus armis minus placabilem victorem relinqueret conjugi ac liberis. Erat illi et fessa aetate parens, quae tamen paucis ante diebus opportuna morte excidium domus praevenit, nihil principatu filii assecuta nisi luctum et bonam famam. Quintodecimo Kalendas Januarii audita defectione legionis cohortiumque, quae se Narniae dediderant, pullo amictu palatio degreditur, maesta circum familia. Simul ferebatur lecticula parvulus filius, velut in funebrem pompam. Voces populi blandae et intempestivae: miles minaci silentio.

LXVIII. Nec quisquam adeo rerum humanarum immemor, quem non commoveret illa facies, Romanum principem et generis humani paulo ante dominum, relicta fortunae suae sede, per populum, per urbem exire de imperio. Nihil tale viderant, nihil audierant. Repentina vis dictatorem Caesarem oppresserat, occultae Caium insidiae; nox et ignotum rus fugam Neronis absconderant; Piso et Galba tanquam in acie cecidere: in sua concione Vitellius, inter suos milites, prospectantibus etiam feminis, pauca et praesenti maestitiae congruentia locutus: "Cedere se pacis et reipublicae causa: retinerent tantum memoriam sui, fratremque et conjugem et innoxiam liberorum aetatem miserarentur:" simul filium protendens, modo singulis, modo universis commendans, prostremo fletu praepediente, assistenti consuli (Caecilius Simplex erat) exsolutum a latere pugionem, velut jus necis vitaeque civium, reddebat. Aspernante consule, reclamantibus qui in concione adstiterant, ut in aede Concordiae positurus insignia imperii domumque fratris petiturus discessit. Major hic clamor obsistentium penatibus privatis, in palatium vocantium. Interclusum aliud iter, idque solum quod in Sacram viam pergeret patebat: tum consilii inops in palatium rediit. Praevenerat rumor ejurari ab eo imperium, scripseratque Flavius Sabinus cohortium tribunis, ut militem cohiberent.

LXIX. Igitur, tanquam omnis respublica in Vespasiani sinum cessisset, primores senatus et plerique equestris ordinis omnisque miles urbanus et vigiles domum Flavii Sabini complevere: illuc de studiis vulgi et minis Germanicarum cohortium affertur. Longius jam progressus erat quam ut regredi posset; et suo quisque metu, ne disjectos eoque minus validos Vitelliani consectarentur, cunctantem in arma impellebant. Sed quod in ejusmodi rebus accidit, consilium ab omnibus datum est, periculum pauci sumpsere. Circa lacum Fundani descendentibus, qui Sabinum comitabantur, armatis occurrunt promptissimi Vitellianorum. Modicum ibi proelium improviso tumultu, sed prosperum Vitellianis fuit. Sabinus re trepida, quod tutissimum e praesentibus, arcem capitolii insedit milite mixto et quibusdam senatorum equitumque, quorum nomina tradere haud promptum est, quoniam, victore Vespasiano, multi id meritum erga partes simulavere. Subierunt obsidium etiam feminae, inter quas maxime insignis Verulana Gratilla, neque liberos neque propinquos, sed bellum secuta. Vitellianus miles socordi custodia clausos circumdedit; eoque concubia nocte suos liberos Sabinus et Domitianum fratris filium in capitolium accivit, misso per neglecta ad Flavianos duces nuntio, qui circumsideri ipsos et, ni subveniretur, arctas res nuntiaret. Noctem adeo quietam egit, ut digredi sine noxa potuerit: quippe miles Vitellii adversus pericula ferox, laboribus et vigiliis parum intentus erat, et hibernus imber repente fusus oculos auresque impediebat.

LXX. Luce prima Sabinus, antequam invicem hostilia coeptarent, Cornelium Martialem e primipilaribus ad Vitellium misit cum mandatis et questu quod pacta turbarentur. "Simulationem prorsus et imaginem deponendi imperii fuisse, ad decipiendos tot illustres viros. Cur enim e rostris fratris domum, imminentem foro et irritandis hominum oculis, quam Aventinum et penates uxoris petisset? Ita privato et omnem principatus speciem vitanti convenisse. Contra Vitellium in palatium, in ipsam imperii arcem regressum; inde armatum agmen emissum; stratam innocentium caedibus celeberrimam urbis partem; ne capitolio quidem abstineri. Togatum nempe se et unum e senatoribus, dum inter Vespasianum ac Vitellium proeliis legionum, captivitatibus urbium, deditionibus cohortium judicatur; jam Hispaniis Germaniisque et Britannia desciscentibus fratrem Vespasiani mansisse in fide, donec ultro ad conditiones vocaretur. Pacem et concordiam victis utilia, victoribus tantum pulchra esse. Si conventionis poeniteat, non se, quem perfidia deceperit, ferro peteret, non filium Vespasiani vix puberem. Quantum occisis uno sene et uno juvene profici? iret obviam legionibus, et de summa rerum illic certaret: cetera secundum eventum proelii cessura." Trepidus ad haec Vitellius pauca purgandi sui causa respondit, culpam in militem conferens, cujus nimio ardori imparem esse modestiam suam. Et monuit Martialem ut per secretam aedium partem occulte abiret, ne a militibus internuntius invisae pacis interficeretur: ipse neque jubendi neque vetandi potens, non jam imperator, sed tantum belli causa erat.

LXXI. Vix dum regresso in Capitolium Martiale, furens miles aderat, nullo duce, sibi quisque auctor: cito agmine forum et imminentia foro templa praetervecti erigunt aciem per adversum collem usque ad primas Capitolinae arcis fores. Erant antiquitus porticus in latere clivi, dextrae subeuntibus; in quarum tectum egressi saxis tegulisque Vitellianos obruebant. Neque illis manus nisi gladiis armatae; et arcessere tormenta aut missilia tela longum videbatur. Faces in prominentem porticum jecere; et sequebantur ignem, ambustasque Capitolii fores penetrassent, ni Sabinus revulsas undique statuas, decora majorum, in ipso aditu vice muri objecisset. Tum diversos Capitolii aditus invadunt, juxta lucum asyli, et qua Tarpeia rupes centum gradibus aditur. Improvisa utraque vis; propior atque acrior per asylum ingruebat: nec sisti poterant scandentes per conjuncta aedificia, quae, ut in multa pace, in altum edita solum capitolii aequabant. Hic ambigitur, ignem tectis oppugnatores injecerint an obsessi, quae crebrior fama, nitentes ac progressos depulerint. Inde lapsus ignis in porticus appositas aedibus: mox sustinentes fastigium aquilae vetere ligno traxerunt flammam alueruntque. Sic Capitolium, clausis foribus, indefensum et indireptum conflagravit.

LXXII. Id facinus post conditam urbem luctuosissimum foedissimumque reipublicae populi Romani accidit nullo externo hoste, propitiis, si per mores nostros liceret, deis, sedem Jovis Optimi Maximi auspicato a majoribus pignus imperii conditam, quam non Porsena dedita urbe, neque Galli capta, temerare potuissent, furore principum exscindi! Arserat et ante Capitolium civili bello, sed fraude privata; nunc palam obsessum, palam incensum: quibus armorum causis? quo tantae cladis pretio stetit? pro patria bellavimus? Voverat Tarquinius Priscus rex bello Sabino, jeceratque fundamenta spe magis futurae magnitudinis, quam quo modicae adhuc populi Romani res sufficerent. Mox Servius Tullius sociorum studio, dein Tarquinius Superbus capta Suessa Pometia hostium spoliis exstruxere. Sed gloria operis libertati reservata: pulsis regibus, Horatius Pulvillus iterum consul dedicavit, ea magnificentia, quam immensae postea populi Romani opes ornarent potius, quam augerent. Iisdem rursus vestigiis situm est, postquam interjecto quadringentorum viginti quinque annorum spatio, L. Scipione, C. Norbano consulibus, flagraverat. Curam victor Sulla suscepit, neque tamen dedicavit: hoc solum felicitati ejus negatum. Lutatii Catuli nomen inter tot Caesarum opera usque ad Vitellium mansit. Ea tunc aedes cremabatur.

LXXIII. Sed plus pavoris obsessis quam obsessoribus intulit. Quippe Vitellianus miles neque astu neque constantia inter dubia indigebat. Ex diverso trepidi milites, dux segnis et velut captus animi, non lingua, non auribus competere; neque alienis consiliis regi, neque sua expedire; huc illuc clamoribus hostium circumagi; quae jusserat vetare, quae vetuerat jubere. Mox, quod in perditis rebus accidit, omnes praecipere, nemo exsequi: postremo abjectis armis, fugam et fallendi artes circumspectabant. Irrumpunt Vitelliani et cuncta sanguine, ferro flammisque miscent. Pauci militarium virorum, inter quos maxime insignes Cornelius Martialis, Aemilius Pacensis, Casperius Niger, Didius Scaeva, pugnam ausi obtruncantur. Flavium Sabinum inermem neque fugam coeptantem circumsistunt, et Quintium Atticum consulem, umbra honoris et suamet vanitate monstratum, quod edicta in populum pro Vespasiano magnifica, probrosa adversus Vitellium jecerat. Ceteri per varios casus elapsi, quidam servili habitu, alii fide clientium contecti et inter sarcinas abditi. Fuere qui excepto Vitellianorum signo, quo inter se noscebantur, ultro rogitantes respondentesve audaciam pro latebra haberent.

LXXIV. Domitianus prima irruptione apud aedituum occultatus, sollertia liberti lineo amictu turbae sacricolarum immixtus ignoratusque, apud Cornelium Primum paternum clientem juxta Velabrum delituit. Ac potiente rerum patre, disjecto aeditui contubernio, modicum sacellum JOVI CONSERVATORI aramque posuit casus suos in marmore expressam. Mox imperium adeptus JOVI CUSTODI templum ingens seque in sinu dei sacravit. Sabinus et Atticus, onerati catenis et ad Vitellium ducti, nequaquam infesto sermone vultuque excipiuntur, frementibus qui jus caedis et praemia enavatae operae petebant. Clamore a proximis orto sordida pars plebis supplicium Sabini exposcit, minas adulationesque miscet. Stantem pro gradibus palatii Vitellium et preces parantem pervicere, ut absisteret. Tum confossum collaceratumque, et absciso capite, truncum corpus Sabini in Gemonias trahunt.

LXXV. Hic exitus viri haud sane spernendi. Quinque et triginta stipendia in republica fecerat, domi militiaeque clarus: innocentiam justitiamque ejus non argueres; sermonis nimius erat: id unum septem annis quibus Moesiam, duodecim quibus praefecturam urbis obtinuit, calumniatus est rumor. In fine vitae alii segnem, multi moderatum et civium sanguinis parcum credidere. Quod inter omnes constiterit, ante principatum Vespasiani decus domus penes Sabinum erat. Caedem ejus laetam fuisse Muciano accepimus. Ferebant plerique etiam paci consultum, dirempta aemulatione inter duos, quorum alter se fratrem imperatoris, alter consortem imperii cogitaret. Sed Vitellius consulis supplicium poscenti populo restitit, placatus ac velut vicem reddens, quod interrogantibus quis Capitolium incendisset, se reum Atticus obtulerat: eaque confessione, sive aptum tempori mendacium fuit, invidiam crimenque agnovisse et a partibus Vitellii amolitus videbatur.

LXXVI. Iisdem diebus L. Vitellius positis apud Feroniam castris excidio Tarracinae imminebat, clausis illic gladiatoribus remigibusque, qui non egredi moenia neque periculum in aperto audebant. Praeerat, ut supra memoravimus, Julianus gladiatoribus, Apollinaris remigibus, lascivia socordiaque gladiatorum magis quam ducum similes; non vigilias agere, non intuta moenium firmare, noctu dieque fluxi et amoena littorum personantes, in ministerium luxus dispersis militibus, de bello tantum inter convivia loquebantur. Paucos ante dies discesserat Apinius Tiro, donisque ac pecuniis acerbe per municipia conquirendis plus invidiae quam virium partibus addebat.

LXXVII. Interim ad L. Vitellium servus Verginii Capitonis perfugit, pollicitusque, si praesidium acciperet, vacuam arcem tradi futurum, multa nocte cohortes expeditas summis montium jugis super caput hostium sistit: inde miles ad caedem magis quam ad pugnam decurrit: sternunt inermos aut arma capientes, et quosdam somno excitos, cum tenebris, pavore, sonitu tubarum, clamore hostili turbarentur. Pauci gladiatorum resistentes neque inulti cecidere; ceteri ad naves ruebant, ubi cuncta pari formidine implicabantur, permixtis paganis, quos nullo discrimine Vitelliani trucidabant. Sex Liburnicae inter primum tumultum evasere, in quis praefectus classis Apollinaris; reliquae in littore captae, aut nimio ruentium onere pressas mare hausit. Julianus ad L. Vitellium perductus et verberibus foedatus in ore ejus jugulatur. Fuere qui uxorem L. Vitellii Triariam incesserent, tanquam gladio militari cincta inter luctum cladesque expugnatae Tarracinae superbe saeveque egisset. Ipse lauream gestae prospere rei ad fratrem misit, percunctatus, statim regredi se an perdomandae Campaniae insistere juberet. Quod salutare non modo partibus Vespasiani, sed reipublicae fuit: nam si recens victoria miles et super insitam pervicaciam secundis ferox Romam contendisset, haud parva mole certatum nec sine exitio urbis foret: quippe L. Vitellio quamvis infami inerat industria; nec virtutibus, ut boni, sed, quo modo pessimus quisque, vitiis valebat.

LXXVIII. Dum haec in partibus Vitellii geruntur, digressus Narnia Vespasiani exercitus, festos Saturni dies Ocriculi per otium agitabat. Causa tam pravae morae, ut Mucianum opperirentur. Nec defuere qui Antonium suspicionibus arguerent, tanquam dolo cunctantem post secretas Vitellii epistolas, quibus consulatum et nubilem filiam et dotales opes pretium proditionis offerebat. Alii, ficta haec et in gratiam Muciani composita. Quidam, omnium id ducum consilium fuisse ostentare potius urbi bellum quam inferre, quando validissimae cohortes a Vitellio descivissent, et abscisis omnibus praesidiis cessurus imperio videbatur. Sed cuncta festinatione, deinde ignavia Sabini corrupta, qui sumptis temere armis munitissimam Capitolii arcem et ne magnis quidem exercitibus expugnabilem adversus tres cohortes tueri nequivisset. Haud facile quis uni assignaverit culpam, quae omnium fuit: nam et Mucianus ambiguis epistolis victores morabatur, et Antonius praepostero obsequio, vel dum regerit invidiam, crimen meruit; ceterique duces, dum peractum bellum putant, finem ejus insignivere. Ne Petilius quidem Cerialis cum mille equitibus praemissus, ut transversis itineribus per agrum Sabinum Salaria via urbem introiret, satis maturaverat, donec obsessi capitolii fama cunctos simul exciret.

LXXIX. Antonius per Flaminiam ad Saxa rubra multo jam noctis serum auxilium venit. Illic interfectum Sabinum, conflagrasse Capitolium, tremere urbem, maesta omnia accepit: plebem quoque et servitia pro Vitellio armari nuntiabatur. Et Petilio Ceriali equestre proelium adversum fuerat: namque incautum et tanquam ad victos ruentem Vitelliani, interjectus equiti pedes, excepere. Pugnatum haud procul urbe inter aedificia hortosque et anfractus viarum; quae gnara Vitellianis, incomperta hostibus, metum fecerant: neque omnis eques concors, adjunctis quibusdam qui nuper apud Narniam dediti fortunam partium speculabantur. Capitur praefectus alae Tullius Flavianus: ceteri foeda fuga consternantur, non ultra Fidenas secutis victoribus.

LXXX. Eo successu studia populi aucta: vulgus urbanum arma cepit. Paucis scuta militaria; plures raptis, quod cuique obvium, telis, signum pugnae exposcunt. Agit grates Vitellius, et ad tuendam urbem prorumpere jubet. Mox vocato senatu deliguntur legati ad exercitus, ut praetexto reipublicae concordiam pacemque suaderent. Varia legatorum sors fuit. Qui Petilio Ceriali occurrerant, extremum discrimen adiere, aspernante milite conditiones pacis: vulneratur praetor Arulenus Rusticus: auxit invidiam, super violatum legati praetorisque nomen, propria dignatio viri: palantur comites, occiditur proximus lictor, dimovere turbam ausus: et ni dato a duce praesidio defensi forent, sacrum etiam in exteras gentes legatorum jus ante ipsa patriae moenia civilis rabies usque in exitium temerasset. Aequioribus animis accepti sunt, qui ad Antonium venerant, non quia modestior miles, sed duci plus auctoritatis.

LXXXI. Miscuerat se legatis Musonius Rufus equestris ordinis, studium philosophiae et placita Stoicorum aemulatus; coeptabatque, permixtus manipulis, bona pacis ac belli discrimina disserens, armatos monere. Id plerisque ludibrio, pluribus taedio: nec deerant, qui propellerent proculcarentque, ni admonitu modestissimi cujusque et aliis minitantibus omisisset intempestivam sapientiam. Obviae fuere et virgines Vestales cum epistolis Vitellii ad Antonium scriptis: eximi supremo certamini unum diem postulabat: si moram interjecissent, facilius omnia conventura. Virgines cum honore dimissae: Vitellio rescriptum Sabini caede et incendio Capitolii dirempta belli commercia.

LXXXII. Tentavit tamen Antonius vocatas ad concionem legiones mitigare, ut castris juxta pontem Mulvium positis, postera die urbem ingrederentur. Ratio cunctandi, ne asperatus proelio miles non populo, non senatui, ne templis quidem ac delubris deorum consuleret. Sed omnem prolationem ut inimicam victoriae suspectabant. Simul fulgentia per colles vexilla, quanquam imbellis populus sequeretur, speciem hostilis exercitus fecerant. Tripartito agmine pars, ut adstiterat, Flaminia via, pars juxta ripam Tiberis incessit; tertium agmen per Salariam Collinae portae propinquabat. Plebs invectis equitibus fusa: miles Vitellianus trinis et ipse praesidiis occurrit. Proelia ante urbem multa et varia, sed Flavianis consilio ducum praestantibus saepius prospera. Ii tantum conflictati sunt, qui in partem sinistram urbis ad Sallustianos hortos per angusta et lubrica viarum flexerant. Superstantes maceriis hortorum Vitelliani ad serum usque diem saxis pilisque subeuntes arcebant, donec ab equitibus, qui porta Collina irruperant, circumvenirentur. Concurrere et in campo Martio infestae acies. Pro Flavianis fortuna et parta totiens victoria; Vitelliani desperatione sola ruebant: et quanquam pulsi, rursus in urbe congregabantur.

LXXXIII. Aderat pugnantibus spectator populus, utque in ludicro certamine, hos, rursus illos clamore et plausu fovebat: quotiens pars altera inclinasset, abditos in tabernis aut si quam in domum perfugerant, erui jugularique expostulantes parte majore praedae potiebantur. Nam milite ad sanguinem et caedes obverso, spolia in vulgus cedebant. Saeva ac deformis urbe tota facies: alibi proelia et vulnera, alibi balineae popinaeque; simul cruor et strues corporum, juxta scorta et scortis similes; quantum in luxurioso otio libidinum, quicquid in acerbissima captivitate scelerum, prorsus ut eandem civitatem et furere crederes et lascivire. Conflixerant ante armati exercitus in urbe, bis L. Sulla, semel Cinna victoribus; nec tunc minus crudelitatis: nunc inhumana securitas, et ne minimo quidem temporis voluptates intermissae: velut festis diebus id quoque gaudium accederet, exsultabant, fruebantur, nulla partium cura, malis publicis laeti.

LXXXIV. Plurimum molis in oppugnatione castrorum fuit, quae acerrimus quisque ut novissimam spem retinebant. Eo intentius victores, praecipuo veterum cohortium studio, cuncta validissimarum urbium excidiis reperta simul admovent, testudinem, tormenta, aggeres facesque, quicquid tot proeliis laboris ac periculi hausissent, opere illo consummari clamitantes. "Urbem senatui ac populo Romano, templa diis reddita: proprium esse militis decus in castris: illam patriam, illos penates: ni statim recipiantur, noctem in armis agendam." Contra Vitelliani, quanquam numero fatoque dispares, inquietare victoriam, morari pacem, domos arasque cruore foedare suprema victis solatia amplectebantur. Multi semianimes super turres et propugnacula moenium exspiravere. Convulsis portis, reliquus globus obtulit se victoribus; et cecidere omnes contrariis vulneribus, versi in hostem. Ea cura etiam morientibus decori exitus fuit.

LXXXV. Vitellius capta urbe per aversam palatii partem Aventinum in domum uxoris sellula defertur, ut, si diem latebra vitavisset, Tarracinam ad cohortes fratremque perfugeret. Dein mobilitate ingenii, et quae natura pavoris est, cum omnia metuenti praesentia maxime displicerent, in palatium regreditur vastum desertumque, dilapsis etiam infimis servitiorum aut occursum ejus declinantibus. Terret solitudo et tacentes loci; tentat clausa, inhorrescit vacuis; fessusque misero errore et pudenda latebra semet occultans, ab Julio Placido tribuno cohortis protrahitur. Vinctae pone tergum manus; laniata veste, foedum spectaculum, ducebatur, multis increpantibus, nullo illacrimante: deformitas exitus misericordiam abstulerat. Obvius e Germanicis militibus Vitellium infesto ictu, per iram vel quo maturius ludibrio eximeret, an tribunum appetierit, in incerto fuit: aurem tribuni amputavit ac statim confossus est. Vitellium infestis mucronibus coactum modo erigere os et offerre contumeliis, nunc cadentes statuas suas, plerumque Rostra, aut Galbae occisi locum contueri, postremo ad Gemonias, ubi corpus Flavii Sabini jacuerat, propulere. Una vox non degeneris animi excepta, cum tribuno insultanti se tamen imperatorem ejus fuisse respondit. Ac deinde ingestis vulneribus concidit: et vulgus eadem pravitate insectabatur interfectum, qua foverat viventem.

LXXXVI. Patria illi Luceria: septimum et quinquagesimum aetatis annum explebat. Consulatum, sacerdotia, nomen locumque inter primores nulla sua industria, sed cuncta patris claritudine adeptus. Principatum ei detulere, qui ipsum non noverant. Studia exercitus raro cuiquam, bonis artibus quaesita, perinde affuere, quam huic per ignaviam. Inerat tamen simplicitas ac liberalitas; quae, ni adsit modus, in exitium vertuntur. Amicitias, dum magnitudine munerum, non constantia morum continere putat, meruit magis quam habuit. Reipublicae haud dubie intererat Vitellium vinci: sed imputare perfidiam non possunt, qui Vitellium Vespasiano prodidere, cum a Galba descivissent. Praecipiti in occasum die, ob pavorem magistratuum senatorumque, qui dilapsi ex urbe aut per domos clientium semet occultabant, vocari senatus non potuit. Domitianum, postquam nihil hostile metuebatur, ad duces partium progressum et Caesarem consalutatum, miles frequens, utque erat in armis, in paternos penates deduxit.

C. CORNELII TACITI

HISTORIARUM

LIBER QUARTUS.

BREVIARIUM LIBRI.

Cap. I. Interfecto Vitellio, milites Flaviani in urbe saeviunt. II. Domitianus, nomen sedemque Caesaris nactus, adulteriis filium principis agit. L. Vitellius interficitur. III. Campania composita, Vespasiano senatus consulatum cum Tito filio, praeturam Domitiano et consulare imperium, decernit. IV. Muciani, Antonii, ceterorum honores. Restituendi Capitolii consilium. Libertati consulit Helvidius Priscus, cujus V, vita et mores, VI—VIII, et cum Eprio Marcello acre jurgium de legatis ad Principem mittendis. IX. De impensis publicis dissensio. X. Musonius Rufus in P. Celerem invehitur. XI. Mucianus urbem ingressus, cuncta in se trahit, Calp. Galerianum caedi curat, Asiaticum libertum servili supplicio tollit.

XII. Germanicae cladis fama. Ejus belli causa in Batavis, XIII, Duce Claudio Civile. XIV—XVI. Is Batavos, Canninefates, Frisios, excitat, statim dolo, mox aperta vi, Romanos superat. XVII. Victoriae hujus fama motae Germaniae auxilia offerunt Civili, qui et Galliarum societatem affectat. XVIII. Hordeonii Flacci segnitia. Victi Romani in Vetera castra fugiunt. XIX. Batavorum et Canninefatium cohortes, jussu Vitellii in urbem pergentes, corruptae, Civili junguntur, et XX, Bonnensi proelio Romanorum aciem perfringunt. XXI. Civilis, consilii ambiguus, suos in verba Vespasiani adigit, hostilia velans; XXII, XXIII, mox Vetera obsidet, frustra. XXIV, XXV. Hordeonius Flaccus, seditione conflictatus, summam rerum Voculae permittit. XXVI, XXVII. Huic additus Herennius Gallus, re male gesta, verberatur. Nova seditio. XXVIII—XXX. Civilis, immensis auctibus ab universa Germania elatus, obsidium Veterum urget, Ubios vexat. Varia certamina.

XXXI. Nuntiato Cremonensi praelio, auxilia Gallorum a Vitellio desciscunt. Suos quoque Hordeonius in Vespasiani verba adigit haesitantes. XXXII. Ad Civilem missus Montanus, ut a bello absistere jubeat, ab ipso tentatur. XXXIII, XXXIV. Cum Vocula confligit

Civilis vario eventu, non sine utriusque ducis culpa. XXXV. Vocula male utitur victoria. Vetera obsidione liberat. XXXVI. Civilis Geldubam capit. Romani milites Hordeonium necant. Vocula per tenebras evadit. XXXVII. Mox a Civile superati Voculam denuo sequuntur, quocum obsidione Magontiacum liberant. Treveri, nunc fidi, mox rebelles.

XXXVIII. Vespasianus cum Tito consulatum init. Falsi pavores in urbe et a L. Pisone. XXXIX. Domitianus praetor. Vis penes Mucianum. Is Primi Antonii potentiam infringit. XL. Restituti Galbae honores. Bareae Sorini manibus, P. Celere damnato, satisfactum. XLI. Alii quoque delatores castigati. XLII. In his Aquilium Regulum, a Messalla fratre defensum, Montanus percellit. XLIII, XLIV. Idem in Marcellum tentat Helvidius, intercedente Caesare, abolendam priorum temporum memoriam rato. Itaque in paucos modo saevitum. XLV. Senenses ob pulsatum senatorem puniti. Antonius Flamma lege repetundarum damnatus. XLVI. Militaris seditio a Muciano repressa. XLVII. Abrogati consulatus, quos Vitellius dederat. Funus censorium Flavio Sabino ductum. XLVIII—L. L. Pisonis, Africae proconsulis, caedes. Servi ejus egregium mendacium. Oeensium Leptitanorumque discordiae compositae. Fusi Garamantes. LI. Parthorum auxilia non recipit Vespasianus. LII. Hunc iratum Domitiano Titus mitigat. LIII. Cura restituendi Capitolii in L. Vestinum collata.

LIV. Audita mors Vitellii duplicaverat bellum per Gallias Germaniasque. Cum incendio capitolii finis imperio adesse creditus. LV—LVIII. Interfecto Hordeonio, conspirant cum Civile et Classico Julius Tutor et Julius Sabinus: nutant reliquae Galliae. Romanae quoque legiones tentantur, frustra renitente Vocula, quo LIX, LX, caeso, vinctisque Herennio et Numisio legatis, istas pro imperio Galliarum sacramento adigit Civilis, Tutor Agrippinenis Classicus obsessos ad Vetera. LXI. Civilis, voti compos, crinem deposuit. Tum et major auctoritas Veledae. LXII. Captarum legionum maestum silensque agmen. Ala Picentina necem Voculae vindicat LXIII—LXV. Colonia Agrippinensis, Transrhenanis gentibus invisa, in summum discrimen adducta, cum Civile societatem init, Veledae Numen donis placat. LXVI. Civilis Betasios, Tungros, Nervios in fidem accipit. LXVII. Fusi Lingones a Sequanis; J. Sabinus victus latet. LXVIII. Mucianus cum Domitiano ad bellum accingitur. LXIX. Remi Gallias in fide Romana conservant, exceptis Treveris atque Lingonibus. LXX. Sed nec iis nec reliquis civitatibus, nec ipsis ducibus, satis consilii ac concordiae. Tutor ad Bingium victus. LXXI. Petilius Cerialis Magontiacum venit, spes Romanorum erigit, Valentinum ducem magna strage affectum capit. LXXII. Treveros intrat. Militibus, exitium urbis poscentibus, resistit. Victas legiones in castra recepit. LXXIII, LXXIV Treveros et Lingonas officii admonet. LXXV. Civilis et Classicus ad Cerialem literas mittunt, ad quas ille nihil. LXXVI. Civilis cunctandum, Tutor et Classicus statim pugnandum, statuunt. LXXVII, LXXVIII. Atrox praelium, quo Cerialis, initio victus, mox victor castra hostium exscindit. LXXIX. Agrippinenses a Germanis desciscunt. LXXX. Mucianus Vitellii filium interficit. Antonius Primus, ad Vespasianum profectus non pro spe excipitur. LXXXI. Multus miraculis coelestis in Vespasianum favor ostensus. Ipse oculorum tabe notum, alium manu aegrum, sanitati restituit. LXXXII. Confirmatur omine in templo Serapidis, cujus LXXXIII, LXXXIV, origo Sinopensis, templum Alexandriae magnificum, nomen. LXXXV. Valentinus supplicio affectus. LXXXVI. Domitianus, frustra tentato Ceriale, an sibi exercitum imperiumque traditurus foret, literarum studium et amorem carminum simulat.

Gesta haec partim eodem anno, partim IMP. VESPASIANO ITERUM, TITO FIL. COSS.

INTERFECTO Vitellio, bellum magis desierat quam pax coeperat. Armati per urbem victores implacabili odio victos consectabantur: plenae caedibus viae, cruenta fora templaque, passim trucidatis, ut quemque fors obtulerat. Ac mox augescente licentia, scrutari ac protrahere abditos; si quem procerum habitu et juventa conspexerant, obtruncare, nullo militum aut populi discrimine. Quae saevitia, recentibus odiis, sanguine explebatur, dein verterat in avaritiam; nihil usquam secretum aut clausum sinebant, Vitellianos occultari simulantes. Initium id perfringendarum domuum, vel, si resisteretur, causa caedis; nec deerat egentissimus quisque e plebe et pessimi servitiorum prodere ultro dites dominos: alii ab amicis monstrabantur. Ubique lamenta, conclamationes, et fortunae captae urbis, adeo ut Othoniani Vitellianique militis invidiosa antea petulantia desideraretur. Duces partium accendendo civili bello acres, temperandae victoriae impares: quippe in turbas et discordias pessimo cuique plurima vis; pax et quies bonis artibus indigent.

II. Nomen sedemque Caesaris Domitianus acceperat, nondum ad curas intentus, sed stupris et adulteriis filium principis agebat. Praefectura praetorii penes Arrium Varum, summa potentiae in Primo Antonio: is pecuniam familiamque e Principis domo, quasi Cremonensem praedam, rapere: ceteri modestia vel ignobilitate, ut in bello obscuri, ita praemiorum expertes. Civitas pavida et servitio parata occupari redeuntem Tarracina L. Vitellium cum cohortibus, exstinguique reliqua belli postulabat. Praemissi Ariciam equites; agmen legionum intra Bovillas stetit. Nec cunctatus est Vitellius seque et cohortes arbitrio victoris permittere, et miles infelicia arma haud minus ira quam metu abjecit. Longus deditorum ordo septus armatis per urbem incessit. Nemo supplici vultu, sed tristes et truces et adversum plausus ac lasciviam insultantis vulgi immobiles: paucos erumpere ausos circumjecti pressere; ceteri in custodiam conditi. Nihil quisquam locutus indignum, et quanquam inter adversa, salva virtutis fama. Dein L. Vitellius interficitur, par vitiis fratris, in principatu ejus vigilantior, nec perinde prosperis socius quam adversis abstractus.

III. Iisdem diebus Lucilius Bassus cum expedito equite ad componendam Campaniam mittitur, discordibus municipiorum animis magis inter semet quam contumacia adversus Principem. Viso milite quies; et minoribus coloniis impunitas. Capuae legio tertia hiemandi causa locatur, et domus illustres afflictae, cum contra Tarracinenses nulla ope juvarentur. Tanto proclivius est injuriae quam beneficio vicem exsolvere, quia gratia oneri, ultio in quaestu habetur. Solatio fuit servus Verginii Capitonis, quem proditorem Tarracinensium diximus, patibulo affixus in iisdem annulis quos acceptos a Vitellio gestabat. At Romae senatus cuncta principibus solita Vespasiano decernit, laetus et spei certus: quippe sumpta per Gallias Hispaniasque civilia arma, motis ad bellum Germanis, mox Illyrico, postquam Aegyptum, Judaeam Syriamque, et omnes provincias exercitusque lustraverant, velut expiato terrarum orbe, cepisse finem videbantur. Addidere alacritatem Vespasiani literae, tanquam manente bello scriptae: ea, prima specie, forma: ceterum ut Princeps loquebatur civilia de se et reipublicae egregia; nec senatus obsequium deerat. Ipsi consulatus cum Tito filio, praetura Domitiano et consulare imperium decernuntur.

IV. Miserat et Mucianus epistolas ad senatum, quae materiam sermonibus praebuere: si privatus esset, cur publice loqueretur? potuisse eadem, paucos post dies, loco sententiae dici: ipsa quoque insectatio in Vitellium sera et sine libertate. Id vero erga rempublicam superbum, erga Principem contumeliosum, quod in manu sua fuisse imperium donatumque Vespasiano jactabat. Ceterum invidia in occulto; adulatio in aperto erant: multo cum honore verborum Muciano triumphalia de bello civium data: sed in Sarmatas expeditio fingebatur. Adduntur Primo Antonio consularia, Cornelio Fusco et Arrio Varo praetoria insignia. Mox deos respexere: restitui Capitolium placuit. Eaque omnia Valerius Asiaticus consul designatus censuit: ceteri vultu manuque, pauci, quibus conspicua dignitas aut ingenium adulatione exercitum, compositis orationibus assentiebantur. Ubi ad Helvidium Priscum praetorem designatum ventum, prompsit sententiam, ut honorificam in bonum Principem, falsa aberant, et studiis senatus attollebatur. Isque praecipuus illi dies magnae offensae initium et magnae gloriae fuit.

V. Res poscere videtur, quia iterum in mentionem incidimus viri saepius memorandi, ut vitam studiaque ejus, et quali fortuna sit usus, paucis repetam. Helvidius Priscus Tarracinae municipio, Cluvio patre qui ordinem primipili duxisset, ingenium illustre altioribus studiis juvenis admodum dedit, non ut plerique, ut nomine magnifico segne otium velaret, sed quo firmior adversus fortuita rempublicam capesseret: doctores sapientiae secutus est, qui sola bona, quae honesta, mala tantum, quae turpia; potentiam, nobilitatem ceteraque extra animum neque bonis neque malis annumerant. Quaestorius adhuc a Paeto Thrasea gener delectus, e moribus soceri nihil aeque ac libertatem hausit: civis, senator, maritus, gener, amicus, cunctis vitae officiis aequabilis, opum contemptor, recti pervicax, constans adversus metus.

VI. Erant, quibus appetentior famae videretur, quando etiam sapientibus cupido gloriae novissima exuitur. Ruina soceri in exsilium pulsus, ut Galbae principatu rediit, Marcellum Eprium delatorem Thraseae accusare aggreditur. Ea ultio, incertum major an justior, senatum in studia diduxerat. Nam si caderet Marcellus, agmen reorum sternebatur. Primo minax certamen, et egregiis utriusque orationibus testatum. Mox dubia voluntate Galbae, multis senatorum deprecantibus, omisit Priscus, variis, ut sunt hominum ingenia, sermonibus moderationem laudantium aut constantiam requirentium. Ceterum eo senatus die, quo de imperio Vespasiani censebant, placuerat mitti ad Principem legatos. Hinc inter Helvidium et Eprium acre jurgium. Priscus eligi nominatim a magistratibus juratis, Marcellus urnam postulabat, quae consulis designati sententia fuerat.

VII. Sed Marcelli studium proprius rubor excitabat, ne, aliis electis, posthabitus crederetur. Paulatimque per altercationem ad continuas et infestas orationes provecti sunt, quaerente Helvidio, "quid ita Marcellus judicium magistratuum pavesceret? esse illi pecuniam et eloquentiam, quis multos anteiret, ni memoria flagitiorum urgeretur. Sorte et urna mores non discerni: suffragia et existimationem senatus reperta, ut in cujusque vitam famamque penetrarent: pertinere ad utilitatem reipublicae, pertinere ad Vespasiani honorem, occurrere illi, quos innocentissimos senatus habeat, qui honestis sermonibus aures Imperatoris imbuant. Fuisse Vespasiano amicitiam cum Thrasea, Sorano, Sentio; quorum accusatores, etiamsi puniri non oporteat, ostentari non debere: hoc senatus judicio velut admoneri Principem, quos probet, quos reformidet: nullum majus boni imperii instrumentum quam bonos amicos esse: satis Marcello, quod Neronem in exitium tot innocentium impulerit. Frueretur praemiis et impunitate; Vespasianum melioribus relinqueret."

VIII. Marcellus, "non suam sententiam impugnari, sed consulem designatum censuisse" dicebat, "secundum vetera exempla, quae sortem legationibus posuissent, ne ambitioni aut inimicitiis locus foret. Nihil evenisse, cur antiquitus instituta exolescerent, aut Principis honor in cujusquam contumeliam verteretur: sufficere omnes obsequio: id magis vitandum, ne pervicacia quorundam irritaretur animus novo principatu suspensus et vultus quoque ac sermones omnium circumspectans. Se meminisse temporum quibus natus sit, quam civitatis formam patres avique instituerint; ulteriora mirari, praesentia sequi; bonos imperatores voto expetere, qualescumque tolerare. Non magis sua oratione Thraseam quam judicio senatus afflictum. Saevitiam Neronis per ejusmodi imagines illusisse, nec minus sibi anxiam talem amicitiam quam aliis exsilium. Denique constantia, fortitudine Catonibus et Brutis aequaretur Helvidius; se unum esse ex illo senatu, qui simul servierit. Suadere etiam Prisco, ne supra Principem scanderet, ne Vespasianum senem triumphalem, juvenum liberorum patrem praeceptis coerceret. Quomodo pessimis imperatoribus sine fine dominationem, ita quamvis egregiis modum libertatis placere." Haec magnis utrimque contentionibus jactata, diversis studiis accipiebantur. Vicit pars, quae sortiri legatos malebat, etiam mediis patrum annitentibus retinere morem. Et splendidissimus quisque eodem inclinabat metu invidiae, si ipsi eligerentur.

IX. Secutum aliud certamen. Praetores aerarii (nam tum a praetoribus tractabatur aerarium) publicam paupertatem questi, modum impensis postulaverant. Eam curam consul designatus, ob magnitudinem oneris et remedii difficultatem, Principi reservabat. Helvidius arbitrio senatus agendum censuit. Cum perrogarent sententias consules, Vulcatius Tertullinus tribunus plebis intercessit, ne quid super tanta re, Principe absente, statueretur. Censuerat Helvidius, ut Capitolium publice restitueretur, adjuvaret Vespasianus. Eam sententiam modestissimus quisque silentio, deinde oblivio transmisit. Fuere qui et meminissent.

X. Tum invectus est Musonius Rufus in Publium Celerem, a quo Baream Soranum falso testimonio circumventum arguebat. Ea cognitione renovari odia accusationum videbantur: sed vilis et nocens reus protegi non poterat. Quippe Sorani sancta memoria; Celer professus sapientiam, dein testis in Baream, proditor corruptorque amicitiae cujus se magistrum ferebat. Proximus dies causae destinatur. Nec tam Musonius aut Publius quam Priscus et Marcellus cetérique, motis ad ultionem animis, exspectabantur.

XI. Tali rerum statu, cum discordia inter patres, ira apud victos, nulla in victoribus auctoritas, non leges, non princeps in civitate essent, Mucianus urbem ingressus cuncta simul in se traxit: fracta Primi Antonii Varique Arrii potentia, male dissimulata in eos Muciani iracundia, quamvis vultu tegeretur. Sed civitas rimandis offensis sagax verterat se transtuleratque. Ille unus ambiri, coli: nec deerat ipse, stipatus armatis, domos hortosque permutans, apparatu, incessu, excubiis, vim principis amplecti, nomen remittere. Plurimum terroris intulit caedes Calpurnii Galeriani. Is fuit filius C. Pisonis, nihil ausus: sed nomen insigne et decora ipsi juventa rumore vulgi celebrabantur, erantque in civitate adhuc turbida et novis sermonibus laeta, qui principatus inanem ei famam circumdarent. Jussu Muciani custodia militari cinctus, ne in ipsa urbe conspectior mors foret, ad quadragesimum ab urbe lapidem Appia via fuso per venas sanguine exstinguitur. Julius Priscus, praetoriarum sub Vitellio cohortium praefectus, se ipse interfecit pudore magis quam necessitate. Alfenus Varus ignaviae infamiaeque suae superfuit. Asiaticus enim (is libertus) malam potentiam servili supplicio expiavit.

XII. Iisdem diebus crebrescentem cladis Germanicae famam, nequaquam maesta civitas excipiebat: caesos exercitus, capta legionum hiberna, descivisse Gallias, non ut mala loquebantur. Id bellum quibus causis ortum, quanto externarum sociarumque gentium motu flagraverit, altius expediam. Batavi, donec trans Rhenum agebant, pars Cattorum: seditione domestica pulsi, extrema Gallicae orae vacua cultoribus, simulque insulam inter vada sitam occupavere, quam mare Oceanum a fronte, Rhenus amnis tergum ac latera circumluit; nec opibus Romanis, societate validiorum, attriti, viros tantum armaque imperio ministrant; diu Germanicis bellis exerciti; mox aucta per Britanniam gloria, transmissis illuc cohortibus, quas vetere instituto nobilissimi popularium regebant. Erat et domi delectus eques, praecipuo nandi studio arma equosque retinens integris turmis Rhenum perrumpere.

XIII. Julius Paulus et Claudius Civilis, regia stirpe, multo ceteros anteibant. Paulum Fonteius Capito falso rebellionis crimine interfecit. Injectae Civili catenae, missusque ad Neronem et a Galba absolutus sub Vitellio rursus discrimen adit, flagitante supplicium ejus exercitu. Inde causae irarum spesque ex malis nostris. Sed Civilis ultra quam barbaris solitum ingenio sollers, et Sertorium se aut Hannibalem ferens simili oris dehonestamento, ne ut hosti obviam iretur si a populo Romano palam descivisset, Vespasiani amicitiam studiumque partium praetendit, missis sane ad eum Primi Antonii literis, quibus avertere accita Vitellio auxilia et tumultus Germanici specie retentare legiones jubebatur. Eadem Hordeonius Flaccus praesens monuerat, inclinato in Vespasianum animo et reipublicae cura, cui excidium adventabat, si redintegratum bellum et tot armatorum millia Italiam irrupissent.

XIV. Igitur Civilis desciscendi certus, occultato interim altiore consilio, cetera ex eventu judicaturus, novare res hoc modo coepit. Jussu Vitellii, Batavorum juventus ad delectum vocabatur; quem, suapte natura gravem, onerabant ministri avaritia ac luxu, senes aut invalidos conquirendo, quos pretio dimitterent; rursus impubes sed forma conspicui (et est plerisque procera pueritia) ad stuprum trahebantur. Hinc invidia; et compositae seditionis auctores perpulere, ut delectum abnuerent. Civilis primores gentis et promptissimos vulgi, specie epularum sacrum in nemus vocatos, ubi nocte ac laetitia incaluisse videt, a laude gloriaque gentis orsus, injurias et raptus et cetera servitii mala enumerat. "Neque enim societatem, ut olim, sed tanquam mancipia haberi: quando legatum, gravi quidem comitatu et superbo cum imperio, venire? tradi se praefectis centurionibusque; quos ubi spoliis et sanguine expleverint, mutari, exquirique novos sinus et varia praedandi vocabula. Instare delectum, quo liberi a parentibus, fratres a fratribus velut supremum dividantur. Nunquam magis afflictam rem Romanam, nec aliud in hibernis quam praedam et senes:

attollerent tantum oculos et inania legionum nomina ne pavescerent. At sibi robur peditum equitumque, consanguineos Germanos, Gallias idem cupientes: ne Romanis quidem ingratum id bellum, cujus ambiguam fortunam Vespasiano imputaturos: victoriae rationem non reddi."

XV. Magno cum assensu auditus, barbaro ritu et patriis exsecrationibus universos adigit. Missi ad Canninefates, qui consilia sociarent. Ea gens partem insulae colit, origine, lingua, virtute par Batavis; numero superantur. Mox occultis nuntiis pellexit Britannica auxilia, Batavorum cohortes missas in Germaniam, ut supra retulimus, ac tum Magontiaci agentes. Erat in Canninefatibus stolidae audaciae Brinno, claritate natalium insigni: pater ejus, multa hostilia ausus, Caianarum expeditionum ludibrium impune spreverat. Igitur ipso rebellis familiae nomine placuit, impositusque scuto more gentis, et sustinentium humeris vibratus, dux deligitur. Statimque accitis Frisiis (transrhenana gens est) duarum cohortium hiberna proxima occupatu, Oceano irrumpit. Nec praeviderant impetum hostium milites; nec si praevidissent, satis virium ad arcendum erat. Capta igitur ac direpta castra: dein vagos et pacis modo effusos lixas negotiatoresque Romanos invadunt. Simul excidiis castellorum imminebat; quae a praefectis cohortium incensa sunt, quia defendi nequibant. Signa vexillaque et quod militum in superiorem insulae partem congregantur, duce Aquilio primipilari, nomen magis exercitus quam robur. Quippe, viribus cohortium abductis, Vitellius e proximis Nerviorum Germanorumque pagis segnem numerum armis oneraverat.

XVI. Civilis dolo grassandum ratus, incusavit ultro praefectos, quod castella deseruissent. "Sese cum cohorte, cui praeerat, Canninefatem tumultum compressurum; illi sua quisque hiberna repeterent." Subesse fraudem consilio, et dispersas cohortes facilius opprimi, nec Brinnonem ducem ejus belli sed Civilem esse patuit, erumpentibus paulatim indiciis, quae Germani, laeta bello gens, non diu occultaverant. Ubi insidiae parum cessere, ad vim transgressus Canninefates, Frisios, Batavos propriis cuneis componit: directa ex diverso acies haud procul a flumine Rheno, et obversis in hostem navibus, quas, incensis castellis, illuc appulerant: nec diu certato, Tungrorum cohors signa ad Civilem transtulit; perculsique milites improvisa proditione a sociis hostibusque caedebantur. Eadem etiam navibus perfidia. Pars remigum e Batavis, tanquam imperitia, officia nautarum propugnatorumque impediebant: mox contra tendere, et puppes hostili ripae objicere: ad postremum gubernatores centurionesque, nisi eadem volentis, trucidant, donec universa quatuor et viginti navium classis transfugeret aut caperetur.

XVII. Clara ea victoria in praesens, in posterum usui; armaque et naves, quibus indigebant, adepti, magna per Germanias Galliasque fama libertatis auctores celebrabantur. Germaniae statim misere legatos auxilia offerentes. Galliarum societatem Civilis arte donisque affectabat, captos cohortium praefectos suas in civitates remittendo, cohortibus, abire an manere mallent, data potestate: manentibus honorata militia, digredientibus spolia Romanorum offerebantur. Simul secretis sermonibus admonebat malorum, quae tot annis perpessi, miseram servitutem falso pacem vocarent. "Batavos, quanquam tributorum expertes, arma contra communes dominos cepisse: prima acie fusum victumque Romanum: quid, si Galliae jugum exuant? quantum in Italia reliquum? provinciarum sanguine provincias vinci: ne Vindicis aciem cogitarent: Batavo equite protritos Aeduos Arvernosque; fuisse inter Verginii auxilia Belgas, vereque reputantibus, Galliam suismet viribus concidisse. Nunc easdem omnium partes, addito, si quid militaris disciplinae in castris Romanorum viguerit: esse secum veteranas cohortes, quibus nuper Othonis legiones procubuerint. Servirent Syria Asiaque et suetus regibus Oriens: multos adhuc in Gallia vivere ante tributa genitos. Nuper certe, caeso Quintilio Varo, pulsam e Germania servitutem, nec Vitellium Principem, sed Caesarem Augustum bello provocatum. Libertatem natura etiam mutis animalibus datam; virtutem proprium hominum bonum. Deos fortioribus adesse. Proinde arriperent vacui occupatos, integri fessos: dum alii Vespasianum, alii Vitellium foveant, patere locum adversus utrumque."

XVIII. Sic in Gallias Germaniasque intentus, si destinata provenissent, validissimarum ditissimarumque nationum regno imminebat. At Flaccus Hordeonius primos Civilis conatus per dissimulationem aluit. Ubi expugnata castra, deletas cohortes, pulsum Batavorum insula Romanum nomen trepidi nuntii afferebant, Munium Lupercum legatum (is duarum legionum hibernis praeerat) egredi adversus hostem jubet. Lupercus legionarios e praesentibus, Ubios e proximis, Treverorum equites haud longe agentis raptim transmisit, addita Batavorum ala, quae jam pridem corrupta fidem simulabat, ut proditis in ipsa acie Romanis, majore pretio fugeret. Civilis captarum cohortium signis circumdatus, ut suo militi recens gloria ante oculos, et hostes memoria cladis terrerentur, matrem suam sororesque, simul omnium conjuges parvosque liberos consistere a tergo jubet, hortamenta victoriae vel pulsis pudorem. Ut virorum cantu, feminarum ululatu sonuit acies, nequaquam par a legionibus cohortibusque redditur clamor. Nudaverat sinistrum cornu Batavorum ala transfugiens statimque in nos versa: sed legionarius miles, quanquam rebus trepidis, arma ordinesque retinebat. Ubiorum Treverorumque auxilia, foeda fuga dispersa, totis campis palantur. Illuc incubuere Germani; et fuit interim effugium legionibus in castra, quibus Veterum nomen est. Praefectus alae Batavorum Claudius Labeo, oppidano certamine aemulus Civili, ne interfectus invidiam apud populares vel, si retineretur, semina discordiae praeberet, in Frisios avehitur.

XIX. Iisdem diebus Batavorum et Canninefatium cohortes, cum jussu Vitellii in urbem pergerent, missus a Civile nuntius assequitur. Intumuere statim superbia ferociaque, et pretium itineris donativum, duplex stipendium, augeri equitum numerum, promissa sane a Vitellio, postulabant, non ut assequerentur, sed causam seditioni. Et Flaccus multa concedendo nihil aliud effecerat, quam ut acrius exposcerent, quae sciebant negaturum. Spreto Flacco inferiorem Germaniam petivere, ut Civili jungerentur. Hordeonius, adhibitis tribunis centurionibusque, consultavit, num obsequium abnuentes vi coerceret. Mox insita ignavia et trepidis ministris, quos ambiguus auxiliorum animus et subito delectu suppletae legiones angebant, statuit continere intra castra militem. Dein poenitentia, et arguentibus ipsis, qui suaserant, tanquam secuturus, scripsit Herennio Gallo legionis primae legato, qui Bonnam obtinebat, ut arceret transitu Batavos: se cum exercitu tergis eorum haesurum. Et opprimi poterant, si hinc Hordeonius, inde Gallus, motis utrimque copiis, medios clausissent. Flaccus omisit inceptum, aliisque literis Gallum monuit, ne terreret abeuntes. Unde suspicio sponte legatorum excitari bellum, cunctaque quae acciderant aut metuebantur, non inertia militis neque hostium vi sed fraude ducum evenire.

XX. Batavi, cum castris Bonnensibus propinquarent, praemisere qui Herennio Gallo mandata cohortium exponeret: "nullum sibi bellum adversus Romanos, pro quibus totiens bellassent. Longa atque irrita militia fessis patriae atque otii cupidinem esse. Si nemo obsisteret, innoxium iter fore; sin arma occurrant, ferro viam inventuros." Cunctantem legatum milites perpulerant, fortunam proelii experiretur. Tria millia legionariorum et tumultuariae Belgarum cohortes, simul paganorum lixarumque ignava sed procax ante periculum manus, omnibus portis rumpunt, ut Batavos numero impares circumfundant. Illi veteres militiae in cuneos congregantur, densi undique et frontem tergaque ac latus tuti. Sic tenuem nostrorum aciem perfringunt. Cedentibus Belgis, pellitur legio, et vallum portasque trepidi petebant. Ibi plurimum cladis: cumulatae corporibus fossae, nec caede tantum et vulneribus, sed ruina et suis plerique telis interire. Victores, colonia Agrippinensium vitata, nihil cetero in itinere hostile ausi, Bonnense proelium excusabant, tanquam petita pace, postquam negabatur, sibimetipsi consuluissent.

XXI. Civilis adventu veteranarum cohortium, justi jam exercitus ductor sed consilii ambiguus et vim Romanam reputans, cunctos qui aderant in verba Vespasiani adigit, mittitque legatos ad duas legiones, quae priore acie pulsae in Vetera castra concesserant, ut idem sacramentum acciperent. Redditur responsum, "neque proditoris neque hostium se consiliis uti. Esse sibi Vitellium Principem, pro quo fidem et arma usque ad supremum spiritum retenturos: proinde perfuga Batavus arbitrium rerum Romanarum ne ageret, sed meritas sceleris poenas exspectaret." Quae ubi relata Civili, incensus ira universam Batavorum gentem in arma rapit. Junguntur Bructeri Tencterique, et excita nuntiis Germania ad praedam famamque.

XXII. Adversus has concurrentis belli minas, legati legionum Munius Lupercus et Numisius Rufus vallum murosque firmabant. Subversa longae pacis opera, haud procul castris in modum municipii exstructa, ne hostibus usui forent. Sed parum provisum, ut copiae in castra conveherentur: rapi permisere; ita paucis diebus per licentiam absumpta sunt, quae adversus necessitates in longum suffecissent. Civilis medium agmen cum robore Batavorum obtinens, utramque Rheni ripam, quo truculentior visu foret, Germanorum catervis complet, assultante per campos equite. Simul naves in adversum amnem agebantur. Hinc veteranarum cohortium signa, inde depromptae silvis lucisque ferarum imagines, ut cuique genti inire proelium mos est, mixta belli civilis externique facie obstupefecerant obsessos: et spem oppugnantium augebat amplitudo valli, quod duabus legionibus situm vix quinque millia armatorum Romanorum tuebantur; sed lixarum multitudo turbata pace illuc congregata et bello ministra aderat.

XXIII. Pars castrorum in collem leniter exsurgens, pars aequo adibatur: quippe illis hibernis obsideri premique Germanias Augustus crediderat, neque unquam id malorum, ut oppugnatum ultro legiones nostras venirent. Inde non loco neque munimentis labor additus: vis et arma satis placebant. Batavi Transrhenanique, quo discreta virtus manifestius spectaretur, sibi quaeque gens consistunt, eminus lacessentes. Post, ubi pleraque telorum turribus pinnisque moenium irrita haerebant et desuper saxis vulnerabantur, clamore atque impetu invasere vallum; appositis plerique scalis, alii per testudinem suorum: scandebantque jam quidam, cum gladiis et armorum incussu praecipitati, sudibus et pilis obruuntur, praeferoces initio et rebus secundis nimii. Sed tum praedae cupidine adversa quoque tolerabant. Machinas etiam, insolitum sibi, ausi; nec ulla ipsis sollertia: perfugae captivique docebant struere materias in modum pontis, mox subjectis rotis propellere, ut alii superstantes tanquam ex aggere proeliarentur, pars intus occulti muros subruerent. Sed excussa ballistis saxa stravere informe opus: et crates vineasque parantibus adactae tormentis ardentes hastae, ultroque ipsi oppugnatores ignibus petebantur, donec desperata vi verterent consilium ad moras, haud ignari paucorum dierum inesse alimenta et multum imbellis turbae. Simul ex inopia proditio et fluxa servitiorum fides ac fortuita belli sperabantur.

XXIV. Flaccus interim, cognito castrorum obsidio, et missis per Gallias qui auxilia concirent, lectos e legionibus Dillio Voculae duodevicesimae legionis legato tradit, ut quam maximis per ripam itineribus celeraret, ipse navibus, invalidus corpore, invisus militibus: neque enim ambigue fremebant, emissas a Magontiaco Batavorum cohortes, dissimulatos Civilis conatus, asciri in societatem Germanos: non Primi Antonii neque Muciani ope Vespasianum magis adolevisse: aperta odia armaque palam depelli: fraudem et dolum obscura, eoque inevitabilia. Civilem stare contra, struere aciem: Hordeonium e cubiculo et lectulo jubere, quicquid hosti conducat. Tot armatas fortissimorum virorum manus unius senis valetudine regi. Quin potius, interfecto traditore, fortunam virtutemque suam malo omine exsolverent. His inter se vocibus instinctos flammavere insuper allatae a Vespasiano literae, quas Flaccus, quia occultari nequibant, pro concione recitavit, vinctosque, qui attulerant, ad Vitellium misit.

XXV. Sic mitigatis animis Bonnam, hiberna primae legionis, ventum. Infensior illic miles culpam cladis in Hordeonium vertebat: "ejus jussu directam adversus Batavos aciem, tanquam a Magontiaco legiones sequerentur; ejusdem proditione caesos, nullis supervenientibus auxiliis. Ignota haec ceteris exercitibus, neque imperatori suo nuntiari, cum accursu tot provinciarum exstingui repens perfidia potuerit." Hordeonius exemplares omnium literarum, quibus per Gallias Britanniamque et Hispanias auxilia orabat, exercitui recitavit instituitque pessimum facinus, ut epistolae aquiliferis legionum traderentur, a quis ante militi quam ducibus legebantur. Tum e seditiosis unum vinciri jubet, magis usurpandi juris quam quia unius culpa foret. Motusque Bonna exercitus in coloniam Agrippinensem, affluentibus auxiliis Gallorum, qui primo rem Romanam enixe juvabant: mox, valescentibus Germanis, pleraeque civitates adversum nos armatae spe libertatis, et, si exuissent servitium, cupidine imperitandi. Gliscebat iracundia legionum, nec terrorem unius militis vincula indiderant: quin idem ille arguebat ultro conscientiam ducis, tanquam nuntius inter Civilem Flaccumque falso crimine testis veri opprimeretur. Conscendit tribunal Vocula mira constantia, prehensumque militem ac vociferantem duci ad supplicium jussit: et dum mali pavent, optimus quisque jussis paruere. Exin consensu ducem Voculam poscentibus, Flaccus summam rerum ei permisit.

XXVI. Sed discordes animos multa efferabant, inopia stipendii frumentique, et simul delectum tributaque Galliae aspernantes, Rhenus incognita illi coelo siccitate vix navium patiens, arcti commeatus, dispositae per omnem ripam stationes quae Germanos vado arcerent, eademque de causa minus frugum, et plures qui consumerent. Apud imperitos prodigii loco accipiebatur ipsa aquarum penuria, tanquam nos amnes quoque et vetera imperii munimenta desererent: quod in pace fors seu natura, tunc fatum et ira dei vocabatur. Ingressis Novesium sextadecima legio conjungitur. Additus Voculae in partem curarum Herennius Gallus legatus; nec ausi ad hostem pergere, loco cui Gelduba nomen est castra fecere. Ibi struenda acie, muniendo vallandoque et ceteris belli meditamentis militem firmabant; utque praeda ad virtutem accenderetur, in proximos Gugernorum pagos, qui societatem Civilis acceperant, ductus a Vocula exercitus. Pars cum Herennio Gallo permansit.

XXVII. Forte navem haud procul castris, frumento gravem, cum per vada haesisset, Germani in suam ripam trahebant. Non tulit Gallus, misitque subsidio cohortem. Auctus et Germanorum numerus, paulatimque aggregantibus se auxiliis acie certatum. Germani multa cum strage nostrorum navem abripiunt. Victi (quod tum in morem verterat) non suam ignaviam, sed perfidiam legati culpabant. Protractum e tentorio, scissa veste, verberato corpore, quo pretio, quibus consciis prodidisset exercitum, dicere jubent. Redit in Hordeonium invidia. Illum auctorem sceleris, hunc ministrum vocant, donec exitium miritantibus exterritus proditionem et ipse Hordeonio objecit; vinctusque, adventu demum Voculae exsolvitur. Is postera die auctores seditionis morte affecit. Tanta illi exercitui diversitas inerat licentiae patientiaeque. Haud dubie gregarius miles Vitellio fidus; splendidissimus quisque in Vespasianum proni: inde scelerum ac suppliciorum vices, et mixtus obsequio furor, ut contineri non possent, qui puniri poterant.

XXVIII. At Civilem immensis auctibus universa Germania extollebat, societate nobilissimis obsidum firmata. Ille, ut cuique proximum, vastari Ubios Treverosque, et alia manu Mosam amnem transire jubet ut Menapios et Morinos et extrema Galliarum quateret. Actae utrobique praedae, infestius in Ubiis, quod gens Germanicae originis, ejurata patria, Romanorum nomen Agrippinenses vocarentur. Caesae cohortes eorum, in vico Marcoduro incuriosius agentes, quia procul ripa aberant. Nec quievere Ubii, quo minus praedas e Germania peterent, primo impune, dein circumventi sunt, per omne id bellum meliore usi fide quam fortuna. Contusis Ubiis gravior et successu rerum ferocior Civilis obsidium legionum urgebat, intentis custodiis, ne quis occultus nuntius venientis auxilii penetraret. Machinas molemque operum Batavis delegat: Transrhenanos proelium poscentes, ad scindendum vallum ire detrusosque redintegrare certamen jubet, superante multitudine et facili damno: nec finem labori nox attulit.

XXIX. Congestis circum lignis accensisque, simul epulantes, ut quisque vino incaluerat, ad pugnam temeritate inani ferebantur. Quippe ipsorum tela per tenebras vana: Romani conspicuam barbarorum aciem, et si quis audacia aut insignibus effulgens, ad ictum destinabant. Intellectum id Civili, et restincto igne misceri cuncta tenebris et armis jubet. Tum vero strepitus dissoni, casus incerti, neque feriendi neque declinandi providentia. Unde clamor acciderat, circumagere corpora, tendere arcus: nihil prodesse virtus, fors cuncta turbare et ignavorum saepe telis fortissimi cadere. Apud Germanos inconsulta ira: Romanus miles periculorum gnarus ferratas sudes, gravia saxa non forte jaciebat. Ubi sonus molientium aut appositae scalae hostem in manus dederant, propellere umbone, pilo sequi; multos, in moenia egressos, pugionibus fodere. Sic exhausta nocte, novam aciem dies aperuit.

XXX. Eduxerant Batavi turrim duplici tabulato, quam praetoriae portae (is aequissimus locus) propinquantem, promoti contra validi asseres et incussae trabes perfregere, multa superstantium pernicie: pugnatumque in perculsos subita et prospera eruptione. Simul a legionariis peritia et arte praestantibus, plura struebantur. Praecipuum pavorem intulit suspensum et nutans machinamentum, quo repente demisso, praeter suorum ora singuli pluresve hostium sublime rapti, verso pondere intra castra effundebantur. Civilis, omissa oppugnandi spe, rursus per otium assidebat, nuntiis et promissis fidem legionum convellens.

XXXI. Haec in Germania ante Cremonense proelium gesta, cujus eventum literae Primi Antonii docuere, addito Caecinae edicto. Et praefectus cohortis e victis Alpinus Montanus, fortunam partium praesens fatebatur. Diversi hinc motus animorum. Auxilia e Gallia, quis nec amor neque odium in partes, militia sine affectu, hortantibus praefectis statim a Vitellio desciscunt: vetus miles cunctabatur. Sed adigente Hordeonio Flacco, instantibus tribunis, dixit sacramentum, non vultu neque animo satis affirmans; et cum cetera jurisjurandi verba conciperent, Vespasiani nomen haesitantes aut levi murmure et plerumque silentio transmittebant.

XXXII. Lectae deinde pro concione epistolae Antonii ad

Civilem suspiciones militum irritavere, tanquam ad socium partium scriptae, et de Germanico exercitu hostiliter. Mox allatis Geldubam in castra nuntiis, eadem dicta factaque, et missus cum mandatis Montanus ad Civilem, ut absisteret bello neve externa armis falsis velaret; si Vespasianum juvare aggressus foret, satisfactum coeptis. Ad ea Civilis primo callide: post, ubi videt Montanum praeferocem ingenio paratumque in res novas, orsus a questu periculisque, quae per quinque et viginti annos in castris Romanis exhausisset, "Egregium," inquit, "pretium laborum recepi, necem fratris et vincula mea et saevissimas hujus exercitus voces, quibus ad supplicium petitus, jure gentium poenas reposco. Vos autem Treveri ceteraeque servientium animae, quod praemium effusi totiens sanguinis exspectatis, nisi ingratam militiam, immortalia tributa, virgas, secures et dominorum ingenia? En ego praefectus unius cohortis et Canninefates Batavique, exigua Galliarum portio, vana illa castrorum spatia excidimus, vel septa ferro fameque premimus: denique ausos aut libertas sequetur, aut victi iidem erimus." Sic accensum, sed molliora referre jussum dimittit. Ille ut irritus legationis redit, cetera dissimulans, quae mox erupere.

XXXIII. Civilis, parte copiarum retenta, veteranas cohortes et quod e Germanis maxime promptum, adversus Voculam exercitumque ejus mittit, Julio Maximo et Claudio Victore, sororis suae filio, ducibus. Rapiunt in transitu hiberna alae Asciburgii sita; adeoque improvisi castra involavere, ut non alloqui, non pandere aciem Vocula potuerit. Id solum, ut in tumultu, monuit, subsignano milite media firmare: auxilia passim circumfusa sunt. Eques prorupit, exceptusque compositis hostium ordinibus terga in suos vertit. Caedes inde, non proelium. Et Nerviorum cohortes, metu seu perfidia, latera nostrorum nudavere. Sic ad legiones perventum: quae, amissis signis, intra vallum sternebantur, cum repente novo auxilio fortuna pugnae mutatur. Vasconum lectae a Galba cohortes ac tum accitae, dum castris propinquant, audito proeliantium clamore, intentos hostes a tergo invadunt, latioremque quam pro numero terrorem faciunt, aliis a Novesio, aliis a Magontiaco universas copias advenisse credentibus. Is error Romanis addit animos, et, dum alienis viribus confidunt, suas recepere. Fortissimus quisque e Batavis, quantum peditum erat, funduntur: eques evasit cum signis captivisque, quos prima acie corripuerant. Caesorum eo die in partibus nostris major numerus et imbellior; e Germanis ipsa robora.

XXXIV. Dux uterque, pari culpa meritus adversa, prosperis defuere. Nam Civilis, si majoribus copiis instruxisset aciem, circumiri a tam paucis cohortibus nequisset, castraque perrupta exscidisset. Vocula nec adventum hostium exploravit, eoque simul egressus victusque; dein victoriae parum confisus, tritis frustra diebus castra in hostem movit, quem si statim impellere cursumque rerum sequi maturasset, solvere obsidium legionum eodem impetu potuit. Tentaverat interim Civilis obsessorum animos, tanquam perditae apud Romanos res et suis victoria provenisset. Circumferebantur signa vexillaque; ostentati etiam captivi, ex quibus unus, egregium facinus ausus, clara voce gesta patefecit, confossus illico a Germanis; unde major indici fides. Simul vastatione incendiisque flagrantium villarum, venire victorem exercitum intelligebatur. In conspectu castrorum constitui signa, fossamque et vallum circumdari Vocula jubet: depositis impedimentis sarcinisque expediti certarent. Hinc in ducem clamor pugnam poscentium; et minari assueverant. Ne tempore quidem ad ordinandam aciem capto, incompositi fessique proelium sumpsere: nam Civilis aderat, non minus vitiis hostium quam virtute suorum fretus. Varia apud Romanos fortuna, et seditiosissimus quisque ignavus: quidam recentis victoriae memores retinere locum, ferire hostem, seque et proximos hortari: et redintegrata acie, manus ad obsessos tendere, ne tempori deessent. Illi cuncta e muris cernentes, omnibus portis prorumpunt. Ac forte Civilis lapsu equi prostratus, credita per utrumque exercitum fama vulneratum aut interfectum, immane quantum suis pavoris et hostibus alacritatis indidit.

XXXV. Sed Vocula, omissis fugientium tergis, vallum

turresque castrorum augebat, tanquam rursus obsidium immineret, corrupta totiens victoria non falso suspectus bellum malle. Nihil aeque exercitus nostros quam egestas copiarum fatigabat. Impedimenta legionum cum imbelli turba Novesium missa, ut inde terrestri itinere frumentum adveherent: nam flumine hostes potiebantur. Primum agmen securum incessit, nondum satis firmo Civile; qui, ubi rursum missos Novesium frumentatores datasque in praesidium cohortes velut multa pace ingredi accepit, rarum apud signa militem, arma in vehiculis, cunctos licentia vagos, compositus invadit, praemissis, qui pontes et viarum angusta insiderent. Pugnatum longo agmine et incerto Marte, donec proelium nox dirimeret. Cohortes Geldubam perrexere, manentibus, ut fuerant, castris, quae relictorum illic militum praesidio tenebantur. Non erat dubium, quantum in regressu discriminis adeundum foret, frumentatoribus onustis perculsisque. Addit exercitui suo Vocula mille delectos e quinta et quintadecima legionibus apud Vetera obsessis, indomitum militem et ducibus infensum. Plures quam jussum erat profecti palam in agmine fremebant non se ultra famem, insidias legatorum toleraturos. At qui remanserant, desertos se abducta parte legionum querebantur. Duplex hinc seditio, aliis revocantibus Voculam, aliis redire in castra abnuentibus.

XXXVI. Interim Civilis Vetera circumsedit. Vocula Geldubam atque inde Novesium concessit. Civilis capit Geldubam. Mox haud procul Novesio equestri proelio prospere certavit. Sed miles secundis adversisque perinde in exitium ducum accendebatur. Et adventu quintanorum quintadecimanorumque auctae legiones donativum exposcunt, comperto pecuniam a Vitellio missam. Nec diu cunctatus Hordeonius nomine Vespasiani dedit. Idque praecipuum fuit seditionis alimentum. Effusi in luxum et epulas et nocturnos coetus, veterem in Hordeonium iram renovant, nec ullo legatorum tribunorumve obsistere auso (quippe omnem pudorem nox ademerat) protractum e cubili interficiunt. Eadem in Voculam parabantur, nisi servili habitu per tenebras ignoratus evasisset. Ubi, sedato impetu, metus rediit, centuriones cum epistolis ad civitates Galliarum misere, auxilia ac stipendia oraturos.

XXXVII. Ipsi, ut est vulgus sine rectore praeceps, pavidum, socors, adventante Civile, raptis temere armis ac statim omissis, in fugam vertuntur. Res adversae discordiam peperere, iis, qui e superiore exercitu erant, causam suam dissociantibus. Vitellii tamen imagines in castris et per proximas Belgarum civitates repositae, cum jam Vitellius occidisset. Dein mutati in poenitentiam primani quartanique et duodevicesimani Voculam sequuntur; apud quem, resumpto Vespasiani sacramento, ad liberandum Magontiaci obsidium ducebantur. Discesserant obsessores, mixtus ex Cattis, Usipiis, Mattiacis exercitus, satietate praedae nec incruenti. In via dispersos et nescios miles noster invaserat. Quin et loricam vallumque per fines suos Treveri struxere, magnisque invicem cladibus cum Germanis certabant, donec egregia erga populum Romanum merita mox rebelles foedarent.

XXXVIII. Interea Vespasianus iterum ac Titus consulatum absentes inierunt, maesta et multiplici metu suspensa civitate, quae super instantia mala falsos pavores induerat, descivisse Africam, res novas moliente L. Pisone. Is praeerat provinciae, nequaquam turbidus ingenio: sed quia naves saevitia hiemis prohibebantur, vulgus alimenta in dies mercari solitum, cui una ex republica annonae cura, clausum littus, retineri commeatus, dum timet, credebat, augentibus famam Vitellianis, qui studium partium nondum posuerant, nec victoribus quidem ingrato rumore, quorum cupiditates, externis quoque bellis inexplebiles, nulla unquam civilis victoria satiavit.

XXXIX. Kalendis Januariis in Senatu, quem Julius Frontinus praetor urbanus vocaverat, legatis exercitibusque ac regibus laudes gratesque decretae: et Tertio Juliano praetura, tanquam transgredientem in partes Vespasiani legionem deseruisset, ablata, ut in Plotium Griphum transferretur. Hormo dignitas equestris data. Et mox ejurante Frontino, Caesar Domitianus praeturam cepit. Ejus nomen epistolis edictisque praeponebatur, vis penes Mucianum erat, nisi quod pleraque Domitianus, instigantibus amicis aut propria libidine, audebat. Sed praecipuus Muciano metus e Primo Antonio Varoque Arrio, quos recentes clarosque rerum fama ac militum studiis etiam populus fovebat, quia in neminem ultra aciem saevierant. Et ferebatur Antonius Scribonianum Crassum, egregiis majoribusque et fraterna imagine fulgentem, ad capessendam rempublicam hortatus, haud defutura consciorum manu, ni Scribonianus abnuisset, ne paratis quidem corrumpi facilis, adeo metuens incerta. Igitur Mucianus, quia propalam opprimi Antonius nequibat, multis in senatu laudibus cumulatum secretis promissis onerat, citeriorem Hispaniam ostentans discessu Cluvii Rufi vacuam; simul amicis ejus tribunatus praefecturasque largitur. Dein postquam inanem animum spe et cupidine impleverat, vires abolet, dimissa in hiberna legione septima, cujus flagrantissimus in Antonium amor. Et tertia legio, familiaris Arrio Varo miles, in Syriam remissa. Pars exercitus in Germanias ducebatur. Sic egesto quicquid turbidum, redit urbi sua forma legesque et munia magistratuum.

XL. Quo die senatum ingressus est Domitianus, de absentia patris fratrisque ac juventa sua pauca et modica disseruit, decorus habitu; et ignotis adhuc moribus, crebra oris confusio pro modestia accipiebatur. Referente Caesare de restituendis Galbae honoribus, censuit Curtius Montanus, ut Pisonis quoque memoria celebraretur. Patres utrumque jussere: de Pisone irritum fuit. Tum sorte ducti, per quos redderentur bello rapta, quique aera legum vetustate delapsa noscerent figerentque, et fastos, adulatione temporum foedatos, exonerarent, modumque publicis impensis facerent. Redditur Tertio Juliano praetura, postquam cognitus est ad Vespasianum confugisse: Gripho honor mansit. Repeti inde cognitionem inter Musonium Rufum et P. Celerem placuit, damnatusque Publius et Sorani manibus satisfactum. Insignis publica severitate dies, ne privatim quidem laude caruit. Justum judicium explesse Musonius videbatur: diversa fama Demetrio, Cynicam sectam professo, quod manifestum reum ambitiosius quam honestius defendisset: ipsi Publio neque animus in periculis neque oratio suppeditavit. Signo ultionis in accusatores dato, petit a Caesare Junius Mauricus, ut commentariorum principalium potestatem senatui faceret, per quos nosceret, quem quisque accusandum poposcisset. Consulendum tali super re Principem respondit.

XLI. Senatus, inchoantibus primoribus, jusjurandum concepit, quo certatim omnes magistratus, ceteri ut sententiam rogabantur, deos testes advocabant nihil ope sua factum, quo cujusquam salus laederetur, neque se praemium aut honorem ex calamitate civium cepisse, trepidis et verba jurisjurandi per varias artes mutantibus, quis flagitii conscientia inerat. Probabant religionem patres, perjurium arguebant. Eaque velut censura in Sariolenum Voculam et Nonium Actianum et Cestium Severum acerrime incubuit, crebris apud Neronem delationibus famosos. Sariolenum et recens crimen urgebat, quod apud Vitellium molitus eadem foret: nec destitit senatus manus intentare Voculae, donec curia excederet. Ad Pactium Africanum transgressi eum quoque proturbant, tanquam Neroni Scribonios fratres concordia opibusque insignes ad exitium monstravisset. Africanus neque fateri audebat neque abnuere poterat: in Vibium Crispum, cujus interrogationibus fatigabatur, ultro conversus, miscendo quae defendere nequibat, societate culpae invidiam declinavit.

XLII. Magnam eo die pietatis eloquentiaeque famam Vipstanus Messala adeptus est, nondum senatoria aetate, ausus pro fratre Aquilio Regulo deprecari. Regulum subversa Crassorum et Orfiti domus in summum odium extulerat. Sponte ex senatus consulto accusationem subisse juvenis admodum, nec depellendi periculi, sed in spem potentiae videbatur. Et Sulpicia Praetextata Crassi uxor quatuorque liberi, si cognosceret senatus, ultores aderant. Igitur Messala non causam neque reum tueri, sed periculis fratris semet opponens, flexerat quosdam. Occurrit truci oratione Curtius Montanus, eo usque progressus, ut post caedem Galbae, datam interfectori Pisonis pecuniam a Regulo, appetitumque morsu Pisonis caput objectaret. "Hoc certe," inquit, "Nero non coegit, nec dignitatem aut salutem illa saevitia redemisti. Sane toleremus istorum defensiones, qui perdere alios quam periclitari ipsi maluerunt. Te securum reliquerat exsul pater et divisa inter creditores bona, nondum honorum capax aetas, nihil quod ex te concupisceret Nero, nihil quod timeret. Libidine sanguinis et hiatu praemiorum ignotum adhuc ingenium et nullis defensionibus expertum caede nobili imbuisti, cum ex funere reipublicae raptis consularibus spoliis, septuagies sestertio saginatus et sacerdotio fulgens, innoxios pueros, illustres senes, conspicuas feminas eadem ruina prosterneres; cum segnitiam Neronis incusares, quod per singulas domos seque et delatores fatigaret: posse universum senatum una voce subverti. Retinete, patres conscripti, et reservate hominem tam expediti consilii, ut omnis aetas instructa sit, et quomodo senes nostri Marcellum, Crispum, juvenes Regulum imitentur. Invenit etiam aemulos infelix nequitia: quid si floreat vigeatque? Et quem adhuc quaestorium offendere non audemus, praetorium et consularem visuri sumus? An Neronem extremum dominorum putatis? Idem crediderant, qui Tiberio, qui Caio superstites fuerunt, cum interim intestabilior et saevior exortus est. Non timemus Vespasianum: ea Principis aetas, ea moderatio. Sed diutius durant exempla quam mores. Elanguimus, patres conscripti, nec jam ille senatus sumus, qui occiso Nerone, delatores et ministros more majorum puniendos flagitabat. Optimus est post malum principem dies primus."

XLIII. Tanto cum assensu senatus auditus est Montanus, ut spem caperet Helvidius posse etiam Marcellum prosterni. Igitur a laude Cluvii Rufi orsus, qui perinde dives et eloquentia clarus nulli unquam sub Nerone periculum facessisset, crimine simul exemploque Eprium urgebat, ardentibus patrum animis. Quod ubi sensit Marcellus, velut excedens curia: "Imus," inquit, "Prisce, et relinquimus tibi senatum tuum: regna, praesente Caesare." Sequebatur Vibius Crispus, ambo infensi, vultu diverso, Marcellus minacibus oculis, Crispus renidens, donec accursu amicorum retraherentur. Cum glisceret certamen, hinc multi bonique, inde pauci et validi pertinacibus odiis tenderent, consumptus per discordiam dies.

XLIV. Proximo senatu, inchoante Caesare de abolendo dolore iraque et priorum temporum necessitatibus, censuit Mucianus prolixe pro accusatoribus: simul eos qui coeptam, deinde omissam actionem repeterent, monuit sermone molli et tanquam rogaret. Patres coeptatam libertatem, postquam obviam itum, omisere. Mucianus, ne sperni senatus judicium et cunctis sub Nerone admissis data impunitas videretur, Octavium Sagittam et Antistium Sosianum senatorii ordinis egressos exsilium in easdem insulas redegit. Octavius Pontiam Postumiam, stupro cognitam et nuptias suas abnuentem, impotens amoris interfecerat; Sosianus pravitate morum multis exitiosus. Ambo gravi senatus consulto damnati pulsique, quamvis concesso aliis reditu, in eadem poena retenti sunt. Nec ideo lenita erga Mucianum invidia. Quippe Sosianus ac Sagitta viles, etiam si reverterentur: accusatorum ingenia et opes et exercita malis artibus potentia timebantur.

XLV. Reconciliavit paulisper studia patrum habita in senatu cognitio secundum veterem morem. Manlius Patruitus senator pulsatum se in colonia Seniensi coetu multitudinis et jussu magistratuum querebatur; nec finem injuriae hic stetisse: planctum et lamenta et supremorum imaginem praesenti sibi circumdata cum contumeliis ac probris, quae in senatum universum jacerentur. Vocati, qui arguebantur, et cognita causa, in convictos vindicatum. Additumque senatus consultum, quo Seniensium plebes modestiae admoneretur. Iisdem diebus Antonius Flamma Cyrenensibus damnatur lege repetundarum, et exsilio ob saevitiam.

XLVI. Inter quae militaris seditio prope exarsit. Praetorianam militiam repetebant a Vitellio dimissi, pro Vespasiano congregati; et lectus in eandem spem e legionibus miles promissa stipendia flagitabat: ne Vitelliani quidem sine multa caede pelli poterant; sed immensa pecunia ferebatur, qua tanta vis hominum retinenda erat. Ingressus castra Mucianus, quo rectius stipendia singulorum spectaret, suis cum insignibus armisque victores constituit, modicis inter se spatiis discretos. Tum Vitelliani, quos apud Bovillas in deditionem acceptos memoravimus, ceterique per urbem et urbi vicina conquisiti producuntur prope intecto corpore. Eos Mucianus diduci, et Germanicum Britannicumque militem, ac si qui aliorum exercituum, separatim assistere jubet. Illos primus statim aspectus obstupefecerat, cum ex diverso velut aciem telis et armis trucem, semet clausos nudosque et illuvie deformes aspicerent. Ut vero huc illuc distrahi coepere, metus per omnes et praecipua Germanici militis formido, tanquam ea separatione ad caedem destinarentur: prensare commanipularium pectora, cervicibus innecti, suprema oscula petere, ne desererentur soli, neu pari causa disparem fortunam paterentur: modo Mucianum, modo absentem Principem, postremum coelum ac deos obtestari, donec Mucianus cunctos ejusdem sacramenti, ejusdem Imperatoris milites appellans, falso timori obviam iret. Namque et victor exercitus clamore lacrimas eorum juvabat. Isque finis illa die. Paucis post diebus, alloquentem Domitianum firmati jam excepere. Spernunt oblatos agros, militiam et stipendia orant. Preces erant, sed quibus contradici non posset: igitur in praetorium accepti. Dein quibus aetas et justa stipendia, dimissi cum honore, alii ob culpam, sed carptim ac singuli; quo tutissimo remedio consensus multitudinis extenuatur.

XLVII. Ceterum verane pauperie an uti videretur, actum in senatu, ut sexcenties sestertium a privatis mutuum acciperetur; praepositusque ei curae Pompeius Silvanus: nec multo post necessitas abiit, sive omissa simulatio. Abrogati inde, legem ferente Domitiano, consulatus, quos Vitellius dederat, funusque censorium Flavio Sabino ductum, magna documenta instabilis fortunae summaque et ima miscentis.

XLVIII. Sub idem tempus L. Piso proconsul interficitur. Ea de caede quam verissime expediam, si pauca supra repetiero, ab initio causisque talium facinorum non absurda. Legio in Africa auxiliaque tutandis imperii finibus, sub divo Augusto Tiberioque principibus, proconsuli parebant. Mox Caius Caesar turbidus animi, ac M. Silanum obtinentem Africam metuens, ablatam proconsuli legionem misso in eam rem legato tradidit. Aequatus inter duos beneficiorum numerus, et mixtis utriusque mandatis discordia quaesita auctaque pravo certamine. Legatorum vis adolevit diuturnitate officii vel quia minoribus major aemulandi cura; proconsulum splendidissimus quisque securitati magis quam potentiae consulebant.

XLIX. Sed tum legionem in Africa regebat Valerius Festus, sumptuosae adolescentiae neque modica cupiens, et affinitate Vitellii anxius. Is crebris sermonibus tentaveritne Pisonem ad res novas an tentanti restiterit, incertum, quoniam secreto eorum nemo affuit, et occiso Pisone plerique ad gratiam interfectoris inclinavere. Nec ambigitur provinciam et militem alienato erga Vespasianum animo fuisse: et quidam e Vitellianis urbe profugi ostentabant Pisoni nutantes Gallias, paratam Germaniam, pericula ipsius, et in pace suspecto tutius bellum. Inter quae Claudius Sagitta praefectus alae Petrinae prospera navigatione praevenit Papirium centurionem a Muciano missum, asseveravitque mandata interficiendi Pisonis centurioni data; cecidisse Galerianum, consobrinum ejus generumque: unam in audacia spem salutis, sed duo itinera audendi, seu mallet statim arma, seu petita navibus Gallia, ducem se Vitellianis exercitibus ostenderet. Nihil ad ea moto Pisone, centurio a Muciano missus, ut portum Carthaginis attigit, magna voce laeta Pisoni omnia, tanquam principi, continuare; obvios et subitae rei miraculo attonitos, ut eadem astreperent, hortari: vulgus credulum ruere in forum, praesentiam Pisonis exposcere. Gaudio clamoribusque cuncta miscebant, indiligentia veri et adulandi libidine. Piso, indicio Sagittae vel insita modestia, non in publicum egressus est neque se studiis vulgi permisit: centurionemque percunctatus, postquam quaesitum sibi crimen caedemque comperit, animadverti in eum jussit, haud perinde spe vitae quam ira in percussorem, quod idem ex interfectoribus Clodii Macri cruentas legati sanguine manus ad caedem proconsulis retulisset. Anxio deinde edicto Carthaginiensibus increpitis, ne solita quidem munia usurpabat, clausus intra domum, ne qua motus novi causa vel forte oreretur.

L. Sed ubi Festo consternatio vulgi, centurionis supplicium, veraque et falsa more famae in majus innotuere, equites in necem Pisonis mittit. Illi raptim vecti, obscuro adhuc coeptae lucis domum proconsulis irrumpunt, destrictis gladiis, et magna pars Pisonis ignari, quod Poenos auxiliares Maurosque in eam caedem delegerat: haud procul cubiculo obvium forte servum, quisnam, et ubi esset Piso, interrogavere. Servus egregio mendacio se Pisonem esse respondit; ac statim obtruncatur: nec multo post Piso interficitur. Namque aderat, qui nosceret, Bebius Massa e procuratoribus Africae, jam tunc optimo cuique exitiosus, et in causas malorum, quae mox tulimus, saepius rediturus. Festus Adrumeto, ubi speculabundus substiterat, ad legionem contendit, praefectumque castrorum Cetronium Pisanum vinciri jussit, proprias ob simultates: sed Pisonis satellitem vocabat, militesque et centuriones quosdam puniit, alios praemiis affecit, neutrum ex merito, sed ut oppressisse bellum crederetur. Mox Oeensium Leptitanorumque discordias componit, quae raptu frugum et pecorum inter agrestes, modicis principiis, jam per arma atque acies exercebantur. Nam populus Oeensis multitudine inferior Garamantas exciverat, gentem indomitam et inter accolas latrociniis fecundam. Unde arctae Leptitanis res, lateque vastatis agris intra moenia trepidabant, donec interventu cohortium alarumque fusi Garamantes et recepta omnis praeda, nisi quam vagi per inaccessa mapalium ulterioribus vendiderant.

LI. At Vespasiano post Cremonensem pugnam et prosperos undique nuntios, cecidisse Vitellium multi cujusque ordinis, pari audacia fortunaque hibernum mare aggressi, nuntiavere. Aderant legati regis Vologesi, quadraginta Parthorum equitum millia offerentes. Magnificum laetumque tantis sociorum auxiliis ambiri neque indigere. Gratiae Vologeso actae, mandatumque ut legatos ad senatum mitteret et pacem esse sciret. Vespasianus in Italiam resque urbis intentus, adversam de Domitiano famam accipit, tanquam terminos aetatis et concessa filio egrederetur. Igitur validissimam exercitus partem Tito tradit ad reliqua Judaici belli perpetranda.

LII. Titum, antequam digrederetur, multo apud patrem sermone orasse dicebatur, ne criminantium nuntiis temere accenderetur, integrumque se ac placabilem filio praestaret. Non legiones, non classes perinde firma imperii munimenta quam numerum liberorum. Nam amicos tempore, fortuna, cupidinibus aliquando aut erroribus imminui, transferri, desinere: suum cuique sanguinem indiscretum, sed maxime principibus, quorum prosperis et alii fruantur, adversa ad junctissimos pertineant: ne fratribus quidem mansuram concordiam, ni parens exemplum praebuisset. Vespasianus haud aeque Domitiano mitigatus quam Titi pietate gaudens, bono esse animo jubet, belloque et armis rempublicam attollere: sibi pacem domumque curae fore. Tum celerrimas navium frumento onustas saevo adhuc mari committit. Quippe tanto discrimine Urbs nutabat, ut decem haud amplius dierum frumentum in horreis fuerit, cum a Vespasiano commeatus subvenere.

LIII. Curam restituendi Capitolii in L. Vestinum confert, equestris ordinis virum, sed auctoritate famaque inter proceres. Ab eo contracti haruspices monuere, ut reliquiae prioris delubri in paludes aveherentur, templum iisdem vestigiis sisteretur: nolle deos mutari veterem formam. Undecimo Kalendas Julias serena luce spatium omne, quod templo dicabatur, evinctum vittis coronisque. Ingressi milites, quis fausta nomina, felicibus ramis: dein virgines Vestales, cum pueris puellisque patrimis matrimisque, aqua vivis e fontibus amnibusque hausta perluere. Tum Helvidius Priscus praetor, praeeunte Plautio Aeliano pontifice, lustrata suovetaurilibus area et super cespitem redditis extis, Jovem, Junonem, Minervam praesidesque imperii deos precatus, uti coepta prosperarent, sedesque suas pietate hominum inchoatas divina ope attollerent, vittas, quis ligatus lapis innexique funes erant, contigit. Simul ceteri magistratus et sacerdotes et senatus et eques et magna pars populi, studio laetitiaque connixi, saxum ingens traxere: passimque injectae fundamentis argenti aurique stipes et metallorum primitiae, nullis fornacibus victae, sed ut gignuntur. Praedixere haruspices, ne temeraretur opus saxo aurove in aliud destinato. Altitudo aedibus adjecta. Id solum religio annuere, et prioris templi magnificentiae defuisse creditum.

LIV. Audita interim per Gallias Germaniasque mors Vitellii duplicaverat bellum. Nam Civilis, omissa dissimulatione, in populum Romanum ruere; Vitellianae legiones vel externum servitium quam Imperatorem Vespasianum malle. Galli sustulerant animos, eandem ubique exercituum nostrorum fortunam rati, vulgato rumore a Sarmatis Dacisque Moesica ac Pannonica hiberna circumsideri: paria de Britannia fingebantur. Sed nihil aeque quam incendium Capitolii, ut finem imperio adesse crederent, impulerat. "Captam olim a Gallis urbem: sed, integra Jovis sede, mansisse imperium. Fatali nunc igne signum coelestis irae datum, et possessionem rerum humanarum Transalpinis gentibus portendi," superstitione vana Druidae canebant. Incesseratque fama primores Galliarum ab Othone adversus Vitellium missos, antequam digrederentur, pepigisse, ne deessent libertati, si populum Romanum continua civilium bellorum series et interna mala fregissent.

LV. Ante Flacci Hordeonii caedem nihil prorupit, quo conjuratio intelligeretur. Interfecto Hordeonio, commeavere nuntii inter Civilem Classicumque praefectum alae Treverorum. Classicus nobilitate opibusque ante alios. Regium illi genus et pace belloque clara origo. Ipse e majoribus suis hostis populi Romani quam socius jactabat. Miscuere sese Julius Tutor et Julius Sabinus, hic Trevir, hic Lingonus. Tutor ripae Rheni a Vitellio praefectus; Sabinus super insitam vanitatem falsae stirpis gloriae incendebatur: proaviam suam divo Julio per Gallias bellanti corpore atque adulterio placuisse. Hi secretis sermonibus animos ceterorum scrutari: ubi quos idoneos rebantur conscientia obstrinxere, in colonia Agrippinensi in domum privatum conveniunt; nam publice civitas talibus inceptis abhorrebat: attamen interfuere quidam Ubiorum Tungrorumque. Sed plurima vis penes Treveros ac Lingonas: nec tulere moras consultandi: certatim proclamant furere discordiis populum Romanum, caesas legiones, vastatam Italiam, capi cum maxime urbem, omnes exercitus suis quemque bellis distineri: si Alpes praesidiis firmentur, coalita libertate dispecturas Gallias, quem virium suarum terminum velint.

LVI. Haec dicta pariter probataque: de reliquiis Vitelliani exercitus dubitavere. Plerique interficiendos censebant, turbidos, infidos, sanguine ducum pollutos. Vicit ratio parcendi, ne sublata spe veniae pertinaciam accenderent: alliciendos potius in societatem; legatis tantum legionum interfectis, ceterum vulgus conscientia scelerum et spe impunitatis facile accessurum. Ea primi consilii forma: missique per Gallias concitores belli. Simulatum ipsis obsequium, quo incautiorem Voculam opprimerent. Nec defuere, qui Voculae nuntiarent. Sed vires ad coercendum deerant, infrequentibus infidisque legionibus. Inter ambiguos milites et occultos hostes, optimum e praesentibus ratus mutua dissimulatione et iisdem quibus petebatur grassari, in coloniam Agrippinensem descendit. Illuc Claudius Labeo, quem captum et extra conventum amandatum in Frisios diximus, corruptis custodibus perfugit; pollicitusque, si praesidium daretur, iturum in Batavos et potiorem civitatis partem ad societatem Romanam retracturum, accepta peditum equitumque modica manu, nihil apud Batavos ausus, quosdam Nerviorum Betasiorumque in arma traxit. Et furtim magis quam bello Canninefates Marsacosque incursabat.

LVII. Vocula Gallorum fraude illectus, ad hostem contendit. Nec procul Veteribus aberat, cum Classicus ac Tutor per speciem explorandi praegressi, cum ducibus Germanorum pacta firmavere. Tumque primum discreti a legionibus proprio vallo castra sua circumdant, obtestante Vocula "non adeo turbatam civilibus armis rem Romanam, ut Treveris etiam Lingonibusque despectui sit. Superesse fidas provincias, victores exercitus, fortunam imperii, et ultores deos. Sic olim Sacrovirum et Aeduos, nuper Vindicem Galliasque singulis proeliis concidisse. Eadem rursus numina, eadem fata ruptores foederum exspectarent. Melius divo Julio divoque Augusto notos eorum animos. Galbam et infracta tributa hostiles spiritus induisse. Nunc hostes, quia molle servitium; cum spoliati exutique fuerint, amicos fore." Haec ferociter locutus, postquam perstare in perfidia Classicum Tutoremque videt, verso itinere Novesium concedit. Galli duum millium spatio distantibus campis consedere. Illuc commeantium centurionum militumque emebantur animi, ut (flagitium incognitum) Romanus exercitus in externa verba jurarent, pignusque tanti sceleris nece aut vinculis legatorum daretur. Vocula, quanquam plerique fugam suadebant, audendum ratus, vocata concione in hunc modum disseruit.

LVIII. "Nunquam apud vos verba feci aut pro vobis sollicitior aut pro me securior. Nam mihi exitium parari libens audio, mortemque in tot malis hostium, ut finem miseriarum, exspecto. Vestri me pudet miseretque, adversus quos non proelium et acies parantur, id enim fas armorum et jus hostium: bellum cum populo Romano vestris se manibus gesturum Classicus sperat, imperiumque et sacramentum Galliarum ostentat. Adeo nos, si fortuna in praesens virtusque deseruit, etiam vetera exempla deficiunt, quotiens Romanae legiones perire praeoptaverint, ne loco pellerentur? socii saepe nostri exscindi urbes suas, seque cum conjugibus ac liberis cremari pertulerunt; neque aliud pretium exitus quam fides famaque. Tolerant cum maxime inopiam obsidiumque apud Vetera legiones, nec terrore aut promissis demoventur. Nobis, super arma et viros et egregia castrorum munimenta, frumentum et commeatus quamvis longo bello pares. Pecunia nuper etiam donativo suffecit, quod sive a Vespasiano sive a Vitellio datum interpretari mavultis, ab imperatore certe Romano accepistis. Tot bellorum victores apud Geldubam, apud Vetera, fuso totiens hoste, si pavetis aciem, indignum id quidem: sed est vallum murique et trahendi artes, donec e proximis provinciis auxilia exercitusque concurrant. Sane ego displiceam: sunt alii legati, tribuni, centurio denique aut miles. Ne hoc prodigium toto terrarum orbe vulgetur, vobis satellitibus Civilem et Classicum Italiam invasuros. An, si ad moenia urbis Germani Gallique duxerint, arma patriae inferetis? Horret animus tanti flagitii imagine. Tutori Trevero agentur excubiae? Signum belli Batavus dabit?

et Germanorum catervas supplebitis? quis deinde sceleris exitus? cum Romanae legiones contra direxerint, transfugae e transfugis et proditores e proditoribus inter recens et vetus sacramentum invisi deis errabitis? Te, Juppiter Optime Maxime, quem per octingentos viginti annos tot triumphis coluimus, te, Quirine Romanae parens urbis, precor venerorque, ut si vobis non fuit cordi me duce haec castra incorrupta et intemerata servari, at certe pollui foedarique a Tutore et Classico ne sinatis. Militibus Romanis aut innocentiam detis, aut maturam et sine noxa poenitentiam."

LIX. Varie excepta oratio, inter spem metumque ac pudorem. Digressum Voculam et de supremis agitantem, liberti servique prohibuere foedissimam mortem sponte praevenire. Et Classicus, misso Aemilio Longino desertore primae legionis, caedem ejus maturavit. Herennium et Numisium legatos vinciri satis visum. Dein sumptis Romani imperii insignibus, in castra venit. Nec illi, quanquam ad omne facinus durato, verba ultra suppeditavere quam ut sacramentum recitaret. Juravere, qui aderant, pro imperio Galliarum. Interfectorem Voculae altis ordinibus, ceteros, ut quisque flagitium navaverat, praemiis attollit. Divisae inde inter Tutorem et Classicum curae. Tutor valida manu circumdatos Agrippinenses, quantumque militum apud superiorem Rheni ripam, in eadem verba adigit, occisis Magontiaci tribunis, pulso castrorum praefecto, qui detrectaverant. Classicus corruptissimum quemque e deditis pergere ad obsessos jubet, veniam ostentantes, si praesentia sequerentur: aliter nihil spei; famem ferrumque et extrema passuros. Adjecere, qui missi erant, exemplum suum.

LX. Obsessos hinc fides, inde egestas inter decus ac flagitium distrahebant. Cunctantibus solita insolitaque alimenta deerant, absumptis jumentis equisque et ceteris animalibus, quae profana foedaque in usum necessitas vertit. Virgulta postremo et stirpes et internatas saxis herbas vellentes, miseriarum patientiaeque documentum fuere, donec egregiam laudem fine turpi macularent, missis ad Civilem legatis vitam orantes. Neque ante preces admissae quam in verba Galliarum jurarent. Tum pactus praedam castrorum dat custodes, qui pecuniam, calones, sarcinas retentarent, ac qui ipsos leves abeuntes prosequerentur. Ad quintum fere lapidem coorti Germani incautum agmen aggrediuntur. Pugnacissimus quisque in vestigio, multi palantes occubuere: ceteri retro in castra perfugiunt, querente sane Civile et increpante Germanos, tanquam fidem per scelus abrumperent. Simulata ea fuerint an retinere saevientes nequiverit, parum affirmatur. Direptis castris, faces injiciunt, cunctosque, qui proelio superfuerant, incendium hausit.

LXI. Civilis barbaro voto, post coepta adversus Romanos arma, propexum rutilatumque crinem, patrata demum caede legionum, deposuit. Et ferebatur parvulo filio quosdam captivorum sagittis jaculisque puerilibus figendos obtulisse. Ceterum neque se neque quenquam Batavum in verba Galliarum adegit, fisus Germanorum opibus et, si certandum adversus Gallos de possessione rerum foret, inclitus fama et potior. Munius Lupercus legatus legionis inter dona missus Veledae. Ea virgo nationis Bructerae late imperitabat, vetere apud Germanos more, quo plerasque feminarum fatidicas et, augescente superstitione, arbitrantur deas. Tuncque Veledae auctoritas adolevit: nam prosperas Germanis res et excidium legionum praedixerat. Sed Lupercus in itinere interfectus; pauci centurionum tribunorumque in Gallia geniti reservantur pignus societatis. Cohortium, alarum, legionum hiberna subversa cremataque, iis tantum relictis quae Magontiaci ac Vindonissae sita sunt.

LXII. Legio sextadecima cum auxiliis simul deditis a Novesio in coloniam Treverorum transgredi jubetur, praefinita die intra quam castris excederet. Medium omne tempus per varias curas egere, ignavissimus quisque caesorum apud Vetera exemplo paventes, melior pars rubore et infamia: "quale illud iter? quis dux viae? et omnia in arbitrio eorum, quos vitae necisque dominos fecissent." Alii, nulla dedecoris cura, pecuniam aut carissima sibimet ipsi circumdare. Quidam expedire arma telisque tanquam in aciem accingi. Haec meditantibus advenit proficiscendi hora, expectatione tristior. Quippe intra vallum deformitas haud perinde notabilis: detexit ignominiam campus et dies. Revulsae imperatorum imagines, inhonora signa, fulgentibus hinc inde Gallorum vexillis; silens agmen, et velut longae exsequiae; dux Claudius Sanctus effosso oculo, dirus ore, ingenio debilior. Duplicatur flagitium, postquam, desertis Bonnensibus castris, altera se legio miscuerat. Et vulgata captarum legionum fama, cuncti, qui paulo ante Romanorum nomen horrebant, procurrentes ex agris tectisque et undique effusi insolito spectaculo nimium fruebantur. Non tulit ala Picentina gaudium insultantis vulgi, spretisque Sancti promissis aut minis, Magontiacum abeunt; ac forte obvio interfectore Voculae Longino, conjectis in eum telis, initium exsolvendae in posterum culpae fecere. Legiones, nihil mutato itinere, ante moenia Treverorum considunt.

LXIII. Civilis et Classicus rebus secundis sublati, an coloniam Agrippinensem diripiendam exercitibus suis permitterent, dubitavere. Saevitia ingenii et cupidine praedae ad excidium civitatis trahebantur: obstabat ratio belli, et novum imperium inchoantibus utilis clementiae fama. Civilem etiam beneficii memoria flexit, quod filium ejus primo rerum motu in colonia Agrippinensi deprehensum honorate custodierant. Sed Transrhenanis gentibus invisa civitas opulentia auctuque. Neque alium finem belli rebantur, quam si promiscua ea sedes omnibus Germanis foret, aut disjecta Ubios quoque dispersisset.

LXIV. Igitur Tencteri, Rheno discreta gens, missis legatis mandata apud concilium Agrippinensium edi jubent: quae ferocissimus e legatis in hunc modum protulit: "Redisse vos in corpus nomenque Germaniae, communibus deis et praecipuo deorum Marti grates agimus; vobisque gratulamur, quod tandem liberi inter liberos eritis. Nam ad hunc diem flumina ac terras et coelum quodammodo ipsum clauserant Romani, ut colloquia congressusque nostros arcerent, vel, quod contumeliosius est viris ad arma natis, inermes ac prope nudi sub custode et pretio coiremus. Sed ut amicitia societasque nostra in aeternum rata sit, postulamus a vobis, muros coloniae, munimenta servitii, detrahatis; etiam fera animalia, si clausa teneas, virtutis obliviscuntur;

Romanos omnes in finibus vestris trucidetis; haud facile libertas et domini miscentur: bona interfectorum in medium cedant, ne quis occulere quicquam aut segregare causam suam possit. Liceat nobis vobisque utramque ripam colere, ut olim majoribus nostris; quomodo lucem diemque omnibus hominibus, ita omnes terras fortibus viris natura aperuit. Instituta cultumque patrium resumite, abruptis voluptatibus, quibus Romani plus adversus subjectos quam armis valent: sincerus et integer et servitutis oblitus populus aut ex aequo agetis aut aliis imperitabitis."

LXV. Agrippinenses sumpto consultandi spatio, quando neque subire conditiones metus futuri neque palam aspernari conditio praesens sinebat, in hunc modum respondent: "Quae prima libertatis facultas data est, avidius quam cautius sumpsimus, ut vobis ceterisque Germanis consanguineis nostris jungeremur. Muros civitatis, congregantibus se cum maxime Romanorum exercitibus, augere nobis quam diruere tutius est. Si qui ex Italia aut provinciis alienigenae in finibus nostris fuerant, eos bellum absumpsit vel in suas quisque sedes refugere. Deductis olim et nobiscum per connubium sociatis, quique mox provenere, haec patria est. Nec vos adeo iniquos existimamus, ut interfici a nobis parentes, fratres, liberos nostros velitis. Vectigal et onera commerciorum resolvimus. Sint transitus incustoditi, sed diurni et inermes, donec nova et recentia jura in vetustatem consuetudine vertantur. Arbitrum habebimus Civilem et Veledam, apud quos pacta sancientur." Sic lenitis Tencteris, legati ad Civilem et Veledam missi cum donis, cuncta ex voluntate Agrippinensium perpetravere. Sed coram adire alloquique Veledam negatum. Arcebantur aspectu, quo venerationis plus inesset. Ipsa edita in turre: delectus e propinquis consulta responsaque, ut internuntius numinis, portabat.

LXVI. Civilis societate Agrippinensium auctus, proximas civitates affectare aut adversantibus bellum inferre statuit: occupatisque Sunicis et juventute eorum per cohortes composita, quo minus ultra pergeret, Claudius Labeo Betasiorum Tungrorumque et Nerviorum tumultuaria manu restitit, fretus loco, quia pontem Mosae fluminis anteceperat: pugnabaturque in angustiis ambigue, donec Germani transnatantes terga Labeonis invasere. Simul Civilis, ausus an ex composito, intulit se agmini Tungrorum, et clara voce: "Non ideo," inquit "bellum sumpsimus, ut Batavi et Treveri gentibus imperent. Procul haec a nobis arrogantia: accipite societatem: transgredior ad vos, seu me ducem, seu militem mavultis." Movebatur vulgus condebantque gladios, cum Campanus ac Juvenalis, e primoribus Tungrorum, universam ei gentem dedidere. Labeo, antequam circumveniretur, profugit. Civilis Betasios quoque ac Nervios, in fidem acceptos, copiis suis adjunxit, ingens rerum, perculsis civitatum animis vel sponte inclinantibus.

LXVII. Interea Julius Sabinus, projectis foederis Romani monumentis, Caesarem se salutari jubet, magnamque et inconditam popularium turbam in Sequanos rapit, conterminam civitatem et nobis fidam. Nec Sequani detrectavere certamen. Fortuna melioribus affuit. Fusi Lingones. Sabinus festinatum temere proelium pari formidine deseruit, utque famam exitii sui faceret, villam, in quam perfugerat, cremavit, illic voluntaria morte interiisse creditus. Sed quibus artibus latebrisque vitam per novem mox annos traduxerit, simul amicorum ejus constantiam et insigne Epponinae uxoris exemplum suo loco reddemus. Sequanorum prospera acie belli impetus stetit. Resipiscere paulatim civitates, fasque et foedera respicere, principibus Remis, qui per Gallias edixere, ut missis legatis in commune consultarent, libertas an pax placeret.

LXVIII. At Romae cuncta in deterius audita Mucianum angebant, ne quanquam egregii duces (jam enim Gallum Annium et Petilium Cerialem delegerat) summam belli parum tolerarent. Nec relinquenda urbs sine rectore. Et Domitiani indomitae libidines timebantur, suspectis, uti diximus, Primo Antonio Varoque Arrio. Varus praetorianis praepositus vim atque arma retinebat. Eum Mucianus pulsum loco, ne sine solatio ageret, annonae praefecit; utque Domitiani animum Varo haud alienum deleniret, Arretinum Clementem, domui Vespasiani per affinitatem innexum et gratissimum Domitiano, praetorianis praeposuit, patrem ejus sub Caio Caesare egregie functum ea cura dictitans: laetum militibus idem nomen, atque ipsum, quanquam senatorii ordinis, ad utraque munia sufficere. Assumuntur e civitate clarissimus quisque, et alii per ambitionem. Simul Domitianus Mucianusque accingebantur, dispari animo; ille spe ac juventa properus, hic moras nectens, quis flagrantem retineret, ne ferocia aetatis et pravis impulsoribus, si exercitum invasisset, paci belloque male consuleret. Legiones victrices, sexta et octava, Vitellianarum unaetvicesima, e recens conscriptis secunda, Penninis Cottianisque Alpibus, pars monte Graio traducuntur: quartadecima legio e Britannia, sexta ac decima ex Hispania accitae. Igitur venientis exercitus fama et suopte ingenio ad mitiora inclinantes Galliarum civitates in Remos convenere. Treverorum legatio illic opperiebatur, acerrimo instinctore belli Tullio Valentino. Is meditata oratione cuncta magnis imperiis objectari solita contumeliasque et invidiam in populum Romanum effudit, turbidus miscendis seditionibus et plerisque gratus vecordi facundia.

LXIX. At Julius Auspex e primoribus Remorum, vim Romanam pacisque bona dissertans, et "sumi bellum etiam ab ignavis, strenuissimi cujusque periculo geri, jamque super caput legiones," sapientissimum quemque reverentia fideque, juniores periculo ac metu continuit. Et Valentini animum laudabant, consilium Auspicis sequebantur. Constat obstitisse Treveris Lingonibusque apud Gallias, quod Vindicis motu cum Verginio steterant. Deterruit plerosque provinciarum aemulatio: "quod bello caput? unde jus auspiciumque peteretur? quam, si cuncta provenissent, sedem imperio legerent?" Nondum victoria, jam discordia erat, aliis foedera, quibusdam opes viresque aut vetustatem originis per jurgia jactantibus. Taedio futurorum praesentia placuere. Scribuntur ad Treveros epistolae nomine Galliarum, ut abstinerent armis, impetrabili venia et paratis deprecatoribus, si poeniteret. Restitit idem Valentinus, obstruxitque civitatis suae aures, haud perinde instruendo bello intentus quam frequens concionibus.

LXX. Igitur non Treveri neque Lingones ceteraeve rebellium civitates pro magnitudine suscepti discriminis agere. Ne duces quidem in unum consulere, sed Civilis avia Belgarum circumibat, dum Claudium Labeonem capere aut exturbare nititur: Classicus, segne plerumque otium trahens, velut parto imperio fruebatur. Ne Tutor quidem maturavit superiorem Germaniae ripam et ardua Alpium praesidiis claudere. Atque interim unaetvicesima legio Vindonissa, Sextilius Felix cum auxiliariis cohortibus per Raetiam irrupere. Accessit ala Singularium, excita olim a Vitellio, deinde in partes Vespasiani transgressa. Praeerat Julius Briganticus sorore Civilis genitus, ut ferme acerrima proximorum odia sunt, invisus avunculo infensusque. Tutor Treverorum copias, recenti Vangionum, Caracatium, Tribocorum delectu auctas, veterano pedite atque equite firmavit, corruptis spe aut metu subactis legionariis; qui primo cohortem praemissam a Sextilio Felice interficiunt, mox ubi duces exercitusque Romanus propinquabant, honesto transfugio rediere, secutis Tribocis Vangionibusque et Caracatibus. Tutor, Treveris comitantibus, vitato Magontiaco, Bingium concessit, fidens loco quia pontem Navae fluminis abruperat, sed incursu cohortium, quas Sextilius ducebat, et reperto vado, proditus fususque. Ea clade perculsi Treveri, et plebes, omissis armis, per agros palatur: quidam principum, ut primi posuisse bellum viderentur, in civitates, quae societatem Romanam non exuerant, perfugere. Legiones a Novesio Bonnaque in Treveros, ut supra memoravimus, traductae, se ipsae in verba Vespasiani adigunt. Haec Valentino absente gesta; qui ubi adventabat furens cunctaque rursus in turbas et exitium conversurus, legiones in Mediomatricos, sociam civitatem, abscessere. Valentinus ac Tutor in arma Treveros retrahunt, occisis Herennio ac Numisio legatis, quo minore spe veniae cresceret vinculum sceleris.

LXXI. Hic belli status erat, cum Petilius Cerialis Magontiacum venit: ejus adventu erectae spes. Ipse pugnae avidus et contemnendis quam cavendis hostibus melior, ferocia verborum militem incendebat, ubi primum congredi licuisset, nullam proelio moram facturus: delectus per Galliam habitos in civitates remittit, ac nuntiare jubet sufficere imperio legiones: socii ad munia pacis redirent, securi velut confecto bello, quod Romanae manus excepissent. Auxit ea res Gallorum obsequium. Nam, recepta juventute, facilius tributa toleravere, proniores ad officia, quod spernebantur. At Civilis et Classicus, ubi pulsum Tutorem, caesos Treveros, cuncta hostibus prospera accepere, trepidi ac properantes, dum dispersas suorum copias conducunt, crebris interim nuntiis Valentinum monuere, ne summae rei periculum faceret. Eo rapidius Cerialis, missis in Mediomatricos qui breviore itinere legiones in hostem verterent, contracto quod erat militum Magontiaci quantumque secum transvexerat, tertiis castris Rigodulum venit; quem locum magna Treverorum manu Valentinus insederat montibus aut Mosella amne septum; et addiderat fossas obicesque saxorum. Nec deterruere ea munimenta Romanum ducem, quo minus peditem perrumpere juberet, equitum aciem in collem erigeret, spreto hoste, quem temere collectum haud ita loco juvari, ut non plus suis in virtute foret. Paulum morae in ascensu, dum missilia hostium praevehuntur: ut ventum in manus, deturbati ruinae modo praecipitantur. Et pars equitum, aequioribus jugis circumvecta, nobilissimos Belgarum, in quis ducem Valentinum, cepit.

LXXII. Cerialis postero die coloniam Treverorum ingressus est, avido milite eruendae civitatis: "hanc esse Classici, hanc Tutoris patriam; horum scelere clausas caesasque legiones. Quid tantum Cremonam meruisse, quam e gremio Italiae raptam, quia unius noctis moram victoribus attulerit? Stare in confinio Germaniae integram sedem spoliis exercituum et ducum caedibus ovantem. Redigeretur praeda in fiscum: ipsis sufficere ignes et rebellis coloniae ruinas, quibus tot castrorum excidia pensarentur." Cerialis a metu infamiae, si licentia saevitiaque imbuere militem crederetur, pressit iras: et paruere, posito civium bello ad externa modestiores. Convertit inde animos accitarum e Mediomatricis legionum miserabilis aspectus. Stabant conscientia flagitii maestae, fixis in terram oculis. Nulla inter coeuntes exercitus consalutatio; neque solantibus hortantibusve responsa dabant, abditi per tentoria et lucem ipsam vitantes; nec perinde periculum aut metus, quam pudor ac dedecus, obstupefecerat, attonitis etiam victoribus, qui vocem precesque adhibere non ausi lacrimis ac silentio veniam poscebant, donec Cerialis mulceret animos, fato acta dictitans, quae militum ducumque discordia vel fraude hostium evenissent. Primum illum stipendiorum et sacramenti diem haberent: priorum facinorum neque Imperatorem neque se meminisse. Tunc recepti in eadem castra, et edictum per manipulos, ne quis in certamine jurgiove seditionem aut cladem commilitoni objectaret.

LXXIII. Mox Treveros ac Lingonas ad concionem vocatos ita alloquitur: "Neque ego unquam facundiam exercui, et populi Romani virtutem armis affirmavi. Sed quoniam apud vos verba plurimum valent, bonaque ac mala non sua natura sed vocibus seditiosorum aestimantur, statui pauca disserere, quae, profligato bello, utilius sit vobis audisse quam nobis dixisse. Terram vestram ceterorumque Gallorum ingressi sunt duces imperatoresque Romani nulla cupidine, sed majoribus vestris invocantibus, quos discordiae usque ad exitium fatigabant; et acciti auxilio Germani sociis pariter atque hostibus servitutem imposuerant. Quot proeliis adversus Cimbros Teutonosque, quantis exercituum nostrorum laboribus, quove eventu Germanica bella tractaverimus, satis clarum. Nec ideo Rhenum insedimus ut Italiam tueremur, sed ne quis alius Ariovistus regno Galliarum potiretur. An vos cariores Civili Batavisque et Transrhenanis gentibus creditis quam majoribus eorum patres avique vestri fuerunt? Eadem semper causa Germanis transcendendi in Gallias, libido atque avaritia et mutandae sedis amor, ut relictis paludibus et solitudinibus suis fecundissimum hoc solum vosque ipsos possiderent. Ceterum libertas et speciosa nomina praetexuntur; nec quisquam alienum servitium et dominationem sibi concupivit, ut non eadem ista vocabula usurparet.

LXXIV. "Regna bellaque per Gallias semper fuere, donec in nostrum jus concederetis. Nos, quanquam totiens lacessiti, jure victoriae id solum vobis addidimus, quo pacem tueremur. Nam neque quies gentium sine armis, neque arma sine stipendiis, neque stipendia sine tributis haberi queunt. Cetera in communi sita sunt. Ipsi plerumque legionibus nostris praesidetis, ipsi has aliasque provincias regitis. Nihil separatum clausumve. Et laudatorum principum usus ex aequo, quamvis procul agentibus: saevi proximis ingruunt. Quomodo sterilitatem aut nimios imbres et cetera naturae mala, ita luxum vel avaritiam dominantium tolerate. Vitia erunt, donec homines; sed neque haec continua, et meliorum interventu pensantur, nisi forte Tutore et Classico regnantibus moderatius imperium speratis, aut minoribus quam nunc tributis parabuntur exercitus, quibus Germani Britannique arceantur. Nam pulsis (quod dii prohibeant) Romanis, quid aliud quam bella omnium inter se gentium exsistent? Octingentorum annorum fortuna disciplinaque compages haec coaluit, quae convelli sine exitio convellentium non potest. Sed vobis maximum discrimen, penes quos aurum et opes, praecipuae bellorum causae. Proinde pacem et urbem, quam victi victoresque eodem jure obtinemus, amate, colite. Moneant vos utriusque fortunae documenta, ne contumaciam cum pernicie quam obsequium cum securitate malitis." Tali oratione graviora metuentes composuit erexitque.

LXXV. Tenebantur victore exercitu Treveri, cum Civilis et Classicus misere epistolas ad Cerialem, quarum haec sententia fuit: "Vespasianum, quanquam nuntios occultarent, excessisse vita. Urbem atque Italiam interno bello consumptam. Muciani ac Domitiani vana et sine viribus nomina. Si Cerialis imperium Galliarum velit, ipsos finibus civitatum suarum contentos; si proelium mallet, ne id quidem abnuere." Ad ea Cerialis Civili et Classico nihil: eum qui attulerat, ipsas epistolas ad Domitianum misit. Hostes divisis copiis advenere undique. Plerique culpabant Cerialem passum jungi, quos discretos intercipere licuisset. Romanus exercitus castra fossa valloque circumdedit, quis temere antea intutis consederat. Apud Germanos diversis sententiis certabatur.

LXXVI. Civilis, "opperiendas Transrhenanorum gentes quarum terrore fractae populi Romani vires obtererentur. Gallos quid aliud quam praedam victoribus? et tamen, quod roboris sit, Belgas, secum palam aut voto stare." Tutor cunctatione crescere rem Romanam affirmabat, coeuntibus undique exercitibus. "Transvectam e Britannia legionem, accitas ex Hispania, adventare ex Italia; nec subitum militem, sed veterem expertumque belli. Nam Germanos, qui ab ipsis sperentur, non juberi, non regi, sed cuncta ex libidine agere; pecuniamque ac dona, quis solis corrumpantur, majora apud Romanos, et neminem adeo in arma pronum, ut non idem pretium quietis quam periculi malit. Quod si statim congrediantur, nullas esse Ceriali nisi ex reliquiis Germanici exercitus legiones, foederibus Galliarum obstrictas. Idque ipsum, quod inconditam nuper Valentini manum contra spem suam fuderint, alimentum illis ducique temeritatis. Ausuros rursus venturosque in manus non imperiti adolescentuli, verba et conciones quam ferrum et arma meditantis, sed Civilis et Classici; quos ubi aspexerint, redituram in animos formidinem, fugam famemque ac totiens captis precariam vitam: neque Treveros aut Lingonas benevolentia contineri; resumpturos arma, ubi metus abscesserit." Diremit consiliorum diversitatem approbata Tutoris sententia Classicus; statimque exsequuntur.

LXXVII. Media acies Ubiis Lingonibusque data; dextro cornu cohortes Batavorum; sinistro Bructeri Tencterique. Pars montibus, alii viam inter Mosellamque flumen, tam improvisi assiluere, ut in cubiculo ac lectulo Cerialis (neque enim noctem in castris egerat) pugnari simul vincique suos audierit, increpans pavorem nuntiantium, donec universa clades in oculis fuit, perrupta legionum castra, fusi equites, medius Mosellae pons, qui ulteriora coloniae annectit, ab hostibus insessus. Cerialis turbidis rebus intrepidus et fugientes manu retrahens, intecto corpore promptus inter tela, felici temeritate et fortissimi cujusque accursu reciperatum pontem electa manu firmavit. Mox in castra reversus, palantes captarum apud Novesium Bonnamque legionum manipulos et rarum apud signa militem ac prope circumventas aquilas videt. Incensus ira, "non Flaccum," inquit, "non Voculam deseritis. Nulla hic proditio; neque aliud excusandum habeo quam quod vos, Gallici foederis oblitos, redisse in memoriam Romani sacramenti temere credidi. Annumerabor Numisiis et Herenniis, ut omnes legati vestri aut militum manibus aut hostium ceciderint. Ite, nuntiate Vespasiano vel, quod propius est, Civili et Classico, relictum a vobis in acie ducem: venient legiones, quae neque me inultum neque vos impunitos patiantur."

LXXVIII. Vera erant, et a tribunis praefectisque eadem ingerebantur. Consistunt per cohortes et manipulos: neque enim poterat patescere acies, effuso hoste et impedientibus tentoriis sarcinisque, cum intra vallum pugnaretur. Tutor et Classicus et Civilis suis quisque locis pugnam ciebant, Gallos pro libertate, Batavos pro gloria, Germanos ad praedam instigantes. Et cuncta pro hostibus erant, donec legio unaetvicesima, patentiore quam ceterae spatio conglobata, sustinuit ruentes, mox impulit. Nec sine ope divina, mutatis repente animis, terga victores vertere. Ipsi territos se cohortium aspectu ferebant, quae primo impetu disjectae summis rursus jugis congregabantur ac speciem novi auxilii fecerant. Sed obstitit vincentibus pravum inter ipsos certamen, omisso hoste, spolia consectandi. Cerialis, ut incuria prope rem afflixit, ita constantia restituit; secutusque fortunam castra hostium eodem die capit exscinditque.

LXXIX. Nec in longum quies militi data. Orabant auxilium Agrippinenses, offerebantque uxorem ac sororem Civilis et filiam Classici, relicta sibi pignora societatis. Atque interim dispersos in domibus Germanos trucidaverant; unde metus et justae preces invocantium, antequam hostes reparatis viribus ad spem vel ad ultionem accingerentur. Namque et Civilis illuc intenderat, non invalidus, flagrantissima cohortium suarum integra, quae e Chaucis Frisiisque composita Tolbiaci in finibus Agrippinensium agebat. Sed tristis nuntius avertit, deletam cohortem dolo Agrippinensium; qui largis epulis vinoque sopitos Germanos, clausis foribus, igne injecto cremavere. Simul Cerialis propero agmine subvenit. Circumsteterat Civilem et alius metus, ne quartadecima legio, adjuncta Britannica classe, afflictaret Batavos, qua Oceano ambiuntur. Sed legionem terrestri itinere Fabius Priscus legatus in Nervios Tungrosque duxit, eaeque civitates in deditionem acceptae: classem ultro Canninefates aggressi sunt, majorque pars navium depressa aut capta. Et Nerviorum multitudinem, sponte commotam ut pro Romanis bellum capesseret, iidem Canninefates fudere. Classicus quoque adversus equites Novesium a Ceriale praemissos secundum proelium fecit: quae modica sed crebra damna famam victoriae nuper partae lacerabant.

LXXX. Iisdem diebus Mucianus Vitellii filium interfici jubet, mansuram discordiam obtendens, ni semina belli restinxisset. Neque Antonium Primum asciri inter comites a Domitiano passus est, favore militum anxius et superbia viri, aequalium quoque, adeo superiorum, intolerantis. Profectus ad Vespasianum Antonius, ut non pro spe sua excipitur, ita neque averso Imperatoris animo. Trahebatur in diversa, hinc meritis Antonii, cujus ductu confectum haud dubie bellum erat, inde Muciani epistolis: simul ceteri ut infestum tumidumque insectabantur, adjunctis prioris vitae criminibus: neque ipse deerat arrogantia vocare offensas, nimius commemorandis quae meruisset. Alios ut imbelles, Caecinam ut captivum ac dediticium increpat. Unde paulatim levior viliorque haberi, manente tamen in speciem amicitia.

LXXXI. Per eos menses, quibus Vespasianus Alexandriae statos aestivis flatibus dies et certa maris opperiebatur, multa miracula evenere, quis coelestis favor et quaedam in Vespasianum inclinatio numinum ostenderetur. E plebe Alexandrina quidam oculorum tabe notus genua ejus advolvitur, remedium caecitatis exposcens gemitu, monitu Serapidis dei, quem dedita superstitionibus gens ante alios colit; precabaturque Principem, ut genas et oculorum orbes dignaretur respergere oris excremento. Alius manum aeger, eodem deo auctore, ut pede ac vestigio Caesaris calcaretur, orabat. Vespasianus primo irridere, aspernari; atque, illis instantibus, modo famam vanitatis metuere, modo obsecratione ipsorum et vocibus adulantium in spem induci: postremo aestimari a medicis jubet, an talis caecitas ac debilitas ope humana superabiles forent. Medici varie disserere: "Huic non exesam vim luminis, et redituram, si pellerentur obstantia; illi elapsos in pravum artus, si salubris vis adhibeatur, posse integrari. Id fortasse cordi deis, et divino ministerio Principem electum: denique patrati remedii gloriam penes Caesarem, irriti ludibrium penes miseros fore." Igitur Vespasianus cuncta fortunae suae patere ratus nec quicquam ultra incredibile, laeto ipse vultu, erecta quae astabat multitudine, jussa exsequitur. Statim conversa ad usum manus, ac caeco reluxit dies. Utrumque, qui interfuere, nunc quoque memorant, postquam nullum mendacio pretium.

LXXXII. Altior inde Vespasiano cupido adeundi sacram sedem, ut super rebus imperii consuleret. Arceri templo cunctos jubet: atque ingressus intentusque numini, respexit pone tergum e primoribus Aegyptiorum nomine Basiliden, quem procul Alexandria plurium dierum itinere et aegro corpore detineri haud ignorabat. Percunctatur sacerdotes, num illo die Basilides templum inisset; percunctatur obvios, num in urbe visus sit: denique missis equitibus explorat illo temporis momento octoginta millibus passuum abfuisse. Tunc divinam speciem et vim responsi ex nomine Basilidis interpretatus est.

LXXXIII. Origo dei nondum nostris auctoribus celebrata. Aegyptiorum antistites sic memorant: "Ptolemaeo regi, qui Macedonum primus Aegypti opes firmavit, cum Alexandriae recens conditae moenia templaque et religiones adderet, oblatum per quietem decore eximio et majore quam humana specie juvenem, qui moneret, ut fidissimis amicorum in Pontum missis effigiem suam acciret: laetum id regno, magnamque et inclitam sedem fore, quae excepisset: simul visum eundem juvenem in coelum igne plurimo attolli." Ptolemaeus omine et miraculo excitus, sacerdotibus Aegyptiorum, quibus mos talia intelligere, nocturnos visus aperit. Atque illis Ponti et externorum parum gnaris, Timotheum Atheniensem e gente Eumolpidarum, quem ut antistitem caerimoniarum Eleusine exciverat, quaenam illa superstitio, quod numen, interrogat. Timotheus, quaesitis qui in Pontum meassent, cognoscit urbem illic Sinopen, nec procul templum, vetere inter accolas fama, Jovis Ditis; namque et muliebrem effigiem assistere, quam plerique Proserpinam vocent. Sed Ptolemaeus, ut sunt ingenia regum, pronus ad formidinem, ubi securitas rediit voluptatum quam religionum appetens, negligere paulatim aliasque ad curas animum vertere, donec eadem species terribilior jam et instantior exitium ipsi regnoque denuntiaret, ni jussa patrarentur. Tum legatos et dona Scydrothemidi regi (is tunc Sinopensibus imperitabat) expediri jubet; praecepitque navigaturis, ut Pythium Apollinem adeant. Illis mare secundum, sors oraculi haud ambigua: "Irent, simulacrumque patris sui reveherent, sororis relinquerent."

LXXXIV. Ut Sinopen venere, munera, preces, mandata regis sui Scydrothemidi allegant. Qui versus animi modo numen pavescere, modo minis adversantis populi terreri; saepe donis promissisque legatorum flectebatur. Atque interim triennio exacto, Ptolemaeus non studium, non preces omittere. Dignitatem legatorum, numerum navium, auri pondus augebat. Tum minax facies Scydrothemidi offertur, ne destinata deo ultra moraretur. Cunctantem varia pernicies morbique et manifesta coelestium ira graviorque in dies fatigabat. Advocata concione, jussa numinis, suos Ptolemaeique visus, ingruentia mala exponit. Vulgus adversari regem, invidere Aegypto, sibi metuere templumque circumsedere. Major hinc fama tradidit deum ipsum appulsas littori naves sponte conscendisse. Mirum inde dictu, tertio die tantum maris emensi Alexandriam appelluntur. Templum pro magnitudine urbis exstructum loco, cui nomen Rhacotis: fuerat illic sacellum Serapidi atque Isidi antiquitus sacratum. Haec de origine et advectu dei celeberrima. Nec sum ignarus esse quosdam qui Seleucia urbe Syriae accitum, regnante Ptolemaeo quem tertia aetas tulit: alii auctorem eundem Ptolemaeum, sedem ex qua transierit Memphim perhibent, inclitam olim et veteris Aegypti columen. Deum ipsum multi Aesculapium, quod medeatur aegris corporibus; quidam Osirin, antiquissimum illis gentibus numen; plerique Jovem, ut rerum omnium potentem; plurimi Ditem patrem, insignibus quae in ipso manifesta, aut per ambages conjectant.

LXXXV. At Domitianus Mucianusque, antequam Alpibus propinquarent, prosperos rerum in Treveris gestarum nuntios accepere. Praecipua victoriae fides dux hostium Valentinus, nequaquam abjecto animo, quos spiritus gessisset, vultu ferebat. Auditus ideo tantum ut nosceretur ingenium ejus, damnatusque, inter ipsum supplicium, exprobranti cuidam patriam ejus captam, "accipere se solatium mortis" respondit. Sed Mucianus quod diu occultaverat, ut recens exprompsit: "quoniam benignitate deum fractae vires hostium forent, parum decore Domitianum, confecto prope bello, alienae gloriae interventurum. Si status imperii aut salus Galliarum in discrimine verteretur, debuisse Caesarem in acie stare: Canninefates Batavosque minoribus ducibus delegandos. Ipse Lugduni vim fortunamque principatus e proximo ostentaret, nec parvis periculis immixtus et majoribus non defuturus."

LXXXVI. Intelligebantur artes; sed pars obsequii in eo, ne deprehenderentur: ita Lugdunum ventum. Unde creditur Domitianus occultis ad Cerialem nuntiis fidem ejus tentavisse, an praesenti sibi exercitum imperiumque traditurus foret: qua cogitatione bellum adversus patrem agitaverit, an opes viresque adversus fratrem in incerto fuit: nam Cerialis salubri temperamento elusit ut vana pueriliter cupientem. Domitianus sperni a senioribus juventam suam cernens, modica quoque et usurpata antea munia imperii omittebat, simplicitatis ac modestiae imagine in altitudinem conditus, studiumque literarum et amorem carminum simulans, quo velaret animum et fratris aemulationi subduceretur, cujus disparem mitioremque naturam contra interpretabatur.

C. CORNELII TACITI

HISTORIARUM

LIBER QUINTUS.

BREVIARIUM LIBRI.

Cap I. Interim Titus cum valido exercitu prope Hierosolyma castra facit. II—V. Judaicae gentis primordia, sacra, instituta, deque iis maligna profanorum judicia. VI, VII. Descriptio terrae finiumque, balsami, Libani, Jordanis, lacus bitumen egerentis, camporum torridorum, fructuum in cinerem vanescentium, Beli amnis, cujus arenae vitro inservientes. VIII. Hierosolyma genti caput. Immensae opulentiae templum. Judaeorum sub aliis gentibus et suis regibus fata IX, varia sors sub Romanis. X—XII. Bellum sub Gessio Floro procuratore ortum. Titus Judaeos, in urbem compulsos, obsidet. Hierosolymorum munitiones, copiae, duces. XIII. Prodigia ante obsidium.

XIV. Interea Civilis, reparato per Germaniam exercitu, bellum renovat. XV. Manum conserit cum Ceriale, satis prospere. Uterque ad maturandum summae rei discrimen erectus, XVI, XVII, aciem instruit, suos alloquitur. XVIII. Fit atrox pugna, qua, proditione cujusdam Batavi, Germani vincuntur. XIX, XX. Civilis, in Batavorum insulam transgressus, praesidia Romanorum invadit, Verace, Classico, Tutore suffultus. XXI. Ambiguum proelium. Subvenit Cerialis fortunamque vertit; XXII, at parum providus ferme opprimitur. XXIII. Civilis navalem aciem ostentat, sed a Ceriale trans Rhenum pellitur. Hic insulam Batavorum populatus, superfuso amne, novum discrimen adit. XXIV, XXV. Tum hostium animos occultis nuntiis labefactat. XXVI. Civilis, petito colloquio, ad deditionem, se pronum profitetur.

EJUSDEM anni principio Caesar Titus perdomandae Judaeae delectus a patre et privatis utriusque rebus militia clarus, majore tum vi famaque agebat, certantibus provinciarum et exercituum studiis. Atque ipse, ut super fortunam crederetur, decorum se promptumque in armis ostendebat, comitate et alloquiis officia provocans, ac plerumque in opere, in agmine gregario militi mixtus, incorrupto ducis honore. Tres eum in Judaea legiones, quinta et decima et quintadecima, vetus Vespasiani miles, excepere. Addidit e Syria duodecimam et abductos Alexandria duoetvicesimanos tertianosque. Comitabantur viginti sociae cohortes, octo equitum alae, simul Agrippa Sohemusque reges, et auxilia regis Antiochi, validaque et solito inter accolas odio infensa Judaeis Arabum manus; multi, quos urbe atque Italia sua quemque spes acciverat occupandi Principem adhuc vacuum. His cum copiis fines hostium ingressus composito agmine, cuncta explorans paratusque decernere, haud procul Hierosolymis castra facit.

II. Sed quoniam famosae urbis supremum diem tradituri sumus, congruens videtur primordia ejus aperire. Judaeos Creta insula profugos novissima Libyae insedisse memorant, qua tempestate Saturnus vi Jovis pulsus cesserit regnis. Argumentum e nomine petitur: inclitum in Creta Idam montem; accolas Idaeos aucto in barbarum cognomento Judaeos vocitari. Quidam, regnante Iside, exundantem per Aegyptum multitudinem, ducibus Hierosolymo ac Juda, proximas in terras exoneratam. Plerique Aethiopum prolem, quos rege Cepheo metus atque odium mutare sedes perpulerit. Sunt qui tradant Assyrios convenas, indigum agrorum populum, parte Aegypti potitos, mox proprias urbes Hebraeasque terras et propiora Syriae coluisse. Clara alii Judaeorum initia Solymos, carminibus Homeri celebratam gentem, conditae urbi Hierosolymam nomen e suo fecisse.

III. Plurimi auctores consentiunt, orta per Aegyptum tabe quae corpora foedaret, regem Bocchorim adito Hammonis oraculo remedium petentem, purgare regnum et id genus hominum ut invisum deis alias in terras avehere jussum. Sic conquisitum collectumque vulgus, postquam vastis locis relictum sit, ceteris per lacrimas torpentibus, Moysen unum exsulum monuisse, ne quam deorum hominumve opem exspectarent utrisque deserti, sed sibimet, duci coelesti, crederent, primo cujus auxilio praesentes miserias pepulissent. Assensere, atque omnium ignari fortuitum iter incipiunt. Sed nihil aeque quam inopia aquae fatigabat. Jamque haud procul exitio totis campis procubuerant, cum grex asinorum agrestium e pastu in rupem nemore opacam concessit. Secutus Moyses conjectura herbidi soli largas aquarum venas aperit. Id levamen: et continuum sex dierum iter emensi, septimo pulsis cultoribus obtinuere terras, in quis urbs et templum dicata.

IV. Moyses, quo sibi in posterum gentem firmaret, novos ritus contrariosque ceteris mortalibus indidit. Profana illic omnia, quae apud nos sacra; rursum concessa apud illos, quae nobis incesta. Effigiem animalis, quo monstrante errorem sitimque depulerant, penetrali sacravere, caeso ariete velut in contumeliam Hammonis. Bos quoque immolatur, quia Aegyptii Apin colunt. Sue abstinent merito cladis, qua ipsos scabies quondam turpaverat, cui id animal obnoxium. Longam olim famem crebris adhuc jejuniis fatentur; et raptarum frugum argumentum panis Judaicus nullo fermento detinetur. Septimo die otium placuisse ferunt, quia is finem laborum tulerit; dein blandiente inertia septimum quoque annum ignaviae datum. Alii honorem eum Saturno haberi, seu principia religionis tradentibus Idaeis, quos cum Saturno pulsos et conditores gentis accepimus, seu quod de septem sideribus quis mortales reguntur, altissimo orbe et praecipua potentia stella Saturni feratur, ac pleraque coelestium vim suam et cursum septimos per numeros conficiant.

V. Hi ritus, quoquo modo inducti, antiquitate defenduntur: cetera instituta sinistra, foeda, pravitate valuere. Nam pessimus quisque, spretis religionibus patriis, tributa et stipes illuc gerebant; unde auctae Judaeorum res, et quia apud ipsos fides obstinata, misericordia in promptu, sed adversus omnes alios hostile odium. Separati epulis, discreti cubilibus, projectissima ad libidinem gens, alienarum concubitu abstinent; inter se nihil illicitum. Circumcidere genitalia instituerunt, ut diversitate noscantur. Transgressi in morem eorum idem usurpant, nec quicquam prius imbuuntur quam contemnere deos, exuere patriam, parentes, liberos, fratres, vilia habere. Augendae tamen multitudini consulitur. Nam et necare quenquam ex agnatis nefas, animosque proelio aut suppliciis peremptorum aeternos putant. Hinc generandi amor et moriendi contemptus. Corpora condere quam cremare, e more Aegyptio; eademque cura et de infernis persuasio: coelestium contra. Aegyptii pleraque animalia effigiesque compositas venerantur; Judaei mente sola unumque numen intelligunt. Profanos, qui deum imagines mortalibus materiis in species hominum effingant: summum illud et aeternum neque imitabile neque interiturum. Igitur nulla simulacra urbibus suis, nedum templis sinunt. Non regibus haec adulatio, non Caesaribus honor. Sed quia sacerdotes eorum tibia tympanisque concinebant, hedera vinciebantur vitisque aurea templo reperta, Liberum Patrem coli domitorem Orientis, quidam arbitrati sunt, nequaquam congruentibus institutis: quippe Liber festos laetosque ritus posuit, Judaeorum mos absurdus sordidusque.

VI. Terra finesque, qua ad Orientem vergunt, Arabia terminantur; a meridie Aegyptus objacet; ab occasu Phoenices et mare; septentrionem a latere Syriae longe prospectant. Corpora hominum salubria et ferentia laborum: rari imbres, uber solum: fruges nostrum ad morem, praeterque eas balsamum et palmae. Palmetis proceritas et decor. Balsamum modica arbor: ut quisque ramus intumuit, si vim ferri adhibeas, pavent venae; fragmine lapidis aut testa aperiuntur: humor in usu medentium est. Praecipuum montium Libanum erigit, mirum dictu, tantos inter ardores opacum fidumque nivibus. Idem amnem Jordanen alit funditque. Nec Jordanes pelago accipitur, sed unum atque alterum lacum integer perfluit, tertio retinetur. Lacus immenso ambitu, specie maris, sapore corruptior, gravitate odoris accolis pestifer, neque vento impellitur neque pisces aut suetas aquis volucres patitur. Incertae undae superjacta, ut solido, ferunt; periti imperitique nandi perinde attolluntur. Certo anni bitumen egerit; cujus legendi usum, ut ceteras artes, experientia docuit. Ater suapte natura liquor et sparso aceto concretus innatat: hunc manu captum, quibus ea cura, in summa navis trahunt. Inde, nullo juvante, influit oneratque, donec abscindas: nec abscindere aere ferrove possis: fugit cruorem vestemque infectam sanguine, quo feminae per menses exsolvuntur: sic veteres auctores. Sed gnari locorum tradunt undantes bitumine moles pelli manuque trahi ad littus: mox, ubi vapore terrae, vi solis inaruerint, securibus cuneisque, ut trabes aut saxa, discindi.

VII. Haud procul inde campi, quos ferunt, olim uberes magnisque urbibus habitatos, fulminum jactu arsisse; et manere vestigia, terramque ipsam, specie torridam, vim frugiferam perdidisse. Nam cuncta sponte edita aut manu sata, sive herba tenus aut flore, seu solitam in speciem adolevere, atra et inania velut in cinerem vanescunt. Ego sicut inclitas quondam urbes igne coelesti flagrasse concesserim, ita halitu lacus infici terram, corrumpi superfusum spiritum, eoque foetus segetum et autumni putrescere reor, solo coeloque juxta gravi. Et Belus amnis Judaico mari illabitur; circa cujus os collectae arenae admixto nitro in vitrum excoquuntur: modicum id littus et egerentibus inexhaustum.

VIII. Magna pars Judaeae vicis dispergitur: habent et oppida. Hierosolyma genti caput. Illic immensae opulentiae templum, et primis munimentis urbs, dein regia, templum intimis clausum: ad fores tantum Judaeo aditus; limine, praeter sacerdotes, arcebantur. Dum Assyrios penes Medosque et Persas Oriens fuit, despectissima pars servientium: postquam Macedones praepotuere, rex Antiochus demere superstitionem et mores Graecorum dare annixus, quo minus teterrimam gentem in melius mutaret, Parthorum bello prohibitus est: nam ea tempestate Arsaces desciverat. Tum Judaei, Macedonibus invalidis, Parthis nondum adultis (et Romani procul erant) sibi ipsi reges imposuere; qui mobilitate vulgi expulsi, resumpta per arma dominatione, fugas civium, urbium eversiones, fratrum, conjugum, parentum neces aliaque solita regibus ausi, superstitionem fovebant, quia honor sacerdotii firmamentum potentiae assumebatur.

IX. Romanorum primus Cn. Pompeius Judaeos domuit, templumque jure victoriae ingressus est. Inde vulgatum, nulla intus deum effigie, vacuam sedem et inania arcana. Muri Hierosolymorum diruti, delubrum mansit. Mox civili inter nos bello, postquam in ditionem M. Antonii provinciae cesserant, rex Parthorum Pacorus Judaea potitus, interfectusque a P. Ventidio, et Parthi trans Euphraten redacti: Judaeos C. Sosius subegit. Regnum ab Antonio Herodi datum victor Augustus auxit. Post mortem Herodis, nihil exspectato Caesare, Simo quidam regium nomen invaserat. Is a Quintilio Varo obtinente Syriam punitus; et gentem coercitam liberi Herodis tripartito rexere. Sub Tiberio quies: dein jussi a C. Caesare effigiem ejus in templo locare, arma potius sumpsere; quem motum Caesaris mors diremit. Claudius, defunctis regibus aut ad modicum redactis, Judaeam provinciam equitibus Romanis aut libertis permisit; e quibus Antonius Felix, per omnem saevitiam ac libidinem, jus regium servili ingenio exercuit, Drusilla Cleopatrae et Antonii nepte in matrimonium accepta, ut ejusdem Antonii Felix progener, Claudius nepos esset.

X. Duravit tamen patientia Judaeis usque ad Gessium Florum procuratorem. Sub eo bellum ortum; et comprimere coeptantem Cestium Gallum Syriae legatum varia proelia ac saepius adversa excepere. Qui ubi fato aut taedio occidit, missu Neronis Vespasianus fortuna famaque et egregiis ministris intra duas aestates cuncta camporum omnesque praeter Hierosolymam urbes victore exercitu tenebat. Proximus annus civili bello intentus, quantum ad Judaeos, per otium transiit. Pace per Italiam parta et externae curae rediere. Augebat iras, quod soli Judaei non cessissent. Simul manere apud exercitus Titum ad omnes principatus novi eventus casusve utilius videbatur. Igitur castris, uti diximus, ante moenia Hierosolymorum positis, instructas legiones ostentavit.

XI. Judaei sub ipsos muros struxere aciem, rebus secundis longius ausuri, et si pellerentur, parato perfugio. Missus in eos eques cum expeditis cohortibus ambigue certavit. Mox cessere hostes, et sequentibus diebus crebra pro portis proelia serebant, donec assiduis damnis intra moenia pellerentur. Romani ad oppugnandum versi; neque enim dignum videbatur famem hostium opperiri; poscebantque pericula, pars virtute, multi ferocia et cupidine praemiorum. Ipsi Tito Roma et opes voluptatesque ante oculos; ac, ni statim Hierosolyma conciderent, morari videbantur. Sed urbem arduam situ opera molesque firmaverant, quis vel plana satis munirentur. Nam duos colles immensum editos claudebant muri per artem obliqui aut introrsus sinuati, ut latera oppugnantium ad ictus patescerent. Extrema rupis abrupta; et turres, ubi mons juvisset, in sexaginta pedes, inter devexa in centenos vicenosque attollebantur, mira specie, ac procul intuentibus pares. Alia intus moenia, regiae circumjecta, conspicuoque fastigio turris Antonia, in honorem M. Antonii ab Herode appellata.

XII. Templum in modum arcis propriique muri, labore et opere ante alios: ipsae porticus, quis templum ambiebatur, egregium propugnaculum. Fons perennis aquae, cavati sub terra montes, et piscinae cisternaeque servandis imbribus: praeviderant conditores ex diversitate morum crebra bella: inde cuncta quamvis adversus longum obsidium: et a Pompeio expugnatis metus atque usus pleraque monstravere. Atque per avaritiam Claudianorum temporum empto jure muniendi struxere muros in pace tanquam ad bellum, magna colluvie et ceterarum urbium clade aucti: nam pervicacissimus quisque illuc perfugerat, eoque seditiosius agebant. Tres duces, totidem exercitus. Extrema et latissima moenium Simo, quem et Bargioram vocabant, mediam urbem Joannes, templum Eleazarus firmaverat. Multitudine et armis Joannes ac Simo, Eleazarus loco pollebat. Sed proelia, dolus, incendia inter ipsos, et magna vis frumenti ambusta. Mox Joannes, missis per speciem sacrificandi qui Eleazarum manumque ejus obtruncarent, templo potitur: ita in duas factiones civitas discessit, donec propinquantibus Romanis, bellum externum concordiam pareret.

XIII. Evenerant prodigia, quae neque hostiis neque votis piare fas habet gens superstitioni obnoxia, religionibus adversa. Visae per coelum concurrere acies, rutilantia arma, et subito nubium igne collucere templum. Exapertae repente delubri fores et audita major humana vox, "excedere deos:" simul ingens motus excedentium. Quae pauci in metum trahebant: pluribus persuasio inerat antiquis sacerdotum literis contineri eo ipso tempore fore, ut valesceret Oriens profectique Judaea rerum potirentur: quae ambages Vespasianum ac Titum praedixerat. Sed vulgus, more humanae cupidinis, sibi tantam fatorum magnitudinem interpretati, ne adversis quidem ad vera mutabantur. Multitudinem obsessorum, omnis aetatis, virile ac muliebre secus, sexcenta millia fuisse accepimus. Arma cunctis qui ferre possent; et plures quam pro numero audebant. Obstinatio viris feminisque par; ac si transferre sedes cogerentur, major vitae metus quam mortis. Hanc adversus urbem gentemque Caesar Titus, quando impetus et subita belli locus abnueret, aggeribus vineisque certare statuit. Dividuntur legionibus munia, et quies proeliorum fuit, donec cuncta expugnandis urbibus reperta apud veteres aut novis ingeniis struerentur.

XIV. At Civilis post malam in Treveris pugnam, reparato per Germaniam exercitu, apud Vetera castra consedit, tutus loco, et ut memoria prosperarum illic rerum augescerent barbarorum animi. Secutus est eodem Cerialis, duplicatis copiis adventu secundae et sextae et quartaedecimae legionum. Cohortesque et alae jampridem accitae post victoriam properaverant. Neuter ducum cunctator. Sed arcebat latitudo camporum suopte ingenio humentium. Addiderat Civilis obliquam in Rhenum molem, cujus objectu revolutus amnis adjacentibus superfunderetur. Ea loci forma, incertis vadis subdola et nobis adversa: quippe miles Romanus armis gravis et nandi pavidus; Germanos fluminibus suetos levitas armorum et proceritas corporum attollit.

XV. Igitur lacessentibus Batavis, ferocissimo cuique nostrorum coeptum certamen; deinde orta trepidatio, cum praealtis paludibus arma, equi haurirentur. Germani notis vadis persultabant, omissa plerumque fronte, latera ac terga circumvenientes: neque ut in pedestri acie cominus certabatur; sed tanquam navali pugna, vagi inter undas aut, si quid stabile occurrebat, totis illic corporibus nitentes, vulnerati cum integris, periti nandi cum ignaris, in mutuam perniciem implicabantur. Minor tamen quam pro tumultu caedes, quia non ausi egredi paludem Germani in castra rediere. Ejus proelii eventus utrumque ducem diversis animi motibus ad maturandum summae rei discrimen erexit. Civilis instare fortunae; Cerialis abolere ignominiam. Germani prosperis feroces; Romanos pudor excitaverat. Nox apud barbaros cantu aut clamore, nostris per iram et minas acta.

XVI. Postera luce Cerialis equite et auxiliariis cohortibus frontem explet; in secunda acie legiones locatae; dux sibi delectos retinuerat ad improvisa. Civilis haud porrecto agmine sed cuneis astitit: Batavi Gugernique in dextro; laeva ac propiora fluminis Transrhenani tenuere. Exhortatio ducum non more concionis apud universos, sed ut quosque suorum advehebantur. Cerialis veterem Romani nominis gloriam, antiquas recentesque victorias: "ut perfidum, ignavum, victum hostem in aeternum exciderent, ultione magis quam proelio, opus esse. Pauciores nuper cum pluribus certasse: attamen fusos Germanos, quod roboris fuerit. Superesse, qui fugam animis, qui vulnera tergo ferant." Proprios inde stimulos legionibus admovebat, domitores Britanniae quartadecimanos appellans; principem Galbam sextae legionis auctoritate factum; illa primum acie secundanos nova signa novamque aquilam dicaturos. Hinc praevectus ad Germanicum exercitum manus tendebat, ut suam ripam, sua castra sanguine hostium reciperarent. Alacrior omnium clamor, quis vel ex longa pace proelii cupido vel fessis bello pacis amor, praemiaque et quies in posterum sperabantur.

XVII. Nec Civilis silentem struxit aciem, locum pugnae testem virtutis ciens: "stare Germanos Batavosque super vestigia gloriae, cineres ossaque legionum calcantes; quocumque oculos Romanus intenderet, captivitatem cladem-que et dira omnia obversari. Ne terrerentur vario Treverici proelii eventu: suam illic victoriam Germanis obstitisse, dum, omissis telis, praeda manus impediunt: sed cuncta mox prospera et hosti contraria evenisse. Quae provideri astu ducis oportuerit, provisa, campos madentes et ipsis gnaros, paludes hostibus noxias. Rhenum et Germaniae deos in aspectu; quorum numine capesserent pugnam, conjugum, parentum, patriae memores: illum diem aut gloriosissimum inter majores aut ignominiosum apud posteros fore." Ubi sono armorum tripudiisque (ita illis mos) approbata sunt dicta, saxis glandibusque et ceteris missilibus proelium incipitur, neque nostro milite paludem ingrediente, et Germanis, ut elicerent, lacessentibus.

XVIII. Absumptis quae jaciuntur, et ardescente pugna, procursum ab hoste infestius: immensis corporibus et praelongis hastis fluitantem labantemque militem eminus fodiebant; simul e mole, quam eductam in Rhenum retulimus, Bructerorum cuneus tranatavit: turbata ibi res, et pellebatur sociarum cohortium acies, cum legiones pugnam excipiunt, suppressaque hostium ferocia proelium aequatur. Inter quae perfuga Batavus adiit Cerialem, terga hostium promittens, si extremo paludis eques mitteretur: solidum illa, et Gugernos, quibus custodia obvenisset, parum intentos. Duae alae cum perfuga missae incauto hosti circumfunduntur; quod ubi clamore cognitum, legiones a fronte incubuere, pulsique Germani Rhenum fuga petebant. Debellatum eo die foret, si Romana classis sequi maturasset. Ne eques quidem institit, repente fusis imbribus et propinqua nocte.

XIX. Postera die quartadecima legio in superiorem provinciam Gallo Annio missa; Cerialis exercitum decima ex Hispania legio supplevit. Civili Chaucorum auxilia venere. Non tamen ausus oppidum Batavorum armis tueri, raptis quae ferri poterant, ceteris injecto igni, in insulam concessit, gnarus deese naves efficiendo ponti, neque exercitum Romanum aliter transmissurum: quin et diruit molem a Druso Germanico factam, Rhenumque prono alveo in Galliam ruentem, disjectis quae morabantur, effudit. Sic velut abacto amne, tenuis alveus insulam inter Germanos-que continentium terrarum speciem fecerat. Transiere Rhenum Tutor quoque et Classicus et centum tredecim Treverorum senatores; in quis fuit Alpinus Montanus, quem a Primo Antonio missum in Gallias superius memoravimus. Comitabatur eum frater D. Alpinus. Simul ceteri miseratione ac donis auxilia concibant inter gentes periculorum avidas.

XX. Tantumque belli superfuit, ut praesidia cohortium, alarum, legionum uno die Civilis quadripartito invaserit, decimam legionem Arenaci, secundam Batavoduri, et Grinnes Vadamque cohortium alarumque castra, ita divisis copiis, ut ipse et Verax, sorore ejus genitus, Classicusque ac Tutor suam quisque manum traherent; nec omnia patrandi fiducia, sed multa ausis aliqua in parte fortunam affore. Simul Cerialem neque satis cautum, et pluribus nuntiis huc illuc cursantem posse medio intercipi. Quibus obvenerant castra decumanorum, oppugnationem legionis arduam rati, egressum militem et caedendis materiis operatum turbavere, occiso praefecto castrorum et quinque primoribus centurionum paucisque militibus. Ceteri se munimentis defendere. Et interim Germanorum manus Batavoduri rumpere inchoatum pontem nitebantur. Ambiguum proelium nox diremit.

XXI. Plus discriminis apud Grinnes Vadamque. Vadam Civilis, Grinnes Classicus oppugnabant: nec sisti poterant, interfecto fortissimo quoque; in quis Briganticus praefectus alae ceciderat, quem fidum Romanis et Civili avunculo infensum diximus. Sed ubi Cerialis cum delecta equitum manu subvenit, versa fortuna praecipites Germani in amnem aguntur. Civilis, dum fugientes retentat, agnitus petitusque telis, relicto equo tranatavit: idem Veracis effugium. Tutorem Classicumque appulsae lintres vexere. Ne tum quidem Romana classis pugnae affuit, ut jussum erat: sed obstitit formido et remiges per alia militiae munia dispersi. Sane Cerialis parum temporis ad exsequenda imperia dabat, subitus consiliis sed eventu clarus. Aderat fortuna etiam ubi artes defuissent: hinc ipsi exercituique minor cura disciplinae. Et paucos post dies, quanquam periculum captivitatis evasisset, infamiam non vitavit.

XXII. Profectus Novesium Bonnamque ad visenda castra, quae hiematuris legionibus erigebantur, navibus remeabat, disjecto agmine, incuriosis vigiliis. Animadversum id Germanis; et insidias composuere. Electa nox atra nubibus, et prono amne rapti, nullo prohibente, vallum ineunt. Prima caedes astu adjuta: incisis tabernaculorum funibus, suismet tentoriis coopertos trucidabant. Aliud agmen turbare classem, injicere vincla, trahere puppes. Utque ad fallendum silentio, ita coepta caede, quo plus terroris adderent, cuncta clamoribus miscebant. Romani vulneribus exciti quaerunt arma, ruunt per vias, pauci ornatu militari, plerique circum brachia torta veste et strictis mucronibus. Dux semisomnus ac prope intectus errore hostium servatur. Namque praetoriam navem vexillo insignem, illic ducem rati, abripiunt. Cerialis alibi noctem egerat, ut plerique credidere, ob stuprum Claudiae Sacratae mulieris Ubiae. Vigiles flagitium suum ducis dedecore excusabant, tanquam jussi silere, ne quietem ejus turbarent: ita intermisso signo et vocibus se quoque in somnum lapsos. Multa luce revecti hostes, captivis navibus, praetoriam triremem flumine Luppia donum Veledae traxere.

XXIII. Civilem cupido incessit navalem aciem ostentandi. Complet, quod biremium, quaeque simplici ordine agebantur. Adjecta ingens lintrium vis, tricenos quadragenosque ferentium: armamenta Liburnicis solita: et simul captae lintres sagulis versicoloribus haud indecore pro velis juvabantur. Spatium velut aequoris electum, quo Mosae fluminis os amnem Rhenum Oceano affundit. Causa instruendae classis, super insitam genti vanitatem, ut eo terrore commeatus Gallia adventantes interciperentur. Cerialis miraculo magis quam metu direxit classem numero imparem, usu remigum, gubernatorum arte, navium magnitudine potiorem. His flumen secundum; illi vento agebantur. Sic praevecti, tentato levium telorum jactu, dirimuntur. Civilis nihil ultra ausus trans Rhenum concessit. Cerialis insulam Batavorum hostiliter populatus, agros villasque

Civilis intactos nota arte ducum sinebat, cum interim flexu autumni et crebris per hiemem imbribus, superfusus amnis palustrem humilemque insulam in faciem stagni opplevit: nec classis aut commeatus aderant, castraque in plano sita vi fluminis differebantur.

XXIV. Potuisse tunc opprimi legiones, et voluisse Germanos, sed dolo a se flexos imputavit Civilis. Neque abhorret vero, quando paucis post diebus deditio insecuta est. Nam Cerialis per occultos nuntios Batavis pacem, Civili veniam ostentans, Veledam propinquosque monebat fortunam belli, tot cladibus adversam, opportuno erga populum Romanum merito mutare. "Caesos Treveros, receptos Ubios, ereptam Batavis patriam; neque aliud Civilis amicitia paratum quam vulnera, fugas, luctus: exsulem eum et extorrem recipientibus oneri; et satis peccavisse, quod totiens Rhenum transcenderint: si quid ultra moliantur, inde injuriam et culpam, hinc ultionem et deos fore."

XXV. Miscebantur minis promissa. Et, concussa Transrhenanorum fide, inter Batavos quoque sermones orti: "non prorogandam ultra ruinam: nec posse ab una natione totius orbis servitium depelli. Quid profectum caede et incendiis legionum, nisi ut plures validioresque accirentur? Si Vespasiano bellum navaverint, Vespasianum rerum potiri; sin populum Romanum armis vocent, quotam partem generis humani Batavos esse? respicerent Raetos Noricosque et ceterorum onera sociorum: sibi non tributa, sed virtutem et viros indici: proximum id libertati; et si dominorum electio sit, honestius principes Romanorum quam Germanorum feminas tolerari." Haec vulgus. Proceres atrociora: "Civilis rabie semet in arma trusos: illum domesticis malis excidium gentis opposuisse: tunc infensos Batavis deos, cum obsiderentur legiones, interficerentur legati, bellum uni necessarium, ferale ipsis sumeretur. Ventum ad extrema, ni resipiscere incipiant, et noxii capitis poena poenitentiam fateantur."

XXVI. Non fefellit Civilem ea inclinatio, et praevenire statuit, super taedium malorum, etiam spe vitae, quae plerumque magnos animos infringit. Petito colloquio, scinditur Nabaliae fluminis pons; in cujus abrupta progressi duces, et Civilis ita coepit: "Si apud Vitellii legatum defenderer, neque facto meo venia, neque dictis fides debebatur. Cuncta inter nos inimica, hostilia, ab illo coepta, a me aucta erant. Erga Vespasianum vetus mihi observantia; et cum privatus esset, amici vocabamur. Hoc Primo Antonio notum, cujus epistolis ad bellum actus sum, ne Germanicae legiones et Gallica juventus Alpes transcenderent. Quae Antonius epistolis, Hordeonius Flaccus praesens monebat, arma in Germania movi, quae Mucianus in Syria, Aponius in Moesia, Flavianus in Pannonia." * * *

NOTES.

NOTES

PRELIMINARY REMARKS.

The historical writings of Tacitus, as we now have them, consist of fragments of two distinct yet not wholly disconnected works, "the Histories" and "the Annals." The former originally comprised fourteen Books, and embraced a period of twenty-eight years, from the second consulship of Galba to the death of Domitian, of which only the first four Books and a small portion of the fifth remain, containing the history of only about one year. The latter consisted, when entire, of sixteen Books, and extended over the space of fifty-four years, from the death of Augustus to the close of the reign of Nero; but four entire Books are lost, from the seventh to the tenth inclusive, and the fifth, eleventh and sixteenth are preserved only in part. The Histories had for their subject the civil wars of Galba, Otho and Vitellius, and the re-establishment of the imperial power under the Flavian family (His. 1, 1). The subject of the Annals was the gradual corruption of morals and manners, and the consequent subversion, *pari passu*, of liberty and law under the Julian and Claudian families, till at length on the death of Nero the military gained the entire ascendency over the civil power, and the commander of the strongest army seated himself on the throne in place of the undisputed hereditary succession of the Cæsars (Ann. 1, 1. 2). If the author's life had been spared, it was his purpose to have written the Life of Augustus, as a sort of introduction to his Annals (Ann. 3, 24), and the Biographies of Nerva and Trajan as a sequel to the Histories (His. 1, 1). But he did not live to execute either of these cherished plans.

In the MSS. and early editions, the Annals and the Histories appear as one work, and the extant Books of both, counted in the same numerical series, bear the common inscription, sometimes of *Annales* or *Historiæ* or *Acta Diurnalia*, and sometimes only of the historian's name. They must have been so arranged and numbered, in some copies at least, as early as the age of Jerome (A. D. 331-420), for in his Commentary on Zachariah, 3, 14, that Christian Father refers to Cornelius Tacitus, as having written the Lives of the Cæsars from the death of Augustus to that of Domitian in thirty Books,* thus comprehending the two works in one, which covers the whole period of time belonging to both. But Tertullian, who flourished in the latter part of

* It is chiefly from this number of Jerome, that we are able to make out the number of Books comprised in the original Histories. The Annals are known to have consisted of sixteen Books, which subtracted from thirty eave fourteen for the Histories.

the second century, cites the speculations of Tacitus touching the origin of the Jews, as occurring in the fifth Book of his Histories, and thus shows, that in his day the works were distinct and the Books were numbered separately, as they are now. And that they were intended to form separate treatises, is demonstrated by incontrovertible evidence external and internal. This is sufficiently apparent from the introductory chapters, which are manifestly prefatory in both, and which mark the limits of the two works, as entirely distinct, though chronologically successive. Tacitus expressly calls his Annals by that name (Ann. 3, 65; 4, 32; 13, 31), while he refers to the Books in which he had composed the history of Domitian, as a separate work (Ann. 11, 11). And Pliny refers with equal explicitness to the latter under the title of Historiae (Ep. 7, 33). There remains therefore no reasonable doubt, that Tacitus himself gave to his two great historical compositions the same distinguishing titles which they now bear. To the question, what distinction he thus intended to mark, different answers are returned by critics and defended with much learning and zeal.

One difference seems to lie on the face of the works, as chronologically related to the author. The Histories cover the age of the historian himself; the Annals embrace a period anterior to his appearance on the stage of active life. And this distinction accords with the original and proper signification of the word history, which in Greek implies personal inspection or investigation, and which many Greek and Latin authors carefully distinguish, not only from tradition and hearsay, but also from the authentic records of bygone days.*

Another obvious difference is suggested by the literal meaning of the word annals, which was originally applied to the yearly register of passing events kept by the Pontiffs (Annales Maximi or Annales Pontificum), and then to the chronicles of Pictor, Piso and others who were the pioneers of the Roman historians, and which in its etymology implies a strictly chronological arrangement of the events that occur year by year. This also accords with the actual difference between the Histories and the Annals of Tacitus. The Histories narrate events according to their geographical connection, or the relation of cause and effect, or they adopt, on rhetorical principles, the arrangement which will produce the most picturesque and striking impression. The Annals, on the contrary, follow strictly the chronological order, relating under each year the events of that year and no other (cf. Ann. 4, 71: *suum quæque in annum referre*), or if they depart from it, they offer such an apology, that the exception demonstrates the rule (cf. Ann. 12, 40).

Other distinctions have been drawn between annals and history, such as these—that annals are a simple detail of facts, while history further investigates the causes and consequences of the events which are recorded; and that, while annals are written in a straight-forward, inartificial and unadorned style, history is composed in a more studied, ornate and flowing diction, descriptions of countries and battles are interwoven with the narrative, fictitious speeches are introduced, such as the speaker or actor might have made whether he did make them or not—in short, history is a work of art, as much so as an oration,

---

* Cf. Plutarch: *ἱστορῆσαι τὴν πόλιν*; Palæphatus: *γέγραφα ταῦτα, οὐχ οἷα ἦν λεγόμενα, ἀλλ' αὐτὸς ἐπελθὼν καὶ ἱστορήσας*; Ælian: *οὐκ ἀκοὴν λέγειν ἀλλὰ ἱστορίαν*; and Verrius Flaccus, as cited by Aulus Gellius, Noct. Att. 5, 18.

or an epic or tragic poem. Both these views have received the sanction of great names (cf. Aulus Gellius, Noct. Att. 5, 18), and the latter is stamped with the authority of Cicero (De Orat. 2, 12; De Legg. 1, 2).* These distinctions doubtless hold in reference to the Roman annals in general as compared with the standard histories, whether of the Romans or the Greeks. But they apply only in a limited measure to the Histories and the Annals of Tacitus. His Annals, not less than his Histories, are marked by profound reflection on the causes and consequences of events—by deep research and penetration into the principles of human action. And though the rigidity of structure, which belongs to the very nature of annals, and the extreme conciseness, which was demanded by so vast and comprehensive a subject as that of the Annals of Tacitus, are unfavorable to ornament, yet they abound in animated descriptions, eloquent speeches and pictures of human conduct and character drawn with great power and true to the life. The Histories have been compared to an epic poem, of which the subject is the fortunes of the Flavian family, and all the collateral topics, that are treated, come in by way of prelude or episode. There is still more of the dramatic element both in the Histories and the Annals, which may well be considered as a prolonged tragedy or a series of tragedies, whether we contemplate the more than tragic horror of most of the incidents, or the consummate art and power with which they are combined and described.

The Annals are the author's last work. That they were written subsequently to the Histories, we learn from the incidental testimony of the historian himself (Ann. 11, 11). That they were not completed till near the close of the reign of Trajan, is inferred from Ann. 2, 61, where he speaks of the boundaries of the Roman empire as already extended to the Red Sea, which was done by Trajan in the 17th year of his reign, A. U. C. 868; A. D. 115. The Histories also were given to the world in the same reign—in what year is not known, though Trajan had already reigned so long and performed such achievements, that Tacitus had formed a purpose of writing his history together with that of the deified Nerva (His. 1, 1). The Biography of Agricola was issued near the commencement of the same reign, as a sort of forerunner to the Histories, of which it contains an announcement (cf. A. 1, and Notes, ibid.), and which must therefore have been already contemplated, if not actually begun at that time. The Treatise on Germania was published not far from the same time with the Agricola (cf. Special Introductions to those Treatises). The Dialogue de Claris Oratoribus, if the work of Tacitus, was doubtless a much earlier production. Accordingly it betrays the author's youth in its playful humor and lively emotions, in its exuberance of fancy and the excessive ornaments of its style. Moreover the other works, though all composed in the full strength of manhood, exhibit a gradual progress in maturity of thought, in depth of feeling and in gravity of expression, in the same order in which they were written. The German Manners and the Life of Agricola abound in poetic fancies, lively conceits and artificial periods, which he afterwards learned, or chose, in a measure to retrench. Besides the one of these was professedly a panegyric, and the other in spirit, though not in form and main design, a satire

* See on this general subject Smith's Dict. of Gr. and Rom. Antiq. under *Annals*; also the Prolegomena of Walther, Ruperti and others.

The former would of course admit of rhetorical flourishes, and the latter of playful sallies and sarcastic cuts, which would not become the dignity of history. In his Annals, the author has pruned off still more of the redundances of his youthful genius, though even there he shows that exuberance was natural to him, that he was endowed by nature with the rhetorical and the poetical element in little less profusion than the historical and the philosophical. It would be instructive and interesting to trace the progressive development of this master-mind, and observe the striking changes, and yet the unequivocal signs of identity, which mark the history of his intellectual life from the commencement of the Dialogue on Oratory to the conclusion of the Annals of the Roman empire. It would be difficult to find a more remarkable example of diversity in unity.

The Histories are on the whole perhaps the most perfect production of the author's genius, as they are also the most finished work of art—the work on which he laid out his strength, and on which he relied to transmit his name to posterity. They were written when he was nearer fifty than forty, in the very prime of life, free alike from the foibles of youth and the feebleness of age, possessing at once imagination in undecayed vigor and judgment in matured perfection. His resources had been accumulating, as the result of long-observation and reflection. His feelings were chastened and yet deepened by suffering, and his eloquence was matured by study and practice. He had spoken at the bar and ruled in the senate. He had served, perhaps commanded in the Roman armies. Whether he writes of civil or military affairs, he seems alike at home, alike familiar with the arts of war and those of peace. At the same time, he was master of all the lore of books, and all the wisdom of the schools. The principles of philosophy were almost the atmosphere he breathed. Like Cicero, he combined the high-toned morals of the Stoics with the more liberal doctrines of the Academy, though he held to the Stoical doctrine of fate and, sometimes, particularly in his Annals, gives utterance to religious opinions bordering on those of the Skeptics and Epicureans (Ann. 3, 18; 6, 22; 16, 33). The Poets, as well as the Philosophers, were his masters. Virgil especially charmed his ear and touched his heart. The image of the Mantuan Bard is stamped on every page, particularly of the historian's earlier writings.* Nor are there wanting reflections of the style and sense and spirit of Horace. He had also caught the living images and winged words of him, "who wandered erst from Scio's rocky isle." The constitution and laws of his country were familiar to him as household words. The civil and political history of Greece and Rome had been his study and his meditation. He was a republican by choice, but by necessity, as he thought, an imperialist (His. 1, 1. 16. et passim). He admired the former state of things at Rome, but he submitted to the present. He loved liberty, but he loved order more, and hoped to find it only under the throne of the Cæsars. He has canonized many a martyr of freedom and damned many a tyrant to eternal infamy. But he abhorred ultraism, censured would-be martyrs and bade the admirers of the impracticable learn from the example of such men as Agricola, that there

---

* Cf. Essay on the style of Tacitus, p. 24. See also Notes passim, particularly those on Agricola and Germania, which often point to examples of Virgilian diction.

may be great and good subjects under such sovereigns as Domitian (A. 42) With the public history and the private life of the period of which he writes, he was of course well acquainted, for it was the period of his own active exertions, and most of the events, which he records, either passed under his own eye at Rome, or were brought directly to his ears as they transpired in the more distant provinces. When with a mind so disciplined and so furnished as we have thus faintly described—in the full maturity of his powers and with the utmost richness of materials—he sat down to write the history of an empire which involved the history of the world—fit author on fit theme—he could say, as Æneas did in beginning the story of his country's fall and his own wanderings:

Quaeque ipse miserrima vidi,
Et quorum magna pars fui.

The parallel holds in more than one particular. The events of Tacitus' history, like those of Æneas' tale, are chiefly sad, disastrous to his country, disgraceful to her rulers and of melancholy interest to himself; he had seen them with his own eyes, mourned over them in his inmost heart,* suffered them in his own person and in the person of his dearest friends; he had acted a somewhat conspicuous part as a senator and an orator in those troublous times; partly by his own prudence, partly by some miracle, as it were, which we cannot understand,† he escaped unharmed and with unsullied reputation; and no sooner has he weathered the storm and found a safe and tranquil harbor, than he gives to the world an able and faithful history of the scenes through which he and his country had passed. Well might the historian felicitate himself on the propitious change in his fortunes and the happiness of that age, in which it was once more lawful for men to think what they pleased and to speak what they thought (His. 1, 1)! Nor have his readers less reason for self-congratulation, that this happy age was preceded by evil times, when the historian experienced bitter trials and when the state passed from the extreme of bloody anarchy to the extreme of despotic cruelty; for to these experiences we are doubtless indebted for much of his wisdom and eloquence; and though other and inferior minds may have been crushed beneath the oppressive sway of Domitian, and almost lost the power of memory together with the gift of speech (A. 2, 3), this long period of forced silence only condensed the swelling thoughts of Tacitus, compressed his glowing emotions and added intensity to the burning words, in which he spoke, as soon as the pressure was removed.‡

Much has been written on the credibility of Tacitus, as a historian. His veracity has been impugned. Provoked by the severity with which he treats the Jews and the Christians, some of the early Fathers pronounce him the most eloquent of liars.§ He has been charged with exaggerating the virtues and the victories of the Romans on the one hand, and on the other, their vices

* Witness the pathetic conclusion of the Biography of Agricola (A. 39–46).

† Witness the absence of Tacitus for four years near the close of Domitian's reign (A. 45), when his tyranny was at its height (A. 44).

‡ Cf. Plin. Ep. 4, 20: Dolori sublimitatem et magnificentiam ingenium, ingenio vim et amaritudinem dolor addit.

§ Cf. Tertullian. Apol. adv. gent. ch. 16: *loquacissimum mendacium.*

and defeats. He has been censured by some as a Machiavelli or a Latin Xenophon, the author of a Tiberiopædia, whose design was to teach the art of tyranny in its perfection, and by others as the rigid, malignant and misanthropic censor of princes and of mankind. Such contradictory accusations may well be left to balance and neutralize each other. No candid reader of Tacitus can regard him as indiscriminate either in censure or in praise.* His worst characters are not without their virtues, and his best show their imperfections. He denies, or holds in suspense, crimes which the public voice unanimously charged upon the emperors, whom he treats with the most unsparing severity, and has not made either Tiberius or Domitian so bad, as some other writers of his age. In short, he manifestly intends to hold the balance of truth and justice with an even hand, and few have better carried out the intention neither to "extenuate aught or set down aught in malice." It is to be regretted that Tacitus did not take the pains to inform himself better touching the Jews and Christians. But in this he erred only in common with all the great writers and great men of his country (cf. Notes, 5, 2), who were born and bred to despise and ridicule the Jews—to hate and persecute the Christians.† Moreover, notwithstanding his national prejudices, Tacitus expressly attests the innocence of the Christians, who suffered under Nero, and commiserates their sufferings (Ann. 15, 44), while he narrates not a little that is true and commendable of the Jews, and ascribes to the whole nation a creed touching the divine nature more pure, more true, more sublime than had ever entered the thoughts of any but the wisest sages of Greece and Rome (His. 5, 5). Tacitus undertakes to write both his Histories and his Annals for the express reason, that no impartial history of that period had been written (His. 1, 1; Ann. 1, 1), but between the parasites and the bitter enemies of those in power, truth and posterity had been forgotten. For himself, he professes perfect candor. From Galba, Otho, and Vitellius, he had received neither benefits nor injuries. The Flavian dynasty was now extinct, and, though they had all conferred honors upon him, he could speak of them all, unswayed by favor and unawed by fear. And nobly, it must be confessed, nobly does he redeem his pledge. He does not spare the besetting sin of the soldier-like and truly imperial Vespasian (His. 1, 50; 2, 5; 2, 84, et al.). He does not conceal the youthful vices of Titus, "delight of the human race" (His. 2, 2; 5, 11). Still less does he withhold his severest animadversions from Domitian (Agr. 39–43), while he bears grateful testimony to the honors which he had received from him (Ann. 2, 11; His. 1, 1). He had abundant means of knowing the facts which he recorded. Besides the extensive personal knowledge of which we have already spoken, he had access to the public archives, to the records of the senate, to the Acta Diurna or public journals of the city, to the Imperial Commentaries, to the histories of Cæsar, Livy, Pliny the Elder, and many other documents or writers, whom he consults as authorities, but whose statements he thoroughly sifts and seldom if ever adopts on mere trust.‡ In short, an air of sincerity, truthfulness and earnestness, a lofty appreciation of the purity and dignity of

* Compare on this subject the Life of Tacitus in Agricola and Germania, p. 11.

† In like manner, Roman writers have all done injustice to the Carthaginians, who might well repeat the complaint of the lions, that the men wrote the history.

‡ See a collection of such authorities and examples of the caution with which he weighs them in Ruperti's Prolegomena, also in Boetticher and others.

history and a sacred scrupulousness to say nothing that shall in the least defile or degrade it, pervades all his historical writings. While therefore we admire them as works of art and study them as lessons of moral and political wisdom, we may also confide in them (with the necessary allowance for human infirmity) as fountains of historical truth, none the less true, but all the more convincing and persuasive, for the skill with which he arranges his facts, the earnestness with which he inculcates his sentiments and the eloquence with which they are adorned.

A glance at the principal events and leading characteristics of the period, which Tacitus has selected for his Histories, may afford an opportunity to observe somewhat more particularly the writer's manner of treating his subject, and may at the same time prepare the reader to follow him through the details with more intelligent interest. The first three emperors reigned in all only about a year and a half, and all came to a violent death. Galba filled the throne only seven months, Otho less than four, and Vitellius about eight, after which little and brief authority, they fell victims successively to the same policy by which they had in succession risen to power—they took the sword, and they perished by the sword. Till the dethronement of Nero, the emperors had been nominally appointed by the senate, though the power of the senate really extended no farther than to confirm the nomination of their successors by those who held the supreme authority. Now this nominal power was wrested from the senate and usurped by the troops. And since one army had as good a right as another to the honor and advantage of placing their commander on the throne, there was a general rush for the city and the spoils from every quarter of the empire. Galba was the first to disclose the secret that an emperor could be nominated in a province as well as in the city, and invested with the imperial purple by the military instead of the civil power (His. 1, 4); and he was the first victim to this disastrous change in the policy of the state. He was named emperor by the legions under his own command in Spain, and when their courage began to falter in so novel and hazardous an enterprise, he was raised to the throne by the Prætorian Guards in the capital, who were inflamed with resentment at the atrocious designs of Nero and further stimulated by the hope of an immense reward which had been promised them in the name, though without the authority, of Galba. But when they saw that the donative was withheld, which could not be bestowed without a renewal of all the extortion and proscription of Nero himself—nay more, when they discovered that Galba would not indulge them in all the licentiousness and crime in which they had revelled under Nero, the same Prætorian Guards hurled him headlong from the throne, severed his head from his body, and left him weltering in his gore. Galba had some apology for his ambition. His only alternative was the scaffold or the throne. Happy for the reputation of the old soldier—happy, we might almost say, for the old soldier himself, if he had chosen the former. "He seemed too great for a private man while he was one," says Tacitus, in one of those pregnant sentences of his which so often body forth a whole character, 'as the cope of heaven is imaged in a dewdrop,' "and the suffrages of all mankind would have pronounced him worthy of empire, had he never made the experiment—*omnium consensu capax imperii, nisi imperasset*" (His. 1, 49).

Otho had no such excuse. He had been the first to espouse the cause of

Galba, and he expected to hold the first place in his counsels. But he was disappointed, and he deserved to be. The old man nominated the virtuous Piso for his successor. And Otho avenged himself in the blood both of the aged emperor and his adopted son. It was Otho's highest recommendation to the degenerate Romans, that he resembled the corrupt and licentious Nero. The rabble, who now ruled at Rome, called him Nero Otho, and were ready at all hazards to follow his fortunes and to defend his throne. Galba had fallen without a blow struck in his behalf. The cause of Otho was maintained with much spirit by followers like himself. In three considerable, though indecisive, battles, his troops were victorious over those of Vitellius. In a fourth, they were defeated with great slaughter. Still they never wavered in their attachment or faltered in hope. They urged and entreated him to summon all his forces and renew the fight. But he had resolved not to survive a defeat. He plunged a dagger to his own heart, and terminated the life of a debauchee by the death, as it seemed to the Romans, of a philosopher—as it appears to us, of a fool. The fortitude and composure, not without real or affected generosity, which he displayed in his last hours, endeared him still more to his soldiers, and many of them made a voluntary sacrifice of their lives at his funeral pile (His. 2, 49).

Vitellius succeeded without further opposition to the vacant throne. But like his predecessors, he had scarcely marched his armies into Rome, before he was obliged to march them out again to meet a formidable competitor. Too lazy and stupid from the first to command his own forces, he had now become yet more drunken and debauched. Leaving all his military operations to those generals whose energies alone had raised him to the throne, he gave himself up to gluttony and intoxication. But one of them, Fabius Valens, had become enervated and diseased by revelling. The other, Alienus Cæcina, marches out at the head of the troops, but proves treacherous and makes an unsuccessful attempt to bring his soldiers over to the allegiance of Vespasian. On the other side, the main force had not yet arrived at the field of action from Syria. Vespasian himself and Mucianus, his commander-in-chief, were still in the East. But the ardor and energy, the conduct and prowess of Antonius Primus, who happened to be located near the northern border of Italy, amply compensated for deficiency of numbers, as the loyalty and zeal of Vitellius' army went far to counterbalance the treachery of one, and the absence of the other, of their generals. And the conflict which ensued, was protracted, furious and sanguinary almost beyond a parallel even in the bloody annals of civil commotion. Fired not only by party passion, but by a thirst for booty and blood, the followers of Antonius fought like tigers, nay like demons, through two days and the intervening night, defeated three successive armies in three successive battles with little intermission, carried two distinct and strongly fortified walls of defence about Cremona, plundered the treasures of that city, took captive its inhabitants and burned its edifices, public and private, sacred and profane, to the ground. The cause of Vitellius was now ruined. He himself had long given up in despair. In the language of Tacitus, he would have forgotten that he had ever been emperor, had not his followers persisted in calling him such. They adhered to him with firmness and fought for him with desperation, when nothing remained to him but Rome and the dregs of its population. And in this last hopeless struggle the Capitol was burned and scenes of horror enacted, little less tragical than the sacking and conflagration of Cremona. Vitellius stalked about his palace, like a ghost, affrighted by its emptiness and desolation, till weary of wandering he took refuge under the bed in the porter's lodge. But he was soon discovered, dragged forth from his *pudenda latebra*, loaded with insults and put to death by repeated wounds. In narrating these scenes of strife and horror, the historian catches the inspiration of his subject, and, like the great epic poet of the Greeks, gathering strength and fervor as he proceeds, rises into unwonted and almost unrivalled eloquence. Witness the series of battles and assaults, which end in the destruction of Cremona by the troops of Antonius. No book of fiction was ever more full of marvellous incidents; and no novelist or poet ever portrayed them in livelier or stronger colors. The whole passage (His. 3, 15–34) can hardly be matched for power in historical description, while for laying bare the workings of the human heart in excited and struggling masses of men, it stands, we believe, without a parallel in history.* See first, how he exposes to the reader's view the secret motives and sordid passions of Antonius' men, when, after having defeated two distinct bodies of the enemy's troops, they came in sight of Cremona (ch. 19). Again, look at the lively and moving picture of the calamities and crimes incident to civil war, which is grouped around the lifeless body of a father slain unintentionally by the hand of his own son in the 25th chapter. It is a truly Homeric episode, full of tenderness and pathos, relieving for the moment and yet enhancing in the end the impression made by protracted scenes of indiscriminate slaughter on the battle-field. Scarcely less Homeric is the description in the 28th chapter of a renewed and desperate assault upon the city, ending in those frightfully energetic words: *integri cum sauciis, semineces cum exspirantibus volvuntur, varia pereuntium forma et omni imagine mortium.* Then to crown the whole, read the description of the sacking and conflagration of Cremona (ch. 33), where "in so vast a multitude, as different in their language as their manners, composed of Roman citizens, allies and foreign auxiliaries, all the fell passions of mankind were crowded together—where nothing was unlawful, nothing sacred, since each soldier had his peculiar notions of right and wrong, and what one scrupled another dared to execute." Yet even this is exceeded by the mingled scorn and pity, bitter sarcasm and tragic pathos, with which our author sets forth the shameful and shocking scenes of burning and pillage, of rioting and revelling, which attended the close of Vitellius' disgraceful reign, in the midst of the imperial city, when "whatever the libidinous passions can inspire in the hour of peace was mixed with all the slaughter and horrors of war—the whole city seemed to be inflamed with frantic rage, and at the same time intoxicated with bacchanalian pleasures—a dreadful carnage was a *spectacle* added to the public *games*—the populace *enjoyed* the havoc; they exulted in the midst of devastation, and without any regard for either of the contending parties, triumphed over the miseries of their country." Those, who cannot read the whole of the Histories, should by all means read the third Book. It is almost the only extant portion of the work, in which his descriptive powers have full scope. It well illustrates also the author's characteristic skill in the delineation of character. Take, for instance, Vitellius, and, while

* Vid. Life of Tacitus, p. 10.

from stage to stage of his history you are made acquainted with his conduct, notice the lights and shades by which his character is brought out more and more distinctly, till at length he stands before you, not so much a perfect picture, as a living man, with not only his entire life but his whole heart naked and open to your view. And do not fail to observe, how much of character is developed often by a word or phrase. For example, in the last quotation: "a dreadful carnage was a *spectacle* added to the public *games*—the populace *enjoyed* the havoc," what an emphasis of meaning there is in the words in italics, and how they probe to the bottom the depths of corruption in the hearts of the city populace! So when Vitellius was met and escorted into the city by an infamous band of pimps, of charioteers, of players and buffoons, "all well known and dear to him by their utility in vicious pleasures," Tacitus adds: "such were the disgraceful connections of the emperor, and he *enjoyed them without a blush*."* How much of Vitellius is exhibited in this single stroke! This is characteristic of Tacitus. No writer ever conveyed so much knowledge of things, and especially so much insight into men, in so few words. In like manner, the finishing stroke in the portraiture of Galba (already mentioned, p. 237) brings out as it were the whole nature of the man with all its greatness and all its infirmities. So of Galba's adopted son, for whom he inspires us with a just reverence and love in half a dozen words: *quasi imperare posset, quam vellet*. In like manner, he shows us the exact condition of the Roman state in half a sentence, when he makes Galba say to Piso: "you are called to rule over men who cannot endure either entire slavery or entire freedom—*qui nec totam servitutem pati possunt, nec totam libertatem*."

With the accession of Vespasian to the throne, closes what is now extant of the Histories of Tacitus. We have not even the record of his arrival at Rome. While he was proceeding deliberately through Egypt towards the imperial city, and busying himself partly in providing for the necessities of the city, partly in discovering his own future fortunes by the aid of the Egyptian priests (His. 4, 81-86), Mucianus exercised all the prerogatives of sovereignty in his stead; Domitian aspiring to usurp power which did not belong to him, and failing in the attempt, gave himself up to dissipation; and Titus, succeeding to his father's command in Judæa, was advancing to the siege of Jerusalem (5, 1-13). Such is the posture of affairs, when the Histories are brought suddenly to a close. The Jewish War is left incomplete. The fragment which remains is invested with peculiar interest to the Christian, because it is so intimately connected at so many points with his holy religion. Tacitus entertained many and violent prejudices against the Jews. It is not strange that he did. They were too exclusive in their politics and too intolerant in their religion, to be appreciated by any foreigners, most of all by the liberal and polytheistic or free-thinking Romans. Accordingly they received little mercy from Roman officers, and little sympathy from Roman scholars. Despised as superstitious by the learned, and hated as seditious by the great at Rome, it is not surprising that Tacitus should denounce them as a sordid, gloomy, unsocial and misanthropic race. It is in fact but the very treatment they have practically met with from the rest of the world ever since. Not only prejudice against their singularities, but

* It will be seen that *this* example is near the close of the 2d Book (ch. 87).

ignorance of their real character and history, as a distinct and isolated people, led him into many errors. Yet some rays of truth may be seen gleaming through nearly all his mistakes, and confirmation of the sacred records may be gathered from all his apparent contradictions. The true account of their origin is given in connection with several other traditionary tales (5, 2). The Exodus from Egypt, the journey through the wilderness, some of the miracles even of Moses are recorded (chap. 3), not as they were, but as they would come to the ears and appear to the eye of a foreigner and a Roman. The rite of circumcision, the abstinence from swine's flesh, the use of unleavened bread, the observance of the seventh day as the sabbath, and the seventh year as a year of rest—all these peculiar features of the Jewish religion are recognised, and referred to their supposed and sometimes their real cause (chap. 4, 5). Our author declares their belief in the immortality of the soul and a future state of rewards and punishments, and gives a sublime description of the one God of the Jews, and the purely spiritual worship which they paid to him (chap. 5), so unlike at once to the polytheism and the idolatry of all the rest of the world, and so unaccountable, except on the supposition of special divine teaching. His geography and topography of the country lead him to notice (chap. 7) the plains of Sodom, the tradition touching the destruction of the once wealthy and populous cities of the plain by fire from heaven, and the utter emptiness of the fruits of the earth in that region, so strikingly alluded to in sacred writ, and hence proverbial to this day, as the apples of Sodom and the clusters of Gomorrah.

But the Christian will regard with the greatest interest the confirmation which Tacitus unwittingly furnishes to the fulfilment of prophecy, in the expected coming of the Messiah and in the circumstances attending the destruction of Jerusalem. He informs us that the Jews cherished a lively expectation, which was derived from prophecies contained in their sacred books, and which all their calamities could not extinguish, that at this very juncture the power of the East would prevail over the nations, and a race of men would go forth from Judæa to extend their dominion over the rest of the world (5, 13). Moreover he gives a graphic picture of those signs and wonders in the heavens above and in the earth beneath, which our Lord predicted should attend the destruction of Jerusalem and its holy temple (Matt. 24, Luke 21)—swords gleaming in the air, embattled armies performing their evolutions in mid-heaven, strange sights and supernatural sounds in the temple, and the like portentous omens of the approaching ruin of the city. It is not easy to say, whether Christianity is more illustrated and confirmed by this historical notice of the general expectation of a mighty king and conqueror from the East, which had been nourished by ancient prophecies of the Messiah, or by the accompanying record of the fulfilment of predictions uttered by the Messiah himself touching the fate of his native land and its devoted metropolis. It cannot but be regarded as truly remarkable, that two celebrated historians, the one a Jew and the other a pagan, both of whom rejected Christianity and hated the Christians, should have recorded so many facts which go directly to authenticate and illustrate the Christian religion.

With the preparations for the siege of Jerusalem the thread of our Histories is broken off. The description of the assault and capture is lost. Only the preface, as it were, is preserved—the principal part of the work, the history of the Flavian Family, has perished. We cannot but mourn over the irreparable loss.* We feel, that we cannot afford to lose any thing from so instructive and attractive a pen. Especially after wading through the chaotic and bloody scenes in the reigns of Galba, Otho and Vitellius, we are unwilling to be denied the pleasure of reaching solid ground once more, and looking on the peace, order and comparative happiness that spring up under the auspices of Vespasian and Titus, as they are painted by the same master hand. The siege of Jerusalem, with its amazing feats of valor and its more amazing scenes of calamity and suffering—what a subject for the pen of Tacitus! We would fain follow the beautiful and brilliant Titus through the glories of his military triumphs to the brighter glories of his virtuous and happy, but too short reign. And we burn to see the fratricide and tyrant Domitian writhing under the just vengeance of the prince at once of historians and of satirists.

Such a period—with such characteristics as our author briefly and vividly sketches in his introductory chapters (1, 2. 3)—is not the most favorable to the excitement of historical interest. The leading characters are for the most part both weak and wicked, at once odious and contemptible. And it is with extreme difficulty, that a history is made to sustain an interest, which does not attach to its leading characters. Still, as Tacitus intimates in the beginning of his third chapter, such a period is the very theatre for the display of the most heroic virtues in those private individuals who have the moral courage to breast the current of the times. And we shall find our historian's pages adorned with biographical episodes and tributes of honor to many such noble souls.

The great Halicarnassian critic would condemn Tacitus, as he did Thucydides (Dion. Halicarn. Epis. ad Cn. Pomp.), for selecting a period so fruitful in disasters and disgrace to his country. But the historian is not responsible for the events which he records, any more than the messenger is for the news he bears. He may be a truer patriot at heart and may render more important services to his country, who sets up beacons at the points of her danger, than he who rears monuments on the fields of her triumph. The patriotism of Herodotus and Livy exults in the glory of their country; that of Thucydides and Tacitus mourns over her shame. The muse of the former is full of buoyancy and hope—she advances in the animated though stately air of a triumphal march, and ever and anon is heard singing pæans. The muse of the latter is grave, thoughtful and melancholy—she sits absorbed in sorrowful meditations and gloomy forebodings—or she moves at a sad and solemn pace and utters "more hearselike harmonies than carols"—or now again, like another Cassandra, she starts up, as in a fit of prophetic phrensy, and pours forth wild and piercing cries of alarm. These warnings came too late for the salvation of their countrymen: but the histories of the commotions and civil wars, which these great masters of their art have composed, are more instructive to posterity, than all the foreign conquests and victories, whether of Greece or Rome, which Herodotus and Livy have recorded. Inferior writers

* The Medicean MS., which alone contains the first six books of the Annals, was found in a monastery of Westphalia, as late as the sixteenth century. Would that we might still cherish the hope of recovering more or less of the lost decade of the Histories.

may thrill their readers with a spirited detail of Roman triumphs; but it required the genius of Tacitus to fathom the depths of Roman degeneracy and corruption, and bring forth instruction and even delight from the shortlived and ill-starred reigns of Galba, Otho and Vitellius. Tacitus himself felt deeply the degradation of his country, and the consequent inferiority of his subject tc the more brilliant and imposing events of Rome's earlier history. "No man will think of comparing these Annals," he says (Ann. 4, 32), and the same remarks are applicable for the most part to the *subject-matter* of the Histories —"No man will think of comparing these Annals with the historians of the old republic. Those writers had for their subject wars of the greatest magnitude, cities taken by storm, kings overthrown and led into captivity; and when from those scenes of splendor, they turned their attention to domestic occurrences, they still had an ample field before them; they had dissensions between the consuls and the tribunes; they had agrarian laws, the price of corn, and the plebeian and patrician orders inflamed with mutual animosity. Those were objects that filled the imagination of the reader and gave free scope to the genius of the writer. The work in which I am engaged, lies in a narrow compass; the labor is great, and glory there is none. A long and settled calm, scarce lifted to a tempest; wars no sooner begun than ended; a gloomy scene at home, and a prince without ambition or even a wish to enlarge the boundaries of the empire: these are the scanty materials that lie before me. And yet materials like these are not to be undervalued; though slight in appearance they still merit attention, since they are often the secret spring of the most important events."

Such is the modest estimate which Tacitus put upon his subject and his treatment of it. Posterity has judged more favorably of both. Lord Monboddo,* the severest of all the critics on his style, has well said: "His subject, I think, is grand and noble. It is the history of the fall of a great people, greater than any that ever existed in arms and government, and in the extent and duration of their empire. Other nations may have been more glorious in their rise or in their prosperity, but *none was ever so great in its fall;* and the period of Tacitus's history affords more extraordinary examples of virtues and vices, sometimes mixed in the same man, than are to be found anywhere else in the history of mankind. For the Romans are great in their vices as well as their virtues, and in both almost exceed humanity. In treating this subject, Tacitus never falls below the dignity of it, nor is it, I think, without reason, that he speaks himself of the gravity of his work. He shows himself everywhere a lover of virtue and of virtuous men, and expresses in the strongest terms his detestation of cruelty and every kind of vice. He speaks with admiration of philosophy and its teachers, knowing that it was philosophy that had produced those extraordinary characters which he celebrates, such as that of Thrasea Pætus and Helvidius Priscus."

"In reading his Annals and Histories,† where we see the baffled and ineffectual efforts by which individuals worthy of a better age strive to bear up against the cruelty of tyrants and the general corruption of morals, and at

---

* Vid. citation in the Life of Tacitus, p. 9.

† This paragraph is translated from Boetticher's Prolegomena to his **Lexicon Taciteum.**

the same time perceive that there may be great and good men even under bad princes—where we behold fortune, fate and the gods themselves, in a manner wonderful and never sufficiently understood by mortals, direct the changeful vicissitudes of human life, contemplating in the Annals the singular fatality that followed the Julian family to its utter extinction, in the Histories the convulsive energies that were put forth to re-establish a vacant and tottering sovereignty, do we not seem to ourselves to be reading some tragedy of Æschylus, Sophocles or Euripides—does not the sorrowful image of Niobe stand before our eyes—are we not stricken through with a kind of horror, as if at the sight of Laocoon struggling in vain to disengage himself from the crushing folds of the serpent? Truly worthy of Tacitus, worthy also of the majesty of the Roman empire, is the design to explain with becoming wisdom and diligence by what fate or fortune or succession of events '*jampridem praevalentis populi vires se ipsae confecerint*'*—what vices of the people or their rulers provoked the justice and the vengeance of the immortal gods, and precipitated the fall of so vast an empire! So, like a second Scipio, we behold Tacitus sitting not now on the ruins of Carthage, but on the soil of Rome herself, already tottering to her fall, and predicting with gushing tears the destruction of his country, and that not in words of elaborate and far-fetched study, but in such obvious and to him spontaneous forms of pathetic eloquence, as to present to the very eye the perfect image of that country convulsed and trembling on the verge of dissolution."

Livy is the only Latin historian who can at all contest the palm with Tacitus. We need not attempt accurately to adjust the balance between them. It were no discredit to either of them to acknowledge the other to be his superior. Indeed their merits are so unlike that they can hardly be brought into direct comparison. There is no ratio between unlike quantities in mathematics; neither can the terms greater and less be predicated in the gross of distinguished but diverse authors. In style, the pre-eminence must be conceded to Livy. His amazing versatility, his infinite variety always pleases and never tires. Unpretending narrative and elaborate description, concise annals and discursive eloquence, succeed and relieve each other with an inexhaustible fertility—as the critics term it, with a *lactea ubertas*, both in thought and language, "always fresh, always sweet, always pure." Tacitus, it must be confessed, is wanting in variety and simplicity.† He does indeed vary his construction and forms of expression infinitely, as Boetticher and Doederlein‡ have well illustrated. But he wants that higher variety and beauty of historical composition, which results from telling a "fine story finely" and "a plain story plainly." He is always treading the stage in his high-heeled tragic buskins, and declaiming to a crowded amphitheatre at the top of his voice. Doubtless his best passages far surpass any thing that can be found in Livy, for coloring and effect. But Livy on the whole is a more pleasing book to the reader, and a safer model for the young writer. Livy is the author to be read continuously; Tacitus, to be taken up at intervals. The one furnishes a wholesome variety of food for the mind; the other serves his reader too exclusively with strong meats and stimulating condiments.

---

* Vid. Preface of Livy. † Vid. Life of Tacitus, p. 9.
‡ Vid. Essay on the Style of Tacitus.

For the sentiments and moral lessons which they convey, the meed of praise must be divided between them. Both are fruitful in instruction. The moral taste of both is pure and elevated. And yet they are very unlike: Livy's sentiments appear to be drawn from books; Tacitus' are obviously the fruit of his own observation and meditation. Tacitus is original and just in his reflections; Livy is varied and beautiful. Livy is the more genial spirit; Tacitus, the more sagacious and profound.

In the delineation of character, Tacitus is greatly the superior. The characters of Livy want individuality. We are not made acquainted with their distinctive features. Still less do we see the very bottom of their hearts. In Tacitus every character stands out distinctly from the surrounding mass, wears his own face, and acts out his own peculiar motives and impulses. His heroes are as diverse as we know heroes are in nature; and in the whole series of tyrants and monsters, whose history he writes, the reader would no more confound their characters, than a contemporary and familiar acquaintance would have mistaken their persons. Tacitus draws characters as Shakspeare does in his dramas; Livy paints them too much like the sophist in his declamations. Livy places before us the statues of heroes and gods; Tacitus conducts us through the crowd of living men.

Livy is little more than an orator and scholar; Tacitus is also a statesman and philosopher. Livy is the greater and better writer; Tacitus the greater and better man. We admire the former: the latter we reverence. Either might inspire us with love; but Tacitus only can impress us with awe and fear. Tacitus selects his incidents with chief regard to their truth and intrinsic value; Livy, with a constant, not to say single, eye to their literary beauty and picturesque effect. Livy is wholly a Roman. To him, the Roman empire is the world. If he loved liberty, it was only Roman liberty. If he extolled the military skill and prowess of Hannibal, it was only that he might exalt Rome herself, with her armies and commanders, to so much the higher glory, as their conquerors. Tacitus is a man and reverences the manly virtues, wherever he finds them. The best speech he ever wrote is put into the mouth of a free and noble Briton. He half prefers the simple virtues of the barbarous but free and independent Germans, to the splendid vices of the cultivated but degenerate Romans. To him Arminius is none the less a hero for being a German; and he complains (Ann. 2, 88), that the Greeks embellished nothing but their own story, while the Romans, absorbed in the veneration of antiquity, did injustice alike to all contemporary achievements. In a word, Livy was born to compose the history of the rise and glory of the Roman empire; Tacitus of its decline and fall. It was the vocation of Livy to compose a great prose epic in honor of his country. It was the mission of Tacitus to write a magnificent historical tragedy for the instruction and warning of mankind.

BOOK I.

Page

31 Chap. I.—It has been conjectured, that this Book, as it now stands is *acephalous*, the words *Populi Romani res enarraturo*, or the like, having been lost from the beginning. But the subject of the work is sufficiently brought out in what follows, and was doubtless prefixed also in a title. *Initium* is pred. after *erunt*.

Line **1. Ser. Galba ... consules** = annus, in quo fuere consules, i. e., the 1st of January, A. U. C. 822, A. D. 69. The *reign* of Galba had commenced in June of the previous year. As Galba was put to death on the 15th of January (cf. chap. 27, seq.), only half a month of his reign is *directly* embraced within the compass of the Histories of our author, who having for his main object to write the history of the Flavian dynasty, commences with the beginning of the civil year, which was nearly coincident with those commotions in the armies of Germany, which led to the assumption of imperial power by Vespasian. The chronology may be seen at a glance in the table on p. 26.—*Consules* means colleagues (those who go together, *con* and *sul*, root of *salio*) or joint presidents of the Roman republic. Cf. Smith's Dict. of Gr. and Rom. Ant., sub voc., and Niebuhr's History, as there cited.

2. Post conditam urbem. Observe the concrete form of expression. The Latin language is very deficient in such abstract words as *foundation, constitution*, &c. The people were marked for *action*, and their language deals in *facts*.—*Octingentos*. Al. septingentos. But the number of years here mentioned, must cover the whole period from the founding of the city to the second consulship of Galba (otherwise the clause, though beginning with *nam*, assigns no reason for commencing the history with that date), and that was 820 years (in round numbers, exactly 822). Cf. 4, 58: *per octingentos viginti annos*. Septingentos is a *conjectural* reading.

3. Dum .... memorabantur. *So long as the history of the Roman people* (i. e. the republic) *was being written*. For after the battle of Actium, it was *res Caesarum*, not *res populi Romani*, that were recorded. So in Ann. 1, 1, *Pop. Rom. prospera vel adversa* is opposed to *temporibus Augusti*. Cf. also G. 37, *Pop. Rom.* vs. *Caesari*.

4. Eloquentia ac libertate. These words limit *retulerunt*.—*Libertate: postquam*. Al. *libertate. Postquam*. But *postquam ... bellatum*, etc., is antithetic to *dum res*, etc. (the antithetic particle *sed* being omitted. Cf. Essay on the Style of T, p. 13); and therefore should not stand at the beginning of a new sentence. The whole passage thus read and pointed may be summed up as follows:— 1. He states the date with which he intends to begin his history, viz. the second consulship of Galba = A. U. C. 822. 2. He gives the reason why he does not commence at an earlier date, viz. that many have written the history of the whole period prior to that date. 3. But he subdivides that whole period into two parts, viz. the Republic and the Empire, the former of which has been treated with as much freedom as eloquence, but not so the latter. Tacitus may have already had in mind the plan, which he afterwards executed (in his Annals), of writing also the history of the latter period, because, though written by many, it had been treated without ability or impartiality. Cf. Ann. 1, 1, a passage which sheds much light on this. Page 31

5. Actium. Where Augustus defeated Antony and established himself in the sole possession of the supreme power.—*Potentiam.* Al. potestatem. Potestas est ἐξουσία, potentia δύναμις. So Wr.,* who argues, that not *omnis potestas,* all lawful authority, but *omnis potentia,* all power and *might* was concentred in one man, that he might preserve peace. For this distinction, cf. His. 1, 13; Ann. 3, 69; Cic. pro domo, 30. See also Or. in loc.

6. Conferri = brought *together, united in one man.*

7. Simul veritas, etc. See a similar passage in Dion, 53, 19.

8. Ut alienae. *Since it was the property of another,* i. e. the emperor, not the people. So Wr., Or. and Död. *As if it were a foreign state;* for they had no more to do with it, and therefore cared and knew no more about it, than if it were a foreign republic. So Ernesti. A truly republican sentiment, according to either interpretation. The former is preferable.—*Rursus.* Cf. note A. 29.

9. Infensos. Sc. *principibus.*

10. Ambitionem. Lit., *going about* to solicit favor. Hence *flattery* to the great, explained below by *adulationi.*

11. Adverseris. So the MSS., Wr. and Död. Al. averseris, Rup., Or. But without good authority or reason. For the accusative after *adversor,* cf. Gr. 224, R. 4; Z. 386. Also Freund's Lexicon, sub voce. For the subjunctive here, cf. Gr. 260, II.; Z. 523. *You may easily withstand* or *resist.* Wr. refers it to the writer: *You (any writer) may easily withstand the temptation to flatter.* This is more pertinent to the connection. But *scriptoris* suggests rather the idea, that the *reader* can easily withstand, etc. So Rup. and most others.—*Pronis auribus,* literally, ears inclining or bending forward = *willing ears.*

---

* The Authorities most frequently cited in these Notes, are cited by their initial letters or syllables, thus: Wr. = Walther, Rup. = Ruperti; Or. = Orelli; Död. = Döderlein, &c Gr stands for Andrews and Stoddard's Grammar; Z. for Zumpt's do

Page 31 **12. Malignitati** = *obtrectatio et livor* above.

15. A Domitiano. Ann. 11, 11. Cf. Life of Tacitus, pp. 5–6.

16. Abnuerim. For the mode and tense, cf. Gr. 260, R. 4 Z. 527.—*Nec .... odio* = neque amore quisquam neque odio. Enallage. Cf. Germania and Agricola passim.

17. Quod si. *And if.* From the tendency to connect sentences by relatives arose the use of *quod* before certain conjunctions, particularly *si*, merely as a copulative. Cf. Z. 807; also Freund's Lexicon, sub voce.—***Principatum***, properly civil government, and hence appropriate to the peaceful reign of Nerva.—***Imperium***, properly military command, and hence equally appropriate to the more warlike Trajan. Cf. Död. in loc.

18. Divi Nervae. This implies that Nerva was already dead, before this paragraph was written and before the history was published. How much labor may have been bestowed on the work previous to the composition of the introduction, we cannot tell. Cf. note, A. 3, *memoriam*, etc.; also Preliminary Remarks, p. 233.

19. Uberiorem. The reign of Trajan was fruitful in great events, in civil and military life, as well as in literature. Cf. Life of T., pp. 6–7.—***Securiorem.*** Wr. renders, *more pleasing*, lit. more free from care (*se-cura*), anxiety, pain. But it may be rendered here, as usual, *more safe, more secure*, not indeed from personal danger, for the historian had nothing to fear for his person in treating either subject, but from the danger of giving offence to bad men or their descendants, of whom there were not so many to be spoken of in the Life of Trajan, as in that for instance of Domitian. Or. and Död. refer to the *periculosae plenum opus aleae* of Horace (Od. 2, 1, 6), as a parallel passage.—***Rara felicitate*** is not abl. abs. but abl. of cause or accompanying circumstance = enjoying as I do that felicity of the times which is so seldom enjoyed, when, etc. Observe that *ubi*, properly an adverb of place, is here and often used as an adverb of time

Ch. II.—This chapter and the next present an outline of the leading events and prominent features of the history. The language is concise as a table of contents, yet it abounds in the disjecta membra poetae.

22. Opus. Lit. a *work.* But the epithets *opimum*, etc., apply only to the *period* to which the work relates. Render: *I propose to write the history of a period*, etc.

23. Ipsa pace instead of *in ipsa pace*, for the sake of conciseness. Cf. Essay on Style of Tacitus, p. 12.—***Saevum.*** Or. and Död. read *saevom*, after the Medicean MS. The MSS. of Tacitus exhibit not a few examples of the old orthography of the Latin language. But they do not preserve consistency. Boetticher thinks that Tacitus resorted to different modes of writing words for the sake of variety. Cf. Prolegomena to his Lexicon Taciteum.

Page

24. Principes. Galba, Otho, Vitellius and Domitian, all of whom came to a violent death.—*Trina,* poetice for *tria.* Cf. Gr. 120, 4. The three civil wars here referred to are those between Otho and Vitellius, between Vitellius and Vespasian, and of L. Antonius against Domitian, on which last vid. Sueton. Dom. 6, Dio Cass. 67, 11. Cf. Or. and Död. in loc. Ruperti would reckon among them that of Otho and Galba, which however hardly amounted to a *war.* Cf. note, chap. 50: *saevae pacis.* 31

25. Permixta, sc. externa cum civilibus, both being carried on at the same time, as, for instance, the war with the Jews by Titus, and with the Gauls and Germans under Civilis by Cerialis, in connection with the civil war between Vitellius and Vespasian.

27. Missa. *Dismissed, neglected* = omissa, the simple for the compound. Cf. Essay, p. 10.

28. Mutuis, i. e. alternis, acceptis et illatis. Rup.—*Dacus.* Cf. note, G. 1; also ibid. *Sarmatae.* Of the wars with the Sarmatians, cf. 1, 79; 3, 5. 24; 4, 54; with the Dacians, cf. His. 3, 46; 4, 54; A. 41. Of the wars with the Suevi we have no other account. The Suevi here meant, says Lipsius, are not the tribe more commonly so called, that dwelt in Germany (Germ. 38, seqq.), but another tribe located beyond the Danube by the Sarmatae, and hence often associated with them, e. g. Ann. 12, 29; Sueton. Dom. 6; Dion Cass. 67, 5. Cf. Or. in loc.

29. Falsi .... ludibrio. *The farce, or game, of the pretended Nero.* T. informs us (His. 2, 8), that inasmuch as there were various reports touching the end of Nero, many pretended and believed that he was still alive. Hence he was personated by several impostors, as late even as the reigns of Titus and Domitian. Cf. Suet. Nero, 57.

30. Jam vero. Cf. note, G. 14.—*Cladibus.* *Calamities,* not slaughters, as just above.

31. Haustae .... urbes. Herculaneum and Pompeii; destroyed by an eruption from Mount Vesuvius in the second year of the reign of Titus, A. U. C. 832. Cf. Pliny's account of the catastrophe and the death of his uncle (Pliny the Elder), in a letter to Tacitus. Epis. 6, 16, 20; and Plut. de Ser. Num. Vind., 42.

32. Ora. Abl. of place without a prep. Wr. connects it with the following clause, and refers the clause to the desolation of the Campanian country by the fires of Vesuvius.—*Incendiis.* Besides that in which the capitol was burnt (3, 71–2), there was another and more dreadful conflagration of the city (Rome) in the reign of Titus, A. U. 833. Cf. Dio. 66, 24. Or.

1. Pollutae caerimoniae, sc. incestis Vestalium. Suet. Dom. 32
8, 22; Plin. Epp. 4, 11, 6.—*Magna adulteria,* i. e. principum virorum. So magnae domus, amicitiae, inimicitiae, etc. = houses, &c., *of the great.*

2. Plenum .... mare. *The sea full of exiles* (*exsiliis* for *exsu-*

Page
32 *libus*) on their way to, or in possession of, those barren rocky islands (*scopuli*), particularly in the Aegean, to which they were banished, and which were afterwards stained with their blood (*infecti caedibus*).

3. Omissi . . . . honores. *Honors, whether declined or accepted.* Dion informs us, that Domitian put Herennius Senecio to death, because he asked no office after having held the quaestorship. Dion, 67, 13.

5. Delatorum. A post-Augustan word, found especially in Tacitus and Suetonius. Cf. Freund's Lexicon, sub voce. The *thing* taking a new form under the emperors, gave rise to a new *word.*

6. Procurationes. The *office of procurator*, or collector of the imperial revenues, afforded ample opportunity for amassing wealth.

7. Interiorem potentiam. *Power at court*, such as was exercised by the freedmen and other creatures of Nero and his successors. —*Agerent verterent.* Compare agere ferre (= Greek ἄγειν καὶ φέρειν) used by Livy to express ravaging with fire and sword; literally, *leading* off the captives and *bearing* off the spoil. The use of *verterent* in this formula is peculiar to Tacitus, if not also to this passage, to which it is peculiarly appropriate, since to the idea of *rapine* expressed by *agere*, it superadds that of *violence and cruelty.* The phrase may be translated (though inadequately), *plundered and destroyed.*—*Odio et terrore. Amid hatred and terror.* Wr. *By reason of the hatred they cherished and the terror they inspired.* Rup.

CH. III.—**11. Prodiderit.** For the subj., cf. Gr. 262, R. 1, Z. 532. For the *perf.* subj. instead of the *imperf.*, cf. note, chap. 24: *dederit.*

14. Supremae . . . . necessitates. *Illustrious men were reduced to the last necessities*, such as precede and threaten death or render it unavoidable, but not (as many suppose) death itself; for they are here distinguished from *exitus*, and, as used elsewhere, the words denote, not death, but the prior necessity, whether imposed by popular indignation, as in the case of Tigellinus, 1, 72, or the loss of imperial favor through calumny, as in the case of Messalina, Ann. 11, 37 (where pl. as here: *supremis necessitatibus*), or the direct command of the emperor, as in the case of Seneca, Ann. 15, 61. Cf. also *necessitate*, His. 4, 11. This clause was probably meant to state only a general fact, introductory to the virtues specified in the next two clauses; though, as Wr. suggests, the bare *existence* of such necessities, when they might have been escaped by obsequious compliance with the tyrant's wishes, was no small proof of virtue. The word *necessitas* properly denotes, that which is *unavoidable* (*ne-cessum*, from *cedo.* Cf. Freund, sub v.).

15. Ipsa . . . . tolerata. This clause has occasioned commentators so much perplexity, that some of the ablest of them, e. g. Ritter

Page 32

and Ruperti, propose to expunge it at once, as a mere gloss. And they have good reason to be dissatisfied with most of the comments, for, almost without exception, they either sacrifice the force of *ipsa*, or make *necessitas* something quite different from *necessitates*, which, though maintained by Död., is not borne out by the usage of Tacitus, and can hardly be supposed in such a juxtaposition as this. But does not the following interpretation avoid both these objections and meet all the demands of the passage? *Illustrious men were reduced to the last necessities* (involving or threatening death); *the necessity itself was endured with fortitude, and the deaths* (which ensued) *were equal to the glorious deaths of the ancients. Ipsa* thus marks the antith. between *necessitas* and *exitus;* while *necessitas* is distinguished from *exitus* and identified with *necessitates*, as it manifestly should be.

16. Exitus. See the word used in like manner in the pl of the *deaths* of Cassius and the Brutuses, Ann. 1, 10, which passage may also illustrate the *kind* of *exitus* that is meant here.

17. Prodigia = prodicia. The letters G and C were originally identical; hence the resemblance in form. See Zumpt's Lat. Gr. So negotium = nec-otium, &c.

20. Justis = *luculentis, manifestis.* Rup. *Magis justis indiciis. More conclusive proofs.*—Before *esse ultionem*, the antith particle *sed* is understood. It is often omitted by T.

Ch. IV.—**22. Repetendum.** *Necessary to go back*, and describe the existing state of things *prior* to the date of the history, i. e. from the death of Nero to the second consulship of Galba, cf. note 1: *Galba .... consules.* For a fuller account of this interval between the close of the Annals and the beginning of the Histories, the reader may consult Suetonius' Nero and Galba; Plutarch's Galba; Dio. 63, 22, seqq. &c.—*Componam.* For the mode and tense, cf. Gr. 263, 3; Z. 576.

25. Quid .... fuerit. Subj. Cf. Gr. 265; Z. 552.

26. Fortuiti. *Inexpectati* et haud promissi, non in se, sed quoad nos. So Brotier. But Tacitus probably means more than this, viz. that *particular events* (as for instance the rise of Otho and Vitellius, rather than any other ambitious men of their day, and the victory of the latter rather than the former), are the result of accident or fortune; but at the same time there were general principles or causes at work, which rendered certain and necessary these or *similar* events: and these causes, even more than those fortuitous events, it is the province of history to investigate. Cf. Wr. in loc. The wonderful sagacity and wisdom with which Tacitus has accomplished this end, constitute a chief merit of his history.

27. Ut ita. *Though .... yet.* Z. 726.

30. Legiones ducesque, sc. in the provinces, *foris* being under-

Page

32 stood in antithesis to *in urbe.—Evulgato .... arcano,* etc. Cf. Liv 26, 2, where the author says, it was deemed by the senate a bad precedent, imperatores legi ab exercitibus, et sollenne auspicatorum comitiorum in castra et provincias, procul ab legibus magistratibusque, ad militarem temeritatem transferri. The emperors might well cherish the same as an established principle. Galba was the first instance of an emperor appointed by the army in one of the provinces, and he was the first victim to the secret thus *evulgato. Evulgato arcano* here denotes the principal *cause* of this excitement.

33. Absentem. Galba was in Spain.

34. Integra = *sound, uncorrupt,* literally untouched (*in* and *tango*).

35. In spem erecti, sc. of a better government, and one under which the families of the condemned and exiled might recover their lost fortunes. *Erecti* is predicate of *pars,* as well as of *clientes. Pars populi,* etc. is antithetic to *plebs sordida,* etc.

36. Sueta for *assueta.* T. prefers the simple to the compound Cf. note, *missa,* 2, supra.

33 Ch. V.—**2. Arte et impulsu.** *Ars* spectat ad dolum quo decipiebantur, *impulsus* ad vim, qua per exemplum ceterorum subito trahebantur. Wr. Roth makes it hendiadys.

5. Praeventam gratiam. They apprehended that the legions that appointed Galba would have the *first place in his favor.*

7. Scelere. *Criminal ambition,* explained by *imperium sibi molientis.—Insuper.* Still further, i. e. besides offering them largesses in the name of Galba, *furthermore plotting to secure the empire for himself.*

8. Praefecti. Commander of the Prætorian Guards (*miles urbanus*).

10. Conscientia, sc. male facti acerrimus stimulus ad odium et res novas moliendas. Ernesti.

11. Senium. Galba was 73 years old at his accession to the throne. Plut. Galba, 8; cf. ch. 49, infra.—*Avaritiam Galbae.* Cf. Suet. Galb. 12.

15. Amarent. Subj. Cf. Gr. 262, R. 1; Z. 531.

16. Verebantur = reverebantur. Simple for compound.—*Accessit .... vox. Add to this the language of Galba,* sc. in reply to the soldiers' demand for the promised largess. Cf. 3, 57: *accessit .... omen.—Pro republica. As it regards the republic.* Most writers would have used the dat. to correspond with *ipsi* in the antithesis. But Tacitus prefers variety.

17. Legi. *Chosen,* hence the very name *legio,* also *delectus.* Cf. Varro de Ling. Lat. lib. 4.—*Nec .... erant.* The language of Galba was unsuited to the times, *nothing else corresponded with it.* The clause is placed by some at the beginning of the next section, and made to express the *inconsistency* between the language of Galba and his conduct, or that of his prime ministers, Vinius and Laco. But that is not so well. 33

CH. VI.—**19. Invalidum senem.** Galba. Cf. Note, 5: *senium.* Concerning *Vinius* and *Laco*, see also Plut. Galb. 7. 10. 12; Suet. Galb. 14; Vitel. 7.

20. Odio flagitiorum, sc. of Vinius transferred to Galba. So also *contemptu inertiae*, primarily of Laco, secondarily of his master.

21. Galbae iter, sc. from Hither Spain, where he had been governor eight years.

22. Cingonio Varrone. Cf. Ann. 14, 45; His. 1, 37; Plut. Galb. 14–16: where we learn that Varro had composed an oration for Nymphidius to address to the Prætorian Guards as a means of securing his elevation to the imperial dignity.

23. Petronio Turpiliano. Ann. 14, 29. 39; 15, 72; A. 16; Plut. Galb. 14–17.

24. Inauditi, in the judicial sense, is post-Augustan. Cf. Boetticher's Lex. Tac. and Freund's Lex. sub v.

25. Tanquam innocentes. Though guilty, yet being put to death without a trial, as innocent persons are by tyrants, they had the sympathies of men, *as if innocent.—Trucidatis .... militum.* Seven thousand marines slain, while pertinaciously demanding admission to the regular service. Cf. His. 1, 87; Suet. Galb. 12; Dio. 64, 3. Dion says the survivors were subsequently decimated. Cf. 37, infra.

29. Numeri = cohortes, manipuli, manus militum. Rup. Cf. A. 18; His. 1, 87; 2, 69. This use of the word is post-Augustan. Cf. Freund. It points to the *composition* and *arrangement* of a body of troops, as it were, *by numbers.*

31. Claustra Caspiarum. A narrow pass in Mt. Taurus near the Caspian sea, called *claustra*, as *closing* or securing the entrance to the country. It was the only passage from the northern part of Western Asia into Persia and India.

32. Vindicis. Cf. note, chap. 8, infra.

CH. VII.—**35. Congruerat.** Casu aliquo *acciderat*, ut *simul* nuntiarentur. Rup.—*Clodii Macri.* An avaricious and cruel governor of Numidia, who on the death of Nero aspired to independence and undertook to cut off supplies of corn from Rome. Cf. His. 1, 11. 37. 73; 2, 97; 4, 49; also Suet. and Plut. Galb.—*Fonteii Capitonis.* Legate (military governor) of Lower Germany. His character is described, His. 1, 52; the cause of his death, 3, 62.

36. Nuntiarentur. For the subj. cf. Gr. 262, R. 3.—*Haud dubie.* Antith. to *fuere qui crederent* below. The whole sentence is made up of studied antitheses.

37. Procurator. Cf. A. 4, and note, 2: *procurationes.*

38. Coeptaret. Subj. Cf. Gr. 263, 5; Z. 577

Page 34 **1. Legati legionum.** Commanders of a single legion each. Cf. *legatus praetorius*, A. 7. Capito was *legatus consularis.* The word *legatus* = any commissioned officer.

2. Juberentur. Subj. Cf. Gr. 263, 3 ; Z. 576.—*Crederent.* Cf Gr. 264, 6 ; Z. 561.—*Ut .... ita. Though .... yet.*

3. Avaritia, etc. Cf. 1, 52.

5. Postquam .... nequiverint. The subj. in a dependent clause of the oratio obliqua. Cf. Gr. 266, 2 ; Z. 603. *Postquam* is usually followed by the indic., unless the subj. is required by some specific reason. For the perf. here, cf. Gr. 258, R. 3 ; Z. 504, Note. The use of the perf. instead of the pluperf. after *postquam,* makes the connection of time closer ; postquam should accordingly be rendered *as soon as.* Arnold's Pr. Intr. 514.

6. Compositum ultro. *Fabricated gratuitously.* Cf. 3, 62.—*Mobilitate .... scrutaretur.* Sub. *utrum,* or *incertum an* before *mobilitate.* T. leaves it uncertain which of the two was the true reason.

7. Quoquo modo acta, is the obj. of *comprobasse : he approved them in whatever way done,* i. e. *whether right or wrong.*

8. Sinistre occurs in Boetticher's list of words belonging to the poets of an earlier age.

9. Facta is subj. nom. to *premunt,* which has for its obj. *eum* understood.

10. Jam = *jam vero, moreover. Now over and above* all that had been previously done, the freedmen of Galba brought every thing into the market. Cf. Död. in loc.—*Afferebant,* according to Wr., is appropriate to those *recently arrived* at power : they *came to* Rome and the palace *bringing* these things in their hands, as it were, and offering them for sale to the highest bidder.—*Cuncta,* e. g. munera, magistratus, jura, judicia. Ernesti.—*Liberti,* sc. Galba's. *Icelus* is specified, § 13, and others are named by Suet. Galb. 14. 15.

11. Subitis avidae. *Eager to avail themselves of their unexpected good fortune ;* highly characteristic of slaves. Död. makes *subitis* abl. of cause.—*Et tanquam,* etc. And *on account of Galba's advanced age, making haste* to enrich themselves, while he afforded them the opportunity.

12. Novae, sc. *Galba's,* in contrast with which understand *veteris,* sc. Nero's.—*Non aeque excusata. Not viewed with equal indulgence.* Quid ita ? Quia Nero ortu et natalibus Princeps, quia juvenis, quia in plebem etiam gratiosus. Itaque plusculum ei licere volebant et ignoscebant. Non sic in Galba qui electus, qui senex erat, ideoque prudens esse debebat, qui denique parcus, tristis et perpaucis grata. Lipsius.

14. Imperatores. *Imperator* was originally the commander of a Roman army. Of course there might be several at a time in the republic. But at length the title was appropriated by the emperor, and thus acquired a new meaning. Cf. Ann. 3, 74. So *princeps* was

at this time applied only to the emperor and his sons. The names 34
and forms of the republic were carefully preserved under the emperors. —*Forma* = beauty of person.—*Decore* = grace of manners. Wr.

CH. VIII.—**16. Tanquam .... multitudine.** *As might be expected in so great a multitude*, sc. that there would be those taking such views of the character of Galba and his friends, as have been described in the previous chapter. This explanation of Or. seems preferable to that of Wr., who interprets the clause thus: so far as it is possible to describe the state of mind in so great and so various a population.

17. E provinciis. *Of the provinces.* Antith. to *Romae.* Notice the emphatic position of both at the beginning of the sentence.

18. Cluvius Rufus. Cf. Ann. 13, 20; His. 1, 76; 2, 65; 4, 43; Suet. Nero, 21. He was a writer of history. Plin. Epis. 9, 19.—*Pacis artibus.* Roth, Rhenanus and others supply *expertus*, as involved by zeugma in *inexpertus*, and render: *experienced in the arts of peace.* See the principle of this interpretation, Essay on the Style of Tacitus, p. 15. But Wr., Rup. and Ernesti make *artibus* abl. of quality (Gr. 211, R. 6), and render: *endowed with the virtues of peace.* Cf. Ann. 1, 19: *Blaesus multa arte dicendi.*

19. Vindicis. Julius Vindex, proprætor of Gaul under Nero, himself descended from a line of Gallic kings though his father was a Roman senator, stirred up the Gauls to revolt from Nero and incited Galba to claim the throne. He was defeated and slain by Verginius, 1, 51; 4, 57. His memory would of course lead the Gauls to favor Galba.

20. Dono .... civitatis. Claudius had conferred the gift of Roman citizenship upon the Gallic chiefs (Ann. 11, 23), but Galba gave it to all who had taken part with Vindex. The wise distribution of this favor was a source of great power and influence to the Roman state, cum id rarum, nec nisi virtuti pretium esset. Of its value to individuals we have a striking example in the life of Paul, Acts, 16, 37. 38; 22, 25–29. Cf. also Cic. in Ver. 5, 62: *civis Romanus sum.* It was now conferred with too unsparing a hand, and finally lost its value when Caracalla bestowed it indiscriminately on all the inhabitants of the Roman empire.

25. Recentis victoriae, sc. over Vindex under the command of Verginius. This victory was of course a source of pride; but it was also a ground of vexation (*irati*), anxiety (*solliciti*) and fear (*metu*), because though a real service to the state for which they deserved reward, it was rendered to Nero, and was more likely to be punished than rewarded by Galba.

26. Metu, tanquam, etc. = *fear, that they would be regarded as having favored another party*, sc. than Galba's, viz. that of **Verginius.** For the subj., cf. Gr. 263, 2; Z. 572.

Page

34 **27. Verginius.** Verginius Rufus, legate of Upper Germany under Nero. See some account of his character and the relation of T to him in the Life of Tacitus. Also Plin. Ep. 2, 1; 5, 3; 6, 10; and Plut. Galb.—*Imperare* = esse imperator.

28. Voluisset. Subj. to denote an indirect question. Cf. Gr. 265; Z. 552. Plup. to correspond with the imperf., on which it depends, and which is used in all this account of the state of things prior to the date of the history.—*Dubium,* sc. *erat: it was a matter of uncertainty* TO THE MEN OF THAT DAY, *whether he wished to be emperor.* So *conveniebat: it was agreed by all authorities* OF THAT DAY.

30. Abducto, sc. by Galba, to whom he had been calumniated by Fabius Valens, 3, 62.

31. Quem .... reum esse. *The fact, that he was not sent back to them and was even called to an account, they construed as a charge against themselves.*

CH. IX.—**33. Superior exercitus.** *The army of Upper Germany,* antith. to *Inferioris Germaniae legiones* just below. The German armies *in general* were the subject of the latter part of the previous section. Here the author *specifies* the two divisions.—*Hordeonium Flaccum.* Appointed legate of Upper Germany by Galba, instead of Verginius recalled. His name will occur often in the subsequent history. See also Plut. Galb.

34. Debilitate pedum invalidum. He was afflicted with the gout. Plut. Galb. 16.

35. Ne .... quidem. *Not even.*—*Quieto milite* = quum quieti essent milites.—*Regimen.* Sub. ejus erat = eos regere poterat. Rup.

36. Adeo = *much more* (lit. in addition to that). Cf. 4, 80: aequalium quoque, *adeo* superiorum intolerantis. So *adeo non* = still less, 3, 39.

37. Inferioris Germaniae. It should be understood, that Upper and Lower Germany here include no part of that Germany proper of which T. treats in his de Germania, and which was not conquered by the Romans; but they are two Roman provinces into which Germania Cisrhenana was subdivided, both on the left or Gallic bank of the Rhine, Upper Germany towards its source, Lower Germany towards its mouth (now Belgium). They were peopled by German tribes.—*Consulari.* Cf. notes supra, chap. 7: *Fonteii Capitonis,* and *Legati legionum.*

38. A. Vitellius. Afterwards emperor. He had been consul (Ann. 11, 23), and of course was now *consularis.* Of Vitellius the father, see Ann. 6, 28; 14, 56; 12, 4. 5. 42. et al.

35 **1. Id satis videbatur,** sc. to Galba and his advisers, who thought that the rank of Vitellius would satisfy the legions, though his gluttony and effeminacy rendered him quite unfit for such a charge Cf. Suet. Vitel. 7: *contemptu magis quam gratia electum.* The rise of such a

Page

man to the supreme power, is doubtless one of the *fortuiti eventus* of which T. speaks in chap. 4. 35

2. Irarum, sc. in Galbam.

4. Hostem potius, sc. quam cives.

5. Excitae. *Called out, raised.* The same troops that are spoken of in § 6.

6. Legationibus adissent. Cf. *legationibus coeunt,* G. 39, note. The purpose of the embassy has been sufficiently intimated in 8: delatum ei imperium, etc. For the subj. after quanquam, cf. note, 5, 21.

Ch. X.—**11. Obtinebat.** Cf. A. 39, note on same word.—*Licinius Mucianus.* Cf. Suet. Vesp. 6, 13. See his character more fully, 2, 5. A prominent man in all the subsequent history, especially under Vespasian.

12. Famosus. In this sense scarcely used, except by poets, before Tacitus. Cf. Boetticher's Lex. Tac.—*Juvenis, when young,* antith. to *mox.*

14. Repositus. Wr. renders *retiring,* as if it were voluntary. But that hardly suits the meaning of the word. Lit. put back, *laid aside,* and hence *buried,* which significations exactly suit the adjuncts *in secretum: buried in an obscure portion of Asia.* So Ritter, Ruperti and Orelli.—*Prope ab.* A peculiar Latin idiom. Cf. Cic. Ver. 2, 52: *tam prope a sicilia.*

15. Postea a principe. The allusion is to the almost imperial power of Mucianus under Vesp. Cf. A. 7, note, and places there cited. —*Luxuria .... mixtus* = in eo mixtae erant luxuria, etc. Cf. A. 4: *locum mixtum.*

17. Vacaret. Subj. after *cum* denoting *cause,* as well as time.—*Expedierat* = in expeditionem sive ad bellum profectus erat. Ernesti. Only T. uses the word thus without an object. It properly means, to clear the way, prepare, &c. See the fuller construction, 2, 99: *expedire ad bellum.*

18. Laudares. Al. laudes. But *laudares* has the better authority and makes a better construction. *You* (any one, men) *would praise his public life* (*palam* acta); so *crederes,* 45; *timeres,* A. 22, &c. Gr. 209, R. 7; Z. 528, N. 2.

19. Collegas. Governors of neighboring provinces. The word means *chosen together;* hence either those chosen at the same election, or those chosen to the same office.

20. Cui = *is, cui* or *talis, ut ei, a man of such a character, that,* etc. Hence followed by the subj. The reference here is to the prominent part which Mucianus acted in conferring the supreme power on Vesp. Cf. 2, 76.

21. Flavius Vespasianus. It was the history of Vesp. and his sons, Titus and Domitian, that T. chiefly intended to write. Hence,

Page
35 from the first, he relates whatever pertains to them, with special care and fulness.

24. Suo loco, sc. 2, 1.

25. Occulta lege fati. Or., after the Medicean MS., omits *lege*.

26. Post fortunam = postquam Imperator factus est. Ernesti.

27. Credidimus = sensim credere didicimus. Rup. There were intimations (*ostentis ac responsis*) enough beforehand; but it was only after their fulfilment that we learned properly to understand and fully to believe them. Of these *ostenta ac responsa*, a fuller account is given, 2, 76; also in Suet. and Josephus.

Ch. XI.—**28. Quibus coerceretur.** *By which it was to be kept in subjection.* The subj. denoting purpose.

29. Loco regum. In the place of their former kings, and hence with *regal power*. Ad rem., cf. Ann 12, 60. Ad verbum, Z. 481.

30. Annonae fecundam. Egypt was the granary of Rome; hence the importance to the emperor of keeping it under his own control.

31. Superstitione. Witness the Egyptian worship of animals, 5, 5.—*Insciam legum.* Because always under absolute government. *Insciam* properly refers to learning, *ignaram* to experience. Död.

32. Domi retinere. *To retain in his own hands*, i. e. *to govern himself*, or by agents directly responsible to him, not to the senate, as most of the provinces were. See *retinere* in the sense of govern in 9: *retinentis*. So Ter. and Cic. use *domi habeo* or *domi est mihi* = I have it with me, I have it myself. Ad rem., cf. Ann. 2, 59. The agents of Augustus in the government of Egypt were the *Romani equites* mentioned above. The provinces were for the most part governed by men of higher than equestrian rank.

33. Tib. Alexander. Cf. Ann. 15, 28; Suet. Vesp. 6.—*Ejusdem nationis*, i. e. an Egyptian, though he was of Jewish descent.

35. Domini minoris. A master of lower rank, sc. Macer, who set up for independence and played the petty tyrant, till they were more than satisfied. See his character above, note, chap. 7.—*Duae Mauretaniae*, sc. Tingitana et Caesariensis, cf. 2, 58.

36. Procuratoribus. Dativus subjectivus. Rup. Cf. Gr. 225, 2. These provinces, having no army stationed in them, were led to favor or oppose the government at Rome, just as the nearest or strongest army in their vicinity took sides.

37. Cohibentur = reguntur. Used in this sense only by Tacitus. Such words (*cohibere, retinere, coercere*) are highly significant of the *nature* of the Roman dominion over the provinces.

38. Inermes provinciae. *Provinces without armies*, such as Achaia, Sicily, &c. So *inermes legati* (2, 81), the legates of such provinces.

2. In pretium, etc. *Were destined to become the prize of the* Page 36
war, i. e. of the victorious party elsewhere. How fallen from the Italy that conquered the world!

CH. XII.—**6. Kal. Januarias.** Al. Cal. The letter K has been superseded by C everywhere except in such abbreviations. See Zumpt, 5. On the reckoning of time among the Romans, see App. to Leverett's Lex. or Gr. 326. The names of the months are always adj., agreeing either with the noun which designates the part of the month (as here with Kal.), or with *mensis* understood, in which case they are of course always masc.

7. Belgica, sc. Gallia.

9. Flagitare. *Demand urgently* or *imperatively,* stronger than *poscere* or *postulare.*

10. Acciperetur. Subj. cf. Gr. 262, R. 9; Z. 536.

12. Adoptione, sc. of a son and successor at his death.—*Proximis. His friends* and advisers. Cf. 10: apud proximos.—*Non sane crebrior. Indeed there was no more frequent topic of conversation,* sc. than Galba's choice of a successor. Cf. *non sane aliae,* 9.

14. Licentia, *unrestrained liberty; libidine, strong passion.* Roth makes them synonyms.—*Fessa aetate. Infirm old age.* Cf. 3, 67.

16. Stulta spe. Al. occulta spe. *Foolish,* i. e. hastily conceived and ill-founded.—*Ambitiosis rumoribus,* i. e. reports designed to gain the favor of Galba for their respective friends and patrons, and thus indirectly to promote their own interest.

17. In .... odium. *To gratify their hatred.* Cf. A. 5: in jactationem, note.

18. Eodem actu. An unusual expression for *idem agendo* = *by this means,* and of course *in the same proportion.* Cf. Or. in loc.

19. Hiantes .... cupiditates. So Cic. in Verr. 2, 54: hians avaritia, *hians* denoting, 1. The outward expression of *hunger;* 2. Any *craving* desire. *In magna fortuna* points to the occasion or exciting cause of the craving.

20. Intendebat. *Was increasing,* lit. stretching, adding *intensity* to.—*Cum .... peccaretur. Since crimes might be committed,* etc. Cum causale followed by the subj., cf. Gr. 263, 5; Z. 577.—*Credulum. Confiding,* explained by *amicorum libertorumque patiens,* etc., chap. 49.

CH. XIII.—**22. Potentia principatus.** *The supreme power,* or *the absolute control of the government.* Cf. potentiam, 1. So Suet. says (Galb. 14): Regebatur trium *arbitrio,* etc.

24. Icelo. Cf. Suet. Nero, 49; Plut. Galb. 7.—*Liberto.* Freedmen ruled the state in this degenerate age, a proof that liberty was extinct, as Tacitus suggests, G. 25.—*Annulis,* sc. aureis, the badge of knighthood.—*Equestri nomine.* "Equestre nomen est nomen no-

Page

36 bilissimarum equestriumque gentium familiare, non deducendum a Marte sed fortasse a Marcus, i. e. Masculus, v. Voss. Etym." Wissowa, cited by Ruperti.

25. Rebus minoribus. *In matters of less importance*, antith. to *circa consilium*, etc. *In* is omitted before the abl. here for the sake of brevity. Cf. Essay on the Style of Tacitus, p. 12.

26. Circa = *in respect to.* Cf. G. 28. "*Circa* apud T. = *de* et *in* apud Cic." Bach.

27. Scindebantur, in this sense, is poetical (cf. Boetticher) and Virgilian. Cf. Virg. Aen. 2, 39.

28. Consensu .... alium. *Agreed in supporting, not so much any particular one* (cf. *unum aliquem*, 6), *as some other*, than Otho.

32. Subisse, sc. animum Galbae. Cf. 37: horror animum subit. Render: *influenced.* The word implies a *silent, secret* influence. Cf. A. 3.

33. Relinqueretur, sc. quasi hereditate. Rup. For the mode and tense, cf. Gr. 261, 1; Z. 524.

34. Otho. Cf. Ann. 13, 45. 46; Suet. Otho; and Plut. Galba and Otho.

35. Eo = ideo.

36. Jam, antith. to *mox*, denotes time = *already.*

37. Octaviam .... amoliretur. He *divorced* her on a charge of adultery, and afterwards put her to death. Ann. 14, 60–64. The subj. after *donec* here is according to the general rule (cf. Gr. 263, 4; Z. 575), for here it refers to a *purpose* or *object* to be attained. But Tacitus disregards this distinction, and uses the subj. after *donec* referring to a mere *fact*, e. g. 4, 35: *pugnatum, donec proelium nox dirimeret;* 1, 35: *donec .... levaretur*, where see note.

38. Suspectum .... Poppaea. Cf. Ann. 13, 46, where the character of this accomplished but depraved woman is sketched, and a full account is given of her relation to Otho and Nero, which however cannot be reconciled with this passage in the Histories. According to the later and doubtless more correct account in the Annals, Poppæa was the *wife* of Otho, from whom she was taken by Nero.

37 **1. Lusitaniam.** A part of Spain, now Portugal. Hence the name which the great Portuguese poet, Camoens, gave his poem in honor of his country, viz. the Lusiad.—*Specie legationis.* He banished him under pretence of conferring upon him an honorable office. Hence Otho speaks of it, as *honor exsilii*, 21. Cf. also Ann. 13, 46. —*Comiter.* Civiliter et populariter.—*Administrata.* 10 years. Suet. Otho, 3.

2. Partes, sc. Galba's.

3. Praesentes, sc. in provincia duces. Rup.

5. Rapiebat denotes the impetuosity with which he seized upon and cherished the hope. Cf. Virg. Aen. 1, 176: *rapuitque flammam.*

Page

Ch. XIV.—**8. Quonam .... erumperet.** Subj. Cf. Gr. 265; 37
Z. 552.

9. Exercituum, sc. Germanicarum.—*Urbano militi.* Whose feelings are described in chap. 5.

10. Comitia imperii. Language borrowed from the usages of the republic (cf. remarks on *imperatores*, 7), and properly denoting an assembly of the people for the choice of a magistrate, but here a council of a few friends and leading men convened for the nomination of a successor to Galba in the empire.

11. Adhibito. *Being called in,* lit. *being had in.* For the number of *adhibito*, cf. Gr. 205, Exc. to R. 2.

12. Praefecto urbis. A different office from the *praefectus praetorii* (13), being a kind of mayorship, to which the emperor appointed from among those who had been consuls.

13. Pisonem Licinianum. Cf. Suet. Galb. 17: nobilem egregiumque juvenem, etc. All accounts give Piso a character worthy of a better fortune and a better age. Cf. also Plut. Galb. 23.—*Arcessi.* A frequentative of *accedo.* Cf. Freund, sub voce. The MSS. here have *accersiri.* Or. and Död. read *accersi.*

14. Propria electione. Suet. (in loc. cit.) makes Piso an old acquaintance and friend of Galba: sibi *olim* probatissimum, testamentoque *semper* in bona et nomen adscitum.

15. Apud Rubellium, etc. *At the house of Rubellius Plautus,* of whose high rank, see Ann. 13, 19; and his death through the jealousy of Nero, Ann. 14, 57. 59.

18. Vultu habituque. Abl. of quality. Gr. 211, R. 6, (1): *with face and mien of the old style.* Cf. *habitus*, G. 4. 17. Here it includes form, dress and deportment, the whole outward man except the face (*vultu*). Or. and Död. have *voltu,* after the older form.

20. Tristior, sc. justo, Gr. 256, R. 9. *Too gloomy, morose.*

21. Quo = *by as much as;* antithetic to *eo magis* understood before *adoptandi,* with the usual conciseness of Tacitus.

Ch. XV.—**23. Privatus.** Antithetic to *ad imperium vocatum. Si* also is antithetic to *nunc.*—*Lege curiata,* i. e. a law passed by the Roman people in their *curiae;* for such a law was originally necessary to ratify an adoption or transfer from one family or gens to another. But long before the age of Galba, the *comitia curiata* (assembly of the *curiae*) had become obsolete (cf. remarks under *comitia imperii,* 14), and all that was now requisite was the presence and sanction of the Pontifex, which office was held by the emperor, so that the *lex curiata* and *the pontificate* were concentrated in Galba.

24. Et mihi. *Et* = *both,* correl. to *et tibi.* The honor would have been mutual.—*Erat.* Ind. for subj. Not uncommon in Lat = our *it were.* Cf. Gr. 259, R. 4; Z. 519, b.

25. Cn. Pompeii. Abavus (great-great-grandfather) to Piso on

Page

37 his mother's (Scribonia) side. Al. Gn. for Cn., cf. note on *prodigia* 3, supra.

26. Sulpiciae ac Lutatiae, sc. gentis. Galba was of the *Sulpician* gens, and his mother was a grand-daughter of Q. *Lutatius* Catulus.

30. Quiescenti. Antith. to *bello adeptus* = in peace. So G. 35: *quiescenti*, et passim.—*Exemplo ... Augusti.* Cf. Ann. 1, 3. A singular fatality attended the efforts of Augustus to provide an heir and successor, one after another of his adopted sons being taken away by natural death or by the arts of Livia, wife of Augustus and mother of Tiberius.

32. Nepotes. C. and L. Caesars, sons of Agrippa. Ann. 1, 3.

34. In domo, sc. *sua*, which is omitted to make *in domo* correspond with *in republica.*—*Non quia .... non* = *non quin.* This use of *quia* is for the most part peculiar to late Latin authors. Cf. Z. 537. Cicero uses *non quia non* rarely, usually *non quod non.* Cf. Tusc. Quæs. 1, 11, and Kühner's note, ibid. All these formulæ are followed by the subjunctive. Cf. Z. 537; Arnold's Prose Introd. 492.

35. Propinquos, *relatives,* such as the adopted sons of Aug. all were to him.—*Socios belli, coadjutors in war,* as Agrippa was to Aug.—*Neque ipse* = *et ipse non,* correlative to *et* before *judicii* Cf. *neque .... ac,* A. 10; *nec .... et,* G. 2, note; also Zumpt, 338.

36. Judicii. *My unbiased judgment* in the choice of a successor. Antithetic to *ambitione.* The logical connection between the two clauses is this: I did not accept imperial power myself from ambitious motives, and in the choice of my successor, I have been governed, not by ambitious or selfish motives, but by sober and unbiased judgment (justis causis et vera aestimatione. Ernesti).

37. Necessitudines = propinqui.

38 **1. Ea** = *such.* Hence followed by the subj. Cf. Gr. 264; Z 556.

2. Praeteritum is not superfluous, but prepares the way for the subsequent exhortation to lead a similar life *in future.*

3. Excusandum habeas. This construction is peculiar to the age of Tacitus. Cf. Boetticher.—*Fortunam .... adversam.* Patre, matre, fratre a Claudio interfectis, fratre altero caeso a Nerone, et ipse diu exsul. Brotier. Cf. 21. 47. 48 in this Book.

4. Acrioribus stimulis. Lit. sharper stings, here *severer tests* Ad rem. Cf. Xen. Mem. 2, 1, 20 Plin. Epis. 9, 26.

8. Imminuent, sc. tuam fidem, libertatem, etc.—*Irrumpet.* Sing. Gr. 209, R. 12, (2).—*Pessimum ... venenum.* In appos. with *utilitas,* Wr.; with *blanditiae,* Rup. Or. decides in favor of the latter, and argues, that if the former were the meaning, it would read *pessimumque,* etc.

9. Et jam = Gr. καὶ δή Wr.

10. Simplicissime. *With the utmost sincerity.* 38

11. Fortuna nostra, ut adulatores cum principibus. Rup. i. e. not caring what we are, but what they may hope to gain by us. Ad verbum ac rem, cf. Ann. 2, 71: *vindicabitis vos* (sc. me meamque mortem) *si me potius, quam fortunam meam fovebatis.*—*Oporteat.* Subj. Cf. Gr. 266, 1; Z. 545, a.

Ch. XVI.—**14. Si .... posset.** The subj. imperf. implies the *im*possibility of the thing supposed. Cf. Gr. 261, 1; Z. 524.—*Librari. In equilibrio quasi retineri.* Rup. From *libra.*—*Eram.* Cf. note, 15: *erat.*

15. Dignus .... inciperet. Gr. 264, 9; Z. 568.

16. Nunc. Antith. to *si.* Cf. 14. = *but now,* i. e. *as things are.*

19. Unius familiae, sc. Claudiae.

20. Fuimus. *We the Roman people.* But *coepimus, we emperors.*

23. Judicium integrum. Cf. *Judicii,* 15, and note ibid.

24. Monstratur, sc. quis eligendus sit.—*Consensu.* So he says of himself, 15: deorum hominumque *consensu* ad imperium vocatum.

26. Inermi provincia. Cf. note on *inermes provinciae,* 11.—*Una legione.* Formerly there were three legions in the Spanish army, Ann. 4, 5; but the spirit of the province was broken, and only one was now necessary, viz. the 6th. His. 5, 16. Cf. also Suet. Galb. 10. Yet three are mentioned again, 2, 97.

28. Adhuc, sc. ante Neronem.—*Nos.* Galba and Piso, raised to the rank of princeps (*asciti*), Galba by the sword (*bello*), Piso by adoption based on merit, and both by men's good opinions (*aestimantibus.*)

30. Ne .... fueris. Subj. perf. with *ne,* for the imperative. Cf. Gr. 260, R. 6; Z. 529. The periphrastic form *ne territus fueris* differs from *ne terreare,* as the aorist subj. in Greek does from the pres. subj. The former means *be not terrified,* and implies that he is not; while the latter would mean *cease to be terrified,* and would imply that he was. Död. *Ne,* like the Greek μή, is usually a subjective negative, followed by the imperative or the subjunctive, to express a prohibition, or an intention or wish negatively. So *ne .... desideretur* just below. *Ut non,* on the contrary, denotes only a negative *result. Ne* appears, however, to have been originally the absolute negative particle of the Latin language, from which non (noenum, ne-unum) and the other negatives were derived. Cf. Freund's Lexicon, sub voce. Of this original use we have a relic in the phrase *ne .... quidem,* which is accordingly followed by the indicative, e. g supra: *ne ipse quidem accessi.*

32. Et audita, etc. *Et* connects the two reasons, why Piso

Page
38 should not be alarmed: 1. The circumstances attending Galba's accession to the supreme power; 2. The fact that the only objection against Galba is now removed.

35. Neque . . . . et. Correlative, as in 15 To exhort you further, *in the first place* suits not the present occasion, and in *the next place* there is no need of it, the necessity being superseded by the happy choice he had made in Piso.

37. Idem ac = *as well as.—Bonarum . . . . rerum,* i. e. *between good and bad measures.*

39 **2. Regnantur.** *Governed by kings.* Poetice. Cf. Virg. Aen. 6, 794; and note, G. 25, et al.

3. Qui nec totam, etc. T. here gives us at a stroke an exact picture of the Romans in that age. His Annals and History are from beginning to end a commentary on this text.

5. Tanquam . . . . faceret, i. e. with deliberation and dignity—*tanquam cum facto,* sc. principe: *the rest talked with Piso as with one already made princeps,* i. e. with eager and servile flattery.

This speech of Galba is worthy to be studied, as a manual of moral and political wisdom. Every sentence is a maxim for the world and all time. Yet it is all especially befitting the aged and experienced Galba in an address to his adopted son. See Life of T., p. 13.

Ch. XVII.—**7. Statim** refers to the time of the ceremony. *Mox* after its close.

10. Vultu habituque. *Vultus* de ore, *habitus* de toto corpore. Wr. Cf. 14, note.

11. Quasi imperare, etc. Another single stroke, that reveals a whole character, and a noble character too, whose self-respect commands our veneration and makes us mourn his misfortunes. For the subj. cf. Gr. 263, 2; Z. 572.

12. Pro rostris, i. e. in the forum, before the people; *in castris,* i. e. to the soldiers of the Praetorian Guard.

13. In castra, for the army had the power, not the senate or the people. Observe the difference between *in castra* and *in castris.* Gr. 235, 2; Z. 316.

14. Ut . . . . ita. Antithetic. Cf. 4. The infinitives in this sentence depend on a verb understood (they said, they thought), and express the motive for going to the camp. The subj. usually stands in the dependent clauses of such sentences (*oratio obliqua*). Cf. Gr. 266, 2; Z. 603.

15. Per bonas artes. Sub. acquisitum.

16. Publica exspectatio . . . . impatiens. Abstract for concrete, poetice, = populus impatienter exspectans.

Ch. XVIII.—**19. Quartum idus.** The fourth *before* (*ante*) the Ides = Jan. 10.

20. Turbaverant. Observe the pluperf. where we with less

exactness use the imperf Cf. Z. 505. The bad weather was prior to 39
the announcement of the adoption in the camp.

21. Observatum. Cf. usitatum, A. 1. The Latin is fond of concrete words. Cf. note 1: *post conditam urbem.*—*Comitiis dirimendis.* For the use of the *gerundive* see Gr. 275, 2; Z. 656. Dat. of the end; lit. observed *for* the dissolving of the assembly, i. e. regarded as a reason why an election should not proceed. Cf. Cic. de Div. In nostris commentariis scriptum habemus: *Jove tonante, fulgurante, comitia populi habere nefas.* The power thus intrusted to the pontiffs and the presiding officers at the elections was greatly abused; elections were deferred or declared null and void on false pretences by patrician officers, whenever they resulted or were likely to result in favor of the plebeians. See Arn. His of Rome, vol. 1, passim.—*Non terruit, quo minus. Did not deter him from proceeding.*

22. Pergeret. *Proceed* (from per-rego, go straight through). For the construction see Gr. 262, R. 9; Z. 543.

25. Imperatoria brevitate, qua imperator uti solet ac debet. Rup. Compare the Queen's Speech in Great Britain.

26. Exemplo militari. "According to a military custom established at an early period of the commonwealth, every Roman soldier chose his favorite comrade, and by that tie of friendship all were mutually bound to share every danger with their fellows. The consequence was, that a warlike spirit pervaded the whole army. Cf. Liv. 9, 39." Murphy. See also Drak. ad loc. cit. in Liv.—*Legeret.* Subj. Cf. Gr. 266, 1; Z. 545, a.

27. Seditio, sc. duarum legionum Germanicarum, 16.—*In majus.* Cf. *in melius, in deterius, in mollius,* a favorite form of expression with T. passim. Sometimes used in the same sense without the *in.* Used with different verbs, e. g. cadere, accipere, credere, trahere, haberi, etc. Ang.: *taken for,* or believed to be, *greater, better,* or *worse,* sc. than the reality, or than it otherwise would be.

29. Verba ac voces. Not exactly synonymous. *Voces* suggests more the idea of *discordant cries and murmurs.* Or. See further in note, 27: *clamore et gaudiis.*

30. In officio fore, lit. would shortly be in (the performance of) their duty, i. e. *would soon return to their duty.*—*Lenocinium. Flattering words, alluring promises.*

33. Usurpatam .... necessitatem. The *donativum* to the soldiers, and the *congiarium* to the plebs, had become so common, even in time of peace, that it was now, as it were, a fixed law or matter of necessity, especially when it was needful to procure their assent to any favorite scheme. Cf. Ann. 12, 41; Suet. Nero, 7. It was peculiarly vexatious to lose this in time of war or revolution, when their rulers were peculiarly dependent on their support.

Page

39 **34. Perdidissent.** The subj. denoting the view of the soldiers, not the sentiments of the author.

35. Nocuit. *Hurt his cause, ruined his popularity.* Cf. ***nocuisse***, 21.

36. Rigor occurs in Boetticher's list of words belonging to the poets of an earlier age. It is not found in Cicero. Cf. Freund sub voce

Ch. XIX.—**37. Inde.** *Thence* or *next*, sc. they proceeded to the senate, of which there is an ellipsis. Tacitus in his conciseness has put two clauses into one. Cf. note, A. 5: *prima . . . approbavit;* also Essay on the Style of Tacitus, p. 18.

40 **1. Multi . . . . obsequio.** Al. pointed and read thus: multi voluntate; effusius qui noluerant; medii, ac plurimi, obvio obsequio. But *medii* is a conjectural reading; and this punctuation destroys the proper antithesis, which is usually the best clue to the understanding of Tacitus: *many out of cordial good-will expressed their approbation* (*favebant* understood) *freely and fully; those who were opposed* (to the nomination), *in moderate* (ordinary, commonplace) *terms; and a still greater number* (the major part) *with ready complaisance, cherishing hopes of personal advantage* (from Piso's elevation) *without regard to the public welfare. Medie*, with the exception of this one passage in Tacitus, occurs only in the brazen or post-classical age. Cf. Or. in loco and Freund sub voce.

7. Cum tristia sunt. Highly descriptive of the morbid state of the public mind.—*Censuerant, had voted*, sc. prior to the discussion which follows.

8. Agitatum secreto. By Galba among his friends and counsellors.

9. Num . . . . proficisceretur. Subj. of the indirect question. Cf. Gr. 265; Z. 552.—*Majore praetextu.* Ut major legationis dignitas esset et auctoritas. Ernesti. So it seems to be explained by the clause which follows. *Praetextus* in this sense (= species, auctoritas) is post-Augustan. Cf. Boetticher.

13. Foeda inconstantia. *With shameful inconstancy* (*want of firmness*), on the part of Galba.

14. Ambitu. Ob ambitum, sive cupiditatem pravam gratia nixam. So it is well explained in the Bipontine edition. Render: *in* (or *through*) *their solicitous desire of going or remaining.*

Ch. XX.—**17. Ubi . . . . causa erat.** Al. *unde*. But that is a mere interpolation, and, as Wr. says, an inappropriate one; for the *cause* of a want of money lay *in* the extravagant donations of Nero, not *from* them.

18. Bis . . . . sestertium. Twenty-two hundred million sesterces. Cf. Roman money, Gr. 327, 6. Summa illa sane grandiuscula, sed digna effusionibus ejus monstri. Lipsius.

19. Singulos, sc. a Nerone donatos. Rup.—*Decuma . . . relicta.*

So Suet. Galb.: non plus decimis concessis They were allowed to Page 40
keep *one-tenth* of what they had received, and were required to refund the remaining nine-tenths.

20. Super .... erant. Separated by tmesis, after the manner of the poets. So 2, 34: jactis super ancoris. Cf. Virg. Aen. 2, 567: *Jamque adeo super unus eram. They scarcely had remaining the tenth parts severally* (*decimae portiones*, pl.), still less the nine-tenths.

23. Instrumenta vitiorum. Gula, balnea, scorta et alia. Rup. What a picture of the times!

24. Exactioni, sc. donationum Neroniarum.—*Triginta* Suet. Galb. 15: quinquaginta. Fortasse primum triginta fuere, et numerus crevit ambitu crescente. Brotier. In numeris libri saepe peccant. Wr.

25. Ambitu .... onerosum. *Burdensome* (to the state) *because of the number of the commissioners and their extensive powers.* So Wr. and Or. But it accords better with prevailing usage to take *ambitu* in the sense of *solicitation, intrigue,* which would be greatly increased by the number of commissioners.—*Hasta.* "It was usual to set up a spear in auctions, a symbol derived, it is said, from the ancient practice of selling under a spear the booty acquired in war."

26. Sector. "Those are called *sectores,* who buy property *publice,*" i. e. sold by public authority. Gaius, 4, 146. Cf. Smith's Dict. of Gr. and Rom. Antiq. sub voce.—*Actionibus. Actions,* i. e. *prosecutions,* against those who refused to repay the sum demanded of them. So Wr., Rup. and Or., with the Medicean and other best MSS. Al. *auctionibus.* But that makes a mere tautology, for what do hasta and sector denote but auctions?

27. Quod .... forent. Subj. = because *in their view* they were as poor, etc. Cf. Gr. 266, 3; Z. 629.—*Donasset.* Cf. Gr. 266, 1; Z. 547.

28. Exauctorati. Strictly, released from the military oath, *dismissed.* But here, in accordance with the prevailing usage of Tacitus and the later times of the empire, dismissed *in disgrace, cashiered.*

29. Praetorio. The *praetorium* was primarily the headquarters of the Roman general (Prae-itor): afterwards more especially the camp of the prætorian cohorts (imperial guards) at Rome. Here put for the *prætorian guards* themselves, which consisted originally of nine cohorts of a thousand men each (Ann. 4, 5), and subsequently (under Vitellius) rose to the number of 16 cohorts, or 16,000 men. His. 2, 93.—*Antonius .... Antonius.* Instead of this repetition, we should have had *Antonii* once before both names, if they had belonged to the same family. The repetition shows that they belonged to different families.

30. Urbanis cohortibus. Three cohorts, the proprius miles urbis. Ann. 4, 5.—*Vigiliis.* Put for *cohortibus vigilum,* like *praetorio* for *praetorianis.* The *vigiliae* consisted of seven cohorts, each having

Page

40 charge of two wards of the city, to suppress and guard against **fires**, and more like fire-companies than regular troops. They were instituted, as were also the prætorian guards, by Augustus. Dio Cass. 55, 26.

32. Omnibus suspectis. Ut Nymphidii sociis Neronive addictis. Cf. 5; also Suet. Galb. 16. It is implied, that all expected to lose their places, as the cashiered tribunes were *driven from* (*pellerentur*) theirs, not however in a mass, for that the emperor was afraid to do, but in detail (*singuli,* one by one). For this use of *pellerentur,* cf. 4, 44: *pulsi* = *banished;* and 4, 46: *pelli* = *dismissed,* removed from office. It is the simple for the compound.

CH. XXI.—**36. Luxuria . . . inopia,** etc. In apposition with *multa.* As to Otho's *inopia,* cf. Suet. Oth. 5, where he says that nothing short of the imperial power could save him from utter ruin, and whether he died in battle or fell a victim to his creditors was immaterial.

41 **1. Lusitaniam . . . . exspectandum.** *He must not wait for the honor of a second banishment to Lusitania.* Cf. 13.

3. Nocuisse. Cf. note on *nocuit,* 18.—*Apud. In the estimation of.*—*Senem.* Galba.

4. Juvenem. Piso.

5. Occidi. Observe the emphatic position of *occidi,* and the emphasis of meaning: Otho might even be *put to death,* not merely banished, as before.

6. Fluxa. *Fluctuating,* ready to be dissolved and pass away—in happy antithesis to *nondum coaluisset.*

7. Nondum coaluisset. *Had not yet become established.* The reader will observe the use of the inf. in the principal clauses, and the subj. in the dependent clauses. Cf. Gr. 266, 2; Z. 603.

8. Transitus rerum. Commutationes principum et imperii, quum ab uno ad alterum transit. Cf. *res translatae,* 29. Ernesti.

11. Acrioris viri. *A man of superior energy and courage.*

12. Merito. *In a manner worthy of himself,* i. e. in bold undertakings. The word is designedly ambiguous.

CH. XXII.—**13. Corpori similis.** Compare what Piso says of Otho's person below, 30, and places cited there.

16. Matrimonia. The frequent marriages of Nero. Cf. 13; Suet. Nero, 28. 35. The same was true of Caligula and Claudius, the former of whom had had four wives and the latter six. Suet. Cal. 24. 25; Claud. 26. 27.—*Regnorum libidines. Vicious pleasures* attendant on the *supreme power;* distinct both from the adulteries and the successive marriages.—*Avido* agrees with *Othoni.*

17. Quiescenti. Antithetic to *si auderet* = *if inactive.*—*Ut aliena.* Antithetic to *ut sua* = *not his, but another's.*

18. Mathematicis. *Astrologers.*

20. Sperantibus. *Aspirants* to power; antith. to *potentibus.*

21. Vetabitur, sc. by law. Cf. Ann. 2, 32; 12, 52.—*Retinebitur* sc. to gratify curiosity and ambition, which are stronger than law. As to the unexpected turn of expression here, cf. Monboddo on Language, 2, 4, 12. Page 41

22. Secreta. *Private apartments,* or *secret conclaves.* It is used in both senses by Tacitus. Cf. notes, A. 22 and 39.—*Pessimum .. instrumentum.* *The basest means of* bringing about *her marriage to the emperor, Nero.* Cf. notes on chap. 13. Burnouf and Orelli render: the *detestable implement of imperial housewifery.*

23. Ptolemaeus. Cf. Plut. Galb. In Suet. Oth. 4. 6, called by mistake Seleucus, which was the name of *Vespasian's* mathematicus.

24. Cum .... promisisset. Plup. subj. in narration. Cf. Gr. 263, R. 2; Z. 578.

25. Postquam .... fides, sc. ei erat. *After confidence* was reposed in him *from its turning out,* as he had predicted.

29. Credendi. Al. credi, which is found in all the MSS., and which, according to Wr., may depend on *cupidine,* as *sequi* does on *natura* in 55: insita mortalibus natura propere sequi. Yet Wr. himself reads *credendi* (as also Död. and Or.), and the active seems much more appropriate here than the passive.

Ch. XXIII.—**30. Et sceleris.** *The criminal act also,* i. e. as well as *the criminal desire* (*ejus modi voto*). *Et* for *etiam* is very rare in Cicero, but common in Livy and later writers. Cf. Z. 698; and Kühner ad Cic. Tusc. Quaes. 1, 17, 40.—*Instinctor* is found only in Tacitus and writers still later than he. Cf. Boetticher.

31. Ad .... transitur states a general principle (as Tacitus always loves to do in connection with historical facts) which Murphy thus freely translates: "The heart, that has formed the wish and conceived the project, has seldom any scruple about the means."

32. Repens. Tacitus alone uses this word in the sense of *recent.* Thus in Ann. 6, 7, it stands opposed to *vetustate obscurum.* So here it is explained by the antithetic *jampridem.* Cf. Or. in loc. and Freund's Lex. sub voce.

33. Successionis, sc. by adoption. Cf. 13.—*Facinoris.* *Acts of violence, forcible seizure of the throne.*

34. In agmine. Ernesti objects, that *in agmine* is identical with *in itinere.* But Wr. replies, that Tacitus uses the words together elsewhere, e. g. Ann. 3, 9: *in agmine atque itinere;* and that in general *agmen* denotes the *troops* on the march, and *iter* the *march* itself. Here, however, he says *in agmine* is antithetic to *in stationibus,* and he explains *in agmine* by ubi copiae essent conjunctae; and *in stationibus* by ubi singuli milites versarentur. Döderlein says: *in itinere,* dum iter faciunt; *in agmine,* dum ambulant, exercendi causa. Orelli has still another way of distinguishing the phrases. Render *in itinere, on the march; in agmine, in the lines; in stationibus, at their quarters.*

23*

Page

41 **35. Vocans, appellando, agnoscere, requirere, juvare, inserendo,** all express the *means* by which Otho courted the favor of the soldiers, and all stand in the same logical relation to *affectaverat*, yet the grammatical forms are strangely varied and intermingled by our author's fondness for enallage. Cf. notes, G. 16 and 18.—*Vocans nomine.* A means of popularity so much relied on at Rome, that great men had a slave called nomenclator, whose business it was to know the name of everybody, and communicate it, as occasion required, to his master. Cf. Beck. Gall. Exc. 2, sc. 2.—*Neroniani comitatus Nero's retinue,* who shared his vicious pleasures and applauded his musical performances in the Roman theatres, and on his excursions through Italy and Greece. Cf. the *Augustani* instituted for this purpose. Ann. 14, 15; also Ann. 15, 33; Suet. Nero, 25.

36. Requirere aliquid is *to inquire after* or into any thing; *agnoscere, to recognise* an old acquaintance. *Agnoscere* refers to persons and things previously known, *cognoscere* to those not previously known.

42 **1. Atrocius accipiebantur.** These words are found together only in Tacitus. So also *aspere accipere.* Ann. 4, 31. Cf. Boetticher.

3. Soliti, sc. sub Nerone (see note above).

4. Eniterentur, sc. duce Galba ex Hispania Romam redeunte. Rup. To justify this contrast, we must suppose, what T. nowhere asserts in his extant works, that some of Nero's prætorians went to meet and escort Galba from Spain. *Eniterentur* is followed by the acc. Cf. Gr. 233, R. 1. It is subj. because *cum* = *since,* denoting a causal connection. Cf. Gr. 263, 5; Z. 577.

Ch. XXIV.—**5. Addiderat.** Pluperfect. Cf. note on *turbaverant,* 18, supra.

6. Proximis = amicis.

7. Novas cupiditates = novarum rerum cupiditatem.

9. Per speciem convivii. "Under pretext of an allowance for an entertainment." Kingsley.—*Quotiens .... epularetur.* Imperf. subj. denoting a repeated action. Cf. Gr. 264, 12; Z. 569.

10. Cohorti .... agenti. Ille mos excubiarum inter epulas originem traxit a Claudio Imperatore. Cf. Dio. 60, 3; Suet. Claud. 35. Wr.

12. Intendebat. Cf. note on it, 12.—*Animosus.* Literally, hearty (from *animus*), hence liberal, *lavish,* one who spares no expense. Cf. Freund, sub voce.

13. Speculatori. *A soldier of the body-guard.* The word (derived from *specula*) properly denotes a watchman, hence used by Tacitus for the emperor's lifeguards, who were chosen from the prætorian bands. The word, in this sense, is post-Augustan. Cf. Boetticher.

15. Dederit. Compare the perf. subj. here with the imperf. subj.

divideret just above. *Divideret* denotes repeated and customary action: he was in the *habit* of dividing *as often as Galba feasted at the house of Otho*. *Dederit* denotes a single, specific act. The distinction is the same which always prevails between the imperf. and the perf. in the *indic.;* but which is not usually observed in the *subj*, where the tenses are less distinctly marked in all languages, and where in Latin the *perf.* is generally used only as a perf. *definite*, and the *imperf.* is used indiscriminately for *completed* and *incomplete* actions. The rule for the succession of the tenses would require the *imperf. subj.* in both places here. Cf. Gr. 258; Z. 516. But certain historical writers, particularly Nepos, Livy and Tacitus, seem to have felt a necessity for the same distinction of time in the subj. as in the indicative. Cf. Z. 504, Note. This distinction, it is believed, will be found applicable to all the examples in *Tacitus*. Thus in 5, 20, the two tenses are brought together in the same sentence, both after *ut* denoting a consequence. The perf. *invaserit* is first used to denote the *simple historical fact* of an attack (like the perf. indefinite of the indic.). But when he proceeds to speak of the *progressive execution* of the assault, he uses the *imperfect* (*traherent*). Compare also *admoverit*, 1, 66, with *occurrerent*, 1, 63; *pedierit*, 3, 51, with *aestimarentur*, 3, 52, &c., &c.—*Praefecti*. Cornelius Laco, ignavissimus mortalium. Cf. chap. 6.—*Nota*, sc. publicae largitiones. 42

16. Occulta, sc. secretiora praemia.

CH. XXV.—**18. Tesserarium.** *Bearer of the watchword*, which in early times was inscribed on a *tessera* or square block (from τέσσαρες), and thus passed through the ranks on the eve of battle, as a *word* by which the soldiers might distinguish friends from foes. Thus Silius Ital: *Tacitum* dat tessera signum. Cf. also Virg. Aen. 7, 637. *Tesserarius*, in the military sense, is post-Augustan.

19. Optionem. The *optiones* were the lieutenants of the centurions (the suc-centuriones of Livy), so called from the time, when (and from the fact that) quem velint, permissum est centurionibus *optare*—previously called *accensi*, according to Festus sub voce *Optio*. Cf. Smith's Dict. of Antiq. under *Centurio*. Render *adjutant*, or retain the Latin word both here and in *tesserarium*.—*Perductos*. *Brought over*, sc. to himself (Otho); in partem deteriorem dictum turpi de causa, ut feminae a lenonibus *perduci* dicuntur. Ernesti. Cf. Horace: perduci poterit pudica.—*Postquam* connects *cognovit* and *onerat*.

22. Manipulares. *Common soldiers*, for such the *tesserarius* and the *optio* must be called, rather than officers. The word is derived from *manus* and *pleo*, since a *handful* of hay on the top of a pole was the original ensign of a Roman maniple.

25. Primores militum, sc. who had been promoted by Nymphidius, when he was præfect of the prætorians, cf. 5; and whom Galba

Page

42 would therefore naturally suspect of cherishing resentment towards himself for putting to death their benefactor. Cf. 6.

26. Vulgus. Antithetic to *primores militum;* hence *common soldiers.*

27. Quos .... accenderet. Subj. in a relative clause after an indefinite general expression.

28. Mutandae militiae. *A change of military service,* i. e. a transfer from the prætorian guards to some less desirable service. The *metus* here is the exact opposite of the *spes honoratioris in posterum militiae,* 87; and is well explained by the language of Suetonius on the same subject. Galb. 16.

Ch. XXVI.—**30. Tabes.** The spreading spirit of revolt is here likened to a *wasting and contagious disease.—Quoque. Also,* i. e. of the legions, &c., as well as the prætorians.

33. Integros. Antithetic to *malos* = *the good,* lit. entire. So our word *holy* from *whole.—Dissimulatio.* Concealment, *neutrality.* Well explained by *paterentur* in 28. It will be observed that *parata* must be taken in a little different sense with *dissimulatio* and with *seditio,* since the latter had been *got ready,* while the former was *found ready, opportunely existing.* Cf. Essay on the Style of Tacitus, p. 16.—*Postero iduum dierum. The day after the Ides days,* sc. of Jan., i. e. Jan. 14. (Gr. 326.) The expression is singular. It seems to be like the Greek ὑστέρᾳ εἰδῶν. There can scarcely be a doubt as to the day meant. Cf. 27, where the author proceeds to the events of Jan. 15. Al. *die,* a conjectural amendment. *Dierum* is found in the Medicean and all the best MSS., but is included in brackets by Or., and entirely omitted by Död.

34. Rapturi fuerint. *They would have carried him off,* sc. to the prætorian camp, to make him emperor. Observe the use of the periphrastic form to denote *intention.* For the subj. perf., cf. note on chap. 24: *dederit.—Incerta* and *castra* are both objects of *timuissent.*

36. Cura is abl., denoting the *cause* why they did not proceed immediately to action.

38. Ut quisque ... oblatus esset. *Any one, who might chance to have fallen in with the soldiers of the Pannonian or the German army.* The plup. is used, because the action expressed by *oblatus esset* is prior to that expressed by *destinaretur.* The subjunctive denotes contingency: *might* perchance *have fallen in.*

43 **1. Ignorantibus plerisque.** *Since most of them were not acquainted* with Otho. Abl. of cause limiting *destinaretur.—Destinaretur* = designaretur salutareturque princeps. Rup.

3. Apud .... aures. *In the hearing of Galba.*

4. Elusit. *Made sport of.—Consilii.* Governed by *inimicus,* which is connected by *que* to *ignarus.*

Page

5. Afferret. Subj. after *quod* in place of *dummodo id.* Cf. Gr. 43
264, 2; Z. 555, = *provided he did not himself propose it.*

CH. XXVII.—**8. Pro aede.** *Before the temple of Apollo. Aedes* = a sacred edifice consecrated by the act of man; *templum* = a temple (or other holy place) sanctioned by the appointment of the gods, who made known their will through the augurs. Cf. Smith's Dict., word *Templum.* The temple of Apollo was on the Palatine Mount. Cf. Horace: *Palatinus Apollo.—Haruspex.* The haruspices were introduced from Etruria, and were different both from the *augures* and the *sacerdotes.* They were regarded by the educated in the age of Cic. as a sort of jugglers (Dio. 2, 24). Claudius attempted to revive their credit. Cf. Ann. 11, 15, where Tacitus speaks of a *collegium haruspicum.*

13. Redemptoribus. *Contractors.*

15. Requirentibus. Dat. after *finxisset,* which is connected by *cum* to *innixus* .... *pergit.—Praedia* signifies an *estate,* whether in the city or the country, and usually implies *buildings* in the city style. Here the idea of the *buildings* is prominent. Hence *vetustate suspecta, of questionable value on account of their age.* Hence also *exploranda,* sc. by the *architect* and the contractors. Suet. (Oth. 6) expresses the same thus: quasi venalem domum inspecturus.

17. Tiberianam domum. A Tiberio domui Augusti additam in occidentali montis Palatini parte. Brotier.—*Velabrum.* Planities inter forum Romanum, et Palatinum, Capitolinum Aventinumque montes. Rup. Varro (Ling. Lat. 5, 5) derives the name from *vehere;* but Döderlein refers it to ἀλεῖφαρ, for it was the locality of the *oil* merchants. —*Milliarium aureum.* Columna aurea ab Augusto in capite fori facta, in quam militares viae omnes ex Italia desinebant. Rup. The milestones along the Roman roads were called *milliaria.* But the miles were not reckoned from the milliarium aureum, but from the gates of the city. Cf. Smith's Dict.; and Kingsley in loco: also Fiske's Man. P. 1, 52.

18. Aedem. Al. Aede. But *sub* here denotes *tendency* to a place near the temple, and requires the acc. Cf. Gr. 235, (2).—*Pergit. He proceeds* (*per* and *rego*). It properly belongs only to the *last stage* of Otho's progress. Cf. *pergeret,* in chap. 18, and note ibid. It applies only by zeugma (Gr. 323, 1, (2); Z. 775) to the first stage, sc. *in Velabrum. Pergit* is historical present, and hence, like the perf. for which it stands, is followed by the pluperf. subj. (*finxisset*). Cf. Gr. 258, R. 1; Z. 501.

20. Sellae. The *sella gestatoria* was a *sedan,* usually covered (*adoperta,* cf. Suet. Aug. 53); it was different from the *lectica,* which was a *litter* or portable bed, and in which the person carried lay in a recumbent posture. Cf. Becker's Gallus and Smith's Dict. of Antiq. Suetonius (Oth. 6) calls this of Otho a *sella muliebris.*

Page 43 **21. Rapiunt.** *They seize and bear him away in haste,* sc. to the camp. Cf. 29: *rapi in castra;* and note, 26: *rapturi.*

22. Gaudiis. Plural to denote the various kinds and sources of joy. Al. *gladiis.* But *clamore et gaudiis* is a much more natural association of ideas, and accords especially with our author's remarkable fondness for *pairs* of words of *kindred signification.* Cf. notes, 1, 84; 3, 20. See also *clamore et gaudio* in 2, 70.—*Miracula.* 1, 23.

23. Animum . . . sumpturi. *Intending to make up their minds* (take sides) *according to the result.*

Ch. XXVIII.—**24. Stationem . . . . agebat.** A cohort of infantry and a company of horse *kept guard* at each gate of a Roman camp. Julius Martialis was *commander* of this guard at the camp of the prætorians. Rup.

25. Tribunus. This word originally denoted the head of a *tribus* (from *tres,* three, the original number of tribes at Rome). Cf. Schmitz's His. Rom. p. 60. It was afterwards applied to several classes of officers, such as tribunes of the commons and tribunes of the soldiers with consular power. Here it denotes one of the *Triburi Militares,* of whom there were at this time six in each legion, whose duty it was to maintain order, keep guard, inspect outposts, &c. Cf. Smith's Dict. *Tribunus.*—*Is. Such,* correlative to *ut,* which is accordingly followed by the subj. denoting result.—*Magnitudine* = propter magnitudinem. It is assigned as one of two possible reasons for the conduct of Martialis, and limits rather the following *sentiment* than any particular *word* = *owing to the greatness of the unexpected crime.* So Wr. and Rup. Orelli and Döderlein supply *perculsus* or some such idea from *metuens* by zeugma = *distracted by the greatness,* etc., *or fearing,* etc. *Metuens* assigns the other reason and governs *castra* as well as *exitium.*

28. Dubiis et honestis. *To measures of doubtful issue, though in themselves virtuous and honorable.* The author's analysis of the *habitus animorum* of the masses here cannot but be admired; and it is capable of a wide application.

Ch. XXIX.—**31. Sacris intentus.** Cf. 27.—*Fatigabat,* sc. precibus votisque = *was importuning.*

32. Alieni jam. *Already another's,* i. e. Otho's.

33. Incertum is neuter gender agreeing with a clause.—*Quem* agrees with *senatorem: a senator, it was uncertain what one.*—*Raperetur. Borne away hastily.* Cf. note, 5, 22: *prono . . . . rapti.* Subj. in oratio obliqua.

34. Ex . . . . urbe, sc. concurrunt ad Galbam.—*Ut . . . . fuerat All those who had fallen in with* Otho on his way to the camp. Cf *ut quisque,* 26.—*Formidine augentes. Through fear exaggerating* (sc. *verum*) the real danger. Al. formidinem. But *formidine* in the Medicean MS., Död., Or., &c. Cf. also 42: *finxit formidine.*

Page

35. Quidam minora. Sub. *dicentes* implied in *augentes.* Zeugma.—*Ne tum quidem.* Not even in such a crisis. Z. 801. 43

36. Igitur. Rarely placed first in Cic. Cf. Z. 357; and Kühner's Cic. Tusc. Qu. 1, 6, 11. Usually first in T., but sometimes in the second place. Cf. note on G. 28.

38. Majoribus remediis, i. e. temporibus, quae majus remedium postularent. Ernesti.

1. Pro gradibus. *From the steps.* So *pro tribunali,* from the tribunal; *pro rostris,* from the rostrum; *pro muris,* from the walls; *pro vallo,* from the rampart, &c. Cf. Z. 311.—*Domus* = palatii. Cf. 27: *Tiberianam domum.* 44

2. Sextus dies. Counting the day of his adoption as the first (as the Romans and also the Greeks and Hebrews always reckoned), and the present as the sixth. Leaving out both, there were but *four* days intervening. Cf. 19: *quatriduo.* On the same principle we may reconcile the 8 days of Luke, 9, 28, with the 6 days of Mat. 17, 1, and Mark, 9, 2. In the same way also we make out the 3 days of our Lord's sepulture.

4. Quo .... fato. Al. quo .... fatum, which is the reading of most of the MSS. The Medicean has *fata.* I have chosen *fato* with Död. and Or., because it makes the sense so much more spirited: ***with what fortune to our family or the state depends on your decision*** (literally, has been placed in your hands).

5. Non quia .... paveam. Cf. note, 15: *non quia .... non. Doleo* is to be supplied before *quia .... paveam* from the antithesis. —*Meo nomine. On my own account = for myself.* Antithetic to *patris et senatus.* Cf. note on *feminarum nomine,* G. 8.

6. Ut qui .... discam. *Since I am such a person .... that I may learn.* Cf. Gr. 264, 8; Z. 565, N. 1; 726.—*Adversas ... expertus.* Cf. note on *fortunam adversam,* 15, supra.

7. Cum maxime = *ut cum maxime* (cf. G. 10, note): *may learn, as when men learn most,* i. e. *may learn most effectually.* The *cum* adds emphasis to *maxime.* Cf. Freund sub *quum.*

8. Patris. Sub. *sed* before it, often omitted by T. Cf. Essay on the Style of Tacitus, p. 13.

10. Proximi motus. When Galba was made emperor.

11. Incruentam urbem. The only sense in which this is true, is, that no blood of *citizens* was shed *in* the city. Thousands of *soldiers* were slain as he was *entering* the city. Cf. chap. 6.

12. Ut ne .... esset. *That not even after Galba* (i. e. at the close of his reign) *there should be room for* (civil) *war. Ne quidem* marks the antith. between *post Galbam* and *proximi motus.* Cf. Gr. 279, 3: *quidem* and *quoque;* Z. 801.

Ch. XXX.—**15. Relatu.** A word now found only in Tacitus. Or

17. Imperatoris, sc. Nero. Cf. 13.—*Ageret. When he was*

Page

44 *acting the part*, by which it is implied, that his friendship for Nero was a mere pretence. Cf. Ann. 1, 4: *specie* secessus, exsulem *egerit*, said of the false Tiberius.—*Habitu .... imperium.* Suetonius (Oth. 12) describes Otho as a man of small stature, ill-set on his feet, with crooked legs, but of almost feminine neatness. *Habitu* here means *person*, as in 14 and 17, where see notes.

18. Illo denotes notoriety. Gr. 207, R. 24; Z. 701.—*Mereretur* est optativus Graecorum = *should he gain?* Wr. Such questions asked by the subj. imply a negative answer. Cf. Z. 530.

19. Specie. Al. *speciem.* But compare Plin. Ep. 2, 6: ne tibi luxuria *specie* frugalitatis imponat.—*Imponit. Deceives,* or *imposes upon.*—*Iste* denotes contempt. Gr. 207 R. 25; Z. 701, = *that wretch,* or *fellow.*

22. Sit. *May be* = though it may be, yet the shame, etc.

26. Vestra. For the case and construction of this word, see Gr. 219, R. 2; also Z. 449.

29. Nero .... destituit. Nero fled from his palace before he was deserted by his palace-guard. The same cohort was now on duty

30. Minus .... transfugae. For the construction of *transfugae,* cf. Gr. 256, R. 6.

33. Commune .... facitis, i. e. become partakers in the guilt.

34. Ad nos .... pertinebunt. Though *the fatal issue of this criminal rebellion will fall upon us, yet to you will remain the calamitous consequences* of the civil *wars* that must ensue.

37. Perinde. Al. proinde. But *proinde, therefore,* has no force; and though it rests on rather better MS. authority, yet the two words are perpetually confounded in the MSS. *Perinde* is correl. to *quam* = *as much as.*—*Donativum.* Al. *donativo plus,* for which reading it is argued, that Piso must offer *more* than Otho, or the offer would be manifestly unavailing. So Wr. and Rup. But Bach replies with great truth and force, that a mind like Piso's could not conceive that the soldiers would not prefer a reward *pro fide* to an *equal* reward *pro facinore.* Död. and Or. read donativom. This entire speech is admirably suited to the character of Piso, as the speech of Galba is to his. Review the character of Piso, as briefly sketched in 14 and 15, and acted out in 17. Then look at the calm dignity, the modesty and yet the conscious worth, the scorn of vice and the contempt for all the low arts of gaining favor with the rabble, which pervade this speech, and you cannot but discern and admire its *fitness.*

45 Ch. XXXI.—**1. Dilapsis.** Having *stolen* away, one by one. They were bribed by Otho. Cf. 27.—*Cetera. The rest,* sc. praeter speculatores.

2. Concionantem. *The speaker,* sc. Piso. Concio = 1. An assembly. 2. An address before it.—*Ut .... evenit* is to be taken with *forte et nullo .... consilio*—it is common in times of commotion for

Page

men to act as chance directs and without plan. *Quam* is omitted in the MSS., and the reading is doubtful in *forte et nullo*. Observe the conciseness of *adhuc: no plan as yet*, sc. matured. 45

5. Electos Illyrici exercitus. Cf. chap. 6. Celsus had been an officer in that army. Ann. 15, 25.—*Vipsania porticu.* A portico built by Vipsanius Agrippa in the field of Mars. Milites, qui extra ordinem in urbe erant, agere plerumque solebant in *porticibus aut templis.* Lipsius.—*Tendentes*, sc. stationem or excubias = *stationed.*

6. Primipilaribus, sc. centurionibus. A post-Augustan word. *The first centurion of the first maniple of the triarii* was called at different times, *primipilaris*, or *primipilus*, or *primi pili centurio* Cf. Liv. 2, 27. He was intrusted with the care of the eagle, and had the right to attend the councils of the general.

7. Libertatis atrio. Where they were quartered, as the Illyrians were in the Vipsanian portico. The word *atrium* denotes, 1. The open area, surrounded by a colonnade, in the private houses of the Romans. 2. A class of public buildings so called from their general resemblance in construction to the *atrium* of a private house, sometimes standing by themselves, but more frequently attached to the front of a temple or some other edifice. The *atrium Libertatis* here meant, was attached to the Aedes Libertatis on the Aventine. Cf. Smith's Dict. of Gr. and Rom. Antiq., word *Atrium.*

8. Diffidebat, sc. Piso. Al. diffidebatur, but without MS. authority

9. Trucidaverat Galba. Cf. note on chap. 6.

11. Si .... flecteretur. Ang. *to see if it might be turned aside.* It denotes both purpose and contingency, and of course requires the subj. So the Greek εἰ, εἴπως. This use of *si* is more frequent in T. than in other Latin authors.

12. Et necdum. The use of *necdum* after *et* is peculiar to the later Latin. Or. A writer of the Augustan age would have omitted the *et.* Cf. Virg. Aen. 11, 70. Död. speaks of the word itself as out of date. Essay, p. 21. But see examples in Freund, from Cicero as well as Virgil.

14. Non ordine militiae. The common explanation of this passage supplies *tribunus factus fuerat:* "Because he had been irregularly promoted to the tribuneship of the prætorian guards." So Brotier, Kingsley and many others. But Wr. thinks such an ellipsis inadmissible, and supplies *suspectus* from the ant. clause: *Because he was not merely suspected,* like Subrius and Cetrius, *on account of his rank and title as tribune* (*ordine = ob ordinem*), *but as a friend of Galba, he was loyal to his prince and* thus *still more an object of suspicion.*

17. Ingestis pilis. Al. infestis. *By pouring in their lances upon him, they drive him away,* compel him to retire.

18. Germanica vexilla. The word *vexillum,* whose meaning,

Page 45 as also that of the corresponding word *vexillarii*, has been much disputed, seems to have denoted, 1. The standard of the cavalry (as *signum* was the standard of the smaller divisions of the infantry, and *aquila* of the whole legion). 2. The standard of a detachment of troops, drafted and dispatched for a specific purpose. 3. The standard of a body of 600 veterans, *attached* (but not *belonging*) to each legion, released from the military oath and free from ordinary duty, but retained *sub vexillo* to render their assistance in the more severe battles, hence technically called *vexillarii*. In each of these three senses, the *vexillum* often stands for the *troops* that served under it. Here the word is used in the second sense = *the German vexillarii*. Cf. 6, where these same troops are called *numeri e Germania*, and are said to have been *electos praemissosque ad bellum in Albanos*. For a full discussion of this subject, see Ruperti's note on *vexilla*, A. 18. See also Smith's Dict. of Antiq., on *Roman Army*.

19. Quod .... refovebat. *Quod* here gives a reason for a state of mind; *quia*, just above, for an outward act. The reason in both cases is an objective fact. Cf. note, 2, 19: *quod ... legisset*. *Quando*, *quandoquidem* and *siquidem*, introduce only subjective reasons; and *quoniam* a motive. Cf. Z. 346. *Quia* and *quoniam* are usually followed by the indic. in Tacitus; *quod* and *quando* by the indic. or the subj., according to the design of the author. *Quandoquidem* and *siquidem* seldom occur, the simple conjunctions being preferred by the author.

20. Inde rursus, sc. *revocatos*, which is implied in *rursus* according to the figure *prægnantia*. Cf. Essay, pp. 16. 17.

Ch. XXXII.—**22. Universa** = all united, all without exception. Cf. Ramshorn and Leverett on the difference between *universus*, *omnis*, *totus* and *cunctus*.

24. Ut si. Between these words there is an ellipsis of *poscerent*. So there is an ellipsis in our *as if*.

25. Judicium .... veritas. Not synonyms, as Ernesti supposed them to be. *Judicium* = *sober reason*, *veritas* = *sincerity*.—*Quippe .... postulaturis*. There is more or less of irony and sarcasm in *quippe* (= *quia-pe*) here; *forsooth* (= *for-true*) *they were about to demand* at a later hour of *the same day the opposite with equal earnestness*. A graphic picture of the corrupt rabble under the Roman emperors.

26. Tradito more limits *adulabantur* or some such verb implied in *adulandi*, or a simple verb of *doing* may be supplied. Cf. Essay, p. 14.

30. Opponenda, sc. against the rebels.—*Servitia*. Abstract for concrete.

31. Daret, sc. Galba. It is the subj. of the oratio obliqua, and would have been expressed by the imperative in the direct address to Galba. Cf. Z. 603, (c); Arnold's Pr. Intr. 460. It depends, like *monendum*, *opponenda*, etc., on *censebat*.

Page

32. Valescere is present to denote a general principle. The word 45
is poetical. Cf. Boetticher.

33. Ultro. Wr. renders: *moreover;* Or.: *at pleasure.*

34. Regressus is genitive after *facultatem* repeated from the foregoing clause.—*Si poeniteat.* Subj. of the dependent clause in oratio obliqua. Gr. 266, 2; Z. 603. Observe the use of the present here, where we must use the imperf., and where the general rule would require the imperf. (as depending on *censebat*). The Latin admits of either in the same sentence and in the same sense. Cf. Arnold's Pr. Intr. 455. 468. We must render it by the imperf.: *if he regretted, or should regret.* We can use the present only with the second person: if *you* regret. So *si ratio sit:* if there *was* or *should be* occasion.

Ch. XXXIII.—**35. Ceteris.** *The rest,* i. e. all but T. Vinius.

37. Ignaros. *Unacquainted with him.* Cf. 26: *ignorantibus.*

38. Cunctatione = *hesitation,* lit. waiting to collect every thing (from *cunctus*); or perhaps trying to do something (conor).—*Segnitia* = *sloth.*—*Terentium* agrees with *nostrum,* sc. *Galbianorum,* understood.—*Imitari principem,* i. e. to act his part as princeps.

1. Discat. Subj. because a dependent clause in the oratio obliqua. 46

2. Capitolium adeat, sc. de more, ut auspicaturus imperium et grates diis acturus sacrificet. Ernesti. Cf. 47: *in capitolium vectus.* For the pres. subj. cf. note, 32: *si poeniteat.* So also *elanguescat* and *necesse sit* just below.

3. Dum . . . . cludit. The ind., contrary to the rule, to represent the shutting up more as a matter of fact and less as a contingency Cf. Gr. 266, R. 5; Z. 575.—*Egregius . . . fortibus.* Spoken ironically

4. Tenus. Properly a noun in the acc. of limit or measure, meaning *as to extent.* Hence it *follows* (not is followed by) the *gen.* and the *abl.* Cf. Freund sub voce. Here it seems to be used pretty much as in the phrases *verbo tenus, nomine tenus, hactenus,* etc., in the sense of *merely: by the gate and threshold merely,* not by *arms,* as truly brave men would do. Cf. Död. in loc. Observe the repetition of kindred words (*janua* and *limine*) for emphasis. Cf. note, 27: *gaudiis,* and places there cited.—*Nimirum* also denotes irony.—*Toleraturus.* Al. toleraturos.

5. Praeclarum, etc. Said in derision of Vinius' proposal: *opponenda servitia,* 33.

6. Quae . . . . valet. The indic. here, contrary to the rule (Gr. 266, 2; Z. 603), affirms the sentiment absolutely and independently of the mere opinion of the speaker.

7. Vel si. *Even if.*

10. Stimulante, sc. Laconem contra Vinium.—*Odii,* sc. in Vinium. Cf. 13.

Ch. XXXIV.—**12. Speciosiora.** Et probabiliora et honestiora. Ruperti.

Page 46 **13. Castra,** sc. praetoriana.—*Juvenis.* Död. places a comma after *juvenis,* thus making his *youth* a separate reason for Piso's being sent before Galba, who, if not too old to meet the danger, was thought less likely to win favor.

14. Nomine and **favore** are abl. of quality.—*Recenti favore* refers to his late adoption, i. e. elevation to imperial favor.

15. Irati. *The enemies* of Vinius, particularly Laco and Icelus, who had now gained the ascendency in Galba's counsels. Vinius had advised not to go to the camp; Galba not only went, but was preceded by one who was thought or hoped to be the personal enemy of Vinius.—*Facilius .... creditur. And the more credible account of the two is, that he was really infensus Vinio.*

17. Ut .... mendaciis, sc. fieri solet, i. e. great lies are apt to gain strength, till at length men are ready to swear to their personal knowledge of their truth.

18. Credula fama. *Credula* is usually taken in a passive sense, here = *readily believed, easily credited.* So Ernesti, Boetticher, Död. and others; though Ernesti suggests also the explanation adopted by Roth., Wr., Rup. and Or., viz. that *fama* is put *poetically* for the *men* who spread and believed the report. Then *credula* may be taken in its ordinary sense, as in 12: *credulum senem. Fama* is not unfrequently personified by T. Cf. A. 9; Ann. 4, 11. Render: *Rumor being credulous where men delight in reports and are indifferent about their truth.*

21. Vulgaverint. Al. *vulgaverant.* The reading we have given follows the Medicean MS. and accords with the general rule for dependent clauses in the oratio obliqua. Cf. Gr. 266, 2; Z. 603.

Ch. XXXV.—**23. In plausus,** sc. *ruere*, or *prorumpere* implied *in ruere* by zeugma: *break forth into shouts of applause.* Cf. Essay on the Style of Tacitus, p. 15.—*Equitum .... senatorum.* Who from their rank might have been expected to be more cautious. *Equites* means, 1. Horsemen, or cavalry. 2. Knights, or men of the equestrian order; for in the early history of Rome men of rank only served in the cavalry, while the plebs made up the infantry. So in Hor. de Ar. Poet.: *quibus est equus = equestres.*

25. Intus. Only the *equites* and *senatores* rushed *in;* the *populus* and *plebs* applauded immoderately without. For the distinction between *populus* and *plebs,* cf. note, A. 43: *vulgus et populus.*

27. Linguae ferocis. Al. linguae feroces, linguis feroces. All the MSS. but one have *linguae ferocis,* which is gen. of quality, and is the more likely to be the true reading, because it is of different construction from *nimii verbis.* Cf. note, G. 16. 18, and Essay, p. 23.

28. Inopia veri = inopia *certorum nuntiorum.* So *veri* is explained by the antithetic *errantium. Inopia* is not, therefore, as Rup. and others say, = ignorantia. Galba was *overcome by the entire*

Page

want of true accounts and the agreement of those who brought false 46
reports.

29. Neque aetate neque corpore. For he was *καὶ γέρων καὶ ἀσθενὴς τὰ νεῦρα.* Xiphil. 64, 3. (The reference is to the abridgment of Dion Cassius by *Xiphilinus,* which alone is preserved in most of this period.)

30. Sistens = resistens, obsistens, as in Virg. Aen. 11, 240. Cf. Essay, p. 10. Vid. Död. in loc. Render: *since he was neither of suitable age nor bodily strength to withstand the now in-rushing multitude.*—*Sella.* Cf. note, 27. The *sella* here, however, appears to have been uncovered (cf. 41), perhaps to suit the military character and taste of Galba.—*Levaretur.* The subj. after *donec,* where a *fact* and not a mere *conception* or *purpose* is expressed. This is contrary to the rule. Cf. note, 13: *donec .... amoliretur.* But it is frequent with Tacitus, who comparatively seldom uses the indic. after *donec, until,* and then without any apparent difference of meaning. Cf. Gr. 263, 4; Z. 575. It is worthy of remark, however, that Tacitus uses the subj. after *donec* where he has occasion for the *imperfect.* Where the sense requires the *perfect,* he uses the indic. The only exception to this usage, so far as I have observed, is in 1, 9: *donec .... aderat. Donec, so long as,* is always followed by the indicative, in oratio recla. Cf. 37: *donec .... dubitabitur.*

33. Quis jussit. "My oath and my duty," replied the soldier. See Plut. Galb. 19. But T. wishing to illustrate only the character of Galba, omits the reply.

CH. XXXVI.—**37. Agmine et corporibus.** Hendiadys for *agmine facto suis corporibus.* Bach. The force of *circumdarent* reaches back to this clause: *not content with surrounding him by their own persons in a body.* Vid. Or. and Duebner in loco. On the mode and tense of *circumdarent,* cf. note, chap. 24: *dederit.*

38. Suggestu = *tribunali,* i. e. at the headquarters of the commander, where the statue of the emperor was always placed. Manual, P. 3, 296. (The reference is to Eschenburg's Manual of Classical Literature: Fiske's Edition.)

1. Signa .... vexillis. The distinction intended between these 47
words in this place is not clear. It *may* be that of their original application, viz. *signa* referring to the infantry, and *vexilla* to the cavalry. More probably, however, *vexillis* is used in the same sense as in 31, where see note. Then *signa* would denote the standards of the cohorts which made up the *legions* (*Hispana* and *Classica*), and *vexilla* those of the *electi Germanici, Britannici et Illyrici exercitus.* Cf. 6.

3. Caveri. Observe the passive form: *should be watched* with a jealous eye.—*Insuper. Furthermore,* i. e. besides precluding the near approach of the tribunes and centurions, they bade each other *beware furthermore* of all their *officers.*

Page 47 **4. Tanquam in .... plebe,** i. e. the formal and heartless adulation of the multitude (cf. 32) was discordant (*variis*) and spiritless (*segni* = se-igni) in comparison with the unanimous and impassioned zeal of the soldiers, which expressed itself not more in words than in actions. Död. supplies, with this clause, *adulabantur* from the noun *adulatione* by brachylogy. Cf. Essay, p. 15.

6. Affluentium = *pouring in.* Cf. A. 29: *affluebat.*

7. Complecti armis denotes a *military* embrace with shield and sword in hand, *armis* being = *armatis brachiis.* Cf. Virg. Aen. 12, 433.—*Juxta,* sc. Othonem.—*Praeire sacramentum. Administer the oath,* lit. *go over it before* them, as they pour in successively. The officer pronounced the words of the military oath, and the soldier repeated the words after him. Hence the former was said *praeire sacramentum,* and the latter *jurāre in verba ejus.* In a regular administration of the oath, only one of the soldiers repeated the words, and the others swore to the same that he had done before them. In the present instance, the soldiers expressed their zeal by volunteering to administer it to each other. Observe the *asyndeton* and the *series of infinitives,* indicative of rapidity. Cf. note, A. 37: *grande .... spectaculum.*

9. Protendens manus. Properly the attitude of supplication, here of respect and reverence.—*Vulgum.* Al. *vulgus,* one MS. The rest *vulgum,* which T. probably used after the example of Virgil. So Wr. and Or.—*Jacere oscula. Throw kisses,* i. e. kiss his hand with an accompanying motion of the hand towards him for whom the kiss was intended. The expression is poetical.

10. Et omnia, sc. *facere.* Cf. Essay on the Style of T., p. 14.

13. Pro vallo. Cf. *pro gradibus,* 29, note.

Ch. XXXVII.—**14. Quis .... processerim.** *In what character I appear before you,* lit. may have appeared. Subj. to soften the expression. Cf. Gr. 260, R. 4; Z. 527.

17. Vestrum .... nomen. *Your title also,* as well as mine: for if I am emperor, you are loyal soldiers; if I am an enemy, you are rebels. An exordium fit for the prince of demagogues: and so is the whole speech.—*Donec dubitabitur.* Cf. note, 35, supra.

18. Habeatis. Subj. Cf. Gr. 265; Z. 552.

19. Auditisne. *Do you not hear,* sc. from the forum, in the *dissono clamore caedem Othonis poscentium,* chap. 32, which could be heard in the prætorian camp, though situated without the walls of the city. So in chap. 39, we read, vice versa, of cries reaching the city from the camp. Vid. Or. in loc.—*Poena* is properly a pecuniary penalty (Gr. ποινή), *supplicium,* capital punishment (*sub* and *plico,* bending under the axe of the executioner). The words are well chosen and well applied here; Otho means to imply, with the falsehood as well as the tact of a demagogue, that a severer punishment awaits

Page

them than him. He exasperates them by arraying before their imagination the terrors of a public execution.—*Postulentur.* Subj. implying the fact, instead of directly asserting it. Render by the ind.: *are demanded.* 47

22. Promisit. *Given promise, furnished an example.* The reader will notice the train of bloody and dismal words that follow: *trucidaverit, horror, feralem,* etc. *Feralis* is a poetical word. Cf. Boetticher's Lex. Tac.—*Ut qui .... trucidaverit.* Cf. note, 29: *ut qui ... discam. Ut qui* is not used by Cic., but *utpote qui.* Cf. Z. 565.

24. Solam .... victoriam. False. Cf. Suet. Galb. 6–8.

25. Decumari. The practice of decimation, i. e. punishing every tenth man of an offending body of soldiers, unfrequent in the early history of Rome, became not uncommon in the civil wars and under the empire. The victims were drawn by lot. Ann. 3, 21. For the fact here referred to, cf. Suet. Galb. 12; and note, 6: *trucidatis .... militum.*

26. In fidem acceperat. *Venire in fidem* alicujus, is to surrender to his discretion, to submit to his will, and *accipere in fidem* is to *receive such submission.* See a parallel passage, Ann. 12, 27.

37. Polycliti .... Aegiali. Polyclitus and Vatinius were favorite freedmen of Nero, who rose to wealth and honor during his reign, and whose very names were ever after synonymous with rapacity and oppression, as T. says, 2, 95: *vetera odiorum nomina.* Polyclitus is mentioned, Ann. 14, 39; Vatinius, 15, 34. The name of *Aegialus* does not occur elsewhere, for which reason, as well as from the obscurity of the Medicean MS., much dispute has arisen as to the reading. The text is that of Or. and Död. Al. *Helii,* and *Helii et Haloti.*

38. Paraverunt. As if they had enriched themselves by their industry and economy, but Icelus by robbery (*rapuit*). Al. *perierunt: rapientes* being supplied by brachylogy from rapuit. Cf. Essay, p. 15.

1. Si ipse imperasset. *If he had been emperor himself,* instead 48
of being prime-minister. In that case, Otho means to imply, Vinius would have felt some interest in us as his subjects. But *now he has us in his power as completely as if we had been his own property, and yet holds us in no estimation as the property of another.*

2. Una illa domus. The single family, i. e. property of Vinius. As to the wealth of Vinius, vid. again chap. 48.

3. Exprobratur, sc. as if an unreasonable demand. Död.

Ch. XXXVIII.—**6. Ab exsilio.** Cf. 21 and 48.

7. Notabili tempestate. Cf. 18.

8. Adversantes. Al. aversantes. Cf. note, 1: *adverseris.—Idem,* sc. the same with the gods, i. e. they too are opposed to it. Accordingly he adds: *vestra virtus,* etc., *your valor alone is further required,* lit. waited for.

Page 48 **13. Nec .... togata.** *And the single, unarmed cohort does not,* etc. The cohort on guard was not fully armed, and wore the *toga* or dress of citizens, not the *sagum* of the regular military service. Lipsius.

15. Quis .... imputet, i. e. quis pro me acrius contendendo efficiat, ut ei plus debeam. Ernesti. Cf. note, G. 21. Used in this sense by poets and later Latin authors. Render: *who can lay me under the greatest obligation.* Subj. in the indirect question. Cf. Gr. 265; Z. 552.

16. Cunctationis. So Rup. and Or. from the Medicean MS. Cf. Liv. 3, 46: *locum seditionis quaerere.* Al. cunctationi.

17. Aperire. Al. aperiri, which is a needless conjecture. *He then ordered them to open the arsenal.* Many of these troops, like the cohort at the palace-gate, were not fully armed, i. e. had no defensive armor, *galeis scutisque,* which were allowed to the prætorian cohorts only at the command of the præfect or tribune. Lipsius. Cf note on *cohors togata.*

18. Ut .... distingueretur. This clause depends on *more et ordine,* and denotes the nature or the object of that military custom. The legionary troops were armed with *pila,* the prætorians with *lanceae,* etc. Ritter.

20. Miscentur ... scutisque. *Prætorian and legionary troops seize indiscriminately on shields and helmets that belong to auxiliaries. Auxiliaribus* agrees with *galeis scutisque. Galea* and *scutum* are among the *few military terms* which have a common etymology in the Greek and the Latin; whereas the names of common things in *agriculture* and *the arts of peace almost all* have a common origin in the two languages, the Pelasgi, who contributed the common element, being an agricultural and pacific people. Cf. Niebuhr's His. of Rome: also Arnold, chap. 2; Keightley, chap. 1; and Schmitz, chap. 1.

Ch. XXXIX.—**24. Exterritus.** *Frightened out* of his purpose of entering the camp.

25. In urbem usque. The prætorian camp was without the city, at the Viminal gate. Rup. Cf. note, 37: *auditisne.—Egressum interim. Who had gone forth* from the palace (cf. 35) *in the mean time,* i. e. the interval between Piso's egress (34) and the events here described.

26. Assecutus erat. *Had come up to, fallen in with.*

27. Marius Celsus. Cf. 31.

28. Redire, sc. Galbam et Pisonem.—*Plerique. Many, very many;* not *most,* for it includes less than *plures.* Cf. 4, 84.

29. Plures. *More.—Contradicerent.* Subj. Cf. Gr. 263, 5, R. 2; Z. 578.

33. Ad postremum vel odio. A conjectural reading, suggested by Rhenanus and adopted by most editors, not because it satisfies, but

because they can think of nothing better. Render: *or finally out of* 48
personal enmity at least.

36. Diffugia. Vocabulum a Tacito effictum, ut alia. Rup. The word, though new, is highly expressive of the *rapid dispersion* of Galba's nearest followers.

37. Primo alacres. Cf. 35: *in periculo non ausurus,* etc.

Ch. XL.—**2. Basilicis.** Strictly an adj., *aula* or *porticus* being 49
understood. The name was derived from the στοά βασίλειος of Athens, where the second archon, ἄρχων βασιλεύς, administered justice. The Roman *basilica* served both as a court of justice and an exchange. There were many of them built around the forum, some of great extent and splendor. The earlier ones were surrounded only by an open peristyle of columns. The later were enclosed by a wall, and the columns were confined to the interior. These were, in many instances, converted at length into Christian churches; and other churches built after the same model were called *basilicae.* Cf. Smith's Dict. of Antiq., *Basilica;* also note on *Libertatis atrio,* 31.

5. Quale .... silentium est. Nam magna ira silet et ardet, levis clamat et tumultuatur. Brotier. Burnouf refers to a very similar passage in Xenophon's Agesilaus, 2, which, he thinks, Tacitus may have had in mind.

7. Occupare. *Praevenire et sic impedire.* Rup.

8. Vologesen .... Pacorum. Kings of the Parthians. Cf. Ann. 12, 14; 13, 9; 15, 14. 24, et al.; His. 5, 9; G. 37.—*Arsacidae* was a common appellation of the Parthian kings, from Arsaces the founder of the state. Cf. note, G. 37: *Arsacis.*

12. Imminentium. *Overhanging* the forum where these scenes were enacted, and which was in a great measure surrounded by temples and porticoes. Cf. 3, 71: *imminentia foro templa.—Priores. The example of former emperors,* who had punished such crimes.—*Futuri. The fear of future emperors,* who would be sure to follow the precedent.

14. Quisquis successit. For no sovereign could trust subjects who had proved so unfaithful. Cf. chap. 44, at the close.

Ch. XLI.—**15. Vexillarius.** Here a *standard-bearer.* For another sense of the word, see note on *vexilla,* 31.—*Comitatae Galbam cohortis.* The same cohort, *quae in palatio stationem agebat,* chap. 29. Al. *Galbae.*

17. Dereptam. *Torn off* from his standard.

20. Curtii lacum. A spot in the middle of the Roman forum, so called from the legend of M. Curtius, who leaped into the yawning chasm and it closed upon him. Cf. note, 3, 69: *lacum Fundani.*

25. Agerent ac ferirent = *age, feri,* a formula of Latin speech The imperatives of the oratio recta become the subjunctives in the

Page

49 oratio obliqua. Z. 603. Cf. the same narrative, Suet. Galb. 20; Plu. Galb. 27.

27. Evocatum. *A veteran soldier.* The *evocati* derived their name from their being *called out* into the field again by the *special invitation* of the general, after they had served out their time.

29. Hausisse. This word properly denotes the *drawing out of the blood,* but here the *piercing of the jugulum, impresso gladio, with the point of his sword.* Render: *cut his throat.*

30. Tegebatur, sc. *thorace.* Cf. chap. 35.

31. Feritate et saevitia. Synonyms brought together for emphasis = *brutal cruelty* (*feritate* from *ferus.* Gr. θήρ).

32. Adjecta. *Superadded,* after the mortal wound.

CH. XLII.—**33. Quo et ipso.** *Et* = *also,* i. e. as well as Galba.

34. Consumpserit. Subj. Cf. Gr 265; Z. 552.

35. Ut occideretur. Cf. Gr. 273, 2; Z. 615.

36. Conscientia. Al. *conscientiam,* which is the easier reading. But the MSS. have *conscientia.*

37. Confessus est has *quod* for its object, thus: *This he either asserted falsely through fear of losing his life, or stated truly by virtue of his participation in the conspiracy.* So Wr. and Död.—*Huc. To the latter.—Ut .... fuerit. That he may have been.* A softened form of the ind., *he was.*

38. Causa erat. Cf. 6: *senem .... destruebant.*

50 **1. Mox.** Antithetic to *primo ictu;* hence = *alio ictu.*

2. In utrumque latus. *In* is omitted in some editions, but found in the MSS. Well explained by Död. as an example of constructio prægnans, or contracta = pierced in (into) both sides, and so pierced through. Cf. Essay, p. 17.

CH. XLIII.—**4. Aetas nostra vidit.** The author means to designate this, as a rare instance of courage and disinterestedness in an age marked by prevailing cowardice and selfishness.

5. Custodiae Pisonis, sc. when Piso was sent forward into the camp. Or. Plut. (Galb. 27) and Xiph. (64, 6) represent this centurion as slain in defence of *Galba.*

6. Exprobrans .... vertendo. Cf. note on *vocans, appellando,* etc., chap. 23.

8. Aedem Vestae. Built by Numa on the declivity of the Capitoline Hill. In ea Palladium, Penates, ignis perpetuus et Vestales Virgines. Rup.

9. Publici servi erant stipatores et ministri sacerdotum, magistratuumve, et publicis sumptibus alebantur. Rup.—*Contubernio.* The dwelling or apartment of the slave, occupied by himself and his fellow-servant (*contubernali*). Only Tacitus uses the word in this sense. Cf. Boetticher and Freund sub voce. The word means *hutting to-*

Page

gether (*con* and *taberna* from *tabula*), *tenting together*, especially in 50
military life.

11. Nominatim. *By name*, i. e. *expressly* for that purpose.

13. Nuper .... donatus. And therefore under obligations to Galba. So also it was the special duty of the *speculator* to *defend* Galba and Piso.

CH. XLIV.—**15. Nullam caedem,** etc. Plutarch says (Galb. 44), that on seeing the head of Galba, Otho cried out: "This is nothing, fellow-soldiers; bring me the head of Piso."

17. Mens (from Gr. μένος) is properly *the intellect; animus* (from Gr. ἄνεμος), *the spirit, the feelings.* The words are used appropriately here, the former referring more to *anxious thoughts,* the latter to a *spirit of sadness.* See a lively picture of the dismal images that disturbed even the sleep of Otho, in Xiph. 64, 7.

18. Amicitiae in T. Vinio. Cf. 13.

19. Confuderat. Our word *confuse.* Often used, as here, to denote *mental disturbance and agitation.*

20. Jus. *Just* in the view of men.

21. Fas. *Right* in the sight of the gods and according to the laws of nature.

22. Signa cohortium ... aquilam legionis. Mark the distinction between *signa* and *aquila.* Cf. also note on *vexilla,* 31. The legion here meant is the *classica,* or *that which Nero had enrolled from the fleet,* chap. 6. The Spanish legion there mentioned had now returned to Spain. Or.

28. Munimentum .... ultionem. Acc. in appos. with the foregoing sentence, instead of a nom. with *quod est.* Roth. Dum occisum principem ulciscuntur, sese ipsi muniunt *ad praesens,* et se *in posterum* vindicant, cum exemplum successoribus ulciscendi principem relinquunt. Vid. Kingsley's Tacitus.

CH. XLV.—**30. Alium crederes,** etc. Their conduct was so changed that you could not have believed it the same *body.* Cf. note, 10: *laudares;* 57: *scires.* Gr. 209, R. 7; Z. 528, N. 2. In all such examples, there is a protasis understood, e. g. *you would have thought,* if you had been present; *men might have known,* if they had considered, etc.—*Ruere, anteire,* etc. Notice the series of infinitives. Cf. 36.

31. In castra, sc. praetoriana, where Otho still was.

37. Ad supplicium. Död. omits *ad,* after the Medicean MS. Cf. Essay, p. 12.

1. Optimo cuique. Dat. after *quaeri.* Rup. Bach calls it dat. 51
for gen. after *perniciem.*

3. Jubere, sc. scelus. He could not *forbid crime,* but he could *command it,* because such a command fell in with the disposition of the soldiers and the spirit of the age. It is one of those many passages

Page 51 in T., in which a single stroke shows us the very age and body of the times.

4. Jussum, sc. esse, depending on *affirmans.*—*Poenas daturum,* lit. *give satisfaction,* cf. note on *poena,* 37; by usage, *suffer punishment.*

Ch. XLVI.—**7. Ipsi legere.** The power of choosing such officers belonged to the senate and people; but was usurped by the emperors, and now conceded by Otho to the soldiers themselves.—*E manipularibus. A common soldier.* Cf. 25.

8. Vigilibus praepositum. This would not make him a regular officer in the army. Cf. note on *vigiliis,* 20. It was, therefore, a sudden elevation to place such a man at the head of the prætorians.

9. Adjungitur .... Proculus, i. e. the prætorians choose Proculus as colleague with Firmus in the præfectship. We should expect *Proculum* in the acc., and connected with Firmum as the object of *legere.* Anacoluthon. Cf. Gr. 323, 3, (5).

11. Urbi .... praefecere. Cf. praefecto urbis, 14, note.

13. Flagitatum. Cf. note on *flagitare,* 12. It is followed by *ut,* with the subj., like other verbs of *demanding.*

14. Vacationes = *pretia vacationum* (Ann. 1, 17), i. e. *fees for exemption from military duty,* or rather *camp* duty, for those who had the *vacatio* were expected to *fight,* if present in time of battle, but were not required to share in the watch, the labor of fortifying, etc. Such exemption had been conferred as an honor in better times; it was now bought with money. The use of *vacatio,* in this sense, is peculiar to Tacitus. Cf. Boetticher.

15. Tributum. Originally the tax of a *tribe* (from *tribus,* cf. Niebuhr, Rom. His.; Keightley and Schmitz. do.); subsequently any tax or tribute.

16. Manipuli. This word denotes properly a *handful* or bunch of hay, then by metonymy a detachment of soldiers serving under the same as an ensign. Cf. note, chap. 25. Under the emperors there were three maniples in each cohort and ten cohorts in each legion, so that the maniple was one-thirtieth of a legion.

17. Dum .... exsolveret. *Provided only, that they would pay,* etc. *Dum,* in this sense, takes the subj. Cf. Gr. 263, 2; and Freund sub voce.

18. Pensi is gen. after *habebat.* Gr. 214, (2); Z. 444, note: *no one cared for the measure of the burden or the kind of gain,* i. e. the source from which he derived his means to pay the fee. Orelli remarks, that *pensi habere aliquid* is a favorite formula with Sallust, whom Monboddo charges Tacitus with imitating, and whom he certainly resembles in style.

20. Tum. *Furthermore* = our *and then.*—*Locupletissimus.* Properly, *rich in real estate* (*locus ... plenus*). Cf. Freund sub voce.

Page

—*Quisque*, after a superlative, = *omnes* with the positive with a little 51
more of the distributive idea. Constructed in Cicero with singular verb; in Tacitus with singular or plural. Z. 367 and 710, b.

21. Fatigari. *Pressed with hard labor* by the centurions.—*Emeret.* Simple for compound (*redimeret*). Cf. Essay, p. 11. Besides avoiding the repetition of *redimere*, *emere* suggests the idea of a *sale* by the centurions for filthy *lucre*. See Or. in loc.

25. Bella civilia is governed by *ad* before *seditiones.* Some editors insert *in;* but it is not necessary to depart from the MSS. See a similar construction in *legiones ducesque*, 4; also Essay, p. 12.

26. Vulgi. *Common soldiers.* In its etymology, *vulgus* is our word *folk*, German, *volk.*—*Largitione*, i. e. *remissione vacationum* *Vulgi* is objective genitive = *in vulgus.*

29. Tanquam .... seponeretur. *Under color of banishment. Seponere* is not used in this sense in the Augustan age. Otho gave out that Laco was banished, but sent a man to put him to death. *Palam* in the next clause is opposed to this clandestine procedure.

31. Confossus. *He was stabbed* on his way from Rome towards his place of banishment. His having left Rome is not *stated*, but *implied* in the *pregnant* style of the author. Cf. Essay, p. 18.

32. Libertum. Ernesti insists on *libertinum.* But in the age of Tacitus, the distinction between these words (for which see note, G. 25) was not observed.

Ch. XLVII.—**33. Novissimum.** Like our word *last*, which = latest, or newest, and also farthest, *last in a series.* Cf. note, G. 24.

34. Vocat .... urbanus. The consuls, Galba and Vinius, were slain; the consul elect also, Marius Celsus, was in irons. The *Praetor Urbanus* was the first in rank of the prætors (of whom there were some twelve or fifteen under the emperors), and the chief magistrate for the administration of justice. His duties confined him to the *city*. In the absence or death of the consuls, he, as in this instance, discharged the functions of a consul. Cf. 4, 39; Cic. Ep. ad Div. 10, 12. *Praetor* was in early times the name for any magistrate or leader (*prae-itor*). Manual, P. 3, 243. The consuls were originally called prætors. Cic. Leg. 3, 3. Cf. Nieb. and Arn. Rom. His.

1. Omisisset. *Passed them over entirely.*—*Distulisset. Deferred* 52
the punishment of them. Subj. Cf. Gr. 265; Z. 552.

4. Permisit and **concedi** are not tautology. He gave permission *to his officers* that the bodies should be yielded *to the friends.*

6. Composuere. *Buried*, properly, arranged or adorned for burial; a sense peculiar to Tacitus with the poets. Cf. Boetticher and Freund sub voce.

Ch. XLVIII.—**8. Explebat.** *Was filling out*, i. e. *had nearly completed*, though Ernesti and Wr. make it = *expleverat.*

11. Ad hoc. *To this end* = *εἰς τοῦτο.*

Page
52 **14. Praetoria familia.** Al. *e praetoria familia.* But cf *eques·tri familia*, 52. The abl. here denotes *rank* and *quality*, not source —*E proscriptis*, sc. by the triumvirate, Octavius, Antony and Lepidus

18. Eadem lascivia. *In the same wanton mood.* Subj. Cf. Gr 263, 5, R. 2; Z. 578.—*Temperasset.* Al. *temerasset, temptasset* and *tentasset. Tentasset* is found in the margin of one MS. All the rest, including the Medicean, have *temperasset,* which when it governs the acc. means *rule, regulate* (Z. 414), as in Suet. Oct. 68: Viden', ut cinaedus orbem digito *temperet.* She went the rounds with the officer of the watch (the *circuitor,* cf. Smith's Dict., *Castra*), and *directed the sentinels and others, who were on duty, in the performance of their exercises.* Such is almost the language of Dion in describing the same occurrence, 59, 18.—*In ipsis principiis.* The *principia* was a large public place in the camp where were the tents of the general (*praetorium*) and of the other principal officers; where also stood the standards, the images of the emperors and the altars of the gods. The emphatic *ipsis* refers to the peculiar boldness of such an act in such a place, sacred by the presence, not only of the officers, but of the gods. —*Stuprum ausa.* Usually said only of males, but peculiarly appropriate to *such* a female. Orelli explains it thus: eo usque impiae temeritatis, ut se stuprari sineret a Vinio.

27. In abruptum. *Upon the brink of a precipice,* i. e. to *a dangerous elevation.* Cf. *per abrupta,* A. 42.

28. Industrius. Ant. to *pravus.* Hence *virtuous.* Compare the Greek σπουδαῖος.

Ch. XLIX.—**31. Galbae.** Emphatic; hence placed first, as also *Pisonis* at the close of the last section.—*Licentia tenebrarum. Under cover of the darkness;* lit. in the unrestrained freedom of the darkness.

32. E prioribus servis. Priores sunt veteres, i. e. qui ante principatum servi Galbae fuere. Wr.

33. Privatis .... hortis, sc. Galbae, ad viam Aureliam. Cf. Suet. Galb. 20.

34. Ante .... tumulum. *Ante* shows the relation between *tumulum* and *repertum.* It had been thrown there in revenge for the death of Patrobius, according to Suetonius (Galb. 20), by a *freedman* of *Patrobius,* who purchased it of the *marketmen* and *camp-boys* (*lixas calonesque*) for a hundred aurei. Of Patrobius, see 2, 95; Plin. 35, 13, et al.

36. Cremato. The Romans burned the bodies of the dead in this age. Cf. note, 5, 5: *corpora.*

37. Hunc exitum. *Such was the death,* etc.

38. Quinque principes emensus, i. e. spatium imperii quinque principum, ut *emetiri spatium.* Ann. 11, 32; 15, 16. Rup.

53 **2. Ipsi medium ingenium.** *He himself had middling talents.*

3. Venditator. *A vain boaster.* Properly, a crier up of wares

for sale, from *vendo.* The word is found only in T *Incuriosus* Page 53
also is peculiar to his age.

5. Avarus, *avaricious; parcus, saving. Avarus* is the stronger word.—*Ubi .... incidisset.* Plup. subj., to denote a repeated action. Cf. Gr. 264, 12; Z. 569.

6. Sine reprehensione = *excusably.* Ant. to *usque ad culpam,* which implies the contrary. As to this *culpa* in Galba, cf. 7 and 12.

8. Quod segnitia .... vocaretur. He was thought to have *prudently* concealed his abilities and repressed his activity, because of the dangers which attended men of *high birth* in those *perilous times,* somewhat as Brutus did under Tarquin. Cf. A. 6: *gnarus sub Nerone temporum, quibus inertia pro sapientia fuit.* See *Döderlein's* note in loc.

9. Pro consule. Al. proconsul. The sense is the same with either reading. A *proconsul* is one who acts *in the place of a consul,* without holding the consular office. It was usual in the later periods of the Roman state, for the consuls, on the expiration of their office, to take the government of a province with consular power. The proconsulship was, therefore, a continuation, though a modified one, of the consulship. Cf. Dict. of Gr. and Rom. Antiq.

11. Continuit, sc. in fide et officio = rexit. Cf. *retinere,* 11.—*Major .... imperasset.* A principle often verified by facts; and here expressed in language which the reader will not soon forget, but which Monboddo censures as affected.

Ch. L.—**14. Paventem.** Properly, *palpitating with fear* (from *pavio,* Gr. παίω). A stronger word than *timens,* or *metuens.*

15. Exterruit. *Ex* only gives emphasis here. But cf. *exterritus,* 39.

16. Superioris .... descivisse. Cf. 12.—*Crederetur.* Impers. The more frequent construction in the early Latin would be *exercitus crederetur.* Cf. note, G. 32: *narratur.*

21. Saevae pacis. Galba fell without a blow struck in his defence. It could not, therefore, be called civil war; but it was a *cruel and bloody peace.* Cf. 2: *ipsa etiam pace saevum.*—*Exempla* is the obj. of *loquebantur,* and *memoria* is abl. abs. with *repetita,* though improperly followed by a colon in the common editions.

23. Pharsaliam. Where Pompey was conquered by Julius Cæsar, A. U. 706.—*Philippos.* Where Brutus and Cassius were defeated and slain by Octavius and Antony, A. U. 712.

24. Perusiam. Where Antony was reduced to submission by Octavius, A. U. 713.—*Mutinam* (now Modena), where the consuls, Hirtius and Pansa, the last who enjoyed with full power the dignity of chief magistrates of Rome, were slain in a battle with the murderers of Julius Cæsar, A. U. 711.

25. Loquebantur = *they talked of.*

Page

53 **26. C. Julio,** sc. victore. *When Julius Cæsar was victorious*

29. Ituros. Direct questions, unless addressed to the second person, are expressed by the acc. with the inf. in the oratio obliqua. Cf Z. 603, c.

34. Ambigua .... fama. *There were contradictory accounts of the character of Vesp.*

35. In melius mutatus est, i. e. became a better emperor than he had been private man. Galba disappointed expectation. Cf. 49. Tiberius, Caligula, Claudius and Nero had each given promise of better things in the early part of those reigns, which have now become the very synonyms of tyranny and cruelty.

Ch. LI.—**37. Caeso .... Vindice.** Cf. note, 8.

38. Ut cui .... evenisset. Cf. note, 37: *ut qui .... trucidaverit.*

54 **1. Expeditionem et aciem.** Al. *quam otium*, which is a conjecture of Lipsius. The MSS. and earlier editions have *et aciem*, and to this reading, the more recent editors have returned. Render thus: *the army* (sc. the German) *now preferred campaigns and battles with their attending rewards* (viz. booty and imperial largesses), *to the regular pay and ordinary service.* Observe the causative sense of *ditissimi: the source of great wealth.* Cf. Tibull.: *divitis auri*

3. Ingenio loci coelique. Cf. G. chap. 2 and 4.

4. Pace. *Tranquillity.* Antith. to *discordiae civium.*

5. Utrimque. *In both parties.*

6. Ad decus. *For ornament,* or *display,* as *ad usum* denotes *for useful purposes.* Al. *ad dedecus* = for disgraceful and criminal uses. The sense is equally good, and the authority nearly equal for either reading. The *viri, arma, equi,* here spoken of, are the prizes of the late victory over Vindex and the Gauls.—*Bellum,* sc. against Vindex.

7. Centurias. Each maniple (cf. note, 46) was divided into two centuries, of which there were, therefore, sixty in each legion, and of course the same number of *centurions.* Cf. Ann. 1, 32. The number of men in a century varied from 50 to 100, as the legion varied from 3000 to 6000. Niebuhr supposes the *century* to have consisted originally of thirty footmen, as the *turma* did of thirty horsemen.—*Noverant. Had been acquainted with.*

9. Se .... expertae, i. e. having found themselves superior to the Gauls, they were now eager for another conflict with them.

11. Vocabant, sc. Gallos.

13. Instigatrix. Only in Tacitus.—*Hoc .... indiderant. For they had given the Gauls this name* (Galbians), *having become weary* (disgusted) *with calling them after Vindex.*

14. Sequanis. Dat. after *infensi.* The Sequani were a people of Belgic Gaul, and derived their name from the Sequana (Seine) about the sources of which they dwelt. Their capital was *Vesontio*

now Besançon.—*Aeduis*. A people of Gallia Lugdunensis, bordering Page 54
on the Sequani. Their capital was *Augustodunum*, now Autun.—*Ac deinde .... erat = ac deinde* aliis *civitatibus, prout opulentia* iis *erat*.

17. Hauserunt animo. *They greedily coveted*, more literally, they already devoured in imagination.—*Super avaritiam*, is to be connected with *irritati*.

18. Remissam .... donatos, sc. with Roman citizenship and the lands of their neighbors. Cf. chap. 8. Instead of *et donatos*, the editions which follow Oberlin and the Bipontines have *eos damnatos*, a mere conjecture.

20. In ignominiam exercitus, sc. Germanici. This clause should be connected with *jactabant*. *The Gauls boasted, to the disgrace of the German army, that a fourth part*, etc. Cf. Orelli's note in loc.—*Accessit*. Cf. note, 5: *accessit vox*.

21. Decumari = decumatum iri. So *dimitti* = *were to be dismissed*, sc. by Galba.—*Legiones*, sc. of Lower Germany.

23. Sinistra. Left hand; hence inauspicious, unfavorable; a poetical sense of the word.—*Lugdunensis colonia*. Now Lyons.

24. Rumoribus. Reports unfavorable to Galba.

CH. LII.—**27. Sub.** *About*, i. e. *shortly before*. Sometimes, though rarely, *shortly after*.—*Superioris* = prioris, i. e. *the preceding year*, A. U. 821.—*Aulus Vitellius .... ingressus*. Cf. 9.

29. Cum cura = cum imperio, ut curaret (i. e. regeret). Rup. and Död. *Cura* (from *quaero*) not unfrequently denotes an office of trust and authority, particularly in the later Latin authors. See examples in the Lexicon.

30. Notae. *Marks of disgrace*, especially those imposed by the censor.

31. In quibus .... mutaverat. *In which* (course of proceedings) *he had entirely changed the state of things which the sordid avarice* (*sordem et avaritiam*, hendiadys) *of Fonteius Capito had produced; by taking away military offices* (from those to whom he had given them), *or restoring them* (to those from whom he had taken them), as the case might require. *Ve* is distributive. Cf. G. 4: *solove*.

33. In majus, i. e. quasi Vitellius non consularis legatus, sed ipse imperator esset. Rup. Cf. note on *in majus*, 18.

34. Et Vitellius. *Et* = *nam*, introduces particular examples of the general fact stated in the foregoing clause. Hence it should not be preceded by a period, as it is in the common editions.—*Ita* = itaque. Cf. 45, where *ita* is used in the same way. Render the whole passage thus: *For in the estimation of strictly impartial judges, Vitellius was abject and mean; so his friends called it condescension: and because without measure and without reason he gave*

Page

54 *away his own* (private) *property and lavished that which was not his* (sc. the public), *they called it goodness* (kindness). *At the same time*, i. e. still further, *in their eagerness for power, the friends of Vitellius construed his very vices* (viz. gluttony and debauchery) *as virtues.* Such is Wr.'s reading and interpretation of this difficult passage. Rup., Död. and Or. insert *ut* between *et* and *Vitellius*, without MS. authority.

36. Donaret. Subj. to express the views of others, not of the author = because, *as they said*, he gave, etc. Cf. Gr. 266, 3; Z. 571.

37. Multi is made the subj. of *interpretabantur* in the previous sentence in the common editions. But such a view of things could hardly be predicated of the *modesti quietique* and the *mali et strenui* in common. Besides that reading destroys the force of *sed* in the next clause. T. has given the character of Vitellius above. He now passes to give a sketch of the army and its officers. He says, *there were in both armies* (sc. of Upper and of Lower Germany) *many peaceable (quieti) and unambitious (modesti) characters; there were also many turbulent (mali,* ill-disposed, cf. *apud malos seditio,* 26) *and restless (strenui) spirits: but Caecina and Valens excelled in,* etc.

55 **3. Tanquam.** *Because in his opinion.* Hence followed by the subj. Cf. note, G. 20: *tanquam.—Cunctationem. Hesitation.* Cf. note, 33. *Indecision* in such a case (sc. when the empire was offered him, cf. 8 and 9) would be construed as a crime against Galba, who would expect of Verginius a prompt and decided negative.

4. Ingrate tulisset. *Had received without due gratitude.* Död. makes *tulisset = retulisset: had made an ungrateful return for.*

5. Ipsum. *Vitellius himself.*

6. Flacco Hordeonio. Cf. 9.

8. Panderet. *A nautical metaphor,* non a sinu togae, sed potius a nautis, qui pandunt sinum velorum. So Rup. But Död. and Or. refer it to the *toga: only let him open his bosom.*

10. Equestri familia, etc. Abl. of quality. Cf. note, 44.

12. Collegium Caesaris. L. Vitellius, the father of the emperor, had been colleague with Claudius Cæsar twice in the consulship and once in the censorship. Cf. Suet. Vitel. chap. 2.

Ch. LIII.—**16. Decora juventa, corpore ingens,** etc. Notice the enallage. These phrases all express the *quality* of Caecina, and at the same time they indirectly denote the *means* of *illexerat. Decora* in the sense of *pulchra* is poetical. Död. follows the Medicean MS. in retaining the antique form *decori* (abl.). Cf. Essay, p. 21.

19. Baetica, sc. Hispania. Galba's command was in Hispania Tarraconensis.

20. Compertum agrees with *Caecinam.*

21. Flagitari = in jus vocari, accusari. *Postulare* is often used in the same sense.

24. Bello .... Vindicem. Cf. 8. 55

26. Praeventus erat. Cf. *praeventam gratiam*, 5.

27. Treveri. A German people between the Meuse and the Rhine, now *Treves.—Lingones.* A people of Gallia Lugdunensis on the Seine, now *Langres.* The reader will be struck with the perpetuity of the names of places. These always outlast spoken languages, and often survive a series of political revolutions. Compare the Celtic names of places in Great Britain, and the Indian names of mountains, rivers and states in America.—*Quas alias civitates.* By attraction for *aliae civitates, quas. Civitates = states,* not cities in our sense of the word. Ad rem. cf. 8.

28. Hibernis .... miscentur. *Lie contiguous to, and have frequent intercourse with, the legions* of Upper Germany *in their winter-quarters.* Expressed with extreme conciseness.

29. Inter .... corruptior, sc. quam in castris. Our word *pagan* comes from *paganus.* The earliest Christian churches were in the cities, while yet the *inhabitants of the country villages* were unconverted. Compare *heathen* from *heath.*

30. Cuicumque alii, sc. quam Verginio, qui imperium sibi delatum respuebat. Cf. 8 and 52. Rup.

Ch. LIV.—**32. Legionibus,** sc. of Upper Germany.

33. Dextras. Quasdam figuras ex auro aut argento. Ernesti. In nummis saepe occurrunt duae manus junctae cum varia epigraphe: Exercituum Fides, Concordia, Consensus. Brotier.—*Squalorem.* Cf. note, G. 31.

34. Compositi. Cf. note, A. 42.—*Principia.* Cf. note, 48.

36. Pronis auribus. Cf. chap. 1.

38. Hordeonius Flaccus. Cf. 9.

4. Per tenebras, etc. = in tenebris, ceterisque insciis, ignaris. Wr. 56

5. Obstringuntur. Like the middle voice of the Greeks. Cf. G. 39: *evolvuntur.*

7. Circumdatis .... alisque is the manner or means of *pararetur,* i. e. *by throwing their cohorts and squadrons around them,* sc. the legions. *Ala* = 1. The wing of a bird; 2. The wing of an army; 3. Any body of cavalry, because the cavalry were usually stationed on the wings of the Roman armies. *Ala,* though indefinite, is usually a larger body than *turma.* Cf. note, chap. 51.

8. Eadem, sc. seditiosa consilia cum legionibus.

Ch. LV.—**12. Sacramento .... adactae.** Död. considers *sacramento* to be *dative* here, as just below: *sacramento advocabant.* Cf. Essay, p. 13. The acc., or acc. with *ad,* is the prevailing construction after *adigere* in Cæsar, Livy and the earlier writers; the abl. in Tacitus, Suetonius and the later authors. Cf. Freund, sub voce.

Page

56 **20. Superiore exercitu.** Cf. note, *superior exercitus*, 9. See also note on *Inferioris Germaniae*, ibid.

22. Dirumpunt. *Break in pieces.* *Di* denotes separation.

23. Duodevicesima. Al. duoetvicesima. *The* 18*th hesitating at first, but afterwards falling in* with the measure.

24. Imperii, sc. Romani. *The Roman empire* or *government.*—*Senatus ..... nomina.* The old republican usage of swearing fidelity to the senate and people of Rome had been superseded by the oath of allegiance to the emperor. It was now in form revived, and those obsolete names were again *called* or *appealed to in the oath* (*sacramento advocabant*). Instead of *sacramento,* some copies have *sacramenta* here.

26. Legatorum. The commander of a legion was called *legatus* (cf. note, 7), also the commander of an entire army, and governor of the province where it was stationed. Cf. A. 7.—*Tribunorum.* Cf. note on *tribunus,* 28.

28. Suggestu. Cf. note, 36. Here put for *de* or *pro suggestu.* Essay, pp. 11, 12.

29. Cui imputaretur. In cujus gratiam fieret. E. Cf. note on *imputet,* 38. Subj. Cf. Gr. 264, 6; Z. 561.

Ch. LVI.—**30. Hordeonius Flaccus.** Cf. 54.—*Consularis legatus.* Cf. note on *legatorum,* 55, and places cited there.

32. Socordia innocens, i. e. he took no part in the *flagitii,* but it was only because he was too inactive.

35. Cum protegerent. *When and because they were protecting.* A combination of *time* and *cause* expressed by the subj. Z. 578.

36. Abrepti. *Torn away* from their post.—*Ultra.* Used in place of an adj. Cf. note, G. 19.

38. Unde. *Ex* vel *in qua parte.* Ernesti.

57 **1. In .... nuntiat.** *Brings word into* or *to* the Agrippinian colony (now Cologne, cf. G. 28).

4. In .... verba jurasse. Cf. notes on *senatus .... nomina,* 55, and *praeire sacramentum,* 36.

5. Inane. *Unmeaning.*—*Occupari.* *Anticipated* (cf. 40), i. e. *seized before* it turned against him, while it was yet *nutantem.*

6. Principem, sc. Vitellius.

7. Qui .... nuntiarent. *Qui* with the subj. denoting the object of the mission. Cf. Gr. 264, 5; Z. 556.

10. Sumi. *Accepted* on the nomination of the *superior exercitus.*

Ch. LVII.—**11. Proxima.** The nearest to the quarters of Vitellius of all the legions of Lower Germany. Probably at Bonna, now Bonn. Cf. 4, 25: *Bonnam, hiberna primae legionis.*—*Promptissimus .... Valens.* Cf. 7.

14. Gressus. Simple for compound (*ingressus*). Compare Virg. Aen. 6, 633: *gressi per opaca viarum.* Cf. Essay, p. 11.

Page

16. Speciosis . . . relictis. Cf. 55. 57

17. Scires. Cf. note, 45: *crederes.*

18. Illum, sc. exercitum. "The men, it now was plain, were never the soldiers of a republic." Murphy.—*Priore biduo. During the two days previous,* while they had been making such a show of patriotism. Cf. 55.

21. Ingenio validus. *Ingenio* is taken in very different senses by different commentators, e. g. *eloquence in enlisting others,* by Pichena; *skill in fabricating arms and implements of war,* by Wr.; *practical tact in general,* by Bach and Rup. Observe throughout this sentence the constant omission of connectives. It is a somewhat striking, though by no means rare specimen of the author's fondness for the asyndeton. Cf. Essay, p. 13.

22. Quibus . . . . spes. *Who had present* resources *in abundance, and who, if victorious, cherished high hopes* of better things in future.—*Ex affluenti* = affluentia, adverbial phrase for adj.

23. Manipuli et gregarius miles. Hendiadys. Gr. 323, 2, (3).

24. Viatica. Pecuniam ad sumptus viae. Cf. Suet. Caes. 68. Brotier.

25. Instinctu, sc. aliorum. Cf. *instinctu decurionum,* 70; *impetu,* sc. proprio, cf. A. 15; *avaritiâ,* hoping to receive in return more than they gave.

Ch. LVIII.—**28. Per libertos . . . . solita.** Cf. note on *liberto,* 13.—*In equites . . . . disponit.* Not however to the exclusion of freedmen, and even buffoons. Cf. 2, 57. 65. 95. Suet. Vitel. 12.

35. Fonteio Capitoni. Cf. 7.—*Struxisset.* Subj. Cf. note, 52: *tanquam.*

36. Occidere palam, etc. See a similar passage in 45, and note on *jubere,* ibid.

38. Post victoriam, sc. Vitellii ad Bedriacum, 2, 40–49.—*Stratis* = compositis, sedatis; lit. *smoothed,* like waves. No other prose writer uses the word so. Cf. Freund, sub voce.

1. Objicitur, sc. militum furori, vel his tanquam feris bestiis. Rup. 58

3. Punienti, sc. Vitellio.—*Vilior. Of less value.* Cf. G. 5: *vilitate.*

Ch. LIX.—**5. Ne . . . . alienaretur** depends on *exemptus,* with which supply *est.* It is *implied* here that the army demanded the punishment of Civilis.—*Et erant* adds a fact which shows the importance of the friendship of Civilis to Vitellius.

6. Tum. *At this time.* So T. uses it passim, e. g. A. 39. 40; His. 1, 70.

10. Supra, sc. chap. 56.—**12. Partibus,** sc. Vitellii.

14. Ala Taurina. So named from a people, whose capital was Augusta Taurinorum, 2, 66, now Turin, and from whom the squadron was enlisted.

Ch. LX.—**17. Trebellius Maximus.** Cf. A. 16.

Page

58 **19. Odium ejus,** i. e. the *hatred* of the army *towards him. Ejus,* obj. gen. Gr. 211, R. 2.

21. Proruperat, sc. Caelius. A less concise writer would have said: qui olim discors fuerat, sed qui, etc.

23. Objectabat. *Was charging* habitually or repeatedly. Gr 145, II. 1.

24. Modestia. Cf. note on *modestiam.* A. 20.—*Eo discordiae.* Cf. Gr. 212, R. 4, N. 3; Z. 434.

25. Auxiliarium quoque. *The auxiliaries also,* i. e. as well as the legion of Caelius. Cf. Gr. 279, 3: *quidem* and *quoque.*

26. Cohortibus alisque, sc. auxiliarium.

28. Consulari, i. e. the governor.—*Legati legionum,* i. e. the commanders of the separate legions. Cf. notes at chapters 7 and 55.

Ch. LXI.—**34. Cottianis Alpibus.** "The Alps are distinguished in different parts by different names: as the *Maritime Alps,* near Genoa; the *Cottian Alps,* separating Dauphiné from Piedmont; the *Graian Alps,* beginning from Mount Cenis, where the *Cottian* end, and extending to Great St. Bernard; the *Pennine Alps,* extending from west to east to the *Rætian Alps,* the *Alpes Noricae,* and the *Pannonian Alps,* as far as the springs of the Kulpe. They are called Alps from alpen, a Celtic term for high mountains." Murphy.

35. Aquila .... alisque, i. e. the entire fifth legion. Of the other legions of Lower Germany, there went only *electi.* Bach.

36. Data agrees with *millia,* as if there were no *ad* in the sentence; *ad* with numerals being often used adverbially, like our *about.* Cf. Z. 296.

59 **2. Tota mole belli.** *With his entire military strength and resources.* Cf. *tota mole regni,* Ann. 6, 36.

Ch. LXII.—**3. Diversitas** is not found in the writers of the Augustan age.

4. Dum .... trepident. The subj. here conveys the sentiments of the army, not of the author. Gr. 266, 3; Z. 549. Otherwise the indic. would follow *dum.*

5. Neque .... moras. Observe the brachylogy: *nor* would they endure *the delays of an inactive peace.*

7. Facto .... consulto. Notice the concrete form of these words. Cf. note, chap. 1: *conditam.* They are much more lively and forcible than our words action and consultation. See the same in Sall. Cat. 1.

10. Medio .... temulentus. So Nero. Ann. 14, 2. Peter argues on the supposition, that it is wellnigh impossible, at least quite incredible, that a man should be drunken at an early hour of the day. Acts, 2, 15.

12. Strenuis .... adderet. Cf. note, G. 4: *minime,* etc.

14. Caesarem .... prohibuit. Cf. 2, 62; Suet. Vitel. 8; Plut. Galb. 22.

Page

15. Laetum augurium is nom. in appos. with *aquila*. 59

17. Meatu. Poetic and post-Augustan. Cf. Freund sub voce. Probably preferred to *volatu*, as more expressive of slow and gentle motion

18. Is is correlative to *ut* = *such .... that*, and accordingly followed by the subj. (Gr. 262, R. 1; Z. 556), which we however must render by the ind. For the imperf. after *ut*, cf. note, chap. 24: *dederit.*

CH. LXIII.—**21. Treviros.** The people of Treves.

22. Divoduri. Now Metz, so called from the name of the people, Mediomatrici.—**23. Pavor.** Cf. note on *paventem*, 50.

24. Ob praedam .... cupidine. Not tautology. Ob praedam is *objective; spoliandi cupidine* subjective: *not because there was booty* to be had in the town, nor because they were fired with a *passion for plunder*. Cf. Döderlein's note in loc.

25. Furore, *fury; rabie, madness. Rabies* implies the privation of consciousness. Ramshorn.

27. Temperavere. *Refrained.* See the same construction and meaning, Virg. Aen. 2, 8: *temperet a lacrimis.* Cf. note, 48: *temperasset.* The radical idea of the word is that of *separation* (*tempus, τέμνω*).—*Caesa.* Cf. note on *data*, 61.

29. Magistratibus et precibus. Hendiadys, = magistratibus, qui deprecabantur exitium imminens. Roth.

30. Occurrerent. *Met* them *successively*, or in a continued series. Observe the force of the imperfect. Cf. notes, 24: *dederit;* and 66: *admoverit.*

31. Placamenta, e. g. infulae et velamenta. Cf. 66: velamenta et infulas praeferentes. The word is post-Augustan.—*Non quidem ... pace*, i. e. though they were not at war with the Romans, they used all the appropriate means of procuring peace. Acute dictum atque acerbe. Wr.

32. Tendebantur = protendebantur. Compare *protendens manus*, 36, with *tendere manus*, 2, 46. Simple for compound.

CH. LXIV.—**35. Volvebat** has *animus militum* for its subject.

37. Proxima. Next south of the Leuci on the way to Rome.

1. Intemperie = propter intemperantiam, immodestiam. Rup. 60

2. Supra, sc. 59.

3. Jurgia. Litigation (from *jure* and *ago*), *altercation.*

4. Rixa. A passionate *quarrel*, which goes to fisticuffs. Cf. G. 22. Ramshorn.

5. Exarsere, ni. Sup. the ellipsis by *et exarsissent.* Cf. *hausisse, ni*, A. 4, note; and Essay, p. 15. Render *ni* by *but.*

6. Animadversione. Cf. note on *animadvertere*, G. 7.—*Imperii* belongs both to *oblitos* and *admonuissent.* Wr.

10. Abductae. *Were withdrawn* from their quarters at Lyons (cf. 59), and joined the army of Vitellius.

Page

60 **11. Lugduni .... hibernis.** Cf. Gr. 204, R. 7; Z. 399.

15. Deciperetur. Subj. Cf. Gr. 262, R. 9; Z. 536.

Ch. LXV.—**16. Viennenses.** The people of Vienna, now Vienne in Dauphiné. This *vetus discordia* goes back to the origin of Lyons, which was founded by exiles from Vienna.

17. Proximum bellum, sc. the war excited by Vindex, in which the Lugdunenses sided with Nero, the Viennenses with Vindex and Galba.—*Invicem.* Adv. for adj. The ellipsis may be supplied by *illatae.* Cf. note, G. 18: *extra;* also A. 6: *longe;* 8: *ultra.*

18. Quam ut .... pugnaretur. *Ut* = *velut* (cf. Essay, p. . 0), or *quasi;* hence followed by the subj. So *ut* is used after *ita* by Cicero in the sense of *quasi.* Cf. Kühner's note, Tusc. Quaes. 5, 28, 81. Or with Död. *pugnaretur* may be taken as equivalent to *pugnari crederes,* in which case *ut* = *sicut.* The sentiment of the clause has reference to the peculiar bitterness of local animosities exceeding even the fury of civil war.

20. Occasione irae. *Taking advantage of the civil discord.* Cf. *irae civiles,* Ann. 1, 43. Wr. But *irae* is doubtless Galba's *resentment,* of which he took *occasion* to enrich himself.

21. Uno amne. *By a river only,* sc. the Rhone. Cf. Essay, p. 17.

22. Connexum = ut inter *connexas,* i. e. finitimas gentes. Cf. solitum inter accolas odium, 5, 1.

25. Referendo = memorando, *reminding.*

29. Cuncta .... Romanam. Vienna was an old town of the Allobroges, built before the Roman conquest. Lyons was a recent colony, established by authority of the Roman senate. Cf. Dio. 46, 50. Both were in fact Roman colonies. Cf. infra: *vetustas .... coloniae.* The Lugdunenses, in the bitterness of their hostility, exaggerate the difference between the two towns.

31. Ne relinquerentur depends on *preces.*

Ch. LXVI.—**36. Arma ..... prensando.** Acts expressive of humble and earnest supplication. Notice the climacteric order beginning with the *armor,* then embracing the *knees* (the Homeric attitude), then the *feet* (*vestigia,* literally, tracks, soles of the feet), of course prostrate on the ground, and following up, as it were, the averted and departing footsteps of the soldiers.

38. Tum, sc. after money had been given them, *then* the soldiers began to think of the *antiquity and dignity of the colony.* The language is somewhat sarcastic. Compare Döderlein's notes both on *vestigia* and *tum.*

61 **1. Salutem** refers to the *continued existence, incolumitatem* to the *uninjured state* of the people. *Salvus incolumisque* = our safe and sound. Roth, Rup. and Wr. call them synonyms.

3. Mulctati = privati.—*Promiscuis copiis.* Frumento vel com meatu communiter ac sine discrimine ordinum ab omnibus dato.

Page

7. Inopi juventa is the *cause* of *prodigus*. 61

8. Ipsa itinerum, etc., i. e. induced by bribes not to encamp at certain towns or country places, but to march farther, or stop short, or take another direction.

11. Luco. Lucus Augusti, now *Luc*. Cf. Plin. 3, 4.

12. Admoverit. Compare the *completed* action expressed by *admoverit* with the *prolonged* anxiety and suspense denoted by *arbitrarentur* at the beginning of the section, or with the continued series of acts denoted by *occurrerent* in chap. 63. Cf. note, 24: *dederit.*—*Donec .... mitigaretur*. Cf. note, 35: *levaretur*.

13. Quotiens .... deesset. The subj. denoting a repeated action. Gr. 264, 12; Z. 569.—*Materia,* i. e. facultas dandae. Ernesti.

Ch. LXVII.—**15. Plus praedae.** More than Valens. The position of *plus* gives it emphasis, = *still more.*—*Hausit* must be taken in a somewhat different sense with these two objects respectively: he *took* more *booty* and *shed* more *blood*. Död. Cf. Essay, 16.

16. Helvetii. The territory of the Helvetii was a part of Celtic Gaul, more extensive than what is now called Switzerland. The people are celebrated by Julius Cæsar for their military virtue and constant warfare with the Germans. Caes. B. G. 1, 1. Murphy.

17. Clara agrees with *gens, ignari* with *Helvetii*. Cf. Gr. 205, R. 3.

19. Avaritia ac festinatio = *avaritia ardens* by hendiadys. So Rup. But *festinatio* may denote *impetuosity.*—*Rapuerant* agrees with *legio,* as a collective noun. Gr. 209, R. 11; Z. 366.

27. Locus .... frequens. Called *castellum* above. Known to the ancients under the name of Aquae Helveticae, or Vicus Aquensis, now Baden (Baths).

28. Ut .... aggrederentur. *To attack.*—*Versos in legionem. While engaged with the legion* (the twenty-first) *in front.*

Ch. LXVIII.—**32. Non arma noscere** = non usum armorum scire. So Wr., Död. and Or. But Rup. prefers another explanation: *non arma noscere* quisque suá, sed promiscue rapere; which accords better with the context and the prevailing usage of Tacitus, who employs *noscere* in the sense of *recognise, distinguish,* cf. 3, 24: *noscere suos noscique;* 1, 90: *genus ipsum orandi noscerent;* or else he employs it in the sense of being or becoming *acquainted* with *persons,* e. g. 1, 51: *centurias .... suas .... noverant.* The former of these uses is hardly found in Cicero. Cf. Freund sub voce.

35. Ipsórum Raetorum juventus, i. e. volunteers, in distinction from those who had enlisted in the Roman army (*alae cohortesque*).

38. Montem Vocetium. Est pars asperrima Jurae. Oberlin.

1. Depulsi. They were *dislodged, driven down.* Supply *sunt.* 62 Cf. Essay, p. 14.

4. Sub corona. The origin of this expression is explained in two

Page

62 ways: 1. That captives wore *coronae* when sold as slaves; 2. That they were surrounded by a body of armed men, called a *corona.* Gellius (N. A. 7, 4) mentions both explanations and prefers the former. See Rup. in loco.—*Aventicum.* Now *Avenches,* near Friburg. Or.

5. Caput. *The chief city. Urbs* is properly the *capital; civitas,* the whole body of *citizens,* the *state.* Cf. Rams. 206.—*Peteretur.* Subj. Cf. Gr. 263, 5, R. 2; Z. 578. Render by the ind.

Ch. LXIX.—**9. Legati.** Sent to Vitellius to propitiate his favor.

10. Invenerint. *Whether they found.* Subj. of the indirect question. Cf. Gr. 265; Z. 552.

12. Minis ac verbis. *Threatening words,* by hendiadys. Roth and Wr. More probably, however, as Död. suggests, *minis* refers to threatening *looks* and *actions.* They are dat. after *temperare,* which with the dat. means to *refrain from,* lit. to restrain himself in respect to. In 63, it is followed by the abl. with *ab* in the same sense; in 48, with acc. in the sense of *to regulate.* Cf. note, 48.

15. Mutabilem agrees with *animum.* Al. *mutabile,* referring to *vulgo,* and about equal in MS. authority with *mutabilem.*

16. Immodicus. This is the reading of Gronovius, Wr., Or., etc. The MSS. have *immodicum,* which does not correspond with *mutabilem,* and cannot agree with *animus* in the nom.

17. Effusis lacrimis. *Copious tears.* Said of any thing unconfined or unrestrained, and particularly frequent after the Augustan age. Cf. Freund. Död. prefers *effusi* with *lacrimis* dative after it. Cf. Essay, p. 12.

Ch. LXX.—**19. Dum .... fieret.** *Till he should become;* i. e. with that object in view. Hence the subj. Cf. Gr. 263, 4; Z. 575.

21. Alam Silianam. Al. Sullanam and Syllanam. The squadron is supposed to have derived its name from C. Silius, legate of Upper Germany under Tiberius. Ann. 1, 31. 72, etc. Cf. *Ala Petrina,* below in this chapter.

22. Padum. Now the Po.—*Proconsulem .... habuerant.* Cf. 2, 97, where Vitellius' proconsular government of Africa is commended as *integrum ac favorabilem.* See also Suet. Vitel. 5.

23. A Nerone .... exciti, etc. Cf. 6, where the same thing is mentioned.

25. Tum. Cf. note on it, 59.—*Instinctu* limits *transiere.* Ad verbum, cf. 57, note.

26. Decurionum. The leader of a decury, i. e. a body of ten men, was called *decurio,* as the commander of a *century* was a *centurio.* Cf. Smith's Dict. Antiq., word *Army.*

28. In partes. *To the party of Vitellius.*

29. Municipia. "*Municipium* is a free provincial city in Italy with its own laws and magistrates, generally also with Roman citizenship; *colonia,* a Roman colonial city, which was granted to Roman citizens for colonization." Rams. 206. Compare both with *urbs, caput* and *civitas,* 68, note. The *coloniae* were also afterwards called *municipia,* from which they differed only in origin. Cf. Smith's Dict., under *Colonia.*—*Mediolanum.* Now Milan. 62

34. Vexillis. Cf. 31, note.—*Ala Petrina.* Supposed to have derived its name from two illustrious Roman knights, who bore the cognomen of *Petra* and were put to death by Claudius. Cf. Ann. 11, 4. It had been stationed in Cumberland, as appears by a lapidary inscription set forth in Camden's Britannia.—*Cunctatus.* Supply est. *Hesitated.*—*Num .... flecteret.* Subj. Cf. Gr. 265; Z. 552.

35. Ibi. This conjectural reading of Lipsius and Brotier is so well supported by the analogy of 2, 16: trierarchum liburnicarum *ibi* navium, that I have ventured to receive it into the text. Rup. and Or. have *urbi,* Wr. and Död. *urbis,* which are the readings of the MSS. But they include the word in brackets and pronounce it a manifest corruption. A procurat[illegible] f a *city* is an office unknown in Roman history.

36. Conciti[illegible] .. pontibus. Abl. abs. denoting the *cause* of *putabatur.* Re[illegible]r: *because he had called together auxiliaries,* etc.

1. Certatu[illegible] foret. Subj. in a subordinate clause of the oratio obliqua. Cf. G[illegible] 266, 2; Z. 603, c. 63

2. Penin[illegible] itinere, i. e. super vel per jugum Alpium Peninarum. Cf. note, 61.—*Subsignanum militem* = *militem sub signis,* or *vexillis,* alias *vexillarios,* for which see note, 31. They are here distinguished from the legions, which served *sub aquila,* and seem to be treated with special indulgence in being allowed to take the easier route. The meaning of the word, which is post-Augustan, has been much disputed, but it probably designates the *veterans* described under No. 3, in the note on *vexilla* at chap. 31. It occurs in only one other passage in Tacitus, 4, 33.

3. Hibernis = hiemantibus, nive conspersis. Rup.

Ch. LXXI.—**7. Composita** implies something *made up, assumed.* Cf. 54, and places there cited.

8. Vitia reditura. Cf. above, 21. 22. and 30.

9. Marium .... subtractum. Cf. 45.

11. Titulus = praetextus. Bach. But Rup. and Or. make it = *laus, gloria.*

13. Ultro imputavit. *He even* (cf. note, G. 20: *ultro*) *reckoned it as a ground of obligation,* or confidence on the part of Otho—in a word, he *claimed credit for it* as an example of good influence on others, and illustrating the steadfastness of his own loyalty. "When an author so expresses himself, we can but guess at his meaning." So Monboddo. But the obscurity results entirely from his lordship's ignorance of the usus loquendi of T., as his criticism on the passage plainly shows.—*Nec Otho,* etc. *Nor did Otho proceed as if he were pardoning* an enemy, *but lest the opposite party should excite* in

Page

63 Celsus *a fear as to the sincerity of the reconciliation, he treated him at once as a most intimate friend,* i. e. as if there were no need of reconciliation. This is substantially Ritter's view of this much disputed passage. Död. follows the same reading and gives essentially the same interpretation, but thinks the text requires some amendment. Other readings and other interpretations have been suggested too numerous to mention. But none of them give so good a sense as this, and none rest on much, if any, better authority of MSS. The reading of Wr., Rup. and Or., with several of the best MSS., is this: sed, ne hostes metueret, conciliationes adhibens.

16. Etiam pro Othone. Ut olim pro Galba. Rup.

17. Integra et infelix. *Unwavering yet unfortunate,* sc. because those to whom he attached himself, were speedily ruined. Observe the *alliteration.*

18. In vulgus instead of *vulgo* for variety.

19. Eandem .... irascebantur. Vera et notabilis gnome atque eadem in Liv. 5, 26: *eandem virtutem et oderant et mirabantur.* Lipsius.

Ch. LXXII.—**21. Sophonius Tigellinus.** Cf. Ann. 14, 48. 51. 57. 60; 15, 50; 16, 17, et al.: also Xiph. 64, 3; Plut. Oth. 2.

23. Vigilum. Cf. note on *vigiliis,* 20.—*Quia velocius erat,* sc. vitiis adipisci quam virtutibus. Alliteration again.

25. Virilia scelera. Facinora vires audaciamque virilis aetatis (virorum) desiderantia, ut caedes et similia. Ernesti.

29. Desiderium. *Regret* for something lost. Cf. *desiderabitur,* chap. 16. *Cupido* is desire of acquisition.

31. Clementia is abl. of cause; *effugium,* acc. in apposition with *eum servaverat.* See a similar enallage in G. 16: *remedium .... inscitia.* Compare also *munimentum,* chap. 44.

37. Fora. *Market-places.* Besides *the* Forum emphatically so called, i. e. the Forum Romanum between the Palatine and Capitoline hills, there were several large *fora* in which public business was transacted, such as the Forum Julii, Forum Augusti, Forum Trajani, etc.; besides which there were smaller market-places set apart each for some particular trade and named accordingly, e. g. forum boarium, olitorium, piscarium, etc. The word *forum* is allied to *foras,* and signifies properly an *open place,* whether *before* some building or *surrounded* by temples, porticoes and other edifices. Cf. Smith's Dict. of Antiq., *Forum.*—*Ubi* refers to *circum ac theatra.*

38. Donec .... foedavit. Here we have *donec, until,* with the ind. according to the rule, but contrary to the prevailing usage of T. Cf. notes, 1, 13. 35; 4, 35. 37.

64 **1. Sinuessanas aquas.** *The baths of Sinuessa.* Sinuessa, a town of Latium, on the confines of Campania, was much frequented for the salubrity of its waters. Cf. Ann. 12, 66; Plin. 31, 4; Mart

Page

11, 8.—*Supremae necessitatis.* Cf. note on these words, chap. 3, 64
also *exitus*, ibid.

Ch. LXXIII.—**6. Galvia Crispinilla.** Cf. Xiph. 63, 12; also Plut. Galb. Al. *Calvia.* Cf. note, chap. 3: *prodigia.*—*Frustrationibus. Artifices*, which is the primary meaning of the word (from *fraus*).—*Adversa . . . . fama. Much to the disgrace of the dissembling emperor. Frustrationibus* is the means of *exempta est*, and *adversa fama* is an accompanying circumstance.

8. In arma, sc. pro Nerone ulciscendo. Ernesti. For Clodius Macer, cf. 7, note.

9. Famem molita, sc. by cutting off the usual supplies from Africa, which furnished Rome with corn for the larger part of every year. Cf. 3, 48, and note ibid.

11. Apud Galbam, i. e. in the reigns of Galba, etc.

12. Orbitate. Cf. note on it, G. 20.—*Bonis temporibus.* Even under Augustus, Tacitus speaks of *childless wealth* as *praevalida.* Ann. 3, 25.

Ch. LXXIV.—**15. Offerebant.** Otho even offered to share the throne with Vitellius and become his son-in-law. Cf. Suet. Oth. 8; Xiph. 64, 10.

17. Legisset. Subj. Cf. note, 70: *certatum foret.*—*Primo* is antith. to *mox.*—*Mollius. In milder terms,* said of both parties in contrast with the reproaches they afterwards heaped upon each other.

18. Quasi rixantes. Döderlein remarks, that the *quasi* is properly prefixed to *rixantes,* because *rixari* strictly implies an *oral* and *personal* quarrel.

20. Legatis. Cf. 19.—**21. Ad . . . . copias.** Cf. 59 and 64.

22. Specie Senatus. *In the name of the senate,* and with a *specious show* of its authority.

23. Quam ut . . . . viderentur. Cf. note, 65: *quam ut . . . . pugnaretur.*

24. Per simulationem officii. *Under pretence of honoring them,* sc. with a retinue, but really to watch over their fidelity.

26. Addidit, sc. to these prætorians.

29. Tanto, sc. tempore. It was in fact only thirteen days before, Vitellius having been nominated on the 2d of Jan. and Otho on the 15th, but this is enough for soldiers to magnify into a long time.

30. Vertissent. The subj. sets forth the sentiments of Fabius Valens: because, as he alleged, etc.

32. Ideo. *By that means;* a sense peculiar to the later Latin. *Ideo* is also more frequently followed by a correlative particle, *quod, quia, quoniam, ut,* or the like.

Ch. LXXV.—**34. Frustra, impune.** Adv. for adj. Cf. 65: *invicem;* and A. passim.

37. Gnaris. Al. ignaris, which is the reading of the MSS. But

Page

64 the antithesis, *mutua ignorantia*, and the force of ***invicem*** **certainly** require *gnaris:* strange faces, *where all knew each other*, would of course betray the Othonian spies. But not so with the Vitellians at Rome, where almost all were mutually strangers.

65 **2. Domus utraque,** sc. Vitellii sub Othone, Othonis sub Vitellio. It so happened, that the family connexions of Vitellius were at Rome, and at the mercy of Otho; while those of Otho were in like manner at the disposal of Vitellius.

Ch. LXXVI.—**4. Primus . . . . . addidit.** *First gave.* The Latins use the adj. where we use the adv. of time. The news from Illyricum was the *first thing* that imparted confidence to Otho.

8. Aquitania. Southwestern Gaul.

9. Diu mansit, sc. in fide. Cited by Döderlein as an example of *praegnantia.* Cf. Essay, p. 16.

11. Provinciam Narbonensem. Southeastern Gaul.

13. Armorum = exercituum.—*Dirimitur*, sc. ab Italia. The reference is to the troops in Egypt, Asia, Africa, &c.

15. Praetexto. Al. praetextu. Cf. *specie senatus*, chap. 74. *The specious name, the pretended authority of the senate. Praetextum* is not found before the age of Tacitus. Cf. Boetticher.

16. Auditus also is a post-Augustan substantive, and is employed here in the unusual sense of *auditio, report.* The distant provinces and armies had heard of Otho's nomination, and acquiesced in it, before they knew of Vitellius', though actually prior in order of time.

20. Neque = *et non, et* connecting the clause, and *non* qualifying *exspectata.*

21. Proconsulis. Cf. note, 49: pro consule.

22. Nam . . . . faciunt. Cf. notes, 13, and G. 25.

24. Pleraque. Intellige ea, quae fieri solent sub initium novi imperii. Wr.—*Festinavit.* Cf. note on *festinantur.* G. 20.

Ch. LXXVII.—**26. Distractis,** sc. in contrarias partes.

27. Quidem gives emphasis to the comparison between Vitellius and Otho, and it shows the impropriety of attaching this clause to the previous section, as in the old editions. The antith. particle *sed* is understood before Otho. Cf. 3, note. Ernesti inserts *at.*

28. Quaedam is the obj. of *obibat, pleraque* of *properando*, which is used instead of *properans.*

30. In . . . . Martias. *Till the 1st of March*, sc. from the commencement of his reign with the death of Galba, on the 15th of January. Cf. 27. For the construction of *Martias*, cf. 12, note. The consulship was originally annual, and elective by the people; but in the reign of Tiberius, the office becoming merely an honor conferred by the emperors (nominally by the senate, Ann. 1, 15), was held for only two months, there being of course 6 *pairs* (*consules* = colleagues, cf. note, 1) during the year, those who held it for the first two

Page

months being called the *ordinary consuls*, and giving their name to 65
the year. Cf. Dic. Ant., Consul. The ordinary consuls for this year were *Galba* and *Vinius*. Cf. 1. But they being slain on the 15th of January, Otho and his brother were substituted (*suffecti*) to fill up their time *to the* 1*st of March*.

33. Praetexto exhibits the reason *alleged* by *Otho*. Cf. 76, note.

34. Viennensium, to whom, therefore, we infer that Vopiscus belonged, though the author nowhere states the fact. Cf. Essay, p. 18.

36. Sabinis attaches to both *Caelio* and *Flavio*, who had the same *cognomen* (cf. note, A. 4), and together with them is dat. after *mansere*. *Flavius Sabinus, consul elect*, is a different man from Flavius Sabinus, brother of Vespasian, who was *præfect of the city*. Cf. 47, and 2, 55, with which compare 2, 36. Or.—*Julias* and *Septembres* agree with *kalendas* understood. Cf. 12.—*Arrio Antonino*. Mentioned by Pliny as a writer of verses in Greek and Latin. Cf. Epis. 4, 3. 18. 5, 10. He was grandfather of Antoninus Pius the emperor. Or. For a synoptical view of the consulships for this year, see the table, p. 26.

38. Pontificatus auguratusque. Acc. pl. in apposition with *cumulum dignitatis*. In the age of the emperors, the number of augurs and pontifices was indefinite, and the offices were conferred by the emperors on whom they pleased, but particularly on those who had already borne the highest civil honors. Though they had lost much of their pristine sanctity and power, still both the pontificate and the augurship were highly esteemed. The emperor himself was always pontifex maximus. For the etymology of the word, and further details, see Dic. Gr. and Rom. Antiq., sub voce.

1. Honoratis .... senibus. Any *aged man who had already* 66
been honored with the consulship and the like civil offices, but had not received the sacred offices of pontifex and augur. Wr. restricts it needlessly to those just mentioned, Caelius, Flavius, &c.—*Aut* distinguishes between the treatment of the *senibus* on the one hand, and the *adolescentulos* on the other. Cf. note on *aut*, A. 17. The common editions have *et*.

3. Recoluit. Iterum honoravit, vel iisdem, quibus avi ac patres fuerant ornati. Rup. Död. makes *sacerdotiis dative* after *recoluit*, which he renders, *restored to*. And this construction seems to be justified by such passages as 3, 7: *recoli imagines Galbae jussit*. *Sacerdotium* includes both the *pontificate* and the *augurship*.—*Cadio Rufo*. Cf. Ann. 12, 22.

5. Repetundarum. *Repetundae*, or in full *pecuniae repetundae*, denotes—1. Such sums of money as provinces or individuals might recover from Roman magistrates, who had improperly received the money in the discharge of any official function; 2. The illegal act for which compensation was claimed. Here render: *extortion*, which is implied in *avaritia*, in the next clause. Cf. Fiske's Man. P. 3. 263

Page 66 **6. Ignoscentibus.** Otho and the senate, or Otho and his advisers.

7. Majestatem, sc. laesam. *Majestas laesa* or *minuta* was, under the republic, any offence against the majesty of the people or the state ; under the emperors, it was especially an offence against the imperial dignity. Anglice: *treason,* though *majestas* is more comprehensive than treason. Cf. Smith's Dic. of Antiq. ; also Man. as above. To pardon the crime of *majestas* was now popular ; to pardon *repetundae* was unpopular. Hence the senators who were now restored to their seats were falsely alleged to have been condemned for the former and not the latter offence.

Ch. LXXVIII.—**9. Civitatum quoque,** etc. *Cities and provinces also,* i. e. as well as Rome, to which the previous section relates

10. Hispaliensibus et Emeritensibus. Hispalis and Emerita were Roman colonies in Spain, now Seville and Merida. The latter was so called from a colony of veteran soldiers (*emeriti*) led thither by command of Augustus. Cf. Dio. 53, 26.

12. Baeticae. A province in the south of Spain.—*Maurorum civitates.* In Mauritania, on the adjacent coast of Africa. These towns of the Mauri were placed under the jurisdiction of the Bætican province, and thus contributed to its revenues.

13. Ostenta. Al. ostentui. These new rights were *presented* rather than *permanent* gifts, because, in the political changes which soon followed, they became null and void.

15. Excusata. Al. excusatus. Cf. same word used in the same way, 7, note.

16. Statuas .... reposuit. They had been thrown down by the populace, and replaced by Nero. Ann. 14, 61. On the death of Nero they were again removed, and now replaced a second time by Otho. On Poppaea, cf. note, 13, and places there cited.

18. Spe .... alliciendi. Nero was popular with the multitude. Cf. 4. and 16. Suet. Ner. 57.—*Qui .... proponerent,* i. e. in locis publicis injussi ponerent. Ernesti. Ad rem, cf. Plut. Otho. Ad verbum, see it used in the same sense by Plin. 35, 4, 7: tabulam pictam *proposuit* in latere curiae Hostiliae. Rup. Subj. Cf. Gr. 264, 6 ; Z. 561.

19. Quibusdam diebus. *On certain days,* i. e. on public occasions.

21. Neroni. Dat. in apposition with Othoni. Gr. 204, R. 8.

22. Metu, pudore. Al. *metum, pudorem.* But the obj. of *tenuit* is understood, sc. the recognition of the title.

Ch. LXXIX.—**24. Rhoxolani.** A people north of the Palus Maeotis (sea of Azof), between the Tanais (Don) and the Borysthenes (Dnieper).—*Sarmatica gens.* Cf. note, G. 1. "The name of the *Russ,* or Russian, is clearly recognised in the *Rhoxolani.*" Introd. to Webst. Dic. Cf. Anthon's Class. Dic. sub voce.

Page

25. Ad denotes the place, quo tenderunt irrumpendo. Wr. 66

26. Irruperant. Taken absolutely, i. e. without a direct obj.: *had made an irruption.*—*Ex* indicat causam originemque rei. Wr.

30. Cupidine praedae shows the reason or motive of *graves . . . sarcinarum*, and explains the *sarcinae* to be not soldiers' packs, but loads of booty. The common reading, *dispersi cupidine praedae*, has no MS. authority. *Dispersi* denotes the scattered and disorderly manner in which the Sarmatians *usually* fight.

33. Extra ipsos, sc. in pernicitate equorum, non in animo et corporis robore, ut hodie fere in tormentis bellicis. Ernesti.—*Nihil.* A strong expression for *nulla alia gens.*

35. Obstiterit. Our potential (Gr. 260, II.), or a softened future. Z. 527.—**36. Usui** is dat. after *erant* understood.

37. Equis and **pondere** are abl. of cause.

4. Facilis lorica. Al. facili. Active ponitur pro agili, habili, 67
i. e. qui in usu alicujus rei sine labore versatur. Sic *sermone promptus et facilis.* Suet. Tib. 71. Wr.—*Lorica, pilo, lanceis, gladio.* Compare these military terms with note on *galea* and *scutum*, 38.—*Ubi . . . posceret.* Cf. note, G. 35. Subj. Cf. note, 66: *quotiens . dcesset.*

12. Bello limits **felix,** with which supply *fuisset*, to which *auxisset* is connected by *et.*

13. Ducibus. *Per duces* would be the ordinary way of expressing the voluntary means or agency. The abl. represents human agents as mere tools. Cf. Gr. 247, R. 4; Z. 455. Note.

Ch. LXXX.—**14. Initio** is abl. of source after *orta.* For the contents of 80–85, cf. Plut. Oth. 3. 4; Suet. Oth. 8.

15. Septimam . . . . cohortem. Cohorts, that did not belong to any legion, were *numbered*, like the legions themselves, and distinguished by their number.

16. Ostiensi. Ostia, formerly a town of note at the mouth of the Tiber, whence its name; at this day it lies in ruins. It was founded by King Ancus. Cf. Liv. 1, 33; Dionys. 3, 44.

17. E praetorianis, sc. tribunis. *One of the prætorian tribunes.*

18. Vacuus. *More free* from disturbance of every kind.—*Quietis castris* denotes *time*, viz. when the watch was set and the rest of the soldiers were in their tents. The *castra* here meant was the camp of the prætorians at Rome, whence arms were to be borne in vehicles to the Tiber and thence by ship to Ostia for the 17th cohort. So the following description shows (though it has been understood differently by some), and so Plutarch (Oth. 3) describes it. Cf. the jealousy of the prætorians towards their officers, 36.

20. Tempus, sc. nox; *causa*, i. e. res ipsa; *affectatio*, i. e. sollers electio; *quietis*, sc. militum in castris. Rup.—*Causa* perhaps rather denotes the *object* or *intention.*

21. Affectatio properly denotes an *aspiring to*, or *earnest seeking*

Page

67 *for.* Cf. Ann. 2, 88: *regnum affectans;* His. 2, 91: *plebis rumorem affectavit.* The *substantive* is nearly confined to the post-Augustan prose.—*Quietis* here is explained by *quietis castris* above.—*Fuit,* rather than *evaluit,* is appropriate to the first two clauses. Render: *the time excited suspicion, the object* aimed at *was made a ground of accusation, and the special pains* taken to find *a quiet time became the occasion of a tumult.*

22. Sui, sc. arma. *Sui* is the gen. pl. of the reflexive. Cf. a similar sentiment in Odys. 16, 292: αὐτὸς γὰρ ἐφέλκεται ἄνδρα σίδηρος, assigned by Ulysses to Telemachus as a reason for removing the armor of the *drunken suitors* out of their *sight.* Lipsius. Död. thinks it an *allusion* to Homer.—*Miles,* sc. praetorianus.

23. Familiae, i. e. servi. Cf. note, G. 15.

25. In occasionem, denotes the *end* or *aim* (cf. A. 8: *in famam,* note), as *ignari* and *cupidum* express the *state of mind* in which the other classes acted. To make the construction regular, supply *intentus* before *in.* Cf. Essay, p. 17. But Tacitus prefers enallage.

Ch. LXXXI.—**31. Celebre.** Properly *crowded* (from cello, κέλλω), *frequented;* hence *distinguished, celebrated.* Either sense would be appropriate here. The former, however, is preferable. The latter signification is not found in Cæsar and Cicero. Cf. Freund sub voce. Observe the use of the imperf. *erat* for an unfinished action.

32. Fortuitusne .... foret. This whole member of the sentence depends on *trepidus,* which means *trembling with uncertainty* whether, etc. Supply *esset* with *furor* and *dolus.* Cf. Essay, p. 14.

35. Detegi, sc. as mere pretenders to firmness.

68 **1. Statim miserat** denotes an act prior to *jussit.* Hence the pluperfect.—**2. Passim.** From the part. of *pando.*

5. Incerta. *Unknown, untraceable.* Cf. A. 38: *incerta fugae vestigia.*

Ch. LXXXII.—**7. Militum .... irrumperent.** Xiphilinus (64, 9) represents this as the natural result of Otho's largesses, flattery and excessive familiarity with the soldiers.—*Foribus* attaches *quidem* to it, as being the emphatic word. The word manifestly has the same root as the Gr. θύρα and the Eng. *door.* The same root is also found in German, Sanscrit, etc. *Fores* is properly the *folds* of the door; *porta* the *aperture.*

9. Martiale. When such adj. as these become proper names, they always have *e* in the abl.: as Juvenale, Martiale, etc. Z. 63, c.

10. Praefecto legionis. An officer who, in the absence of the *legatus legionis,* took his place in the command, called elsewhere *legioni praepositus.* 2, 86; 3, 52.

15. Toro. *Couch;* properly a soft cushion or pillow, then the whole sofa, couch, or bed. Rams. refers it to *torqueo* (622), where see it distinguished from *lectus, cubile,* etc.

Page

18. Populus, plebs. Cf. 35, and note, A. 43, where *vulgus* = *plebs* here.—**20. Licinius Proculus et Plotius Firmus.** Cf. 46. 68

22. Ut, with the subj. denoting result.—*Quina .... nummum. Five thousand sesterces apiece. Nummum* is gen. pl. for nummorum.

23. Tum. *Then at length, then only.* Used just as in chap. 66, where see note.

25. Otium et salutem. Nam tribunus et centuriones a militibus obtruncati. Cf. 80. Brotier. Dōderlein takes it as a request to be discharged, which derives some support from the *abjectis .... insignibus,* as well as from the frequent use of *otium* by T. as the opposite of war. Cf. note, A. 11. But the use of *salutem* rather favors the interpretation of Brotier and Rup. They demanded *safety* for their persons, and *order, tranquillity,* in the camp. Otherwise (as they intimated by casting off their badges) they could not retain their offices.—*Sensit invidiam. Felt the odium,* or reproach, thus brought upon themselves. *Invidia*—quod verbum ductum est a nimis intuendo fortunam alterius. Cic. Tusc. Quaest. 3, 9.

26. Compositus. Used here and in 65, nearly in the sense of our word *composed, quieted, calmed.* For other senses, cf. 47 and 71; also A. 42 and 45, notes.

Ch. LXXXIII.—**28. Quanquam** non spectat ad sequens *sed,* ut videtur Ernestio; consequens (apodosis) potius est inde a verbis: *postremo ita disseruit.* Wr. Ante *postremo* intelligendum *tamen.* Rup. *Quanquam turbidis rebus* = quanquam turbidae res erant, etc.

30. Et plures = iique plures. Ernesti. "Always the greatest number." Murphy.—*Ambitioso imperio. Imperial power obtained by solicitation of the multitude.* Cf. note on *ambitionem,* 1.

32. Non posse .... retineri. Cf. the same sentiment prophetically uttered in the speech of Galba, 30.

34. Sed .... anxius. Antithetic to *simul reputans.* Wr.

1. Tumultus .... initium, sc. excitatum est, implied in the an- 69
tithetic clause *nimia .... excitavit.* So *veni* above is understood in the first clause, and expressed only in the antithesis.

4. Acrius .... considerate. Al. consideratius. T. uses both constructions. Cf. A. 4: *vehementius quam caute;* 2, 24: *avidius quam consultius.* The regular Latin construction is that with two comparatives. Cf. Z. 690.

11. Etiam .... tribunosque. *Even the centurions and tribunes,* much more common soldiers.—*Tantum juberi. Receive commands only,* without reasons.

13. Et illic. *Even there,* i. e. *under such circumstances,* as have been described.

15. Neque .... crediderim. *For I cannot believe—would not willingly,* i. e. will not, *believe.* Cf. 79: *obstiterit.* The subj. perf. used to soften an assertion. Gr. 260, 11, R. 4; Z. 527.

Page

69 CH. LXXXIV.—**18. Pro.** Primarily *before;* hence, as here, *in defence of,* or *in behalf of.* Observe the conciseness, *fecistis* being omitted. Cf. Essay, p. 14.

26. Fortissimus . . . . . quietissimus. Ad rem., cf. Hom. Il. 2, 8; 4, 429.

33. Non hercule illi . . . . Germani. *Not even those German barbarians,* still less you. *Hercule* is voc.; sometimes *mehercule,* which is an ellipsis for *ita me, Hercule, juves* (cf. Z. 361, note); or, according to Freund, the *me* is only a demonstrative prefix for emphasis. Cf. Freund sub voce *ce.—Cum maxime.* Cf. note on it, 29.

35. Depoposcerint. Cf. 83: *crediderim;* 79: *obstiterit.* This use of the subj. is much more frequent in the later than in the earlier Latin. "The perf. subj., when used independently, usually has the meaning of a softened future." Z. 527. Zumpt suggests, by way of explaining this meaning, that the same form is probably used both for the subj. perf. and the subj. of the fut. perf., e. g. *depoposcerim* = subj. both of *depoposci* and *depoposcero.* It does not necessarily imply doubt. Cf. Cic. Brut. 6: Hoc sine ulla dubitatione confirmaverim, etc. In such questions as this it implies a negative answer. Cf. note, 30: *mereretur.* The use of the *perf.* subj. after *ut* and *ne* (as in *utque sic dixerim,* G. 2) is entirely peculiar to the silver age.

37. Praestringimus = obumbramus. Al. perstringimus, which is the reading of the MSS., and is retained by Rup. in the sense of *hebetamus.* The departure from the MSS. is justified by Wr., from the frequent and easy confounding of those two syllables.—*Nationes, imaginem . . . . exercitus, senatus.* Notice the position of these emphatic words in their respective clauses.

70 **2. Constiterint.** Subj. as usual after the impers. verb. Cf. Gr. 262, R. 3.

3. Domibus. Properly generic, = *buildings; tectis, roofs.* Accumulated here for emphasis, rather than for distinction. This speech abounds in such emphatic accumulation of words nearly synonymous, e. g. *seditionem et discordiam, sanguinem et caedem, splendore et gloria, sordes et obscuritatem.*

4. Stare = constare, consistere. Cf. Essay, pp. 10. 11. Ad sententiam, compare Liv. 5, 54; Dio. 56, 5.

5. Promiscua sunt, agreeing with *muta ista* in the nom.; instead of *promiscuum est* agreeing with the *clause.* Render: *whether these mute and inanimate objects fall or are rebuilt is a matter of indifference.* It is a case of *attraction,* resembling the *Greek.* Cf. Essay, p. 18.—*Aeternitas rerum. The perpetuity of the empire.*

7. Auspicato. The Romans undertook no great enterprise without first ascertaining the will of the gods by auspices. Religion, deeply seated in the breasts of the people, was the most powerful engine both of war and of state. This speech is highly characteristic, and plays upon the passions and the prejudices of the soldiers with much of the same skill as that recorded in 37–8. Page 70

CH. LXXXV.—**12. Et oratio.** *Et* is correlative to *et* before *severitatis.* Both his address and his moderation were well received. Observe *accepta* nom. pl. neuter agreeing with two subs., one masc, the other fem.

16. Strepitus .... militibus. Such is the reading of the best MSS. Al. *strepitus telorum et facies belli erat militibus,* which is adopted in the common editions with a colon after *erat.* Various other emendations have been suggested. But it may be read as it is, and the conciseness and enallage of the text go to substantiate its genuineness. *Strepitus .... belli* is one reason for *non quies redierat ; et militibus,* etc., is another. The former is expressed in the nom., the latter is the regular abl. of cause.

18. Occulto habitu, i. e. in the guise of citizens or countrymen, and acting the part of spies.—*Maligna cura. Evil intentions.* Död. refers *occulto habitu* also to the concealment of their *feelings, animi* being understood by *prægnantia.* Cf. Essay, p. 16.

23. In publico. Ant. to *secreta domuum.*

24. Attulisset. Subj. Cf. Gr. 264, 12 ; Z. 569.—*Conversis.* Al. *conversi.* But *conversis* is found in the Medicean and nearly all the other MSS. It is abl. of cause or manner with *hominibus* understood: *But there was the greatest agitation in public, when* (or *since*) *men changed* (lit. men being changed as to) *their feelings and countenances with every report which rumor brought,* sc. from Vitellius.

26. Modus. The *juste milieu,* happy mean. What follows is thus paraphrased by Lipsius: Taceres? silentium pro contumacia esset. Diceres libere? invisa libertas. Ad gratiam loquerere? non faceres fidem, quia privatus nuper Otho peritus harum rerum et iisdem adulationibus exercitus.

27. Ne for the more common but less concise *ut non.* Cf. Essay, p. 10.

29. Sententias. Their *opinions* given in the senate-house.

CH. LXXXVI.—**34. Auctoribus.** For *ab auctoribus.* Cf. Gr. 225, 11.

35. Omissas, i. e. dropped from the hands of the goddess, as if she were unable to hold them. Cf. Plut. Oth. 4. See also, touching these prodigies, Suet. Oth. 8 ; and Xiph. 64, 7.

36. Cella. Primarily a storeroom (from *celo*). Secondarily the interior of a temple. In the Capitoline temple there were three distinct *cellae* under the same roof, with common partition-walls, viz. that of Jupiter in the centre, that of Minerva on the right, and that of Juno on the left. Render: *chapel of Juno.*

38. Immoto. Undisturbed by earthquake, or storm, or any natural cause of such a phenomenon. Cf. Plut. in loc. cit.—*In Orientem.*

Page

Betokening the elevation of Vespasian, in whose reign this prodigy was doubtless fabricated. Cf. Plut. as above.

71 **3. In metu.** Sic *in pace, in bello,* de tempore. Igitur *in metu* = eo tempore, ubi metuitur. Wr. *In time of danger.* Ad rem, cf note, 4, 26: *quod ..... vocabatur.—Audiuntur.* The subj. here would make this clause a part of the common talk (*vulgata*) at Rome The ind. is used to set forth the views of the author.

5. Proruto. Al. *prorupto.* But the following words show that the *bridge* had *fallen into* the river.—*Ponte sublicio.* A bridge of *beams,* resting on piles, built over the Tiber by Ancus Marcius. The Romans felt a religious scruple about driving a nail in it. Plin. 36, 15; Liv 1, 33. 37; 2, 10. 40. 51.

10. Insularum. Blocks of buildings, detached from other edifices (hence their name) and rented to several occupants. The word sometimes denotes simply *hired* buildings. Cf. Smith's Dict.

13. Via Flaminia. The great northern road (as the Appian was the southern), reaching from Rome to Ariminum on the Gulf of Venice; made by Flaminius, A. U. C. 533.

14. Esset obstructum. The subj. sets forth the view of the multitude.

CH. LXXXVII.—**17. Lustrata urbe.** The city of Rome, and other towns within its dominion, always underwent a *lustratio* after they had been visited by some great calamity, such as civil bloodshed, awful prodigies and the like. *Lustratio* was originally a purification by ablution in water (from luo, Gr. λούω). But in the lustration of Roman cities, armies, fields, etc., as left on record, the chief thing was the offering of sacrifices, which were carried three times round the persons or things to be purified. Cf. Smith's Dict. of Antiq., under *Lustratio.—Expensis.* Lit. weighed out, hence pondered, considered, matured.

19. Narbonensem Galliam, which had revolted to Vitellius. Cf 76, where see note.

21. Reliquos, sc. *classicorum.—Caesorum.* Cf. note, 6.—*Pontem Mulvium.* Al. Milvium. A bridge over the Tiber, two miles from Rome, on the Via Flaminia, now *Ponte-Molle.* It is not agreed whether the name denotes the bridge of Mulvius, or the Kites-bridge.

22. Habitos in custodiam. Observe the acc. after *habitos in,* like our *had into custody.* Compare *adhibito,* 1, 14, and note ibid. *Habeo* (from ἅπω, ἅπτω) strictly implies *motion,* and hence may be followed by *in* with the acc. Cf. Död. Synonyms, where he makes *habere* = *geben, give.* Boetticher makes this clause = *in custodiam datos et in ea habitos* by zeugma.—*Numeros.* Cf. note on it, 6.—*Composuerat. Had enrolled.*

23. Et ceteris, sc. classicis. *To the rest of the marines also.*

24. Plerosque. *Very many.—E praetorianis. Selected from the praetorian cohorts,* [illegible] vexillarii. Cf. 31.

Page

25. Consilium = consiliarios, abs. for conc. *Consilium* and *custodes*, like *vires* and *robur*, are in appos. with *plerosque*. The select prætorians were sent to advise and watch the commanders, as in the case of the ambassadors above, 74. 71

26. Summa expeditionis. *The whole enterprise*, i. e. the supreme command of both army and navy.

27. Aemilio Pacensi. Dismissed by Galba. Cf. 20.

29. Retinebat. *Continued to hold.* Appointed probably to *repair the fleet* (*curam navium*). But his office, which would properly have ceased when the fleet sailed, was *prolonged.* Gronovius.—*Comitatus.* Al. *immutatus, invitatus, incitatus, impositus, simul datus*, etc., etc. The reading is mere guesswork. The sense is obvious with or without either of the words.

34. Maturitatem. *Ripeness* of judgment and experience. This accords with his subsequent history, e. g. 2, 23. 33. 44. *Ut cuique erat. According to their several characters.* Proculus seized upon their characteristic virtues and misrepresented them as vices.

Ch. LXXXVIII.—**37. C. Dolabella.** Cf. 2, 63–4; Plut. Galb. 23; Suet. Galb. 12.

38. Coloniam Aquinatem. Aquinum, a town of the Volsci, in Latium; now Aquino, but almost in ruins.—*Neque obscura. Yet manifest.*

4. L. Vitellium. Brother of the emperor Vitellius. Cf. note 72
on *domus utraque*, 75.

6. Motae .... curae. Al. *mota .... cura.* The MSS. are about equally divided between the two readings. Wr. prefers *motae .... curae*, as less ambiguous, and expressing definitely the thing here meant, viz. the *anxieties of the citizens.*

7. Metu aut periculo = *metu et periculo*, i. e. by hendiadys *metu periculi.* So Roth. But *aut* implies a specific difference: fear *or* real danger, or inverting the order, as we should, real danger on the one hand, or at least the fear of it on the other. So Wr. and Rup.

13. Irritamenta libidinum. Cf. *delenimenta vitiorum*, A. 21. —*Mercarentur.* Subj. Cf. Gr. 264, 6; Z. 561.

15. Afflicta fide. Abl. of quality equivalent to an adj. and used as predicate of *multi: Many had lost their credit in time of peace* (tranquillity).

16. Per incerta. *In an unsettled state of things.*

Ch. LXXXIX.—**17. Vulgus .... populus.** Cf. note, 82: *populus, plebs.*—*Magnitudine nimia* is the *cause* of *expers: and the people too numerous to share in the concerns of the public.*

19. Intentis. *Increased.* Cf. 24: *intendebat*, note.

20. Haud perinde. *Not so much*, as now. *Haud* is the Gr. οὐδ'.

23. Res .... composuit = potentiam domus Caesareae fundavit. Rup.—*Unius*, sc. principis.

Page

72 **25. Pacis .... reipublicae.** *Pacis* is objective, and *reipublicae* subjective gen. after *adversa* (cf. *proditionis ira militum,* 3, 10): *those evils which the republic experiences in time of peace,* i. e. popular commotions and imperial cruelty. *Reipublicae* cannot be dat. after *pertinuere,* which always takes *ad* or *in* with the acc. after it. Hence some read *in rempublicam;* others expunge *reipublicae,* though found in all the MSS. *Pertimuere* is found instead of *pertinuere* in several MSS., but not the best. *Pertinuere* = duravere according to Wr. But why not take it in the more usual sense of *reached, belonged to,* or *affected,* sc. the people? Tacitus' use of *pertinere* may be seen in 3, 19: Expugnatae urbis praedam ad militem, deditae ad duces, pertinere. Död. makes *reipublicae* dat. (for acc. with *ad*) after *pertinuere.*

26. Scriboniani .... incepta. Cf. Ann. 12, 52; Suet. Claud. 13; Dio. 60, 15.

30. A tergo. The East *followed* Otho; the West, Vitellius.

32. Nondum .... ancilium. The sacred shields, made in imitation of the golden ones sent down from heaven to Numa by the nymph Egeria. At different times, during the month of March, these were borne through the streets by the Salii, and finally *laid up* (*conditorum*) in the curia of the Salii, on the Palatine mount. The days set apart for this ceremony were sacred, and no public business might be transacted. Cf. Ovid, Fast. 3, 260, seq.; Plut. Numa, etc.

Ch. XC.—**37. Reliquias .... sectionum.** Cf. 20.

73 **2. Usu sterili.** Al. sterile. Parum interest; sed maneat veteribus libris sua auctoritas. Wr. *Sterili usu* is abl. of quality after *donum.* Cf. *sterilis pax,* Ann. 1, 17.

6. Ipsius. *His own.—Scriptor orationis,* sc. Galerius Trachalus, who was an orator and joint consul with Silius Ital. A. U. C. 821. Cf 2, 60. 64; Suet. Vitel. 6; Quintil. 10, 1, 119, et al. Sic Nero Senecae *ingenio utebatur.* Ann. 13, 3. Rup..

9. Othonem uti credebatur. A Greek construction, not uncommon with Tacitus, for *Otho uti credebatur.* Cf. note, 50: *crederetur*

10. Genus .... orandi, sc. Trachali.

11. Latum. *Copious.* Opposed by Cic. (Brut. 31) to *contractum.*

13. Dictatorem. Julius Cæsar.

15. Ut in familiis, sc. servorum. Cf. G. 15, note. The passage is well explained by Ernesti. Populus serviendi amore eadem faciebat, quae in privatis aedibus familia servorum solet: utilitatis cura est singulis, nulla dignitatis ac decoris.

BOOK II.

Page

CH. I.—**2. Laetum,** sc. under Vespasian and Titus; *atrox,* under Domitian; *prosperum,* to Vespasian; *exitio,* to Titus and Domitian, who both died a violent death. The *dynasty* of Vespasian is here meant by *imperio.* 76

5. Maturam . . . . juventam. Titus was now in his twenty-eighth year.

6. Ferebat = *praeferebat, set forth, exhibited.*

7. Disperserat. Only T. applies this word to the *spreading of reports.*

9. Donec . . . . eligatur. Cf, note, 1, 13: *donec . . . . amoliretur.*—*Destinandi.* Objective gen. after *intemperantia.*

11. Majestate. Titus was brought up in the court with Britannicus, the son of Claudius. Cf. Suet. Tit. 2.

12. Praesaga responsa. Suet. ibid. *Praesaga* is a poetical word.

13. Corinthi . . . . urbe. Cf. Gr. 204, R. 7; Z. 399. This use of the gen. is explained by some as an old form of the dat. (Corinthoi, Gr. Κορίνθοι=Κορίνθῳ), the original *where*-case. Compare the *locative* case in Sanscrit, which ends in *i. Urbe* = *capital,* 1, 68.

16. Adhibitis. Cf. note on *adhibito,* 1, 14; and on *habitos,* 1, 87.—*Pergeret.* Cf. note on *pergit,* 1, 27.

19. Incerta . . . . victoria is abl. of cause with *excusatum,* with which supply the auxiliary for the fut. pass. infin., viz. *iri.* Cf. Essay, p. 14.

21. Rempublicam susciperet, sc. under his protection and government.

CH. II.—**23. Jactatum,** sc. Titum. Al. jactato, because hope prevailed not over Titus, but over fear. But in thus prevailing, it also *bore sway* in the breast of Titus.

1. Berenices. The Bernice of Scripture (Acts, 25, 13. 23; 77
26, 30); famed for her beauty and incest (Suet. Tit. 7; Juv. 6, 156). She was daughter of Agrippa the Elder, wife of her uncle Herod, and at the time she heard Paul, was probably living in incest with her brother Agrippa the Less.

5. Igitur = Gr. οὖν; *Under these circumstances.* Cf. note on it, A. 13.

6. Ac laeva maris. Exegetical of *oram Achaiae et Asiae,* which lay to *the left,* as Titus sailed from Corinth towards Syria.—*Praevectus. Coasting along.* Al. praetervectus. But T. uses *prae* for *praeter* in such combinations. Cf. A. 26.—*Cyprum.* Copper derives its name from *Cyprus,* where it is found in great abundance.

Page
77 **7. Audentioribus spatiis.** *With bolder courses.* With this poetical use of *spatiis* compare Cicero's use of it for *turns* or *courses* in *walking*. Cic. de Or. 1, 7, 28. Antith. to *praevectus .... oram.* Previous to the invention of the compass, sailors *feared* to lose sight of the shore. Titus was daring because he was impatient.

8. Templum .... inclitum. Cf. Strabo, 14; and Herod. 1, 105. also Virg. Aen. 1, 415. There was also in the island another less famous temple of Venus, who took the epithet Cyprian from the extent of her worship by the pleasure-loving Cyprians.—*Paphiae Veneris.* Paphos, in the isle of Cyprus, was sacred to the worship of Venus.

9. Haud fuerit. *It will not be,* etc. Cf. note, 83: *neque crediderim;* and 84: *depoposcerint.*

10. Templi ritum. Al. situm, but the site of the temple T. does not describe. On the word *templum,* cf. notes, 1, 27; and G. 9: *cohibere parietibus.*

11. Habetur, sc. religio, templi ritus et forma deae. Murphy avails himself of this digression to vindicate T. from the charge of irreligion.

Ch. III.—**14. A Cinyra.** De Cinyra, vid. Athenaeus, 1, 10 Aelian, G. 36. Rup.

15. Conceptam mari. *Sprung from the* (foam of the) *sea,* hence her name 'Αφροδίτη.—*Appulsam. Wafted.*

16. Haruspicum. Cf. note, 1, 27.—*Accitam. Introduced from abroad.*—**17. Familiae utriusque,** i. e. of Cinyras and Thamiras.

19. Hospites. *The foreigners.* Ad verbum, cf. note, G. 21.

20. Cinyrades. The descendant of Cinyras.—*Hostiae.* Slain for inspection of the entrails, not to be burned upon the altar, which was prohibited. Cf. the use made of the *compluribus hostiis* slain by Titus, 4.

22. Haedorum, animalium libidinosorum. Rup.—*Fibris. Entrails.* Virg. Aen. 10, 176. He avoids the usual word *exta.*

23. Adolentur. Adolere proprie est olentem reddere cremando, et hinc cremare. Bach. It is also used poetically in the sense to *load with offerings.* The sentence does not bear a literal translation into English. Render: *Supplications and a pure flame of fire are the only offerings on the altar.* The distinction between *ara* and *altare* (for which see Lexicon) is not here observed.—*Nec ullis imbribus,* etc Pliny makes the same statement, N. H. 2, 96.

25. Continuus orbis, etc. Stripped of its verbiage (cf. note on description of Britain, A. 10), this description imports simply: *in the shape of a rude cone.* Max. Tyr. (8, 7) likens it to a *white pyramid.* On the position of *in,* cf. Z. 324. *Continuus,* uninterrupted by arms, neck, head, etc., like most idols.

26. Ratio in obscuro. Probably there was no reason for it, but the rudeness of the early times in which it originated. Ernesti.

Page

CH. IV.—**29. De navigatione primum.** Antith. to *de se.* 77

30. Per ambages. *In terms properly guarded.* Murphy.

34. Petito secreto. *At a secret interview.* Murphy. Lit. seeking a retired apartment. Cf. note, A. 39.

36. Fiducia = causa fiduciae. So *fides* is used, chap. 5, and 4, 85.—*Profligaverat. Had almost finished.* Cf. note on it, G. 13.

1. Superstitionis. Ad verbum, cf. note, 3, 57.—*Quo.* Al. quod. 78
But *quo* = eo quod. Cf. Cic. Fin. 4, 2. Subj. after *quam.* Gr. 264, 4; Z. 560.

7. Inexperti ... labor. Al. *inexpertus,* but without MS. authority. One MS. has *labores.* Intellige severitatem disciplinae in pace inexorabilem (1, 51). The two things contrasted are the labors and dangers of war, and the toil and discipline of an uninterrupted peace. Wr.

CH. V.—**11. Si .... posceret.** The imperf. subj. follows the historical inf., and even the present ind., when used for the historical tense.

12. Fortuito = Gr. τῷ τυχόντι. Such as chanced to fall in his way, hence *common.*

16. Sermone. Al. *sermoni.* But *aptior sermone* = perfectior in dicendo. Rup.—*Dispositu provisuque.* Words found only in Tacitus. Cf. Boetticher.—*Peritus.* Cf. Gr. 213, R. 4, (5).

17. Si .... miscerentur. *If they had been united.* Imperf. subj. used, as it often is, where we use the plup. Cf. Gr. 260, R. 2; Z. 525. The writer transports his reader into the past and represents it as present.

19. Vicinis provinciarum, instead of *vicinarum provinciarum.*

25. Industria .... per voluptates, are the various *motives* by which they were influenced, all characters finding something to attract them either in Vespasian or in Mucianus. Notice the *pairs.*

26. Asciscebantur. *Were brought over,* or *attached* to their party.

CH. VI.—**31. Civium arma.** *Civil wars.*

33. Trans mare. Across the Mediterranean and into the East.

36. Minae. *Slight conflicts.* Ad rem, cf. Ann. 15, 24. 27.—*Proximo .... bello.* Between Vindex and Nero.

37. Inconcussa is not found prior to the age of T. Cf. Boetticher and Freund.

3 Septem legiones. The four of Mucianus and the three of 79
Vespasian. Cf. 1, 10.—*Statim. On the spot* (*sto*); *inde, on that side; hinc, on this:* these three words are correlative.

4. Continua = contermina.

5. Quicquid .... Armeniis. *And all the forces,* lit. camps, that stretch along the *frontier of the Armenias,* sc. the Greater and the Less.

Page

79 **6. Praetendere** is little used in this literal and physical sense, except by the poets. Prose writers use it chiefly in the sense of *to cover* or *cloak*.

7. Nec virorum, etc. *Nec* = *et non,* and correl. to *et* before *pecuniae*. Cf. note on *neque .... et,* 1, 15.—*Pecuniae* is gen. Gr. 213. —*Quantum .... cingitur. All the islands of the sea,* i. e. the Mediterranean. The predicate is omitted here (as it is also in several of the foregoing clauses), viz. were on their side.

8. Interim, sc. between the present and the time of decisive action.

Ch. VII.—**11. Victores,** etc. The reader will perceive, that these are the *considerations* that influenced the Flavian leaders to *delay.* The *motives* of men's conduct are set forth by T. with no less distinctness and fulness than their actions.

13. Faceret. Subj. Cf. Gr. 265; Z. 552.

14. Etiam egregios duces. *Even illustrious commanders,* still more those, who, like Oth. and Vitel., were *discordes, ignavi* and *luxuriosi.*

17. Nuper. Ant. to *olim,* and like *olim* limiting *mixtis* consiliis. —*Mixtis consiliis, amore reipublicae, dulcedo praedarum,* etc., are the motives which influenced them, not to *delay,* but to *watch an opportunity for action.*—*Optimus quisque,* sc. stimulabantur. Cf. note on *tumultus initium,* 1, 83.

19. Stimulabat is to be connected logically, not with *distulere,* but with *in occasionem.*—*Ambiguae .... res* need not be confined to pecuniary circumstances, it may include all private occasions of discomfort or danger.

Ch. VIII.—**22. Velut,** in Cic., means *for example.* By the later writers, it is used in the same sense as *quasi,* and followed by the subj. Cf. Z. 282. 572; Gr. 263, 2. The imperf. subj. here implies, that Nero was *not* to make his appearance. Ad rem, cf. note on *falsi Neronis ludibrio,* 1, 2.—*Vario .... rumore.* Cf. Xiph. 63, 27. 29; Suet. Ner. 48. 49. *Super,* in the sense of *de, concerning,* requires the ablative. Z. 320.

24. Ceterorum, sc. falsorum Neronum.—*In contextu operis. In the course of this work,* now lost.

26. Unde .... fides. For Nero valued himself more on his skill in music than in government. Cf. Ann. 14, 14; 15, 44, et al. *Propior* here, as often in T., denotes tendency. The credulity of the multitude was the *more easily imposed upon,* because this slave besides resembling Nero in his looks, was also a skilful musician.

29. Cythnum. One of the Cyclades in the Ægean.

30. Et militum. Correlative to *et negotiatoribus.* He took measures to procure *both* men *and* money.

80 Ch. IX.—**3. Datae.** *Assigned him* (at his setting out for his provinces), *ad prosequendum* to attend him as an escort.—*Misenensi.*

Page

Misenum was the principal naval station of the Romans on the west, 80
as Ravenna was on the east.

4. Tenuit. Reached, *arrived at.* Cf. *portum tenuit,* A. 38. Calpurnius happened to touch at the island on his way east, just at this time.

5. Trierarchos. The captains of the *triremes.—Accirent.* Subj Cf. Gr. 264, 6; Z. 561.—*In maestitiam compositus.* Cf. 1, 54. Also A. 42.

7. Ut eum for the more common *ut se,* to avoid ambiguity. Död.

8. Dolo. Enallage for *dolosi,* or dolose agentes. Rup.

9. Firmaverunt for *affirmaverunt.* Cf. Essay, pp. 10, 11.

11. Navis. Qua falsus Nero pervenerat, quamque conscenderat inde abiturus. Rup.—**12. Oculis, etc.,** marked features in Nero.

Ch. X.—**16. Vibius Crispus.** A celebrated orator, Dial. de Or. 8. 13; Quintil. 5, 13. 6, 2. et al.; and informer, Suet. Dom 3; Juv. 4, 81, and at the close of this section. He accumulated immense wealth.

23. Ad hoc terroris. *In addition to this source of terror,* sc. the *senatus consultum.—Et propria vi. With his personal influence also,* i. e. *pecunia, potentia, ingenio.*

24. Sui fratris, sc. *Vibius Secundus,* convicted of extortion. Ann. 14, 28.

26. Aeque .... quam. Cicero says *aeque .... et* or *ac.* In like manner T. uses *perinde .... quam;* Cic. *perinde .... et* or *ac.*

Ch. XI.—**36. E Dalmatia Pannoniaque.** Cf. 1. 76.

2. Rebellione .... compressa is the cause of *praecipui.* Al. 81
praecipue.

7. Quinque .... cohortes. Comprising 5000 men. Cf. note on *praetorio,* 1, 20.—*Equitum vexilla.* Cf. note on *vexilla,* 1, 31.

8. Legione prima. That which Nero enlisted from the marines, 1, 6.; called prima Adjutrix below, 43.

11. Vestricio Spurinna. Egregius et dux et poeta. Plin. Ep. 2, 7. 3, 1. 10.

12. Quoniam (= quum jam), properly introduces a *motive,* rather than a *logical reason.* Cf. note, 1. 31: *quia.*

15. Lecta corpora. *Picked men.* *Corpora* used like Gr. σώματα. Cf. Xen. Mem. 3, 5, 2. Demosth. de Cor. 23.—*Ceteris praetoriis,* i. e. four cohorts, for there were nine in all. 1, 20.—*Veterani e praetorio.* Distinguished from the praetorians, for though attached to that body, they did not belong to it; same as the vexillarii. Cf. 1, 31.

18. Horridus refers to the *person; incomptus* to the *dress.* Död. In *virium ac roboris* above, Or. refers *vires* to *number; robur* to *valor.—Famae.* Cf. 1, 22. 71.

Ch. XII.—**20. Mare et naves.** Hendiadys for *naves mare tenentes.* Roth.

Page

81 **21. Maritimarum Alpium.** Cf. note, 1, 61. *Maritime Alps* was the name, not only of the mountains, but of a province in North-western Italy, bordering on Gallia Narbonensis, of which see notes, 1, 76. 87.

22. Tentandis. Lit. *testing them,* i. e. their friendship and enmity, and then treating them accordingly.

27. Adversus .... corruptus, i. e. sacrificing rigid discipline to his desire of popularity.

28. Loca sedesque. A pair of kindred words for emphasis.

31. Occursantes .... liberos. *The owners, going forth together with their wives and children, to meet* the invaders, etc.

36. Quibus. Dat. after *esset.* For the subj. cf. note, 1, 29: *ut qui,* etc.; also 1, 37.

82 Ch. XIII.—**2. Albium Intemelium.** Now Vintimiglia, south-west of the territory of Genoa, with a port on the Mediterranean. Or. has Albintimilium, as approaching nearer to the reading of the Medicean MS.

5. Femina Ligus. *A Ligurian woman.* Intemelium was in Liguria.

6. Cum, *when* in narration, is followed by the subj. Observe the accurate discrimination of time in the plup. (*credidissent*) and the imp. (*interrogarent*), where we should use the imperf. in both places. The plup. denotes the original motive, and the imp. the subsequent action. *Occuleret* is the subj. in an indirect question.

8. Latere. Inf. of *lateo.* MS. Agr. *hic latere.* Sed illud *hic* inutile est juxta verba *uterum ostendens.* Wr. The mother of Agricola was put to death by this same party. Cf. A. 7. But our author makes no allusion to it in his history.

Ch. XIV.—**11. In verba .... adactae.** Ad rem, cf. 1, 76. Ad verba, 1, 36. The full formula is found in Cæsar, e. g. B. C. 2, 18: *provinciam omnem in sua et Pompeii verba jusjurandum adigebat.* The shorter form (omitting *jusjurandum*) is peculiar to Tacitus and Suetonius. Cf. Freund, sub *adigo.*

16. Forojuliensi. Cf. A. 4, note. The mole and entrance-tower of the old harbor now rise out of a plain of grass. Arnold's Letters, 206.

17. Vacuo mari. The Vitellians had no fleet; hence they must leave some of their land forces to defend their seaports from the attacks of Otho's fleet.

20. Nondum sub signis. Milites auxiliarii in Pannonia a Vitellio nuper conscripti, sed *nondum in cohortes divisi.* Rup.

21. Acie .... instructa, sc. Othonianorum. This clause, together with *ut .... praetenderetur,* is the protasis, and *Vitelliani .... locant* the apodosis.

22. Qu ntum is the subject of *esset* understood, and its antece

Page

dent is the object of *expleret*. Observe the emphatic position of *in* 82
ipso mari before *ut*.

24. Conversa et minaci fronte, ita, ut non puppes obverteret litori ut in pace, sed proras et rostra, ut in proeliis et oppugnationibus fieret. Ernesti.

26. Alpinos here includes, according to Wr. and Dōd., both the Pannonians and the Ligurians mentioned above.

31. Audebant. The ind. is used in this clause (though it follows the subj.), because it stands in so slight a dependence being a mere additional remark.

34. Attinuisset. *Checked.*—*Obtentui fugientibus. Obtentui*, instead of *obtentus* in apposition with *obscurum.* Supply *quod esset: had not the victorious army been checked by the darkness of the night, which afforded a cover for the retreating.*

Ch. XV.—**36. Socordius agentem.** *Neglecting to guard their encampment. Agentem* is used absolutely, like *tendentem*, for *agentem excubias* or *stationem.* Cf. 1, 31. A. 18.

38. Sidente. Al. cedente. Metus multo exquisitius rectiusque dicitur *sidere* quam *cedere.* Wr. *Sidere* is found, however, in this tropical sense only in the poets, and those not till the age of Tacitus.

3. Ne .... quidem. Cf. note, 1, 16: *ne .... fueris.* The em- 83
phatic word always stands between these particles.—*Quorum. Some of whom.*

5. Hinc classis, sc. on the side of Otho; *inde eques*, on the side of Vitellius, *quibus .... in equite robur*, 14.

6. Antipolim. Now Antibes, on the coast of Provence.

7. Albigaunum. Now Albenga, to the west of the territory of Genoa. The editions for the most part read Albingaunum. But Or and Dōd. Albigaunum, from the Medicean MS.

Ch. XVI.—**10. Tenuit** = retinuit. Cf. Essay, pp. 10, 11.

12. In summam. *To the issue of the whole war.* Cf. 1, 87: *summa expeditionis.* Or. reads *in summa*, with the MSS.

16. Liburnicarum .... navium. Cf. note G. 9.—*Ibi* used as an adj. or rather elliptically for a phrase: quae *ibi* erant. Cf. 1, 65: *invicem*, note.

20. Inconditos. Undisciplined, unused to military service.

25. Et aversi = itaque aversi sunt. Observe the concise and elliptical structure of the whole sentence.—*Aperta vi* strictly limits some verb understood, and *sed* is omitted before *aptum*, as often in T.

27. Balineis. The writers of the silver age imitate the poets in a more frequent use of the abl. without a prep. to designate the place where. Z. 482.—*Comites*, sc. from Rome, whereas those, *qui Pacarium frequentabant*, and who made their escape, were residents of the island.

Page

83 **30. In multa .... permixtos.** In cumulo aliorum, qui majoribus flagitiis tenebantur, oblivione transmissos. Pichena.

Ch. XVII.—**33. Supra,** sc. 1, 70.

34. Mallent. *Would prefer,* sc. if it were left to their choice The protasis is not expressed, but implied. Cf Gr. 261, R. 4.

35. Occupantibus. Cf. note, 40: *occupare.—Melioribus incuriosos.* Non curantes, utrum sint hi an illi meliores. Dat. pro *ad* cum acc. Wr. Cf. Essay, p. 12.

38. Praemissae .... cohortes. Cf. 1, 70.

84 **1. Cremonam.** Still Cremona, a flourishing city in the duchy of Milan.

2. Placentiam. Now Placenza, in the duchy of Parma.—*Ticinum.* Cf. note, 27, below. All in the valley of the Po, and important places in history.

4. Irritabat. Incitabat ad transgrediendum. Rup.—*Quin etiam. Nay,* it *even,* etc.

Ch. XVIII.—**10. Nec dum** = *et nondum,* correlative to *et* before *si:* Spurinna had made up his mind (*certum* from *cerno,* to decide) *both that* Cæcina had *not yet* arrived, *and,* if he should approach, to keep, etc.

14. Signis vexillisque. Cf. notes, 1, 31. 36; also Ramshorn's Synonyms, 930.

15. Prodi Othonem. Al. proditionem. But the name of Otho occurs in all the MSS. Ad rem, cf. Plut. Oth. 5.

16. Fit .... comes, i. e. *falls in with,* from prudential considerations.

Ch. XIX.—**20. Urbano militi.** The prætorians, who were not used to rearing fortifications.—*Contundit.* Jam attende ad singularem temporum orationisque variationem (enallage): *placuit . . . contundit .... castigare, ostendere, laudari .... reduxit.* Bach.

21. Vetustissimus quisque. All the veteran soldiers; probably the *mille vexillarii,* 18.

22. Metum ac discrimen = quantum discriminis metuendum esset; hence followed by the subj. plup. (*circumfudisset*).

26. Quod .... legisset. The subj. here gives the sentiments of the officers, and not of the writer = *because, as they said. Laudo* and the like verbs, denoting the outward expression of feeling, are commonly followed by *quod* with the ind. or subj.; while those significant of the inward feeling are usually followed by the acc. with the infinitive. Cf. Z. 629. *Quia* does not properly follow either of these classes of verbs. Cf. note, 1, 31.—*Coloniam .... validam,* sc. Placentia.—*Virium. Men.*

28. Relictis exploratoribus, sc. in the camp which they had begun to fortify.

30. Solidati in prose is post-Augustan. Cf. Boet. and Freund.

Pag

33. Haud poeniteret. *They were not deficient in bravery.* 84
Cf. A. 33: *neque poenituit.* Subj. after *cum causalis.*

Ch. XX.—**36. Quod .... alloqueretur.** Cf. note, 19: *quod ... legisset.*

37. Versicolori sagulo. Cf. note, G. 6. The particolored *sagum,* as well as the *braccae,* was characteristic of *barbarians.* Cf. 5, 23; G. 17; Caes. B. G. 5. 42. *Gallia Narbonensis* was called also *Gallia Braccata.—Togatos. Men clad in the toga,* which was characteristic of *Romans* and *Italians.*

38. Autem. *But* they were still more displeased with the pomp of his wife, as if a wrong done to themselves. Some copies read *quoque.—Quanquam ... veheretur.* Cf. note, 5, 21: *quanquam .. evasisset.*

1. Equo ostroque = equus ostro stratus, by hendiadys. Roth. 85

3. Acribus oculis. *With sharp,* i. e. *jealous eyes.* Al. *aegris.*

5. Viderunt. So the MSS. The early editions have *viderc,* which form (in *ere*) is much more frequent in T., but not therefore necessarily universal.

7. Jactata sunt. Cf. Gr. 205, R. 2 (2). Note.

9. Ut .... provenissent. *Ut* = prout. Cf. A. 18: *prout ... cessissent.* Cf. Essay, p. 10.

Ch. XXI.—**12. Aperti.** Non tecti pluteis, cratibus vineisque. Rup.

15. Glandes. Not of lead, but of iron, and thrown red hot.—*Missilem ignem.* Such as the *falaricae* and the *malleoli,* of which, as well as all the engines and arts employed in a siege, cf. Fiske's Man. P. 2, 299. Observe the author's avoidance of technical terms. Cf. Essay, p. 20.

19. Quod .... foret depends on *invidia et aemulatione.* Cf. note, 19: *quod .... legisset;* also Gr. 273, 5; Z. 629.

23. Nox .... assumpta, i. e. not even the night put an end to the preparation; *the night was added* to the labors of the day. Al. absumpta, by conjecture.

24. Pluteos .... vineas. Cf. Manual as above.

26. Perfringendis, sc. *pluteis et vineis,* supplied from above. So Död. Cf. Essay, p. 15. But it may be taken with *hostibus: for breaking through the ranks of the enemy.*

27. Gloria = gloriae cupido by *prægnantia.* Cf. Essay, p. 16

30. Segnem is the opposite of *promptus; desidem* the opposite of *strenuus.* Död.

33. Uberioribus ..... stimulabantur. Two things seem to be implied in this clause: that there was more to blame than to praise in Otho and Vitellius; and that their followers were more readily excited by hatred than by love.

Ch. XXII.—**36. Legionum** must be taken here in the general.

Page

85 sense of legionary troops (cf. *legionarius* below), for Cæcina had but one full legion, together with several thousand picked men from other legions. Cf. 1, 61.

37. Murorum. *Murus,* as here, properly denotes the *wall* of the city; *moenia,* the *towers* and *bulwarks* upon it.

86 **1. Librato magis.** Better balanced, hence *truer* and *surer* aim. Cf. 1, 16: *librari.*—**2. Cantu truci,** etc. Cf. A. 33; G. 3: *baritum.*

4. Legionarius, sc. miles Caecinae.

5. Aggerem. A mound reared to a level with the walls, and serving as a basis for towers and engines. Cf. Smith's Dic. sub verbo; also Fiske's Man. P. 3, 299.—*Contra. On the other side,* sc. of the besieged under Spurinna. In this animated description, the scene changes several times from the walls to the plains beneath, and vice versa.—**11. Irrisus ac vanus.** *Mocked and baffled.*

12. Intendit. Cf. *animo intendit,* A. 18. For its literal meaning, cf. note, 1, 12.—**13. Julius Briganticus.** Cf. 4, 70.

15. Primipilaris. Cf. note, 1, 31.—*Haud alienus. Not a stranger,* or, as others take it, *not averse. Haud* is used by later writers, and even by Livy, without distinction from *non.* The authors of the best age limit it to certain combinations, such as *haud multum,* and the like. Cf. Z. 277.

Ch. XXIII.—**20. Ducebat.** *Was leading,* sc. at the time he received the letters of Spurinna.—*Paucitate.* Cf. Gr. 245. II.

25. Vicus, sc. Bedriacum, which was 20 miles from Cremona, now Caneto. *Vicus* from Gr. οἶκος, a villa or village.—*Duabus . . . cladibus,* sc. Othonis, 39, and Vitellii, 3, 15. The defeat of Vitellius was *between* Bedriacum and Cremona, and is referred sometimes to the one, sometimes to the other.

27. Prospere pugnatum. On the side of Otho.

29. Effudit. Said properly of a *stream;* implies here the *rapidity* and *force,* and also the *disorder* with which the troops were landed. Cf. Ann. 1, 23: *effunderentur.*

33. Certatim. They vied with each other in their abuse of their commanders.—**35. Eos . . . . praefecerat.** Cf. 1, 87.

36. Incesserant. *Had assailed,* sc. before *Otho Titianum . . . . praeposuit.* Al. *incessebant.*

87 **3. Inter adversa melior** refers to the firmness and fortitude of Otho near his end. Cf. 46, seq.

Ch. XXIV.—**8. Per concursum exploratorum,** by enallage for concurrentibus exploratoribus: *worsted even in the engagement of the scouts.*—**10. Illuc,** sc. to Valens.

11. Avidius quam consultius. Cf. note, 1, 83.—*Duodecimum,* sc. lapidem or milliarium.

12. Castorum, i. e. Castoris et Pollucis. Cf. Plin. 7, 22; Suet. Oth. 9. Rup.

Page

13. Viae, sc. Postumiae.—*Lucis.* Cf. note, ad verbum. G. 9. 87

18. Vexillum, i. e. the vexillaries of the 13th legion.

19. Aggerem viae. *The high-way,* the elevated road. Cf. Fiske's Man. 1, 52, where see the construction of Roman roads.

20. Dextra fronte, i. e. dextro cornu. Cf. Curt. 4, 13. Observe, that auxiliaries were placed on either wing, as the Roman allies were in the earliest wars of the republic.

Ch. XXV.—**25. Prudens** = providens, which has the same etymology

26. Exsurgentes, sc. ex insidiis, i. e. lucis viae imminentibus, 24.

27. Ultro = insuper, *furthermore;* so Rup. But better perhaps: of their own accord, i. e. *by their own act.* Cf. note, G. 28.

28. Adversa frons. This is the reading of Wr., Bach, Rit., Rup., Död., Or. and the best MSS. Al. fronte. The sense is the same. Supply *erat:* literally, *the opposing front was* (composed) of *legionary soldiers,* for so we must take *legionum* here as in 22 (where see note), for there was but one entire legion under command of Paullinus, viz. the first. Cf. 24.

30. Cui ..... placerent = *talis, ut,* etc. Cf. Gr. 264, 1; Z. 556.

31. Fossas. Wr. and Bach understand this of the ditches by the roadside, and refer to 41: *praeruptis utrimque fossis,* etc. But most editors understand it of agricultural ditches for draining, and refer in proof to 3, 21: *agresti fossa.* The latter accords better with *aperiri campum,* which denotes the *clearing and levelling of the fields.*

34. Vineas .... impeditas. *Vineyards thick with interwoven branches.* Murphy. Or. remarks that even now, in that part of Italy, vines are planted between trees, and interlock their branches.

37. Rex Epiphanes. Non proprie rex, sed Antiochi regis Commageni *filius* (crown prince). Cf. Joseph. B. 9. 7, 7. Sic et infra, 5, 9, *rex Pacorus* pro *regis filio.* Wr.

Ch. XXVI.—**5. Abriperet.** Observe the force of *ab:* bore *away,* 88
i. e. along with the panic-stricken fugitives. Subj. after *cum causalis.*

6. Quod .... ducerentur. Cf. note, 19: *quod .... legisset.*—*Praefectus castrorum.* There was one præfect of the camp to each legion, whose duty it was to attend to the making of the camp, and its whole internal economy. (Vegetius, 2, 10). This office is first mentioned in the reign of Augustus. Cf. Smith's Dic.

7. Fratri .... ageret. For the more common expression: *cum fratre de proditione ageret.*

13. Percrebruerit. *It was a general remark.* For the perf. subj. cf. note, 1, 24: *dederit.*

14. Insuper = additional. Adv. for adj.

Page

88 **17. Adverso rumore.** Ant. to *probata: generally condemned*

Ch. XXVII.—**19. Apud Caecinam,** i. e. in the army of Cæcina. Observe the omission of *sed* before *Fabii.* Cf. Essay, p. 13. It is inserted in many editions.

22. Ticinum. On the river Ticinus, near its confluence with the Po. Now Pavia in Milan.

24. Alioquin. Literally, in other respects, i. e. *but, besides.*—*Altiore initio* = altius et ab initio. Död. Cf. Essay, p. 18.

29. Retulimus. Cf. 1, 59.—*Ut .... accessissent.* Subj. Cf Gr. 264, 12; Z. 569.

33. Jurgiis .... rixis. Cf. note on these words, 1, 64.

34. Ad postremum, etc. *At last, Valens was suspicious that out of this quarrelsome spirit would grow* something, worse *even open mutiny. Suspectare* is not found in writers of the age of Augustus. Cf. Freund, sub voce.

Ch. XXVIII.—**36. Pulsam ..... circumiri.** Ad rem, cf. 14, seq.

89 **7. Sanitas.** *Completeness.*—*Sustentaculum. Prop.* It is a new word, invented so far as appears by T.—*Columen.* Allied to *columna, culmen,* and our word *column* = *stay, support.*

8. In .... verteretur. Lit. *turns in* (we say *on*) *Italy,* i. e. the whole question is to be decided there. *Verteretur* is appropriate to *sustentaculum* and *columen,* but not to *sanitas,* which properly means health. Död. takes *columen* in the sense of *summit,* and says: *sanitas* ad plenitatem, *sustentaculum* ad stabilitatem, *columen* ad gloriam victoriae spectat.

Ch. XXIX.—**14. Sarcinis,** sc. Valentis. The word properly denotes a *pack* (from *sarcio,* to sew); hence private baggage, *camp-equipage.*

16. Decurionem equitum. Cf. note, 1, 70; also Fiske's Man. P. 3, 290.

17. Praefectus castrorum. Cf. note, 26.—*Deflagrante. Subsiding,* lit. burning out.—*Addit consilium,* i. e. *adopts a plan for quelling it still further.* This plan is expressed by the ablatives which follow: *vetitis,* &c., instead of *vetuit enim,* &c., which would be less concise.

18. Obire vigilias. *To visit the watch,* go the rounds of inspection. Cf. note, 1, 48; also Fiske's Man. P. 3, 298.—*Omisso . . . sono.* Nam *tuba* initio, *cornu* seu buccina in fine vigiliarum cani solebat. Veget. 3, 8; Polyb. 6, 37. Rup.

28. Plus .... licere. Guilt, when widely spread, levels all distinctions. Lucan truly observes (Pharsal. 5, 290): Facinus, quos inquinat, aequat. Murphy.

Ch XXX.—**32. Nolle requiem.** Observe the series of infinitives, indicative of rapidity. Cf. note, 1, 36: *complecti armis,* etc

Page

34. Improspera. This word is found only in Tacitus. Cf. Essay, p. 22. 89

36. Simul .... et. Correlatives, though, as usual in Tacitus, the clauses are of different construction: *in suam excusationem* being put, by enallage, for *se excusantes.*

38. Despectarentur is found in this sense (look down upon, despise) only in Tacitus and the later writers. Cf. Freund and Boet.

1. Duplicatus .... Valenti. See the original numbers, 1, 61; 90
and the large additions to the army of Valens, 1, 64. *Duplicatus* = duplex.

3 Promptior. *Promptus* Tacito paene id, quod *pronus.* Rup.

5. Inani favore. *Groundless partiality.*

6. Foedum .... maculosum, sc. libidine ac rapacitate. Cf. 1, 66. The words agree with *Valentem* understood; as *vanum* and *tumidum* do with *Caecinam.* Observe the brachylogy. Cf. Essay, p. 15.

9. Cum duces .... abstinerent. Thus indicating less confidence of victory than the leaders of the army of Vitellius.

Ch. XXXI.—**15. Contra illi initium,** etc. He was pushed on by others. Cf. 1, 53.—*Vitellius .... inhonestus. Vitellius by his gluttony (ventre) and his drunkenness (gula) was a disgrace to himself.* Al. ipse hostis.

21. Qua = quatenus, *since.* Död. Cf. Essay, p. 10.

Ch. XXXII.—**25. Galliae tumeant.** *The Gauls are ready to break forth in rebellion.*

27. Distineri, by a species of zeugma (cf. Essay, p. 16), is used in a double sense: *occupied* by the *enemy* and *separated* by the *sea.* Döderlein.

30. Nullo maris subsidio. *Want of naval succor,* for the fleet was on the side of Otho.—**34. Fluxis corporibus.** Cf. note, 1, 21.

2. Obumbrentur. *Cast into the shade.* Found in this sense 91
in no other classic.

4. Objacere .... Padum; tanquam munimentum. Rup.

7. Duceret. *He would protract.* This speech, or rather argument, suits well the character of Paullinus. Cf. 25: *cunctator natura,* etc.

Ch. XXXIII.—**14. Decertandum.** *A decisive battle.*

16. Numen Othonis. So the flatterers of Tiberius were fain to dignify his administration with the epithet of *divine,* while he yet lived (Ann. 1, 87). *Divus* was a common appellation of the emperors after their death. Cf. G. 28.

17. Neu quis = et nequis. Zumpt, 535.

20. Objectare periculis. Sumptum ex Virg. Aen. 2, 751. Ernesti. Cf. Essay, p. 24.—**21. Deterioris consilii,** sc. pugnari.

22. Perpulere. *Prevailed on him* (Otho).—*Brixellum.* Now Bresello, in the territory of Reggio.

Page
91 **23. Summae .... imperii.** *For the general good and the supreme command.* Cf. notes on *summa,* 1, 87; 2, 16.

29. In incerto, etc., i. e. effecerat, ut nemo militum esset certus, penes quem summum imperium esset. Wr. Död. omits *in,* after the Medicean MS., and according to the analogy of 1, 68: ipsi *medio* vagi. Cf. Essay, p. 12.

Ch. XXXIV.—**31. Diversa.** The measures of the opposite party. Cf. *ex diverso,* 75, note.

33. Quando depends on *intenti.*—*Quod* refers to *alienam . . . opperiebantur.*

36. Ac ne .... tereret. There were two reasons for commencing the bridge: 1. To make a feint of crossing the river; 2. To keep the soldiers occupied. *Otium tereret* is a concise expression for *otio tempus tereret.* Död. gives it the name of structura contracta. Cf. Essay, p. 17.

37. Adversum .... dirigebantur. *Were set with their prows against the current.*—*Super* for *insuper* (cf. Essay, p. 10): *anchors moreover being cast,* sc. *besides* the support of the timbers on either side. So Or. and Död.

92 **1. Non extenti** = laxi.—**2. Inoffensus.** *Without obstruction.*

3. In extremam .... educta. *Erected on the last ship* in the line. T. uses *educere* in the sense of *erect.* Cf. 4, 30: *eduxerant Batavi turrim;* Ann. 2, 61: *eductae pyramides.* So Wr. and Rup. Or. and Död. take *educta* in the sense of *drawn out* or *pushed forward,* as a moveable tower. But cf. Virg. Aen. 2, 460: turrim sub astra eductam.

4. Tormentis ac machinis. See these, as also the towers described and illustrated, in Man. P. 3, 199, 4. 5.

Ch. XXXV.—**7. Gladiatores** is taken by Rup. as acc. after *praelabebantur.* But Or. and Död., with better reason, make it the subject of a verb implied (by zeugma) in *praelabebantur: into which the gladiators toiling with ships endeavored to pass, but the Germans by swimming slipped over before them.*

12. Vulnera dirigebant. Poetic for *tela* dirigebant. Cf. Virg. Aen. 2, 529. See Essay, p. 24.

Ch. XXXVI.—**19. Abreptis** = raptim abductis. Wr., Or., etc., after Gronovius. The MSS. have *abruptis.*

20. Macer ... poscebatur. Yet he had been successful in a like conflict with these same gladiators, 23. Cf. A. 27: *adversa* (bellorum) *uni imputantur,* etc.—*Ad exitium.* Död. omits *ad,* after the Medicean MS. Cf. Essay, p. 12.

25. Flavium Sabinum. Not Vespasian's brother of the same name, who was now at Rome. Cf. note, 1, 77.

27. Infestam = *periculosam.* Rup. For the active sense of *infestus*, cf. note, A. 25 Derived from *in* and the obsolete *fendo*. Cf. *of-fendo*, *de-fendo*. Page 92

CH. XXXVII.—**30. Flagitia** refers to character, *dedecus* to reputation.

32. Vel .... vel. *Either .... or*, as they chose (from *volo*).—*In medium. In common, for the common weal.* Cf. Freund sub v.

34. Spe Paullini, sc. se lectum iri imperatorem. Rup.

35. Gloriam nomenque. By hendiadys for *nomen gloriosum*, or synonymous, like *spatium ac moras* just above. Roth.

3. Caritate. Lit. *scarcity* (from *careo*) ; hence *dearness, affection*, as here, and at length *charity*. 93

6. Magna ex parte. *Ante, contra, inter* and *propter, ob, post, de, ex* and *in* are frequently placed between the adj. and subs. Z. 324. Cf. chap. 3: *tenuem in ambitum.*

7. Pollutum .... meritis. *Defiled and laid under obligation by their* criminal *favors. Meritis* must be taken in this bad sense with *pollutum.*

CH. XXXVIII.—**10. Rebus modicis.** *When the* (Roman) *republic was small.*

11. Regibusve. Al. *que.* Cf. note, 1, 44: *quive;* G. 4: *solove. Ve* distinguit aemulos sive fuerint urbes sive reges. Wr. *Rivals, whether cities* (i. e. free states) *or kings, having been cut off.*—*Securas.* Safe from external violence.

12. Prima certamina must be taken in a modified sense. The strife between the orders commenced almost with the foundation of the city ; but it *blazed out* into a fiercer flame just in proportion as the state was exempt from the assaults of foreign enemies.

15. Nobilium saevissimus. According to Arnold, "the most sincere of aristocrats." Cf. Rom. His.

17. Occultior. Magis celans potentiae cupidinem. Rup. After *Pompeius*, we may supply *idem fecit* with Död., or simply *fuit.*

18. Nunquam .... quaesitum. *And ever after the only question* in dispute *was, who should be princeps.*

19. Pharsalia ac Philippis. Cf. note, 1, 50.

21. Illos refers to *exercitus*, which though the latter mentioned word, is the more remote idea. Cf. Gr. 207, R. 23.

The commentators remark a close resemblance between this chapter, particularly at the beginning, and Thucyd. 3, 82, and a fragment of the History of Sallust. Cf. Död. in loc.

CH. XXXIX.—**29. Uteretur.** Subj. Gr. 263, 5 ; Z. 577.—*Inani ... praetendebantur. With the empty name of general served only as a screen for* (literally, were stretched before) *the faults of others*, sc. Titianus and Proculus.

30. Ambigui. *Undecided*, i. e. they hesitated which to obey.

Page

93 **32. Interpretari.** *Discuss.—Mallet.* For the subj. cf. Gr. 264, 1; Z. 558.

33. Adeo imperite. There is an obvious ellipsis of *quod factum est*, or the like: *which was done with so little skill.* Cf. Plut. Oth. 11, of which Lipsius says: totum hunc locum verbatim Plutarchus expressit, ut pleraque alia, etsi haud multum aetate Nostro inferior.

38. Perinde, followed by *quam,* is peculiar to post-Augustan writers. Cf. Freund and Boetticher, Lex. Tac.

94 Ch. XL.—**3. Non . . . bellandum.** *Not as if to battle, but as if to a* (protracted) *war*, i. e. encumbered with baggage (*gravem sarcinis*) and in marching, not fighting, order. On the contrary, the Vitellians are said (45) to have been *expediti et tantum ad proelium egressi.* See *proelium* and *bellum* contrasted in like manner, G. 30.

4. Inde refers to the encampment *ad quartum a Bedriaco.*

5. Spatio. Abl. Cf. Gr. 236, R. 4; Z. 396.

7. Admissuro. Al. amissuro, omissuro. Literally, who would not allow but that he would attack, i. e. *would not fail to attack. Non admitto* is equivalent to a verb of *hindering*. Z. 543.

10. Ad jus . . . . transibant. *They had recourse to their authority as commanders-in-chief.* Strictly, they *were* having recourse, sc. at the very time when Otho's courier arrived.

11. Numida. People of wealth and fashion at this time were habitually attended by a train of *Numidians,* mounted on the swift horses of their country, to ride before them and announce their approach. Cf. Sen. Epist. 88 and 124; Suet. Ner. 30; Beck. Gall. Sc. 4.

13. Aeger . . . . impatiens. "Hope deferred maketh the heart sick."

Ch. XLI.—**14. Operi . . . . intentum.** Cf. 34.

16. Conditiones. *Proposals.*

18. Insidias. *To lay a snare* for the Vitellians: *proditionem, to betray* their own party.

23. A . . . . Othonianis belongs with *impingerentur,* being placed before *quo minus* for emphasis. Or. and Död. trace the form of expression here to Virg. Aen. 5, 805: Cum Troia Achilles . . . . impingeret agmina muris.

29. Mixta, sc. with the soldiers.—*Lixae.* Cf. note, 1, 49: *ante . . . . tumulum.*—**30. Fossis.** Cf. note, 25.

34. Aut relabebantur. Al. *vel revehebantur.* But *vel* suits not the place. Wr. *Aut* is found in the best MS. together with *relabebantur, fell back,* literally, glided back, flowed back, like a wave. Cf. Virg. Aen. 10, 307: *unda relabens.*

Ch. XLII.—**38. Dispersus** = utrum dispersus sit. The author leaves it *uncertain whether the report was spread abroad by spies of Vitellius, or originated in the party of Otho,* and, in the latter case *whether it was by accident or by treachery.* Suetonius (Oth. 9) de-

Page

clares that Otho was defeated by a stratagem: his soldiers were called out to be present at a general pacification, and were suddenly attacked in the very act of saluting the Vitellian army.

2. Salutavere. Armies were wont to salute each other and join 95
hands at a friendly meeting. Cf. 3, 25; 4, 72.

8. Cominus eminus. Notice the asyndeton and its effect. Cf. note, 1, 36.—*Catervis et cuneis. In the form of a wedge* (cf. note, G. 6), *and in less regular masses* (cf. Rams. 624). Rup. takes *cuneis* here as a general term = divisions, as in Ann. 1, 51. But *non una ... facies* requires here the more distinctive sense.

9. Collato gradu. *Foot to foot,* as we say. It is a technic for a close engagement.—*Niti,* sc. hostibus, which is the object. *Corporibus* and *umbonibus* are the instrument.

11. Noscentes inter se. *Being mutually acquainted,* sc. the soldiers on opposite sides. They are called *fratres et propinqui,* 45 Cf. γνωρίζοντες ἀλλήλους. Xiph. 65, 12.—*Ceteris conspicui,* i. e. those, who fought on the highway, were *conspicuous in the view of their comrades.*

Ch. XLIII.—**16. Prima Adjutrix.** Cf. note, on *prima legione,* chap. 11.

18. Principiis. Intellige προμάχους, primam aciem. The word is used in the same sense by Livy (e. g. 2, 65; 3, 22). Cf. also Plutarch ad rem eandem: πάντας τοὺς προμάχους αποκτείναντες.

20. Signa vexillaque. Cf. notes, 1, 31. 36.—*A parte alia. In another part of the field.*

Ch. XLIV.—**29. Immensum spatium,** i. e. for a flying army. The distance was sixteen miles.

30. Strage corporum. According to Xiph. (64, 10), forty thousand men fell on both sides in this battle. Cf. also Plutarch's account of the carnage, Oth. 13.—*Neque .... vertuntur.* Hence no quarter was given. Cf. 3, 34.

32. Castra vitavere. Nimirum φοβούμενοι τοὺς στρατιώτας. Plut. Oth. 13. Wr.

34. Multo adhuc die. *While much of the day still remained.* Non noctu et furtim, ut Titianus et Celsus. Rup.

1. Excubiis. Cf. Manual, P. 3, 298; Smith's Dict. of Antiq., 96
under *Army.*—**9. Militum, quod.** Cf. *frugum, quod,* G. 15, note.

13. Truces refers to the *praetoriani; pavidi* to *ceteri* above. *His cogitationibus* limits *truces* only, not *pavidi.*

Ch. XLV.—**17. Sed expeditis .... victoria.** They neglected the usual precaution of fortifying their camp, because they had not the requisite implements. *But their arms and their recent victory were a sufficient defence.*

21. Missa legatio, sc. by the army of Otho, asking peace of the Vitellian officers, who had no hesitation about granting it, though they

Page

96 retained the ambassadors a little while, and thus occasioned an anxious suspense to the Othonians.

24. Vallum, sc. of the Othonians; *patuit,* sc. to receive the Vitellians.

31. Ceterum vulgus = *ceteri,* sc. *vulgus,* by attraction: *the rest,* namely *the common soldiers.* Cf. Essay, p. 17.

The concluding portion of this section presents a very lively and touching picture of the evils of civil war.

Ch. XLVI.—**33. Nequaquam trepidus** = fearless; hence the propriety of *et* after it, where Rhenanus proposed *sed.*

34. Consilii certus. *Firm of purpose,* sc. to meet any result with composure. Tacitus resembles the poets in a more frequent use of the gen. after such adjectives as *certus.* Cf. Z. 437.

36. Haberet. Observe the omission of *ut.* Cf. Essay, p. 14. Al. habere.

97 **1. Excitare.** Literally, *to rouse it up,* as it were out of sleep, quasi jacentem ac dormientem genium. Död.—*Furore . . . instinctu.* By hendiadys for *furore quodam instincti.* Ernesti. Cf. *instincti,* A. 16. 35; *instinctu,* 1, 73. T. has a marked fondness for such pairs of kindred words, e. g. in this section: *fortes et strenuos, timidos et ignavos.* Cf. also note on *domibus,* etc., 1, 84.

2. Tendere manus. Cf. notes on *protendens manus,* 1, 36; and *tendebantur,* 1, 63.

3. Prensare genua. Cf. 1, 66, note.—*Plotio Firmo.* Cf. 1, 46.

8. Flexerat. Antithetic to *induraverat;* hence = *softened,* indicative of compliance.—*Ut* for *prout.* Cf. Essay, p. 10.

9. Clamor, sc. ubi *flexerat; gemitus,* ubi *induraverat.*

11. Aquileiam. A large city of the Veneti, and formerly a Roman colony.

12. Ut dubitet potuisse. Observe the tenses: *so that no one can* (now) *doubt, that the war could* (then) *have been renewed.*

Ch. XLVII.—**14. Ipse . . . . inquit.** Compare this speech with Suet. Oth. 10; Plut. 15. *Inquam* is used only *between* the words of a quotation, while *ait, aiunt,* are found most frequently in the *oratio obliqua.* Z. 219.

18. Experti . . . . sumus. *Have made trial of each other, found each other out.* Otho had found out all there was in good fortune by his elevation to the highest seat of power; and good fortune had tried him and found him moderate in the exercise and enjoyment of it.—*Fortuna* = felicitas.—*Nec . . . . computaveritis. And you may not have estimated* aright, the short *time* of my reign; the shorter the time, the greater the temptation to abuse power, and therefore the severer the trial.

23. Fruetur . . . . liberis. Cf. note on *domus utraque,* 1, 75; also 1, 88.

Page

30. Extremis. *My last hours, my death.* Lipsius compares 97
the sentiments of this speech with those of Ajax when about to terminate his life. Soph. Aj. 852, seq.

CH. XLVIII.—**35. Irent.** Cf. note, 1, 41: *agerent.*

36. Asperarent for *exasperarent,* simple for compound. Scarcely found in this sense in any other prose writer.

38. Naves. Otho was at Brixellum, i. e. at the confluence of the Po and the Nicia.

2. Nec ut periturus. *Nor yet with the profusion of a man* 98
quitting the world. Murphy.

3. Fratris filium, sc. of Salvius Titianus, who had fled to the camp, according to T. (44); Suetonius makes him to have been present on this occasion (Oth. 10), and his son to have been slain (Dom. 10). Plutarch agrees with T. (Oth. 10).

11. Julios, sc. Augustus, Tiberius and Caligula.—*Claudios,* sc. Nero and Claudius.—*Servios,* sc. Galba.

12. Familiam = gentem, sc. Salviam. Rup.

13. Capesseret = frueretur.—*Neu ..... meminisset.* Translated by Plut. Oth. 16. Cf. note on *adeo imperite* above, 39.

CH. XLIX.—**15. Dimotis,** i. e. jussis abire.

17. Avertit, sc. ab his curis.

19. Verginium. Cf. 1, 8. 9. Brotier suggests, that the example of Verginius in declining the imperial dignity, may have been regarded by the soldiers as a cause of Otho's undervaluing and resigning it.

22. Allatis pugionibus. After the example of Nero. Cf. Suet. Ner. 49. Some MSS. and most editions add *duobus.* But it is not in the best MSS. and is quite superfluous. Cf. Or. in loc.

23. Cum .... pertentasset. *When he had carefully (per) tried the points of both*—for some time, adds Plutarch (Oth. 17): πολὺν χρόνον.

27. Unum vulnus. Indicative of intrepidity in the act of suicide.

28. Ambitiosis. *Earnest,* like those of the candidate soliciting popular favor. Nero had made the same request (Suet. Ner. 49). Alike in their manner of life, in death they were not dissimilar, though Otho died with the greater dignity.

31. Exosculantes. *Ex* gives emphasis: *kissing fondly, repeatedly.* This compound is not found earlier than the age of T.

32. Non noxa neque ob metum. Hendiadys according to Wr. But Oberlin and Rup. refer *noxa* to Otho, and *metum* to Vitellius as its object: not through remorse for any unfaithfulness to Otho, nor through fear of punishment from Vitellius. And so it is expressly rendered by Plutarch (Oth. 17).

34. Celebratum. Saepe et a multis peractum. Rup. Cf. note, 1, 81: *celebre.*

Page

98 **35. Sepulcrum .... mansurum,** sc. ob modestiam: *and therefore likely to last.* So Murphy translates, and adds the following note: Plutarch tells us (Oth. 18) that he himself visited Otho's tomb at Brixellum. Those perishable monuments have long since mouldered away; but the epitaph written by Martial will never die. The poet admits that Otho led a dissolute life, but adds that in his end, he was no way inferior to Cato. Cf. Mart. 6, 31.

Ch. L.—**36. Hunc finem.** Cf. note on *hunc exitum,* 1, 49.—*Septimo et tricesimo.* The 38th according to Suet. (Oth. 11), who always includes in such computations both the year of birth and of death. Wr. Cf. note on *sextus dies,* 1, 28.

37. Origo, i. e. of his family, not his own birthplace.—*Ferentio.* A town of Etruria, different from the Ferentinum so often mentioned by Livy, though confounded with it by many commentators. Cf. Suet. Oth. 1.

38. Maternum ... impar, etc., viz. Equestrian. Cf. Suet. Oth. 1.

99 **1. Qualem monstravimus.** Cf. 1, 13.

2. Altero flagitiosissimo, sc. the dethronement of Galba, with its accompanying crimes.—*Altero egregio,* sc. his voluntary death, with a view to terminate the civil war. It scarcely need be said that the Christian, while he approves the motive (if this were the motive), will condemn the means.

4. Fabulosa. T. relates few prodigies in comparison with Suetonius.

5. Crediderim .... ausim. Cf. note on *crediderim,* 1, 83.

7. Invisitata = antea non visa. Al. inusitata.—*Regium Lepidum.* A town of Gallia Cispadana, not far from Brixellum; called Lepidum from Aemilius Lepidus (Strab. 5); now *Reggio.*—*Celebri luco.* Al. loco. But the MSS. all have *luco.* *Celebri* may be either *frequented* or *celebrated.* Cf. note, 1, 81.

12. Competisse, in the sense of agreement, is not found prior to the age of Tacitus, and the word is very rarely used by the earlier Latin authors.

Ch. LI.—**13. Luctu ac dolore.** *Grief and pain. Grief* for Otho, *pain* for their own calamities. Cf. Död. in loc.

14. Modo .... nunc. Correlatives = *modo ... modo.* A. 25.

17. Aversam .... partem, sc. posticam et secretam. Rup.

18. Preces .... tulit, sc. to Cæcina and Valens.

19. Concedentibus is abl., denoting not the *cause,* but the *concomitant* of *venia impetrata.* Cf. note on *expulsis ... professoribus.* A. 2.

20. Flavium Sabinum. Prefect of the city and brother of Vespasian. Cf. 1, 46, 77; 2, 36, and notes ibid.

Ch. LII.—**23. Mutinae.** Cf. 1, 50. The fact that the senators were left at Mutina, was not mentioned in its place, though we are told (1, 88) that they left Rome with Otho, *comitum specie.*

Page

26. Vultum habitumque. Cf. note, 1, 17. 99

27. In deterius. Cf. *in majus*, 1, 18.

32. Tutior agrees with *quisque* implied in *nemo*, which = *quisque non.* In like manner *quisque* is implied in *quisquam* in 1, 1: neque amore quisquam et sine odio dicendus est.

33. Ordo Mutinensis. Senatus sive decuriones Mutinensium. Ernesti. The senators of the municipia were called decuriones. Man. P. 3, 268, 2. (2.); and the senate *ordo decurionum,* afterwards simply *ordo.* Smith's Dic. under *Colonia.*

34. Patres Conscriptos. See the origin of this double title explained, Liv. 2, 1.—***Intempestivo honore.*** *Ill-timed* enough always under the emperors, but especially ill-timed now, when the senators were assembled only in part, out of the city and without their princeps.

Ch. LIII.—**36. Ambigua.** Vacillating between Otho and Vitellius.

37. Invisum . . . . nomen. Marcellus had been a notorious informer under Nero (cf. 4, 7. 43); and the inveterate enemy of the virtuous Paetus Thrasea. Ann. 16, 22. 28.

1. Novus adhuc, sc. homo, i. e. without distinction by birth. Cf. 100
Cic. passim.

2. Magnis inimicitiis. Cf. note on *magna adulteria*, 1, 2.

3. Bononiam. Now Bologna. It was a colony. Ann. 12, 58.

5. Recentissimum. Last from the scene of action.

8. Sola . . . . cura, i. e. caring only for his reputation with posterity.

Ch. LIV.—**11. Consiliis,** sc. senatus.

13. Superventu . . . . legionis. This legion was in fact hemmed in by superior numbers (cf. 43), though it is alleged by the soldiers (cf. 66), that their main body was not present. Superventus is a post-Augustan word.—**15. Causa.** *The design, motive.*

16. Diplomata. Well explained in Leverett; more fully in Smith's Dic. sub voce. Cf. Plin. Ep. 10, 14. 54. The *diploma* consisted of two leaves, or tablets folded together; hence the name (from Gr. διπλόω). These writs, being given by the emperor, and sealed with his seal, were of course disregarded (*negligebantur*) after his death, as null and void; but would recover their force (*revalescerent*), if Otho were again believed to be alive.

18. Paucos post dies. Cf. note on *magna ex parte*, 37.—***Poenas luit.*** Literally, *he paid the penalty.* Cf. note, 1, 37: *poena.*

21. Publici . . . . discessum. Cf. 53: *rediere . . . consiliaturi.* —***Partes,*** sc. Othonis.

22. In commune. Cf. note on it, G. 27.

Ch. LV.—**26. Ex more.** In the usual manner and at the usual time, viz. the 19th of April. Ann. 15, 53.

Page

100 **27. Cessisse.** *Cedo* is followed by the dat. of the person and acc. or abl. of the thing. Cf. Z. 413. Tacitus uses it here without either, *vita* being understood. So *concedo*, Ann. 4, 38. 13, 30.

29. Certi auctores. *Credible witnesses.* The opposite of *incertis auctoribus*, 73.

30. Vitellio plausere, sc. the multitude. Compare a similar scene of servility, 1, 32.—**32. Lacum Curtii.** Cf. note, 1, 41.

33. Cuncta. All the honors and prerogatives.

34. Composita. *Contrived, invented.* A satire on the age so fertile in new methods of obsequiousness.

35. Missa legatio, sc. to Vitellius. Cf. 69: *senatus legatione*, etc.

36. Quae .... fungeretur. *To offer their congratulations.* The expression implies a mere *official* and heartless congratulation. Cf. Or. ad loc. See also Essay, p. 16.

37. Gratior .... scripsisset. It had already become a prevailing custom, that none but the emperors should write to the consuls or senate, but all others should write to the emperor. Cf. Lipsius ad loc.

101 Ch. LVI.—**2. Municipia et colonias.** Cf. note on *municipia*, 1, 70.

3. Vi et stupris = stupris violentis by hendiadys. Roth.—*Fas nefasque*, i. e. *right and wrong*, without distinction. Cf. note on *fas*, 1, 44.

4. Avidi aut venales. Either eager under the impulse of their own passions, or influenced by bribes from others.

5. Inimicos. *Private enemies; hostes*, public do.—*Specie militum*, quasi milites Othonis essent et hostes. Rup.

6. Refertos, sc. frugibus.

8. Obnoxiis .... ausis. *The generals being liable to be called to account for their own crimes* (ob noxam), *and therefore not daring to forbid the crimes of others.*

9. Plus ambitionis. Sub. *sed: but more desire of popularity;* for which reason he was as ready to connive at the faults of the soldiers, as Valens was in order to gratify his avarice.

11. Tantum .... injuriae = tantum peditum equitumque cum vi, damnisque et injuriis, quibus per illos afficiebantur. Wr.

Ch. LVII.—**15. Pauci .... relicti,** sc. to bear up the *names* of their respective legions (which had been withdrawn by Vitellius), and to serve as a nucleus about which the full number was to be gathered by *hasty levies from the Gauls.* This explains *remanentium . . nomina: the empty names of legions which remained behind.* Cf. 4, 14: *inania legionum nomina.*

17. Cura .... permissa, sc. ne Germani transirent. Lipsius.—*E Britannico ..... millia.* Called *vexillis .... Britannicarum legionum*, 3, 22.

Page

Ch. LVIII.—**27. Utramque Mauretaniam.** Cf. duae Mauretaniae, 1, 11. *Uterque* is plural in its meaning, but seldom used in a plural form, when only two persons or things are spoken of. 101

31. Decem novem. For *decem et novem.* Al. undeviginti (Wr.), and novendecim (Oberlin and the common editions). But neither of these is found in the MSS. Zumpt says (115, N. 2), that such forms as *octodecim* and *novendecim* are not supported by any authority.

34. Hispaniae. Spain had espoused the cause of Vitellius.

2. Jubae nomen. Quod erat illustre inter Maurorum reges. Brot. 102

Ch. LIX.—**7. Appulsu littoris.** *Immediately on his approach to the shore.* Al. appulsus.

9. Quae fierent. *Which might* (chance) *to be done*, i. e. whatever they might be.

12. Arare. Now the Saone. Cf. Ann. 13, 53.—*Paratu* = apparatu. Död.—*Vetere egestate.* For the extreme poverty of Vitellius at his setting out for the province, from which he returned an emperor, cf. Suet. Vitel. 7.

14. Par opibus. *With resources equal* to his liberality.

16. Ingratus, sc. because he outshone Vitellius—a crime which he finally expiated with his blood. Cf. 3, 39.—*Quamvis. Although*, followed by the subj. Cf. Gr. 263, 2; Z. 574; and note below, 79: *quamvis .... jurasset.*

19. Curuli, sc. sellae. *Chair of state,* occupied originally only by the kings (Liv. 1, 20: *curuli regia sella*); under the republic by all the principal magistrates; under the emperors again more restricted, viz. to themselves, the Augustales and the prætor in the administration of justice. Cf. Smith's Dict. of Antiq., *Sella.*

20. Infanti filio. Qui titubantia oris prope mutus fuit. Cf. Suet. Vitel. 6. Brotier.—*Perlatum. Brought to him.*

23. Rebus .... cessit. It was some solace that the child had once worn princely robes. So when Vitellius was insulted by a tribune and expected every moment to be put to death, he said: "but yet I have been your sovereign" (3, 85). The passage has been made the subject of much needless censure by the commentators.—*Rebus adversis.* The son, as well as the father, was ere long put to death. Cf. 4, 80.

Ch. LX.—**26. Contactu.** *Under their influence,* spreading from one to another like a *contagious disease.*

30. Ultro imputabant. Cf. note on *ultro imputavit*, 1, 71.

33. Fidem absolvit. *Pardoned their fidelity* to Otho, as if a *crime.* Cf. 1, 59: fidei crimine, gravissimo inter desciscentes. Observe the satire on Vitellius, who is represented as pardoning virtue and rewarding crime.

36. Creditum fama. *It was believed on the ground of mere rumor.*

Page

102 **38. Restitit.** *Resisted* the offer of Simplex. Others understand denied the report.—*Dedit .... consulatum.* Cf. 3, 68.

103 **1. Trachalum.** The writer of Otho's speeches, 1, 90.

2. Galeria was of the same gens as *Galerius* Trachalus. Women at Rome had no *prænomen* or *cognomen;* but only the *nomen* or *gentile name* (cf. note on the name of Agricola, A. 4). They were further distinguished only by the name of the father or husband, as here: *uxor Vitellii.*

Ch. LXI.—**4. Inserere .... fortunae.** *To thrust himself in as an aspirant to fortune,* sc. inter magnorum virorum discrimina.

5. Simulatione numinum. Simulans se deum esse, vel a diis missum ad patriam liberandam. Rup. The latter is preferable.

6. Assertor. *Liberator.*—*Nam id,* etc Al. nomen id, but without MS. authority. Of course *nomen* is understood by a not unfrequent ellipsis.

7. Proximos Aeduorum. In quorum finibus Caesar post bellum Helveticum Boios collocavit. Cf. Caes. B. G. 1, 28. Ryckius.

8. Trahebat, sc. in suas partes. Wr. Others make it = *vastabat.*—*Gravissima. Most dignified, most prudent.* Opposed to *fanaticam multitudinem.* So Or., Dōd. and Wr. According to Ernesti = potens, valida.

10. Feris objectus. Quae erat seditiosorum poena. Brotier.

Ch. LXII.—**13. Defectores.** The partisans of Otho, viewed as rebels against Galba. Wr. refers it to the followers of Mariccus. But that is quite too *pudendum dictu!*

14. Rata is the pred. of *lex* as well as of *testamenta.*

15. Si temperaret .... timeres. *If he had refrained from,* etc., *you would not have feared,* etc. Imp. subj., where we use the plup. both in the protasis and the apodosis. This is not unfrequent. Cf. Z. 525. It has the effect of transferring completed past actions to the present.—*Luxuriae.* Al. luxuriam. But then *temperaret* would have a different meaning. Cf. note, 1, 69. As to the luxury of Vitel. cf. 95. 3, 36. 63; Suet. 10, 13.

18. Utroque mari. The Upper or Adriatic and Lower or Tyrrhenian.

22. Differret . non reciperet. These honors were voted him in the decree of the senate (57), to which this edict must be a response. The subj. denotes the object or design of the edict.

23. Cum = *although.* Cf. Gr. 263, 5.—*Pulsi .... mathematici.* Cf. 1, 22; Xiphil. (65, 1) differs from T. and Suet. (Vitel. 14) as to the *time* when this act was issued.

24. Ludo et arena. *The stage and the gladiatorial arena.* Dōd. makes it = gladiatoriis ludis by hendiadys.

25. Priores .... perpulerant, e. g. J. Caes. (Suet. 39), Aug. (do. 43), et in primis Nero (do. 11. 12; His. 2, 71; 3, 62, et Ann.

passim). *Perpulerant* is structura prægnans for perpellendo impetra- 103
verant. Död.

Ch. LXIII.—**28. Fratris.** Cf. 54.—*Dominationis magistris Masters in the art of tyranny.* So the *courtiers* of that age might well be called.—**31. Retulimus.** 1, 88.

32. Praetura functus. Ex-prætor; hence a man of prætorian rank. Cf. *consulatu functus,* Ann. 1, 39, et al.

35. Quae .... ageret. Subj. in a dependent clause of the oratio obliqua. Cf. Gr. 266, 2; Z. 603, c.

36. Nec .... probationibus. *When he could furnish no proof to substantiate such weighty charges,* he repented, etc.; but it was too late—Dolabella was ruined.—*Veniam,* sc. for Dolabella.

38. Super ..... re. *Super* with abl. = *concerning,* belongs chiefly to the silver age. Z. 320.

4. Impulit ruentem. *Precipitated his fall. Allevasse* is ex- 104
actly antith. to *ruentem,* meaning, lit. *to lift up.*

Ch. LXIV.—**5. Quod .... accepisset.** The subj. here assigns the alleged reason for Vitellius' hatred. The ind. would give the true reason in the view of the author. Cf. Z. 549. See an example of the ind. after *quod* in 72: *quod .... manebat.*—*Petroniam.* The first wife of Vitellius, whom he divorced. Cf. Suet. Vitel. 6.

8. Interamnium. Al. Interamnam, which is the more common form. Cf. 3, 61. A town of Umbria, not far from the river Liris—the supposed birthplace of Tacitus (cf. Life, p. 1), now *Terni.*

9. In .... taberna. *At an inn on the road,* by hendiadys.

12. Onerabat. *Rendered more odious, aggravated* (*ad* and *gravis*).

13. Non immixta. *Taking no part in.* Witness her protection of Trachalus, 60.—*Probitate, moris.* Cf. Gr. 211, R. 6.

14. Sextilia. Cf. Suet. Vitel. 3.—*Quin etiam. Nay,* she was *even* said, etc. Observe the position of these particles after the verb. T. is fond of anastrophe. Cf. note, G. 14: *quin immo.*

16. Nec .... evicta. *Nor by any subsequent* (*postea* = an adj.) *allurements of fortune, or flattering solicitations of the public, was she prevailed upon to join in the general rejoicings.* A fine example of moderation (*modestum exemplum*) indeed! And how touching is the historian's *intimation* of the concluding scene in the drama: *domus suae tantum adversa sensit. Evincere* is a favorite word with Tacitus and with the poets Virgil and Ovid. Cf. Or. in loco.

Ch. LXV.—**21. Ferens** = praeferens. Cf. Essay, pp. 10. 11.

24. Diplomatibus. Cf. note, 54.—*Nullum principem,* sed suum ipsius nomen.

25. Praescripsisset. The name of the author of a diploma or decree, as also of a letter, was *prefixed* by the ancients, by us it is *subscribed.*

Page

104 **27. Puniri ultro.** *Punished even,* i. e. not only not rewarded, but *furthermore punished.* Cf. notes on *ultro,* 25. 1, 71.

33. E praesentibus. One of the followers of Vitellius, in distinction from one already abroad in the provinces.

105 Ch. LXVI.—**4. Augustae Taurinorum.** Cf. note on *ala Taurina,* 1, 59.

8. Arsisset. Al. *exarsisset,* ex uno codice. Wr. Cf. note, 1, 2: *missa;* and Essay, pp. 10. 11.

12. Vitarent. The histor. pres. (*jubet*) is followed often by the subj. imp. Cf. Z. 501.

17. Ferebant denotes a mere *attempt* or *preparation* to march to Vienne. Cf. Gr. 145, II. 4.

Ch. LXVII.—**20. Separati,** sc. into small parties. Al. *separatae.* But it agrees with *cohortes* ad sensum. Cf. Gr. 205, R. 3; Z. 368.

21. Lenimento is post-Augustan. Cf. Freund.—*Arma . . . deferebant. They were preparing to lay down* or perhaps *were gradually* (one division after another) *laying down their arms.* Cf. note on *ferebant,* 66.

22. Crebresceret. *Became at length* (lit. was becoming) *a matter of common remark.*

Ch. LXVIII.—**29. Partes,** sc. victae, which need not be expressed; for it is *the* party of which he has just been speaking, and is further defined by *victores* in the antithesis.—*Modeste. By mild measures,* such as have been described in the previous section.

31. Bello. *The fight,* the quarrel in question. So Wr. But it may be taken of the whole *civil war,* which was rendered more odious by the number slain on this trivial occasion.—*Discubuerat.* Lit. had reclined, i. e. *was banqueting.*

33. Tempestivis. Seasonable, early, earlier than usual, and so *unusually luxurious.* Cf. Note, 1, 62: *medio . . . . temulentus.*

34. Intentus . . . . agit. Cf. note, A. 5: *intentus agere.*

35. Indisposita. A word found only in T. Cf. Boet. Lex. Tac. The adv. *indisposite* is found in Seneca.—*Pervigiliis. Pervigilia,* quanquam res sacra (cf. Ann. 15, 44), a corruptis posterioris aetatis moribus malam famam habebant, ideoque *pervigilia* et *Bacchanalia synonyma* esse coeperunt. Wr. Render: *bacchanalian vigils,* by hendiadys. So *disciplinae et castris* = *military discipline.*

106 **7. Agminis coactores.** *The rearguard,* whose duty it was to gather up (*cogere*) stragglers, reclaim deserters, etc. The word is found in this sense only in this single passage. Cf. Or. and Boetticher.

12. Quondam . . . . sui. Cf. 1, 8.

15. Fastiditi. Quorum preces bis fastidivisset—a quibus imperium bis oblatum accipere noluisset. Cf. 1, 52; 2, 51.

Ch. LXIX.—**16. Senatus legatione.** Cf. 55.

17. Pietatem. *Loyalty.*

Page

21. Principium .... fatis. The foreign war was with the Batavians under Civilis (Books 4 and 5, passim): the domestic with Vespasian. 106

23. Inania belli. *The empty parade of war.* Ad rem, cf. 1, 61. Ad verba, cf. A. 6: *inania honoris*, etc.

25. Amputari .... numeros. *The companies to be cut down*, i. e. so as to reduce the number of soldiers without diminishing the number of cohorts.

30. Apud .... stetit. *In whose day the republic was in a better condition, and that not because there was more money, but because there was more virtue.* Two sentences in one. Cf. Essay, p. 18.

Ch. LXX.—**32. Munere** = spectaculo gladiatorum (cf. 67); called *munus*, as a *present* to the people. Ramshorn, 944.

35. Intra .... diem. *Within forty days after the battle;* of course, before the bodies had gone wholly to decay—putrid, but still wearing the human form.

36. Formae. The general *forms.* The minute and distinguishing features were lost.

37. Tabo. This form (viz. after the 2d declension) is found only in poetry and post-Augustan prose. Cf. Freund.

38. Inhumana. *Shocking to humanity.* Cf. 3, 83: *inhumana securitas.* The Postumian way, *now strewed with roses and laurels and lined with altars smoking with victims, as if in honor of some despotic prince*, had been obstructed with heaps of slain in the disastrous flight to Bedriacum (cf. 44), and must have been still thickly strewn with their putrid corses. The *contrast* was truly *monstrous.*

2. Quae .... fecere. Cf. 3, 18, seq., and 3, 27–34. 107

8. Clamore et gaudio. *Shouts of joy.* So *lacrimae et misericordia = tears of compassion*, by hendiadys. *Foedum et atrox*, just above, is still another instance of the fondness of Tac. for such *pairs.* Cf. note, 1, 84: *domibus*, etc.

10. Et erant. *There were also.—Varia fors rerum. The vicissitudes of life.*

11. Subiret. Cf. note, 1, 13: *subisse.* A more simple writer would have said: affected even to tears, making *fors* only the subject of *subiret.* For the subj. cf. Gr. 264, 6; Z. 561.—*Flexit.* Cf. note, 46: *flexerat.* Observe the emphatic separation of *non* from the verb, to mark the contrast between Vitellius and others.

12. Tot millia. Cf. note, 44: *strage corporum.—Laetus ultro.* Nay, he was *joyful even.* Cf. note, 65: *puniri ultro.* Suetonius reports a remark almost too monstrous to be imputed even to Vitellius, and too vile and vulgar to be recorded by Tacitus: optime olere occisum hostem, et melius civem. Cf. Vitel. 10, where, as also in Xiph. 65, 1, see further of this visit to the field of battle.

Ch. LXXI.—**17. Iter,** sc. Vitellii ad Romam.

Page

107 **18. Cetero . . . ingenio.** *And all the other ingenious inventions of Nero's court.*

19. Admiratione celebrabat. *He used to attend also upon Nero's person out of admiration for his character.* Suetonius says (Vitel. 4, 12), Vitellius passed his time under Nero among buffoons, charioteers and wrestlers.

20. Necessitate, qua, etc. Cf. 62: *priores . . . . perpulerant.*

21. Luxu. Dat. in *u* instead of *ui,* used exclusively by Cæsar (Gell. 4, 19), sometimes by the poets, and in several unequivocal instances by T., e. g. Ann. 3, 30: *luxu propior.* Cf. Gr. 89, 3; Z. 81; Essay, p. 21.—*Luxu . . . emptusque = sold and given up to appetite and luxury,* lit. bought and handed over to it, as to a master and owner.

23. Dissimulatus. Silentio praetermissus, quasi non destinatus. Rup. Cf. A. 39: dissimulari.—*Martii Macri.* Cf. 23. Nothing is said there however or anywhere of his being designated consul. It is only *implied* here. Cf. Essay, pp. 18. 19.

26. Omittitur. Nomen ejus in catalogo consulum a Galba destinatorum deletur. Rup. Cæcina and Valens were designated consuls for the last two months in the year, beginning with the Kal. of Nov. Cf. 3, 37. Compare on this whole subject, note, 1, 77: *In . . . martias;* also Table, p. 26.

Ch. LXXII.—**31. Scribonianum Camerinum.** The same with Sulpicius Camerinus put to death, together with his son, by Helius, Nero's freedman. Xiph. 63, 18. So Wr., Or., Mur., etc. Others (from the mention of the Crassi below) identify him with M. Licinius Crassus, consul, A. U. C. 817, slain by Nero (Ann. 15, 33), called Scribonianus (4, 39). So Brotier and Ryckius.

33. Histria. A peninsula near the head of the Adriatic.—*Quod . . . . manebat.* Cf. note, 64: *quod . . . . accepisset.*

36. Errore veri. *Veri* adds more to the sound than to the sense. Död. says it is added to preserve concinnity with the antithetic clause. Cf. Essay, p. 23.

38. Quisnam . . . . esset. Subj. Cf. Gr. 265; Z. 552.

108 **1. Geta.** Geta and Davus were common names for slaves at Rome (cf. Ter., Plaut. and Hor. passim), both derived from the Getae or Daci, who were led captive and sold into slavery at Rome in great numbers. Cf. Anthon, Class. Dic. sub voce. So, according to some, our word *slave* is derived from the old Slavi of the North.

2. In servilem modum. Slaves were crucified. Cf. Ann. 3, 50: *serviles cruciatus.*

Ch. LXXIII.—**3. Quantum . . . . adoleverit.** Subj. Cf. Gr. 265; Z. 552.

4. Speculatores. The speculatores, besides being the body-guard of the commander-in-chief (cf. note, 1, 25), were the official *messen-*

Page

gers of the legion or army to which they belonged. Cf. Suet. Cal. 44. 108
Each legion had its division of *speculatores*. Cf. Freund sub voce.

7. Plerumque .... excitabatur. *Was sometimes roused from his lethargy.* Highly descriptive of the character of Vitellius. So 1, 53: *quatiebatur segne*, etc.

9. In externos mores, i. e. externorum regum, qui non legibus sed ut libitum regnant. Wr.

Ch. LXXIV.—**15. De Syria.** Al. *e Syria. De* with the better authority is also better suited to the place. *De* plus dicit quam *e:* nempe indicat legionem illam prius stationem suam habuisse in Syria; *e* simpliciter significat locum, unde discessum sit. Wr.

16. Transisset. Observe the force of the subj. *because*, as he said within himself, *it had passed.* Cf. note, 64: *quod . . . accepisset.* —*Ceterae .... sperabantur.* Observe the attraction, instead of *ceteras .... secuturas sperabatur.* Cf. Essay, p. 18.

18. Flammaverat. This verb is found only in poetry and post-Augustan prose.

22. Sexaginta annos = se sexagenarium. Rup.

24. Progressum. *Et regressum* is implied, but not necessary to be expressed. Cf. Essay, p. 15.

Ch. LXXV.—**30. Fluxam.** Cf. note on the word, 1, 21.

32. Praesenti facinori. Al. *facinore.* Either makes a good sense, and indeed essentially the same. *Facinori* is dat. after *paratum*, and *praesenti* according to Wr. is antith. to *ex diverso: if one or two* (solitary individuals) *covet the reward which ever awaits a crime easily perpetrated* (lit. at hand, on the spot) *from the opposite party.*

33. Petat. Subj. in a dependent clause of the oratio obliqua.—*Scribonianum.* Cf. 1, 89, note.—**35. Singulos,** sc. assassins.

Ch. LXXVI.—**1. Coram.** *In their presence*, sc. of the *legati* 109
amicique. Cf. chap. 78. Observe the brachylogy. Wr. makes it = palam, quasi in publico.

2. An .... sit. Subj. in an indirect question. Cf. Gr. 265; Z 552. So *adjiciat* and *acquiratur* below.

4. Ipse .... considerandus est. Cf. Essay, p. 18.

8. Juxta. *In connection with, under.* Cf. note, G. 21.

9. Expaveris ... fuerit. *Nor should you fear ... it would be*, etc. Cf. notes, 1, 84: *depoposcerint.*—*A .... propius.* Cf. note, G. 43: *protinus .... ab;* also 1, 10: *prope ab.*

12. Caii aut Claudii vel Neronis. *Aut* implies a greater difference than *vel: Of Caligula* on the one hand, *or* on the other *of Claudius or Nero.* Cf. Rams. Syn. 138; and note, A. 17, G. 15: *vel .... vel.*—**13. Exsurgimus,** tanquam ex insidiis. Rup.

14. Galbae imaginibus = Galbae propter antiquitatem nobilitatemque generis. Cf. Suet Galb. 2.

17. Transvectum est. Cf. A. 18. Only T. uses the word in

Page

109 reference to time. Observe here, as in so many other places, the pairs of words nearly synonymous: *abiit et transvectum est, sopor et ignavia, ardoris ac ferociae, popinis et commissationibus.* The sentiment of this and the following clause is: it is too late for you to hope that you will merely *seem* (*videri* is emphatic) to have coveted the throne; nobody doubts that you have, and now the throne is your only place of refuge and safety.

18. Excidit, sc. de memoria tua. Rup. Corbulo was put to death by Nero, though, had he ventured on it, he might have dethroned the fiddling emperor. Cf. Xiph. 63, 17.

23. Nullis stipendiis. *Without military experience.—Galbae odio.* The hatred of the soldiers towards Galba.

24. Ne Othonem .... fecit. Two distinct thoughts are blended in this sentence: 1. Otho was not conquered by the skill of Vitellius or the power of his army, but, etc.; 2. Even Otho is now regretted and honored in comparison with Vitellius. Cf. note, chap. 69: *apud .... stetit.*

26. Spargit .... ministrat. Cf. 66 and 67. The disarmed prætorians and disbanded legions carried with them the spirit of disaffection.

Ch. LXXVII.—**37. Triumphale nomen.** Awarded by Claudius for his services in Britain. Cf. A. 13; Suet. Vesp. 4. *Nomen* = honor, decus.—*Duo juvenes.* Titus and Domitian.

38. Alter. Titus.—*Capax jam imperii.* He was now 27 years old.

110 **2. Cedere imperio.** *Cedere, to give up,* takes the dat. of the person with either the acc. or abl. of the thing. Cf. Z. 413.

8. Hos .... illi. *Hos* here refers to the former, *illi* to the latter. Cf. Gr. 207, R. 23.

10. Aperiet .... bellum. Almost a translation of Demos. Phil. 1, 44. *Recludet* is peculiar to poetry and post-Augustan prose.

12. Parsimonia. *Economy,* which provides the sinews of war. Cf. 84.

14. Qui deliberant, desciverunt. Cf. A. 15; Plut. Galb. 4, same sentiment. This speech well befits a *politician,* such as Mucianus is described to be, chap. 5.

Ch. LXXVIII.—**17. Vatum.** Used here in its primary sense: *prophets, diviners.* The secondary and more frequent sense is: sacred poets, bards.—**18. Intactus,** sc. Vespasian.

19. Rerum dominus, i. e. emperor.—*Mathematicum.* Cf. note, 1, 22.

22. Repente. Suet. (Vesp. 5) says: sine ulla vi. Xiph. (66, 1), on the contrary, says, it was by a violent wind. "Tam parum sibi constant prodigia." Brotier.—**24. Haruspicum.** Cf. note, 1, 27.

28. Judaeam inter. The position of the prep. here is a pecu-

Page

liarity of T. (cf. *insulam inter*, 4, 19; Z. 324); though the best prose 110
writers frequently place the prep. between the adj. and subs. Cf. note, 2, 37: *magna ex parte.—Carmelus.* A mountain in Galilee on the Mediterranean. Two others in Palestine bore the same name, which properly denotes a garden-like fertility and beauty. Cf. Isaiah, 35, 2: "the excellency of Carmel."

29. Deumque, sc. cujus oraculum in monte fuit. Cf. Suet. Vesp. 5; Oros. 7, 9. Or. thinks it was the old Philistine god of war.

30. Sic tradidere, etc. Al. *situm* tradidere, etc., by conjecture. The passage, as it stands in the text and in the MSS., is elliptical and concise = sic tradidere majores, i. e. tradidere aram tantum, etc. Wr.

34. Ampliare servitia = augere numerum servitiorum. Rup. *Ampliare* and *prolatare* are both used here in a sense peculiar to poetry, or to the age of T.

35. Has ambages. *These obscure prophetic intimations.* Cf. 4: per ambages. Cf. Suet. Vesp. 5. 7, for a fuller and somewhat different account of these and other oracles and prodigies.

36. Et statim . . . et tunc. Cf. note, 1, 17: *statim . . . et mox.*

CH. LXXIX.—**1. Haud . . . . destinatione,** i. e. *with a settled* 111
plan or *purpose.*

2. Antiochiam, Caesaream. Places familiar to us in sacred, even more than in profane history. Cf. Acts, passim.—*Illa,* the former; *haec,* the latter. Död. follows the Medicean MS. in reading *hoc,* agreeing with *caput.*

3. Initium . . . . coeptum. Cf. note, G. 30: *initium inchoare.* Wr. says: *coepisse* Tacito est ἐπιχειρεῖν. See Essay, p. 20.—*Ferendi.* Ernesti prefers *deferendi.* But cf. note, 1, 2: *missa.*

7. Quinto Nonas Julias = July 3d. Suet. (Vesp. 6) says: quinto *idus* Jul. T. is proved to be correct.—*Jurasset.* Subj. after *quamvis,* as usual in T. and Cic., though most of the later writers construe *quamvis* with the ind.

10. Non parata concione. *Without any formal harangue;* such as it was usual for new aspirants or nominees to the throne to make, e. g. Otho, 1, 36; Galba, Suet. Galb. 18; and others.

CH. LXXX.—**13. Prima vox.** *The first salutation* or *nomination.—Spes . . . casus.* Observe the *asyndeton* and the antith. *pairs: hope, fear; principle, chance,* i. e. the principles to be adopted and the chances to be met.

15. Assistentes, sc. cubiculo; the guards of the bedchamber.

16. Caesarem . . . . cumulare. Observe the zeugma. Cf Essay, p. 16.

17. Mens. Cujus mens? Vespasiani. Ernesti. Amicorum Vespasiani. Wr. and Or. Militum ceterorum praeter illos, qui salutavere. Rup. Ruperti is right; for *ceteri* doubtless refers to the *soldiers;* and the transition from them to Vespasian himself is marked by *in ipso.*

Page

111 The whole army, having sworn allegiance to Vitellius, feared to utter the *prima vox;* but that having been uttered by a few, *they passed from fear to the enjoyment of their unexpected good fortune.*

18. In ipso, etc. Josephus (B. J. 4, 36), writing under the influence of the Flavian dynasty says, that Vespasian was forced to accept the throne by the threats and violence of the soldiers. This may serve to illustrate the impartiality of T., who has been sometimes thought too partial to Vespasian and Titus.

20. Mutationis. Al. multitudinis, altitudinis, vicissitudinis, etc. Mutationis is the only reading which resembles the Medicean MS. and at the same time makes a good sense.—*Militariter. In the language of a soldier,* i. e. rough and unpolished.

21. Laeta . . . excepit. *Found* (in return for his speech) *every thing auspicious, and resources flowing in upon him from every side.* Cf. A. 29: *affluebat.*

23. Ubi . . . . mos est. The Greeks transacted public business not unfrequently in the theatre. Cf. Demos. pro Cor. 53; Cic. pro Flac. 27; Acts, 12, 21; 19, 29–31.

25. Graeca facundia. He addressed them in the Greek language, which had been diffused by the conquests of Alexander over all southwestern Asia.

34. Stipendiorum. 1. Soldiers' pay; 2. *Military service,* as here.

Ch. LXXXI.—**37. Sohemus,** king of the country called Sophene. Ann. 13, 7.—*Antiochus,* king of Commagene. Ann. 12, 55.—*Agrippa* II., king of part of Judea. Ann. 13, 7.—*Berenice.* Cf. note, chap. 2, above.

112 **2. Ab urbe.** From Rome, whither he set out to go with Titus, and continued his journey when Titus turned back at Corinth. Cf. chap. 1, supra; also 1, 10.

5. Quidquid . . . . patescit. *The several maritime provinces, with Asia and Achaia and the whole inland country between Pontus and the two Armenias.* Murphy. Ad verba, cf. 6: *quantum . . . . cingitur;* and G. 30: *in . . . . patescit.*

9. Beryti. An ancient and illustrious city of Phœnicia, with a port on the Mediterranean (cf. Strab. 16; Plin. N. H. 5, 20); familiar in modern history and the history of missions, as Beirût (Beyroot) in Syria.

12. Decora is used in a poetical sense for *corpora.* Cf. Boetticher

Ch. LXXXII.—**30. Instare Judaeae,** i. e. *prosecute the war in Judea.*

33. Ac . . . . fatis. And this fact, or *this consideration, that nothing is too hard for destiny.* By attraction for *ac quod nihil arduum esset fatis.* Cf. Essay, p. 18.

113 Ch. LXXXIII.—**1. Majora . . . . absentibus.** Compare A. 30 omne ignotum pro magnifico est.

Page

2. Vexillariorum. Cf. note, 1, 31: *vexilla.* 113

3. Classem e Ponto. A fleet of forty ships (Heg. 2, 9), which guarded the coast of Pontus. Lipsius.

4. Adigi. *To be conducted.—Dyrrhachium, Brundisium, Tarentum.* These were the principal seaports on the Upper Sea, or Adriatic—Dyrrhachium in Illyricum, Brundisium in Calabria, and Tarentum in Lucania. Securing possession of these, the first by his land-forces, the other two by his fleets, Mucianus could protect Achaia, Asia and all the East. Brundisium was connected with Rome by the Appian Way. Cf. Hor. Sat. 1, 5.

5. Longis navibus. *Ships of war.* (Greek, νῆες μάκραι). The proper merchant-vessel was broader and rounder (στρογγύλη).—*Versum in.* Cf. note on *versus*, G. 1; also 1, 76: *versae in* = lying towards, *bordering on. Versum . . . mare. Seas of Italy.* Murphy.

9. Sibi = a se, sc. Muciano. Gr. 225, II. Cf. Essay, p. 12.

Ch. LXXXIV.—**13. Eos . . . . nervos.** *Eos* for *eas.* Cf. Z. 372. Ad rem, cf. Cic. Phil. 5, 2: nervi civilis belli pecunia infinita.

18. Ad . . . . iniquitates. *To secure unjust gains.* Cf. Liv. 29, 1: pertinaces ad obtinendam injuriam.

19. Haud . . . obstinante, &c., sc. se, or animum: *not applying himself so perseveringly,* sc. as he did at a later period in his reign. Avarice is mentioned by Suet. (16. 22) and Xiph. (66, 14) as the only vice of Vespasian, and this is excused on the ground of his liberality in adorning Rome with grand and useful works.

21. Largus . . . . sumeret. *Liberal of his private property, because he might take* (as he argued, subj.) *more freely* (sc. than he gave, lit. more greedily) *from the public purse.*

23. Rarissimus quisque. *Very few.*

Ch. LXXXV.—**25. Coepta.** Cf. note, 79: *initium . . . coeptum.*

27. Erat. Gr. 209, R. 12, (2.) Render: *these* (the other legions) *were the eighth and seventh.* Lit. *it was*, etc.

29. Aquileiam progressae. Ad rem, cf. 46.—*Proturbatis* = spretis, rejectisque. Rup.

30. Qui . . . . nuntiabant, sc. his defeat and death. Cf. Suet. Vesp. 6.

31. Pecunia here refers to the treasury of the army.

4. Ex nuntiis. *According to the news* he received. Cf. G. 7: 114 *ex virtute*, note.

Ch. LXXXVI.—**9. Falsi.** *Forgery.* A very common crime among the later Romans. Cf. Smith's Dic. sub voce. Antonius was banished by Nero, and recalled by Galba and raised to the rank of senator. Ann. 14, 40. Xiph. 65, 9. Yet he is greatly praised by Martial, 9, 101; 10, 23.

16. Raptor. Ant. to *largitor. A plunderer and a prodigal.* Mur.

19. Consularibus legatis. The governors named in the next sentence.

Page

114 **20. Tenebant** = obtinebant. Cf. 1, 11, and Essay, pp. 10, 11.

21. Procurator, fortasse utriusque provinciae. Rup.—*Aderat.* Favored Vespasian. **24. Coloniae suae.** *Of his native colony.*

115 Ch. LXXXVII.—**2. Procacissimis . . . ingeniis.** *Of all classes of slaves even, the camp-servants being the most riotous. Lixarum* seems to be used as a synonym with *calonum,* to avoid repetition. Cf. Essay, p. 23. *Calones* were properly wood-carriers (from *cala,* Gr. κᾶλα, fire-wood), and *lixae,* water-drawers (from *lixa,* obs. for *aqua*). The former = camp-servants, the latter = cooks. The words are usually associated together, e. g. 1, 49; 3, 20; 3, 33.

9. Amicitiarum dehonestamentis = amicis inhonestis.

11. Ipsi . . . arvaque = ipsa cultorum arva, by hendiadys. Rup. This section contains a highly graphic description, in few words, of a very ludicrous yet sad scene.

Ch. LXXXVIII.—**14. Seditionem Ticini.** Cf. 68.

15. Ubi . . . . consensu. *Whenever they* had to *contend with the country people,* they (the legions and auxiliaries) *acted in concert.* The language is very concise. *Consensu* is ant. to *discordia.* The subj. imp. is here used to denote an action of repeated occurrence. Cf. Gr. 264, 12; Z. 569.

19. Vernacula . . . . urbanitate. *They were practising the refinement* (trickery) *characteristic of homebred slaves,* sc. in cutting the belts of the soldiers, &c. *Vernacula* more commonly means native, vernacular. But cf. Ann. 1, 31: *vernacula multitudo* = a multitude of slaves. Al. *ut rebantur* for *utebantur.* But the latter is found in all the MSS.

23. Caesus, non a filio, sed ab alio quodam milite, ira in omnes paganos accensa.

24. Agnitus, sc. non esse e scurris illis (paganis), sed militis pater. Wr.

26. In quo . . . . jacuisset. The subj. here denotes not the mere fact that Galba had fallen, but the influence it had on the minds of the soldiers.

28. Cum . . . . vitarent. *Cum* causalis = since, and followed by the subj.

Ch. LXXXIX.—**33. Ponte Mulvio.** Cf. note, 1, 87, and Essay, p. 20.

34. Paludatus accinctusque. Military attire, in which Vitellius proposed to enter the city, but which, at the instance of his friends, he exchanged for the robe of state (*sumpta praetexta*). Suetonius makes him to have *entered* the city *paludatus ferroque succinctus* (Vitel. 11).

116 **3. Ante aquilam,** i. e. before the eagle of *each legion* (there were four) marched the præfects, tribunes, &c. of *that legion.* So Wr and Död. explain the singular number.

Page

7. Non .... dignus, sed alio meliore principe. Rup. 116

Ch. XC.—**10. Alterius civitatis.** *Another city,* i. e. a foreign one, where his vices were unknown. *Alterius = alius.* Cf. A. 17.

15. Adulationes = adulationis formulae. Wr.

16. Astrepebat is post-Augustan and particularly frequent in T. Cf. Freund sub voce.

17. Tam frustra. *To as little purpose,* sc. because he enjoyed it for so short a time. The language here is very concise and elliptical, two clauses being thrown into one, thus: they forced him to accept it; he did accept it, but to as little purpose, etc. Cf. note, 76: *ne ... Othonem fecit.* Död. connects *frustra* with *expressere* in the sense of *falso,* thus: *they extorted* from him an acceptance *with as little sincerity* as *he had* previously *declined* the honor.

Ch. XCI.—**19. Interpretantem.** *Putting a superstitious construction upon.*

20. Quod .... edixisset. Cf. note, 74: *transisset.*

22. Cremerensi clade. The defeat and slaughter of the 300 Fabii at the river Cremera, A. U. C. 277.

23. Alliensi. The same of the Roman army at the river Allia, A. U. C. 364, by the Gauls under Brennus.

The day on which these disasters befell the Romans, was ever after deemed unlucky; and on such days no important business might be transacted.

24. Expers. *Ignorant* or *regardless.—Pari. Equal,* sc. to that of Vitellius.

25. Comitia consulum. Cf. note, 1, 14: *comitia imperii;* also Smith's Dic. Ant. sub voce. Render: *But frequenting the consular elections with his* (favorite) *candidates, just like a common citizen* (*civiliter*), i. e. soliciting votes for them, &c. This was in the *senate,* who at this time had the nominal power, and went through the form of electing consuls. The remainder of the sentence introduces *another* illustration of his excessive condescension, viz. his conduct in the *theatre* and the *circus,* among the *common people.* In a less concise writer it would have been thrown into a distinct sentence or clause.

29. Vitae prioris. Cf. notes, chap. 71.

31. Priscus Helvidius. Cf. A. 2, note.—*Praetor designatus,* i. e. *prætor elect,* but not yet inducted into office.

32. Non .... ultra. Ellipsis of *saeviit,* or some other verb: *did not, however, proceed further than to call*—lit. no more than called.

37. Thraseae. Cf. note, A. 2.

38. Quod legisset. Cf. *quod .... dissentirent* and *quod .. edixisset,* just above.

Ch. XCII.—**3. A .... cohortis,** i. e. from being commander of 117 a cohort. This clause, and the corresponding one, *tum centurionem,*

Page

117 are added to denote a sudden elevation from a lov to a high post. Cf. 1, 46: *e manipularibus*, etc.

11. Nec .... potentia. *Nor indeed is power ever very secure when it is excessive;* a general remark, suggested by the balance of power wavering between Cæcina and Valens, as Vitellius inclined to favor the one or the other.

12. Simul. *At the same time* (that Vitellius vacillated between them) *they in turn both despised and feared Vitellius himself, who capriciously indulged in sudden bursts of displeasure* or *extravagant expressions of attachment,* according to his humor. Död. makes *offensis* and *blanditiis* datives.

16. Patriae .... reddiderat, but not to the possession of their estates. Hence *flebilis et egens.*

17. Gratum is acc., agreeing with the object of *approbavit,* viz. the clause, *quod .... concessisset.*

19. Jura libertorum. Cf. Essay, p. 12. *Their rights over their freedmen.* Patrons were entitled to service, and if necessary, support, from their freedmen; also to inherit one-half of their estates. Lipsius.

20. Servilia ingenia = liberti, quibus servile ingenium est. Rup. —*Abditis .... sinus. By concealing their wealth in obscure places, or depositing it in the custody of the great.* So Död. Or. understands by *occultos sinus* the hands (lit. bosoms) of obscure *persons.*

Ch. XCIII.—**28. Infamibus.** *Notorious,* sc. for their unhealthy air, as the Vatican is to this day. The pontifical palace stands there; but the pontiffs seldom reside in it. Cf. Arnold's chap. on the climate, &c. of Italy, His. Rom. vol. 1, chap. 23.

29. Germanorum .... corpora, sc. because accustomed to a colder climate.

30. Fluminis is objective gen. = bibendi ex flumine aviditas.

32. Sedecim praetoriae, etc. An increased number. Cf. note, 1, 20.

33. Quis . .. inessent. *In which there were to be,* when the levy was complete. They were now *being enrolled* (*scribebantur*). The subj. here denotes an intention, not a fact.

35. Sane. *In truth;* justifying in some measure the claim of Valens. Cf. note on *sane,* 1, 12.

38. Unde .... fluitasse. Cæcina proved a traitor. Cf. 100.

118 Ch. XCIV.—**7. Convulsum ... decus.** *The order and beauty of the* prætorian *camp was destroyed,* viz. by the very same means which withdrew from the legions and squadrons abroad their main strength.

10. Quod .... bellassent. Observe again the force of the subj. to denote the reason *assigned* by the soldiers.

14. Liberti principum. *The freedmen of* former *emperors,* who, as belonging to the state, passed from one imperial family to

Page

another So Wr. Lipsius and Ernesti understand by *principum* the principal men. 118

15. Stabula ... circum, etc. Agreeably to his early life and habits. Cf. note, chap. 71.

CH. XCV.—**19. Tota urbe vicatim.** *Through all the streets of the city,* of which there were 424. Brotier. The abl. with the adj. *tota* is generally used without *in*. Cf. Z. 482.

21. Invidiae. By enallage for *invidiosum.—Quod ... fecisset.* Ad rem, cf. Suet. Vitel. 11. Xiph. 65, 7 ; also above, 71.

24. Ut .... regi. As Romulus had instituted one (not the same order, but the Titienses) in honor of King Tatius. For the Titienses and the Augustales, cf. Smith's Dic. sub voce.

26. Polyclitos, etc. Cf. note, 1, 37.—*Vetera .. nomina. And other odious freedmen of former emperors.*

33. Vinios .... Asiaticos. Titus Vinius and Icelus. Cf. 1, 13. —*Fabios,* i. e. Fabius Valens.

35. Marcellus. Cf. 53, above. He was the favorite minister of Vespasian, as Vinius and Icelus of Galba, and Fabius and Asiaticus of Vitellius.

CH. XCVI.—**38. Aponio Saturnino.** Cf. 85.

1. Neque = et non, correlative to *et amici.* 119

3. Mollius. Cf. note, 1, 18: in *majus,* and Essay, p. 12.

4. Constare = constantem, firmam esse. Rup.

6. Exauctoratos. Ad verbum, cf. note, 1, 23. Ad rem, 67. 82, above.—*Dispergi.* Cf. note, chap. 1.

8. Qui .... coercerent = *to restrain.*

9. Id .... erat. Compare the sentiment with 1, 17: *male .... augebant.*

CH. XCVII.—**11. Perinde ... cunctabantur.** The commanders and the provinces were as tardy in their movements as Vitellius. The reasons for this follow.

14. Ambigui. *Wavering in their allegiance. Uterque* takes a pl. pred. sometimes in T., never in Cic. Z. 367. Cf. note, chap. 50.

21. Favorabilem. *Popular.* A word not used in the Augustan age.

22. Famosum .... egerat. Suet. (Vesp. 4) gives a more favorable account of Vespasian's government in *Africa.* But he felt obliged to flatter the Flavian dynasty, being one of the *scriptores temporum.* Cf. 100, below. Compare also note, 80: *in ipso.*

23. Proinde. Hence, *accordingly,* i. e. the Africans augured worse of the reign of Vespasian than of that of Vitellius. Al. *perinde.*

CH. XCVIII.—**25. Legatus,** sc. legionis in Africa. Cf. 4, 49.

35. Etesiarum flatu. *The trade-winds,* lit. the *annual* winds (ἔτος, ἐτησίαι). Sufficiently explained in Leverett and Liddell and Scott.

Page

119 Ch. XCIX.—**38. Expedire.** MSS. expediri. But the active is used elsewhere by T., when *officers* get ready for a campaign, cf. 1, 10, note, 1, 88 ; the passive only when *troops* are dispatched, Ann. 15, 10.

120 **9. Meditato.** Al. *meditanti,* and *meditantis.* But *meditato* is nearest to the MSS. which read *meditatio;* and it accords with the usage of T. who often puts the past part. of dep. verbs in an aorist sense for the present. Cf. 3, 25: *placatos manes.* So Wr and Död.

Ch. C.—**18. Vexilla.** Cf. note, 1, 31. The MSS. differ much, and are manifestly corrupt in the specification of the legions to which these vexillaries belonged. The reading given in the text is that of Bekker, Ritter, Ruperti and Duebner, and accords with the enumeration in 3, 22, where there are no various readings.

24. Immutatum. This word is sometimes used as an adj., when it means *unchanged;* here it is a part. and means *changed.* Cf. Z. 328.

26. Cremonam. Cf. note, 2, 17. The legions ordered to Cremona were Rapax and Italica, as appears infra, 3, 14. The rest went to Hostilia. Cf. 3, 21.

27. Hostiliam. A village on the Po; now Ostiglia, in the neighborhood of Cremona.—*Ravennam.* Cf. note, 9 : *Misenensi.*

28. Patavii. The birthplace of Livy ; now Padua.

Ch. CI.—**38. Corruptas . . . adulationem.** *Exhibited in false colors for the sake of flattery.*—*Causas,* sc. proditionis illius Caecinae et Bassi.

121 **1. Nobis** = mihi.—*Super* = praeter.

3. Ipsum videntur, sc. Cæcina and Lucilius. *Ipsum* is ant. to *apud :* that they might not be surpassed by others *in the estimation* of Vitellius, they appear to have ruined Vitellius *himself.* Al. *anteiretur* and *videtur,* with Cæcina alone for the subject. But why in that case should the name of Cæcina be repeated at the beginning of the next sentence ? The text is that of Or. and the Medicean MS.

BOOK III.

124 Ch. I.—**2. Poetovionem.** A town in the borders of Noricum and Pannonia, on the river Drave ; now Pettau.

3. Obstrui . . . . Alpes, i. e. more fully guarded, *closed up ;* they were already *praesidiis insessae* (cf. 2, 98), but only so as to intercept the passage of messengers: *nuntios retinebant.*

4. Consurgeret. Rise up together, i. e. *accumulate* near the field of action.

Page

5. Constantius foret. *Would be the firmer* (*bolder*) *course.* 124
Subj. of the indirect question. Cf. Gr. 265. Z. 552.

7. Advenisse .... Vitellio. *Arrived* (sc. in Italy) *subsequently* (sc. to the arrival of the German legions) *with Vitellius* (i. e. under his command in person). The German legions were under command of Valens and Caecina, 1, 61; the Briton troops followed under Vitellius in person, 1, 61, cf. 2, 57. The advocates of delay are here enumerating the forces with which, *at the outset*, Vitellius *entered upon the war with Otho*, and which, of course, he still had at his disposal.

13. Velut .... belli. *As if for another war*, than one with Vitellius, i. e. the Jewish. Cf. note, 2, 90: *alterius civitatis.*

Ch. II.—**18. In procinctu.** *In readiness for battle;* lit. girt up for action.

22. Et his. *Both these* (already in the field) *would recover their strength, and Germany was not far distant, whence they might draw fresh forces. Et* correl. to *neque* = et non. Cf. note, 1, 15: *neque ipse.*

24. Utrimque, sc. ab Germania Britanniaque, et e Galliis Hispaniisque.

26. Si .... velint. Cf. note, 1, 32: *si poeniteat.*—*Duas classes,* sc. Misenensem et Ravennatem. 2, 100.

27. Illyricum mare. That part of the Adriatic which washes the shore of Illyricum.

29. Quin interrog. = qui (old abl.) ne (non): *why not;* used with the ind., the subj. 1st pl., and the imp. by way of *exhortation*, and, unlike *cur non*, expects no answer. Cf. Z. 542.

31. Integras. Non fractas bello. Brotier. The Mœsian troops were not in the battle at Bedriacum.

33. Putetur for *computetur.* Cf. Essay, pp. 10, 11. It is implied here, that the legions of Vitellius were not full.

2. Pulsu, sc. armorum, *sonitu* equorum, *nube* pulveris. 125

4. Idem .... ero. *I will execute, as well as propose the plan.*

5. Vos . .. est. *You, whose fortune is unimpaired.* That of Antonius was already ruined, so that he had nothing to lose. Cf. 2, 86.

Ch. III.—**11. Permoveret** is stronger than *moveret; deeply, thoroughly* (i. e. *throughly*) moved.

13. Sui. *In regard to himself.* Objective gen. Cf. note, G 28: conditoris sui.—*Ea .... concione. In that original assembly.* The reference is to a former meeting of the mass in Pannonia. Cf. 2, 86.

15. Huc .... interpretatione. *Intending to put this or that construction on his language, as might be expedient.* Al. interpretationem. Cf. Essay, p. 17

16. Conduxisset is plup. to correspond with *commoverat.* Gr. 258.—*Descendisse in causam* seems to be an allusion to the *arena.*

17. Gravior .... socius. *And for that reason, he had more*

Page

125 *weight with the soldiers,* (since he was) *a sharer* with them *whether of* their *guilt or* their *glory.* So *levior* = of less weight, 4, 80. See Ritter, ad loc. Al. *gratior,* with this sense: And for that reason, he was more popular with the soldiers, since he shared with them their guilt or glory, as the result might be. Either makes a good sense. I have preferred *gravior,* as the reading of the *best* MSS. and the more difficult reading.

Ch. IV.—**19. Cornelii Fusci.** *Titus ... Flavianus.* Cf. 2, 86. —*Is quoque. He also,* i. e. he, as well as Antonius.

22. Cunctatior, sc. than Fuscus and Antonius. Al. *cunctator.*

23. Affinitatis. Flavianus was related to Vitellius. Cf. 10, infra. —*Coeptante ... motu.* Cf. 2, 86.

24. Perfidiae .... credebatur, i. e. he was believed to have returned to Pannonia with the design of betraying the cause of Vespasian, which he professed to espouse.

26. Discrimini exemptum is added to show that he was under no necessity of returning: he returned from love of change, when he was already beyond the reach of danger.

Ch. V.—**31. Ut impune .... foret.** That it might be safe and advantageous. Observe the enallage.

32. Aponio Saturnino. Governor of Mœsia. Cf. 1, 79. Observe the omission of *ut* before *celeraret.* Cf. Gr. 262, R. 4.

34. Iazygum. A people of Sarmatia Europæa, on this side of the Palus Mæotis. Murphy.

35. Plebem quoque, sc. as well as their own services.

36. Remissum. *Declined.* Cf. 4, 11: *remittere nomen.*

37. Externa molirentur. *Build up a foreign interest,* hostile to the Roman.—*Ex diverso.* From the opposite party, sc. the Vitellian.

126 **1. Sido** is mentioned Ann. 12, 29. 30. Italicus was perhaps the son of Sido, and called *rex* only by birth. Cf. note, 2, 25: *rex Epiphanes.*

2. Fidei .... patientior. Lit. *more susceptible of confidence reposed in them,* and by implication more observant of their own plighted faith. Cf. Or. ad loc.—*Posita in latus. Posted on the confines,* sc. of Rætia, *because it was hostile* (*infesta Rætia*).

5. Ala Auriana. So called either from Auria, a city in Spain, or from an unknown præfect (Aurius). Cf. notes on *ala,* 1, 59. and 1, 70.

6. Aeni. The river Inn, a branch of the Danube.

7. Nec qualifies *tentantibus* only; it does not limit *transacta.*

Ch. VI.—**9. Vexillarios,** etc., i. e. he took only the veteran infantry and a portion of the cavalry, leaving the legions as he proposed, 2, supra.

10. Rapienti. Hurrying on, marching with rapidity.

11. Quam gloriam, sc. viri bello strenui.—*Et ... Corbulo Both his service under Corbulo,* etc. Corbulo was a distinguished commander in the reigns of Claudius and Nero, in Germany (Ann. 11, 18), in Armenia (Ann. 13, 8), Syria and Parthia (14, 24; 15, 25. et al); put to death by Nero. H. 2, 76.

12. Secretis .... sermonibus. In private interviews with Nero. Al. *rumoribus,* with less authority and a less appropriate sense.

14. Primum pilum. Cf. 1, 31: *primipilaribus,* note: *having obtained the office of first centurion through the scandalous favor* (of Nero) *thus gained* (*unde,* i. e. criminando Corbulonem), *his present prosperity, ill acquired, afterwards proved his ruin,* perhaps under Domitian, who married the daughter of Corbulo. Ryckius.

16. Occupata ... quaeque. Al. *occupantes Aquileiae proxima quaeque. Having gained possession of Aquileia, they are received into all the neighboring places,* etc. *Aquileia, Altinum* and *Opitergium* were towns at or near the head of the Adriatic, in the territory of the Veneti. The names of the last two are still preserved in *Oderzo* and the ruined tower of *Altino.*—*In* is not found in any MS. Baiter would supply *per* instead of it. Död. leaves *proxima quaeque* without a preposition, as acc. of place.

19. Patavium. Cf. note, 2, 100.—*Ateste* was near Patavium, in the territory of Venice; now Este.

21. Forum Allieni. Now Ferrara on the Po.

22. Id quoque, sc. that they were off their guard, as well as that they were there.

23. Praedictum = praeceptum, mandatum. Cf. note, 4, 53: *praedixere.*

Ch. VII.—**27. Vulgata victoria** limits *veniunt,* and together with *post principia ... Flavianos* assigns the reason for the coming of the two legions: *When this victory was published abroad, now that* (*post,* lit. after) *the commencement of the war was favorable to the Flavian party.*

28. Duae legiones. Al. datae legiones. These two legions belonged in Pannonia (2, 86), the 7th under the command of Antonius (ibid.), the 13th under that of Vedius Aquila (2, 44). Antonius had left them behind at first (cf. 2, supra: *continete legiones*); but now they were glad to share with him in his victories, agreeably to his prediction: *juvabit sequi,* etc.

31. Praefectus castrorum. Cf. note, 2, 26.—*Adductius. With tighter rein.* Cf. note, G. 43. The use of the adv. in this sense is peculiar to T. Boetticher.

33. Desiderata .... res, sc. the restoration of Galba to due honor; for his memory became dear after the crimes and calamities of the next two reigns. Död., Rup. and Rit. refer *res* more specifically to the *military discipline* of Galba, suggested by the samo severity just mentioned of Minucius Justus.

Page

126 **36. Si .... crederentur.** Lit. *if the reign of Galba were believed to please him* (Antonius), *and the party of Galba to be revived by him.*—*Principatus* and *partes* are both subj. nom. of *crederentur.*

Ch. VIII.—**38. Verona.** An ancient city on the Adige, near Bedriacum (cf. 2, 23); still called Verona. It was the birthplace of Catullus.

127 **3. In .... videbatur.** *It seemed to be for their interest and their honor.*—*Possessa. Was taken,* from *possido,* not *possideo.*

4. Vicetia. Now Vicenza.

7. Pretium fuit. *They reaped solid advantages,* not a mere name, as at Vicetia.—*Exemplo,* sc. influencing others to join the party.

8. Et .... exercitus, etc. *And* (as an additional result of the acquisition of Verona) *the army was thrown in through Rætia and the Julian Alps* (cf. 5, supra: *ad occupandam .... missus*), and had thus closed up the entrance against the German armies.—*Interjectus.* Sub. *erat.* Cf. Essay, p. 14.

10. Quae. All these movements subsequent to the occupation of Aquileia.

12. Consilium. *His policy,* his reasons for such a course.—*Quando, since,* like *quoniam* (cf. note, 2, 11), introduces a subjective reason or motive. Cf. Z. 346.

13. Claustra annonae. Egypt was the Roman granary for corn, and the Egyptians prided themselves on thus holding in their hands plenty or famine for Rome. Cf. Plin. Panegyr. 31, and note, 48, infra.—*Vectigalia .... provinciarum,* sc. of the East.

Ch. IX.—**31. Aponius .... advenit.** From Mœsia, 2, 85.

32. Vipstanus Messala. A distinguished orator, hence one of the interlocutors in the Dial. de Clar. Orat. 14–23; also a writer of the history of his age. Chaps. 25. 28. infra.

33. Qui .... attulisset. *Qui* = talis, ut. Hence followed by the subj. Cf. Gr. 264, 1; Z. 558. So *quod .... corrumperet* below.

128 **2. Prioris fortunae.** Their defeat under Otho.

4. De exercitu. Al. *de exitu,* but that idea is involved in *pro causa: Touching the* (much vaunted German) *army fearless.* Cf. Or. ad loc.—*Praesumpsere. Dared to speak out beforehand,* before the result could be known, before the usual or proper time. See Död.'s explanation, Essay, p. 15.

5. Facta .... spe. *The hope being held out, in addition, to the tribunes and centurions,* of Vitellius' party.

Ch. X.—**14. In .... fronte,** i. e. on the side fronting the enemy —*Valli,* sc. struendi; gen. after *opus.*

16. Ut .... militum. *The anger of the soldiers as if for*

Page

treachery. *Proditionis* is obj. gen. after *ira*. Cf. Liv. 5, 33: *ira corruptae uxoris*. The subj. gen. (*militum*) is also added. Cf. Cic. de N. 6: *canum adulatio dominorum*. See another construction, Essay, p. 14.—**21. Quanquam . . . tenderet.** Cf. note, 5, 21: *quanquam*. 128

22. Pectus . . . . quatiens = *convulsed with sobbing*. The expression is Virgilian. Cf. Aen. 5, 199. 200: *creber anhelitus artus Aridaque ora quatit.*

28. Crudescere. Ad verbum, cf. Virg. Geor. 3, 504; Aen. 7, 788.

30. Ludibrium. *The artifice*, sc. to rescue Flavianus.—*Tribunal.* Cf. note, 1, 36: *suggestu;* also Smith's Dict., under *Castra*.

35. Signa . . . . deos. By hendiadys for: the gods of war on the standards.

36. Donec with subj. Cf. note, 1, 13: *amoliretur*. *Donec* never occurs in Cæsar, and but once in Cicero. Z. 350.—*Fatisceret*, lit. fell to pieces, like the earth yawning and falling asunder. The word is poetical. Cf. Boetticher.

1. Obviis . . . . exemptus est. Not immediately, but some time 129
after, as he journeyed slowly towards Vespasian.

Ch. XI.—**5. Exarserant.** The ind. after *quod* gives the author's reason.—**6. Vulgatis epistolis** is the *cause* of *exarserant*.

10. Pannonicorum ultionem, sc. on *Flavianus*, 10.

11. Velut absolverentur. Cf. note, 2, 8: *velut*.—*Aliorum seditione*, sc. of the Mœsians.

17. Consularium. Flavianus and Aponius.

19. Collegis, sc. the other *legati legionum*, Vedius, Aponianus, Messala, etc.

Ch. XII.—**22. Ne** limits *quietae* only, and does not extend to *turbabantur*.—**24. Lucilius Bassus.** Cf. 2, 100. 101.

26. Vespasiano. Dat. for abl. with *ab;* a poetical construction. Gr. 225, II.; Z. 419.—**28. Principia.** Cf. note, 1, 48.

33. Classis . . . . destinat. The antith. particle (*but*) is understood before *classis*. *Lucilius* was willing to place himself at their head, when the revolt had been consummated without his help. *But* the fleet preferred a man of more decision and zeal in the cause of Vespasian. Cf. the account of Cornelius Fuscus, 2, 86. I can see no necessity for supposing with Wr. that there is a *lacuna* between *praebet* and *classis*.

35. Atriam. A town on the river Tartarus near the Po, once so important as to give name to the Adriatic sea. Touching the orthography, cf. Anthon's Class. Dict. sub voce; Plin. 3, 16, 20.

38. Is . . . . habebatur. Sarcastic. Cf. note, G. 25.

Ch. XIII.—**3. Secretum . . . . affectans.** *Eagerly courting a* 130
military council, i. e. striving to draw the proper persons into it. On this disputed passage, see Or. ad loc. and Freund sub voce, No. 4. Al. secreta, secretiora, etc.

Page

130 **9. Imagines dereptae.** Cf. note, 1, 41; also Xiph. 65, 10.

11. Praescriptum .... projectas. Observe the asyndeton and its effect. Cf. note, 1, 36: *praeire sacramentum*, etc.

18. Ut .... darentur. Some connect this clause back to *ut ... traderent*, as depending on *huc cecidisse*, and enclose *quas enim .... straverintque* in a parenthesis. Wr., Bek., Död. and Or. connect it closely with the preceding clause, on which it depends thus: *whom however they had routed and overwhelmed in those very fields, only that* (i. e. with no better reward than that) *thousands of armed men should be given*, etc.; said in bitter irony. This is certainly the most natural construction, and I see no reason for seeking any other. Rup. makes here a succession of broken and disconnected exclamations, which is preferable to the parenthesis of the common editions.—*Exsuli Antonio.* Cf. 2, 86, note.—**19. Nimirum** denotes irony.

20. Accessionem. *Quite an accession!* Cf. Liv. 7, 30; 30, 12: *accessio fortunae.*

21. Militibus .... auferre. Al. principi auferri militem But the reading of the text is found in all the MSS. and earliest editions, and makes even a better sense, or at least a more Tacitus-like antithesis, than the emendation.

23. Quid .... adversa. *What shall we say to those who hereafter question us touching our successes or reverses*, sc. in this war, in which we shall have met with neither—with nothing worthy of mention. *Prospera aut adversa* breviter dictum pro *rationem prosperorum aut adversorum.* Död. Cf. Essay, p. 16.

Ch. XIV.—**26. Initio .... orto.** Cf. note, 2, 79: *initium coeptum.*—*Quinta legione.* This legion had been particularly forward in rebelling against Galba, 1, 55. Xiph. (65, 10) gives the same account of this scene of commotion, and adds, that it was increased by an accompanying eclipse of the moon.

30. Trucidant, sc. out of resentment for the revolt of the fleet, in which however they had no concern.

32. Ut .... jungerentur. Before the junction was *effected*, Antony had defeated first the cavalry (16. 17, infra), then the two legions stationed at Cremona (18); and these troops came up only to share in the disaster.—**33. Quas .... praemiserat.** Cf. 2, 100.

131 Ch. XV.—**3. Britannia .... acciverat.** Cf. 2, 97.

4. Immensam .... luem = immensam multitudinem, quae multam luem (perniciem) excitare poterat. Wr.

6. Secundis .... castris. *Two days' march*, castris bis positis. Cf. *σταθμοὺς δύο, τρεῖς*, etc. Xen. Anab. passim.

11. Octavum, sc. lapidem, or milliarium.—*A Bedriaco. From*, i. e. *beyond Bedriacum;* of course within twelve miles of Cremona. Cf. note, 2, 23.—*Quo .... popularentur*, sc. without danger from the enemy.

Page

12. Exploratores . . . . curabant. *The scouts, as usual, per-* 131
formed their duty (i. e. *explored the country*) *still further.*

Ch. XVI.—**14. Quinta . . . . hora,** i. e. near eleven o'clock, A. M. Cf. Man. P. 3, 228. 1; also Lev. App. I.—*Adventare . . . . praegredi . . . . audiri.* Observe the asyndeton.

22. Diductis . . . . turmis. *Drawing off his companies of horse to the flanks.* Antonius had on hand only cavalry to the number of 4000. The legions were engaged in fortifying their camp, and the cohorts were sent out to forage and plunder the country. Cf. 15.

25. Qua . . . . proximum limits *occurreret: the signal was given* (to the cohorts) *over the country, that, leaving their booty, they should betake themselves by the nearest route* (*qua* via) *to the battle.*

26. Turbae suorum, sc. the main body under the immediate command of Antonius.

Ch. XVII.—**33. Ardoris** is gen. after *eo,* which is the old dative. Cf. A. 28: *eo . . . . inopiae.*—*Vexillarium* is here a standard-bearer, as the context shows.

37. Rivi. Now *Dermona,* about midway between Cremona and Bedriacum. Rup.—*Incerto alveo. The fordable places being unknown.* Murphy. Rup. compares it with *certum alveo,* G. 32, where see note.

2. Effusos. Cf. note, 2, 23: *effudit.* 132

Ch. XVIII.—**8. Laeto . . . . proelio** denotes the *cause* of their march. It was the *cavalry* only that took part in the battle just described, 16. 17.

9. Provecta, sc. from Cremona, where they were stationed. Cf. 14.

12. Forte victi, i. e. virtually conquered by the previous misfortune of their comrades, not really defeated in a fair trial of strength.—*Haud . . . . desideraverant. They had not felt the want of their general* (Cæcina) *so much in their former prosperity as now in adversity,* etc.

16. Quos . . . . aequabant. *Whom, though brought into the field by rapid marches, military experience was rendering equal to the legionary soldiers.*—*Militiae.* Nom. pl. to denote the number and variety of their *services.* Cf. Suet. Claud. 25, et al.

19. Minorem. Al. *tanto minorem.* But *tanto* is not in the MSS. and is not necessary in T., who is fond of omitting one of two antithetic particles.

Ch. XIX.—**24. Cumulos super.** Cf. note, 2, 78: *Judaeam inter.* Observe also the prægnantia, cumulos = cumulos corporum. Cf. Essay, p. 16.—**27. In medio** = palam. Cf. in medium, G. 46, note.

28. Illa. *The following* considerations, with the additional idea however of their being kept in the *background,* while *haec* denotes the arguments which were put *forward* to public view; thus according with the general principle, that *hic* refers to what is *near,* and *ille* to

Page

132 what is remote. Gr. 207, R. 23. *Haec* is far more frequently used to denote *the following* than *illa*. Z. 700.

30. Quod si. If then, *if now*. Cf. note, 1, 1.—*Jam* = *then, in that case.*

31. Clementiam et gloriam = *clementiae gloriam* by hendiadys. So Roth. But the pl., *inania*, shows that the ideas are distinct. Better thus with Död.: an opportunity to show mercy, and the honor of showing it, both alike empty of solid advantage.

133 Ch. XX.—**3. Duces .... prodesse,** e. g. Q. Fabius Cunctator, M Minucius Rufus, etc. Rup.

4. Pro ... portione. Cf. note, A. 45.

5. Armis ac manu .... ratione et consilio. Cf. notes, 1, 84; 2, 46. 76, etc., on pairs of kindred words.

6. Neque .... occurrant. *For there can be no question as to the obstacles that await our progress.* So Pliny uses *occurrit* of Mt. Taurus, as *meeting* and *obstructing* the course of the Euphrates.

8. Nisi explorato. *Without reconnoitering. Explorato* is an impers. part. So Livy: *ante explorato*, an exploration having been previously made. Cf. Gr. 257, R. 9; Z. 647.

10. Quis ... foret. All this depends on *adempto ... prospectu.*

11. Tormentis et telis. *By engines and missiles*, i. e. from a distance.—*Operibus et vineis. With breastworks* (mounds, turrets, etc.) *and mantelets* (so called from resemblance to a vine arbor), i. e. by regular approaches and a nearer assault.

13. Secures dolabrasque. *Hatchets and pickaxes.* The *dolabra* was half axe or adze (Man. P. 3, 269, 2), for cutting, and half pick for digging. So it is pictured on the column of Trajan. Smith's Dict. (sub voce) makes it a kind of chisel, which was inserted between the stones to loosen the clay and thus destroy the wall.

16. Aggerem, pluteis, cratibus. For these and the other terms relating to a siege in this section, cf. Man. P. 3, 299; and Smith's Dict. sub vocc.

18. Quin .... ferimus. *Why not rather*, etc. Cf. note, 3, 2· *quin.*

Ch. XXI —**23. Prope seditionem.** *Prope* used as a prep. with acc. Cf. Z. 411, also 267 and 323.

26. Qui .... egerat. Ad rem, cf. 9 and 14: *ut .... jungerentur*, note. Ad verbum, cf. note, A. 18: *in finibus agentem.*

27. Millia. Our word *mile.*—*Comperta .... clade* gives the reason for *accingi*, not, as Murphy strangely makes it, for *emensum.*

28. Accingi .... affore. *Were arming themselves, and would soon be on the spot.*

29. Tertiam decimam. Al. tertiam. So below for *tertiam*, some read *tertiam decimam.* The text accords with the order of Antony's address to the legions (24, infra), supposing Antony to have begun at

Page
the centre, as usual, and proceeded first through the left wing and 133
then through the right. So Wr. and Rup.

30. Ipso . . . . aggere. Cf. note, 2, 24.

32. Agresti fossa. Cf. note, 2, 25.

33. Apertum limitem. Brotier, Or., and many others understand this of the *cleared border* of the *via Postumia* (cleared in opposition to the *densis arbustis*, a little further back); Rup. and Wr. of an *open cross-road* through the country.

34. Aquilarum signorumque = legionum auxiliariumque. Rup. Cf. 1, 44: *signa cohortium, aquila legionis.*

35. Praetorianum vexillum. The prætorians dismissed by Vitellius (2, 67. 93), but invited to resume the service under Vespasian (2, 84; 4, 46). This is the first mention we have of them as actually *sub vexillis.*—**37. Sido . . . Italicus.** Cf. 5, supra, note.

Ch. XXII.—**3. Ratio fuit.** *It would have been reasonable and* 134
expedient.

4. Tertia . . . . hora. About nine o'clock at night. Cf. note, 16: *quinta . . . . hora.*

7. Dextro . . . . cornu. *Were on the right of their troops; suorum,* on *their* side, in antith. to the Flavian army just described. We cannot suppose that this one legion formed the right wing alone. Tac. stated all that he found on the subject. Wr.

11. Laevum cornu. Al. *cornum,* in some of the best MSS. and editions. And grammarians are now abandoning the doctrine, that neuters in *u* are indeclinable. Cf. Z. 80, and Freund's pref., App. III.

13. Varium refers to the *form* and *aspect* of the battle; *anceps* to its results from stage to stage.

16. Pugnae signum. The *tessera.* Cf. note, 1, 25. The watchword became known to both armies, and thus increased the confusion.

21. Primipili centurio. Cf. note, 1, 31: *primipilaribus.*

Ch. XXIII.—**26. Vacuo atque aperto.** *From a place open and clear,* sc. of *arbusta.*

27. Magnitudine eximia. Abl. of quality. Gr. 211, R. 6. The *abl.* (not the gen.) must be used to denote an *accidental* quality. Cf. Z. 471, N. The gen. expresses only the inherent.

28. Balista. See this warlike engine described by Vegetius, 4, 22; also Man. P. 3, 299; and Smith's Dict., under *Tormentum.*

30. Arreptis . . . . ignorati. *Disguised by shields taken from the slain,* sc. of the Vitellians.

33. Adulta nocte. *At midnight.* *Adulta* was used by the Romans to designate the second of the three parts, into which they divided the night and also the several seasons. Cf. Servius at Virg. Georg. 1, 43.

34. Falleret refers to the optical *illusion,* which follows.

35. Aequior. *More favorable; a tergo, being behind their backs.*

Page

134 —*Hinc majores*, etc. The sense of this concise passage is very well expressed by Murphy thus: *hence the shadows of men and horses projected forward to such a length, that the Vitellians, deceived by appearances, aimed at a wrong mark. Their darts by consequence fell short of their aim. The moonbeams, in the mean time, played on the front of their lines and gave their bodies in full view to the adverse army, who fought behind their shadows as if concealed in obscurity.*

135 CH. XXIV.—**3. Cur.** Interrogative particle = *cui rei?* Z. 276, 2.—*Rursus*, sc. after having been already defeated in that very field of Bedriacum, as he goes on to say.

8. Tolerent. Al. tolerarent, a mere conjecture of Ernesti. *If you cannot bear*, as it *now appears* you cannot; it is not a mere supposition or conception as *tolerarent* would denote, but a fact. So Wr., Rup. and Bek.

10. Sub .... Parthos. A. U. C. 710. Cf. Dio. 49, 22–33.

11. Sub .... Armenios. Cf. Ann. 15, 26; also note, 6, supra.—*Nuper Sarmatas.* 1, 79.

12. Infensus. So all the MSS. The common editions have *infensius*. But *infensus* of itself in the connection denotes peculiar violence in the manner of addressing these troops, bearing down upon them and striking against them, as it were (*in-fendo*). So Bach and Wr.

13. Pagani. *Peasants*, not soldiers, for if defeated here, who will employ such troops. *Paganus*, from *pagus*, a term of reproach, somewhat like *villain* from *villa*.

14. Illic. *There*, among the followers of Vitellius, to whom you resigned them, when you were dismissed. Cf. 2, 67: *arma... deferebant. There are your standards and arms*, and you may regain them or die, as you please—there is no other alternative; *for you have already exhausted ignominy* in all its forms, and if *conquered* now, it is certain *death.* Such is the meaning of this singularly sententious and energetic address.

16. In Syria, where the third legion had served under Corbulo, as intimated above, before they were transferred to Mœsia.

CH. XXV.—**18. Vagus.** Flying, *accidental*, antith. to *consilio .... subditus.*

21. Ut .... contraheret, etc. The subj. here assigns a *reason* for *rariore.* Gr. 264, 8; Z. 564.

22. Pulsos. So all the MSS. Al. *impulsos* and *repulsos.* But cf. note, 1, 2: *missa;* and Essay, p. 11.

25. Per limitem viae. Cf. note, chap. 21, supra.

26. Eo is correl. to *quia.* *For this reason*, viz. *because.*

27. Vipstano Messalla. A cotemporary historian and eye-witness. Cf. note, 9, supra.

33. Placatos .... manes. Al. *piatos.* But *placatos*, with the

Page

best MS. authority, gives also the most appropriate sense; for the 135
manes of the dead were *appeased* by prayers, but *expiated* by sacrifices. Ernesti. *Placatos* = *ut placati essent* neve-aversarentur.

This little incident, like some of Homer's episodes, is exceedingly touching, and conveys a more affecting sense of the evils of civil war, than even the author's matchless description of the blood and carnage of the battle-field. The concluding clause (*factum esse .... faciuntque*) is cited by Monboddo (On Lang. 2, 4, 12) as an example of affected smartness in the turn of expression; but it brings out in a very striking light a singular trait in depraved human nature: *they talk of the wicked deed that has just been done, and still go on to do it.*

Ch. XXVI.—**11. Munire castra.** Followed by a mark of inter- 136
rogation in the common editions, at the suggestion of Ernesti. But this is unnecessary. The sentence begins just like the one above: *incipere*, etc. The only difference between the two is, that here *id quoque* is thrown in by apposition with *munire* to indicate deliberation. Wr. makes *munire* depend on *si juberent* implied in *quid juberent* above. *Quid juberent* is the subj. of the indirect question.

15. Ex temeritate. Al. *et ex*, etc. But cf. note, 1, 3: *esse ultionem.*—*Caedes .... sanguis.* Synonyma hoc loco poetarum more junguntur. Rup.

Ch. XXVII.—**19. Librabantur.** Cf. note, 2, 22: *librato.*

22. Bedriacensi viae. The way from Cremona to Bedriacum. So *Brixianam portam* = the gate of Cremona opening towards Brixia, now Brescia, south of the Po.

24. Impetus. *Their own ardor* (cf. note, 1, 57); hence our word impetuosity.

25. Ligones. *Grub-hoes.* Cf. Smith's Dict. sub voce.

26. Dolabras. Cf. note, 20, supra. Observe the asyndeton.—*Falces scalasque. Hooks and ladders.* The latter for scaling the walls, and the former for tearing down the upper breastwork. Cf. Man. P. 3, 289, and Smith's Dict. sub vocc. See also the same under *testudo.*

29. Disjectam fluitantemque. Both these words denote a separation of the shields that formed the *testudo;* but the former a *lateral severance*, the latter an opening produced by *unequal elevation.*

31. Multa cum strage. Cf. note, 2, 37: *magna ex parte.* This clause is placed in some MSS. at the beginning of the next section.

Ch. XXVIII.—**32. Incesserat ... ni ... monstrassent.** There is an ellipsis before *ni*, which may be supplied thus: *hesitation had begun to prevail* (and would have prevailed still further), *had not*, etc. But *ni* is more readily translated in such passages *but: The soldiers began to hesitate, but*, etc. Cf. note, A. 4: *hausisse, ni.* This usage abounds in T., but is rarely found in Cic. Cf. Z. 519, b; Essay, p. 15.

Page

136 It will be seen that *monstrassent* here implies offering the town to the *cupidity* of the soldiers.

34. Hormine .... ingenium. *Whether this expedient was the invention of Hormus* (the offspring of his wit, spoken ironically), etc. Al. *ad ingenium*. But what is gained by this departure from all the MSS. I cannot perceive.—*Hormi.* Cf. note, 12, supra.—*Messalla.* Cf. notes, 9 and 25, supra.

35. Plinius. Known as the elder Pliny, who, besides his Natural History, wrote a history of the German wars (cf. G. and A. p. 79), and also of his own times (cf. Plin. Ep. 3, 5), both of which are lost.—*Haud facile.* This is one of the combinations in which *haud* appears with special frequency.

36. Nisi quod. Cf. note, A. 6; also Z. 627. *Except that (but) neither Antonius nor Hormus degenerated from his former life and character in this act, criminal and flagitious as it was,* i. e. it was no worse than they had always been in the habit of doing.

37. Degenerare non solum a bono, sed et a vitiis Latini dicunt, ut Cic. Verr. 3, 68. Bipontine. Cf. note, G. 42: *degenerant.*

137 **1. Iteratam testudinem.** *Upon the renewed testudo.* The *testudo* had been completely broken up. Cf. 27: *soluta compage scutorum.*

3. Integri ..... mortium. This sentence gives the finishing stroke to a frightful picture of blood and carnage, and is marked by a truly Homeric brevity and energy. In the next section, after the manner of Homer, the author enters more into detail. *Omni imagine mortium* resembles very nearly Thucyd. 3, 81, and Virg. Aen. 2, 369. Orelli.

Ch. XXIX.—**9. Testudine** for *a testudine.* Cf. Essay, p. 11.—*Laberentur. Glanced from it,* without effect.

11. Quos inciderat, i. e. in quos ceciderat. Wr. But Zumpt (386) says *quos* is not governed by *in,* but is a real acc. of the object, *incidere* by composition having acquired a trans. meaning. No other classic writer uses it with the acc. Cf. Boetticher, p. 15.

12. Simul juncta turris. *At the same time, an adjoining tower.*—**13. Tertianus,** sc. miles = tertiani.

17. Conclamavit. Properly, *cried out together,* said of a number. Here of one: *shouted aloud,* as with the voice of a multitude. Cf. Virg. Aen. 9, 375: *conclamat .... Volscens.*

19. Completur caede. Josephus says (B. J. 4, 11), that above 30,000 of the Vitellians were put to the sword in this series of engagements, while there fell of Vespasian's army about 4,500. Cf. also Xiph. (65, 15), who makes the number of the slain in all 50,000.

Ch. XXX.—**20. Ac.** Al. *at.* But *ac* is in all the best MSS. and need not be changed.—*Nova laborum facies.* The language of Virg. Aen. 6, 103–4.

Page

23. Stato . . . mercatu. *By reason of a fair held annually at that season.* 137

25. Rapi. *To be instantly brought.* Cf. 1, 27: *rapiunt,* note.

27. Si = our *to see, if.* So the Greeks use εἰ, especially Homer. Cf. Kühner's Gram. 344, R. 9; Matthiæ, 526; and note, 1, 31, supra.

29. Moenium. Not exactly synonymous with *muris.* Cf. note, 2, 22.—*Egressa . . . altitudinem. Exceeding the height,* etc. *Egredi* acquires a transitive force by a modification of its original signification, and hence is followed by the acc. Cf. Z. 387. So A. 33: *egressi terminos.*

30. Trabibus tegulisque. Tectorum ipsorum materie. Rup.

Ch. XXXI.—**33. Ut quis . . . . anteibat.** *All the men of the first rank.* Cf. note, 1, 29: *ut quisque . . . . fuerat.* Al. *quisque,* ex interpretamento. Rup.

36. Reverteretur. According to Wr. the *re* is antith. to *non: should not fall upon the poor common people, but fall back from them upon,* etc.

2. Nam . . . vinctus. *For he was still in bonds.* Cf. 14, supra. 138

5. Extremum malorum. This *last of evils* consisted in the reduction of *so many brave men* to the necessity of *imploring the aid of a traitor.* Hence the impropriety of a comma after *viri,* as in the common editions.

6. Velamenta et infulas. Cf. note, 1, 63.—*Pro muris.* Cf. note, 1, 27: *pro aede.*

10. Ut praeberi, etc. Constructione variata inter infin. histor. et tempus finitum. Orelli.

15. Adeo . . . . sunt is to be connected with what follows: *nay more, so odious are crimes, they even charged him with perfidy,* though that was a crime which had conduced greatly to their interest.

Ch. XXXII.—**22. In neutrum.** He said *nothing either way,* favorable or unfavorable. "To make the last member of the sentence as short and abrupt as possible, he has made it obscure." Monboddo on Lang. 2, 4, 12.

25. Mox . . . . illuserant. Cf. 2, 67.

29. Feminae . . . . progressae. The extreme zeal for the cause of Vitellius thus manifested, displeased the opposite party.

34. Excepta . . . . incalescerent. *The voice* (of Antonius) *was heard, while he complained that the baths were not sufficiently warm,* adding, *that they would* soon *become warm* enough.

35. Vernile dictum. *This wanton speech,* lit. slave-like, worthy of a slave. Some, however, interpret it as the *remark of a slave* attending the bath, in response to Antonius' complaint, which remark was considered as showing that his master, Antony, was privy to the conflagration.

Page

Cʜ. XXXIII.—**38. Calonum .... corruptior.** Cf. note, 2, 87

139 **5. Ubi.** *Whenever.* Followed by the subj. plup. denoting a repeated occurrence. Cf. Gr. 264, 12; Z. 569.—*Quis ... conspicuus,* sc. puer, as the gender and the antithesis of *virgo* sufficiently indicate without inserting the word. So Ernesti. Gronovius would read *aut puer* instead of *aut quis.* What a state of morals is here shadowed forth!

9. Truncabantur pro *obtruncabantur.* Rup. and Död. Cf. Essay, pp. 10. 11.

11. Faces in manibus. Acc. after *habentes* understood, as the Greeks omit the part. of ἔχω. Matthiæ, p. 588, Ed. 1. Rup. So we say in English, " torch in hand."

13. Utque exercitu, etc. Sententia: utque evenit, ubi exercitus est varius, etc. Abl. abs. Wr.

14. Interessent. For the subj., cf. Gr. 264, 8; Z. 564.

16. Suffecit, sc. incendio, ad alimenta igni praebenda. Render, *continued to burn.*

17. Mefitis was the goddess that was worshipped in all places that sent forth noxious exhalations. Hence we read in Virgil: Sacramque exhalat opaca Mefitim. Aen. 7, 64. Murphy.

This portion of the history furnishes a very good illustration of our author's characteristic power of description. The rapid succession of bloody battles and sieges, in which Antonius and his followers fought like tigers, nay like demons, through two days and the intervening night, defeated three separate armies in three successive encounters without intermission, and carried two distinct and strongly fortified lines of defence—walls, towers and bulwarks—around Cremona, is sketched with a rapidity and force fully adequate to the subject. The outward movements and the inward motives of the men are set before the eye of the reader with equal distinctness. And finally the burning and sacking of the city presents a picture of unrestrained passions, of unbounded crimes, of dreadful calamities and sufferings, of utter desolation and ruin, to which history and even the drama with all its wild license of imagined horrors can furnish few parallels. The student, who has failed to perceive the historian's power, has read the passage to little purpose, and will do well to read it again. In default of all other means of appreciating it, he will find the passage well represented in Murphy's translation, though not with all the conciseness, force and fire of the original. Cf. Life of T. pp. 9–10; and Preliminary Remarks, p. 238.

Cʜ. XXXIV.—**20. Condita erat.** It was established, sc. as a colony. The town existed before. Brotier.—*Tiberio ... consulibus,* i. e. ᴀ. ᴜ. ᴄ. 536. Cf. Liv. 21, 6.

23. Rueret. Al. *irrueret.* Cf. Essay, pp. 10. 11. As to this design of the colony, cf. Liv. 21, 25; Polyb. 3, 40.

Page

24. Opportunitate fluminum. Padi, Adduae, Ollii, aliorumque 139
plurium, sed minorum. Rup. See Cremona on the map.—*Annexu connubiisque. Connection by marriage.* Hendiadys. Wr. and Or. It is quite as well, however, to take *annexu* in the wider sense of *intercourse.*

25. Gentium. *With foreign nations. Gentium* antith. to *urbs,* as Hor. Od. 1, 2, 2: terruit urbem, terruit gentes. Wr.

32. Munificentia municipum. *By the liberality of the inhabitants,* sc. of Cremona. Al. *magnificentia.*

Ch. XXXV.—**34. Sepultae.** *Buried,* sc. in ashes, incendio deletae. Ruperti.

3. Trevir .... Aeduus. *A Trevir* (native of Treves) . . . *an* 140
Æduan. These were Gallic people.

4. Ostentui. *For display,* as trophies of victory.

Ch. XXXVI.—**7. At Vitellius.** The historian now returns to 2, 101. Or. *At* often serves as a transition particle.

8. Curis .... obtendebat. *Concealed his anxiety under the veil of pleasure,* lit. stretched luxury over against his anxieties. Leverett sub voce gives a little different sense.

13. Nemore Aricino. A grove famous for the nightly meetings of Numa and the nymph Egeria. Cf. Liv. 1, 19. 21.

16. Mixtus .... dolor = nuntius et tristis et laetus. Rup.

19. Publium Sabinum. Cf. 2, 92.

21. Alfeno Varo. 2, 29. 43. In 2, 43, it is Varus Alfénus.

Ch. XXXVII.—**22. In magnificentiam.** *To set forth his greatness,* or *his grand prospects.*

24. Initium .... factum. *The motion was made for,* etc.

25. Composita indignatione. *Affected, hypocritical* seems to be the main idea of *composita* here, though not exclusively of the other idea, viz. *studied.—Consul, dux,* etc., sc. Cæcina.

28. Suum dolorem, sc. for the private and public injuries they had received from Cæcina.

32. Is .... supererat. *For so much* (one day) *remained for Cæcina's substitute,* sc. to fill out his time.

33. Eblandiretur. *Obtained by flattery,* lit. *flattered it out of* Vitellius. The subj. is required after the indefinite *nec defuit.* Cf. Gr. 264, 7; Z. 561.

35. Nunquam .... suffectum. *Never before had another been put in the place of a magistrate, till the office was first declared vacant, and a law enacted to that end.*

36. Nam consul, etc. See the fine vein of humor in which Cic. indulges on this subject, Ep. ad Div. 7, 30. In that consulship, he says, no man had time to dine, and no kind of mischief happened. The consul was a man of so much vigilance, that he did not allow himself a wink of sleep!

Page 141 CH. XXXVIII.—**1. Junii Blaesi.** Cf. 2, 59, where see note on *ingratus.*

2. Accepimus. Pro *accepi,* i. e. audivi ab aliis relata. Rup. Cf. note, G. 27, ad vocem.

3. Servilianis hortis. Abl. of *place where,* without a prepos. characteristic of poets and later prose writers. Cf. note, 2, 16: *balineis.* These gardens were occupied by Nero and the succeeding emperors. Ann. 15, 55; Suet. Nero, 47. It is not agreed from whom they derived their name (perhaps M. Servilius, Ann. 6, 31; 14, 19), or what was their exact location in the city.—*Turrim. A tower,* i. e. a lofty and splendid edifice reared in a garden, or a part of a palace raised several stories above the rest of the building for the sake of the *prospect,* like the tower of Mæcenas (Suet. Ner. 38), and the tower of Hannibal (Liv. 33, 48; Plin. N. H. 2, 71). Cf. Rup. ad loc. and Beck. Gall. Sc. 7, N. 2.

8. Quod .... ageret. Notice the difference between the subj. here and the ind. in *quod .... anteibat* below. The latter is stated as a fact by the historian, while the former is an allegation.

9. Asperatum for exasperatum. Cf. note, 2, 48.

20. Junios .... jactantem, etc. Blæsus was descended from Octavia the sister of Augustus (hence *imperatoria stirpe*) and Marc Antony the Triumvir. In like manner Nero compelled Torquatus Silanus to put an end to his own life for no other reason, than because he united to the splendor of the Junian family the honor of being great-grandson to Augustus. Ann. 15, 35.

21. Qui .... ostentet. The subj. here assigns a *reason* why Blæsus is to be guarded against. So also *quem .... arceat* above.

23. Amicorum .... negligens. *Making no distinction between friends and enemies* (*inimicorum,* always *personal* enemies).

24. Labores. Morbum, ejusque dolores et cruciatus. Rup.

27. Si quid .... accidat. Notus εὐφημισμὸς pro: si moriatur. Rup. Cf. Ann. 14, 47: si quid fato pateretur. Cic. Or. Cat. 4, 2: si quid obtigerit. The *fato* added by T. makes it more specifically a *fatal* accident in the course of *nature.* See the same euphemism in Greek, Hom. Il. 5, 567; ἤν τι πάθῃ; Dem. Phil. 1, 11.

CH. XXXIX.—**28. Inter .... metumque.** *Between horror of the crime and fear of danger.*—*Ne .... ferret.* This clause gives the reason for *veneno grassari.*

30. Addidit .... fidem. *He confirmed the general belief* that he was accessory *to the crime.*

31. Nobili = notabili, which some editions substitute, though found in no MS.

34. Fidei obstinatio. *Inflexible fidelity* to Vitellius.

35. Integris ... rebus. *Even when the reign of Vitellius was secure,* without a rival.—**36. Ambitus.** *Solicited.*

37. Inturbidus. Only in T.—*Adeo non* = nedum, *still less.* 141
Cf. note, 1, 9, ad vocem.

38. Parum .... crederetur. Compare the Greek: παρ' ὀλίγον ἐξέφυγε τοῦ μὴ ἀξιοῦσθαι.

Ch. XL.—**3. Proditam .... classem.** Cf. 12 and 36, supra; 142
also 2, 100–1.

7. Vitata Ravenna. On account of the defection of the fleet.—*Hostiliam Cremonamve*, sc. to take command of the troops at those places left without a leader by the treachery of Cæcina. Cf. 9. 14. 21, etc. supra.—**12. Dum media,** etc. Mark the sentiment.

Ch. XLI.—**15. Neque .... aptus,** etc., i. e. too large to escape notice and too small to break through by force.

19. Ruentis ... libido. Qui diu frui non sperat, avidius fruitur. Ryckius. See the same principle, 1, 7: *tanquam apud senem, festinantes.* Död. makes *pecunia* = pecuniae cupido, and *novissima* = quod vitium ultimum exuitur. Cf. Essay, pp. 16. 17.

24. Avidos periculorum. *Eager for danger*, i. e. enterprising and restless. Cf. 26: *periculi quam morae patientior.*

25. Dedecoris securos. *Reckless (se-cura) of dishonor.*—*Eo ... comitantibus. Fearing this* (i. e. the perfidy of his soldiers), *and having but few among his immediate attendants whose fidelity was not shaken by misfortune.* Two reasons for the course he pursued.

26. Ariminum. A town of Umbria, on the Gulf of Venice.

31. Exercitus, sc. in Gallia, octo legiones. Rup.

Ch. XLII.—**34. Cornelius Fuscus.** He was now commander of the fleet. Cf. 12. See also 4, note.

36. Adria. The Adriatic. Cf. note, 12, supra.

38. Segnitia maris. *By a calm at sea.* Al. saevitia. But that is involved in *adversante vento. Aut* does not leave it doubtful *which* (that would require *an*), but denotes *sometimes* by a calm, *sometimes* by a storm. *Depellitur* is applicable to *segnitia* only by zeugma. *Impeditur* is rather required. Cf. Wr. and Or. ad loc.

1. Portum .... Monoeci. Now Monaco near Genoa. There 143
was a temple of Hercules Monœcus there. Cf. Strab. 4; Plin. Nat. Hist. 3.

6. Infracta. *Impaired*, the part. not the adj. Cf. note, 2, 100: *immutatum.*

7. Namque = Gr. καὶ γάρ, *and* with reason, *for.*

Ch. XLIII.—**10. Exauctorati.** Ad verbum, cf. note, 1, 20. Ad rem, cf. 2, 67. They are called *praetorianos* just below.

11. Forojuliensem. Cf. note, 2, 14.—*Claustra maris. Forum Julii* was as it were the *key* to that part of the Mediterranean, being an important naval station.

12. Gravior auctor. *A more influential leader.* Cf. note, 3: *gravior.*

Page

143 **14. Ipsi .... municipali.** *And the people from the country out of friendship to their townsman, and in the hope of* advantage from *his future power* under Vespasian. Cf. Or. and Död. ad loc.

16. Paratu .... rumore. Cf. a like ant. of *paratu* and *fama*, A. 25, with the same collocation of words, viz. the noun standing first in the first clause, but the adj. or part. in the second clause, as the emphasis requires: in *reality* (the real array) strong, and made still *stronger* by report.

19. Maturo .... volentibus fuit = *Maturus ceterique* volebant. Cf. note, A. 18: *volentibus erat.* Z. 420.

22. Stoechadas. Three islands in a *row,* hence their name (from Gr. *στοῖχος*). Now the *Hieres* on the coast of Provence.

23. Insulas affertur. Cf. Essay, p. 12.

24. Oppressere. *Overcame* him and took him prisoner. Cf. 44: *capto Valente.*

Ch. XLIV.—**26. Prima Adjutrice.** This legion fought for Otho with great zeal in the battle at Bedriacum (2, 43), and after his defeat was sent into Spain (2, 67). The 6th and 10th were also in Spain. Cf. note, 1, 16: *una legione.*

29. Inditus. Al. inclitus, indictus, insitus, &c. But *inditus* has the best MS. authority, and accords well with the reason which follows: *conceived, because* (occasioned by the fact that) *he had,* etc.

30. Clarus egerat. Cf. A. 13.

31. Ceterarum. The other three legions in Britain, sc. except the second.

Ch. XLV.—**34. Venutio.** Cf. Ann. 12, 40.

36. Cartismanduam .... Caractaco. Ann. 12, 32–36.

38. Instruxisse .... videbatur. Caractacus was taken prisoner some years after the triumph of Claudius (cf. Suet. Claud. 17: Ann. 12, 36) ; but by his capture, Cartismandua added new brilliancy to it. Cf. Wr. ad loc.

144 **8. Petita .... praesidia,** sc. by Cartismandua.

9. Exemere tamen. *Though the battles were of various issue* (i. e. not decidedly successful in re-establishing Cartismandua on the throne), *yet they at least rescued the queen from personal danger.* There is an ellipsis of a verb and particle ant. to *exemere tamen* in the first clause, so that *tamen* really stands here, as usual, near the beginning of its own member of the sentence.

Ch. XLVI.—**12. Perfidia sociali.** *By the treachery of the states in alliance.*

14. Etenim .... provectum est. *For it was prolonged to a later period.* The reference is to the war with Civilis the Batavian, for which see 4, 2, infra.—*Etenim.* Compare *καὶ γάρ.*

15. Abducto .... exercitu is the *cause* of *sine metu.*

20. Ni. *But.* Cf. notes, chap. 28; A. 4. 13; Z. 519. 144

21. Ac ne. Sub. *metuens,* connected by *ac* to *gnarus,* and expressing an additional motive for opposing the Dacians.

24. Et quod .... transegimus. This fact also was favorable (*affuit*). For *transegimus*, cf. note, A. 34: *transigite.*

25. Pro consule. Cf. note, 1, 49.

26. Annuo imperio. Cf. note, A. 22: *annuis copiis.*

Ch. XLVII.—**32. Polemonis.** Polemon II. was made king of Pontus by Caligula, and after his death the kingdom was changed by Nero into a Roman province. Suet. Ner. 18.

34. Verterat. Intrans. Cf. note, G. 31.

37. Trapezuntem. Now Trebizond, an important city and seaport in Asia Minor, on the Euxine.—*A Graecis . . . conditam.* Cf. Xen. Anab. 4, 6, 17; Strab. 12.

38. Subitus for *subito.* Gr. 205, R. 15.

1. Donati .... Romana. By granting the freedom of the 145
city, the Romans drew distant colonies into a close alliance. Cf. note, 1, 8.

2. Desidiam .... Graecorum. Notice the Roman contempt for the now degenerate Greeks.

3. Classi. A fleet left by Mucianus unmanned and unprotected in the harbor of Trebizond. Or. Al. classis.

5. Barbari. Non Aniceti milites, sed *alii homines barbari,* qui utebantur, ut fit, turbatis rebus, ut *piraticam* exercerent. Wr.

6. Camaras .... connexam. Al. *quas camaras .... lata alvo .... connexa.* But the acc. of the last three words is found in all the MSS. *Alvum* is in appos. with *camaras.* Gr. 230: *they call by the name of camaræ a broad hold with narrow sides, and bound with neither brass nor iron.* A similar kind of boats is described, G. 44. Like the canoes of the American Indians, these camaræ were borne on the shoulders of the natives. The word *camaræ* is found in no Latin author earlier than T. It occurs in the Greek of Strabo.

11. Indiscretum . . . est. *It is alike safe, and indeed a matter of indifference,* etc.

Ch. XLVIII.—**17. Cohibi.** A river of Colchis, called *Cobus,* Plin. N. H. 6, 4; now Khopi.

21. Fluxa .... fide. Cf. note, 1, 21: *fluxa.*

26. Urbem quoque. *The city* (Rome) *also,* i. e. as well as the army. Al. *urbemque.* But in that case *que* = *quoque* in abbreviated form.

27. Et Africam. *Africa also,* as well as Egypt. These were the two principal granaries of Rome, the former supplying the city for eight months, the latter for the remaining four months of the year. Cf. notes, 8, supra, and 1, 73.

29. Facturus denotes purpose, like the fut. part. in Greek. **As**

Page

145 to the object of Vespasian's stay in Egypt, see further Josep. B. J 4, 37; Suet. Vesp. 7.

Ch. XLIX.—**30. Nutatione.** Al. mutatione. We have given the reading of Wr., Rup., Bach, Död. and the Medicean MS. Cf Plin. Panegyr. 5: *nutatio reipublicae.*

31. Post Cremonam, sc. deletam. Censured by Lord Monboddo as excessively concise and abrupt. But cf. also Flor. 1, 7, 1; 3, 1, 1: *post Carthaginem,* et al.

32. Ex facili = *facilia.* Cf. A. 15. = *facile.* So Livy and the best Latin authors ad Graecorum consuetudinem, e. g. Thucyd. 1, 34: ἐκ τοῦ εὐθέος. Cf. Walch ad A. 15.

35. Viam .... struere. The MSS. read *vim,* which Wr. defends, but does not restore.

37. Ordines .... offerebat, i. e. allowed the soldiers to choose their own centurions, instead of appointing them himself, as was usual for the commander.

38. In arbitrio. *Under the sovereign command.*

146 **2. Corrumpendae disciplinae.** Dat. of end, or tendency.—*In vertebat. Converted into a means of enriching himself by plunder.*

Ch. L.—**6. Expeditum agmen.** *The light-armed troops.* Cf. note, A. 29.

12. Pompeius Silvanus. Cf. 2, 86. Al. Poppæus.

15. Ad omniaque. *Ad* is not in MS. Med. Cf. Essay, p. 12.

19. Fanum Fortunae. Oppidum Umbriae, quod aliis simpl Fanum et colonia Julia Fanestris, nunc Fano dicitur. Rup.

20. Quod .... audierant. The ind. after *quod* here directs attention to the cause, as an historical fact stated by the author; the subj. in *quod defuisset* above directs the attention more to the reason, as it lay in the minds of others. Cf. note, 36: *quod .... ageret.*

23. Clavarium. Lit. *nail-money,* i. e. originally a small sum given to soldiers to provide nails for their shoes. The word occurs only in T. So *calcearium* from *calcei.* Suet. Vesp. 8. *Unguentarium* from *unguentum.* Plin. Ep. 2, 11.

25. Accipi. *Received as a free gift.* Ant. to *rapiuntur* = *taken by force.*

Ch. LI.—**28. Fas nefasque.** Cf. note, 2, 56.—*Irreverentiam* Found only in T. Essay, p. 22.

29. Praemium .... petierit. As if it were proof of great zeal for the party, to have slain a brother on the opposite side. For the *perf.* subj. cf. note, 1, 24: *dederit*

30. Jus hominum. *The law of nature,* as we call it. Cf. note, G. 21: *jus hospitis.* So Cic. Tusc. Qu.: *jus hominum.*

31. Ratio belli. *The kind of the war,* i. e. civil.—*Distulerant* Sententia est: *distulerunt et dilatus manebat.* Ita plup. contrahit vim imp, Wr.

Page

32. Meritum agrees with *equitem* understood. For the subj. in *exsolverentur*, cf. Gr. 264, 4; Z. 560. 146

37. Sisenna. An orator and historian, whose work was continued by Sallust. Cf. Man. P. 5. 511, 2; Sal. B. Jug. 95.

Ch. LII.—**6. Commeatibus,** i. e. ships laden with provisions. 147

8. Nimius = nimio potens et rapax. Rup.—*Certiora . . . sperabantur*, sc. *praemia*. Spem majorem praemiorum habebant in Muciano, majoris virtutis, dignitatis et gratiae apud Vespasianum viro. Ernesti. Ritter supplies *mandata*.

9. Ni praesens . . . . ratus. *Thinking, that if he were not present at the taking of the city, he should have no share in the war and its glory.*

11. Media. *Ambiguous expressions.—Scriptitabat.* Observe the frequentative.—*Instandum* (sc. esse) depends on *scriptitabat.*

12. Edisserens (*setting forth at length*) governs only *utilitates.* —*Compositus. Studied*, guarded in his language.

14. Plotium Griphum. Cf. 4, 39 40, infra.

17. Volentia. *Pleasing.* Taken intransitively.

Ch. LIII.—**21. Eviluissent.** *Had been depreciated.* Compare *vilis*, 3, 33, et passim. The subj. after *cujus* here denotes the *cause* of Antonius' complaints.

22. Lingua. Al. *linguae*, without MS. authority. Cf. note, 1, 35: *linguae*. For the position of *lingua* and *obsequii* in their respective clauses, cf. note, 43: *paratu . . . rumore.*

30. Bello imputandum, i. e. it was not *his* fault.

31. Majore . . . . stetisse. Cf. notes, A. 16, and chap. 72, below.

34. Asiam composuerint. Cf. 2, 79. For the subj. cf. Gr. 266, 2; Z. 603. For the perf. cf. Gr. 258, 1; Z. 516.

35. Moesiae pacem. Cf. 46, supra. It will be seen that all along here Antonius draws the contrast between his own achievements and those of Mucianus, but without mentioning his rival's name.

38. Si . . . . assequantur. If, as is now the fact, etc. Cf. note, 24: *tolerent.*

2. Simplicius. Cf. note, G. 22: *simplices.* 148

3. Implacabilius is found only in T. Cf. Boet. and Freund.

Ch. LIV.—**8. Ingravescebat.** *He grew worse* (weaker, like a sick man) *under these false reports.* So the word is used, Cic. de Sen. 11; Plin. Ep. 2, 20; and so most of the commentators understand it here.

11. Nec . . . . augendae . . . . deerant = non omittebant neque cessabant augere. Rup.

23. Ultro. *Furthermore.*

25. Cui credas. *Cui* = talem, ut; hence followed by the subj. Cf. Gr. 264; Z. 558.

Page

148 **26. Voluntaria morte.** In the characteristic spirit of the old Roman soldier, ever ready to die for his country or his commander.

CH. LV.—**30. Quatuordecim .... cohortibus.** There were sixteen in all. Cf. 2, 93.

32. E .... legio. Not the same with Otho's *legio classicorum* (1, 6. 31, 36. et al.) that was sent into Spain (2, 67), but probably a new legion enrolled from the fleets at Ravenna and Misenum.—*Tot millia.* Each cohort numbered a thousand men. Cf. note, 1, 20.

33. Pollebant. Ind. for the subj. found seldom in Cic. but often in T. and late writers, especially after *ni* and in the plup. Cf. note, 28: *incesserat . . . ni.*

36. Quibus .... destinabat. Carrying still further the policy of Otho. Cf. 1, 77, note.

37. Latium, *Latinitas,* and *jus Latii* were different expressions used to denote a standing or state intermediate between citizens and foreigners. Cf. Dic. of Ant., *Latinitas.* Arn. His. Rom.

149 **2. Aderat.** *Was present,* eager to receive and applaud.

5. Mevaniam. A city in Umbria, now Bevagna.

CH. LVI.—**11. Accessit.** Cf. note, ad vocem, 1, 5.

12. Nec ubi. Al. *nec ut.* The reading is doubtful. Either makes the omen inauspicious.

13. Sed praecipuum, etc. A description of great power, showing a master in severe yet truthful satire. Cf. Life of Tacitus, p. 11.

14. Quis ordo, etc. These clauses depend on *improvidus consilii*: *without forethought to consider what should be the order of march,* etc.

15. Quantus modus = quantopere bellum vel urgendum esset vel trahendum. Rup.

21. In aperto. *Easy.* Cf. note, A. 1.

25. Arcuere. Prohibuere aditu ad principem. Rup. The MSS. have *arguere.* Cf. note, 1, 3: prodigia.

26. Aspera, sc. essent. Al. aspere, limiting *acciperet.*

CH. LVII.—**28. Misenensem.** Cf. note, 2, 9. *Misenum* was near Puteoli, Cumæ, Mount Vesuvius, &c., and not far from Capua, as is implied below.

33. Praetura functus. Cf. note, 2, 63.

34. Minturnis. A town north of Misenum, near the mouth of the Liris; now in ruins.

150 **3. Ut .... castra.** Julianus *pitched his camp over against* that of the revolters, as if with hostile intentions, but soon went over himself to their side.

6. Ipsorum ingenio. *The spirit of the people themselves,* sc. of Tarracina—the people being implied in the place.

CH. LVIII.—**7. Narniae.** A city of Umbria, on the river Nar (a branch of the Tiber), now Narni.

15. Tribus. The *three* original *tribes* (from *tres*) at Rome were

Page

confined to the patricians. But the number was at length increased 150
to thirty-five, which, as the right of suffrage was extended, included all classes of Roman citizens. Cf. Nieb. and Arn. His. Rom. In the age of the *Emperors* the tribes were chiefly made up of the middling classes, and did not include those of senatorial and equestrian rank on the one hand, nor the lowest rabble on the other.—*Dantes . . . partitur.* He at first summons the tribes in a body, and administers the oath to all who gave in their names (i. e. all who consented to serve in the army) indiscriminately; but finding the number too great, he afterwards assigns to the consuls the duty of *drafting* a portion of them by a regular levy (*delectus*).

17. Indicit. *Assesses.* Cf. G. 25: *injungit.*

20. Favorem. *Attachment* to Vitellius, or rather zeal for his cause, as is implied in the following clause.

24. Aspernatus antea. Cf. 1, 62.

25. Superstitione nominis. As if there were a talismanic power in the mere name. The word *superstitio* properly denotes a sentiment, rite, or usage, that has *survived* (from *supersto*) and been handed down from an earlier age.

30. Quae .... remisit, e. g. money, slaves, titles, &c.

Ch. LIX.—**32. Ut .... ita.** *Though .... yet.* Observe the difference between *ita* and *tam*, which = to such a degree.

35. Erectus. *Roused up.—Samnis ... et Marsi.* T. is particularly fond of interchanging the singular and the plural, as here. *The Samnite,* the old enemy of Rome in the famous Samnite wars, dwelt near the borders of Campania. The *Peligni* and the *Marsi* were farther north.

36. Campania praevenisset, sc. in going over to Vespasian. Cf. 57, supra.—*Ut .... obsequio. As is usually the case in the service of a new master.*

38. Nives eluctantibus. Compare *difficultates eluctari,* A. 17, and *elapsum custodias,* just below. Cf. Z. as cited, note 29: *quos .... inciderat. Eluctantibus* is dat. after *patuit.*

2. Quae .... affuit. Ind. because it is a remark of the his- 151
torian, and not what was evident to the Flavian army.

3. Obvium .... habuere. *They met.* Compare our common idiom, they *had met.* So *habeo dictum* = *dixi*, etc. Z. 634.—*Petilium Cerialem.* Cf. A. 8, and often in the ensuing history.

7. Sabino .... Domitiano. The brother and the son of Vespasian.

Ch. LX.—**15. Partium,** sc. Flavianarum.—*Carsulas.* Not far from Mevania and Narnia; now in ruins.

16. Assequerentur. Observe the imp. subj. after the histor. pres. Cf. Gr. 258, R. 1; Z. 501.

22. Opperiebantur. Imp. to denote an unaccomplished effort or

Page

151 wish.—*Praedae . . . periculorum.* *Potius* omitted. Cf. note, G. 6 *consilii quam formidinis.* They thought but little danger remained; and they chose to have the booty to themselves.

24. Si deliberarent . . . . si desperassent. Notice the change of tense: *if they should be allowed still to deliberate—when once they had been reduced to despair.*

28. Tarracinam. A city of the Volsci in Latium, famed as a border town in the Volscian wars. It was about as far south from Rome as Narnia was north, i. e. about sixty miles. Now Terracina on the Tuscan Sea.

Ch LXI.—**37. Suas centurias turmasque.** Their respective companies of infantry and cavalry. Cf. note, 1, 51.—*Donum . . . . gratiam.* Acc. of the end. *Gratiam* praegnanter for gratiae causam. Döderlein.

152 **1. Interamnam.** Cf. note, 2, 64.

2. Varus, sc. Arrius. Cf. 6, supra, et al.

10. Induruerat. See the phrase under induresco, Lev. Lex.

Ch. LXII.—**13. Urbini.** Urbinum was a town in the territory of the Senones, not far from the Adriatic; now Urbino, famous as the birthplace of Raphael.—*In custodia.* His capture is related above, 43.

18. Immane, quantum animo. Lit. it is wonderful how much in the ardor of their feelings = with wonderful ardor, with very great confidence. Cf. Hor. Od. 1, 27, 6. So *mirum, quantum; incredibile, quantum,* etc. See a different explanation, Essay, p. 17.

19. Anagniae. A town of ancient Latium; now Anagni, thirty-six miles to the east of Rome.

20. Absurdus ingenio. *By no means despicable for talent.* So *absurdum ingenium,* Ann. 13, 45. Sall. Bell. Cat. 25, and *absurde,* Ann. 13, 14. Often used with a negative, like *non ineptus* and our *not bad.*

21. Ludicro juvenum. The Juvenalia, a licentious festival, instituted by Nero. Cf. Ann. 14, 15, where see it described. Cf. also Ann. 16, 21. T. avoids the technical name. Cf. Essay, p. 20.

22. Actitavit. Compare what is said of Vitellius, 2, 71. Observe the frequentative.

24. Fonteium . . . . interfecit. Cf. 1, 7.

26. Aliorum . . . . illustratus. And by that only, not by his own virtues. We have here a specimen of Tacitus' manner of summing up a character, as he takes leave of it—concise, antithetic, candid; yet, if need be, piquant and severe.

Ch. LXIII.—**28. Decore.** Al. dedecore. But *decore* in the oldest and best MSS. And with the Romans, as with us, it was an *honor* to march out (as we say) under arms and colors flying. Moreover, *id quoque non sine decore* corresponds with the previous conduct

Page

of the Vitellian soldiery. Cf. 62: *gregarius miles induruerat pro* 152
Vitellio.

30. Ornatus, sc. omni instrumento militari. *Equipped.*

36. Secreta Campaniae. *A retreat in Campania,* deemed the richest and most beautiful part of Italy. Cf. 66: *Sinus Campaniae beati;* also 1, 2: *fecundissima Campaniae ora.*

37. Seque ac liberos. Poetice. So 4, 2: *seque ac cohortes;* Ann. 1, 61: *visuque ac memoria.* Al. *se ac liberos.*

38. Permisisset. Notice the plup. = *if* (when) *he should* first *have surrendered up. Permisisset* instead of *dedidisset* to avoid offence.

4. Oblivisceretur. Imp. in the apodosis, where we use the 153
plup. Cf. note, 2, 62: *si temperaret.*

Ch. LXIV.—**5. Flavium Sabinum.** Cf. 1, 46.—*Praefectum urbis.* Cf. 1, 14, note.

7. Cohortium urbanarum. Cf. note, 1, 20.—*Vigilum.* Ibid.

8. Servitia ipsorum. *Their own slaves,* sc. of the speakers, primorum civitatis.

12. Si .... praebuisset. When once he had presented himself, etc. So *si . . . permisisset,* 63.—**14. Adeo.** Cf. note, 1, 9.

Ch. LXV.—**23. Affectam .... fidem.** *Impaired credit.* Cf. note, 1, 88: *afflicta fide.—Praejuvisse* is a word peculiar to T., formed after the analogy of Gr. *προβοηθεῖν*: *helped beforehand,* i. e. before Vespasian had completely failed—before it was called for.

24. Pignori. Cf. Gr. 227, R. 2. Ad rem, cf Suet. Vesp. 4.

25. Offensarum operta = offensae opertae. A form of expression abounding in T., peculiar to poets and prose writers later than Cic. Cf. Z. 435; also note, G. 43: *pauca campestrium.* The idiom is Greek, as well as poetical. Ibid.—*Melior interpretatio. A more charitable construction.*

29. Aede Apollinis. Cf. note, 1, 27.—*Pepigere.* Cf. Suet. Vitel. 15.

30. Verba vocesque. *The words* of the contract, *and the expressions* used in the whole conversation. So Död.—*Cluvium Rufum.* Cf. note, 1, 8.

31. Silium Italicum. The poet; consul, A. U. C. 821; commended by Pliny (Ep. 3, 7) for his discreet conduct as the friend of Vitellius.

Ch. LXVI.—**38. Fidem .... victoris.** *That the fulfilment of the pledge* (given by Sabinus) *would depend on the sovereign will of the conqueror.—Tantam .... superbiam. So much conscious superiority* and consequent security.

2. Victos, sc. themselves. They threaten that they would put 154
Vitellius to death with their own hands, rather than see him in private life; and *so danger* to him would arise *from their very compassion* for him.

Page

154 **5. Beatos .... sinus.** Cf. note, 63: *secreta campaniae.* Ad verbum, cf. notes, G. 29, A. 30.

8. Aemulatore. Al. aemulato (Wr.), aemulatu (Lip., Ober.), aemulo (Rhen.). All with the same sense.—*Captivum.* And therefore less dangerous.

9. Casibus .... reservatum, sc. when his favor might be of service to them, if vanquished.

13. Nisi forte. There is quite an ellipsis, as there often is, before *nisi.* Cf. note, A. 6. Nor would Vespasian spare Vitellius, unless you can suppose that one of inferior rank will rise above jealousy of one greatly his superior.

14. Vitellius collega. Vitellius the father. Cf. 1, 52, near the close, and note ad idem.

16. Accingeretur. Subj. Cf. note, 1, 41: *agerent.*

Ch. LXVII.—**25. Erat .... parens,** etc. Cf. 2, 64; also Suet. Vitel. 14.

27. Quinto .... Januarias, i. e. Dec. 18, A. U. C. 822. Ad verba, cf. note, 1, 12.

29. Pullo amictu. The usual dress of mourners at Rome was black; though under the emperors, white, having grown into disrepute, became the mourning apparel of females. Cf. Man. P. 3. 340, 4; Dic. of Antiq. under *funus,* at the end of the Art.; Beck. Gall. Exc. Sc. 12.

31. Lecticula. Cf. note, 1, 27: *sellae.* On this whole scene, cf. Suet. 15; also Juv. 3, 213, who makes the mother of Vitellius also one of the melancholy train.

Ch. LXVIII.—**33. Rerum humanarum.** *Of the instability of human affairs.*

38. Caesarem. Julius Cæsar, who was assassinated by Brutus and Cassius.—*Caium.* Caligula, who was put to death by the tribunes Chaerea and Sabinus. Cf. Suet. Cal. 56, 57.—*Nox ... absconderant.* Cf. note, 1, 2: *falsi Neronis;* also Suet. Ner. 48.

155 **2. Cecidere.** Observe the transition from the plup. (*absconderant*) to the *perf.*, designed, as Wr. suggests, to mark the fact that the end of Piso and Galba is narrated in this history, whereas that of Nero *preceded* the date with which it begins.

9. Caecilius Simplex. Cf. 2, 60.

10. Jus .... civium. Of which the sword is everywhere the symbol. *Nex* is always a violent death; *mors* is death as the common destiny of men (μόρος).

11. In aede Concordiae. In qua senatus haberi solebat, in clivo Capitolino sita. Brotier.

12. Domum fratris. Imminentem foro (cf. 70) vicinamque aedi Concordiae. Brotier

Page

13. Obsistentium .... privatis. *Opposing his entrance to a private house.* 155

CH. LXIX.—**19. Respublica .... cessisset.** Ad verba, cf. Plin. Pan. 6, 3: *confugit in sinum tuum concussa res publica.*

28. Lacum Fundani. A Fundane lake, now called Lago di Fundi, is mentioned by Pliny (N. H. 3, 9). But this lake now in question was in the city of Rome, near the *Mons Quirinalis.* Brotier says there were at least a thousand of those lakes at Rome, which ought more properly to be called fountains. Murphy. Cf. 1, 41: *Curtii lacum.*

31. Re trepida. *In this unexpected and critical emergency.*

32. Arcem capitolii. The relative position of the *arx* (*citadel*) and the *Capitolium* proper (i. e. the temple of Jupiter) has given rise to much discussion, some maintaining that the *Capitolium* was within the *arx,* others that they stood on distinct summits or points of the Mons Capitolinus. Cf. Dic. Antiq. under *Capitolium.* Cic. and Liv. always say arx *et* Capitolium. *Capitolium* seems to be used here by T. as it often is by others, for the whole mount. In the next section he calls the citadel *arx Capitolina.*—*Mixto milite,* etc., i. e. soldiers mingled with citizens of senatorial and equestrian rank. Cf. 2, 14: *pars classicorum mixtis paganis.*

35. Simulavere. *Falsely claimed.*

2. Neglecta, i. e. non obsessa a Vitellianis. Rup. 156

4. Digredi. Al. degredi, a conjecture of Ernesti. But as Wr. says, the thing intended is not so much *going down* from the Capitolium, as *going away and escaping* from the enemy.

CH. LXX.—**11. Simulationem .... fuisse.** He said *it was a mere pretence and show,* (sc. his appearance) *of abdicating the throne. Simulationem* and *imaginem* are predicates. Cf. Essay, pp. 14, 15.

12. Cur enim .... petisset. *Else why should he have gone,* etc. Compare ἢ γὰρ ἄν, etc. in Greek.—*E rostris,* i. e. from the assembly of the people. Cf. 68: *sua concione.*

13. Irritandis .... oculis. Dat. of the end after *petisset: and so as* (or *with a view*) *to attract the eyes of men.* Or dat. after *aptum* implied in *domum imminentem:* a house fitted to attract, etc. Cf. Essay, pp. 16, 17.—**19. Togatum.** Cf. notes, 1, 38; A. 9.

21. Judicatur. So the Greeks use κρίνω of deciding disputes by arms.—**22. Hispaniis,** etc. Spain and Germany were divided, Britain was *one.*

24. Utilia. *Useful things,* like the Greek, with χρήματα understood. The general rules of Latin construction would require *utilem.* Cf. Z. 376, *a.* But exceptions are not wanting in Cic. and Liv. (Z. 377), and are not unfrequent in T., e. g. 2, 20: *pax et concordia jactata sunt.*

CH. LXXI.—**1. Erigunt aciem.** Cf. note, A. 18: *erexit aciem.* 157

2. Capitolinae arcis. Cf. note, 69: *arcem Capitolii.*

Page 157 **3. Porticus.** Cf. notes, 1, 40: *Basilicis*, and *imminentium*, ibid

10. Diversos .... aditus. This implies that there were at least three approaches from the forum to the Mons Capitolinus. Cf. Dic. Antiq., *Capitolium.*

11. Lucum asyli. The Asylum opened by Romulus for the indiscriminate reception of foreigners, as described by Livy (1, 8) and Dion. Hal. (2, 15), was situated *between two groves.* Only one remained in the age of T., here called *lucum asyli*, which was situated between the two summits of the Capitoline Hill. Cf. note, 69: *arcem Capitolii.—Tarpeia rupes.* The whole Capitoline Hill was originally called *Mons Tarpeius*, from the virgin Tarpeia, who was killed and buried there by the Sabines. Liv. 1, 11. But the name *Tarpeia* was afterwards confined to the rock which was the immediate scene of her destruction, and whence criminals were thrown headlong into the Tiber. Cf. Dic. Antiq. as above.

16. Quae crebrior fama. Al. *fama est.* Pliny (N. H. 34, 7) and Josephus (B. J. 4, 11) charge the conflagration to the Vitellians. But they lived in the reign of Vespasian, Tacitus under Trajan, quum veritati, non adulationi locus esset. Brotier.

17. Nitentes .... depulerint. Al. *quo ... depellerent.* But the reading of the text, though less obvious, gives the same sense, and rests on better authority.

18. Porticus .... aedibus, i. e. to the temple of Jupiter Capitolinus, which had a triple row of columns in front, and a double row on each side (Dionys. 4, 61), and which T. calls *aedibus*, perhaps because it contained within one enclosure and beneath one roof, three *aedes*, sacred severally to Jupiter, Juno and Minerva. Brotier. Cf. Dic. Antiq. as above.—*Sustinentes .... aquilae.* The ornaments and supports of the pediment (vulgarly called the gable-end). These were usually in public edifices wrought into the form of eagles with outstretched wings. Cf. Rup. ad loc.

20. Indireptum. Josephus (B. J. 4, 11, 4) says that the Vitellians plundered the temple.

Ch. LXXII.—**25. Pignus imperii** = ut pignus imperii esset. Rup. Cf. Gr. 204, R. 1.

26. Porsena. Al. Porsenna. The penult. is short in Mart. 1, 22; Hor. Epod. 16, 4; Sil. Ital. 8, 391, et al.; but long in Virg. Aen. 8, 646. The best authorities are at variance touching the orthography and the prosody of the word. Cf. Macaulay's Lays of Ancient Rome —*Dedita urbe.* T. is charged by many with error here, or at least with speaking rhetorically, rather than what was historically true. But Niebuhr and Arnold argue with great force from the circumstances and results of the war with Porsena, that the common history is falsified by Roman pride, and that T. has preserved the only true account, and Rome was really surrendered to the Etruscans.

Page

27. Galli capta. A. U. C. 364. Cf. Liv. 5, 43; Ann. 11, 24.—*Exscindi* depends on *accidit*, or rather is in appos. with *facinus;* though some copies place a pause after *accidit*. 157

28. Arserat .... bello. A. U. C. 671, in the civil war between Sylla and Marius. Cf. Flor. 3, 21; Cic. in Cat. 3, 4. This conflagration is referred to again below.—*Fraude privata.* Privati hominis et auctoris ignoti. Rup.

30. Quo .... stetit. T. more suo duo momenta in unam enuntiationem contrahit. Plenius scripsisset: quod pretium tantae cladis fuit, quo illa res stetit? i. e. what was the price of so great a calamity, how much did it stand us in? So Wr. and Bach. Cf. note, A. 16: *seditio ... stetit.* Others take *stetit* in the sense of *evenit, locum habuit.*—**31. Voverat Tarquinius,** etc. Cf. Liv. 1, 38.

33. Mox Servius Tullius, etc. Quod alibi haud legere memini Rup.—**34. Dein Tarquinius Superbus.** Cf. Liv. 1, 53. 55. 56.

36. Libertati, i. e. temporibus liberae rei publicae.—*Horatius .. dedicavit.* A. U. C. 247, about three years after the expulsion of Tarquin. Cf. Liv. 2, 8; 7, 3. Dionys. 5, 35.

37. Ea magnificentia refers rather to the grandeur of the work, than to the pomp and ceremony of the dedication, as the next clause shows.—**38. Ornarent.** Subj. Cf. Gr. 264, 1; Z. 556.

2. Viginti quinque. All the MSS. have *quindecim*, or ccccxv., and Wr. and Or. follow them. But Lipsius, Ruperti, and most editors think it more probable that an x may have been omitted in the MSS., than that T. could have erred or departed from the established chronology by a period of ten years. 158

4. Hoc .... negatum. Pliny (N. H. 7, 44, 137) reports this as the language of Sylla himself.

5. Lutatii ..... nomen, i. e. Lutatius Catulus (consul with Aemilius Lepidus, A. U. C. 676, A. C. 78) had the honor of dedicating the Capitol, and so of inscribing his name upon it, where it remained visible, notwithstanding all the improvements the Capitol had received from the Cæsars (*inter tanta Caesaris opera*), till the edifice itself was consumed by fire, in the reign of Vitellius.

CH. LXXIII.—**10. Ex diverso.** *In the opposite party.* Cf. note, 5, supra.

11. Captus animi. Ut alibi *captus animo*, i. e. ejus usu privatus. Rup.—*Non lingua .... competere.* See the phrase in Lev. Lex., under *competo*. The same words are cited by the grammarian Nonius from Sallust's History, now lost.

19. Martialis. Cf. 70, above.—*Pacensis.* Cf. 1, 20. 87; 2, 12. The other two (Niger and Scaeva) are not mentioned elsewhere.

22. Quinctium Atticum. Consul suffectus with Caecilius Simplex. Cf. 68, supra.—*Umbra .... vanitate.* Usu insignium consularium quae amovenda in tali periculo erant. Ernesti.

Page

158 **24. Jecerat,** i. e. *secretly scattered abroad,* instead of openly posting them up according to custom. Wr.

26. Excepto .... signo. *Having caught the watchword.* Cf. note, 22: *pugnae signum.*

28. Audaciam .... haberent. Cf. Sall. B. Cat. 58: *audacia pro muro habetur.*

Ch. LXXIV.—**33. Disjecto** = destructo.—*Contubernio.* Cf. note, 1, 43.—Jovi Conservatori = Διὶ Σωτῆρι.

34. Aram casus .... expressam. Dictio poetica ac Graeca, quales T. amat, pro *aram marmoream* in qua casus sui expressi erant. Rup. Gr. 234, II.

36. Sabinus, etc. Eutropius (7, 12) and Victor (Caes. 8) make Sabinus to have perished in the burning of the Capitol; while Suet. (Dom. 10) says he was put to death by Domitian. Xiph. (65, 17) agrees with T.

159 **1. Enavatae.** So the MSS. The common editions have *navatae.* Ritter observes a fondness in T. for the use of *e* in composition to denote *consummation.* Cf. *evicta,* 2, 64.

5. Absciso is omitted in the common editions, but is found in all the MSS., and is not superfluous: *his head having been cut off, they drag his mutilated body.*

6. Gemonias, sc. scalas. Cf. Lev. Lex. and Anthon's Class. Dic sub voce.

Ch. LXXV.—**8. In republica.** As we say, *in the service of his country,* not of a civil faction, or a military chieftain. Ernesti thought the words superfluous, or at least misplaced.

13. Quod .... constiterit. Subj. Cf. Gr. 264, 3; Z. 559. Or., following Duebner, makes it = constitit, ni fallor.

18. Consulis. Quinctius Atticus, named with Sabinus, 73 and 74, supra.

19. Velut .... reddens. *Reciprocating, as it were, the favor* of Atticus in assuming the responsibility of having fired the capitol.

Ch. LXXVI.—**24. Feroniam.** A town of Latium, celebrated for the grove and the worship of Feronia, the Latin goddess of liberty. Brotier. Cf. Hor. Sat. 1, 5, 24.

25. Tarracinae. Cf. note, 60, supra.

27. Periculum is the object of *audebant,* which takes an acc. Cf. Gr. 229, R. 2. In the other clause, *audebant* is followed by an inf. (*egredi*). For the case of *moenia,* cf. Gr. 233, R. 1. It is peculiar to the age of T. to use the acc. after verbs compounded with *e* or *ex.* Sall. and Liv. use the abl.; Cic. the abl. with *ex* repeated. Cf. Z. 386.—*Ut .... memoravimus.* Cf. 57, supra.

28. Lascivia .... similes. The common editions connect this clause with the next sentence, to the manifest injury of the sense and spirit

Page

30. Intuta moenium, amoena litorum. Cf. note, 65: *offen-* 159
sarum operta.

31. Personantes. Sono vocum musicorumque instrumentorum implentes. Rup. Cf. Virg. Aen. 6, 171.

33. Apinius Tiro. Cf. 57, supra.

Ch. LXXVII.—**37. Perfugit,** sc. from the garrison of Tarracina.

38. Tradi futurum. Al. *traditurum.* The slave *promised that it would come to pass that the citadel would be delivered up,* not that he himself would deliver it up. So Wr., Ober. and Bach, after the Medicean MS.—*Multa nocte. In the dead of night;* more lit. deep in the night; *when the night was far advanced.*

12. In ore ejus. *In his presence.—Triariam.* Cf. 2, 63. 160

13. Incesserent. Al. incesserint. Cf. 78: *arguerent.*

15. Lauream. A letter bound with bay leaves. Cf. note, A. 18: *laureatis.* Pliny employs the word in the same unusual sense, Panegyr. 8.—**17. Juberet.** Subj. Cf. Gr. 265; Z. 552.

Ch. LXXVIII.—**24. Digressus Narnia,** etc. Cf. 58 and 63, supra.

25. Festos .... dies. The Saturnalia began on the 17th of December. It was the Roman Thanksgiving, or Christmas, or both combined, especially to the rustic population, who having now finished their agricultural labors, were ready to celebrate a joyous harvest-home. Cf. Dic. Antiq., *Saturnalia.*

26. Ocriculi. A town of Umbria, near the confluence of the Nar and the Tiber, now *Otricoli.*

33. Quando. Cf. note, 8, supra. It is here followed, first by the subj., to denote the motive of the generals, as reported by *quidam,* and secondly by the ind., to convey an additional thought of the historian.

34. Cessurus imperio. Cf. note, 2, 55: *cessisse.*

38. Nequivisset. Subj. after *qui* = talis, ut = *such a man that he could not.—Haud facile.* Cf. note, 28, supra.

2. Antonius .... meruit. *Antonius, with illtimed submission,* 161
or with the design of retorting the odium (sc. offsetting the affair at Cremona by those of Rome and the Capitol) *deserved censure.*

6. Salaria via. A road leading from the *salt-works* at Ostia through the country of the Sabines to Rome, which it entered through the Colline gate.

Ch. LXXIX.—**9. Flaminiam,** sc. viam. Cf. note, 1, 86.—*Saxa rubra.* A place on the Flaminian road in Etruria, nine miles from Rome.—*Multo noctis.* Cf. note, 77: *multa nocte.*

19. Nuper .... dediti. Cf. 63, supra.

21. Fuga consternantur. Intelligenda *consternatio cum foeda fuga conjuncta.* Wr.

Ch. LXXX.—**24. Raptis .... telis.** Omnes rapiunt *tela,* sed unusquisque quod sibi obvium. Hence the sing. *quod.* Wr. Ernesti

Page

161 compares Virg. Aen. 7, 507: quod cuique repertum rimanti telum ira fecit.—**31. Arulenus Rusticus.** Cf. A. 2, and note, ibid.

32. Propria . . . . viri. *The personal merit*, or *peculiar worth, of the man.*

33. Palantur is considered by Död. to be passive here. Cf. Essay, p. 10.—*Proximus lictor.* The lictors went before the magistrates, one by one in a line. He who went last, or next to the magistrate, was called *proximus lictor.* Cf. Dict. Antiq., *Lictor.*

35. In . . . gentes. Al. *inter.* Bach., Rup., Or. and Död. explain *in = apud: sacred even with* (or *to*) *foreign nations.* Wr., Ober. and Bip. connect *in gentes* with *legatorum: ambassadors to foreign nations.* The former gives the better sense and accords with the use of *in* by Tac. and even Cicero, e. g. Verr. 4, 11: *in exteras nationes*, where *in = apud*, though with more of the idea of (motion and) gradual extension.

162 Ch. LXXXI.—**1. Musonius Rufus.** Named as a philosopher of Tuscan origin, Ann. 14, 59; 15, 71.

2. Placita from *placeo = dogmas* from *δοκέω.*

7. Obviae fuere. *Met* them, sc. the Flavian troops.

8. Virgines Vestales. Ad rem, cf. Suet. Vitel. 16. The vestal virgins not unfrequently acted the part of intercessors, as for instance with Sylla for Julius Cæsar. Suet. Jul. 1; Cic. pro Font. 17. Cf. also Ann. 3, 69; 11, 32; Dict. Antiq., *Vestales.*

9. Certamini. Al. *certamine.* Utrumque probum; sed illud Tacito usitatius. Rup.—*Unum diem.* Al. *unam.* Cf. Gr. 90; also Lexicon, sub *dies.* We should say: *he earnestly requested that the final conflict be put off for one day.*

12. Belli commercia. *Negotiations.* Compare the reply of Æneas to Turnus, Aen. 10, 532: *Belli commercia Turnus sustulit.*

Ch. LXXXII.—**14. Pontem Mulvium.** Cf. note, 1, 87.

17. Delubris. This word denotes a temple, as a place of purification and atonement. Rams. 38; Freund, sub voce.

23. Trinis. Poetice for tribus. Cf. Gr. 120, 4.

24. Praesidiis. Used for agminibus, to avoid repetition.

27. Sallustianos hortos. These famous gardens were in the suburbs of Rome near the Colline gate. They derive their name from the historian Sallust, who constructed and adorned them with every attraction which the plundered treasures of Numidia could purchase. They became, after his death, a favorite residence of the emperors.

32. Desperatione sola, sc. adjuti, or pro suis partibus. Cf. Essay, p. 17.

163 Ch. LXXXIII.—**4. Scortis similes,** i. e. pathici. Rup.—*Quantum . . . . libidinum. All the licentious pleasures of a luxurious peace.* It is to be borne in mind, that this was the period of the Saturnalia. Cf. 78. Hence *festis diebus* below.

5. Prorsus. *In a word.*

9. Inhumana securitas. *Inhuman indifference.* Cf. note, 2, 70. 163

10. Velut . . . . accederet. *As if this pleasure also* (sc. of seeing the fight) *were added to the usual entertainments of these festive days.* The punctuation of the last clause is different in different editions, some placing a semicolon after *exsultabant*, others after *fruebantur*, and others still, allowing no such pause. *Exsultabant* implies more outward demonstrations of pleasure; *fruebantur*, inward enjoyment. Imagination never portrayed a more vivid and moving picture of mingled ferocity and voluptuousness than the pen of our historian has sketched. Its credibility has been called in question. But Florus (3, 21) affirms the same of the civil war between Marius and Sylla. The last grievous calamity that befell the Romans, was a war waged by parricides within the walls of Rome, in which citizens were engaged against citizens with the rage of gladiators exhibiting a spectacle in the forum.

Ch. LXXXIV.—**13. Oppugnatione castrorum.** The camp of the prætorian guards, a little way out of the city, where it was first located by Sejanus in the time of Tiberius. Ann. 4, 2. Cf. Dict. Antiq. sub voce, *Praetoriani*, and note, 1, 39: *vocibus in urbem.*

21. Recipiantur, sc. *castra.* The *veteres cohortes,* i. e. the old prætorians discharged by Vitellius, might with special propriety speak of *re*taking their old camp.

24. Suprema . . . . solatia. These words are in appos. with *inquietare, morari* and *foedare*, all which depend on *amplectebantur;* these acts of vengeance were the last solace of the conquered. Ernesti understands by *suprema . . . solatia* their wives and children!

27. Contrariis vulneribus. *With wounds in front. Versi in hostem* (a superfluous clause in the view of some), gives the cause of this: *since they faced the enemy* to the last. So Wr.

Ch. LXXXV.—**30. Sellula.** Dim. of *sella,* on which see note, 1, 27.

31. Diem stands opposed to *noctu* understood, when he would have fled to Tarracina, had he escaped the *peculiar dangers of the day.*

37. Pudenda latebra. A dog's kennel, according to Xiph. 65, 20; according to Suet. Vitel. 16, the porter's lodge.

3. E . . . militibus. Doubtless one of the emperor's body-guard. 164

4. Per iram, etc. T. here adverts to three distinct suppositions: 1. That the soldier aimed a hostile blow at Vitellius out of resentment; 2. That he did it out of compassion, to rescue him from further insults; 3. That the blow was intended for the tribune. According to Xiph. 65, 21, the soldier said, I will give you the best assistance in my power, and thereupon he stabbed Vitellius and dispatched himself.

11. Una vox. Al. *vox una.* *Una vox* has the authority of all the MSS. and lays the emphasis, where it belongs, on the *number.*

Page

164 **13. Concidit.** Cf. Suet. Vitel. 17, where the account is more full and particular.

Ch. LXXXVI.—**15. Patria .... Luceria.** The various readings here are many. But this is, with a slight alteration, the reading of the best two MSS. and accords with Suet. Vitel. 1. Luceria was an ancient city of Apulia, now Lucera. Cf. Anth. Class. Dict.—*Septimum .... annum.* So Suet. 18; Eutrop. 7, 12; Vict. Caes. 10. But Xiph. (65, 22) says, he lived 54 years and 89 days.

18. Cuncta ... adeptus. Foedis quoque in Caligulam, Claudium et Neronem obsequiis. Brotier.

23. Continere. Al. *contineri.* But it is a needless conjecture. The remark refers to what Vitellius vainly expected to do for himself, not to what he laid down as a general principle.

24. Meruit .... habuit. *He earned friends, rather than had them,* as is usually the case with those who seek to buy them.

25. Imputare. Cf. note, 1, 71. Praetendere non possunt, se reipublicae causa Vitellium prodidisse. Pichena

---

BOOK IV.

167 Ch. I.—**2. Per urbem.** Notice the position of these words. They do not limit *consectabantur,* but *armati victores:* armed victors in every quarter of the city.

6. Procerum .... juventa. The German soldiers were *tall* (cf. G. 4: *magna corpora*) and *youthful;* and under pretence of slaying them, they slew indiscriminately, soldier and citizen, all whom they could in any way contrive to confound with them.

8. Recentibus odiis. *When their hatred was fresh,* i. e. in the heat of battle.—*Dein verterat. Had soon after changed.* The plup. denotes the suddenness and completeness of the change. Z. 508.

11. Nec deerat .... prodere. *Prodere* depends on *deerat.* In the common editions it is separated from it by a colon. But *deesse* usually takes after it either an inf. or a dat. or a pred. nom. to limit its meaning. Cf. 3, 58: *deerat elicere,* 1, 23: *deerat instinctor.*

14. Fortunae. The vicissitudes, all the varied fortunes. Compare the Gr. τύχαι, συμφοραί. Al. *forma* and *fortuna. Forma* is a mere conjecture.

17. Turbas et discordias .... pax et quies. Notice the pairs of synonyms, or rather kindred words. Cf. note, 1, 84.

Ch. II.—**20. Sedem.** *Residence,* sc. the imperial palace. At first he was conducted to the private house of his father. 3, 86.

Page

21. Stupris et adulteriis. Cf. A. 7; Suet. Dom. 1 and 22; 167
Xiph. 66, 3. 26, etc.

22. Agebat. Cf. note, 1, 30.

4. Occupari = praeveniri. Cf. note, 1, 40.—*Tarracinu.* Cf. 168
note, 3, 60.

5. Ariciam. An ancient town of Latium, at the foot of Mons Albanus, about 16 miles from Rome. The *Aricinum Nemus* (cf. note, 3, 36) was near, whence the present name of the place, *Nemi.*

6. Bovillas. An ancient town 10 miles from Rome. It was on the Appian Road, as was also Aricia.—*Nec* = et non, correl. to *et* miles.

16. Adversis abstractus. *Ruined* (lit. dragged down, swept away) *by his adversity.*

Ch. III.—**17. Lucilius Bassus.** Whose treachery is described, 3, 12.

18. Discordibus animis, as well as *contumacia,* is abl. of cause limiting *mittitur.*

21. Capuae, etc. That is, of the larger towns (opposed to *minoribus coloniis*), Capua was punished for its fidelity to Vitellius (3, 57); but Tarracina was not rewarded, though it favored the party of Vespasian (3, 76); which gives rise to the striking and yet just reflection which follows.

25. Quem .... diximus. Cf. 3, 77. The crucifixion of this slave was some consolation to the people of Tarracina for not being rewarded as they deserved. Observe the Latin idiom, the concrete, *servus affixus,* where we use the abstract, *crucifixion.*

27. Annulis. The badge of knighthood (cf. note, 1, 13) still on his hands was now only a mark of derision.

28. Cuncta .... decernit. So at the accession of Otho (1, 47) and of Vitellius (2, 55), where see note on *cuncta.*

32. Lustraverant has for its subject *civilia arma.*

34. Tanquam .... bello, i. e. he did not write like a conqueror dictating his own terms, but as if peace was yet to be established; *such at least was the first aspect of the letter* (*ea .... forma*), yet on closer inspection his language was that of an emperor, uttering modest sentiments (those becoming a citizen) touching himself, and excellent sentiments in regard to the republic.

37. Consulare imperium. It was usual to confer perpetual consular authority on the emperor's sons. Wr. It should be added, that his father and brother, the consuls for the year, were both absent.

Ch. IV.—**3. Publice.** Rei publicae nomine, in causis publicis. 169
Ernesti. To address the senate thus (on the general interests of the state) was not in character for a private citizen. Cf. note, 2, 55: *gratior .... scripsisset.*—*Paucos ... dies,* sc. on his arrival at Rome. —*Loco sententiae,* sc. in his place as a senator.

Page

169 **8. Multo cum honore.** Cf. note, 2, 37 : *magna ex parte.*

9. Triumphalia. Cf. note, A. 40.—*De bello civium,* i. e. really for his agency in dethroning Vitellius, but nominally for his defeat of the Sarmatians, or the Dacians as they are called, 3, 46, where the victory of Mucianus is narrated. The Sarmatians and Dacians often acted in concert. Cf. 54, below. A triumph was never granted for a victory over Roman citizens.

12. Mox, sc. after honoring *men,* thus reversing the proper order. Gall. 14, 7.

16. Ubi ventum, i. e. in calling on the senators to give their opinions in the order of their rank and honors. Cf. Dict. Antiq., *Senatus.*—*Helvidium Priscum.* Cf. note and text, 2, 91; also note, A. 2.

18. Falsa aberant = ita falsis carentem, i. e. *though respectful to the emperor, yet devoid of false adulation.* The enallage is very bold.

19. Praecipuus = praecipue. Död.

Ch. V.—**21. Iterum.** Cf. 2, 91. Helvidius Priscus is often mentioned in the Annals. But the Annals were not composed till after the History. At the time of writing this, therefore, he could say *iterum incidimus, we have happened to mention a second time.*

23. Quali .... sit usus. Subj. of the indirect question.—*Repetam.* Cf. note, 1, 4: *repetendum.*

24. Primi pili. Cf. note, 1, 31: *primipilaribus.* For the subj. (*duxisset*), cf. Gr. 264, 1; Z. 558.

28. Doctores ... qui ... annumerant. The Stoics. Cf. note, A. 44: *vera bona;* also Cic. de Fin. 3, 7, et al.

31. Quaestorius. Helvidius quaestor fuit sub Nerone et Achaiam administravit. Lipsius.—*Paeto Thrasea.* Cf. note, A. 2.

32. Libertatem, etc. Dion. (66, 12) says, it was an illtimed imitation of Thrasea's freedom of speech.

34. Pervicax is not found in Cic. or Cæs. Cf. Freund, sub voce. It is rarely used in a good sense, as it is here.

Ch. VI.—**36. Appetentior.** Cf. Gr. 256, R. 9.—*Videretur.* Subj. Cf. Gr. 264, 6; Z. 561.—*Quando .... exuitur.* De sententia, cf. A. 9: *famam, cui etiam saepe boni indulgent.* Valer. Flac. 1, 76; Cic. Or. pro Archia, 11. Plato and Epictetus both denominate love of glory *the last garment* (χιτών) that we put off.

38. Marcellum Eprium. Cf. notes, 2, 53. 95.

170 **1. Delatorem Thraseae.** Cf. Ann. 16, 28. 29; and note, 1, 2· *delatorum.*

2. Major, sc. in its consequences. Cf. *nam si caderet,* etc.

5. Testatum. *Attested* to T. and his cotemporaries by the orations of both, which were still preserved. Wr.

11. Priscus .... juratis. *Priscus demanded that they* (the

Page

ambassadors) *should be chosen expressly for the purpose by magistrates under oath.* Cf. note, 1, 43: *nominatim.* Besides the oath of office, senators and magistrates were sometimes put under oath to be faithful in a particular duty. Cf. Ann. 4, 21: *jurati senatus;* also Dict. Antiq., *Oaths.* 170

12. Urnam. An urn was used to receive the names in *drawing lots.* Cf. Hor. Od. 3, 1, 16; Virg. Aen. 6, 432. Hence *urnam* = *sortem.* Cf. 7: *sorte et urna.*—*Quae consulis designati,* etc. It was usual to call on the consuls elect, if present, for their opinion first. Cf. Dict. Antiq., *Senatus.*

Ch. VII.—**20. Suffragia.** Observe the etymology of the word. Cf. Lev. Lex.—*Existimationem senatus* = *judicio senatus* below.

23. Occurrere. *Meet him* and escort him with due honor to Rome, as Vitellius, 2, 59; Agricola, A. 40; Cic. pro Mil. 35.

25. Sorano, who shared the hatred of Nero with Thrasea. Ann. 16, 21, seq.—*Sentio.* The name of an unknown person. The text is disputed. *Senecio* occurs in two or three MSS. But he belonged to a later generation. Cf. A. 2. *Seneca* has been suggested, but it is without MS. authority.

29. Satis Marcello, sc. sit or esse. Cf. Essay, p. 14.

30. Frueretur. Cf. note, *agerent,* 1, 41.

Ch. VIII.—**34. Censuisse.** *Had advanced the opinion,* sc. which Helvidius impugned.—*Vetera exempla.* Cic. Epis. ad Att. 1, 17; Suet. Aug. 35; Dio. 59, 23.

1. Animus . . . suspensus. *The mind* of Vespasian, *at the commencement of his reign, still unsettled.* 171

3. Se meminisse, etc. He remembered the spirit of the age in which he lived, the form of government which their fathers and grandsires had established, sc. the imperial, which had originated about two generations previous.

8. Per . . . . imagines, i. e. the forms of law and justice, such as a prosecutor and a board of judges.

10. Se unum esse. *He was but one member of that senate, which, like himself, had submitted* to the reigning despot. An admirable speech for a demagogue.

18. Mediis patrum. Neutri parti faventibus, inter duas partes medium quasi tenentibus. Rup.

Ch. IX.—**21. Nam tum . . . . aerarium.** The treasury of the Roman republic was under the care of the quæstors. Augustus transferred it to the prætors and those who had been prætors. Suet. Oct. 36. Claudius restored it to the quæstors, and Nero again transferred it to the prætors. Ann. 13, 29; Suet. Claud. 24. Hence the propriety of Tacitus' stating how it was at this time (*tum*).

24. Consul . . . . reservabat. The consul elect (in the exercise of his prerogative to give his opinion first, cf. note 6) proposed to re-

Page

171 serve (was inclined to reserve) the treasury for the emperor. For this use of the imperf., cf. Gr. 145, II. 4.

26. Perrogarent. Subj. Cf. 263, 5, R. 2; Z. 578. Observe the force of *per*, asked *through*, i. e. *all round* in order.

27. Intercessit. *Interposed his veto.*

31. Oblivio. Abl. from *oblivium* which in the sing. occurs only in T., though the poets use the pl. *oblivia.—Meminissent. Remembered it* and reported it to Vespasian to the ruin of Helvidius. Cf. note on Helvidius, A. 2. The proposal to repair the Capitol at the expense and by the authority of the commonwealth (*publice*) with the *help of Vespasian,* was deemed derogatory to the honor of the emperor. *Meminissent.* Subj. Cf. Gr. 264, 6; Z. 561. Plup. Gr. 183, 3, Note; Z. 221.

Ch. X.—**33. P. Celerem.** A Stoic philosopher, the client, friend and master of Soranus, and also his betrayer.

38. Amicitiae, cujus. Such is the reading of all the MSS. The common editions have, *amici et cujus,* an emendation of Lipsius. But the reading of the MSS. has the same meaning. *Amicitiae* is the friendship between Soranus and Celer, of which Celer was the *master* by having trained Soranus for it, but which he afterwards *betrayed and violated* (*proditor corruptorque*). So Wr. and Or.

172 **3. Exspectabantur,** i. e. their participation in the cause was looked to as giving it its chief interest.

Ch. XI.—**8. Dissimulata .... iracundia** is abl. of *cause* limiting *fracta.—Quamvis .... tegeretur.* Cf. Gr. 263, 2; Z. 574.

12. Excubiis. Guards. See these set down as characteristic of sovereignty, Ann. 1, 7: *excubiae, cetera aulae.*

13. Calpurnii Galeriani. Son of Caius Calpurnius Piso (Ann. 14, 65; 15, 48–59), and son-in-law of Lucius Piso (49, infra). His only crime was his high birth (*nomen*) and his personal attractions (*decora juventa*).

15. Ipsi. Dat. for gen. = *his own,* in distinction from the name which he inherited from his ancestors.

18. Ne .... foret gives the reason for putting him to death forty miles from the city. Ibi villa monumentumque Calpurniorum erat, et adhuc reperiuntur inscripti lapides, qui ad gentis hujus libertos pertinent. Brotier.—**20. Julius Priscus.** Cf. 2, 92; 3, 55.

21. Pudore, sc. for their cowardly flight, 3, 61.

22. Necessitate. Cf. note, 1, 3: *necessitates.—Alfenus Varus.* Colleague of Priscus. Cf. 3, 36. 55. 61.—*Ignaviae .... suae.* Dat. of the end = to lead a life of inaction and infamy.

23. Asiaticus. The favorite freedman of Vitellius. Cf. 2, 57 95.—*Enim* refers to a suppressed clause of this purport: but not so with Asiaticus, *for he,* etc.—*Is libertus* gives the reason why Asiaticus was punished like a slave (crucified), viz. that he had been a slave.

Page

CH. XII.—**30. Batavi.** See the same account of the origin of 172
the Batavi and of their country, in different language, G. 29.

32. Inter vada sitam, i. e. *interpenetrated by shallow waters.* Cf. our author's description of the island, 5, 23: *palustrem humilemque insulam.* Al. *juxta sitam,* Wr., Rup. and Or.; *nunc Bataviam,* Oberlin; and many other conjectural readings. The MSS. differ much. The Medicean here has no meaning. The only reading in which there is any agreement, is that given in the text, which is adopted by Wr. and Död.

33. Mare Oceanum. *Oceanum* is an adj. Cf. Caes. B. G. 3, 7. Al. *Oceanus.*—*Tergum ac latera.* The object of *circumluit* by enallage, instead of *a tergis ac lateribus.*

34. Opibus Romanis. *By Roman power.*—*Societate validiorum* explains *opibus Romanis: by Roman power,* that is, *by alliance with a more powerful nation,* which usually exhausted and ruined (*attriti*) the weaker party. The Batavians fared better than the allies of Rome usually did.

35. Viros tantum, etc., i. e. they do not pay tribute. Cf. 17: *tributorum expertes;* also G. 29. On *ministrant,* see note G. 44.

38. Praecipuo .... studio. Cf. A. 18: *patrius nandi usus,* etc. *Perrumpere* depends on *studio,* and denotes the result=*so as to break,* etc.

CH. XIII.—**3. Paullus** and **Civilis** were brothers; compare with 173
this the words of Civilis below, 32: *necem fratris et vincula mea.*

4. Fonteius Capito. Cf. 1, 7.

10. Simili .... dehonestamento. Sertorius and Hannibal were blind of one eye. Cf. Plut. Sertor.; and Liv. 22, 2.—*Ne .... iretur. Lest he should be met as an enemy.*

14. Vitellio. Al. a Vitellio. Cf. note, 1, 86: *auctoribus.*

16. Animo et ... cura. Two reasons for the advice of Flaccus.

17. Adventabat. *Would have come,* was already coming as it were. Cf. notes, 3, 46: *coeperant, ni;* A. 13: *ni .... fuissent.* Z. 519.

CH. XIV.—**23. Avaritia ac luxu.** *Avaritia* showed itself in *drafting the aged or invalids* and exacting money for their release; *luxus* in the scandalous abuse of *the young and the beautiful,* who were particularly numerous among the Batavians. Cf. note, 3, 33: *quis .... conspicuus.*

29. Nocte ac laetitia. Hendiadys. *By the pleasures* (festivities) *of the night.* See in G. 22, the German custom of deliberating on great questions at feasts prolonged through the day and the night.

31. Neque societatem. *Nor was it an alliance, as formerly.*

32. Quando .... venire. Plenius T. scripsisset: quando legatum venire? quanquam legatum molestum gravi comitatu et superbo imperio: sed ne venire quidem; tradi se, etc. Wr.

35. Novos sinus. *New plunderers,* lit. new laps or bosoms to

Page

173 be filled. Cf. 2, 92: *ambitiosos sinus;* 3, 19: *opes in sinu praefectorum legatorumque fore.*

174 **4. Cujus .... reddi,** i. e. if unsuccessful, they could claim a reward from Vespasian for their (pretended) zeal in his service; but if successful, no account need be rendered of their conduct.

Ch. XV.—**7. Qui .... sociarent.** Cf. Gr. 264, 5; Z. 567.

11. Ut ... retulimus, sc. 2, 69. These Batavian cohorts had long served in *Britain* as *auxiliaries* of the 14th legion. Cf. 1, 59. 64. Hence they are here called *Britannica auxilia.*—*Magontiaci.* A town of Belgic Gaul, now *Mentz,* situated at the confluence of the Rhine and the Maine.

12. Brinno. This word probably has the same root as *Brennus,* the name of the commander of the Gauls when they sacked Rome. It seems to be the official designation of a prince or leader among the Gauls, like Pharaoh in Egypt.

14. Caianarum .... ludibrium. *The ridiculous campaigns of Caligula.* Cf. G. 37; Ann. Books 7 and 8; also note, A. 39: falsum .... triumphum.

15. Ipso .... placuit. *The people were pleased with* (lit. he pleased them by) *the very name of a rebel family,* i. e. with the very fact, that like *his father,* he had rebelled against the Romans. Orelli. Al. *omine* for *nomine.*

16. More gentis. This custom was afterwards adopted from the Gauls and Goths by the Romans. Cf. Or. in loc.

24. Quod militum, sc. erat = *what few soldiers they had. Signa, vexilla* and *quod militum* make up the subject of *congregantur,* and *nomen* is in apposition with them.

28. Nerviorum. A Gallic tribe, who aspired to the honor of being Germans. Cf. note, G. 28.—*Germanorum,* sc. cis Rhenum colentium.—*Segnem numerum.* Cf. Hor. Epis. 1, 2, 27: *nos numerus sumus* = a mere number, that *count,* but cannot *do.*

29. Oneraverat is very expressive, implying that their arms were a burden.

Ch. XVI.—**38. Propriis cuneis.** In the wedge-form masses peculiar to those tribes. The Germans usually arranged their troops in form of a wedge. Cf. note, G. 6. Död. makes *cuneis* dat. for *in .... cuneos,* Essay, p. 13.

175 **1. Ex diverso.** *On the opposite side,* sc. that of the Romans, *the line of battle was drawn up not far from the river Rhine, and with the ships facing the enemy. Diversus* is very often used for *adversus.* Cf. note, A. 11: *in diversa.*

3. Certato. Cf. Gr. 257, R. 9; Z. 647; and note, 3, 20: *explorato.*

6. E Batavis, i. e. *being Batavians.*

9. Volentis = *volentes.* Cf. Z. 2.

Page

Ch. XVII.—**15. Germaniae.** Upper and Lower Germany, not 175
Germany proper. Cf. note, 1, 9.

26. Vindicis aciem. Cf. note, 1, 8. Civilis artfully calls it a *battle* (*aciem*), not, as it really was, a defeat and slaughter (*cladem*). And he proceeds immediately to impute the success of the opposite army to the valor of the Batavian horse, who were now under his command: *it was by the Batavian horse* (under Verginius) *that the Ædui* (under Vindex) *and the Arverni* (hodie, Auvergne) *were trampled under foot.*—**27. Verginii.** Cf. note, 1, 8: *Vindicis.*

29. Addito agrees with the following clause, which is thus put in the abl. abs.: *with the addition of all the discipline,* etc.

30. Esse secum .... procubuerint. Observe the *present* and *perfect* here in the *oratio obliqua.* We can use only the imperfect and pluperfect (if we use the present and perfect, we must say *we* and *us,* in other words adopt the *oratio recta*); the Latins may use either class of tenses with the same subject, *se.* Cf. note, 1, 32: *si poeniteat.*

33. Ante tributa. The reference here is to the census and tribute imposed on the Gauls by Augustus, A. U. C. 727. Cf. Ann. 1, 31. 33.—**34. Caeso .... Varo.** Cf. G. 37, note.

Ch. XVIII.—**5. Flaccus Hordeonius.** Observe the inverted or- 176
der of the names *Flaccus Hordeonius.* Cf. 1, 9: *Hordeonius Flaccus,* which in early times was always the order, but often disregarded in later times. Cf. Z. 797, and note on the names of Agricola, A. 4.

7. Romanum nomen = Romanos omnes. So Livy, passim.

10. E praesentibus. *Of those on the spot.* *E proximis.* *Of those nearest at hand.*—**11. Agentis.** Cf. note, 16: *volentis.*

15. Ut .... gloria. Sub. esset. Cf. Essay, p. 14.

19. Nequaquam .... clamor. Ominous of defeat. Cf. note, G. 3: *terrent.*

24. Totis campis. The abl. with *totus,* denoting place, usually stands without a prep. Cf. Z. 482.

27. Oppidano certamine. In *their competition, as townsmen, for the* pre-eminence.—**29. Avehitur,** sc. by Civilis.

Ch. XIX.—**30. Batavorum .... cohortes.** Auxiliares Romanorum ex istis populis scriptas. Ernesti.

33. Pretium .... donativum. These words are in apposition: *they demanded as the price of their march, a donative, double pay, and an increase of the number of horse* (the cavalry had easier service and better pay); *all which had, in fact (sane), been promised them by Vitellius.*

2. Mox .... ministris. *Presently influenced by his natural* 177
sluggishness (cf. 1, 9) *and by the fears of his subordinates.* Abl. of cause, limiting *statuit.*

5. Dein .... ipsis. *Afterwards changing his purpose and censured by the very persons who,* etc. *Dein* is correlative to *mox.*

Page

177 **7. Bonnam.** Now Bonn. This is the earliest mention of Bonn in history. Cf. Rup. in loc.—*Transitu. Crossing*, sc. the Rhine at Bonn.

Ch. XX.—**19. Si obsisteret .... sin occurrant.** Cf. note, 75, infra: *si velit .... si mallet.*

21. Experiretur. Al. *ut .... experiretur.* But *ut* is wanting in all the MSS. Of course it is to be supplied, as in so many other exhortations, e. g. 2, 46: *haberet;* 3, 64: *capesseret.* Ang. *to try.*

24. Rumpunt for *erumpunt.* Essay, pp. 10. 11.

31. Interire. Histor. infin. Al. *interiere.—Colonia Agrippinensium.* Now Cologne. Cf. G. 28, and note there on *conditoris;* also infra, 28: *Romanorum nomen.*

33. Sibimetipsi consuluissent. *They had fought in self-defence.*

Ch. XXI.—**35. Justi.** Suitable, *sufficient.* So Livy often.

178 **5. Arbitrium .... ageret.** *Take upon himself the sovereign disposal.* Al. *arbitrum.* But cf. Liv. 24, 45: *arbitria agere;* also Ann. 13, 49.

Ch. XXII.—**10. Concurrentis** may be taken either with *belli* = *gathering*, or with *minas* for *concurrentes* = *simultaneous.* The former is the better.

12. Subversa, etc. *They* (the *legati*) *demolished the works which during a long peace had been built up in the neighborhood of the camp into something like a town.* These appendages of camps were not uncommon, especially on the borders where camps were permanent. They were frequented by merchants, mechanics, and all men of business.

15. Rapi. *Seized* by force and in haste, instead of being procured in the regular way.

17. Medium .... obtinens. *Commanding the centre in person at the head of the flower of the Batavians.*

18. Quo .... foret gives the reason for placing the *Germans* who were peculiarly *truculenti,* on both banks of the Rhine, viz. that he (Civilis) might appear the more formidable.

20. In .... agebantur. *Advanced against the current.*

21. Depromptae ... imagines. The standards of the Germans. Cf. G. 7: *effigies .... detracta lucis, in prœlium ferunt.*

24. Duabus .... situm. *Built* (lit. located) *for two legions.*

25. Armatorum Romanorum stands opposed to *lixarum,* who were *unarmed* and for the most part *provincials.*

Ch. XXIII.—**30. Neque ... malorum,** sc. *fore crediderat: nor had he anticipated that there would ever be such a depth of misfortunes.*

32. Satis placebant = sufficere ei videbantur. Rup. Per attractionem pro *vim et arma satis fore placebat.* Död.

Page

33. Transrhenani. The Germans mentioned, 21, supra. 178

38. Scalis, testudinem. Cf. notes, 3, 27; and Man. and Dict Antiq. sub vocc. for these and other military terms which follow.

1. Armorum incussu. *The dashing of shields and bucklers.* 179 *Arma* = defensive armor, properly for the *shoulders* (*armi*). *Incussu* is post-Augustan. Cf. note, G. 3: *repercussu.*

9. Crates, vineas, tormentis. Cf. notes, 3, 20, and references there.

10. Ardentes hastae = falaricae, but T. avoids the technical name. Cf. Essay, p. 20.

Ch. XXIV.—**15. Obsidio.** Cf. note, 9: *oblivio.*

18. Ipse navibus, sc. celeraturus: *himself intending to go by ship, because he was feeble,* etc. Cf. Essay, p. 15. Al. ipse pavidus.

20. Dissimulatos. *Connived at.*

27. Quin. Cf. note, 3, 20: *quin ferimus.*

28. Traditore. *Traditorem* pro *proditore* apud veteres dici negant interpretes. At imitator noster Graecorum, qui plane sic usurpant verbum παραδίδωμι, παράδοσις: nec inepte Hordeonius *traditor* dici poterat, quia videbatur *traditurus esse* Vespasiano imperium exercitusque. Wr.—**29. Flammavere.** Cf. note, 2, 74.

Ch. XXV.—**1. Tot provinciarum** = auxiliorum ex tot provinciis. 180 —*Repens* = recens. Cf. note, 1, 23.

2. Exemplares instead of *exemplaria,* which is the reading of the common editions, but not of the best MSS. *Exemplares* is found in other late writers.

7. Usurpandi juris, sc. *causa,* which is not unfrequently omitted by T. before the gen. of the gerundive. Cf. Ann. 2, 59: *cognoscendae antiquitatis;* 3, 9: *vitandae suspicionis.* It is a deviation from Latin syntax, and imitation of the Greek idiom. Cf. Z. 663; Gr. 275, III. (5).

13. Quin, etc. *Nay more, that very soldier even charged conscious guilt upon his general.*

Ch. XXVI.—**24. Commeatus** is, properly, *supplies brought in,* by convoy or forage. These were *straitened* (*arcti*) by the circumstances mentioned in the context. Död. takes *commeatus* in the sense of *liberty to go and come,* to avoid tautology with *inopia frumenti.* But cf. 3, 13: *in arcto commeatum.*

28. Amnes .... munimenta. Hendiadys, or rather *vetera .... munimenta* is epexegetical of *amnes.* Cf. G. 29: *ultra Rhenum ultraque veteres terminos;* A. 41: *de limite imperii et ripa.*

29. Quod ... vocabatur. The observation which T. has compressed into a maxim, is explained by Cicero in his more open style. Having mentioned a number of prodigies, he says: Atque haec in bello plura et majora videntur timentibus; eadem non tam animadvertuntur in pace. Accedit illud etiam, quod in metu et periculo, cum credentur facilius, tum finguntur impunius. Cic. de Div. 2, 27. This

Page

180 may account for the many portents and prodigies recorded in the Roman historians, who are often said to be superstitious, when they are giving a true picture of the public mind. See the phenomena of this kind, 1, 86: supra. Murphy.

30. Novesium. A town of the Ubii in Belgic Gaul, not far from Bonn and the Rhine, now Nuys. It derived its name from the *Nova Castra* of the Romans. Cf. *vetera,* 18, supra.

31. Additus .... curarum, i. e. he was associated with Vocula in the command by Hordeonius, the governor of the province.

32. Gelduba was near *Novesium,* now Gelb.

34. Meditamentis (preparations) is post-Augustan.

181 Ch. XXVII.—**6. Quod .... verterat** refers, not to *victi,* but to *culpabant.*

10. Illum refers to Hordeonius at a distance; *hunc* to Herennius Gallus, who was on the spot.

16. Quisque. For its position, cf. Gr. 279, 14; Z. 800. For pl. pred. (*proni*), cf. Gr. 209, R. 11, (4); Z. 367.

Ch. XXVIII.—**22. Alia manu.** Sic MSS. et editiones omnes ante Bipontinos et Oberlinum, qui ediderunt *aliam manum.* Wr. It is a marked case of enallage. *Civilis gives orders* (to his subordinates) *that the Ubii and Treveri be laid waste,* each country by the troops *that happened to be nearest* to it, *and that with another division* they *cross the Meuse and harass the Menapii,* etc.

23. Morinos et extrema. Cf. Virg. Aen. 8, 727: extremique hominum Morini. They dwelt by the British Channel.—*Utrobique.* On both sides, i. e. in both the above expeditions.

25. Romanorum nomen. In appos. with *Agrippinenses,* so called from the empress Agrippina (the Younger), who was born there and sent thither a colony. Ann. 12, 27. Al. *nomine.* But cf. G. 6: *id ipsum* (nomen) *vocantur.* It is a Greek construction. Cf. Essay, p. 23. Ritter encloses it in brackets.

26. Marcoduro. Now *Duren.*

27. Quia .... aberant. Their distance from the *German frontier* made them feel secure.

31. Obsidium legionum, sc. at Vetera, 22. 23, supra.

182 Ch. XXIX.—**1. Quippe .... vana** gives the reason for *inani.*

6. Unde .... acciderat. *From whatever direction a shout happened to have proceeded, in that direction they turn their bodies and draw their bows.* The propriety of *arcus* here has been much disputed, but with little reason.

12. Propellere .... sequi. *They thrust them back with the shield,* and *then follow them up* (and transfix them) *with the lance* For the position of *umbone* and *pilo,* cf. Gr. 279, 5; Z. 798.

Ch. XXX.—**15. Eduxerant.** Cf. note, 2, 34: *in extremam ... educta.*—*Turrim.* See the description of *moveable towers,* Dic. Antiq.

Page

sub voce; also Man. P. 3, 299, 4.—*Duplici tabulato.* *With two* 182
floors or *stories.* Towers were oftener 10, 15 or 20 stories.

16. Praetoriae portae. Every Roman camp had four gates, one on each side, of which the front gate was called the prætorian. Cf. Man. P. 3, 297; Dic. Antiq., *castra.*

21. Suspensum .... machinamentum. Describitur hic *tollenon,* de quo vid. Veget. 4, 21; Liv. 38, 5. Wr. The old-fashioned well-sweep is a rude illustration of the principle of the *tollenon,* though the sweep must of course have had a horizontal as well as a vertical motion. Archimedes employed a similar machine against the Roman fleet. Liv. 24, 34.

22. Praeter .... rapti. *One or more at a time* (observe the force of the distributive, *singuli*) *being caught up and borne aloft in the face of* (lit. past, *praeter* = παρὰ) *their comrades,* etc.

Ch. XXXI.—**28. Caecinae edicto.** Cæcina was consul (cf. 2, 71, and note there), and probably issued an edict for submission to Vespasian. —*Alpinus Montanus.* Cf. 3, 35.—**33. Adigente.** *Administering it.*

34. Dixit. *Said it,* as a necessary form, *without looks or feelings to correspond* (*non vultu,* etc.).

35. Conciperent. *Repeated.* *Concipere verba* is a technic both for *drawing up* and *taking up* a form of words.

Ch. XXXII.—**1. Tanquam ad,** etc., i. e. recognising Civilis 183
as a friend of Vespasian, and regarding the German legions as enemies.

5. Externa .... velaret. And not disguise hostility to the Roman empire under a false pretence of fighting for Vespasian. Cf. *externa* in the same sense, 1, 79; 3, 5.

6. Satisfactum coeptis. *His object was accomplished.*

10. Necem fratris, etc. Cf. 13. *Necem* is a violent death. Cf. note, 3, 68: *jus .... civium.*

15. Dominorum ingenia. And the like *inventions of tyrants.* Cf. *ingenium* in the same sense, 3, 28; 2, 71. Or. renders it *caprices.*

19. Iidem erimus. We shall be as well off as we are now.

Ch. XXXIII.—**23. Parte .... retenta,** sc. to press the blockade of Vetera. Vocula with his army was among the villages of the Gugerni. Cf. 26. 27.—**27. Asciburgii.** Now Asburg.

29. Subsignano milite. Cf. note, 1, 70.

30. Auxilia, etc. *The auxiliaries gathered hastily* (confusedly) *around* the subsignani.

31. Terga .... vertit, i. e. *turn their backs* to the enemy, and retreat *towards their comrades.*

34. Sternebantur. Observe the force of the imperfect: *were being overthrown.*

36. Vasconum. A people of Spain, at the base of the Pyrenees; afterwards settled in *Gascony* in France, to which province they gave their name. Rup.—*A Galba,* sc. when proconsul in Spain. Cf. 1, 49.

Page

184 **4. Quisque** with superl. Cf. note, 1, 46; A. [illegible]9.

5. Prima acie. *In the first part of the battle.* Cf. Gr. 205. R. 17.—*Funduntur* = *sternuntur.* Ritter.

Ch. XXXIV.—**11. Vocula nec .... dein** = Vocula et primum non .. et dein = *Vocula in the first place did not .. in the next place.*

12. Simul .... victusque. *Was defeated as soon as he went out* to battle.—**13. Castra .... movit.** *Marched.*

21. Simul .... intelligebatur, i. e. while the besieged could not doubt the testimony of the witness, given at the price of his life, they were confirmed in the belief that the Romans were victorious, by the sight of burning villages.—**23. Constitui signa.** *To halt.*

25. Certarent depends on *jubet, ut* being understood.

36. Immane quantum. Cf. note, 3, 62.

185 Ch. XXXV.—**2. Corrupta ..... malle.** *Justly suspected, on account of his frequent failures to profit by his victories* (lit. on account of victory so often spoiled), *of preferring a protracted war.*

4. Impedimenta. Baggage-wagons and beasts of burden.

7. Firmo, i. e. not yet having recovered from his fall, 34.

8. Rursum. Again.

14. Manentibus .... castris describes the state in which the cohorts found the camp at *Gelduba,* viz. the same state in which it had been left, as described 26, supra.

15. Non erat dubium, etc., gives the reason why Vocula strengthens his own troops by a detachment from the legions (now relieved from the siege by the retreat of Civilis), and goes to succor the cohorts and foragers.—**19. Indomitum.** *Ungovernable.*

Ch. XXXVI.—**25. Circumsedit,** i. e. returns to the siege. Monboddo complains with some reason of the rapidity and abruptness of the narrative here.

37. Nisi .... evasisset. *But he made his escape,* &c.

186 **2. Stipendia.** Money to pay their wages.—*Oraturos.* *To ask* Cf. Z. 639.

Ch. XXXVII.—**3. Ipsi,** i. e. the soldiers in distinction from the centurions spoken of at the close of the last section.

6. Superiore exercitu. Cf. note, 1, 9. The troops of Upper Germany seem to have favored Vespasian, and refused to act in concert with those of Lower Germany in their zeal for Vitellius. Yet (*tamen,* notwithstanding this refusal) the latter go forward and replace his images.

11. Liberandum .... obsidium. Structura contracta for *liberandum Magontiacum obsidio.* Cf. Essay, p. 17.

13. Satietate .... incruenti. *Satiated with booty, yet not without bloodshed,* as described in what follows: *in via,* etc.

15. Quin et, etc. Commentators find it difficult to discover the connection here. May it not be this: Besides the success of the Ro-

Page
mans in raising the siege of Magontiacum, and slaying many of the 186
enemy on their retreat, the Treveri also (*quin et*) constructed a breast-work (*loricam*) along their border, and fought strenuously against the common enemy (the Germans) for a season.

17. Donec with subj. Cf. note, 1, 35.

Ch. XXXVIII.—**19. Consulatum.** For the chronology, see table, p. 26.

22. Descivisse, etc., depends on *pavores*, or on something implied in *pavores*, e. g. it being rumored that, etc.—*L. Pisone.* Cf. Ann. 13, 31; 15, 18.

24. Naves. The ships that conveyed corn to Rome from Africa, the granary of the city.—*Vulgus*, sc. at Rome. *Vulgus* is subject of *credebat*, on which *clausum*, sc. esse, and *retineri* depend. *Littus* is the shore of Africa.

28. Nec .... rumore. *And not even the victors* (the Flavians) *being averse to the rumor.* Al. *ne victoribus quidem*, etc.

Ch. XXXIX.—**32. Praetor .... vocaverat.** It was his duty in the absence of the consuls. Cf. note, 1, 47.

33. Regibus. Those who had espoused the cause of Vespasian. Cf. 2, 81.

36. Ejurante. *Resigning, retiring from*, sc. the city-prætorship.

6. Majoribusque. T. imitates the poets in annexing *que* to the 187
former of two words, connected by *et*. Cf. 1, 51: *seque et Gallias;* 3, 63, et al. *Que* is omitted here in some copies.

7. Fraterna imagine. *The image* (i. e. the rank and station) *of his brother* Piso, who was adopted by Galba. Cf. 1, 14.

9. Adeo. *Still more.*

18. Egesto has the clause *quicquid turbidum* for its subject, which with *egesto* forms an abl. abs. Cf. Z. 647; Gr. 257, R. 8.

Ch. XL.—**22. Crebra ... confusio.** *Frequent blushing.* This seems at length to have become a settled redness of face, which precluded a blush. Cf. note, A. 45: *rubor.* This use of *confusio* is peculiar to T.

23. Referente Caesare. It was the office of Domitian, as city prætor (cf. 39), in the absence of the consuls, to convene the senate and propose to them business.

27. Quique .... figerentque. *And to examine and replace the brazen tablets of the laws which had fallen down through age.* These tablets were affixed to the statues and the walls in the temples and the forum.

28. Fastos .... exonerarent. *To disburden the calendar defiled by the adulation of the times*, sc. with games and religious festivals in honor of unworthy men, voted and registered especially in the days of Nero. To erase and annul these would of course reduce the public expenses (*modum ... facerent*). Cf. Wr. in loc.

Page

187 **30. Redditur .. praetura.** Cf. 39.—*Postquam .... confugisse.* Cf. 2, 85.

32. Honor. *The honor* without the office. Or as Or. explains, he remained prætor extraordinarius or honorarius.—*Repeti. Resumed* Cf. 10, supra, and notes ibid.

35. Privatim, i. e. out of the senate, in private and social life The particular fact in private life which shed lustre on the day, is mentioned in the next sentence, viz. that Musonius was honored and Demetrius disgraced, as they deserved to be.—*Justum judicium. A just process* or *impeachment.* Al. indicium.

36. Explesse. *To have accomplished* or *carried out.*—*Diversa fama,* sc. *erat,* after which *Demetrio* is dative Demetrius attended Thrasea in his last moments (Ann. 16, 35). Now the same man defends the prosecutor of Soranus: such was the consistency of a philosopher by profession! Brotier.

188 **2. Junius Mauricus.** Cf. note, A. 45: *visus.* Plin. Epis. 4, 22.

Ch. XLI.—**6. Inchoantibus primoribus.** *On the motion of some of the leading members.* Cf. note, 3, 37: initium .... factum. —*Concepit.* Drew up. Cf. note, 31.

7. Certatim is antith. to *ut rogabantur.* The magistrates were innocent, and hence *emulously* volunteered to take the oath; while the rest, some of whom were guilty, waited till *called on for their assent.*

12. Probabant .... arguebant. *The senate approved the religious scruples, but censured the false swearing,* for after all the change of phraseology, it was perjury still. Observe the order: the emphatic word (*probabant*) first, the contrasted words (*religionem, perjurium*) near each other.

19. Scribonios fratres. Cf. Ann. 13, 48. The two Scribonii, whose names were Rufus and Proculus, were put to death by Nero at the instigation of Pactius Africanus, A. U. C. 820.

22. Vibium Crispum. Cf. note, 2, 10.

Ch. XLII.—**26. Messala.** Cf. note, 3, 9.—*Senatoria aetate,* i. e. 25, as fixed by Augustus; in earlier times, 32.

27. Aquilio Regulo. A practised informer. Cf. Plin. Epis. 1, 5; 2, 20; 4, 2; 6, 2; Mart. 2, 74.

28. Crassorum. M. Crassus Camerinus, brother of Piso (1, 48), and Scribonianus Camerinus were accused by Regulus in the reign of Nero. Plin. Epis. 1, 5.—*Orfiti.* Cf. Ann. 12, 41; 16, 12.

29. Sponte ex senatus consulto, i. e. the accusation having been decreed in general by the senate was voluntarily prosecuted by Regulus. The reading is generally thought to be corrupt.

30. Depellendi periculi. Cf. note, 25: *usurpandi juris.*

37. Appetitum ... caput, i. e. Regulus had bitten the lifeless head of Piso in malicious spite.

Page

3. Reliquerat has for its subject all the following clauses of the sentence.—**5. Hiatu,** in the sense of *eager desire,* is peculiar to T. 189

7. Ex funere . . . . raptis. *Torn from the dead body of the republic.*

8. Consularibus spoliis. *The spoils of consular men,* sc. Crassus and Orfitus.—*Septuagies . . . . saginatus. Pampered with seven millions of sesterces. Sestertio* is abl. limiting *saginatus,* the word being constructed just as if it stood without the numeral. Cf. Dict. Antiq., *Sestertius.*

13. Retinete, etc. A beautiful imitation of Cic. in Verr. 2, 31. Ernesti.

15. Marcellum, sc. Eprius. Cf. chaps. 6. 7, supra.—*Crispum* sc. Vibius. Cf. 41.

22. Sed . . . . mores. *But examples last longer than characters* or men. Hence let us establish a precedent for the punishment of informers, which, though not needed under such a prince as Vespasian, will live after he is dead.

Ch. XLIII.—**29. Cluvius Rufus.** Cf. note, 1, 8.—*Perinde. No less,* sc. than Marcellus, touching whose wealth and eloquence, cf. Dial. de Clar. Orat. 5. 8.

30. Sub Nerone. Cluvius Rufus attended Nero in his musical itinerations (Xiph. 63, 14; Suet. Ner. 21), but made no bad use of his influence.

31. Crimine. *With his own guilt,* as an informer, particularly in accusing Thrasea. Cf. 6, supra.—*Exemploque, and the better example of Cluvius.*

34. Regna . . . Caesare. Observe the tact of the court-flatterer, by which he afterwards intrenched himself in the favor of Vespasian.

Ch. XLIV.—**1. Proximo senatu.** At the next meeting of the senate, i. e. on the next day. 190

6. Postquam . . . . itum. *As soon as they met with opposition.*

9. Egressos exsilium. Cf. note, 3, 30: *altitudinem egressa.*—*Octavius . . . . interfecerat.* Ad rem, cf. Ann. 13, 44.

11. Sosianus . . . . exitiosus. Cf. Ann. 13, 28; 14, 48. 49; 16, 14. 21.

13. Pulsi = expulsi. Cf. note, 1, 20: *omnibus suspectis.*

Ch. XLV.—**20. Colonia Seniensi.** A colony established by Augustus in Etruria, now Sienna in Tuscany.

22. Supremorum imaginem. *A mock funeral.*

27. Cyrenensibus. Dat. of the agent. At their instance or accusation.—**28. Repetundarum.** Cf. note, 1, 77.

Ch. XLVI.—**30. Dimissi . . . . congregati.** Cf. 2, 67. 82.

31. Lectus . . . . miles. *Soldiers chosen out of the legions for this privilege* (lit. hope, *spem*). Al. illectus.

32. Promissa stipendia, sc. of prætorians.—*Ne . . . . quidem.*

Page

190 *Not even the Vitellians,* i. e. the prætorians of Vitellius, who were a third class of competitors for the same office.

33. Pelli. *Dismissed.* Cf. note, 1, 20: *omnibus suspectis.—Ferebatur.* A lacuna in the Medicean MS. makes the reading here doubtful.—**35. Stipendia.** *Services.* Cf. note, 3, 75.

37. Quos .... memoravimus. Cf. 2, supra.

191 **1. Intecto** is post-Augustan. So is *commanipulares* below.

4. Primus statim. *The very first.* Cf. note, A. 20: *statim. Statim* here is antith. to *ut vero.*

10. Cervicibus innecti. Poetice for *cervices amplecti.*

17. Firmati jam. Non amplius trepidi, jam confirmato animo. Ruperti

20. Quibus aetas. Those who were 50 years of age and had served 20 campaigns. Orelli.

Ch. XLVII.—**23. Uti videretur,** i. e. that the new government might have the credit of finding the treasury exhausted and so of restoring it. A policy not yet obsolete!

24. Sexcenties sestertium. Six hundred times a hundred thousand sesterces, i. e. *sixty millions of sesterces. Sestertium* is subject nom. of *acciperetur.* Cf. note, 42: *septuagies,* and 1, 20.

27. Legem .... Domitiano. Cf. note, 40: *referente Caesare.—Consulatus .... dederat.* Cf. 2, 71: 3, 55.

28. Censorium. *Due to a censor.—Flavio Sabino.* Brother of Vespasian, slain by the Vitellians, 3, 74.

29. Instabilis fortunae. Compare the insults heaped on his lifeless body (3, 74), with the honors now paid to it.

Ch. XLVIII.—**31. L. Piso.** Cf. 38, and note, ibid.—*Proconsul.* Al. pro consule. Cf. note, 1, 49.

32. Verissime here means *faithfully* and *fully.* Non opponitur *mendacio.* Wr.—*Si .... repetiero. After having gone back and stated a few prior circumstances.* Cf. note, 1, 4: *repetendum.—Supra* = superiora. Cf. note, 1, 65: *invicem.*

33. Talium facinorum = *talis facinoris* by enallage of number. Wr.—**34. Finibus.** Dat. of the *end* after *auxilia.*

36. M. Silanum. Father-in-law of Caligula, by whom he was put to death. Cf. note, A. 4.

38. Duos, sc. the proconsul and the legate.—*Beneficiorum. Offices in their gift.* So Liv. 9, 30: *consulum beneficia* = offices in the gift (not of the people, but) of the consuls.

192 **2. Diuturnitate officii.** The office of proconsul was *annual,* like the original tenure of the consulship, while that of the legate might continue from year to year.

3. Minoribus, sc. the legates, who were of lower rank than the proconsuls.

Ch. XLIX.—**6. Valerius Festus.** Cf. 2, 98; Plin. Epis. 3, 7 12.

8. Affinitate . . . . anxius. His relationship to Vitellius made 192
him the more anxious to avert the displeasure of Vespasian by such services as the death of Piso.

12. Erga in T. denotes either a friendly or *un*friendly relation.

15. Suspecto. Lit. *and to him suspected in peace, war more safe,* sc. than peace itself. Al. suspecta.

16. Alae Petrinae. Cf. note, 1, 70.

19. Galerianum. Cf. 11, and note, ibid.

24. Continuare. Lit. *prolongs* all things favorable, i. e. *proclaims* every thing *still* favorable, in opposition to the *adverse* rumors that had gone abroad. Ritter makes it = *continuo clamare.*

Ch. L.—**1. Consternatio.** Confusion, *disorder.* 193

10. Bebius Massa. Afterwards an infamous informer. Cf. note, A. 45. Hence what follows: *jam tunc . . . . rediturus.*

13. Festus . . . . contendit. *From Adrumetum, where he had stopped to watch* the issue from a place near by, *Festus proceeds rapidly to the legion.* Observe the force of *sub* in *substiterat* = had stood near, and of *con* in *contendit:* stretches all his energies at once towards. Al. tendit. Adrumetum was a Phœnician colony in Africa.

18. Oensium Leptitanorumque. *The people of Oea and Leptis,* two large towns between the Syrtes, now *Tripoli* and *Lebeda.*

21. Garamantas. A people of the interior of Africa, little known, mentioned however, Ann. 3, 74; 4, 23; Plin. N. H. 5, 5, etc.

26. Mapalium is a Punic word: huts or hamlets of the Africans.

Ch. LI.—**27. Vespasiano.** Vespasian was tarrying at Alexandria. Cf. 2, 82; 3, 48; 4, 81.

29. Aggressi. *Adventuring upon.*

30. Vologesi. Cf. note, 1, 40, where the acc. occurs after the form of the third declension (one among many examples of our author's fondness for variety).

32. Ambiri. To be solicited by, to have urged upon his acceptance. Cf. note, G. 18.

Ch. LII.—**1. Titum . . . . dicebatur.** *Titus dicebatur* is the 194
usual construction in the early Latin. Cf. note, 1, 50: *crederetur,* and G. 33: *narratur.*

3. Integrumque, etc. Enallage for *et ut integrum . . . praestaret. Integrum. Unprejudiced* (lit. untouched, entire). Cf. 1, 16: *judicium integrum.*

11. Pietate. *Fraternal affection.* Dom. rewarded Titus for it by hatred, perhaps by poison.

15. Nutabat. *Was balancing,* as it were, on a pivot. Compare with this Vespasian's original plan of starving the city to submission, if necessary, by cutting off supplies from Egypt and Africa, 3, 7. 48, and notes ibid. on *claustra annonae* and *et Africam.*

Ch. LIII.—**18. Restituendi.** *Rebuilding.* The Capitol had

Page

194 been burned down in the civil war. Cf. 3, 71. The senate had voted the rebuilding, under the direction of Vespasian, chap. 9, supra.

20. Contracti. *Brought together* from without, as well as within the city, particularly perhaps from Etruria, their mother country.—*Haruspices.* Cf. note, 1, 27.

23. Serena luce. *On a clear day,* or *with an unclouded sun.*

25. Fausta nomina. Such as Faustus, Salvius, Longinus, etc The Romans attached great importance to auspicious names on solemn occasions (cf. Cic. de Div. 1, 45, 102), as the Greeks did to auspicious words.

26. Patrimis matrimisque. *Whose parents had been married by* the solemn religious rite of *confarreatio* = *confarreatis parentibus genitos,* Ann. 4, 16. Dict. Antiq. sub vocc. Others understand by it: *whose parents were living.*

28. Praeeunte, sc. verba sive formulam precationis. Rup. Cf. note, 1, 36: *praeire.*—*Lustrata .... area,* sc. by leading the victims (a pig, a sheep and a bull) around the area and then sacrificing them. Cf. note, 1, 87.

29. Cespitem, i. e. an altar of turf.—*Redditis. Offered.*—*Jovem .... Minervam.* These were the Capitoline divinities. Cf. note, 1, 86: *cella Junonis.*

36. Stipes. *Masses.*

37. Primitiae. The first ores taken from the mines.—*Ut gignuntur. In their native state.*—*Praedixere* = praecepere. Cf. note, 3, 6: *praedictum.*

195 **1. Annuere** depends on *credita* implied in *creditum.* Wr. *Id* is object of *annuere* and subject of *defuisse creditum.*

Ch. LIV.—**15. Druidae.** Touching the Druids, cf. Ann. 14, 30; Caes. B. G. 6, 13; Turner's Hist. Ang. Saxons, B. 1, chap. 5.

16. Primores Galliarum. Intellige primores Galliarum in urbe praesentes et inde ab Othone missos, ut populares suos adversus Vitellium concitarent. Wr.

Ch. LV.—**20. Flacci .... caedem.** For the murder of *Hordeonius,* cf. 36, supra. For the order of the two names, cf. note, 18, supra.

24. Illi, i. e. Classicus. *Ipse* also refers to the same, and introduces what he *himself* said *of* himself.—*Origo* = stock, *ancestry.*

25. Hostis is *pred. nom.* after *esse* understood. It is a Greek construction and unusual in the Latin. Cf. Hom. Il. 13, 54: ὃς Διὸς εὔχεται παῖς εἶναι. Buttman's Gr. Gr. 179; Kühner, 307, 4; Essay, p. 18. It occurs rarely in the poets, e. g. Virg. Aen. 2, 377: sensit medios delapsus in hostes. Render, *he himself boasted that, from his ancestry* (by birth), *he was more* (*magis* understood as usual with T.) *an enemy of the Roman people than an ally.*

26. Miscuere sese. *Attached themselves to* Civilis and Classicus.—*Hic .... hic,* instead of *ille ... hic.* So Virg. Ecl. 4, 56; Cic

Page

Epis. ad Div. 9, 16. Both are thus brought near, and, as it were, into the presence of the reader. Bach. 195

27. Lingonus. So the best MSS. Al. Lingon But T. uses it as a heteroclite for the sake of variety. Boetticher.

30. Corpore atque adulterio = corpore in adulterium. Roth.

34. Attamen, i. e. notwithstanding the state was averse, still some of the people took part. Agrippinensis was the capital of the Ubii.

38. Capi .... urbem. *The city was on the very eve of being taken*, sc. by the Flavian army.

1. Distineri. *Were kept away.* Al. detineri. 196

2. Dispecturas. *Would decide*, lit. look into, discover.

Ch. LVI.—**4. Haec ... probataque.** See the impetuosity of the Gallic character; so described by Cæs. B. G. 3, 10, and characteristic of the French to this day.—*Pariter* = at the same time, i. e. *no sooner said than approved.*

9. Ceterum vulgus. *The rest*, viz. *the common soldiers.* Essay, p. 17.

18. Quem ... diximus, sc. 18, supra.—*Extra conventum.* This may mean *without the bounds of the confederacy*, or *without the limits of the judicial district.* Cf. note, A. 9. Al. confinium, continentem, etc.

Ch. LVII.—**33. Sacrovirum.** Ann. 3, 40. 46. *Sacrovir* was a leader of the Ædui in a rebellion.—*Vindicem.* Cf. note, 1, 8.

35. Melius, sc. than Galba and his successors, who had treated the Gauls too gently.

37. Infracta tributa. *The reduction of their tribute.* Cf. 1, 8: *tributi levamento.*—*Induisse. Had excited,* or inspired.

2. Novesium. Cf. note, 26, supra. 197

6. In externa verba, i. e. allegiance to a foreign or hostile nation. Boet. instances this use of *externus*, as peculiar to T. Cf. note, 32.

Ch. LVIII.—**11. Pro me.** *Pro* = de. Cf. note, A. 26.

12. Hostium. So all the MSS. The common editions have *honestam*, a conjecture of Lip., to which Wr. objects that the very same death is called *foedissimam* in the next chapter. On the other hand, it is objected to *hostium*, that *the evils arising from the enemy* were not the only nor the chief evils by which Vocula was encompassed. Various other readings have been proposed, but *hostium* still stands in the best editions, though enclosed in brackets in several.

32. Sane ... displiceam. *Sane* = concedo et doleo. Ruperti. Al. *sin.*

34. Toto .... orbe. Hence a monstrous prodigy, for only such would be so widely proclaimed.

37. Tutorin, i. e. Tutorine. *Ne* is the enclitic interrogative particle. The most recent editions do not mark the elision by the apostrophe.

Page

This speech well illustrates the spirit of a Roman soldier, and breathes all the national pride and martial energy of the Roman people.

198 Ch. LIX.—**15. Herennium,** sc. Gallum. Cf. 19. 26, etc.

16. Numisium, sc. Rufum. Cf. 22, supra.—*Sumptis . . . insignibus. Assuming the insignia of a Roman commander,* sc. the fasces, lictors, etc.

20. Altis ordinibus. *Altis* = primis. He made him first centurion.

21. Flagitium navaverat. Praegnanter for operam in flagitio perpetrando navaverat.

23. Agrippinenses. The inhabitants of this colony were opposed to the rebellion. Cf. 55, supra.

24. Superiorem . . . . ripam. *The* (Gallic) *bank of the Upper Rhine.*

25. Pulso. *Driven away,* sc. in flight.

27. Obsessos, sc. at Vetera. Cf. 18 and 35, supra.

Ch. LX.—**35. Donec . . . . orantes.** Observe the high standard of military duty, allowing no extremity of suffering to be an apology for surrender.

199 **2. Leves** = *stripped* of all but clothes and armor.

3. Germani, sc. of the party of Civilis.—*Incautum agmen,* sc. of the Roman captives.

5. Perfugiunt. *Fly for refuge.* Al. profugiunt, which means *flee away,* and is less appropriate with *retro in castra.*

Ch. LXI.—**11. Barbaro voto.** Cf. G. 31.—*Post coepta . . . . arma* limits *propexum rutilatumque : his hair, which, in accordance with a vow common among barbarians, had been suffered to grow long and was stained red* (*rutilatum* = reddened, *rutilum* = red) *ever after the commencement of hostilities with the Romans.* It was not uncommon for the Gauls and Britons to color their hair before entering battle. The custom of letting the hair and beard grow long, till they had slain an enemy or accomplished some act of vengeance, prevailed also among the Germans (cf. G. 31) and was imitated by Cæsar himself (Suet. Caes. 67).

15. Ceterum neque se, etc. A Gallic empire was a mere pretence on the part of Civilis in order to secure the co-operation of the Gauls. His real object was independence and supremacy for himself and his countrymen, the Batavians.

17. Possessione rerum. *Supremacy.*—*Inclitus . . . potior. He had a distinguished reputation and superior power.*—*Fama* is abl. limiting *inclitus.*

19. Nationis limits *virgo.* Cf. 1, 11 : *ejusdem nationis.*

20. More quo, etc. Cf. G. 8, where also *Veleda* is specified. That passage and this taken together show, that in the opinion of T. the Germans actually deemed some of their women divine, and did

Page

not suppose they raised mortals to the rank of goddesses: nec tanquam 199
facerent deas.

27. Quae .... sunt. These were still in the hands of the Romans.—*Vindonissae.* Now Windisch in the canton of Berne, in Switzerland.

Ch. LXII.—**32. Rubore et infamia.** Hendiadys and enallage for *rubentes infamia* = *blushing for shame.*

2. Revulsae = *dereptae,* 1, 41, where see note.—*Inhonora* = 200
squalida; opposed to the *fulgentibus vexillis Gallorum.* Post-Augustan.

5. Debilior. This word usually means maimed or lame. Cf. 81, infra: *debilitas. More disfigured and disabled in mind,* sc. than in looks

13. Initium. Implying that he paid the full penalty afterwards. —*Exsolvendae. Expiating,* lit. paying off.

Ch. LXIII.—**25. Disjecta** instead of *disjectio ejus,* the Latins using few abstract nouns. Cf. Gr. 274, R. 5; Z. 637, and notes supra, 3: *servus affixus;* 1, 1: *conditam urbem,* et al.

Ch. LXIV.—**26. Discreta.** *Separated,* sc. from the Ubii and Agrippinensis their capital.

29. Corpus. Cf. note, G. 39.

34. Inermes. A special indignity to Germans, who did every thing armed. G. 13.

35. Sub custode, sc. a Roman soldier.—*Pretio.* On condition of paying for the privilege.

5. Lucem diemque = light of day, by hendiadys. Observe the 201
author's extreme fondness for pairs of synonyms: *lucem diemque, amicitia societasque, colloquia congressusque.*

8. Quibus .... valent. Cf. A. 21.

10. Ex aequo agetis. Cf. note, A. 20.

Ch. LXV.—**20. Deductis olim.** The original Roman colonists.

21. Provenere = e nobis nati sunt. The sense is post-Augustan.

23. Vectigal et onera. Cf. note, G. 29: *oneribus et collationibus.*

31. Ipsa .... turre, sc. erat, habitabat.—*Edita* is abl. agreeing with *turre.*

Ch. LXVI.—**3. Ausus ... composito.** *Either under a sudden* 202
impulse or according to a preconcerted plan.

8. Movebatur .... condebant. Observe the change of number, representing the *emotion* more as a *common* feeling, and the *sheathing* of their *swords* more as separate, *individual* acts.

11. In fidem acceptos. Cf. note, 1, 37: *in fidem acceperat.*

Ch. LXVII.—**14. Projectis .... monumentis.** *Casting down the monuments of their alliance with the Romans,* i. e. the columns or tablets on which the treaty was inscribed. Touching such **monuments,** cf. Dion. Hal. 4, 26; Liv. 2, 33; 26, 24.

Page

202 **15. Caesarem.** He pretended to have sprung from Julius Cæsar Cf. 55, supra.—**16. Sequanos.** Cf. note, 1, 51.

18. Melioribus. Rup. and Or. say = fortioribus. But rather = *better,* more faithful.

24. Suo loco reddemus, sc. in one of the lost books of this history. Ad rem, cf. Xiph. 63, 3; Plut. in Erot. 25. Sabinus and his wife lay concealed nine years in a subterranean tomb, where she bore him two children. They were at length discovered, brought to Rome and put to death by Vespasian.

25. Resipiscere. *Began to recover their senses.* An inceptive verb.

26. Principibus. Taking the lead.—*Remis.* Hence the modern *Rheims.*

Ch. LXVIII.—**29. In deterius.** Cf. note, 1, 18: *in majus.*

30. Ne .... duces. *Lest the generals, although* (or *however*) *excellent.*—*Gallum Annium.* Cf. 1, 87; 2, 11. 23. 33, &c., in all which the name is *Annius Gallus.* Cf. note, 18: *Flaccus Hordeonius.*—**31. Petilium Cerialem.** Cf. 3, 59, and note, ibid.

33. Libidines here refers to *lust of power,* rather than to his licentiousness. Cf. *spe .... properus* and *flagrantem,* below. See also his ambition, 39 and 51, supra.

203 **4. Utraque munia.** Both of senator and commander of the prætorian guards. It was usual in this age to appoint only men of *equestrian* rank to this office.—*Assumuntur .... ambitionem.* The men of distinction were obliged to follow in the train of Mucianus because he was jealous of leaving them behind, and others attached themselves to him voluntarily from ambitious motives.

6. Accingebantur. *Were preparing* for the war, as we say *were buckling on* (lit. *girding to,* ad and cingere) their armor. Observe the middle sense. Cf. note, G. 39: *evolvuntur.*

8. Si .... invasisset. If he should once enter the army and take the command.

11. Penninis .... Graio. Cf. note, 1, 61.

Ch. LXIX.—**22. Sumi .... geri.** See a similar passage, Sall. Jug. 54. Observe the juxtaposition of the contrasted words *ignavis* and *strenuissimi.* Cf. Gr. 279, 5; Z. 798.

24. Super caput. *Near at hand,* just ready to fall upon them.—*Reverentia fideque.* *Respect for authority,* and a sense of duty.

25. Periculo ac metu. *Danger and the fear of it,* 1, 88, note.

29. Quod .... caput = quis belli dux? Rup. *Quod* is neuter to agree with *caput.*—*Unde ... peteretur* = quis imperator in Gallia. *Rightful authority* (*jus*) and *religious ceremonies* (*auspicia*) were quite inseparable in the view of the Romans. Hence, in their writers, they are often named together, e. g. Liv. 22, 1: *justum imperium et auspicium.* Ernesti.

Page

CH. LXX.—**7. Superiorem . . . ripam.** The banks of the Upper Rhine. 204

9. Vindonissa. From or by way of Vindonissa.—*Sextilius Felix* Cf. 3, 5.

10. Singularium. The meaning of this term is left wholly to conjecture. E. understands by it, troops *in high rank,* next to the prætorians, like *extraordinarii* or *selecti* = *elite.* Wr. horsemen fighting not in companies but as individuals, each for and by himself = *μονομάχους.*—**27. Ut . . . . memoravimus.** Cf. 62.

31. Mediomatricos. Cf. note, 1, 63 : *Divoduri.*

CH. LXXI.—**1. Delectus . . . . habitos,** i. e. the troops levied in 205 Gaul.

5. Recepta juventute. *Having received back* their young men, sc. the levies sent back by Cerialis.

6. Facilius toleravere. They were better able to pay their tribute with the help of their young and able-bodied men.

11. Ne . . . . faceret. *Not to hazard a decisive battle.*

14. Tertiis castris. *After three days' march.*—*Rigodulum.* A town of the Treveri on the Moselle, now *Rigol* or *Réol,* near *Treves.*

16. Insederat. *Had taken possession of.*—*Montibus aut Mosella,* i. e. partly by the mountains and partly by the river. So G. 1: *metu aut montibus.*

19. Aciem . . . . erigeret. Cf. notes, 3, 71, and A. 18: *erexit aciem.*

20. Quem . . . . juvari, sc. putabat, or dicebat.

21. Dum . . . . praevehuntur. *While they are passing by the missiles of the enemy,* i. e. so long as they are exposed to them. *Missilia,* acc. after *prae.* So Wr. and Or. Rup. makes it nom.: while the missiles are flying past them.

22. Ut . . . . manus. *When they came to a close engagement.* Cf. *in manus,* 76, infra; also the Greek, *εἰς χεῖρας ἐλθεῖν.* *Ad manus* is more common.

CH. LXXII.—**27. Eruendae.** *Utterly destroying.* Poetice for evertendae. So Virg. Aen. 2, 611: *totamque ab sedibus urbem Eruit.*

30. E gremio Italiae. Hence particularly dear to the Romans. The colony of the Treveri, on the contrary, was on the confines of Germany.

35. A metu. From, i. e. through fear. The Latins more commonly omit the preposition.

6. Qui . . . . poscebant. The victors asked pardon for their 206 comrades. Al. quis, quia, quos, etc. etc. But *qui* is found in all the MSS. and earliest editions, and it accords with the sympathizing spirit above ascribed to the victors (*solantibus,* etc.) to suppose, that *they* asked pardon for their erring and guilty comrades.—*Vocem preceesque* = *loud entreaties* by hendiadys. So with the other pairs:

Page

206 *lacrimis ac silentio* = *silent tears: pudor ac dedecus* = the shame of their disgrace. *Periculum aut metus.* Cf. note, 1, 88.

12. Ne .... objectaret. *That no one should reproach his fellow-soldiers with their revolt or their* (subsequent) *calamities.*

This section, like 58 and 61 supra, shows the high sense of honor and duty which marked, and in a great measure *made* the Roman soldier.

CH. LXXIII.—**16. Neque ego unquam ... et** = ego et nunquam ... et. Cf. notes, G. 2 *nec ... et,* H. 1, 15: *neque ipse.*

17. Armis affirmavi. *I have demonstrated by arms,* not by words. The address accordingly bespeaks the soldier, rather than the orator.

20. Profligato bello. *Now the war is finished.*

22. Nulla cupidine. Is this said of the *Romans!* Compare the speech of Calgacus, A. 30.

25. Quot proeliis, etc. On the German wars, cf. G. 37 and notes ibid.

26. Teutonosque. This word contains the element of the modern name of the Germans, sc. Deutsche (D is pronounced like T). For the Teutonic war, cf. Vell. Paterc. 2, 8. 12; Plut. Marius.

29. Alius Ariovistus. *A second Ariovistus.* This is the name of a German conqueror of large portions of Gaul, who was himself defeated by Julius Cæsar. Cf. Cæs. B. G. 1, 31–52.

37. Ut non for *quin* or *qui non.* Cf. Z. 539.

207 CH. LXXIV.—**3. Id solum .... quo.** *We have imposed only that* tribute, *by which.*

6. Cetera .... sita sunt. *Every thing else* (except the necessary tributes) *is held in common* by the Romans and the Gauls.

8. Laudatorum principum. *Praiseworthy rulers.* Ant. to *saevi,* sc. principes. In like manner *procul agentibus* is ant. to *proximis.* The design is to set forth the advantages of being governed *by the Romans at a distance,* rather than by *their own princes at home.* See the same argument used by Sulla (Sal. Jug. 102): in quo (sc. the distance of the Romans) offensae minimum, gratia par ac si prope adessemus.

12. Sed neque .... et. *Neque* correl. to *et,* and = et non: in the first place, these are not perpetual, and in the next, they are counterbalanced by the better rulers that intervene.

17. Quid aliud quam bella, etc. So Sallust represents the Roman empire under Julius Cæsar as the universal bond of peace and safety, and Plutarch speaks of it as the anchor of a fluctuating world.

19. Compages haec. *This fabric,* more exactly *bond, enclosure.*

26. Composuit erexitque. Allayed their fears and revived (lit. raised) their hopes.

CH. LXXV.—**27. Tenebantur .... Treveri.** *The country of*

Page
the Treveri was occupied by the victorious army of Cerialis. 207
Cf. 72.

29. Quanquam ..... occultarent. *Although they* (the Romans) *were endeavoring to conceal the news.* Al. nuntii.

32. Si velit .... si mallet. Observe the change of tense. Ernesti proposes to make the reading conform. But the difference in the tense is designed to set forth a difference in the conception. *Si velit* implies a direct offer of the empire with the apparent expectation of its acceptance: *if he will accept,* etc. *Si mallet* expresses a more remote and less anticipated contingency: *if he should prefer,* etc. Cf. Gr. 261; Z. 524. So 20, supra: *si ... obsisteret = if no one shoula oppose them,* a contingency which they could hardly anticipate; *sin ... occurrant = but if arms* (battle) *await them,* as they suppose to be the fact.

35. Ipsas epistolas. Asyndeton for *ipsasque epistolas:* he sent the bearer *and the letters themselves.* There is no force in the *ipsas,* if *epistolas* is connected with *attulerat,* as in the edition of Oberlin.

37. Passum jungi denotes the *ground* on which they censured Cerialis = *for having suffered,* etc.

1. Intutis. *Not fortified.* 208

CH. LXXVI.—**3. Civilis,** sc. censebat, affirmabat. The verb is expressed with *Tutor* below.

5. Gallos is placed before *quid* for emphasis: *the Gauls* alone, *what would they be but a prey,* etc.?

9. Accitas, sc. legiones.—*Adventare,* etc. Cf. 68.

19. Venturos in manus. Cf. note, 71: *ut ... manus.*

20. Adolescentuli .... meditantis. Such as Valentinus.—*Quam.* Sub. magis.

23. Precariam. Cf. note, G. 44: *precario.*

CH. LXXVII.—**29. Viam inter.** Cf. note, 2, 78: *Judaeam inter.*

33. Perrupta ... castra. This and the following clauses are the items of the *universa clades* which Cerialis saw. Hence they should not be separated from it by a period, as they are in many editions.

7. Aut militum .... aut hostium. Flaccus and Vocula had 209
fallen by the hands of their soldiers (36 and 59); Numisius and Herennius by the enemy (70).

CH. LXXVIII.—**13. Consistunt.** *They rally* (lit. stand together).

14. Acies. *A regular line of battle,* ant. to *cohortes et manipulos.*—*Effuso hoste.* Since the enemy were spread out on all sides. Cf. note, G. 30: *effusis.*

24. Sed obstitit assigns the true reason for the defeat of the Gauls, in opposition to the reason which they alleged: *ipsi .. ferebant,* etc.

CH. LXXIX.—**32. Justae .... invocantium.** *Reasonable entreaties of those invoking aid* (lit. calling it in).

33. Ad spem, etc. *To the hope of victory or the purpose of*

Page

209 *revenge.—Namque* = Greek κἀι γάρ. The *que* belongs to some clause that is to be supplied, thus: *and* they had reason to fear, etc., *for Civilis also* (*et*) was in motion as wel as they.

34. Intenderat, sc. animum, as in 1, 48, or oculos, as in 5, 17, = *had directed his attention.* The word means to *increase* in 1, 12, and to *resolve* (our *intend*) in 2, 22, at which places see notes.—*Flagrantissima . . . integra* is abl. abs., denoting the cause (Gr. 257) and limiting *invalidus:* he felt himself strong, notwithstanding his recent defeat, *because his bravest* (lit. most ardent) *cohort was* still left *unharmed.*

36. Tolbiaci. Now *Zülpich,* in the diocese of Cologne.

37. Avertit. *Turned him back,* or *away.*

38. Germanos, sc. Chaucos Frisiosque.

210 **6. Ultro** est *insuper.* Wr. Immo, est *sponte,* non instincti a Civile Classicove aut injuria. Rup. and Or.

Ch. LXXX.—**14. Obtendens.** *Alleging.* Cf. note, 3, 36.

17. Adeo. Cf. note, 1, 9.

19. Averso. Al. adverso. Although Antony was not received according to his expectations, yet neither was he met with coldness or aversion.

22. Prioris vitae criminibus. Cf. 2, 86.

23. Vocare = provocare. Cf. note, G. 14: *vocare hostem,* and Virg. Geor. 4, 76.

Ch. LXXXI.—**28. Statos . . . dies.** *The proper season* (lit. set days) *for the summer winds.—Certa maris.* Connect this with *statos . . . dies* by hendiadys, and render: *when navigation is safe.—Multa miracula.* T. relates only *two* with his usual cautious and incredulous spirit. See others in Suet. Vesp. 7; Xiph. 66, 8.

31. Genua. Cf. note, 1, 66: *arma . . . prensando.—Advolvitur* = se advolvit. Cf. note, G. 39: *evolvuntur.*

32. Monitu Serapidis. In case of sickness, it was the custom of the common people, by the advice of the Egyptian priests, to abstain from food and lie in the temple of Serapis, stretched on the skins of victims slain at the altar. Hence the distempered visions of crazed imaginations, which were considered as light divine and prophecy. Brotier.

33. Superstitionibus. Ad verbum, cf. note, 3, 58. As to the superstition of the Egyptians, cf. 1, 11, and note, ibid.

35. Oris excremento. T. avoids the technical vulgar word *saliva.* Cf. Essay, p. 20.—*Manum aeger.* According to Suet. (Vesp. 7), it was a paralytic *leg.* The testimonies do not agree.

36. Pede ac vestigio = *the step* or *sole of his foot,* by hendiadys. Cf. 1, 66: *vestigia prensando,* and note, ibid.

211 **2. Debilitas.** Here *disease in the hand, impotence.* Cf. note, 62, supra: *debilior.*

Page

3. Medici. The physicians, the priests and the emperor were 211
doubtless in collusion to impose upon the superstitious people, who were equally ready to *be* deluded. The miracles of Christ and his apostles, on the contrary, were wrought in the face of prejudice in the popular mind, and of envy and hatred on the part of all the leading men.

8. Igitur. Cf. note, 1, 29.

10. Laeto ... vultu, erecta ... multitudine. These statements show how ready all parties were to believe the miracle.

12. Utrumque .... pretium. The dynasty of Vespasian was no longer on the throne, so that the imperial favor could not now be the motive of the witnesses. But how was it when they first told the story, and for a long time afterwards? That is the main question. The fact here stated only proves, that having once told the story, the witnesses still persisted in it. Voltaire pronounces these the best authenticated miracles that are to be found in history, sacred or profane. Hume also adduces them with great confidence, as an offset against the Christian miracles. But look at the circumstances above adverted to,—the discrepancy in the written records—the conspiring interest of the emperor, the priests and the physicians to get up a miracle—the readiness of the people to believe it—and the motive of the original witnesses in the first place to tell the story, and then to persist in it. Moreover, the cases are expressly declared to have been such in their outward appearance, that a deception might easily have been practised. The language of T. (*dedita superstitionibus gens*, etc.) makes it more than doubtful whether he believed in any miracle, though he leaves no room to doubt some of the facts. On this subject, see Paley's Evidences, prop. 2, chap. 2.

CH. LXXXII.—**15. Sacram sedem,** sc. Serapidis.

17. Intentusque numini. Consequently with his back towards the door.—***Respexit*** *pone tergum*, i. e. quum ... capturus auspicium ... tandem se convertisset. Suet. Vesp. 7.

18. E primoribus. Suetonius makes Basilides a freedman.

24. Ex nomine Basilidis, i. e. as prophetic of royal dignity or imperial power (βασιλεὺς, king).

CH. LXXXIII.—**26. Celebrata.** *Treated, handled.*

27. Antistites. *Priests* (præstites); those who stand before or preside over religious rites.

28. Qui .... primus, i. e. Ptolemy I. There were 13 Ptolemies in the Macedonian line of Egyptian kings. Ptolemy III. is mentioned in the next section (*quem tertia aetas tulit*).

38. E gente Eumolpidarum. Of the family of the Eumolpidae. Eumolpus was the founder of the Eleusinian Mysteries. Cf. Dic. Ant., Ευμολπίδαι.

1. Eleusine. *From Eleusis*, a town of Attica, near the right 212
bank of the Cephissus at its mouth, where the Eleusinian Mysteries

Page
212 were celebrated, and from which they derive their name Now a mere pile of rubbish, bearing the name of *Lefsina*.

4. Jovis Ditis. Pluto. According to Cic. de Nat. De. 2, 26, Dis = Dives, rich, as Gr. Πλούτων from Πλοῦτος. According to others, = Gr. Δὶς, Ζευς.—*Namque. And* with reason is it considered the temple of Pluto, *for* an image of Proserpine stands by the side of the image of the god.

13. Pythium .... adeant. And consult the oracle.

14. Sors oraculi. Nam responsa plurimorum oraculorum per sortes (*lots*) dabantur. Rup. So also Freund explains it. But Död. considers *response* to be the primitive meaning of *sors* (serere, ἐρεῖν). —*Patris sui. His* (Apollo's) *father*, sc. Jupiter. More properly his uncle, if Jupiter Dis is Pluto.—**15. Sororis.** *Proserpine.*

Ch. LXXXIV.—**17. Allegant.** *They send*, sc. by the servants of Scydrothemis.—*Versus animi. Changeable in his feelings*, wanting in decision of character, lit. turned, or turning himself this way and that. The genitive of *animus* is used in this construction by the later much more than by the earlier prose writers.

23. Destinata deo. *The honors destined for the god.* Or it may be, as Rup. suggests, for *destinata a deo* = the purposes of the god.

26. Adversari regem. Al. aversari. Cf. note, 1, 1: *adverseris.*

28. Circumsedere is the inf. of circumsedeo. Al. circumsidere. —*Major fama.* E. and Wr. make *major* = *more wonderful:* Or. = *better attested.*

32. Rhacotis. A promontory and village, afterwards a part of Alexandria, overhanging the naval station.—*Fuerat sacratum.* The name of Serapis was therefore previously known in Egypt, and the image brought from Sinope now began to be worshipped under the ancient name. Wr. Cf. Dic. Myth. and Biog., *Serapis;* also Man. P. 2, 96, 4.

33. Advectu. *Importation.* Cf. G. 9: *advectam religionem. Advectus*, as a subs., occurs only in T. Al. adventu.

35. Quem tertia aetas, etc. Cf. note, 83: *qui ... primus.*

36. Eundem Ptolemaeum, i. e. Ptolemy III. or Euergetes.— *Ex qua transierit*, sc. to Alexandria. Memphis declined after the foundation of Alexandria.

37. Memphim. The ancient capital of Egypt, situated at the apex of the Delta, whose magnificent ruins are so often visited by travellers; now *Gizeh,* opposite Cairo.

38. Columen. *Capital*, our word column.

213 **3. Plurimi .... conjectant.** *Most conjecture from evident signs in the deity himself, or by indirect inference that the god is Pluto. Plurimi* comprehends more than *plerique.* Cf. 1, 39.

4. Per ambages is ant. to *insignibus ... manifesta.* Observe

Page

the enallage. Cf. note, G. 15: *venatibus, per otium.* See also Essay, p. 17. 213

Ch. LXXXV.—**6. Rerum in Treveris.** Cf. 69–78.

7. Fides. In appos. with *Valentinus.* Cf. the same, 2, 5; also *fiducia,* 2, 4, and note, ibid.

14. Decore is an adv. limiting *interventurum.*

16. In . . . verteretur. *Were at stake,* lit. turned on a critical point.—**18. Ipse.** Domitian.

Ch. LXXXVI.—**21. Intelligebantur,** sc. by Domitian. The real object of Mucianus is explained, 68, supra, viz. to keep Domitian from entering the army, where so ambitious and unprincipled a youth might do great mischief.—*Pars . . . . deprehenderentur. It was the part of submission in him* (Domitian) *not to expose* these arts, i. e. he chose to pursue a submissive course, and thus not appear to understand the motives of Mucianus.

22. Ita Lugdunum ventum. Silius Ital. (3, 607) and Josephus (B. J. 7, 4, 2) give Domitian the credit of bringing this war to a close. They wrote under the Flavian dynasty. Cf. notes, 2, 80 3, 71.—**24. Praesenti.** *If present.*

25. Cogitatione. *Secret counsel.*

30. In altitudinem conditus = in altitudinem animi, tanquam in latebram se condens simulando, tacendo. Bipontines. *Retiring within the depths of his own spirit.* See also Essay, p. 16.

31. Studiumque literarum. Domitian is highly praised for his love of literature by Quintilian (10, 1), and by Sil. Ital. (3, 616). Suetonius (Dom. 2) agrees with Tacitus in ascribing it all to affectation.

33. Contra, sc. to what it really was.

BOOK V.

Ch. I.—**1. Principio** limits *delectus,* not *agebat.* Titus was *selected* to complete the conquest of Judæa at *the beginning of the year* (A. D. 70), as was stated in its proper place, 4, 51.—*Tum* qualifies *agebat,* and refers to the period now reached in the history = *at this time.* 214

2. Privatis . . . . rebus. *When both were private men.* Al. praelatis. But see the same form of words in 3, 65.

3. Certantibus . . . . studiis. *The provinces and armies emulating each other in their zeal.*

Page

214 **4. Super fortunam.** Non modo par, sed etiam superior fortuna imperatoria. Rup. Cf. 2, 1: *quantaecunque fortunae capax.*

5. Decorum. *Elegant* in person and manners. Cf. 2, 1: *decor oris cum quadam majestate,* said of Titus. Wr. takes it in the more general sense of *propriety of conduct,* Ritter connects it with *in armis.*

215 **1. Comitate et alloquiis** = *affability of address,* by hendiadys.

2. In opere. *In the labor* of the camp. Cf. 3, 10: *valli opus.* —*In agmine. In* the fatigue of *the march.*—*Incorrupto . . . honore. Without impairing the dignity of a commander.*

7. Agrippa, etc. For these kings, cf. notes, 2, 81.

9. Multi is the subject of *comitabantur.*

10. Occupandi . . . . vacuum. These words are exactly correlative in signification: the hope of *gaining a prior hold* on the favor of a prince whose affections were *not yet preoccupied.*

Ch. II.—**16. Creta insula.** We find mentioned (1 Sam. 30, 14, Ezek. 25, 16, Zeph. 2, 5) a nation, in the south of Palestine, called *Crethim* (Cherethites in the English version, in the Septuagint, Κρητὰς, Cretans), who were probably connected with the inhabitants of Crete, and who were perhaps confounded with their Jewish neighbors by the authorities from which Tacitus drew. The supposition of a Cretan origin of the Jews may also have been confirmed by a similarity of customs between the two nations, e. g. abstaining from swine's flesh.—*Novissima. Remotest.*

17. Qua tempestate. Poetical for *quo tempore.* Cicero declares, however (De Or. 3, 38), that he should not hesitate to use the expression in prose.—*Saturnus . . . pulsus.* For the dethroning and banishment of Saturn by his son Jupiter, see Dic. Myth. and Biog., *Saturnus;* Man. P. 2, 15, etc. Ad verbum *pulsus,* cf. note, 1, 20.

20. Regnante Iside. Cf. Dic. Myth. and Biog.; also Man. P. 2, 96. 2.—*Exundantem.* Lit. *overflowing,* to which answers *exoneratam, discharged;* the figure being drawn from a stream. *Exundare* is a post-Augustan word.

24. Tradant. Al. tradunt. Cf. Gr. 264, 6; Z. 561.—*Assyrios,* etc. The tyro at the present day hardly need be informed, that this is the only tradition which accords at all with the *facts,* though there are circumstances giving plausibility to some of the others here recorded by T.

25. Proprias urbes. *Cities of their own,* ant. to *parte Aegypti potitos;* or *cities* previously *their own* in Canaan. Gen. 1, 31.

26. Propiora Syriae. The adjacent parts of Syria. Cf. 16, infra: *propiora fluminis.*

27. Clara is taken by Wr. and Rup. in the sense of *clear, manifest,* implying that this is the *true* origin. Others take it in the sense of *illustrious.*—*Initia* is in appos. with *Solymos.*—*Carminibus Homeri.* Il. 6, 184. 204; Odys. 5, 283.

Page 215

28. Conditae .... fecisse. *Gave to the city which they built the name Jerusalem, from their own name.* Al. conditam urbem ... nomine suo.—*Hierosolymam.* Al. Hierosolyma, acc. pl. Both forms are used. See Lexicon. But *Hierosolymam,* though less common in T., stands here in nearly all the MSS. The plural form of this name, as of the names of Athens, Thebes, and many other places, seems to have originated in the incorporation of two or more adjacent towns or fortresses (in this case, Mount Moriah and Mount Zion) into one. For the true etymology of *Hierosolyma,* cf. Kitto's Bib. Cyclopædia, and Rup. ad loc.

It cannot but strike us, familiar as we are with the origin and history of the Jews, as very singular that Tacitus should have contented himself with throwing together such a crude jumble of contradictory fables, instead of going to the original records, or consulting Jewish authorities, in all of which he would have found the same consistent and true story. But it is important for us to bear in mind, in reading this or any other Roman history of the Jews, that they were a secluded and peculiar people; that their neighbors consequently knew little of them, and were prejudiced against them; and that at Rome especially, they were hated by the great for their insubordination, and despised by the learned for their superstition, bigotry and intolerance. It should also be remembered, that the same prejudice extended to the early Christians, who were regarded as a Jewish sect, and are often spoken of by Roman writers in the same terms of hatred and contempt as the Jews. See the famous passage in the Annals (15, 44), where T. calls Christianity an *exitiabilis superstitio.* Yet on both these subjects we find traces of the truth in nearly all our author's errors, and those errors need not destroy our confidence in his veracity as a historian, on subjects about which he was better informed and less prejudiced. Similar and even worse absurdities are found in the other Latin authors respecting the Jews, e. g. Justin, 36, 2, Juv. 14, 96. seq., Martial, Diodorus, &c. Cf. Preliminary Remarks, p. 236.

CH. III.—**30. Orta .... tabe.** Justin (36, 2) speaks of this disease and calls it *scabiem et vitiliginem,* i. e. the leprosy. T. as usual omits the common technical name. Cf. Essay, p. 20. We have here manifestly a corruption, and at the same time an indirect confirmation of the history of the plagues that attended the exodus of the Israelites from Egypt. Ex. 9.

31. Quae .... foedaret. For the subj., cf. Gr. 264; Z. 558. —*Hammonis oraculo.* The original oracle of Ammon was in Lybia (where his worship originated), twelve days' journey west of Memphis. Cf. Plin. 5, 9. But the oracle here referred to was probably in Thebes, which was a city sacred to Ammon, and hence called in the scriptures, No-Ammon, the abode of Ammon. Cf. Nahum, 3, 8, in the Hebrew.

Page

215 **35. Vastis locis,** sc. the wilderness or deserts of Arabia.—***Pet** lacrimas* = inter lacrimas. Wr.—*Torpentibus. Sunk in inaction.*

37. Sed sibimet . . . pepulissent. The reading and the meaning of this difficult passage have been much disputed. It is particularly a question whether *sibimet* refers to Moses or to the exiles, and whether *duci* should be read in the dative or the ablative. *Pepulissent* is also referred by some to the past and by others to the future. Without dwelling on the reasons for it, the following is given as on the whole the most satisfactory version: *but they should trust to himself, a celestial leader, by whose aid first* (the first offered them) *they would soon avert their present calamities.* It will be seen, that in this version *pepulissent* is taken as the subj. of the oratio obliqua used for the future perfect of the oratio recta, and that fut. perf. used for the simple fut. for the sake of implying rapidity, i. e. in the oratio recta, it would be *pepuleritis.* Cf. Z. 511 and 496, 5.

216 **5. Conjectura . . . . soli.** *Led by inference from the grassy soil.*

8. Dicata. Al. dicata sunt. Dicata is nom. pl. neut. Cf. Gr. 205, R. 2, (2); Z. 376, b. The clause is a concise expression for urbs condita et templum dicatum est, with the additional implication, however, of the sacredness of the city as well as the temple.

Ch. IV.—**9. Quo sibi . . . . firmaret.** Rather to preserve them from the idolatry which the rest of the world practised. Put *Deo* instead of *sibi* here (as after *crederent* in the previous section), and T will be quite correct.

12. Effigiem animalis, sc. asini. Cf. 3. This charge of holding sacred the image of an ass is reiterated by very many classic writers. Cf. Rup. ad loc. It gained currency perhaps for no other reason so much, as that it was a convenient topic of ridicule and satire on a despised people. T. expressly declares, in the very next section, that they allowed no images in their temple. The Bipontines explain away the contradiction by supposing that *sacrare penetrali* does not here mean to consecrate as an object of worship, but to preserve as a sacred memorial. But? It may not be amiss to observe, in this connection, that the ass was held in high esteem by the Jews, insomuch that kings and princes rode on asses and were forbidden to multiply horses. Deut. 17, 16; 2 Sam. 8, 4; Mat. 21, 5.—*Errorem sitimque,* i. e. sitim, qua errabundi cruciabantur, by hendiadys. Wr.

13. Caeso ariete. *While the ram is slain* (sacrificed).

14. In contumeliam Hammonis. Ammon was represented and worshipped under the image of a ram's head (Herod. 2, 42), the original idea of the god being that of a protector and leader of the flocks. Cf. Dict. Mythol. and Biog., *Ammon.*

15. Quia. Al. quem.—*Apin.* Apis was a sacred bull at Memphis, which received the highest honors as a god among the Egyptians

For the manner in which the animal was selected, served and worshipped, cf. Dict. of Mythol. and Biog. sub voce.—*Merito* = culpa and causa. Död. and Or. Al. memoria. Pag 216

16. Qua .... turpaverat. T. probably hits here upon a true reason, though not the only one, for the prohibition of swine's flesh to the Israelites. The eating of it exposes to the leprosy, that dreadful scourge of the East. The Levitical law was founded more in reason and the nature of things than is generally supposed.

17. Longam olim famem. Cf. 3. *Olim* here = an adj., *former.*

18. Raptarum .... detinetur. *As a proof of their seizure of grain* (to relieve their hunger), ***Jewish bread is carefully kept without leaven.*** This is true only of the bread used at the feast of the Passover. As to the thing signified by the unleavened bread, T. approximates the truth. Cf. Ex. 12, 15, seq.; Deut. 16, 3. Al. *retinetur.* Cf. Ann. 6, 23: *detinuisset. Detinetur* denotes care and effort.

20. Quia .... tulerit. Cf. close of previous section. *Laborum* refers to their fatiguing journey.

24. De septem sideribus. *Of the seven planets.* Al. *e.* But *de* has the better authority and is often used for *e* or *ex.* Cf. Cic. pro Flac.: *quis de nostris hominibus.*—*Quis .... reguntur.* A doctrine taught by ancient philosophers, as also by modern astrologers.—*Altissimo orbe feratur. Revolves in the highest orbit.* So the Gr. *φέρομαι* is used in the sense of *revolve.* The day of the Jewish sabbath was sacred to *Saturn* among the Greeks and Romans, and is even now called *Saturday.*

26. Vim .... conficiant. *Exert their influence and perform their revolutions by the number seven.* Some recondite astrological notion is concealed here. The number seven was a sacred number with the Jews, as also with many other nations. The principal MSS. instead of *conficiant* read *commearent,* which Wr. retains and considers to be used like the Greek optative.

Ch. V.—**30. Pessimus ... gerebant.** This refers to those Jews and proselytes who dwelt in foreign lands; for, though dispersed over the world, the Jews still retained their nationality, and annually sent contributions (*tributa et stipes*) to support the temple worship at Jerusalem. Cf. Cic. pro Flac. 28; Joseph. B. J. 6, 6, 2. *Patriis* must of course refer to their adopted countries.

31. Et quia, etc. Sub. praeterea auctae. *And* their wealth was still further increased, *because among themselves* they cherished *an inflexible fidelity and lively* (in promptu = an adj.) *compassion, but towards all other nations, hatred as if they were enemies.* The passage is pointed and read differently by different editors. We have given that of Or. and many others, which seems to make the connection more natural than any other.

Page

216 **34. Alienarum** = alienigenarum, *the women of foreign nations.* For the reason of this exclusiveness, see note, 4: *quo sibi*, etc.

35. Inter .... illicitum. But compare the precepts of the dec alogue, Exod. 20, 14. 17; also the severe punishment of adulterers, Deut. 22, 13–29.—*Circumcidere .... noscantur.* Yet we are by no means to understand, that circumcision was entirely peculiar to the Jews. It prevailed among the Egyptians, Ethiopians, Colchians, Arabs, Armenians and other oriental nations. Cf. Herod. 2, 36. 104; Diod. 1, 28; Strab. lib. 17; Joseph. Ant. Jud. 8, 10; 12, 5. Its extensive prevalence implies a physical reason for it, which doubtless exists in those warm climates. On this subject, see a good collection of facts and authorities in Kitto's Bib. Cyclop., art. *Circumcision.*

36. Transgressi .... eorum. *Proselytes.*

37. Idem, sc. circumcision.—*Quicquam .... imbuuntur.* This verb usually and properly takes an abl. after it. But it is here followed by an acc., as if a verb of teaching: *nor are they taught any thing.*

38. Parentes is the object of *habere.*—*Vilia. Worthless things.*

217 **2. Et necare.** *Et* = *both,* correl. to *que,* for both the clauses of this sentence stand related to the increase of population and the desire of offspring among the Jews.—*Agnatis.* Superfluous children, i. e. those born after there was already a sufficient number of heirs, which were put to death by the Romans. Cf. note, G. 19.

3. Animos .... aeternos. So Medicean MS., Or. and Död. Al. animas aeternas.—*Proelio ... peremptorum.* Those who fell in battle or were put to death by their Greek and Roman oppressors were especially incited by the hope of immortality, e. g. the Maccabees and their followers. Cf. 2 Mac. 7. 9. 36. But those Jews who held the doctrine in respect to any, doubtless held it in respect to all.

4. Corpora ... Aegyptio. *They bury their dead after the manner of the Egyptians, rather* (*magis* understood) *than burn them.* Burning was the custom of the Romans under the emperors and in the latter ages of the republic. The earlier Romans buried their dead. Both usages prevailed among the Greeks. Cf. Dict. Antiq., *Funus.* The Jews embalmed (like the Egyptians, though with less care) and buried. Cf. Gen. 50, 2. 26; John, 19, 39. 40; Kit. Bib. Cycl., *Burial.*

5. Eademque ... persuasio. *And* they have *the same anxiety and firm belief touching the lower world,* sc. as the Egyptians.

6. Coelestium contra, sc. persuasio est. *In respect to the gods, their belief is opposite* to that of the Egyptians. For a similar use of *contra,* cf. 2, 97: *experimentum contra fuit.* Wr. joins these words to the following, and governs *coelestium* by *pleraque.*

7. Pleraque. *Very many.* Cf. note, 1, 39, and A. 1.—*Animalia.* Such as the bull of Memphis, the crocodile of Arsinoe, the ibis, the ichneumon, etc. Cf. Juv. 15, 1, seq.; Herod. 2, 40.—*Effigies compositas.* Images made up of the parts of different animals put together Look

Page

at the grotesque and monstrous figures in Egyptian sculpture and painting, and you will be at no loss to understand the force of *effigies compositas*. Cf. note on *Hammonis*, 4, supra.—*Judaei mente*, etc. Cf. G. 9 : *sola reverentia*, and note ibid. We have here a sublime idea of one great, supreme and governing Mind ; of one omnipotent, eternal God. It is astonishing that T. did not pause in deep reflection upon what he could so well describe. Murphy. Ad verba, cf. Essay, p. 17. 217

10. Imitabile. The common editions have *mutabile.* But that is included in *interiturum*. Cf. Wr. in loc.

13. Sed quia. The force of *quia* extends to *reperta,* and the apodosis commences with *Liberum.*

14. Hedera. The Jews had not so much as a name for ivy in their language. But they bore branches of willow and other trees at the feast of Tabernacles. Cf. Rup. in loc.—*Vitisque aurea.* A vine wrought in pure gold of a thousand talents' weight is mentioned by Josephus, as an ornament. Cf. Ant. J. 15, 11.—*Templo* for *in templo.* Cf. Essay, p. 12.

15. Liberum Patrem. Properly the old Italian god of planting, particularly of the vine, though the name is often applied by the Roman poets to the Greek Bacchus, as it is here by T. The name is probably derived from *liberare*. Cf. Dict. Biog. and Mythol. Others derive it from *libare.*

Ch. VI.—**19. Terra finesque** = fines terrae. *The boundaries of the country.*

20. Phoenices. The people put for the country, as *Gallis,* etc. G. 1.

21. Septentrionem .... prospectant, sc. *terra finesque,* lit. the frontiers look towards the north for a great distance alongside of Syria, i. e. *the northern frontier stretches for a long distance on the confines of Syria.* Cf. 3, 60 : *locus late prospectans.* Notice the etymology of *septentrionem* in the lexicon.

23. Rari imbres. True of the summer. The winter is the rainy season in the East.

24. Palmetis. Dat. of possession after *sunt* understood.

26. Pavent venae. A fiction of course. Till the present century, the East has always been to Europeans the land of romance.

27. Praecipuum .... erigit, sc. terra. *Libanum* is acc. after *erigit.* Cf. G. 27: *sepulcrum caespes erigit.* The reader will observe the highly poetical turn of expression in this, as also in many other phrases here, e. g. *pavent venae, fidumque nivibus, Jordanem alit, volucres patitur, fugit cruorem.* T. is very fond of poetical descriptions. Compare that of Britain, A. 10, and notes ibid. It may be attractive, but it is one of those dulcia vitia which should not be imitated. Far preferable is the simplicity of Cæsar and the Greek historians.

Page

217 **29. Fidumque nivibus.** Faithful to the snow, i. e. affording a safe and permanent resting-place.—*Idem*, sc. Libanus.

32. Sapore corruptior. *In taste more offensive*, sc. than the sea

33. Neque vento impellitur. Compare with this the following from the letters of Lieut. Lynch of the recent U. S. Exploring Expedition: "The boats, heavily laden, struggled sluggishly at first, but when the wind freshened to a gale, it seemed as if the bows, so dense was the water, were encountering the sledge-hammers of the Titans, instead of the opposing waves of an angry sea. . . . . When we were near the shore, and while I was weighing the practicability of landing the boats through the surf, the wind suddenly ceased, and with it the sea rapidly fell, the ponderous quality of the water causing it to settle as soon as the agitating power had ceased. Within five minutes, there was a perfect calm, and the sea was unmoved even by undulation."

34. Suetas . . . volucres. A pure fiction.—*Incertae . . . ferunt. The waves, if waves they may be called, bear up things thrown upon them, as if placed on a solid structure*, e. g. on a boat. *Incertae*, lit. of a *doubtful nature*, sc. because they exhibit so imperfectly the *motion* of waves, or the fluidity of water. The great specific gravity of the Dead Sea is well authenticated, and explains the remarkable buoyancy attributed to its waters. Cf. Robinson's Researches in Palestine, vol. ii. p. 213.

35. Periti imperitique . . . perinde. The use of *perinde* with *que* as a connective between the things compared is peculiar to T. and writers of his age. Cf. Freund and Boet. Lex. Tac.

36. Certo anni. In the autumn.—*Bitumen.* Hence the name of the lake, Asphaltites. Cf. Plin. N. H. 5, 16.—*Egerit.* It sends up, casts forth, from *e* and *gero*.

218 **4. Sic veteres auctores,** e. g. Plin. N. H. 7, 13; 28, 23; Joseph. B. J. 4, 8. But how absurd, as T. fully perceived.

Ch. VII.—**10. Fulminum jactu.** The use of *jactu* here has been objected to, and *ictu* and *tactu* have been substituted for it. But *jactu* is justified by the example of Cic. in Cat. 3, 8; de Div. 2, 18; Liv. 28, 27, et al. Ad rem, cf. Gen. 19, 24. 25.

11. Vestigia, sc. of ruined cities. Strabo (16, 2) and Josephus (4, 8, 4) both testify to the existence of these ruins. See the names of the five principal cities of the plain, Gen. 14, 2.

12. Nam cuncta, etc. *For all* the productions of the soil, *whether of spontaneous growth or cultivated by the hand of man, either in the state of herbage or of blossom, or when they have grown to maturity with their usual outward appearance*, etc. Al. *herbae tenues aut flores.*

14. Atra . . . vanescunt. See a similar account in Joseph. B. J 4, 8, 4. Compare also the allusion to the vine of Sodom and the fruit of Gomorrah, Deut. 32, 32. The apples and grapes of Sodom are a proverb among the Arabs to this day. Modern travellers find in that 218 vicinity a plant or tree (the Solanum) whose fruit answers in many respects to the description of T. and other ancient writers, and bears the popular name of the grapes of Sodom. Cf. Robinson, ii. p. 236. 472.—*Ego.* Inserted for emphasis, like our *for my part.*

15. Sicut .... concesserim, ita. *While* (though) *I might admit,* etc. *yet,* etc. For *concesserim,* cf. note, G. 2: *crediderim.*

16. Halitu lacus is emphatic, as its position shows, and it limits not only *infici* but *corrumpi.*—*Infici. Poisoned,* as it were, i. e. made unfruitful. *It is by the exhalations of the lake that the soil is made unfruitful, and the surrounding* (lit. poured over or lying above) *atmosphere rendered unwholesome, and for that reason the crops and fruits decay.*

18. Juxta = pariter.—*Judaico mari.* The Mediterranean. It was on this coast that the manufacture of glass was accidentally discovered by some mariners, who having a cargo of nitre used lumps of it for andirons, which being melted in connection with the sand formed glass. See the account of the discovery and a description of the country at the mouth of the Belus, corresponding with this of T., in Plin. N. H. 36, 65–67.

20. Excoquuntur is poetical.—*Modicum.* According to Pliny, half a mile; according to Josephus (B. J. 1, 2, 10), only a hundred cubits.—*Et* = et tamen.—*Egerentibus,* sc. arenam.—*Inexhaustum. Inexhaustible.* Cf. G. 20: *inexhausta pubertas;* Virg. Aen. 10, 174: *inexhausta metalla.* So invictus = invincible. Z. 328. A. 33, note.

Ch. VIII.—**22. Magna .... dispergitur.** *A large part of Judæa is sprinkled over with villages.* A more simple and usual mode of expression would have been: villages are scattered over a large part of Judæa.

23. Genti caput. Al. gentis. *To the nation,* i. e. in their estimation.—*Immensae .... templum.* Touching this temple, which was built by Herod the Great, and which exceeded even Solomon's in magnificence, cf. Joseph. Ant. J. 15, 11, 1–7; B. J. 5, 5, 2–6; Kit. Bib. Cyclop., *Temple;* John, 2, 20: Forty and six years was this temple in building, i. e. in being completed. The principal part of the work was done in eight years.

24. Primis .... clausum, i. e. there were three distinct walls: the first enclosing the whole city, the second the palace, and the third or inmost the temple. Cf. 11: *alia intus moenia regiae circumjecta;* and 12: *templum .... propriique muri.* Observe the author's fondness for variety of expression, *dein* for *secundis,* adv. for adj.

26. Arcebantur, sc. all, Jews as well as Gentiles. At the time this history was written, the temple had been destroyed. Hence the propriety of the past tense, for which Ernesti would substitute *arcentur.* The imp. here denotes customary past action. Compare with

Page

218 this passage of T., Luke's account of the people praying without, while Zachariah went into the temple to burn incense (L. 1, 9. 10).—*Assyrios penes.* Observe the anastrophe, of which T. is peculiarly fond.

27. Despectissima, etc. See remarks at close of notes, 2, supra, and Preliminary Remarks, p. 236.

28. Macedones. Alexander and his successors, who reigned in Syria till its conquest by the Romans.—*Praepotuere.* Observe the force of the *prae :* before others, pre-eminently.—*Rex Antiochus.* Antiochus Epiphanes, the cruel enemy and persecutor of the Jews, king of Syria, A. C. 176–164.

31. Nam.... desciverat. This passage involves so serious a chronological difficulty, that the commentators resort to emendations of the text to effect a solution. Arsaces, the founder of the Parthian state, revolted from Antiochus II. almost a century before the war of Antiochus Epiphanes with the Jews. Wr., Or. and Död. suppose that T. confounded the two Antiochi, and thus fell into an anachronism. Ernesti regards the passage as an interpolation. Brotier and Rup. suggest emendations. The Bipontines understand by Arsaces, one of the successors of Arsaces I., for it became the family name. Cf. note, 1, 40: *Arsacidarum.* This will remove the difficulty, if we may also take *desciverat* in a sense applicable, not to the original revolt, but to the continued rebellion and war; for that Antiochus Epiphanes was engaged in a war with the Parthians appears from the first and second Books of the Maccabees, where, as in the poets, they are called Persians.

32. Macedonibus invalidis. The successors of Antiochus Epiphanes were comparatively feeble sovereigns.—*Nondum.* *Not yet.* The Parthians afterwards got possession of Judæa. Cf. 9.

33. Sibi.... imposuere. The Maccabees, having thrown off the yoke of Syria, at length made the high-priesthood hereditary in the Asmonæan family, and finally assumed the *name* of kings, and transmitted it together with the regal power (which they had long exercised) to several generations. Kingly power, however, corrupted the truly virtuous and heroic character which originally belonged to the family, and they became for the most part monsters in crime and cruelty, and reigned only amid commotions till the Romans extended their conquests over Judæa. Cf. Joseph. B. J., B. 1.

219 CH. IX.—**1. Romanorum.** Placed first in emphatic opposition to the Macedonians, Parthians, etc., spoken of in the last section.—*Domuit.* A. U. C. 691; B. C. 63. Pompey was invited to Jerusalem by the rival claimants of the kingdom.

2. Templum, etc. He entered not only the outer temple, but the holy of holies, abstaining however from plunder and content with imposing an annual tribute. Cf. Joseph. Ant. J. 14, 4; Flor. 3, 5; Cic. pro Flac. 28.

3. Nulla.... effigie. Al. nullas effigies. Ad rem, cf. 5: *nulla* *simulacra . . . templis sinunt;* and note, 4: *effigiem animalis.—Sedem*, sc. dei. The seat or throne, which in Greek and Roman temples was occupied by the image of the god.—*Arcana* = penetralia. It suggests, however, a little more of the idea of secrecy and mystery.

5. Provinciae, sc. Orientis, Judæa and the neighboring provinces. These fell to Antony in the division of the Roman empire between the Triumviri—Octavius, Antony and Lepidus, B. C. 36.

6. Rex Parthorum. Cf. note, 2, 25: *rex Epiphanes.—Interfectus . . . . Ventidio.* Cf. notes, G. 37: *amisso . . . . Pacoro,* and *Ventidium;* also, Ant. J. 14, 13. 14. 15.

7. Redacti is here used in its original sense: *driven back.*

8. C. Sosius. Appointed to the command in Syria by Antony, B. C. 34.—*Herodi.* Herod the Great was raised to the throne by Antony and Octavius (then acting in concert), with the approbation of the senate, B. C. 40.

9. Victor Augustus, i. e. having gained the victory over Antony in the battle of Actium.—*Auxit. Enlarged* its boundaries. Herod is said to have gained the favor of Augustus by magnanimously avowing and dwelling on the warmth of his attachment to Antony, and the great services he had rendered him. He had not, however, taken an immediate part in the civil war, being happily employed during that time by Antony in a war with the king of Arabia. Cf. Dict. Biog. and Mythol., *Herodes.—Nihil . . . . Caesare. Without waiting for* the sanction of *Augustus.*

10. Simo quidam. A servant of Herod, not the Simon Bargioras mentioned in 12, infra, though Rup. confounds the two, and thus involves T. in a contradiction with other authorities touching the execution of that chief at Rome. Simon was a very common name among the Jews.

11. Quintilio Varo. Afterwards defeated and slain with his army in Germany. Cf. note, G. 37.—*Obtinente Syriam.* Governor of Syria.

12. Tripartito. Herod left his kingdom by will to his three sons —Archelaus, Antipas and Philip, and the will was confirmed by Augustus, though without the regal title. Joseph. Ant J. 17, 8–11.—*Sub Tiberio quies.* Cf. Ann. 2, 42.

13. C. Caesare. Caligula. See the full account of this by Philo (Legatio ad Caium), who was sent on an embassy to divert the tyrant from his purpose; also Joseph. Ant. J. 18, 8, 2–9.

15. Regibus. The descendants of Herod.—*Ad modicum redactis.* Reduced to narrow limits.

16. Judaeam provinciam. Judæa was united with Syria, as a Roman province, with Cesarea for the governor's residence. Cf. Ann. 12, 23; Acts, 23, 23–4, and 25, 1. 4. 6.—*Equitibus . . . permisit,* i. e. he intrusted it to their government, with the title of Procurator. Cf.

Page
219 10: *Florum procuratorem.* Among the procurators, previous to the age of Claudius, was Pontius Pilate. Ann. 15, 44; Joseph. Ant. J. 18, 3. 4; Matt. 27, etc.

17. Per omnem .... libidinem. We see in the character here given of Felix, a good reason why he trembled while Paul reasoned before him of *justice, continence and a judgment to come* (Acts, 24, 25), as well as a striking illustration of the Apostle's boldness in thus indirectly arraigning his own judge.

20. Progener. *Grandson-in-law,* sc. by marriage to his granddaughter (*nepte*) Drusilla. The word is post-Augustan.—*Claudius nepos.* Claudius was son of Antonia, the daughter of Antony.

Ch. X.—**21. Patientia.** *Submission.*

22. Procuratorem. Cf. note, 9: *equitibus . . . permisit.* Florus was a wicked and cruel governor. Cf. Joseph. Ant. J. 20, 9. 10; Suet. Vesp. 4.—**23. Cestium Gallum.** Joseph. A. J. 20, 10; Suet. Vesp. 4.

24. Fato aut taedio. *In the course of nature or from weariness of life,* i. e. by his own hand.

25. Missu Neronis. Cf. 1, 10.—*Fortuna . . . ministris.* These are all the *means* of his success.

27. Hierosolymam. Cf. note, 2. Al. Hierosolyma. But in both these places, the best authorities have Hierosolymam.

28. Civili bello, sc. of Galba, Otho, Vitellius and Vespasian.

29. Pace .... parta. By the triumph of Vespasian's arms.—*Et* = etiam. *The care of foreign affairs also,* as well as Italian.

30. Iras, sc. of Vespasian.—*Cessissent,* sc. to his authority.

33. Hierosolymorum. Here the pl. form occurs in all the MSS T., with his usual fondness for variety, interchanges the two forms. Cf. note, 2.

Ch. XI.—**35. Rebus secundis** instead of *si* res secundae forent, to vary the expression from the ant. clause, *si pellerentur.*

37. Ambigue certavit. Josephus says (B. J. 5, 2), that Titus was almost routed and the tenth legion was driven from its camp.

220 **1. Proelia serebant.** *Joined battle.* Cf. Essay, p. 17. Al. ferebant.

5. Roma .... voluptatesque. Compare the character of Titus, as given, 2, 2.

6. Morari videbantur. *Those* (treasures and pleasures) *seemed to linger.*

7. Arduam situ. On the site of Jerusalem, cf. Joseph. 5, 4. 1. 2; Jahn's Archæol. 23. 24; Kitto's Bib. Cyclop.

8. Duos colles. Four in all, but two principal ones. Cf note, 2, supra: *Hierosolymam,* and places just cited.

9. Obliqui .. sinuati. *Projecting outward or retiring inward* This was a common way of building walls among the Romans, for the reason which T. assigns. Cf. Veget. 4, 2.

11. Sexaginta pedes. Al. *sexagenos.* But the distribution is required only in the valleys: *centenos vicenosque* = *a hundred and twenty feet in each.*

13. Procul .... pares. *Appearing of equal height* (whether on higher or lower ground) *to those who beheld them from a distance.*

14. Regiae. Built by Herod on Mount Zion. Cf. Joseph. Ant. J. 1, 20, 7.—*Turris.* Arx potius dicenda quam turris. In ea enim atria, balneae, aulae; ipsaque in angulis cincta quatuor aliis turribus. Brotier.

Ch. XII.—**16. Proprii muri,** sc. templo sunt: *it has walls of its own,* besides those which encompass the whole city. Cf. note, 8 *primis .... clausum.*—*Labore* ad magnitudinem murorum, *opere* ad eorundem qualitatem et artem referendum est. Död.

18. Fons perennis. Jerusalem has always been found to possess an inexhaustible supply of water for the most protracted siege, even when the besieging armies, as for instance that of the crusaders, have suffered intolerably from thirst. A mystery still overhangs the source of this supply. Large cisterns are known to exist. But "there is also good ground to believe, that there has also been from very ancient times an unfailing source of water derived by secret and subterranean channels from springs to the west of the town, and communicating by other subterraneous passages with the pool of Siloam and the fountain of the Virgin in the east of the town." Cf. Kitto's Cyclopædia, art. *Jerusalem, Waters of;* Strab. Geog. 16, 2, 40.

19. Cavati .... montes, i. e. the mountains, on which the city was built, were scooped out into subterranean caverns. These were used for places of concealment, as well as for cisterns of water. Cf. Xiph. 66, 4; Ammian. Marcel. 19, 5, 4. Here as usual T. avoids the technical expression, *specus subterranei.*—*Piscinae cisternaeque.* Immense cisterns of great antiquity still exist within the area of the temple, supplied partly by rain-water and partly by an aqueduct from Solomon's pools, and which of themselves would furnish a tolerable supply in case of a siege. Cf. Bib. Cyclop., art. *Cisterns.* See also for many interesting and instructive details on this whole subject, Robinson's Researches, vol. i. pp. 479–516, and Olin's Travels, vol. ii. pp. 168–181.

25. Magna colluvie. *A great conflux* from the country, as well as from the cities already destroyed by the Romans. The siege of Titus took place at the time of the annual feast of the Passover, when all the adult male population were expected to go up to Jerusalem.

27. Tres duces, etc. Cf. Joseph. B. J. 5, 1–6.

28. Quem ..... Bargioram, i. e. son of Gioras. This clause stands after Joannes in the Medicean MS. and the earliest editions. It may perhaps have been written so by T. through ignorance. But that the surname belongs to Simon is evident from Joseph. B. J. 2, 23, and 4, 7.

Page

220 Ch. XIII.—**37. Prodigia.** Ad verbum, cf. note, 1, 3. Ad rem, compare the fuller account of these prodigies in Josephus (B. J. 6, 5, 3; 7, 31), and with both histories compare the predictions of Christ (Mat. 27, 45. 51; Luke, 23, 44. 45). The Roman and the Jewish historians both strikingly confirm the prophetic character and divine mission of the great Teacher, in whom neither of them believed.

38. Superstitioni. See the etymology of the word in note, 3, 58. It is commonly used by T. in a bad sense, as here.

221 **2. Exapertae ... fores.** These doors or gates were of brass, and could scarcely be opened by twenty men. Cf. Joseph. B. J. 6, 5, 3. *Exapertae* is found in no other classic writer. It appears in Jerome's confessions.

3. Delubri. Probably from *de* and *luo* = the place of expiation. Freund.—*Excedere deos. That the gods* (the guardian divinities of the temple) *were departing*. Compare with this the Roman custom of *evoking* the gods from the cities which they besieged. Plin. 28, 4.

4. In metum trahebant. *Construed as a ground of fear*, i. e. as ominous of evil. So Ann. 14, 32: *ad metum trahebant. Trahere* is used in the same sense in 3, 3.

5. Antiquis .... literis, i. e. the books of the prophets, which are full of prophecies of the Messiah, and some of which, e. g. Daniel, fix with great definiteness the time of his coming (*eo ipso tempore*). The Jews understood these to promise a temporal deliverer and conqueror. Hence the universal expectation, that at this very time *the East should become powerful, and persons proceeding from Judæa should become masters of the world.* Language happily descriptive of the spiritual conquests of Christ and his apostles! Josephus and Suetonius use very similar language. B. J. 6, 5, 1; Suet. Vesp. 4.

7. Quae ambages .... praedixerat. *Which oracle was to be accomplished in Vespasian and Titus,* who had command in the East, and thence marched to the sovereignty of Rome. Such an interpretation would be easily adopted by a Roman historian, especially one who had received favors from the Flavian dynasty (cf. 1, 1). It is even countenanced by Josephus, in compliment doubtless to the same princes. B. J. 6, 5, 1. Al. praedixerant. *Ambages* is used by other writers only in the pl. and the abl. sing. Cf. Ann. 6, 46.

10. Ne adversis .... mutabantur. Nor have they been by all the calamities that have befallen them through eighteen centuries of persecution

12. Sexcenta millia. Josephus (B. J. 6, 9, 3. 4) and Zonaras (6, 26) estimate the number who *perished* in and after the siege at eleven hundred thousand. Others make it still larger. Ernesti remarks, that the number of the slain in battles and sieges is the most frequent subject of discrepancy in all history.

Page

13. Plures quam pro numero, i. e. more than the fourth or fifth part, that are usually reckoned able to bear arms. 221

15. Hanc adversus urbem. *Hanc* is put first, as the emphatic word: *such* was the city against which, etc. T. allows himself in such liberties oftener than most Latin authors.

16. Subita belli, lit. sudden modes of warfare. Cf. A. 37. Here it manifestly refers to *carrying the city by storm,* in contradistinction to the gradual approaches of a regular siege. The use of *abnuere,* in the sense of *forbidding a thing,* belongs to the later Latin, and is a favorite usage of T. Cf. Boet. Lex. Tac.

The foregoing thirteen sections are all that remain of our author's history of the Jewish war. The major part of his entire Histories is lost (cf. Preliminary Remarks, p. 231), and, with the rest, his narrative of the destruction of Jerusalem, a tragic scene which T. must have described with great power—fit theme for such a master, as he was a master fully adequate to such a theme.

Ch. XIV.—**21. Malam .... pugnam.** *The unsuccessful battle,* or defeat, described 4, 77. 78

23. Tutus loco. The security of the situation involves the first reason. Observe the varied grammatical construction, by which T. chooses to express the same logical relation.—*Et ut .... animi.* This clause assigns a second reason why Civilis encamped at Vetera (which he had previously taken and plundered, 4, 60).

24. Eodem. Old dat. used adverbially = *to the same place.*

26. Post victoriam, sc. that gained by Cerialis and the 21st legion over Civilis. Cf. 4, 78.

28. Arcebat. *Hindered,* sc. an engagement. Observe the author's conciseness.

29. Addiderat, i. e. had interposed as an *additional* obstacle to an engagement, over and above the *natural wetness* of the plains (*camporum suopte ingenio humentium*).—*Molem* = a dam of wood or stone; *agger,* a dike of earth. Or.

30. Ea .... forma. *Such was the nature of the country* (locality).—**33. Proceritas corporum.** Cf. G. 4: *magna corpora.*

Ch. XV.—**35. Ferocissimo cuique.** Dat. of the agent = a ferocissimo quoque. Cf. notes, 1, 86: *auctoribus,* and 3, 12: *Vespasiano.*

37. Arma, equi. Notice the asyndeton. The arms were first dropped by the horsemen in their trepidation, and then they sunk to the bottom (*haurirentur*).

1. Pedestri acie. *A land fight* in opposition to a naval battle (*navali pugna*). So *pedestris* is often used by the best Latin authors, like πεζοὶ, πεζομαχία, etc., in Greek. 222

6. Egredi paludem. Cf. note, 4, 44: *egressos exsilium.*

Ch. XVI.—**17. Propiora fluminis.** *The parts nearer the river. Propior* and *proximus* may be followed by the gen. in this sense. Cf

Page

222 3, 42: *proxima litorum;* Ann. 3, 1: *proxima maris;* Sall. Jug. 48: *fluminis propinqua loca;* Lucr. 4, 339: *propior caliginis aer.* So Wr. Others take *propiora fluminis* to mean *the parts of the river nearer the bank,* where the Germans could fight to advantage (cf. 14), and whence they might annoy the flank of the Romans. So Freund seems to understand it. Vid. sub voce. Cf. note, 2: *propiora Syriae.*

19. Cerialis, sc. memorat.

20. Ut . . . exciderent. Al. exscinderent. Wr., Dōd. and many others place a colon after *exciderent,* and make it depend on a verb of entreaty or command understood. But such a verb is not appropriate to the previous clause; and in such a case the *ut* would be omitted. Cf. 3, 5: *celeraret;* 3, 10: *injicerent;* 3, 68: *retinerent,* et passim.

23. Quod roboris fuerit. This clause is in app. with *Germanos.* The Germans constituted *all the real strength* of Civilis.

25. Proprios . . . . legionibus. We learn from 4, 68, that the 14th legion had been summoned from Britain; the 6th from Spain, where it seems to have taken the lead in proclaiming Galba emperor (cf. 1, 4); and the 2d was a recently enlisted legion—hence *illa primum acie . . . . nova signa,* etc.

29. Praevectus. Passing along the lines, before (*prae*) the legions.—*Manus tendebat.* As a sign of entreaty. Cf. 1, 36.

Ch. XVII.—**34. Silentem . . . aciem,** i. e. he not only addressed his troops, as Cerialis had addressed the Romans, but they responded with shouts. Or. Ita dicimus *silens* vel *tacitum* iter facere. Wr.—*Locum,* sc. Vetera. Cf. 14, and notes there.

223 **2. Dum . . . . impediunt.** The general rule requires the subj. in such dependent clauses in the oratio obliqua. Cf. Gr. 266, 2; Z. 603. But when the dependent clause expresses a *fact* independent of the speaker's opinion, it is put in the ind. Gr. 266, 2, R. 5; Z. 603.

5. Gnaros, in the passive sense (known to) is found only in T.—*Rhenum . . . . deos.* Probably Civilis means to speak of the Rhine as a divinity, and so it is represented on some ancient coins. See a similar appeal to the sun and stars, as divinities, by a German chief, in Ann. 13, 55, and Grote's note on the same, Hist. Greece, vol. i. p. 465. The word Rhein = a stream, in Celtic or old German.

6. Capesserent. Subj. for the imp. of the oratio recta. Z. 603, c.

9. Ita . . . . mos. Cf. G. 11.

11. Neque . . . . et. Correl. Our soldiers *on the one hand* not entering the marsh (cf. 14. 15, supra), *and* the Germans *on the other* assailing them (*saxis glandibusque*) to draw them off, sc. into the marsh.

Ch. XVIII.—**16. Quam . . . . retulimus.** Cf. 14, supra, where and in 15, see incidents similar to and illustrative of those here narrated.

20. Terga . . . . promittens. Lit. *promising him the rear of the*

Page

enemy, i. e. to bring the cavalry upon their rear, if sent agreeably to his suggestion. Others take *terga* in the sense of *flight, rout*. 223

21. Extremo paludis. Abl. of the way. Cf. 4, 15: *Oceano;* 4, 68: *Alpibus.*—**22. Illa,** sc. parte.

27. Institit, sc. fugientibus Germanis.

Ch. XIX.—**29. Superiorem provinciam.** Upper Germany. Cf note, 1, 9: *inferioris Germaniae.*

30. Gallo Annio. See 4, 68, and note, ibid.

32. Oppidum Batavorum. These words have greatly perplexed the commentators. Some take *oppidum* to be a proper name; others a common noun; but what walled town is referred to, they cannot agree. Several editors, and Ukert in his Geography, adopt the reading *oppida.*

33. Insulam. Formed by the mouths of the Rhine, and constituting the chief territory of the Batavi. Cf. G. 29.

35. Molem .... factam. Cf. Ann. 3, 53.

38. Abacto amne. The *river* was *drawn off* by its steeper (*prono alveo*) and more natural channel on the Gallic side of the island, as soon as the dam on that side was broken down.—*Insulam inter.* Observe the position of *inter.* Cf. notes, 2, 78; 4, 77.

3. Senatores. We find a senate instituted among the Frisii. 224
Ann. 11, 19.

4. Quem .... memoravimus, sc. 3, 35. There, however, Montanus is said to have been sent into Germany, by which, if we understand Germany Cisrhenana or Belgica, which was properly a part of Gaul, there will be no real contradiction. Cf. note, 1, 9: *inferioris Germaniae.* So Brot. and Wr.

Ch. XX.—**8. Superfuit.** *Remained,* sc. after the defeat of Civilis, as related in the foregoing section.

9. Quadripartito, sc. exercitu. Cf. Ann. 13, 39.

10. Arenaci, Batavoduri, etc. Walled towns of the Batavians, whose exact position is so disputed, that we shall not attempt to identify them. Cf. Rup., Or. and Ukert's and Walckenaer's Geog. of Gaul.

13. Traherent. Compare with this imperf. the perf. *invaserit,* and note, 1, 24: *dederit.*

14. Affore and **posse .... intercipi** depend on *fiducia,* or some kindred word to be supplied.

16. Obvenerant. *Had been allotted.* Cf. A. 6: *jurisdictio obvenerat.*—**17. Decumanorum.** The soldiers of the 10th legion.

18. Materiis. *Wood* for building, fortifying, etc. Wood, considered as to its nature and substance, is *lignum;* in reference to its uses, *materia.* Cf. Rams. Syn. 638. Wood intended expressly for burning, is also usually called *lignum.*

21. Rumpere. So nearly all the editions. Wr., with most of the MSS. and earliest editions, reads *irrumpere,* which he takes in the

Page

224 sense *interrupt.* But T. uses *irrumpere* in the sense of break in or rush into (cf. 3, 9: *stationes . . . irrumpit*), and the *ir-* may easily have attached itself to *rumpere* by mistake from the last syllable of the previous word.

Ch. XXI.—**27. Quem . . . . diximus,** sc. 4, 70. Cf. also 2, 22.

29. Versa fortuna is abl. abs.

33. Ne tum quidem . . . . classis, etc. *Not even at this time did the fleet,* etc. The emphatic *ne tum quidem* has reference to a like failure of the fleet to do its duty in a former battle. Cf. 18.

34. Sed. *But,* i. e. notwithstanding their orders.—*Et remiges,* etc. Observe the attraction for *et quod remiges,* etc. = *and the fact that the rowers,* etc. Cf. Essay, p. 18.

35. Sane. *Indeed,* or *the fact is.*

37. Defuissent. Subj. after *ubi* = *cum* in the sense of *although.* Gr. 263, 5, R. 1; Z. 577. Notice the effect of the *plup.:* fortune favored even, though skill *had not been* used.

38. Paucos post dies, sc. as described in the next section. For this way of designating a definite time, cf. Gr. 253, R. 1. Zumpt (477) gives eight different modes of expressing the same time.

225 **1. Quanquam . . . evasisset.** *Quanquam* seldom with Cic., but usually with T., is followed by the subj. Z. 574, Note. Wr. says, that when followed by the subj. it denotes a closer causal connection, than when followed by the ind. *Tamen* is omitted in the beginning of the antith. clause, as it often is by T.

Ch. XXII.—**3. Novesium.** Cf. note, 4, 26.—*Bonnam.* Cf. note, 4, 19.

6. Germanis. Dat. for abl. with *a,* so often used by T.—*Composuere. Planned,* lit. put together.

7. Prono . . . . rapti. *Borne rapidly down the current of the stream.* This is a frequent sense of *rapio.*—*Vallum,* sc. where the troops of Cerialis had encamped for the night, with the fleet moored at the bank near by.

11. Utque . . . . silentio. Supply by zeugma some verb correlative to *miscebant: And as they* approached *in silence in order to escape observation, so when the slaughter was begun,* etc.

13. Exciti. *Awaked out of sleep.*

16. Praetoriam navem. *The ship of the commander, praetor* originally denoting any leader (prae-itor).

17. Abripiunt. *They hurry it away,* sc. from the fleet. Cf notes, 2, 26. 36; 4, 27. Compare *rapti* above.

20. Silere. Here, as usual, opposed to all *noise. Tacere* is opposed to speech.

21. Signo et vocibus. *The sound of the trumpet and the watchwords,* though some take them by hendiadys, as both relating to watchwords.—*Se . . . . lapsos* depends on *excusabant.*

Page

22. Multa luce. *In broad daylight.* 225

23. Luppia. A branch of the Rhine, now the Lippe in Westphalia.—*Veledae.* Cf. 4, 61, and note, ibid. on *more, quo,* etc.

Ch. XXIII.—**24. Incessit.** Invades, *seizes.* Cf. 2, 63: *ubi formido incessisset.*

25. Complet. Furnishes with sailors and soldiers, *mans.* So in Greek, πληροῦν ναῦς. Cf. Herod. 8, 43.—*Quod .... agebantur. All his galleys with two banks of rowers, and those which were propelled by a single bank.* This is referred to as a test passage, as to the meaning of *biremes, triremes,* etc. Cf. Ernesti and Rup. in loc.

26. Tricenos. Observe the distributive force = *three hundred men each.*

27. Armamenta. *The rigging* of these boats *was similar to that of the Roman liburnæ.* But the *captured boats* were fitted out in a unique manner, *sagulis versicoloribus.—Captae lintres,* sc. those taken from the Romans. Cf. 22: *captivis navibus.* Al. aptae lintres. The reading of the whole sentence is doubtful and perplexed.

28. Juvabantur, sc. in cursu. Rup.

29. Velut aequoris, i. e. *a sea-like expanse* at the mouth of the river Meuse.

32. Gallia for *ex Gallia.* Cf. Essay, p. 11.—*Miraculo ... metu. More in wonder than in fear,* lit. *from the wonderfulness,* sc. of the fact that Civilis should venture on such an engagement. Cf. 1, 27: *miraculo.*

35. His. The latter, sc. Cerialis and his followers.—*Illi.* The former, sc. the partisans of Civilis.

1. Intactos. Al. intactas.—*Nota arte. According to a well-* 226
known policy, with a view to excite the jealousy of Civilis' followers, as if he must have some understanding with the Roman general. Hannibal pursued the same policy in reference to the estates of Fabius in Italy. Liv. 22, 23.—*Flexu autumni. Near the close of autumn,* lit. at its turning point. Cf. Cic. pro Cael.: *flexu aetatis;* Ann. 1, 16: *flexo in vesperam die.*

5. Differebantur = dirimebantur, were separated, *torn asunder.* This is the primary meaning of *differo.* See Freund, sub voce. Cf. also Hor. Epod. 5, 99: *insepulta membra different lupi.* Al. deferebantur.

Ch. XXIV.—**6. Potuisse .... Civilis.** *That the legions might at this time have been destroyed, and that the Germans wished* it done, *but were diverted from* the purpose *by a fraudulent device of his own, Civilis claimed should be set down to his credit.* Cf. note, 1, 71: *ultro imputavit.*

7. Neque abhorret vero. *Nor is this irreconcilable with the truth.* Observe the omission of *a* before *vero.* See the more common construction in 2, 2: neque abhorrebat *a* Berenice. But in Ann. 1, 54, we have *abhorrebat studiis* without *a* Poetical, Z. 468.

Page

226 **10. Veniam.** Properly access (venio, cf. Freund, sub voce), favor, here *pardon.*—*Veledam propinquosque. Veleda* (cf. note, 22), *and her connections,* who served as *internuntii numinis.* Cf. 4, 65: *delectus e propinquis.*

12. Caesos Treveros. Cf. 4, 71. 72.—*Receptos Ubios.* The Ubii had been received back, i. e. had submitted and returned to their former friendly relation to the Romans.

14. Exsulem . . . et extorrem. *An exile and an outcast.* These words have a similar etymology (*extorris* from ex-terra, *exsul* from ex-solum) and do not differ essentially in meaning. They are used together by T. for emphasis, and with his usual fondness for pairs of kindred words. *Exsul* denotes more frequently a legal banishment; *extorris* a forcible expulsion.

17. Inde. *On their side. Hinc. On his side,* sc. that of Cerialis. Observe the pairs of substantives in these two clauses. The sense may be expressed by hendiadys thus: the guilt of injustice . . . the revenge of the gods; though the connection in which they are placed by the author, is more lively and energetic.

CH. XXV.—**21. Quid profectum.** Al. perfectum. Cf. A. 17: *nihil profici;* A. 14: *parum profici,* etc.

24. Armis for *ad arma.* So T. often; earlier writers seldom. Cf. Essay, pp. 12. 13.

26. Non tributa . . . . indici. Cf. G. 29: *nec tributis contemnuntur,* etc.—*Virtutem et viros.* The valor of their men. Cf. note, 24, at the close.

29. Germanorum feminas. Such as Veleda, who were virtually their sovereigns, though not formally; for a female *sovereign* was for the most part deemed a disgrace by the Germans. Cf. G. 8 and 45.

30. Atrociora. Al. *atrociore* with *rabie* in the next clause. But then the *comparative* has no force.

227 CH. XXVI.—**1. Nabaliae.** This name occurs nowhere else, and it seems impossible to determine what river is meant. Brotier refers it to the channel made by Drusus from the Rhine to the Yssel, Walckenaer to the Yssel itself, etc. Cf. Ann. 2, 8.—*Abrupta. Extremities,* where the bridge was *broken off.*

2. Defenderer. Notice the middle sense.

3. Debebatur. Imp. ind. for imp. subj. Cf. Gr. 259, R. 4; Z. 519, b.

4. Inimica, hostilia. Inimicus, qui nos odit, hostilis qui oppugnat. Facciolati and Forcellini's Lexicon.

7. Actus = incitatus. Al. *accitus.*

The concluding sentence is incomplete. The much vaunted Gallic empire soon came to an end. The subsequent fortunes of Civilis are not known. But from the offers made him (cf. chap. 24), it is inferred that he received a full pardon.

INDEX OF PERSONS AND PLACES.

B.

C.

S.

T.

U.

V.

INDEX TO THE NOTES.

J.

K.

L.

T.

U.

V.

Z.

Latin Classical Works.

Lincoln's Livy.

SELECTIONS FROM THE FIRST FIVE BOOKS, TOGETHER WITH THE TWENTY-FIRST AND TWENTY-SECOND BOOKS ENTIRE: WITH A PLAN OF ROME, A MAP OF THE PASSAGE OF HANNIBAL, AND ENGLISH NOTES FOR THE USE OF SCHOOLS.

BY J. L. LINCOLN,

PROFESSOR OF THE LATIN LANGUAGE AND LITERATURE IN BROWN UNIVERSITY.

12mo. 329 pages. Price $1 25.

The publishers believe that in this edition of Livy a want is supplied which has been universally felt; there being previous to this no American edition furnished with the requisite aids for the successful study of this Latin author. The text is chiefly that of Alschefski, which is now generally received by the best critics. The notes have been prepared with special reference to the grammatical study of the language, and the illustration of its forms, constructions, and idioms, as used by Livy. They will not be found to foster habits of dependence in the student, by supplying indiscriminate translation or unnecessary assistance; but come to his help only in such parts as it is fair to suppose he cannot master by his own exertions. They also embrace all necessary information relating to history, geography, and antiquities.

Lincoln's Livy has been highly commended by critics, and is used in nearly all the colleges in the country.

From PROF. ANDERSON, *of Waterville College.*

"A careful examination of several portions of your work has convinced me that for the use of students, it is altogether superior to any edition of Livy with which I am acquainted. Among its excellencies you will permit me to name the close attention given to particles, to the subjunctive mood, the constant reference to the grammars, the discrimination of words nearly synonymous, and the care in giving the localities mentioned in the text. The book will be hereafter used in our college."

BEZA'S LATIN VERSION

OF

The New Teftament.

12mo. 291 pages. Price 75 cents.

The now acknowledged propriety of giving students of languages familiar works for translation—thus adopting in the schools the mode by which the child first learns to talk—has induced the publication of this new American edition of Beza's Latin Version of the New Testament. Ever since its first appearance, this work has kept its place in the general esteem; while more recent versions have been so strongly tinged with the peculiar views of the translators as to make them acceptable to particular classes only. The editor has exerted himself to render the present edition worthy of patronage by its superior accuracy and neatness; and the publishers flatter themselves that the pains bestowed will insure for it a preference over other editions

Latin Classical Works.

The Works of Horace.

WITH ENGLISH NOTES, FOR THE USE OF SCHOOLS AND COLLEGES
BY J. L. LINCOLN,

PROFESSOR OF THE LATIN LANGUAGE AND LITERATURE IN BROWN UNIVERSITY

12mo. 575 pages. Price $1 50.

The text of this edition is mainly that of Orelli, the most important readings of other critics being given in foot-notes. The volume is introduced with a biographical sketch of Horace and a critique on his writings, which enable the student to enter intelligently on his work. Peculiar grammatical constructions, as well as geographical and historical allusions, are explained in notes, which are just full enough to aid the pupil, to excite him to gain a thorough understanding of the author, and awaken in him a taste for philological studies, without taking all labor off his hands. While the chief aim has been to impart a clear idea of Latin Syntax as exhibited in the text, it has also been a cherished object to take advantage of the means so variously and richly furnished by Horace for promoting the poetical taste and literary culture of the student.

From an article by PROF. BAHR, *of the University of Heidelberg, in the Heidelberg Annals of Literature.*

"There are already several American editions of Horace, intended for the use of schools; of one of these, which has passed through many editions, and has also been widely circulated in England, mention has been formerly made in this journal; but that one we may not put upon an equality with the one now before us, inasmuch as this has taken a different stand-point, which may serve as a sign of progress in this department of study. The editor has, it is true, also intended his work for the use of schools, and has sought to adapt it, in all its parts, to such a use; but still, without losing sight of this purpose, he has proceeded throughout with more independence. In the preparation of the Notes, the editor has faithfully observed the principles (laid down in his preface); the explanations of the poet's words commend themselves by a compressed brevity which limits itself to what is most essential, and by a sharp precision of expression; and references to other passages of the poet, and also to grammars, dictionaries, &c., are not wanting.

SALLUST'S

Jugurtha and Catiline

WITH NOTES AND A VOCABULARY

BY NOBLE BUTLER AND MINARD STURGUS.

12mo. 397 pages. Price $1 25.

The editors have spent a vast amount of time and labor in correcting the text, by comparison of the most improved German and English editions. It is believed that this will be found superior to any edition hitherto published in this country. In accordance with their chronological order, the "Jugurtha" precedes the "Catiline." The Notes are copious and tersely expressed; they display not only fine scholarship, but (what is quite as necessary in such a book) a practical knowledge of the difficulties which the student encounters in reading this author, and the aids that he requires. The Vocabulary was prepared by the late WILLIAM H. G. BUTLER. It will be found an able and faithful performance.

www.ingramcontent.com/pod-product-compliance
Lightning Source LLC
LaVergne TN
LVHW021125110826
845150LV00005B/947

* 9 7 8 1 4 2 5 5 5 1 2 9 2 *